THE
unofficial GUIDE®
TO Disneyland
2018

COME CHECK US OUT!

Supplement your valuable guidebook with tips, news, and deals by visiting our websites:

theunofficialguides.com
touringplans.com

Also, while there, sign up for The Unofficial Guide newsletter for even more travel tips and special offers.

Join the conversation on social media:

 @theUGSeries   theUnofficialGuides

 theUGSeries   theUGSeries

#theUGseries

Other Unofficial Guides

Beyond Disney: The Unofficial Guide to SeaWorld, Universal Orlando, & the Best of Central Florida

The Disneyland Story: The Unofficial Guide to the Evolution of Walt Disney's Dream

Mini-Mickey: The Pocket-Sized Unofficial Guide to Walt Disney World

Universal vs. Disney: The Unofficial Guide to American Theme Parks' Greatest Rivalry

The Unofficial Guide Color Companion to Walt Disney World

The Unofficial Guide to Disney Cruise Line

The Unofficial Guide to Las Vegas

The Unofficial Guide to Mall of America

The Unofficial Guide to Universal Orlando

The Unofficial Guide to Walt Disney World

The Unofficial Guide to Walt Disney World with Kids

The Unofficial Guide to Washington, D.C.

THE *unofficial* GUIDE*
TO Disneyland*

2018

SETH KUBERSKY *with* BOB SEHLINGER, LEN TESTA, *and* GUY SELGA JR.

Disneyland is officially known as the Disneyland Resort*.

Please note that prices fluctuate in the course of time and that travel information changes under the impact of many factors that influence the travel industry. We therefore suggest that you write or call ahead for confirmation when making your travel plans. Every effort has been made to ensure the accuracy of information throughout this book, and the contents of this publication are believed to be correct at the time of printing. Nevertheless, the publishers cannot accept responsibility for errors or omissions, for changes in details given in this guide, or for the consequences of any reliance on the information provided by the same. Assessments of attractions and so forth are based upon the author's own experience; therefore, descriptions given in this guide necessarily contain an element of subjective opinion, which may not reflect the publisher's opinion or dictate a reader's own experience on another occasion. Readers are invited to write the publisher with ideas, comments, and suggestions for future editions.

Published by:
AdventureKEEN
2204 First Ave. S, Ste. 102
Birmingham. AL 35233

Unofficial Guide is a registered trademark of Google Inc. in the United States and other countries and may not be used without written permission. Used under license. All other trademarks are the property of their respective owners. Google Inc. is not associated with any product or vendor mentioned in this book.

Cover design by Scott McGrew

Text design by Vertigo Design with updates by Annie Long

For information on our other products and services or to obtain technical support, please contact us from within the United States at 888-604-4537 or by fax at 205-326-1012.

AdventureKEEN also publishes its books in a variety of electronic formats. Some content that appears in print may not be available in electronic formats.

ISBN: 978-1-62809-071-0; eISBN: 978-1-62809-072-7

Manufactured in the United States of America

5 4 3 2

CONTENTS

LIST *of* MAPS

ACKNOWLEDGMENTS

A BIG SALUTE TO OUR WHOLE UNOFFICIAL TEAM, who rendered a Herculean effort in what must have seemed like a fantasy version of Jean-Paul Sartre's *No Exit* to the tune of "It's a Small World." We hope you all recover to tour another day.

Special thanks to Disney historian Jim Hill; cartoonist Tami Knight; Unofficial Guide research director Len Testa; dining contributor Erin Mahoney Harris; child psychologist Karen Turnbow, PhD; Unofficial Guide statistician Fred Hazleton; "Unheralded Treasures" writer Lani Teshima; and Unofficial friend Genevieve Bernard.

Amber Kaye Henderson and Annie Long both contributed energetically to shaping this latest edition. Much appreciation also goes to editorial-production manager Molly Merkle, cartographer Steve Jones, and indexer Rich Carlson.

—*Bob Sehlinger*

INTRODUCTION

▌ WHY "UNOFFICIAL"?

DECLARATION OF INDEPENDENCE

THE AUTHORS AND RESEARCHERS OF THIS GUIDE specifically and categorically declare that they are and always have been totally independent of the Walt Disney Company, Inc., of Disneyland, Inc., of Walt Disney World Company, Inc., and of any and all other members of the Disney corporate family.

The material in this guide originated with the authors and researchers and has not been reviewed, edited, or in any way approved by Walt Disney Company, Inc., Disneyland, Inc., or Walt Disney World Company, Inc.

This guidebook represents the first comprehensive *critical* appraisal of Disneyland. Its purpose is to provide the reader with the information necessary to tour the theme parks with the greatest efficiency and economy and with the least amount of hassle and standing in line. The researchers of this guide believe in the wondrous variety, joy, and excitement of the Disney attractions. At the same time, we realistically recognize that Disneyland is a business, with the same profit motivations as businesses all over the world.

With no obligation to toe the Disney line, we represent and serve you, the reader. The contents were researched and compiled by a team of evaluators who are completely independent of the Walt Disney Company, Inc. If a restaurant serves bad food, if a gift item is overpriced, or if a ride isn't worth the wait, we say so. And in the process, we hope to make your visit more fun, efficient, and economical.

DANCE TO THE MUSIC

A DANCE HAS A BEGINNING AND AN END. But when you're dancing, you're not concerned about getting to the end or where on the dance floor you might wind up. In other words, you're totally in the moment. That's the way you should be on your Disneyland vacation.

You may feel a bit of pressure concerning your vacation. Vacations, after all, are very special events, and expensive ones to boot. So you work hard to make your vacation the best that it can be. Planning and organizing are essential to a successful Disneyland vacation, but if they become your focus, you won't be able to hear the music and enjoy the dance.

So think of us as your dancing coach. We'll teach you the steps to the dance in advance, so when you're on vacation and the music plays, you will dance with effortless grace and ease.

THE IMPORTANCE OF BEING GOOFY

JACOB, DISNEY MARKETING'S HEAD of social media, stared perplexed at a new report. "Since Donald Trump was elected, our characters are losing followers across the board, but they're really getting trounced on Twitter," he remarked.

"Which characters?," quizzed his assistant, Roy.

"The number of Twitter followers are down just a little for most of our characters, but wow, bird characters like Donald, Daisy, Huey, Dewey, Louie, and Uncle Scrooge have totally tanked."

"Is it just duck characters then?" Roy asked.

"No," Jacob replied. "Among our bird characters, José Carioca, Iago, Scuttle, and Zazu are losing followers by the minute. Non-Disney characters, including Woody Woodpecker, Foghorn J. Leghorn, Daffy Duck, and Road Runner, are also way down."

"Where are all the followers going? Do you see an uptick for anyone?"

"No. Well, wait a minute! There's a huge gain in Twitter followers in the Looney Tunes column, but not for all of them. One character seems to be picking up all the defected followers," Jacob responded.

"Who?!"

"Good grief, it's Tweety Bird!" Jacob exclaimed. "He's gained thousands of followers because of a string of tweets with Donald Trump arguing about cats' rights."

"Huh? Like what?"

"Whether a cat has to use the litter box corresponding to the gender on its birth certificate, for example."

"Well, that's a weighty matter, all right," Roy remarked.

"Tweety told the president that he's pooped from tweeting all night, but that he's on call 24/7 for matters of national security, which he prefers to tweets about cats."

And so it goes. . . .

The Death of Spontaneity

One of our all-time favorite letters is from a man in Chapel Hill, North Carolina. He writes:

> Your book reads like the operations plan for an amphibious landing: Go here, do this, proceed to Step 15. You must think that everyone is a hyperactive, type-A theme park commando. What happened to the

satisfaction of self-discovery or the joy of spontaneity? Next you will be telling us when to empty our bladders.

More recently, a reader from Seattle, Washington, wrote online:

We skipped the touring plans and instead took our time to smell the flowers and truly take in the entire experience of Disney—isn't that what it is all about! Our friends decided to strictly follow the touring plans. We felt sorry for their 7-year-old daughter, who had a fever and was pumped up with Tylenol just so her parents could follow this plan. Their whole family was quite exhausted at the end.

Once we were actually there, we realized that maximizing the number of rides/events one does is NOT the same as maximizing one's true enjoyment of Disney.

As it happens, we at The Unofficial Guides are a pretty existential crew. We are big on self-discovery when walking in the woods or watching birds. Some of us are able to improvise jazz without reading music, while others can whip up a mean pot of chili without a recipe. When it comes to Disneyland, however, we all agree that you either need a good plan or a frontal lobotomy. The operational definition of self-discovery and spontaneity at Disneyland is the "pleasure" of heat prostration and the "joy" of standing in line.

It's easy to spot the free spirits at Disneyland Park and Disney California Adventure, especially at opening time. While everyone else is stampeding to Space Mountain or Radiator Springs Racers, they're standing in a cloud of dust puzzling over the park map. Later, they're the folks running around like chickens in a thunderstorm trying to find an attraction with less than a 40-minute wait. Face it: Disneyland Resort is not a very existential place. In many ways it's the ultimate in mass-produced entertainment, the most planned and programmed environment imaginable. Self-discovery and spontaneity work about as well at Disneyland as they do on your tax return. One mother of two young boys had this to say about our book:

Your book was invaluable in giving us the tools to plan a great day. We had a magical day thanks to being able to prioritize our goals. Thank you for the full descriptions of rides—with only one day, you really need to pick your battles.

We're not saying that you can't have a great time at Disneyland. Bowling isn't very spontaneous either, but lots of people love it. What we *are* saying is that you need a plan. You don't have to be inflexible about it. Just think about what you want to do—before you go. Don't delude yourself by rationalizing that the information in this modest tome is only for the pathological and superorganized. For those who truly want to stop and smell the roses at Disneyland, we recommend our Anti-Touring Plan (see page 279), which guarantees a day without stress, waiting in queues, or bouncing around the park. You won't actually get on many (if any) rides, but you can enjoy a full day of live entertainment and people-watching without sticking to a strict schedule. Just step out of the way when guests stampeding toward their next E-ticket rush by.

HOW *This* GUIDE WAS RESEARCHED *and* WRITTEN

WHILE MUCH HAS BEEN WRITTEN CONCERNING Disneyland Resort, very little has been comparative or evaluative. In preparing this guide, nothing was taken for granted. The theme parks were visited at different times throughout the year by a team of trained observers who conducted detailed evaluations, rating the theme parks along with all of their component rides, shows, exhibits, services, and concessions according to formal, pretested rating criteria. Interviews with attraction patrons were conducted to determine what tourists of all age groups enjoyed most and least during their Disneyland visit.

unofficial **TIP**
The Unofficial Guide to Disneyland maintains a researcher whose job it is to be in one of the two Disneyland Resort parks several days each week.

Though our observers are independent and impartial, we do not claim special expertise or scientific backgrounds relative to the types of exhibits, performances, or attractions viewed. Like you, we visit the Disneyland parks as tourists, noting our satisfaction or dissatisfaction. Disneyland offerings are marketed to the touring public, and it is as the public that we have experienced them.

The primary difference between the average tourist and the trained evaluator is that the latter approaches attractions equipped with professional skills in organization, preparation, and observation. The trained evaluator is responsible for much more than simply observing and cataloging. While the tourist is being entertained and delighted by the *Enchanted Tiki Room,* the professional evaluator seated nearby is rating the performance in terms of theme, pace, continuity, and originality. The evaluator also checks out the physical arrangements: Is the sound system clear and audible without being overpowering; is the audience shielded from the sun or rain; is seating adequate; can everyone in the audience clearly see the stage? Similarly, detailed and relevant checklists are prepared by observer teams and applied to rides, exhibits, and concessions, as well as to the theme park in general. Finally, observations and evaluator ratings are integrated with audience reactions and the opinions of patrons to compile a comprehensive profile of each feature and service.

In compiling this guide, we recognize the fact that a tourist's age, gender, background, and interests will strongly influence his or her taste in Disneyland offerings and will account for his or her preference of one ride or feature over another. Given this fact, we make no attempt at comparing apples with oranges. How, indeed, could a meaningful comparison be made between the serenity and beauty of the Storybook Land Canal Boats and the wild roller coaster ride of California Screamin'? Instead, our objective is to provide the reader with a critical evaluation and enough pertinent data to make knowledgeable decisions according to individual tastes.

The essence of this guide, then, consists of individual critiques and descriptions of each feature of the Disneyland parks, supplemented with some maps to help you get around and several detailed touring plans to help you avoid bottlenecks and crowds. Because so many Disneyland guests also visit Universal Studios Hollywood to see The Wizarding World of Harry Potter, we have included comprehensive coverage and a touring plan for that park as well.

A WORD TO OUR READERS ABOUT ANNUAL REVISIONS

SOME OF YOU WHO PURCHASE EACH NEW EDITION of *The Unofficial Guide to Disneyland* have chastised us for retaining examples, comments, and descriptions from previous years' editions. This letter from a Grand Rapids, Michigan, reader is typical:

> *Your guidebook still has the same little example stories. When I got my new book, I expected a true update and new stuff, not the same old, same old!*

First, *The Unofficial Guide to Disneyland* is a reference work. Though we are flattered that some readers read the guide from cover to cover, and that some of you find it entertaining, our objective is fairly straightforward: to provide information that enables you to have the best possible Disneyland vacation.

Each year during our revision research, we check every attraction, restaurant, hotel, shop, and entertainment offering. Though there are many changes, much remains the same from year to year. When we profile and critique an attraction, we try to provide the reader with the most insightful, relevant, and useful information, written in the clearest possible language. It is our opinion that if an attraction does not change, then it makes little sense to risk clarity and content for the sake of freshening up the prose. Disneyland guests who try the Mad Tea Party or Pinocchio's Daring Journey today, for example, experience the same presentation as guests who visited Disneyland in 2013, 1995, or 1986. Moreover, according to our extensive patron surveys (about 1,000 each year), today's guests still respond to these attractions in the same way as prior-year patrons.

The bottom line: We believe that our readers are better served if we devote our time to that which is changing and new as opposed to that which remains the same. The success or failure of this *Unofficial Guide* is determined not by the style of the writing but by the accuracy of the information and, ultimately, whether you have a positive experience at Disneyland. Every change to the guide we make (or don't make) is evaluated in this context.

WE'VE GOT ATTITUDE

SOME READERS DISAGREE with our attitude toward Disney. One, a 30-something woman from Golden, Colorado, lambasted us, writing:

I read your book cover to cover and felt you were way too hard on Disney. It's disappointing, when you're all enthused about going, to be slammed with all these criticisms and possible pitfalls.

A reader from Little Rock, Arkansas, also took us to task:

Your book was quite complimentary of Disney, perhaps too complimentary. Maybe the free trips you travel writers get at Disneyland are chipping away at your objectivity.

And from a Williamsport, Pennsylvania, mother of three:

Reading your book irritated me before we went because of all the warnings. I'm used to having guidebooks pump me up about where I'm going. But once I arrived, I found that I was fully prepared and we had a great time. In retrospect, I have to admit you were right on the money. What I regarded as you being negative was just a good dose of reality.

A Vienna, Virginia, family chimed in with this:

After being at Disney for three days at the height of tourist season, I laughed out loud at your "Death of Spontaneity" section. We are definitely free spirit types who don't like to plan our days when we are on vacation. A friend warned us, and we got your guidebook. After skimming through it before we left, I was terrified that we had made a terrible mistake booking this vacation. Thanks to your book, we had a wonderful time. If it had not been for the book, we definitely would have been trampled by all the people stampeding to Space Mountain while we were standing there with our maps.

Finally, a reader from Phoenixville, Pennsylvania, prefers no opinions at all, writing:

Though each person has the right to his or her own opinion, I did not purchase the book for an opinion.

For the record, we've always paid our own way at Disneyland Resort: hotels, admissions, meals, the works. We don't dislike Disney, and we most definitely don't have an ax to grind. We're positive by nature and much prefer to praise than to criticize. Personally, we have enjoyed the Disney parks immensely over the years, both experiencing them and writing about them. Disney, however, as with all corporations (and all people, for that matter), is better at some things than others. Because our readers shell out big bucks to go to Disneyland, we believe that they have the right to know in advance what's good and what's not. For those who think we're overly positive, please understand that *The Unofficial Guide to Disneyland* is a guidebook, not an exposé. Our overriding objective is for you to enjoy your visit. To that end we try to report fairly and objectively. When readers disagree with our opinions, we, in the interest of fairness and balance, publish their point of view right alongside ours. To the best of our knowledge, The Unofficial Guides are the only travel guides in print that do this.

THE SUM OF ALL FEARS

EVERY WRITER WHO EXPRESSES an opinion is quite accustomed to readers who strongly agree or disagree. It comes with the territory. Troubling in the extreme, however, is the possibility that our efforts to be objective have frightened some readers away from Disneyland, or stimulated in others a state of apprehension. For the record, if you enjoy theme parks, Disneyland and Walt Disney World are as good as they get: absolute nirvana. They're upbeat, safe, fun, eye-popping, happy, and exciting. Even if you arrive knowing nothing about the place and make every possible touring mistake, chances are about 90% that you'll have a wonderful time anyway. In the end, guidebooks don't make or break great destinations. They are simply tools to help you enhance your experience and get the most vacation for your money.

As wonderful as Disneyland is, however, it is nevertheless a complex destination. Even so, it's certainly not nearly as challenging or difficult as visiting New York, San Francisco, Paris, Acapulco, or any other large city or destination. And, happily, there are numerous ways, if forewarned, to save money, minimize hassle, and make the most of your time. In large measure, that's what this guide is about: giving you a heads up regarding potential problems and opportunities. Unfortunately, some folks reading *The Unofficial Guide* subconsciously add up the various warnings and critical advice and conclude that Disneyland is altogether too intimidating or, alternatively, too expensive or too much work. They lose track of the wonder of Disneyland and become focused instead on what might go wrong.

Our philosophy is that knowledge is power (and time and money too). You're free to follow our advice or not at your sole discretion. But you'd be denied the opportunity to exercise that discretion if we failed to fairly present the issues.

With or without a guidebook, you'll have a great time at Disneyland. If you let us, we'll help you smooth the potential bumps. We are certain that we can help you turn a great vacation into an absolutely superb one. Either way, once there, you will get the feel of the place and quickly reach a comfort level that will allay your apprehensions, as well as allow you to have a great experience.

THE *UNOFFICIAL GUIDE* PUBLISHING YEAR

WE RECEIVE MANY QUERIES each year asking when the next edition of *The Unofficial Guide to Disneyland* will be available. Usually our new editions are published and available in stores by late August or early September. Thus the 2019 edition will be on the shelves in fall 2018.

WHERE'S THE INDEX?

TO ELIMINATE YOUR HAVING TO CARRY this tome around the theme parks, the touring plans are located on tear-out pages at the end of the book. Consequently, the index immediately precedes the plans instead of being at the end of the book, where an index is typically located.

LETTERS, COMMENTS, AND QUESTIONS FROM READERS

MANY OF THOSE WHO USE *The Unofficial Guide to Disneyland* write to us, asking questions, making comments, or sharing their own strategies for visiting Disneyland. We appreciate all such input, both positive and critical, and encourage our readers to continue writing. Readers' comments and observations are frequently used in revised editions of *The Unofficial Guide to Disneyland* and have contributed immeasurably to its improvement.

Reader Survey

Please fill out our reader survey online by visiting **touringplans.com /disneyland-resort/survey.** You can rest assured that we won't release your name and address to any mailing-list companies, direct mail advertisers, or other third parties. Unless you instruct us otherwise, we will assume that you do not object to being quoted in a future edition.

How to Contact the Author

Write to Seth Kubersky at this address:

> *The Unofficial Guide to Disneyland*
> 2204 First Ave. S, Ste. 102
> Birmingham, AL 35233

Or e-mail him at **unofficialguides@menasharidge.com.** When you write, put your address on both your letter and envelope; sometimes the two get separated. It is also a good idea to include your phone number and e-mail address. If you e-mail us, please tell us where you're from. Remember, as travel writers, we're often out of the office for long periods of time, so forgive us if our response is slow. Unofficial Guide e-mail is not forwarded to us when we're traveling, but we will respond as soon as possible when we return.

Questions from Readers

Questions frequently asked by readers are answered in an appendix at the back of this *Unofficial Guide*.

DISNEYLAND RESORT: *An* OVERVIEW

IF YOU HAVEN'T BEEN TO DISNEYLAND for a while, you'll hardly know the place. First, of course, there is **Disneyland Park,** which in 2015 marked its 60th year as the original Disney theme park; it's also the only park that Walt Disney saw completed in his lifetime. Much more than the Magic Kingdom at Walt Disney World, Disneyland Park embodies the quiet, charming spirit of nostalgia that so characterized Walt himself. The park is vast yet intimate, steeped in the tradition of its creator yet continually changing.

Disneyland opened in 1955 on a 107-acre tract surrounded almost exclusively by orange groves, just west of the sleepy and little-known Southern California community of Anaheim. Constrained by finances and ultimately enveloped by the city it helped create, Disneyland operated on that same modest parcel of land until 2001.

Disneyland Park is a collection of adventures, rides, and shows symbolized by the Disney characters and Sleeping Beauty Castle. It's divided into nine subareas, or "lands," arranged around a central hub. First encountered is **Main Street, U.S.A.,** which connects the Disneyland entrance with the central hub. Moving clockwise around the hub, the other lands are **Adventureland, Frontierland, Fantasyland,** and **Tomorrowland.** Two major lands, **Critter Country** and **New Orleans Square,** are accessible via Adventureland and Frontierland but do not connect directly with the central hub. Another land, **Mickey's Toontown,** connects to Fantasyland. Finally, the huge **Star Wars: Galaxy's Edge** is scheduled to open in 2019 on 14 acres of former backstage areas behind Critter Country and Frontierland, making it the biggest expansion in Disneyland Park's history. All nine lands will be described in detail later.

Growth and change at Disneyland (until 1996) had been internal, in marked contrast to the ever-enlarging development of Walt Disney World near Orlando, Florida. Until recently, when something new was added at Disneyland, something old had to go. The Disney engineers, to their credit, however, have never been shy about disturbing the status quo. Patrons of the park's earlier, modest years are amazed by the transformation. Gone are the days of the "magical little park" with the Monsanto House of the Future, donkey rides, and Captain Hook's Pirate Ship. Substituted in a process of continuous evolution and modernization are state-of-the-art fourth-, fifth-, and sixth-generation attractions and entertainment. To paraphrase Walt Disney, Disneyland will never stop changing as long as there are new ideas to explore.

Disneyland Park was arguably Walt Disney's riskiest venture. It was developed on a shoestring budget and made possible only through Disney's relationship with ABC Television and other corporate sponsors. The capital available was barely sufficient to acquire the property and build the park; nothing was left over for the development of hotels or the acquisition and improvement of property adjoining the park. Even the Disneyland Hotel, connected to the theme park by monorail, was owned and operated by a third party until 1989.

Disneyland's success spawned a wave of development that rapidly surrounded the theme park with mom-and-pop motels, souvenir stands, and fast-food restaurants. The steady decline of the area encircling Disneyland continued to rankle Walt. After tolerating the blight for 30 years, the Walt Disney Company (finally flush with funds and ready for a good fight) set about putting Disneyland Park right. Quietly at first, then aggressively, Disney began buying up the mom-and-pop motels, as well as the few remaining orange and vegetable groves near the park.

In June 1993 the City of Anaheim adopted a Disney plan that called for the development of a new Disney destination resort, including a second theme park situated in what was once the Disneyland parking lot; a Disney-owned hotel district with 4,600 hotel rooms; two new parking facilities; and improvements, including extensive landscaping of the streets that provide access to the complex. Infrastructure changes required to support the expanded Disney presence included widening I-5, building new interchanges, moving a major power line, adding new sewer systems, and expanding utilities capacity.

By the end of 2000, all of the changes, modifications, and additions were finished, and Disneyland began the new century as a complete multi–theme park resort destination. The second and newest park, **Disney California Adventure** (or DCA to the initiated), celebrated its grand opening on February 8, 2001.

DCA is an oddly shaped park built around a lagoon on one side and the Grand Californian Hotel on the other, with one of Disney's trademark mountains, **Grizzly Peak,** plopped down in the middle. **Buena Vista Street,** an entranceway evoking 1920s Los Angeles, leads to six "lands." Inside the front gate and to the left is **Hollywood Land** (formerly Hollywood Pictures Backlot), a diminutive version of the Disney's Hollywood Studios theme park at Walt Disney World. Then there are **Grizzly Peak** (which absorbed the former Condor Flats area) and **Pacific Wharf,** a pair of lands (originally known collectively as Golden State) celebrating California's industry, cuisine, and natural resources. Next is **A Bug's Land,** with characters and attractions based on the Disney-Pixar film *a bug's life*. **Cars Land** is dedicated to the desert town of Radiator Springs from Disney-Pixar's *Cars*. Finally, **Paradise Pier/Pixar Pier** recalls the grand old seaside amusement parks of the early 20th century.

The entrances to Disneyland Park and DCA face each other across a palm-studded pedestrian plaza called the **Esplanade,** which begins at Harbor Boulevard and runs west, between the parks, passing into **Downtown Disney,** a dining, shopping, entertainment, and nightlife venue. From Downtown Disney, the Esplanade continues via an overpass across Downtown Drive and past the monorail station to the **Disneyland** and **Paradise Pier Hotels.**

Sandwiched between the Esplanade and Downtown Disney on the north and DCA on the south is the 1,019-room **Grand Californian Hotel,** which includes the 50-unit **Grand Californian Villas.** Designed in the image of rustic national park lodges, the Grand Californian Hotel supplanted the Disneyland Hotel as Disneyland's prestigious lodging property.

Disney struck a deal with the City of Anaheim in 2015 to invest at least $1.5 billion—including building a new 6,800-spot parking structure to the east of the resort—by 2024 in exchange for a 45-year moratorium on ticket taxes. Additionally, a new 700-room four-diamond luxury hotel, featuring a rooftop restaurant with views of Disneyland Park, has been proposed to open by 2021 on 10 acres of the current Downtown Disney parking lot. The rumor mill has been rumbling for several years about a third theme park, possibly to be built on an outlying parking lot, but Disney CEO Bob Iger has publicly downplayed any such plans.

North of the hotels and across West Street from Disneyland Park is a huge multistory parking garage that can be accessed directly from I-5. This is where most Disneyland guests park. Tram transport is provided from the garage, from the adjacent oversize-vehicle lot, and from outlying lots to the Esplanade. Kennels are to the right of the Disneyland Park main entrance. Ticket booths are situated along the Esplanade.

SHOULD I GO TO DISNEYLAND PARK IF I'VE SEEN WALT DISNEY WORLD?

DISNEYLAND PARK IS ROUGHLY COMPARABLE to the Magic Kingdom theme park at Walt Disney World near Orlando, Florida. Both are arranged by "lands" accessible from a central hub and connected to the entrance by a main street. Both parks feature many rides and attractions of the same name: Space Mountain, Jungle Cruise, Pirates of the Caribbean, It's a Small World, and Dumbo the Flying Elephant, to name a few. Interestingly, however, the same name does not necessarily connote the same experience. Pirates of the Caribbean at Disneyland Park is much longer and more elaborate than its Walt Disney World counterpart. The Haunted Mansion is more elaborate in Florida, and the *Enchanted Tiki Room* is about the same in both places.

Disneyland Park is more intimate than the Magic Kingdom, not having the room for expansion enjoyed by the Florida park. Pedestrian thoroughfares are narrower, and everything from Big Thunder Mountain to the castle is scaled down somewhat. Large crowds are more taxing at Disneyland Park because there is less room for them to disperse. At Disneyland Park, however, there are dozens of little surprises, small unheralded attractions tucked away in crooks and corners of the park, which give Disneyland Park a special charm and variety that the Magic Kingdom lacks. And, of course, Disneyland Park has the stamp of Walt Disney's personal touch.

A Minnesota couple who have sampled Disney both east and west offered this observation:

> We have been to WDW in Florida several times. This was our first visit to Disneyland. For parents with children 10 years of age and younger, I highly recommend Disneyland instead of WDW. Its size is much more manageable. You can stay within walking distance of the front gate. That makes it practical and easy to get to the gates early in the morning (an absolute imperative) and get away in the afternoon for a break (always helpful). The size and scale of WDW make this impractical.

A Salem, Massachusetts, family who had visited WDW three years prior to their Disneyland trip, agreed:

> We heard from many that Disneyland was small and that the castle was underwhelming. But the Disney magic was there, and we had a great time exploring what was unique about each park. We spent three

CRITICAL COMPARISON OF ATTRACTIONS FOUND AT BOTH PARKS

ADVENTURELAND

- *Enchanted Tiki Room* Similar at both parks; slightly longer show at Disneyland but more advanced rainstorm effects at Walt Disney World.
- **Jungle Cruise** Updated Audio-Animatronic (robotic) animals and funnier narrators at Disneyland but longer ride at Walt Disney World.

CRITTER COUNTRY

- **The Many Adventures of Winnie the Pooh** Longer and with more motion at the Magic Kingdom.
- **Splash Mountain** Longer ride and a bigger drop at Magic Kingdom, but California has more animatronic animals.

FANTASYLAND

- **Carrousels** About the same at both parks.
- **Castles** Far larger and more beautiful at Magic Kingdom; Disneyland has walk-through display.
- **Dumbo the Flying Elephant** About the same, but WDW version has double the capacity and an interactive circus-themed queue.
- **It's a Small World** Disneyland version is longer with hidden Disney characters, and it gets a holiday overlay.
- **Mad Tea Party** Disneyland's is open-air; otherwise the same at both parks.
- **Peter Pan's Flight** Shorter but with upgraded special effects at Disneyland.
- **Royal Hall at Fantasy Faire/Princess Fairytale Hall** About the same, but Disneyland doesn't have FastPass.

FRONTIERLAND

- **Big Thunder Mountain Railroad** More monumental mountain and an interactive queue at Magic Kingdom; smoother track and explosive special effects at Disneyland.
- **Tom Sawyer Island** Comparable; pirate theme with more elaborate effects at Disneyland but more caves and play structures to explore at Magic Kingdom.
- **Various river cruises (canoes, boats, and such)** More interesting sights at Disneyland, and only Disneyland offers canoes.

MAIN STREET, U.S.A.

- **Railroads** The Disneyland Railroad is far more entertaining by virtue of the Grand Canyon diorama and the primeval world components not found at the Magic Kingdom.

NEW ORLEANS SQUARE

- **The Haunted Mansion** Longer ride and high-tech hitchhiking ghosts give Magic Kingdom the edge. Holiday version is offered only at Disneyland.
- **Pirates of the Caribbean** Far superior at Disneyland.

TOMORROWLAND

- **Astro Orbitor** About the same at both parks, but much higher in the air at the Magic Kingdom.
- **Autopia/Tomorrowland Speedway** Disneyland version is superior.
- **Buzz Lightyear** More mobile guns and better game play at Disneyland.
- **Space Mountain** Much better effects and smoother track at Disneyland but a wilder ride with sharper drops at Magic Kingdom. Only Disneyland offers seasonal versions like Ghost Galaxy.

*It should be noted that several of the attractions at Disney California Adventure, such as *It's Tough to Be a Bug!*, Toy Story Midway Mania!, and *Turtle Talk with Crush,* appeared first at one of the Walt Disney World theme parks. Versions of Ariel's Undersea Adventure, Soarin' Around the World, and Star Tours have been exported to Walt Disney World. None of the remaining DCA attractions are found at Disney World.

days at the parks and wished that we had planned to be there longer. The parks may be smaller, but there is still plenty to see and do.

And these die-hard Disney veterans from Pleasantville, New York, praised the Anaheim resort's employees:

Disneyland is such a wonderful alternative to the traditional trip to Walt Disney World. We particularly were impressed with the cast members. The Disneyland cast members consistently went above and beyond for us, even compared to Orlando's cast members.

To allow for a meaningful comparison, we have provided a summary of those features found at Disneyland Park and not WDW's Magic Kingdom (listed alphabetically below), accompanied by a critical look at the attractions found at both parks on the opposite page.

ATTRACTIONS FOUND ONLY AT DISNEYLAND PARK

ADVENTURELAND

• Indiana Jones Adventure • Tarzan's Treehouse

CRITTER COUNTRY

• Davy Crockett's Explorer Canoes

FANTASYLAND

• Alice in Wonderland • Casey Jr. Circus Train • Fantasyland Theatre
• Matterhorn Bobsleds • Mr. Toad's Wild Ride • Pinocchio's Daring Journey
• Royal Theatre at Fantasy Faire • Sleeping Beauty Castle Walk-Through
• Snow White's Scary Adventures • Storybook Land Canal Boats

FRONTIERLAND

• *Fantasmic!* (at Disney's Hollywood Studios) • The Golden Horseshoe
• Sailing Ship *Columbia*

MAIN STREET, U.S.A.

• *The Disneyland Story,* presenting *Great Moments with Mr. Lincoln*

MICKEY'S TOONTOWN

• Chip 'n Dale Treehouse • Gadget's Go Coaster • Goofy's Playhouse
• Mickey's House • Minnie's House • *Miss Daisy,* Donald's Boat
• Roger Rabbit's Car Toon Spin

TOMORROWLAND

• Disneyland Monorail System • Finding Nemo Submarine Voyage • *Jedi Training: Trials of the Temple* (at Disney's Hollywood Studios) • Star Tours—The Adventures Continue (at Disney's Hollywood Studios) • Star Wars Launch Bay (at Disney's Hollywood Studios) • Tomorrowland Theater

PART ONE

PLANNING *Before* YOU LEAVE HOME

■ GATHERING INFORMATION

IN ADDITION TO THIS GUIDE, we recommend that you first visit our website, **touringplans.com,** which offers essential tools for planning your trip and saving you time and money. Our blog, **blog.touringplans .com,** lists breaking news for the Disneyland Resort and Disney theme parks worldwide. Our other website, **theunofficialguides.com,** is dedicated to news about our guidebooks, as well as a blog with posts from Unofficial Guide authors. You can also sign up for the "Unofficial Guide Newsletter," containing even more travel tips and special offers.

Touringplans.com also offers computer-optimized touring plans for Disneyland and Disney California Adventure (DCA). With these, you choose the attractions you want to experience, including character greetings, parades, fireworks, meals, and midday breaks, and we'll give you a step-by-step itinerary for your specific dates of travel, showing you how to see everything with minimal waits in line. The touring plans can incorporate any FastPasses you retrieve.

You can update the touring plans when you're in the parks too. Let's say that your touring plan calls for riding The Haunted Mansion next, but your family really needs an ice cream break and 30 minutes out of the sun. Get the ice cream and take the break. When you're done, click the OPTIMIZE button on your plan, and it will be updated with what to do next. The ability to redo your plan allows you to recover from any situation while still minimizing your waits for the rest of the day.

Another really popular part of **touringplans.com** is our Crowd Calendar, which shows crowd projections for Disneyland and DCA for every day of the year. Look up the dates of your visit, and the calendar will not only show the projected wait times for each day but will also indicate for each day which theme park will be the least crowded. Historical wait times are also available, so you can see how crowded the parks were last year for your upcoming trip dates.

The website also has complete dining menus, including wine lists, for every food cart, stand, kiosk, counter-service restaurant, and sit-down restaurant in the Disneyland Resort. The whole thing is searchable too, so you can find every restaurant in DCA that serves steak (and its prices), or see which snacks are available in New Orleans Square. Updated constantly, these menus represent the most accurate collection of Disney dining information available anywhere.

The touring plans, menus, Crowd Calendar, and more are available in Lines, our mobile application, which provides continuous real-time updates on wait times at Disneyland. Using in-park staff and updates sent in by readers, Lines shows you the current wait and FastPass distribution times at every attraction in every park, as well as our estimated actual waits for these attractions for the rest of today. For example, Lines will tell you that the posted wait time for Space Mountain is 60 minutes, and that based on what we know about how Disney manages Space Mountain's queue, the actual time you'll probably wait in line is 48 minutes. Lines is the only Disney app that shows you both posted and actual wait times.

Lines also has an online chat feature, where folks can ask questions and give travel tips. Hundreds of "Liners" interact every day in discussions that stay remarkably on-topic for an Internet forum, and the group organizes regular in-park meets. We're thrilled with it. One couple from Easton, Pennsylvania, found Lines especially useful:

> I don't know what we would have done without The Unofficial Guide to Disneyland and the Lines app. This was our first and possibly only trip to Disneyland. We were able to do everything we wanted and ride many big attractions like the Matterhorn several times. We also enjoyed using the menu feature on the site and app. I was able to plan all our meals before arriving at a restaurant instead of realizing later that there were no good vegetarian options.

As did this family from Folsom, California:

> The Lines app proved to be absolutely invaluable on our trip. Without Lines, there is no way we could have accomplished nearly as much as we did. We consulted it constantly. We used Lines to find out what was offline and what had a reasonable wait time. For instance, we were going to give up on Radiator Springs Racers until we noticed that the single-rider line had a reasonable wait. I cannot recommend Lines highly enough to anyone going to the Disney parks!

Lines is available free to **touringplans.com** subscribers for the Apple iPhone and iPad at the iTunes Store (search for "TouringPlans") and for Android devices at the Google Play Store. Owners of other phones can use the Web-based version at **m.touringplans.com**.

As long as you have that smartphone handy while visiting the parks, we and your fellow *Unofficial Guide* readers would love it if you could report on the actual wait times you get while you're there. Run Lines, log in to your user account, and click +TIME in the upper right corner to help everyone out. We'll use that information to update the wait times for everyone in the park, and make everyone's lives just a little bit better.

Much of our Web content—including the menus, resort photos and video, and errata for this book—is completely free for anyone to use. Access to part of the site, most notably the Crowd Calendar, touring plans, and in-park wait times, requires a small subscription fee (current-book owners get a substantial discount). This nominal charge helps keep us online and costs less than a souvenir bucket of popcorn at Disneyland. Plus **touringplans.com** offers a 45-day money-back guarantee.

A subscriber from Arvada, Colorado, wrote in to say:

> *I purchased a membership to your website approximately one month before we went to Disneyland in the summer. I would never go without it again. I knew what kind of crowds to expect in advance, and not having to ask nine people what they wanted to do or go on next was great. Lunch and dinner were planned at certain times, and we even made adjustments to your recommended plan, so my 4½-year-old niece got to ride a couple of the kids' rides right away.*

In addition we recommend that you obtain copies of the following publications:

1. DISNEYLAND RESORT VACATION-PLANNING VIDEOS Disney has discontinued mailing DVD-based vacation-planning toolkits, instead shifting to online videos advertising the resort's offerings. To view them, you'll need to fill out a short survey at **disneyplanning.com.** You can also access videos about Walt Disney World, Disney Cruise Line, and other Disney destinations from the same website.

2. _DISNEYLAND GUIDEBOOK FOR GUESTS WITH DISABILITIES_ If members of your party are sight- or hearing-impaired or partially or wholly nonambulatory, you will find this small guide very helpful. Special guides are also available for guests with cognitive disabilities, including autism spectrum disorders. Disney does not mail them, but copies are readily available at the park. You can also download the guides at **disneyland .disney.go.com/guest-services/guests-with-disabilities.**

3. _HOTELCOUPONS.COM SOUTHWEST GUIDE_ A good source of lodging discounts throughout California, the *HotelCoupons.com Southwest Guide* can be downloaded for free at **hotelcoupons.com.** You can also obtain a printed copy by calling ☎ 800-222-3948, Monday–Friday, 8:30 a.m.– 5:30 p.m. Eastern time, or e-mailing **custserv@travelmediagroup.com;** you will be charged $4 ($6 Canadian) for postage and handling. Similar guides to other states are also available.

Disneyland Main Information Phone and Website

The following website and phone numbers provide general information. Inquiries may be expedited by using phone numbers specific to the nature of the inquiry (other phone numbers are listed elsewhere in this chapter, under their relevant topics, and in the table on the next page). If you don't mind interacting with an artificial intelligence, you can call

IMPORTANT DISNEYLAND RESORT PHONE NUMBERS	
Anaheim Travel Information	☎ 714-765-8888
Ask Otto Automated Attraction Info	☎ 714-520-7090
Dining Reservations	☎ 714-781-3463, Option 3
Disability Services	☎ 407-560-2547
Disney Cruise Line	☎ 800-951-3532
Disney Guided Tours	☎ 714-781-8687
Disneyland Hotel	☎ 714-778-6600
Disneyland Resort Room Reservations	☎ 714-956-6425
Disneyland Vacation Packages	☎ 714-520-5060
Foreign Language Assistance	☎ 714-781-7290
Grand Californian Hotel	☎ 714-635-2300
Lost & Found	☎ 714-781-4765
Paradise Pier Hotel	☎ 714-999-0990
Premium Viewing Dining Packages	☎ 714-781-3463, Option 2

☎ 714-520-7090 and Ask Otto, Disneyland's automated information hot line, about ride wait times and upcoming shows.

Disneyland Guest Relations
☎ 714-781-4565 for recorded information;
☎ 714-781-7290 for live operator; **disneyland.com**

The Phone from Hell

Sometimes it is virtually impossible to get through on the Disneyland information numbers listed above. When you get through, you will get a recording that offers various information options. If none of the recorded options answer your question, you will have to hold for a live person. Eat before you call—you may have a long wait. If, after repeated attempts, you get tired of a busy signal in your ear or, worse, 20 minutes' worth of singing mice warbling "Cinderelly" in alto falsettos while you are on hold, call the Disneyland Hotel at ☎ 714-778-6600.

RECOMMENDED WEBSITES

A NUMBER OF GOOD Disneyland information sources are online. The following are brief profiles of our favorites:

BEST OFFICIAL THEME PARK SITES The official Disneyland website, **disney land.com,** has been upgraded in recent years to finally catch up with its sister site, **disneyworld.com,** in areas such as online dining reservations. You must create an account before booking or log in with an existing My Disney Experience account if you've visited Walt Disney World. There's a ton of information, though it usually takes a lot of clicks to find what you're looking for.

The Universal Studios website is **universalstudioshollywood.com.** Like the Disneyland site, it has a lot of information, though there are no online dining reservations or registration process. Both sites are filled with photos and videos that can be slow to load, so as far as your Internet connection is concerned, be high-speed or be gone.

BEST OFFICIAL AREA WEBSITE   Anaheimoc.org is the official website of the Anaheim–Orange County Visitor & Convention Bureau. You'll find everything from hotels and restaurants to weather and driving directions on this site.

BEST GENERAL UNOFFICIAL WEBSITES We recommend the following websites for general information related to the Disneyland Resort.

Mouseplanet.com is a comprehensive resource for Disneyland data, offering features and reviews by guest writers, information on the Disney theme parks, discussion groups, and news. The site includes an interactive Disney restaurant and hotel review page, where users can voice opinions on their Disney dining and lodging experiences. We particularly enjoy the weekly Disneyland update column.

Disneytouristblog.com, run by park photographer extraordinaire and Touring Plans contributor Tom Bricker, hosts a comprehensive introduction to planning a Disneyland vacation, along with reporting on more exotic Disney destinations in France, China, and Japan.

Deb Wills's **allears.net,** which maintains a fantastic site for Walt Disney World, also has a growing Disneyland sister site. It includes extensive information about the Disney resorts and attractions, including reader reviews. The site is updated several times a week and includes Disney restaurant menus, ticketing information, maps, and more.

Wdwinfo.com has a vibrant Disneyland section that includes up-to-date dining menus, attraction reviews, touring tips, and more.

BEST DISNEYLAND HISTORY WEBSITE At **yesterland.com** you can visit the Disneyland of the past, where retired Disneyland attractions are brought back to life through vivid descriptions and historical photographs. Yesterland attraction descriptions relate what it was once like to experience the Flying Saucers, the Mine Train through Nature's Wonderland, the *Tahitian Terrace*, and dozens of other rides, shows, and restaurants.

BEST WEBSITE FOR RUMORS AND THE INSIDE SCOOP   Jimhillmedia.com is perfectly attuned to what's going on behind the scenes—Jim Hill always has good gossip. He works with The Unofficial Guides as our resident historian and contributes sidebars and anecdotes to our Disney titles.

BEST DISNEYLAND NEWS SITES   Micechat.com, with a dedicated group of local editors, is the definitive on-the-ground coverage of the Disneyland Resort. Be sure to check out Dusty Sage's regular update columns that stay on the pulse of the parks, complete with photos. **Mouseplanet.com** and Robert Niles's **themeparkinsider.com** are other great sources for breaking Southern California theme park news, as is Brady MacDonald of the *Los Angeles Times* (**latimes.com/travel/themeparks**). For official news, the Disney Parks Blog (**disneyparks.com/blog**) covers news from all Disney resorts. For Universal Studios Hollywood updates, check out **insideuniversal.net** and **ushtoday.com.**

BEST MONEY-SAVING SITE Mousesavers.com specializes in finding you the deepest discounts on hotels, park admissions, and rental cars. Mouse-Savers does not actually sell travel but rather unearths and publishes special discounts that you can use. It's the first place we look for deals when we go to Disneyland Resort.

BEST DISNEY DISCUSSION BOARDS The best online discussion of all things Disney can be found at **micechat.com/forums, mousepad.mouseplanet .com,** and **disboards.com.** With tens of thousands of members and millions of posts, they are the most active and popular discussion boards online. There is also a rousing chat room inside our own mobile application, Lines (learn more at **touringplans.com/lines**).

BEST DISNEY PODCASTS Our favorite Disneyland-centric podcast is *Mousetalgia,* found at **mousetalgia.com,** which covers Disneyland, Disney California Adventure, and everything else Disney. The hosts appreciate the history of the resort while maintaining balanced coverage of new Disneyland developments. **Seasonpasspodcast.com** has breaking news and in-depth interviews with theme park designers and executives from Disneyland and parks around the world. Hosted by industry veterans (and fans!), the show provides detailed discussions about how and why theme parks work. And if you want warts-and-all tales from behind the scenes of Mickey's kingdoms, don't miss *The Unofficial Guide Disney Dish Podcast with Jim Hill,* hosted by coauthor Len Testa.

BEST DISNEY TWITTER FEEDS If you want your Disney news and rumors in 140 character bites, follow these prolific park Tweeters:

@datelinedisneyland   @thedisneyblog   @disneyland   @disneylandcats
@disneylandtoday   @disneyparks   @latimesfunland   @micechat   @ocregister
@touringplans   @guyselga   @skubersky

BEST DISNEYLAND YOUTUBE CHANNELS We don't necessarily advocate spoiling attractions you haven't yet experienced in person, but YouTube videos can be very useful for assuaging anxious children (see page 146) or reliving the magic once you return home. The TouringPlans YouTube channel (**you tube.com/touringplans**) hosts a wealth of clips from every Disney park, including nifty 360-degree virtual-reality videos that can be used with a Google Cardboard viewer for an immersive park visit without leaving your living room. Other good sources for Disney park videos are the official Disney Parks channel (**youtube.com/disneyparks**), *Attractions* Magazine (**youtube.com/attractionsmagazine**), and SoCal Attractions 360 (**youtube .com/socalattractions360**), which uploads 4K ultra-low-light footage of dark rides that look sharper and brighter than actually being there.

BEST DISNEYLAND MOBILE APPS Smartphone apps are a great way to stay up to date on Disneyland info inside and outside the parks. First and foremost, we suggest installing our Lines app, which is free from the Apple and Google app store; certain features require an active subscription to **touringplans.com.** Additionally, Disneyland offers a fairly robust free app with official park hours, attraction wait times, show schedules, restaurant menus, and interactive maps. You can even use it to purchase or store admission tickets and link to all your PhotoPass pictures; you'll need to register for a free Disney online account to use these features. It's best to download this app in advance via Wi-Fi, so you don't waste time and bandwidth inside the park.

ADMISSION OPTIONS

THEME PARK ADMISSION OPTIONS can be a bit complicated at Disneyland Resort. For starters, you have three things to decide:

1. How many days admission you'll need.
2. What date you wish to attend, if only visiting for one day.
3. Whether you want to go to both Disneyland Park and Disney California Adventure on the same day. This is known as park hopping.

Multiday tickets expire 13 days after the first use, so you don't want to buy more days than you'll need. Needless to say, tickets expire after you've used the number of days purchased even if 13 days haven't passed yet. Finally, all passes must be used before they expire at the end of the year after they were purchased; passes purchased in 2018 expire in December 2019. That means you can't stockpile current tickets as a hedge against future inflation, but Guest Services will let you pay the difference and upgrade a wholly unused expired ticket to a new one at current prices, as long as it costs the same or more than you originally paid.

All admissions can be purchased at the park entrance, at the Disneyland Resort hotels, from the Walt Disney Travel Sales Center, on

ADMISSION OPTIONS	ADULT (age 10 and UP)	CHILD (ages 3–9)
One-Day, One Park (depending on season)	$97–$124	$91–$118
One-Day Park Hopper (depending on season)	$157–$174	$151–$168
Two-Day, One Park Per Day	$199	$187
Two-Day Park Hopper	$244	$232
Three-Day, One Park Per Day with Magic Morning	$270	$258
Three-Day Park Hopper with Magic Morning	$315	$303
Four-Day, One Park Per Day with Magic Morning	$290	$275
Four-Day Park Hopper with Magic Morning	$335	$320
Five-Day, One Park Per Day with Magic Morning	$305	$290
Five-Day Park Hopper with Magic Morning	$350	$335
Southern California Select Annual Passport (many blockout dates; only available to residents of certain zip codes)	$339	$339
Southern California Annual Passport (some blockout dates)	$469	$469
Deluxe Annual Passport (some blockout dates)	$619	$619
Signature Annual Passport (a few blockout dates; parking included)	$849	$849
Signature Plus Annual Passport (no blockout dates; parking included)	$1,049	$1,049
Disney Premier Passport (no blockout dates; valid at all California and Florida parks)	$1,439	$1,439

the Disneyland website, and at most Disney stores in the western United States. You can also now purchase single and multiday tickets through your smartphone using the Disneyland app, though these passes don't include any discounts. One- and 2-year-olds are exempt from admission fees.

Admission Costs and Available Discounts

It's possible to obtain discounts on all multiday tickets, but only in the 1%–7% range. You can purchase tickets in advance with Magic Morning Hours for full gate prices at **disneyland.com**. These

unofficial TIP
The money you can save makes researching Disney's dizzying array of ticket options worthwhile.

tickets allow you to enter only Disneyland Park on select days 1 hour earlier than the general public one time during your visit. The feature is offered only on three-, four-, and five-day tickets purchased in advance of your visit. You can learn about any special seasonal discounts offered directly from Disney at **disneyland.disney.go.com/offers-discounts.**

If you purchase tickets on the Disneyland website, you can choose between "hard" tickets, which will be shipped to you, or e-tickets, which can be downloaded as PDF files and printed at home or scanned from your mobile device. An e-ticket printed from your home computer will show two bar codes. A cast member will scan these at the turnstiles. Once the bar codes are read, the cast member can issue your actual ticket.

The deepest discounts we've found are from **ARES Travel** (**arestravel.com**). ARES usually beats the Disney advance purchase price by $2–$10 per ticket and also includes the Magic Morning feature. Guests may pick up their tickets at any main entrance window; a $2-per-ticket convenience fee applies. You can order online or call ☎ 800-434-7894. You must provide the first date you intend to visit when purchasing the ticket, and exchanging the voucher for your ticket requires waiting in line at a ticket booth, which can be a bit of a hassle. Another option is **The Cleaver Brothers' Discount Tickets & Tours** (**discountticketsandtours.com**), located at The Grand Legacy at the Park hotel on Harbor Boulevard and at Anaheim GardenWalk. It sells legitimate multiday tickets that can be taken straight to the turnstiles for $2–$10 under Disney's gate price. Whatever you do, never buy cheap Disney tickets on eBay, Craigslist, or off the street. The passes are probably partially used and not authorized for resale, and Mickey will not give you your money back if you are turned away at the turnstiles.

If you plan to visit other Southern California attractions in addition to Disneyland, you might want to consider a **CityPass.** CityPass includes a Three-Day Park Hopper for Disneyland Park and DCA, including early entry to a designated park for one day. Also included are one day's admission each to Legoland California and SeaWorld San Diego. Costing $353 for adults and $324 for children ages 3–9, the pass is valid for 13 days after the first use. If you plan to visit all these parks, it will save you about 25% on admissions. If you don't use all of the admissions, however, you will save little or nothing by purchasing the CityPass. The pass does not include dining or shopping discounts. Details concerning other CityPass destinations are available at **citypass.com/southern-california.**

Military discounts are available for all Disney theme parks, usually in the 7%–25% range; in 2017 a Three-Day Park Hopper was offered for less than the regular price of a One-Day Park Hopper. Check with your base Morale, Welfare, & Recreation office for info. Be aware that one member of your party must show military ID at the park turnstiles to use the tickets, so you can't purchase them for friends or relatives you won't be traveling with. Learn about current military discount offers at **disneyland.disney.go.com/offers-discounts /military-tickets-discount.**

Disneyland Resort and other area attractions sometimes offer discounted afternoon and evening tickets for conventioneers. See **disney meetings.com.**

Admission prices increase from time to time. For planning your budget, however, the table on page 20 provides a fair estimate. Note that Walt Disney World tickets are *not* valid for admission to Disneyland, with the sole exception of bicoastal Premier Annual Passports.

Single-Day Tickets with Variable Pricing

In 2016 Disney radically revamped its prices for single-day visits to its California and Florida theme parks by introducing a new demand-based variable pricing structure. In the past, a one-day admission to Disneyland cost the same whether you were visiting on an empty off-season weekday or the busiest holiday of the year. Now, Disney has followed the lead of airline and ski resort industries by instituting three seasonal tiers— value, regular, and peak—for all single-day tickets, charging more money for tickets on the busiest days and offering a modest discount during periods of lower attendance.

The price difference between a value and peak single day is currently $27 for one-park tickets or $17 for park hoppers. That's probably not enough of a premium to dictate plans for most out-of-state visitors, whose vacation schedules are dictated by school and work schedules, but it does encourage locals to shift their visits toward cheaper days, perversely pumping up crowds when the parks would otherwise be empty, without significantly shrinking them on peak days.

Because of the tiered pricing structure, you must be certain of which date you will visit Disneyland when buying your ticket, or risk buying a more expensive ticket than you need. A peak day ticket is valid on any day of the year, while a regular one is good during regular or value season. Value tickets are only accepted on those select days, but they (or any other admission) can be upgraded to any more expensive pass, presuming the park isn't sold out.

With a one-day ticket, you may exit and return to the park on the same day as many times as you like. Disneyland now photographs every guest upon first entry for identification purposes; be prepared to have your pass (and face) scanned shortly before passing the turnstiles, with your picture replacing the old exit handstamps for readmission.

Multiday Tickets

These are good for two, three, four, or five days, respectively. Multiday tickets are not affected by the single-day pricing seasons and can be used on any day of the year. These multiday tickets do not have to be used on consecutive days, but they do expire 13 days after their first use, which must happen on or before the last day of the year after purchase (currently December 31, 2019, for tickets bought in 2018). If you mistakenly bought multiday tickets because you were not aware of the 13-day expiration, call ☎ 714-781-7290 or ☎ 714-781-4565 and ask to be connected to Guest Communications, which has the authority to issue you a voucher for the unused days on your ticket.

All three-, four-, and five-day Disneyland tickets also include one Magic Morning, which entitles you to enter Disneyland early on Tuesday, Thursday, or Saturday; see page 30 for more details.

Any time before a pass expires, you can apply the full original value of the ticket toward the cost of a higher-priced ticket. If you buy a Four-Day Park Hopper ticket, for example, and then decide you'd rather have an Annual Passport, you can apply the full original value of the former toward the purchase of the latter. The maximum number of days you can purchase on a standard Disneyland ticket is five. After that you have to upgrade to an annual pass or buy another ticket, which makes a six- or seven-day visit extremely cost-ineffective. Upgraded passes expire on the same 13-day deadline date as the original ticket; annual passes expire one year from the first usage of the original ticket.

Park Hopper Tickets

By default, tickets without Park Hopper require you to choose one park or the other to visit each day. All single and multiday tickets may be purchased with the Park Hopper option, which allows you to visit both Disneyland Park and Disney California Adventure during the same day. The Park Hopper premium on a single-day admission is quite pricey (currently $50–$60, depending on season), but on a five-day pass that drops to only $9 per day.

If you are spending more than two days at Disneyland Resort, we strongly encourage you to spring for the park-to-park access. The ease of walking from one park to the other makes the Park Hopper premium more than worth it.

Annual Passports

Disneyland Resort also revamped its annual pass offerings, apparently in an attempt to tame its legions of local pass holders. The Signature Plus Passport (which replaced the former Premium pass) is the only Disneyland annual pass that is good for an entire year with no block-out dates, and it includes self-parking in the theme park garages and lots. The pass costs $1,049 and is good for admission to both parks 365 days a year during normal operating hours, with use of all attractions (excluding arcades), up to 15% discounts at most resort dining locations, and 20% off most merchandise. Signature Passports ($849) are valid every day except for the week before Christmas to New Year's Day; it includes the same free parking and discounts as Signature Plus. If you are a bicoastal Disneyphile for whom price is no object, the Disney Premier Passport ($1,439) permits unlimited access to any Disney theme park or water park in Anaheim or Orlando, along with free parking and 15%–20% discounts. Premier, Signature, and Signature Plus passes also include free unlimited PhotoPass digital picture downloads (see page 107 for details).

Disney Deluxe Annual Passports ($619) are valid 312 days of the year, with 53 blockout dates around Easter, Thanksgiving, Christmas, and most Saturdays. Deluxe pass holders get a 10% discount on most food and merchandise but have to pay full price for parking.

Disneyland offers a Southern California Select Annual Passport ($339) valid 170 days per year to residents in qualifying zip codes. Locals can purchase any passport on an installment plan, paying $97 up front and making interest-free payments starting at $20.17 a month.

unofficial **TIP**
If you are a local who visits Disneyland five or more days each year, or a tourist making at least two five-day trips, an annual pass is a potential money saver.

Prices for children are the same as those for adults on all annual passports.

If you purchase your annual passport in July of this year and schedule your visit next year for June, you'll cover two years' vacations with a single pass. Admission passes can be ordered by calling ☎ 714-781-4565 or visiting the Disneyland website. They can also be purchased in advance from Disneyland Resort hotels, Disney Stores in the western United States, and the Walt Disney Travel Sales Center at ☎ 800-854-3104.

Rides and Shows Closed for Repairs or Maintenance

Rides and shows at Disneyland parks are sometimes closed for maintenance or repairs. In particular, visitors to Disneyland Park from late 2017 through 2019 may find certain attractions—especially around Frontierland—disrupted due to construction on the Star Wars expansion. If a certain attraction is important to you, call ☎ 714-781-7290 before your visit to make sure that it will be operating. We also maintain an unofficial schedule of current and upcoming closures at **touringplans .com/disneyland-resort/closures**. A mother from Dover, Massachusetts, wrote us, lamenting:

> We were disappointed to find Space Mountain and the Riverboat closed for repairs. We felt that a large chunk [of the park] was not working, yet the tickets were still full price and expensive!

Even if an attraction isn't on the disabled list, unplanned outages may prevent you from riding, as a woman from Antioch, Illinois, discovered:

The biggest drawback of the whole trip was the numerous break-downs of the rides. We were aware of Big Thunder Mountain and a few other rides closed for long-term scheduled maintenance, but a lot of the rides broke down as soon as we headed to them! The only thing that didn't have any breakdowns were the cash registers!

HOW MUCH DOES IT COST TO GO TO DISNEYLAND FOR A DAY?

LET'S SAY THAT WE HAVE A FAMILY OF FOUR—Mom, Dad, Tim (age 12), and Tami (age 8)—driving their own car. Because they plan to be in the area for a few days, they intend to buy the Three-Day Park Hopper tickets. A typical day would cost $683.43, excluding lodging and transportation. See the table below for a breakdown of expenses.

HOW MUCH DOES A DAY COST?	
Breakfast for four at Denny's with tax and tip	$40.09
Disneyland parking fee	$20.00
One day's admission for four on a Three-Day Park Hopper Pass	$416.00
Dad: *Adult three-day is $315 divided by three days = $105*	
Mom: *Adult three-day is $315 divided by three days = $105*	
Tim: *Adult three-day is $315 divided by three days = $105*	
Tami: *Child three-day is $303 divided by three days = $101*	
Morning break (soda or coffee)	$14.61
Fast-food lunch (burger, fries, and soda), no tip	$52.34
Afternoon break (soda and popcorn)	$34.34
Dinner in park at counter-service restaurant with tax	$58.64
Souvenirs (Mickey T-shirts for Tim and Tami) with tax*	$47.41
One-day total (without lodging or transportation)	**$683.43**

* Cheer up—you won't have to buy souvenirs every day.

TIMING *Your* VISIT

SELECTING THE TIME OF YEAR FOR YOUR VISIT

unofficial **TIP**
You can't pick a less crowded time to visit Disneyland Resort than late August through September.

CROWDS ARE LARGEST at Disneyland during the summer (Memorial Day–Labor Day) and during specific holiday periods throughout the rest of the year. The busiest time of all is December 25–January 1. Thanksgiving weekend, the week of Presidents Day, spring break for schools and colleges, and the two weeks around Easter are also extremely busy. To give you some idea of what *busy* means at Disneyland, more than 88,000 people have toured Disneyland Park in one day! While this level of attendance is far from typical, the possibility of its occurrence should prevent all but the ignorant and the foolish from challenging this mega-attraction at its busiest periods.

TOP 10 AMERICAN THEME PARKS		
THEME PARK	ANNUAL ATTENDANCE	AVERAGE DAILY ATTENDANCE
Walt Disney World's Magic Kingdom	20.4 million	55,877
Disneyland Park	17.9 million	49,159
Walt Disney World's Epcot	11.7 million	32,088
Disney's Animal Kingdom	10.8 million	29,710
Disney's Hollywood Studios	10.8 million	29,523
Universal Studios Florida	10.0 million	27,392
Universal Orlando's Islands of Adventure	9.4 million	25,649
Disney California Adventure	9.3 million	25,466
Universal Studios Hollywood	8.1 million	22,153
SeaWorld Florida	4.4 million	12,060

Source: Themed Entertainment Association

Historically, after Thanksgiving weekend until the week before Christmas was the least-busy time of all, but recently late August–September has taken that title. The next slowest times are January 8–early March (excepting Martin Luther King Jr. Day and Presidents' Day weekends) and the week following Easter to Memorial Day weekend. At the risk of being blasphemous, our research team was so impressed with the relative ease of touring in the fall and other off-season periods that we would rather take our children out of school for a few days than do battle with the summer crowds. Though we strongly recommend going to Disneyland in the fall or in the spring, it should be noted that there are certain trade-offs. The parks often close earlier on fall, winter, and spring days, sometimes early enough to eliminate evening parades, fireworks, and other live-entertainment offerings such as *Fantasmic!* Also, because these are slow times of the year at Disneyland, you can anticipate that some rides and attractions may be closed for maintenance or renovation. Finally, if the parks open late and close early, it's tough to see everything, even if the crowds are light.

unofficial TIP
In our opinion, the risk of encountering colder weather and closed attractions during an off-season visit to Disneyland is worth it.

Most readers who have tried Disney parks at varying times of the year concur. A wintertime visitor from Sacramento, California, agrees:

Though there was a torrential storm on two days of our four-day visit, I can safely say that I will never visit in high season again. Yes, we were wet. Yes, attractions and rides were closed for refurb. BUT the longest line we waited in was 25 minutes to see the princesses. Characters were EVERYWHERE, and access to them was easy as pie. There were no issues with heat or sunburn. And we saved a boatload of money.

Not to overstate the case: We want to emphasize that you can have a great time at the Disneyland parks regardless of the time of year or crowd level. In fact, a primary objective of this guide is to make the parks fun and manageable for those readers who visit during the busier times of year. Since late 2015, we've noticed that crowds at both parks during the fall and late winter/early spring have far surpassed the attendance of previous years. A New Orleans couple describes their experience:

> Everything we read led us to believe October after Columbus Day and before Halloween week would be relatively less crowded. Nothing prepared us for the crowds we experienced. I may not have understood the crowd estimates, but barely being able to move was not what I expected.

The basic rule of thumb is that Disneyland is more crowded when school is out and less crowded when kids are in school. However, Disney has become increasingly adept at loading slow periods of the year with special events, conventions, food festivals, and the like. Discounts on rooms, variable pricing for single-day tickets, and annual pass holder blockouts also figure in. We initially thought the larger off-season crowds were an anomaly, but they have persisted into winter and spring of 2017. The increased attendance has not gone unnoticed by long-time visitors, like this family from Redmond, California:

> For the first time, Disneyland felt like an amusement park—just a collection of rides—rather than a pleasant, away-from-reality, immersive environment. Most likely because it was so crowded, so consistently, that I couldn't see, hear, or smell much aside from a sea of people. So while I recommended Disneyland or DCA to others in the past, I'd now instead recommend that they consider Universal or a different park if there were a potential for smaller crowds.

However, there are still some periods of more moderate attendance, such as late summer, as one family from Vancouver, Canada, found:

> With many California schools starting in late August, we found a sweet spot to visit during the second-to-last week of August when our kids are still on vacation. The parks were still open late and all entertainment was still running, but the crowds were down from the summer peak.

The bottom line is that Disneyland can be packed at any time, and you need to dig a little deeper than merely the time of year to pinpoint the least-crowded periods. For a calendar of scheduled Disney events, see **touringplans.com/disneyland-resort/events.** Other factors affecting crowding and long lines include a combination of closed rides and an improving US economy. As a result, we've added more data about ride closures and economic indicators to our crowd level forecasts.

Of course, crowds are not the only consideration when deciding what time of year to visit Disneyland. Holidays are celebrated at Disneyland like nowhere else, and the festive decor is almost worth the price of admission. The parks are decked out for Halloween from late September until the end of October. Be aware that after-hours extra-cost Halloween parties (tickets are $72–$99) cause Disneyland (and possibly DCA in 2018) to close early to day guests on several evenings in the fall, as a Tucson, Arizona, family found:

> The Halloween event from mid-September to the end of October changes the low season to a zoo. Every local with an annual pass showed up in the afternoon. The park closed early for this event, and DCA backed up because of the early closure of Disneyland Park.

Christmas trappings transform Disneyland Park from mid-November until after New Year's Day. There's also a Christmas parade, and several attractions such as The Haunted Mansion and It's a Small World offer a special holiday version. Some holiday entertainment (such as the special parade and fireworks) may require a special ticket to an after-hours event, if long-running rumors of Orlando's popular Mickey's Very Merry Christmas Party migrating westward ever pan out. Finally, beware of Grad Night late-night parties for high school seniors on select days each May and June. The kids have after-hours access to Disney California Adventure, but they also get admission to both parks during the daytime and make their presence known in the crowded queues starting midafternoon.

unofficial **TIP**
If it's not your first trip to Disneyland and you must join the holiday-weekend crowds, you may have just as much fun enjoying Disney's fantastic array of shows, parades, and fireworks as you would riding the rides.

THE SPOILER

SO YOU CHOOSE YOUR OFF-SEASON DATES and then find it almost impossible to find a hotel room. What gives? In all probability you've been foiled by a mammoth convention or trade show at the Anaheim Convention Center. One of the largest and busiest convention venues in the country, the convention center hosts meetings with as many as 100,000 attendees and was recently expanded in a $180-million project that added 200,000 square feet to the center. The sheer numbers alone guarantee that hotel rooms will be hard to find. Compounding the problem is the fact that most business travelers don't have room-mates. Thus a trade show with 8,000 people registered might suck up 13,000 rooms (including people who registered late)! The final straw, as you might expect, is that room rates climb into the stratosphere based on the high demand and scarcity of supply. In regard to increased crowds at the theme parks, it's estimated that less than 10% of convention attendees will find time to enjoy the parks. It's also true, however, that business travelers are more likely to bring their spouse and even kids to a convention held in Anaheim. The bottom line is that you don't want to schedule your vacation while a major event is going on at the convention center. To help you avoid major trade shows and conventions, we've created a calendar of meetings scheduled through February 2019, showing the number of expected attendees of each (see the opposite page). In addition, the Disney parks can sometimes be overrun by events not associated with the convention center, such as RunDisney

ANAHEIM CONVENTION and SPECIAL EVENTS CALENDAR

DATES	CONVENTION/ EVENT	NUMBER OF ATTENDEES
2017		
Oct. 4–11	Medical Group Mgmt. Ass. Annual Meeting	10,000
Oct. 28–Nov. 6	BlizzCon	35,000
Nov. 6–17	American Heart Association Scientific Sessions	25,000
Nov. 10–12	Run Disney Avengers Super Heroes Half Marathon	51,000
Nov. 19–20	Ass. of Christian Schools Int'l Prof. Development Conf.	15,000
Nov. 23–26	ESPN Events Wooden Legacy	5,000
Dec. 3–12	Playstation Experience	15,000
Dec. 10–18	Milton H. Erickson Foundation Evolution of Psychotherapy	7,000
2018		
Jan. 15–31	The NAMM Show	100,000
Feb. 1–9	UBM Advanced Manufacturing Expo & Conference	42,000
Feb. 20–26	United Spirit Association Spirit Nationals	22,800
Feb. 21–Mar. 2	Commodity Classic	10,000
Mar. 7–10	Natural Products Expo West	71,000
Mar. 13–19	Archdiocese of Los Angeles RECongress	40,000
Mar. 13–19	United Spirit Association All Star Nationals	6,800
Mar. 20–26	WonderCon Anaheim	40,000
Apr. 5–9	American Championships American Showcase	22,000
May 15–20	California Dental Ass. The Art & Science of Dentistry	30,000
May 28–June 4	Pri-Med Western Conference and Exhibition	7,000
July 3–7	AVID Center Summer Institute	5,000
July 9–15	LifeVantage Corp. Elite Academy	12,000
July 13–22	Amateur Athletic Union National Jr. Olympic Games	5,000
Aug. 2–9	Tom Ferry—Your Coach Success Summit	6,000
Aug. 31–Sep. 11	The Home Entertainment (T.H.E) Show Newport	10,000
Sep. 20–29	Solar Power International	10,000
Oct. 18–24	ARMA International Annual Meeting	5,000
Nov. 28–Dec. 7	American Soc. of Health-System Pharmacists Annual Meeting	20,000
2019		
Jan. 14–30	The NAMM Show	100,000
Feb. 2–9	UBM Advanced Manufacturing Expo & Conference	42,000
Feb. 12–18	United Spirit Association Spirit Nationals	22,800
Feb. 12–18	United Spirit Association Dance Nationals	9,500
Feb. 15–21	American Rental Association Annual Convention	6,000

footraces (January, May, August, and November; **rundisney.com**) and unofficial fan gatherings like Dapper Day (April and November; **dapper day.com**) and Bats Day (May; **batsday.net**). Schedules vary each year, so check the respective websites when planning your trip.

SELECTING THE DAY OF THE WEEK FOR YOUR VISIT

THE CROWDS AT WALT DISNEY WORLD in Florida comprise mostly out-of-state visitors. Not necessarily so at Disneyland Resort, which, along with Six Flags Magic Mountain, serves as an often-frequented recreational resource for the greater Los Angeles and San Diego communities. To many Southern Californians, Disneyland Park and Disney California Adventure are their private theme parks. Yearly passes are available at less cost than a year's membership to the YMCA.

What all this means is that weekends are usually packed. If you have to go on a weekend, your best bet is to go on Sunday in the morning or after 5 p.m., or visit on a Saturday when most annual pass holders are blocked out from attending (visit **disneyland.disney .go.com/passes/blockout-dates** for details).

During the summer, Monday and Friday are very busy, Tuesday and Wednesday are usually less so, and Thursday is normally the slowest day of all. During the off-season (September–May, holiday periods excepted), Thursday is usually the least crowded day, followed by Friday and Wednesday.

Disneyland Park usually hosts crowds 50% larger than those at Disney California Adventure, but because DCA is smaller, crowd conditions are comparable. Expressed differently, the most crowded and least crowded days are essentially the same for both Disneyland parks. However, if you are ineligible for early admission (see below), we advise visiting the park that does not offer early entry, as the other will be busy by the time ordinary guests arrive.

EARLY ENTRY

ANYONE WHO BUYS in advance a three-or-more-day ticket with Magic Morning admission may enter Disneyland Park 1 hour before the park is opened to the general public on one morning of their vacation. You can exercise your early-entry privilege on Tuesday, Thursday, or Saturday. Guests at the Paradise Pier, Grand Californian, and Disneyland Hotels can also enter on any early-entry day, as long as they have any valid ticket; this privilege is referred to as Extra Magic Hour. During this early-entry hour, most of the Fantasyland attractions—along with Astro Orbitor, Buzz Lightyear Astro Blasters, Finding Nemo Submarine Voyage, Space Mountain, and Star Tours: The Adventures Continue in Tomorrowland—will usually be open. The rest of the park's attractions (and all FastPass machines) will remain off-limits until the official opening time. Disney California Adventure (DCA) also offers its own Extra Magic Hour exclusively for hotel guests, offering access to all of Cars Land, along with select attractions in Hollywood Land, Paradise Pier/Pixar Pier, and Grizzly Peak, on four mornings (Sunday, Monday, Wednesday, and Friday).

Security checkpoints can be painfully understaffed during Extra Magic Hour, so even on-site guests should plan on departing their hotel room up to an hour before the park opens to take full advantage of early entry. Also, so many guests are eligible for Magic Mornings at Disneyland that early-entry wait times in Fantasyland can exceed those during regular hours; if you can't be among the first through the turnstiles, you may want to avoid Disneyland Magic Mornings entirely. Magic Mornings at DCA, on the other hand, are only available to hotel guests, so queues are far less crowded, making it one of the most valuable perks of staying on-site.

If you plan on driving to Disneyland, be advised that the Mickey & Friends parking structure opens only 30 minutes before the park opens for Magic Morning. Due to this, we recommend arriving at the parking structure at least an hour before Magic Morning starts. You'll spend a bit of time waiting in your car for the parking structure to open, but it's necessary to get to Disneyland in time for the start of Magic Morning. It's also important to note that the Toy Story parking lot does not open early for Magic Morning. That means Mickey & Friends is your only option for parking that early in the day.

This reader from Tulsa, Oklahoma, wrote:

We tried to get to the turnstiles as you recommended on a Magic Morning 45 minutes before opening but were stuck in Mickey & Friends parking structure waiting for it to open. It finally opened 30 minutes before Magic Morning. Needless to say it ruined the touring plan as we were well behind the mob at the turnstiles by the time we got a tram and went through security.

OPERATING HOURS

DISNEYLAND RESORT RUNS a dozen or more different operating schedules during the year, making it advisable to visit **disneyland.disney .go.com/calendar** or call ☎ 714-781-4565 the day before you arrive for exact hours of operation.

PACKED-PARK COMPENSATION PLAN

THE THOUGHT OF TEEMING, jostling throngs jockeying for position in endless lines under the baking Fourth of July sun is enough to wilt the will and ears of the most ardent Mouseketeer. Why would anyone go to Disneyland Park or DCA on a summer Saturday or during a major holiday period? The Disney folks, however, feel kind of bad about those interminably long lines and the basically impossible touring conditions on packed days and compensate patrons with an incredible array of first-rate live entertainment and happenings throughout the park.

Throughout the day, the party goes on with shows, parades, concerts, and pageantry. In the evening, there is so much going on that you have to make some tough choices. Musical acts sometimes perform on the Tomorrowland Terrace stage in Disneyland and in Hollywood Land at DCA. There are always parades and fireworks, and the Disney characters make frequent appearances. No question about it—you can go to the Disneyland parks on the Fourth of July (or any other crowded extended-hours day), never get on a ride, and still get your money's worth. Even on the busiest days, there are attractions at each park that rarely require more than a 15-minute wait: *Great Moments with Mr. Lincoln,* the *Enchanted Tiki Room,* the railroad and monorail, and Star Wars Launch Bay at Disneyland Park, as well as Disney Animation and the Bakery Tour at DCA.

If you decide to go on one of the parks' big days, we suggest that you arrive 1 hour and 20 minutes before the stated opening time. Use the touring plan of your choice until about 1 p.m., and then take the monorail to Downtown Disney for lunch and relaxation. Southern Californian visitors often chip in and rent a room for the group (make reservations well in advance) at the Disneyland Resort hotels, thus affording a place to meet, relax, have a drink, or change clothes before enjoying the pools at the hotel. A comparable arrangement can be made at other nearby hotels as long as they are within walking distance or furnish a shuttle service to and from the park. After an early dinner, return to the park for the evening's festivities, which really crank up at about 8 p.m.

GETTING THERE

WHILE MANY DISNEYLAND VISITORS HAIL from California and drive to the resort area, if you are flying in from across the country (or globe), you have three options for your arrival airport. With domestic and international service from nearly every airline known to man, Los Angeles Airport (LAX) is one of the largest and busiest in the world, and one of the more frustrating to navigate. LAX is also located 34 miles west of Anaheim, a 45-minute drive along the busy I-105 and I-55 freeways at the best of times, or an hour and a half or more in typical terrible traffic. Unless you are starting or ending your Disneyland vacation with a visit to Hollywood, we recommend looking at flights into John Wayne Airport (SNA) or Long Beach Airport (LGB), both of which are significantly calmer and closer to Disneyland. John Wayne (also known as Orange County Airport) is only 14 miles southeast of Disneyland on CA 55 and I-5 and is serviced by Alaska, American, Delta, Frontier, Southwest, United, and WestJet airlines. Long Beach (our personal favorite airport) is 24 miles west of Disneyland but can be reached using surface streets, making it the shortest drive when the highways are halted. Long Beach is only serviced by American, Delta, JetBlue, and Southwest, but it boasts the most painless on-site rental car return and security screening we've ever experienced; going from the airport parking lot to sitting at your departure gate usually takes about 15 minutes.

If you're arriving at LAX or John Wayne, Coach USA's official Disneyland Resort Express will take you and your luggage directly from the airport to your Disneyland-area hotel, then back to the airport when it's time for your flight home. Unlike Walt Disney World's Magical Express, this service is not free. Prices from LAX are $30 one-way, $48 round-trip for adults, and $22 one-way, $36 round-trip for children. Prices for John Wayne Airport are $20 one-way, $35

Southern California at a Glance

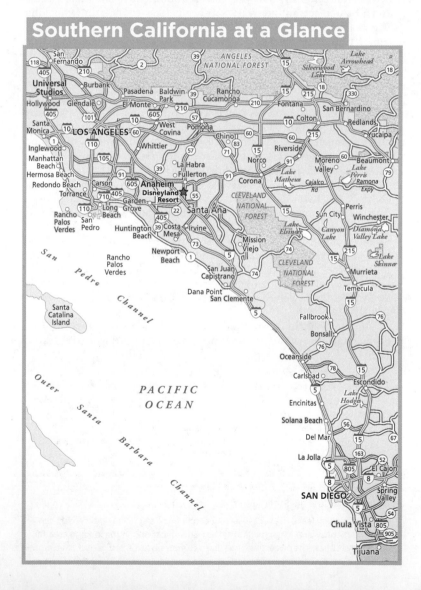

round-trip for adults and $15 one-way, $26 round-trip for children. Reservations can be made in advance at **dre.coachusa.com** or by calling ☎ 800-828-6699.

Another transportation option is a third-party airport shuttle, such as SuperShuttle (**supershuttle.com**), PrimeTime (**primetime shuttle.com**), or Karmel Shuttle (**karmel.com**). SuperShuttle charges $17 per person one-way, $32 per person round-trip from LAX; $35 per person one-way, $66 per person round-trip from Long Beach; and $11 per person one-way, $20 per person round-trip from John Wayne. PrimeTime charges $16.95 per person one-way, $32.50 per person round-trip from LAX; $43.95 per person one-way, $83.80 per person round-trip from Long Beach; and $11.95 per person one-way, $23 per person round-trip from John Wayne. Karmel charges $24.75 per person each way from LAX or Long Beach, and $18.10 per person each way from John Wayne. None of the shuttle prices include tip ($5 per person each way is suggested), and all are for shared van service, so you may spend an extended time picking up or dropping off other passengers before arriving at your destination. The Disneyland Resort Express bus does not require child seats, but if you're riding a shuttle van, you'll need to provide your own.

Rental cars are also available at all local airports, as are taxis, but the price of a cab can become extremely expensive after sitting in Los Angeles traffic on the way to Disneyland Resort. We've heard reports from people who have paid almost $150 to get from LAX to their Anaheim hotel. Less expensive ride-share services (such as Uber and Lyft) are also readily available to and from Los Angeles International, John Wayne, and (as of mid-2017) Long Beach Airport Airports. At LAX, look for designated Ride Share Pickup locations on the upper Departures level. We've had great results using Uber from the airports and Disney hotels.

Once in Anaheim, Disney patrons can drive directly into and out of parking facilities without becoming enmeshed in surface-street traffic. To avoid traffic problems, we recommend the following:

1. Stay as close to Disneyland as possible. If you are within walking distance, leave your car at the hotel and walk to the park using the pedestrian entrance on the east side of the resort, along Harbor Boulevard between Disney Way and Manchester Avenue, or through the security checkpoint near Downtown Disney's ESPN Zone if walking from the west side along Disneyland Drive. If your hotel provides efficient shuttle service (that is, will get you to the parks at least 30 minutes before opening), use the shuttle.

2. If your hotel is more than 5 miles from Disneyland and you intend to drive your car, leave for the park extra early, say 1 hour or more.

3. If you must use the Santa Ana Freeway (I-5), give yourself lots of extra time.

4. Any time you leave the park just before, at, or just after closing time, you can expect considerable congestion in the parking lots and in the loading area for hotel shuttles. The easiest way to return to your hotel (if you do not have a car in the Disneyland Resort parking lot) is to take the monorail to the Disneyland

Hotel or walk to the Grand Californian Hotel, and then take a cab to your own hotel. While cabs in Anaheim are a little pricey, they are usually available in ample numbers at the Disneyland hotels and at the taxi stand in Downtown Disney behind ESPN Zone. When you consider the alternatives of fighting your way onto a hotel shuttle or trudging back to your hotel on worn-out feet, spending $5–$10 for a cab often sounds pretty reasonable. Ride-share services (such as **Uber** and **Lyft**) are an even cheaper option, costing about half the price of an equivalent taxi ride. The easiest places for ride-share drivers to access are the drop-off points on the west side behind ESPN Zone, and off Harbor Boulevard to the east, as well as the driveways outside the main lobbies of the Disneyland Hotel and Grand Californian.

5. The Orange County Transit District provides very efficient bus service to Disneyland with several different long-distance lines. Running about every 30 minutes during the day and evening, service runs 10 a.m.–midnight, depending on the season and your location. Buses drop off and pick up passengers at the east shuttle loop off Harbor Boulevard. From there, guests can walk to the park entrance. Bus fare is about $2 and children age 5 and under ride free. A bus day pass is available for $4; 30-day passes are $69 for adults, $40 for children ages 6–18. For additional information, call ☎ 714-636-7433 or visit **octa.net.** For public transportation in the immediate area surrounding Disneyland, see our discussion of the Anaheim Resort Transit (ART) system on page 38.

DISNEYLAND PARKING

DISNEYLAND HAS FOUR PARKING AREAS. The main parking facility, the Mickey & Friends parking garage, can be accessed directly from I-5, Disneyland Drive, or Ball Road. One of the largest parking structures in the world, the garage is connected to Downtown Disney and the theme parks by Disney tram. Non-collapsible strollers are permitted on trams only in the first or last car where there are extra-large sections for strollers and wheelchairs. If you'd rather hoof it, the walking distance to the park gates is about a mile, cutting south through the Downtown Disney parking lots until you reach the rear of ESPN Zone. You'll have to pass through Disney's metal detectors and baggage screening immediately after exiting the garage if you want to ride the tram; if the checkpoint is overcrowded, there is usually a shorter wait outside Downtown Disney where walkers are inspected.

The secondary parking areas are the Simba lot behind the Paradise Pier Hotel and the Toy Story lot south of the corner of Katella Avenue and Harbor Boulevard (a favorite of local pass holders and our top pick for the most convenient place to park). From Simba (available only on the busiest of days) you can walk through Downtown Disney to the parks or alternatively walk to the Downtown Disney Monorail stop and take the monorail into Disneyland Park (not Disney California Adventure). Toy Story offers shuttles to and from the bus loop east of the Esplanade, or you can walk (about 0.5 mile). The Pumbaa lot off Disney Way across from the Anaheim GardenWalk is usually used as cast member or special event parking. It is scheduled to be replaced

Around Disneyland

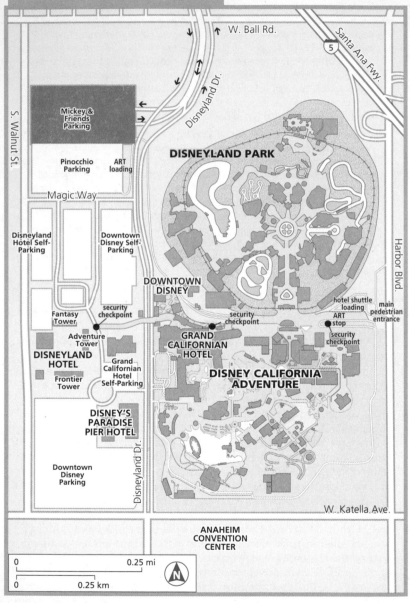

W. Ball Rd.

Santa Ana Fwy.

5

Disneyland Dr.

S. Walnut St.

Mickey & Friends Parking

Pinocchio Parking

ART loading

DISNEYLAND PARK

Magic Way

Disneyland Hotel Self-Parking

Downtown Disney Self-Parking

Harbor Blvd.

DOWNTOWN DISNEY

hotel shuttle loading

main pedestrian entrance

ART stop

Fantasy Tower

security checkpoint

security checkpoint

security checkpoint

Adventure Tower

GRAND CALIFORNIAN HOTEL

DISNEYLAND HOTEL

Grand Californian Hotel Self-Parking

Frontier Tower

DISNEY CALIFORNIA ADVENTURE

DISNEY'S PARADISE PIER HOTEL

Disneyland Dr.

Downtown Disney Parking

W. Katella Ave.

ANAHEIM CONVENTION CENTER

0   0.25 mi

0   0.25 km

N

with a new parking structure that will connect with the Disneyland Resort via a pathway replacing Harbor Boulevard's former Carousel Inn, which was purchased by Disney in 2015. The Pinocchio parking lot between the main parking structure and Disneyland Hotel is used for overflow and for oversize vehicles and buses. Parking fees for all lots are $20 for cars and motorcycles, $25 for RVs and oversize vehicles without trailers, and $30 for buses and tractors with extended trailers. For $35 (or a $15 upgrade if prepaid) you can get Preferred Parking, which puts you in the first three rows of each level closest to the elevators and escalators; we'd rather spend the money on churros and use the extra yards to walk off the calories. After parking your car, save yourself a frantic search at the end of your day by taking a digital photo of the lot name and section number.

You can park for free for up to 2 hours in the Downtown Disney parking lot and get 2 additional free hours with validation from AMC Theatres or select table-service dining restaurants. Additional half hours cost $6 each up to a $36 daily maximum. Valet parking is no longer offered at Downtown Disney but is available anytime at the resort hotels ($30 plus $10 per hour, up to $100 daily for non-guests). If you have money to burn, valet parking at the Grand Californian puts you closest to the parks.

TAKING A TRAM OR SHUTTLE BUS FROM YOUR HOTEL

TRAMS AND SHUTTLE BUSES are provided by many hotels and motels in the vicinity of Disneyland. Usually without charge, they represent a fairly carefree means of getting to and from the theme parks, letting you off near the entrances and saving you the cost of parking. The rub is that they might not get you there as early as you desire (a critical point if you take our touring advice) or be available at the time you wish to return to your lodging. Also, some shuttles are direct to Disneyland, while others make stops at other motels and hotels in the vicinity. Each shuttle service is a little bit different, so check out the particulars before you book your hotel. If the shuttle provided by your hotel runs regularly throughout the day to and from Disneyland and if you have the flexibility to tour the parks over two or three days, the shuttle provides a wonderful opportunity to tour in the morning and return to your lodging for lunch, a swim, or perhaps a nap; then you can head back to Disneyland refreshed in the early evening for a little more fun.

Be forewarned that most hotel shuttle services do not add more vehicles at the parks' opening or closing times. In the mornings, your biggest problem is that you might not get a seat on the first shuttle. This occurs most frequently if your hotel is the last stop for a shuttle that serves several hotels. Because hotels that share a shuttle service are usually located close together, you can improve your chances of getting a seat by simply walking to the hotel preceding yours on the pickup

unofficial **TIP**
Warning: Most shuttles don't add vehicles at park-opening or park-closing times. In the mornings, you may not get a seat.

route. At closing time, and sometimes following a hard rain, you can expect a mass exodus from the parks. The worst-case scenario in this event is that more people will be waiting for the shuttle to your hotel than the bus will hold and that some will be left. While most (but not all) hotel shuttles return for stranded guests, you may suffer a wait of 15 minutes–1 hour. Our suggestion, if you are depending on hotel shuttles, is to exit the park at least 45 minutes before closing. If you stay in a park until closing and lack the energy to deal with the shuttle or hike back to your hotel, go to the Disneyland Hotel and catch a cab or Uber from there. A cab stand is also behind the ESPN Zone in Downtown Disney and another is at the Grand Californian Hotel.

The shuttle-loading area is located on the Harbor Boulevard side of the Disneyland Park's main entrances. The loading area connects to a pedestrian corridor that leads to the park entrances. Each hotel's shuttle bus is color-coded yellow, blue, red, silver, or white. Signs of like color designate where the shuttles load and unload. You'll also find a passenger drop-off loop (parking strictly prohibited) off Harbor; taxis may deposit here, but they are not supposed to pick up. If you are staying near the corner of Harbor and Katella, you can walk into the Toy Story parking lot and use its park shuttle for free.

Anaheim Resort Transit

Anaheim Resort Transit (ART) provides shuttle service to the Disneyland Resort, Anaheim GardenWalk, and the convention center. The service operates 20 routes designated 1–21 (excluding 13). There are just three to nine well-marked stops on each route, so a complete circuit on any given route usually takes about 20 minutes, but some take up to 1 hour. All of the routes originate and terminate at Disneyland's bus loop east of the Esplanade near Harbor Boulevard. There is also service from Disneyland to Knott's Berry Farm, Discovery Cube Orange County, and Angel Stadium in case you want to catch an afternoon ballgame. To continue on to the convention center, you must transfer at Disneyland to Route 1, 3–6, 9, 12, or 17–20.

The colorful buses are wheelchair accessible. They ideally run every 10 minutes on peak days during morning and evening periods but can take up to 30 minutes when it's really busy, every 20 minutes during the less busy middle part of the day, and every 20 minutes all day long on off-peak days. Service begins 100 minutes before park opening and ends 30–90 minutes after park closing (may vary seasonally). If you commute to Disneyland on ART and then head to Downtown Disney after the parks close, you'll have to find your own way home if you stay at Downtown Disney more than 90 minutes. All shuttle vehicles and respective stops are clearly marked with the route designation.

Vending kiosks and hotels served by ART sell one-day, three-day, and five-day passes for $5.50, $14, and $23, respectively. You'll also find an ART vending kiosk at the Disneyland bus loop, but you may not want to depend on them, as one Melbourne, Australia, reader discovered:

The ART buses around the Disneyland area were great; however, the ticket machine at Disneyland wasn't functioning well, and we couldn't find other machines easily.

The most convenient option is to use the free smartphone app, which can be found by searching for "ART Ticketing" on the Apple or Google Play app stores.

Children age 2 years and under ride free with a paying adult. Day passes for children can be purchased for $2, a three-day pass for $3, and a five-day pass for $5. One-way cash fares are $3 for adults, $1 for children. Children must be taken out of strollers to ride. Passes cannot be purchased from the driver. For more information, call ☎ 888-364-ARTS (2787) or check **rideart.org**. Passes are also available at ART's website.

A **WORD** *About* **LODGING**

TRAFFIC AROUND DISNEYLAND, and in the Anaheim–Los Angeles area in general, is so terrible that we advocate staying in accommodations within 2–3 miles of the park. Included in this radius are many expensive hotels as well as a considerable number of moderately priced establishments and a small number of bargain motels.

READERS' DISNEYLAND RESORT REPORT CARD

ON PAGE 40 IS THE READERS' DISNEYLAND RESORT Report Card. Room quality indicates cleanliness, bed comfort, and room size. Check-in efficiency rates how quickly and accurately the hotel staff get you into your room. Quietness of room considers soundproofing from neighbors and exterior noise. The pool rating includes the size of the pool, how crowded it gets, and how clean the pool and pool area are. The staff category assesses how friendly and effective the hotel staff are at handling problems and special requests. Our hotel dining rating applies to any on-site counter-service dining, and the overall rating is the summary for every category.

Readers rate Disneyland hotels better than neighboring hotels, continuing a years-long trend. Much of the lodging around Disneyland consists of motels with aging rooms, many in need of refurbishment, content to trade on their proximity to the park rather than the quality of their rooms.

Readers indicate that Disneyland's hotels are substantially better than nearby hotels. In this year's reader report card, Disney's highest grades are in room quality and staff friendliness—two things you'd expect to see, given the premium Disney charges for its lodging.

Each of the Disneyland hotels fare poorly in the dining category, but some context is necessary. Each of the hotels offers decent choices for breakfast, from quick grab-and-go options to table-service meals. And the hotels' short walk to Downtown Disney and surrounding neighborhoods provides plenty of options for good lunches and dinners.

READERS' DISNEYLAND RESORT REPORT CARD							
HOTEL	ROOM QUALITY	CHECK-IN EFFICIENCY	QUIETNESS OF ROOM	POOL	STAFF	HOTEL DINING	OVERALL RATING
Disneyland Hotel	A	B+	B	B+	B	C	B
Grand Californian	B	B	B–	B	B	C	B
Paradise Pier	A	B	C	C	A	F	B

WALKING TO DISNEYLAND FROM NEARBY HOTELS

WHILE IT IS TRUE THAT MOST DISNEYLAND area hotels provide shuttle service, or are on the ART routes, it is equally true that an ever-increasing number of guests walk to the parks from their hotels. Shuttles are not always available when needed, and parking in the Disneyland lot has become pretty expensive. A pedestrian walkway from Harbor Boulevard provides safe access to Disneyland for guests on foot. This pedestrian corridor extends from Harbor Boulevard west to the Disneyland Hotel, connecting Disneyland Park, Disney California Adventure, and Downtown Disney.

Close proximity to the theme parks figures prominently in the choice of a hotel. Harbor Boulevard borders Disneyland Resort on the east, and Katella Avenue runs along the resort's southern boundary. The closest non-Disney hotels, and the only ones really within walking distance, are on Harbor Boulevard from just south of I-5 to the north to just south of the intersection with Katella Avenue, and along Katella Avenue near Harbor. Disney has plans to build a new Eastern Gateway, including a pedestrian bridge over Harbor, by the end of 2018 and shift its security checkpoint behind the motels, with the new parking complex's entrance located at the corner of Disney Way and Clementine Street. Disneyland says guests at the hotels on Harbor will have direct access to the resort without backtracking eastward, but skeptical neighboring property owners are still protesting the project, so stay tuned as the proposal works its way through the approval process.

Farther south on Harbor are some of the best hotels in the area, but they are a little far removed for commuting to the parks on foot. Additionally, these hotels are close to the Anaheim Convention Center and tend to cater, though certainly not exclusively, to business travelers. While the hotels near Disneyland Drive appear close to Disney property on a map, pedestrian access to the parks from the west is a bit more circuitous. If staying along Katella Avenue to the west of the convention center, you can walk north on Disneyland Drive and cut through the hotel parking lot across from the Grand Californian to Downtown Disney's security checkpoint. From West Ball Road, you can enter the Mickey & Friends garage from its north side through the employee gate on West Place, ascend to Level 2, and walk south about 6 minutes to reach the trams to the parks.

WALKING TIMES TO THE THEME PARK ENTRANCES AND SWIMMING POOL RATINGS

HOTEL	MAP NUMBER (pgs. 60-61)	OVERALL QUALITY RATING	COST ($=$50)	WALKING TIME	POOL RATING
Alpine Inn	2	★★½	$$$	13:00	2
Anaheim Camelot Inn & Suites	4	★★★½	$$$+	7:15	2
Best Western Plus Anaheim Inn	12	★★★	$$$+	7:15	2
Best Western Plus Park Place Inn	13	★★★	$$$+	5:45	2
Best Western Plus Stovall's Inn	16	★★★½	$$$$-	22:00	6
Candy Cane Inn	19	★★★	$$$$-	10:30	4
Castle Inn & Suites	20	★★★	$$$+	12:30	1
Country Inn & Suites	24	★★★½	$$$$$+	14:30	3
Courtyard Anaheim Theme Park Ent.	25	★★★½	$+ x 7	11:15	9
del Sol Inn Anaheim Resort	30	★★½	$$$$$+	7:00	3
Desert Inn & Suites	31	★★★	$$$+	6:40	3
Desert Palms Hotel & Suites	32	★★★	$$$$+	13:00	2
Disneyland Hotel	33	★★★★	$+ x 10	10:00–12:00	10
Disney's Grand Californian Hotel	34	★★★★½	$- x 12	4:00*	10
Disney's Paradise Pier Hotel	35	★★★★	$+ x 7	12:00	7
Eden Roc Inn & Suites	39	★★★	$$$+	22:00	2
Fairfield Inn Anaheim Resort	43	★★★	$$$$+	9:30	4
Grand Legacy at the Park	45	★★½	$$$	8:20	8
Holiday Inn Express & Suites: Anaheim Resort	50	★★★½	$$$$$	12:30	5
Hotel Indigo Anaheim	54	★★★½	$$$$	15:00	2
Howard Johnson Anaheim Hotel	55	★★★½	$$$$+	10:15	8
Hyatt House at Anaheim Resort	57	★★★★	$$$$$	15:00	4
Park Vue Inn	63	★★★½	$$$$-	6:40	6
Portofino Inn & Suites	65	★★★½	$$$$	16:30	7
Quality Inn & Suites	66	★★½	$$$	13:30	2
Ramada Plaza Anaheim Hotel	68	★★★	$$$$$-	14:30	2
Red Lion Hotel Anaheim	69	★★★	$$$$$-	16:45	4
Residence Inn Anaheim-Maingate	70	★★★½	$- x 6	16:30	4
Residence Inn at Anaheim Resort	71	★★★½	$$$$$+	15:45	3
Sheraton Park Hotel at Anaheim Resort	74	★★★★	$$$+	17:00	7
SpringHill Suites Anaheim Resort	76	★★★★	$$$$+	15:30	5
Super 8 Anaheim Near Disneyland	80	★★½	$$$+	15:30	2
Tropicana Inn & Suites	83	★★★	$$$+	6:15	3

To Disneyland Park. The Grand Californian has an on-site entrance to DCA.

For families, a second important consideration is the quality of the hotel swimming pool. We mention this because, unfortunately, many of the non-Disney hotels closest to the theme parks have really crummy pools, sometimes just a tiny rectangle on a stark slab of concrete surrounded on four sides by a parking lot. To bring pool quality and proximity to the theme parks together, we've developed a table (see page 41) that lists the hotels, both Disney and non-Disney, within walking distance of the theme parks.

The table shows the walking time from each hotel to the theme park entrances. The times provided are averages—a couple of fit adults might cover the distance in less time, and a family with small children will likely take longer. Also on the table we rate the swimming areas of the hotels listed on a scale of 1–10, with 10 being best. As a rule of thumb, any pool with a rating less than 5 is not a place where most folks would want to spend much time. Any hotel not listed is, in our opinion, too far away for walking. Note that several non-Disney hotels are closer than the Disneyland Resort hotels, except for the Grand Californian.

The table and the above discussion might lead you to wonder whether there's any real advantage to staying in a Disney-owned hotel. The Disney hotels, of course, are very expensive, but if you can handle the tariff, here are the primary benefits of staying in one:

1. You are eligible for early entry at Disneyland Park three days each week and DCA on the other four days.
2. Dozens of full- and counter-service restaurants are within walking distance.
3. The Disney hotels offer the nicest rooms of any of the hotels within walking distance.
4. The Disney hotels offer the nicest swimming pools of any of the hotels within walking distance.
5. Numerous entertainment and shopping options are in Downtown Disney.
6. It's easy to retreat to your hotel for a meal, a nap, or a swim.
7. You don't need a car.
8. You can charge purchases at most Disney-owned shops and restaurants to your hotel account, and have packages delivered to your room.

DISNEYLAND RESORT HOTELS

DISNEY OFFERS THREE ON-SITE HOTELS: the **Grand Californian Hotel,** the **Disneyland Hotel,** and the **Paradise Pier Hotel.** The Grand Californian, built in the rustic stone-and-timber style of the grand national park lodges, is the flagship property. Newer, more elaborately themed, and closer to the theme parks and Downtown Disney than the other two on-property hotels, the Grand Californian is without a doubt the best place to stay . . . if you can afford it.

The next most convenient is the sprawling Disneyland Hotel, the oldest of the three, though repeatedly renovated. Comprising three guest-room towers, the hotel is lushly landscaped with a new vintage Disneyana theme and offers large, luxurious guest rooms. Walking time to the monorail station, with transportation to Disneyland Park, is about 3–6 minutes. The Grand Californian and Disneyland Hotels both offer club-level rooms with luxury amenities, such as nightly turndown service and access to a private club, but one reader from Ontario, Canada, didn't feel that it was worth the extra money:

> The club lounge was open 6:30 a.m.–8:30 p.m. each day. The early-morning park hours began at 7 a.m., and one needs to be at the park at least 45 minutes before park opening, so breakfast in the lounge was not possible. The lounge was also closed too early in the evening, not allowing us to stop and pick up a water or soda on our way back from the parks.

The east side of the third Disney hotel overlooks the Paradise Pier section of Disney California Adventure theme park, hence the name Paradise Pier Hotel. Though the guest rooms and public areas have a beach-and-boardwalk flavor, the hotel is not themed. The guest rooms here are large. Walking to the monorail station and Downtown Disney takes about 5–10 minutes.

Guests at all three Disney-owned hotels can use their keys to charge dining and shopping within the resort to their room. Third-party vendors (including most Downtown Disney restaurants) are excluded, and you'll need to show photo ID along with your room key. Parking for registered resort guests at any of the Disney-owned hotels is $20 per night for self-parking (free for Disney Vacation Club members) or $30 per night for valet (☎ 714-635-2300). On the plus side, none of the hotels charge a resort fee, and all provide safes, mini-fridges, coffee makers, and free Wi-Fi (supposedly high-speed, but don't plan on streaming high-definition video) in rooms and public areas.

Disney's Grand Californian Hotel & Spa

The Grand Californian Hotel is the crown jewel of Disneyland Resort's three hotels. With its shingle siding, rock foundations, cavernous hewn-beam lobby, polished hardwood floors, and cozy hearths, the hotel is a stately combination of elements from Western national park lodges. Designed by architect Peter Dominick (who also designed the Wilderness Lodge at Walt Disney World), the Grand Californian is rendered in the Arts & Crafts style of the early 20th century, with such classic features as "flying" roofs, projecting beams, massive buttresses, and an earth-tone color palette. In 2017 Disney gave the Grand Californian a face-lift, refreshing the lobby and concierge Craftsman Club with new artisanal furnishings. We strongly encourage visitors with an interest in architecture to take the fascinating (and free) hour-long Art of the Craft walking tour of the resort, offered several times each week through the Guest Services desk. Most reminiscent of The Majestic Yosemite Hotel (formerly The Ahwahnee) at Yosemite National Park, the Grand Californian combines rugged craftsmanship and grand scale with functional design and intimate spaces. Pull up a vintage rocker in front of a blazing fire, and the bustling lobby instantly becomes a snug cabin.

The hotel's main entrance off Downtown Drive is primarily for vehicular traffic. Two pedestrian-only entrances open into Downtown Disney and DCA; this last makes it a cinch to return to the hotel from DCA for a nap, a swim, or lunch.

The features we like in the 948 guest rooms include excellent light for reading in bed, more than adequate storage space, a two-sink vanity outside the toilet and bath, and, in some rooms, a balcony. All guest rooms were renovated in 2017 with new hardwood flooring, brighter carpets, white soft goods, orange tree-inspired wall art, and oak furnishings featuring headboards inlaid with Chip 'n' Dale (not Chippendale) designs. Views from the guest rooms overlook the swimming pool, Downtown Disney, or Disney California Adventure theme park. Ranging $417 (for a standard view) to more than $2,100 (for a three-bedroom suite) per night, guest rooms are the most expensive at Disneyland Resort.

Disney's time-share condo enterprise, the Disney Vacation Club, premiered its first West Coast property as part of the 2009 expansion of the Grand Californian. The Villas at Disney's Grand Californian consist of 48 two-bedroom equivalent villas and two Grand Villas. *Equivalent* is the term used to describe single units that can be sold (or rented) as studio suites or combined to make two- and three-bedroom villas. All villas except studio suites include kitchens, living rooms, and dining areas, as well as washers and dryers. Master bedrooms offer a king bed, while other bedrooms provide two queen beds. Studio suites come with a single queen bed. All bedrooms have a flat-panel TV, private bath, and private balcony. Though studio suites don't have full kitchens, they do include a small fridge, a microwave, and a coffee maker. Two-bedroom villas consist of a one-bedroom villa joined to a studio suite. Three-bedroom Grand Villas are two-story affairs with the living area, kitchen, and master bedroom on the lower level and two bedrooms on the upper level. Rates for various villas range from $272 for a studio suite during the off-season to more than $3,580 for a three-bedroom Grand Villa on New Year's weekend. Other elements of the Grand Californian include a swimming pool for the villas and an underground parking garage.

The resort's beautiful High Sierra–themed pool complex, which was completely renovated in 2017, features three pools surrounded by handlaid stone, private cabanas that can be rented by the day or half-day, and a 90-foot waterslide that wraps around a redwood stump. The on-site Mandara Spa is one of Disney's best, offering a wide selection of treatments and a state-of-the-art fitness facility. Rounding out the Grand Californian's amenity mix are two clubby lounges.

GOOD (AND NOT-SO-GOOD) ROOMS AT GRAND CALIFORNIAN HOTEL Grand Californian's rooms are large and attractive, but unless you're willing to pay extra, you'll be stuck looking at a parking lot or the backs of buildings. Standard rooms that don't have a great view but are close to the hotel's exclusive entrance into DCA are rooms 2336, 2338–2346, 3334, 3336, and 3338.

Avoid even-numbered rooms X240–X260, as these are directly next to a loud roller coaster. Also avoid even-numbered rooms 3240–3252, as these are expensive premium-theme-park-view rooms but don't offer a great view of the park.

For the best views of DCA we like even-numbered rooms 5424–5448 (which view the Grizzly Peak area of the park) or the ultra-expensive concierge-level rooms, which are even-numbered rooms 6402–6412 and 6416. Odd-numbered rooms 4419–4447 and 5419–5447 are the expensive Downtown Disney or deluxe view room types, but these offer views of Disneyland's fireworks show.

The Disneyland Hotel

Walt Disney barely managed to finance the construction of the Disneyland theme park. He certainly didn't have the funds to purchase adjacent property or build hotels, though on-site hotels were central to his overall concept. So he cut a deal with petroleum engineer and TV producer Jack Wrather to build and operate Disneyland Hotel. The deal not only gave Wrather the rights to the Disneyland Hotel but also allowed him to build other Disneyland Hotels within the state of California until 2054. It always irked Walt that he didn't own the hotel that bore his name, but Wrather steadfastly refused to renegotiate the rights. After Jack Wrather died in 1984, the Walt Disney Company bought the entire Wrather Corporation, which among other things held the rights to the *Lone Ranger* and *Lassie* TV series and, improbably, the RMS *Queen Mary,* docked at Long Beach. By acquiring the whole corporation, the Walt Disney Company brought Disneyland Hotel under Disney ownership in 1988. If you want to learn more about the hotel's history, sign up with the concierge for the free Happiest Hotel on Earth tour, held at 1 p.m. Wednesday and Saturday.

Disneyland Hotel consists of three towers facing each other across a verdant landscaped plaza, as well as a swimming complex, restaurants, and shops. The hotel was originally connected to Disneyland Park by monorail, but a portion of the hotel was demolished during the construction of DCA and Downtown Disney, and the station was rebuilt on its original location. Guest registration for all three towers is situated in the Fantasy Tower (previously called the Magic Tower, and the Marina Tower before that), which is connected to the Disneyland Convention Center and Disneyland Hotel's self-parking garage. Though all three towers share restaurants, shopping, and recreational amenities, the Fantasy Tower is most conveniently located. It and the Adventure Tower (formerly Dreams, née Sierra) are closest to Downtown Disney and the theme parks. The Frontier Tower (formerly Wonder, formerly Bonita) is the farthest from the action.

Rack rates for the Disneyland Hotel range from around $405 for a city view in the off-season to $674 for a theme park view during holiday periods (and more than $1,350 for a three-bedroom suite).

Disneyland Hotel embraces the retro-nostalgia of baby boomer Disneyland devotees with decorative elements evoking the park's early years; look for 1950s-style signage outside each tower and a tribute to Frontierland's long-gone Old Unfaithful geysers. The main lobby evokes Mary Blair's It's a Small World designs and features a blown-up fun map of the original park. The check-in area sports early attraction concept artwork and seating styled after the spinning teacups, whimsical touches that stand in stark contrast with the ultramodern sculpted steel behind the front desk. Peek inside the Frontier Tower lobby to see an amazingly detailed model of Big Thunder Mountain. Large windows, specially designed to filter outside noise, give the facade a glistening sky-blue tint.

The rooms have a sleek monochromatic contemporary look. Each room has one king-size or two queen-size beds, along with a pullout couch; one-bedroom suites with a wet bar and living room are also available. Features include a headboard with a carving of Sleeping Beauty Castle; fiber optics in the headboard create a skyline with fireworks (accompanied by a tinny rendition of "When You Wish Upon a Star") at the flick of a switch. Other decorative touches include black-and-white photography depicting the history of Disneyland and hidden Mickey designs in the carpet, though the overall feel is more business modern than Disney whimsy. Each room has a flat-panel HDTV, perfect for connecting a laptop or video game console. Other room amenities include mini-refrigerators; coffee makers; safes large enough for laptops; and high-tech phone, cable, and wireless Internet connections.

If the standard rooms aren't pixie-dusted (or pricey) enough for you, five different elaborately themed Signature Suites allow big spenders to sleep in a pirate's lair, the Big Thunder mine, or Mickey's penthouse. A night in one of these rooms can easily run into the mid-four figures; if you have to ask how much, you probably can't afford it.

The bathrooms are small for an upscale hotel, but there is a sink and vanity outside the bathrooms. As in most family hotels built in the 1950s and '60s, a connecting door, situated by the closet and the aforementioned single sink, leads to an adjoining room. Soundproofing around the connecting doors is nonexistent, so be prepared to revel in the sounds of your neighbors brushing their teeth, coping with indigestion, and arguing over what to wear. Fortunately, these sounds don't carry into the sleeping area.

The swimming complex's centerpiece is a pair of waterslides (187 feet and 112 feet long, respectively) themed to resemble vintage monorail trains, topped by the classic Disneyland block-letter logo. There's also a 19-foot kiddie slide and bubble jets for the little ones; family films are screened here in the evenings, and guests of the other on-site hotels may attend. A 4-foot-deep pool separates the 4,800-square-foot E-ticket Pool and the waterslides, with a footbridge allowing easy passage from one side of the water to the other. On sunny days expect long inefficient lines for the slides, as well as a severe shortage of lounge chairs and elbow room.

Tangaroa Terrace and Trader Sam's, a casual restaurant and bar, bank on fond memories of Adventureland's 1960s-era *Tahitian Terrace* dinner show. Disneyland Hotel's other restaurants include Steakhouse 55 and Goofy's Kitchen, the hotel's character-meal headquarters. (All Disneyland Hotel restaurants are profiled in full in Part Four.)

As concerns practical matters, parking is a royal pain at the Disneyland Hotel. The self-parking garage is convenient only to the Fantasy Tower, and even there you'll probably have a long walk. To reach the other two towers, you must pass through the Fantasy Tower and navigate across the hotel's inner plaza and pool area. The Frontier Tower on the southern end of the property has a small parking lot to the rear, accessible via Downtown Drive and Paradise Way. Unfortunately, many of the already limited spaces are reserved for the adjacent Disney Vacation Club time-share sales office. Even so, if you're staying at the Frontier Tower, it's your best bet. If there's no room in the Frontier lot, you're better off parking in the Paradise Pier Hotel's lot than in the Disneyland Hotel parking garage. The only valet parking is at the Fantasy Tower, so even if you valet park, you'll still have to hoof it to the other towers.

While the nearby monorail station is convenient, you can't always count on it for transportation into Disneyland Park, as this Buffalo, New York, woman discovered:

> I found it annoying that the monorail closed with the rest of the park (or before!) and could not be used for transportation back to the hotel in the evening. It also shuts down if it's too hot in the afternoon because there is no A/C.

GOOD (AND NOT-SO-GOOD) ROOMS AT DISNEYLAND HOTEL There are three guest-room buildings at Disneyland Hotel: Fantasy, Adventure, and Frontier Towers. Each tower has three room view types: standard (of trees or parking lots), deluxe (of the resort's pool complex), and premium (facing Disneyland Park and Downtown Disney, or the pool). The best views can be had from the east-west-facing Adventure Tower, which overlooks the hotel's inner plaza and pool area on the west and Downtown Disney and the theme parks to the east. The most lackluster views are the north-facing vistas of the Fantasy Tower.

The Fantasy Tower's north side looks out onto several massive parking lots, but you can catch a glimpse of Disneyland Park if you crane your neck to the right. Rooms facing south in Fantasy Tower look out onto the pool and are categorized as deluxe view rooms. If you opt for standard view and want a slightly better view of Disneyland, go for odd-numbered rooms XX25–XX35 on floors 7–11. If you want to avoid views of parking lots but don't want to drop the extra cash on a room upgrade, even-numbered rooms XX00–XX34 on floors 2–3 on the tower's south side are categorized as standard.

Adventure Tower faces Disneyland and Downtown Disney on the east and the pool complex on the west. Standard view rooms on Adventure Tower's east side (odd-numbered rooms XX37–XX67 on floors 2–6) are better than the equivalently priced rooms in the other towers—instead of parking lots you'll mostly see trees. Almost all of the other rooms in

Adventure are categorized as deluxe or premium and carry a hefty price tag. If you're willing to pay the extra money, go for odd-numbered rooms XX37–XX51 on floors 7–10 for the best views of Disneyland.

Rooms on Frontier Tower's north side face the hotel's pool, and most above the fourth floor are categorized as deluxe or premium views. Avoid any standard rooms facing south (odd-numbered rooms XX69–XX99, floors 2–14) in Frontier, as these are the worst views of any of the Disneyland Hotel's rooms.

Paradise Pier Hotel

Disney acquired the independent Pan Pacific Hotel just south of the Disneyland Hotel in 1997 and changed its name to the Disneyland Pacific Hotel. Just before Disney California Adventure opened in 2001, the hotel was rechristened as the Paradise Pier Hotel in recognition of the Paradise Pier district of DCA that the hotel overlooks.

The 481-room property makes a mostly successful attempt to merge the hotel's original South Seas flavor with a vintage seaside amusement theme inspired by the attractions across the street. The sunny lobby sports a stunning glass-enclosed exterior elevator with high-tech touch screen controls (interior ones are available if it induces vertigo) and a statue of Goofy holding a surfboard. Guest rooms are furnished with blond wood furniture and the usual pastel soft goods, including bedspreads with a hidden Mickey pattern. Somewhat more whimsical than rooms at the Disneyland Hotel or the Grand Californian, Paradise Pier rooms include accents such as Mickey Mouse table lamps, beach ball pillows, and seashell-patterned carpets. Rates range $269–$1,003, depending on season and view.

For dining, the informal Disney's PCH Grill serves a breakfast (with characters) and dinner buffet daily. Next to the restaurant you'll find the Surfside Lounge, perfect for unwinding after an exhausting day of family fun. Amenities include a fitness center, conference rooms, a kids' game room, and an often breezy rooftop pool complete with a waterslide (the view from the top of the slide is killer). Self-parking in Paradise Pier's on-site garage is fast and convenient. Somewhat isolated on the Disneyland Resort property, the hotel is a 12-minute hike to the theme park entrances, farther away than most non-Disney hotels lining Harbor Boulevard on the east side of the resort, if you walk through Downtown Disney. Crossing Disneyland Drive and going through Grand Californian Hotel used to cut the walk in half, but Paradise Pier guests must now walk through the parking lot to the security check on the west side of Downtown Disney instead, making the hotel's location even less attractive.

Many guests overlook the Paradise Pier, but this Superior, Colorado, family had a positive experience:

> *It was great with one exception: the tiny pool (especially compared to the other two Disney hotels). Staff was awesome, room was nice, restaurant was fun. We would definitely stay again.*

GOOD (AND NOT-SO-GOOD) ROOMS AT PARADISE PIER HOTEL There are two guest-room buildings at Paradise Pier Hotel. Rooms facing east have excellent views of the Paradise Pier area of Disney California Adventure. Rooms facing west look out onto parking lots and a nearby residential neighborhood. There are two room-view categories at Paradise Pier, standard and premium. All rooms facing west are tagged as standard, while all rooms facing east on the sixth floor and above are premium. Request rooms 300–318 and 326–345 if you want to be on the same floor as the pool. If you want to catch a small glimpse of DCA but don't want to pay the extra cost for a premium room, even-numbered rooms 502–518 are standard view rooms facing the park. Even-numbered rooms 1200–1218, 1300–1318, 1400–1418, 1500, and 1510 are premium rooms that offer the best views of DCA.

HOW TO GET DISCOUNTS ON LODGING AT DISNEYLAND RESORT HOTELS

SO MANY GUEST ROOMS ARE in and around Disneyland Resort that competition is brisk, and everyone, including Disney, wheels and deals to keep them filled. The recession compounded this, leading to a more flexible discount policy for Disneyland Resort hotels, but rack rates are rising with the recovery. Here are tips for getting price breaks:

1. DISNEYLAND RESORT WEBSITE Disney has become more aggressive about offering deals on its website. Go to **disneyland.com** and check the page for "Special Offers." When booking rooms on Disney's or any other site, be sure to click on "Terms and Conditions" and read the fine print *before* making reservations.

2. SEASONAL SAVINGS You can save $15 to more than $200 per night on a Disneyland Resort hotel room by visiting during the slower times of the year. Disney uses so many adjectives (regular, holiday, peak, value, and such) to describe its seasonal calendar, however, that it's hard to keep up without a scorecard. To confuse matters more, the dates for each season vary from hotel to hotel. Understand that Disney seasonal dates are not sequential like spring, summer, fall, and winter. For any specific resort, there are sometimes several seasonal changes in a month. This is important because your room rate per night is determined by the season prevailing when you check in. Let's say that you checked in to the Disneyland Hotel on April 20 for a five-night stay. April 20 is in the more expensive holiday season that ends April 21, followed by the less pricey regular season beginning April 23. Because you arrived during a holiday season, the holiday season rate will be applied for your entire stay, even though almost half of your stay will be in regular season. Your strategy, therefore, is to shift your dates (if possible) to arrive during a less expensive season.

3. ASK ABOUT SPECIALS When you talk to Disney reservationists, inquire specifically about special deals. Ask, for example, "What special rates or discounts are available at Disney hotels during the time of our visit?" Being specific and assertive paid off for an Illinois reader:

DISNEY LODGING FOR LESS

The people at **mousesavers.com** (see opposite page) know more about Disney hotel packages than anyone on the planet. Here are their money-saving suggestions.

• **BOOK ROOM-ONLY.** It's frequently a better deal to book a room-only reservation instead of buying a vacation package. When you buy a package, you're typically paying a premium for convenience. You can often save money by putting together your own package—just book room-only at a resort and buy passes, meals, and extras separately.

Disney prices its standard packages at the same rates as if you had purchased individual components separately at full price. However, what Disney doesn't tell you is that components can usually be purchased separately at a discount—and those discounts are not reflected in the brochure prices of its packages. (Sometimes you can get special-offer packages that do include discounts; see below.)

Disney's packages often include extras you are unlikely to use. Also, packages require a $200 deposit and full payment 45 days in advance; plus, they have stringent change and cancellation policies. Generally, booking room-only requires a deposit of one night's room rate with the remainder due at check-in. Your reservation can be changed or canceled for any reason until five days before check-in.

Whether you decide to book a Disney vacation package or create your own, there are a number of ways to save:

• **BE FLEXIBLE.** Buying a room or package with a discount is a little like shopping for clothes at a discount store: if you wear size XX-small or XXXX-large, or you like green when everyone else is wearing pink, you're a lot more likely to score a bargain. Likewise, resort discounts are available only when Disney has excess rooms. You're more likely to get a discount during less-popular times (such as value season) and at larger or less-popular resorts.

• **BE PERSISTENT.** This is the most important tip. Disney allots a certain number of rooms to each discount. Once the discounted rooms are gone, you won't get that rate unless someone cancels. Fortunately, people change and cancel reservations all the time. If you can't get your preferred dates or hotel with one discount, try another one (if available) or keep calling back first thing in the morning to check for cancellations—the system resets overnight, and any reservations with unpaid deposits are automatically released for resale.

I called Disney's reservations number and asked for availability and rates. [Because] of The Unofficial Guide *warning about Disney reservationists answering only the questions posed, I specifically asked, "Are there any special rates or discounts for that room during the month of October?" She replied, "Yes, we have that room available at a special price." [For] the price of one phone call, I saved $440.*

Along similar lines, a Warren Township, New Jersey, dad chimed in with this:

Your tip about asking Disney employees about discounts was invaluable. They will not volunteer this information, but by asking we saved almost $500 on our hotel room.

4. LEARN ABOUT DEALS OFFERED TO SPECIFIC MARKETS The folks at **mouse savers.com** keep an updated list of discounts for use at Disney resorts. The discounts are separated into categories such as "for anyone," "for residents of certain states," "for Annual Passport holders," and so on. For example, the site once listed a deal targeted to residents of the San Diego area published in an ad in a San Diego newspaper. Dozens of discounts are usually listed on the site, covering almost all Disneyland Resort hotels. Usually anyone calling the Disneyland Resort Reservations Office (call ☎ 714-956-6425 and press 1 on the menu) can cite the referenced ad and get the discounted rate.

Disney has moved away from room discounts that anyone can use. Instead, Disney is targeting people with PIN codes in e-mails and direct mailings. PIN-code discounts are offered to specific individuals and are correlated with that person's name and address. PIN-code offers are nontransferable. When you try to make a reservation using the code, Disney will verify that the street or e-mail address to which the PIN code was sent is yours.

*un*official **TIP** For the best rates and least crowded conditions, try to avoid visiting Disneyland Resort when a major convention or trade show is in progress.

To enhance your chances of receiving a PIN-code offer, you need to get your name and street or e-mail address into the Disney system. One way is to call the Disney Resort Travel Sales Center at ☎ 714-520-5060 and request that info be sent to you. Or go to **disneyplan ning.com** and fill out the short survey to have offers and news sent automatically to your e-mail address. If you've been to Disneyland previously, your name and address will already be on record, but you won't be as likely to receive a PIN-code offer as you would by calling and requesting to be sent information. The latter is regarded as new business. Or, expressed differently, if Disney smells blood, they're more likely to come after you.

Mousesavers.com also features a great links page with short descriptions and URLs of the best Disney-related websites and a current-year seasonal rates calendar.

5. KAYAK.COM This search engine compares discounts offered by hotel chains and Internet travel sellers. With Kayak's help you can see photos and descriptions of Disneyland-area hotels and determine which seller is offering the best discounts.

6. ANNUAL PASSPORT HOLDER DISCOUNTS Annual pass holders are eligible for discounts on dining, shopping, and lodging. If you visit Disneyland Resort once a year or more, or if you plan on a visit of five or more days, you might save money overall by purchasing an annual pass. We've seen resort discounts as deep as 30% offered to annual pass holders. It doesn't take long to recoup the extra bucks you spent on an annual pass when you're saving that kind of money on lodging. Discounts in the 10%–15% range are more the norm.

7. TRAVEL AGENTS Travel agents are active players in the market and are particularly good sources of information on time-limited special programs and discounts. In our opinion, a good travel agent is the best friend a traveler can have. And though we at The Unofficial Guides know a thing or two about the travel industry, we always give our agent a chance to beat any deal we find. If our agent can't beat the deal, we let her book it if she can receive commission from it. In other words, we create a relationship that gives her plenty of incentive to really roll up her sleeves and work on our behalf.

As you might expect, some travel agents and agencies specialize, sometimes exclusively, in selling Disneyland and Walt Disney World. These agents have spent an incredible amount of time at both resorts and have completed extensive Disney education programs. They are usually the most Disney-knowledgeable agents in the travel industry. Most of these specialists and their agencies display the Earmarked logo indicating that they are Authorized Disney Vacation Planners. These Disney specialists are so good that we use them ourselves. They save us time and money, sometimes lots of both. The best of the best include **Sue Pisaturo,** whom we've used many times and who is a contributor to this guide (**sue@wdwvacations.com**), **Magical Vacations Travel** (**magicalvacationstravel.com**), **Mouse Fan Travel** (**mousefan travel.com**), and **The Magic for Less** (**themagicforless.com**).

8. ROOM UPGRADES Sometimes a room upgrade is as good as a discount. If you're visiting Disneyland Resort during a slower time, book the least expensive room your discounts will allow. Checking in, ask very politely about being upgraded to a pool view room. A fair percentage of the time, you will get one at no additional charge.

NON-DISNEY HOTELS

MANY OF THE HOTELS AND MOTELS near Disneyland were built in the early 1960s, and they are small and sometimes unattractive by today's standards. Quite a few motels adopted adventure or fantasy themes in emulation of Disneyland. As you might imagine, these themes from five decades ago seem hokey and irrelevant today. There is a disquieting (though rapidly diminishing) number of seedy hotels near Disneyland, and even some of the chain properties fail to live up to their national standards.

If you consider a non-Disney-owned hotel in Anaheim, check its quality as reported by a reliable independent rating system such as those offered by The Unofficial Guides, AAA Directories, Forbes Guides, or Frommer's guides. Also, before you book, ask how old the hotel is and when the guest rooms were last refurbished. Be aware that almost any hotel can be made to look good on a website, so don't depend on websites alone. Locate the hotel on our street map (see pages 60–61) to verify its proximity to Disneyland. If you will not have a car, make sure that the hotel has a shuttle service that will satisfy your needs.

GOOD NEIGHBOR HOTELS

A GOOD NEIGHBOR HOTEL is a hotel that has paid Disney a marketing fee to display that designation. Usually a ticket shop in the lobby will sell full-price Disney tickets. Other than that, the Good Neighbor designation means little to nothing for the consumer. It does not guarantee quality or proximity to Disneyland. Unlike at Walt Disney World, Disneyland does not require Good Neighbor hotels to provide free shuttle service to the park, though many do. You can book Good Neighbor hotels in a package with park tickets through the Walt Disney Travel Co.; prices are the same as if booked à la carte, though they toss in a free on-attraction photo, a card for discounts at select Downtown Disney locations, and a free collectible pin lanyard. In our opinion, you shouldn't let the presence or absence of the Good Neighbor designation influence your hotel choice.

GETTING A GOOD DEAL AT NON-DISNEY HOTELS

FOLLOWING ARE SOME TIPS and strategies for getting a good deal on a hotel room near Disneyland. Though the following list may seem a bit intimidating and may refer to players in the travel market that are unfamiliar to you, acquainting yourself with the strategies will serve you well in the long run. Simply put, the tips we provide for getting a good deal near Disneyland will work equally well at just about any other place where you need a hotel. Once you have invested a little time and have experimented with these strategies, you will be able to routinely obtain rooms at the best hotels and at the lowest possible rates.

Remember that Disneyland Resort is right across the street from the Anaheim Convention Center, one of the largest and busiest convention centers in the country. Room availability, as well as rates, are affected significantly by trade shows and other events at the convention center. To determine whether such an event will be going on during your projected dates, check out the convention calendar on page 29.

1. MOUSESAVERS.COM is a site dedicated to finding great deals on hotels, admissions, and more at Disneyland Resort and Walt Disney World. The site covers discounts on both Disney and non-Disney hotels and is especially effective at keeping track of time-limited deals and discounts offered in a select market—San Diego, for example. However, the site does not sell travel products.

2. KAYAK.COM AND MOBISSIMO.COM are travel search engines that search the better hotel-discount sites, as well as chain and individual hotel websites. (As an aside, Kayak used to be purely a search engine but now sells travel products, raising the issue of whether products not sold by Kayak are equally likely to come up in a search. Mobissimo, on the other hand, only links potential buyers to provider websites.)

3. EXPEDIA.COM AND TRAVELOCITY.COM sometimes offer good discounts on area hotels. We find that Expedia offers the best deals if you're booking within two weeks of your visit. In fact, some of Expedia's last-minute deals are amazing, really rock-bottom rates. Travelocity frequently beats Expedia, however, if you reserve two weeks to three months out. Neither site offers anything to get excited about if you book more than three months from the time of your visit. If you use either site, be sure to take into consideration the demand for rooms during the season of your visit, and check to see if any big conventions or trade shows are scheduled for the convention center.

4. PRICELINE.COM allows you to tender a bid for a room. You can't bid on a specific hotel, but you can specify location ("Disneyland Vicinity") and the quality rating expressed in stars. If your bid is accepted, you will be assigned to a hotel consistent with your location and quality requirements, and your credit card will be charged in a nonrefundable transaction for your entire stay. Notification of acceptance usually takes less than an hour. We recommend bidding $35–$55 per night for a three-star hotel and $55–$80 per night for a four-star property. To gauge your chances of success, check to see if any major conventions or trade shows are scheduled during your preferred dates.

5. *HOTELCOUPONS.COM SOUTHWEST GUIDE* is a book of discount coupons for hotels throughout California and is available free of charge at many restaurants and motels along the main interstates in and leading to California. However, because most folks make reservations before leaving home, picking up the coupon book en route does not help much. But for $4 ($6 Canadian) the company will mail you a copy, allowing you to examine the discounts offered before you make your reservations. The guide is free; the charge is for the postage. To order call ☎ 800-222-3948, Monday–Friday, 8:30 a.m.–5:30 p.m. Eastern time. You can also download the guide from **hotelcoupons.com** or have it e-mailed to you at no charge.

6. SPECIAL WEEKEND RATES If you are not averse to about an hour's drive to Disneyland, you can get a great weekend rate on rooms in downtown Los Angeles. Most hotels that cater to business, government, and convention travelers offer special weekend discounts that range 15%–40% below normal weekday rates. You can find out about weekend specials by calling the hotel or by consulting your travel agent.

7. WHOLESALERS, CONSOLIDATORS, AND RESERVATION SERVICES Wholesalers and consolidators buy rooms, or options on rooms (room blocks), from hotels at a low negotiated rate. They then resell the rooms at a profit through travel agents, tour packagers, or directly to the public. Most wholesalers and consolidators have a provision for returning unsold rooms to participating hotels, but they are disinclined to do so. The wholesaler's or consolidator's relationship with any hotel is predicated on volume. If they return rooms unsold, the hotel might not make as many rooms available to them the next time around. Thus, wholesalers and consolidators often offer rooms at bargain rates, anywhere from 15%–50% off rack, occasionally sacrificing their profit margin to avoid returning the rooms to the hotel unsold.

When wholesalers and consolidators deal directly with the public, they frequently represent themselves as reservation services. When you call, you can ask for a rate quote for a particular hotel or, alternatively, ask for their best available deal in the area where you prefer to stay. If there is a maximum amount you are willing to pay, say so. Chances are that the service will find something that will work for you, even if they have to shave a dollar or two off their own profit. Sometimes you will have to prepay for your room with your credit card when you make your reservation. Most often, you will pay when you check out. Listed below are two services that frequently offer substantial discounts in the Anaheim area.

ANAHEIM AREA WHOLESALERS AND CONSOLIDATORS
Hotel Reservations Network ☎ 800-780-5733   cheap-discount-hotels.com
Hotels.com ☎ 800-246-8357   hotels.com

8. CLUBS AND ORGANIZATIONS If you belong to AAA, AARP, or a number of other organizations, you can obtain lodging discounts. Usually the discounts are modest, 5%–15%, but occasionally higher.

9. IF YOU MAKE YOUR OWN RESERVATION As you poke around trying to find a good deal, there are several things you should know. First, always call the hotel in question as opposed to the hotel chain's national toll-free number. Quite often, the reservationists at the national numbers are unaware of local specials. Always ask about specials before you inquire about corporate rates. Do not be reluctant to bargain. If you are buying a hotel's weekend package, for example, and want to extend your stay into the following week, you can often obtain at least the corporate rate for the extra days. Do your bargaining before you check in, however, preferably when you make your reservations. Work far enough in advance to receive a confirmation.

HOW TO GET THE ROOM YOU WANT

MOST HOTELS, INCLUDING DISNEY'S, won't guarantee a specific room when you book but will post your request on your reservations record and try to accommodate you. Our experience indicates that if you give them your first, second, and third choices, you'll probably get one of the three.

unofficial **TIP**
Request a renovated room at your hotel— these can be much nicer than the older rooms.

When speaking to the reservationist or your travel agent, it's important to be specific. If you want a room overlooking the pool, say so. Similarly, be sure to clearly state such preferences as a particular floor, a corner room, a room close to restaurants, a room away from elevators and ice machines, a nonsmoking room, a room with a balcony, or any other preference. If you have a list of preferences, type it up in order of importance, and e-mail or fax it to the hotel or to your travel agent. Keep in mind that Disney's reservations computer is limited to storing a short block of text, so keep your request as brief and specific as possible. Be sure to include your own contact information and, if you've already booked, your reservation confirmation number. If it makes you feel better, call back in a few days to make sure that your preferences were posted to your reservations record.

About Hotel Renovations

We have inspected almost 100 hotels in the Disneyland Resort area to compile the lodging choices presented here. Each year we phone each hotel to verify contact information and inquire about renovations or refurbishments. If a hotel has been renovated or has refurbished its guest rooms, we reinspect that hotel along with new hotels for the next edition of this book.

Most hotels more than five years old refurbish 10%–20% of their guest rooms each year. This incremental approach minimizes disruption of business but makes your room assignment a crapshoot. You might luck into a newly renovated room or be assigned a threadbare room. Disney resorts will not guarantee a recently renovated room but will note your request and try to accommodate you. Non-Disney hotels will often guarantee an updated room when you book.

Our hotel ratings are provided starting on page 67.

TRAVEL PACKAGES

PACKAGE TOURS THAT INCLUDE LODGING, park admission, and other features are routinely available. Some packages are very good deals if you make use of the features you are paying for.

Finally, here's a helpful source of regional travel information:

ANAHEIM–ORANGE COUNTY VISITOR & CONVENTION BUREAU
☎ 714-765-8888; **anaheimoc.org**

How to Evaluate a Disneyland Travel Package

Hundreds of Disneyland package vacations are offered to the public each year. Some are created by the Disney Resort Travel Sales Center, others by airline touring companies, and some by independent travel agents and wholesalers. Almost all Disneyland packages include lodging at or near Disneyland and theme park admission. Packages offered by the airlines include air transportation.

Package prices vary seasonally, with mid-June–mid-August and holiday periods being the most expensive. During the off-season, forget packages; there are plenty of empty rooms, and you can negotiate great discounts (at non-Disney properties) yourself. Similarly, airfares and rental cars are cheaper at off-peak times.

When considering a package, choose one that includes features that you are sure to use. Whether you use all the features or not, you will most certainly pay for them. Second, if cost is of greater concern than convenience, make a few phone calls and see what the package would cost if you booked its individual components (such as airfare, rental car, and lodging) on your own. If the package price is less than the à la carte cost, the package is a good deal. If the costs are about the same, the package is probably worth it for the convenience.

If you buy a package from Disney, do not expect Disney reservationists to offer suggestions or help you sort out your options. As a rule they will not volunteer information but will only respond to specific questions you pose, adroitly ducking any query that calls for an opinion. A reader from North Riverside, Illinois, wrote to *The Unofficial Guide*, complaining:

> I have received various pieces of literature from Disney, and it is very confusing to try and figure everything out. My wife made two phone calls, and the [Disney] representatives were very courteous. However, they answered only the questions posed and were not very eager to give advice on what might be most cost-effective. The reps would not say if we would be better off doing one thing over the other. I feel that a person could spend 8 hours on the phone with [Disney] reps and not have any more input than you get from reading the literature.

If you cannot get the information you need from the Disney people, try a good travel agent. Chances are that the agent will be more forthcoming in helping you sort out your options.

Information Needed for Evaluation

For quick reference, visit **disneyplanning.com** and fill out a short survey to view video footage and descriptions for all Disneyland lodging properties. In addition, you can call the Disney Resort Travel Sales Center at ☎ 714-520-5060 and ask for a rate sheet listing admission options and prices for the theme parks. With this in hand, you are ready to evaluate any package that appeals to you. Remember that all packages are quoted on a per-person basis, two to a room (double occupancy). Good luck.

VISITING OTHER LOS ANGELES–AREA ATTRACTIONS

If your travel plans include a stay in the area of more than two or three days, lodge near Disneyland Resort only just before and on the days you visit the parks. The same traffic you avoid by staying close to the park will eat you alive when you begin branching out to other Los Angeles–area attractions. Also, the area immediately around Disneyland is uninspiring, and there is a marked scarcity of decent restaurants.

VACATION HOMES

SOME OF THE BEST LODGING DEALS in the Disneyland Resort area are vacation homes. Prices range from about $195 a night for two-bedroom condos and town homes to $200–$600 a night for three- to five-bedroom vacation homes.

Forgetting about taxes to keep things simple, let's compare renting a vacation home with staying at a three-star hotel near Disneyland. A family of two parents, two teens, and two grandparents would need three hotel rooms at the Fairfield Inn Anaheim Resort. At the lowest rate obtainable, they'd be spending $159 per night per room, or $566.56 total with tax and parking. Rooms are 228 square feet each, so they'd have a total of 684 square feet. Each room has a private bath, TV, and mini-fridge. The hotel has a pool and whirlpool tub, but parking costs extra.

At the same time of year, they can rent a 1,350-square-foot, three-bedroom, two-bath vacation home with a private pool within easy walking distance of Disneyland for $467.65—a saving of $98.91 per night over Fairfield Inn (a total saving of $494.55 on a five-night stay). But that's not all: the home comes with a washer and dryer; an outdoor hot tub; a grill; lounge chairs; a game room with pool table; a family room with a 52-inch HDTV, DVD player, and surround sound; a stereo system; a dining room with seating for eight, plus a covered patio dining area; and off-street parking. The only trade-off for our hypothetical family would be having two bathrooms instead of three.

You can see the specific home described above at **vrbo.com /175261**. VRBO stands for **Vacation Rental by Owner,** a listing service for owners of vacation properties nationwide. The VRBO website offers detailed information, including a good number of photos of each specific home. When you book, the home you've been looking at is the actual one you're reserving. On the other hand, some vacation-home rental companies, like rental car agencies, don't assign you a specific home until the day you arrive—these companies provide photos of a "typical" home instead of making information available on each of the individual homes in their inventory. In this case, you have to take the company's word that the typical home pictured is representative and that the property you'll be assigned will be just as nice.

Location is everything, especially in Southern California with its legendary traffic. Before renting a home, contact the owner and get the address. Then, using **google.com/maps,** obtain exact directions from the home to Disneyland. This will tell you how long and how complicated your commute will be. Avoid homes for which it's necessary to drive on a freeway for more than a couple of miles. Don't worry if the home isn't in Anaheim per se; it's the distance to Disneyland that counts.

The only practical way to shop for a rental home is online. Going online makes it relatively easy to compare different properties and rental companies. The best sites are easy to navigate, let you see what you're interested in without having to log in or divulge any personal information, and list memberships in such organizations as the Better Business Bureau. Before you book, ask about minimum stays, damage deposits, cleaning charges, and pets, as well as how any problems will be addressed once you're in the home.

In July 2016 the Anaheim City Council voted to impose a moratorium on new short-term rentals (including services like VRBO and Airbnb) and begin an 18-month phaseout of existing rentals, terminating them all by February 2018. The city is currently in the process of settling a lawsuit over the ordinance and has extended the phaseout to 2 years for some owners, but if restrictions aren't ultimately overturned, area visitors may have fewer lodging options in the future. Thankfully, short-term rentals are still legal in neighboring towns like Buena Park, where we found a room near Knott's Berry Farm through Airbnb for about $100 a night, gourmet whiskey included.

HOTELS *and* MOTELS:
Rated and Ranked

WHAT'S IN A ROOM?

EXCEPT FOR CLEANLINESS, STATE OF REPAIR, and decor, most travelers do not pay much attention to hotel rooms. There is, of course, a discernible standard of quality and luxury that differentiates Motel 6 from Holiday Inn, Holiday Inn from Marriott, and so on. In general, however, hotel guests fail to appreciate that some rooms are better engineered than others.

Contrary to what you might suppose, designing a hotel room is (or should be) a lot more complex than picking a bedspread to match the carpet and drapes. Making the room usable to its occupants is an art, a planning discipline that combines both form and function.

Decor and taste are important, certainly. No one wants to spend several days in a room where the decor is dated, garish, or even ugly. But beyond the decor, there are variables that determine how livable a hotel room is. In Anaheim, for example, we have seen some beautifully appointed rooms that are simply not well designed for human habitation. The next time you stay in a hotel, pay attention to the details and design elements of your room. Even more than decor, these are the things that will make you feel comfortable and at home.

ROOM RATINGS

TO SEPARATE PROPERTIES ACCORDING to the relative quality, tastefulness, state of repair, cleanliness, and size of their standard rooms, we have grouped the hotels and motels into classifications denoted by stars. Star ratings in this guide apply to Anaheim properties only and do not necessarily correspond to ratings awarded by Forbes, AAA, or other travel critics. Because stars have little relevance when awarded in the absence of commonly recognized standards of comparison, we have tied our ratings to expected levels of quality established by specific American hotel corporations.

Star ratings apply to *room quality only* and describe the property's standard accommodations. For most hotels and motels, a standard accommodation is a hotel room with either one king bed or two queen beds. In an all-suite property, the standard accommodation is either a studio or one-bedroom suite. In addition to standard accommodations, many hotels offer luxury rooms and special suites that are not rated in this guide. Star ratings for rooms are assigned without regard to whether a property has a restaurant, recreational facilities, entertainment, or other extras.

In addition to stars (which delineate broad categories), we also employ a numerical rating system. Our rating scale is 0–100, with 100

Continued on page 62

Disneyland-Area Hotels

1. Alo Hotel
2. Alpine Inn
3. America's Best Value Astoria Inn & Suites
4. Anaheim Camelot Inn & Suites
5. Anaheim Carriage Inn
6. Anaheim Express Inn Maingate
7. Anaheim Marriott
8. Anaheim Marriott Suites
9. Ayres Hotel Anaheim
10. Ayres Hotel Orange
11. Best Western Courtesy Inn
12. Best Western Plus Anaheim Inn
13. Best Western Plus Park Place Inn & Mini-Suites
14. Best Western Plus Pavilions
15. Best Western Plus Raffles Inn & Suites
16. Best Western Plus Stovall's Inn
17. Budget Inn
18. Candlewood Suites Anaheim Resort
19. Candy Cane Inn
20. Castle Inn & Suites
21. Clarion Hotel Anaheim
22. Comfort Inn & Suites
23. Cortona Inn & Suites
24. Country Inn & Suites
25. Courtyard Anaheim Theme Park Entrance
26. Courtyard by Marriott Anaheim
27. Days Inn Anaheim Maingate
28. Days Inn Anaheim West
29. Days Inn & Suites Anaheim at Disneyland Park
30. del Sol Inn Anaheim Resort
31. Desert Inn & Suites
32. Desert Palms Hotel & Suites Anaheim Resort
33. Disneyland Hotel
34. Disney's Grand Californian Hotel & Spa
35. Disney's Paradise Pier Hotel
36. Dolphin's Cove Resort
37. DoubleTree Anaheim–Orange County
38. DoubleTree Suites Anaheim Resort–Conv. Ctr.
39. Eden Roc Inn and Suites
40. Embassy Suites Anaheim–Orange
41. Embassy Suites Anaheim–South
42. Extended Stay America Orange County–Anaheim Conv. Ctr.
43. Fairfield Inn Anaheim Resort
44. Four Points by Sheraton Anaheim
45. Grand Legacy at the Park
46. Hampton Inn & Suites
47. Hilton Anaheim
48. Hilton Garden Inn Anaheim–Garden Grove
49. Holiday Inn–Anaheim Resort Area
50. Holiday Inn Express & Suites: Anaheim Resort
51. Holiday Inn Hotel & Suites Anaheim
52. Homewood Suites Anaheim–Main Gate Area
53. Homewood Suites Anaheim Resort–Conv. Ctr.
54. Hotel Indigo Anaheim
55. Howard Johnson Anaheim Hotel & Water Playground
56. Howard Johnson Inn Fullerton Hotel and Conference Center
57. Hyatt House at Anaheim Resort/Conv. Ctr.
58. Hyatt Place Anaheim Conv. Ctr.
59. Hyatt Regency Orange County
60. La Quinta Inn & Suites Anaheim
61. Majestic Garden Hotel
62. Motel 6 Anaheim Maingate
63. Park Vue Inn
64. Peacock Suites
65. Portofino Inn & Suites
66. Quality Inn & Suites Anaheim at the Park
67. Ramada Anaheim Maingate North
68. Ramada Plaza Anaheim Hotel
69. Red Lion Hotel Anaheim
70. Residence Inn Anaheim–Maingate
71. Residence Inn Anaheim Resort Area
72. Residence Inn at Anaheim Resort/Conv. Ctr.
73. Sheraton Garden Grove–Anaheim South Hotel
74. Sheraton Park Hotel at the Anaheim Resort

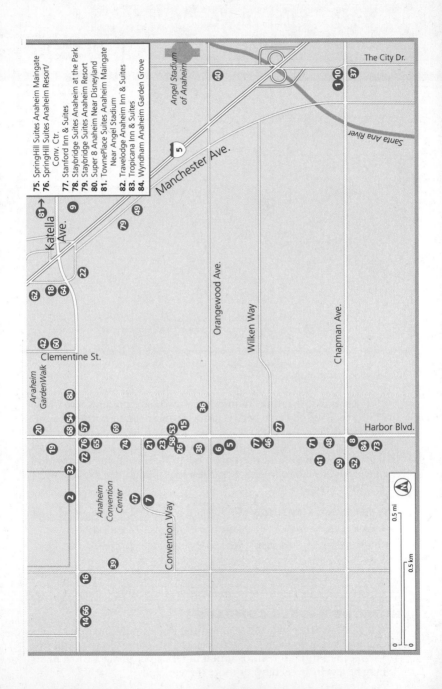

75. SpringHill Suites Anaheim Maingate
76. SpringHill Suites Anaheim Resort/ Conv. Ctr.
77. Stanford Inn & Suites
78. Staybridge Suites Anaheim at the Park
79. Staybridge Suites Anaheim Resort
80. Super 8 Anaheim Near Disneyland
81. TownePlace Suites Anaheim Maingate Near Angel Stadium
82. Travelodge Anaheim Inn & Suites
83. Tropicana Inn & Suites
84. Wyndham Anaheim Garden Grove

Hotels near Universal Studios

ACCOMMODATIONS
1. Best Western Hollywood Plaza Inn
2. Chamberlain West Hollywood
3. Colony Inn
4. Hilton Los Angeles at Universal City
5. Holiday Inn Burbank–Media Center
6. Marriott Los Angeles Burbank Airport
7. Sheraton Universal Hotel
8. Tilt Hotel Universal/Hollywood

Continued from page 59

as the best possible rating. Numerical ratings are presented to show the difference we perceive between one property and another. Rooms at the Hotel Indigo and Park Vue Inn are both rated as three and a half stars (★★★½). In the supplemental numerical ratings, the Hotel Indigo is rated an 82 and the Park Vue a 78. This means that within the three-and-a-half-star category, the Hotel Indigo has slightly nicer rooms than the Park Vue.

OVERALL STAR RATINGS		
★★★★★	Superior rooms	Tasteful and luxurious by any standard
★★★★	Extremely nice rooms	What you'd expect at a Hyatt Regency or Marriott
★★★	Nice rooms	Holiday Inn or comparable quality
★★	Adequate rooms	Clean, comfortable, and functional without frills—like a Motel 6

HOW THE HOTELS COMPARE

COST ESTIMATES ARE BASED on the hotel's published rack rates for standard rooms. Each "$" represents $50. Thus, a cost symbol of "$$$" means a room (or suite) at that hotel will be about $150 a night (it may be less for weekdays or more on weekends).

On pages 64–66, we list a hit parade of the nicest rooms in town. We've focused strictly on room quality and have excluded any consideration of location, services, recreation, or amenities. In some instances, a one- or two-room suite can be had for the same price or less than that of a hotel room.

If you used an earlier edition of this guide, you will notice that many of the ratings and rankings have changed. In addition to the inclusion of new properties, these changes are occasioned by such positive developments as guest room renovation or improved maintenance and housekeeping. A failure to properly maintain guest rooms or a lapse in housekeeping standards can negatively affect the ratings.

Finally, before you begin to shop for a hotel, take a hard look at this letter we received from a couple in Hot Springs, Arkansas:

> *We canceled our room reservations to follow the advice in your book [and reserved a hotel highly ranked by* The Unofficial Guide*]. We wanted inexpensive but clean and cheerful. We got inexpensive but dirty, grim, and depressing. I really felt disappointed in your advice and the room. It was the pits. That was the one real piece of information I needed from your book!*

Needless to say, this letter was as unsettling to us as the bad room was to our reader. Our integrity as travel journalists, after all, is based on the quality of the information we provide to our readers. Even with the best of intentions and the most conscientious research, however, we cannot inspect every room in every hotel. What we do, in statistical terms, is take a sample: we check out several rooms selected at random in each hotel and base our ratings and rankings on those rooms. Though it would be unusual, it is certainly possible that the rooms we randomly inspect are not representative of the majority of rooms at a particular hotel. Another possibility is that the rooms we inspect in a given hotel are representative but that by bad luck a reader is assigned to an inferior room. When we rechecked the hotel that our reader disliked so intensely, we discovered that our rating was correctly representative but that he and his wife had unfortunately been assigned to one of a small number of threadbare rooms scheduled for renovation.

The key to avoiding disappointment is to do some snooping around in advance. We recommend that you ask to get a photo of a hotel's standard guest room before you book, or at least a copy of the hotel's promotional brochure. Be forewarned, however, that some hotel chains use the same guest room photo in their promotional literature for all hotels in the chain, and that the guest room in a specific property may not resemble the photo in the brochure. When you or your travel agent call, ask how old the property is and when the guest room you are being assigned was last renovated. If you arrive and are assigned a room inferior to that which you had been led to expect, demand to be moved to another room.

Continued on page 72

HOW THE HOTELS COMPARE

HOTEL	MAP NUMBER (pgs. 60-61)	OVERALL QUALITY RATING	ROOM QUALITY RATING	COST ($ = $50)
DISNEYLAND AREA				
Disney's Grand Californian Hotel & Spa	34	★★★★½	90	$- x 12
Disneyland Hotel	33	★★★★	89	$+ x 10
Hyatt Regency Orange County	59	★★★★	89	$$$$$
SpringHill Suites Marriott at Anaheim Resort/ Convention Center	76	★★★★	88	$$$$+
Staybridge Suites Anaheim at the Park	78	★★★★	88	$$$$-
Embassy Suites Anaheim-Orange	40	★★★★	87	$- x 7
Disney's Paradise Pier Hotel	35	★★★★	86	$+ x 7
DoubleTree Suites by Hilton Hotel Anaheim Resort-Convention Center	38	★★★★	86	$$$$
Hyatt Place Anaheim Convention Center	58	★★★★	86	$$$$
SpringHill Suites Anaheim Maingate	75	★★★★	86	$$$$$+
Wyndham Anaheim Garden Grove	84	★★★★	86	$$$$-
Anaheim Marriott Suites	8	★★★★	85	$$$$+
DoubleTree by Hilton Hotel Anaheim-Orange County	37	★★★★	85	$$$$$
Hyatt House at Anaheim Resort/ Convention Center	57	★★★★	85	$$$$$
Homewood Suites by Hilton Anaheim Resort-Convention Center	51	★★★★	84	$$$$$
Ayres Hotel Orange	10	★★★★	83	$$$$+
Embassy Suites Anaheim-South	41	★★★★	83	$$$$$+
Sheraton Park Hotel at the Anaheim Resort	74	★★★★	83	$$$+
Ayres Hotel Anaheim	9	★★★½	82	$$$$
Best Western Plus Stovall's Inn	16	★★★½	82	$$$$-
Candlewood Suites Anaheim Resort	18	★★★½	82	$$$+
Holiday Inn-Anaheim Resort Area	49	★★★½	82	$$$$-
Hotel Indigo Anaheim	54	★★★½	82	$$$$
Staybridge Suites Anaheim Resort	79	★★★½	82	$$$$-
Homewood Suites by Hilton Anaheim-Main Gate Area	52	★★★½	81	$$$$+
Howard Johnson Anaheim Hotel & Water Playground	55	★★★½	81	$$$$+
Majestic Garden Hotel	61	★★★½	81	$$$+
Peacock Suites	64	★★★½	81	$$$
Residence Inn at Anaheim Resort/Convention Center	72	★★★½	81	$$$$$+
Anaheim Marriott	7	★★★½	80	$$$$+

HOW THE HOTELS COMPARE (continued)

HOTEL	MAP NUMBER (pgs. 60-61)	OVERALL QUALITY RATING	ROOM QUALITY RATING	COST ($ = $50)
DISNEYLAND AREA (continued)				
Country Inn & Suites	24	★★★½	80	$$$$$+
Sheraton Garden Grove–Anaheim South Hotel	73	★★★½	80	$$$$$–
Hilton Anaheim	47	★★★½	79	$$$$+
Hampton Inn & Suites	46	★★★½	78	$$$$$+
Park Vue Inn	63	★★★½	78	$$$$–
Residence Inn Anaheim-Maingate	70	★★★½	78	$- x 6
TownePlace Suites Anaheim Maingate Near Angel Stadium	81	★★★½	78	$$$$$
Anaheim Camelot Inn & Suites	4	★★★½	77	$$$+
Four Points by Sheraton Anaheim	44	★★★½	77	$$$$
Holiday Inn Express & Suites: Anaheim Resort	50	★★★½	77	$$$$$
Courtyard Anaheim Theme Park Entrance	25	★★★½	76	$+ x 7
Residence Inn Anaheim Resort Area	71	★★★½	76	$$$$$–
Courtyard by Marriott Anaheim	26	★★★½	75	$$$$+
La Quinta Inn & Suites Anaheim	60	★★★½	75	$$$$
Portofino Inn & Suites	65	★★★½	75	$$$$
Alo Hotel	1	★★★	74	$$$$–
Best Western Plus Anaheim Inn	12	★★★	74	$$$+
Best Western Plus Pavilions	14	★★★	74	$$$
Candy Cane Inn	19	★★★	74	$$$$–
Cortona Inn & Suites	23	★★★	74	$$$$–
Fairfield Inn Anaheim Resort	43	★★★	74	$$$$+
Hilton Garden Inn Anaheim-Garden Grove	48	★★★	74	$$$$$–
Holiday Inn Hotel & Suites Anaheim	51	★★★	74	$$$$
Ramada Anaheim Maingate North	67	★★★	74	$$$
Ramada Plaza Anaheim Hotel	68	★★★	74	$$$$$–
Red Lion Hotel Anaheim	69	★★★	74	$$$$$–
Best Western Plus Raffles Inn & Suites	15	★★★	73	$$$$–
Comfort Inn & Suites	22	★★★	72	$$$+
Dolphin's Cove Resort	36	★★★	72	$$$$+
Castle Inn & Suites	20	★★★	71	$$$+
Clarion Hotel Anaheim	21	★★★	71	$$$+
Desert Palms Hotel & Suites Anaheim Resort	32	★★★	69	$$$$+
Stanford Inn & Suites	77	★★★	69	$$$$

HOW THE HOTELS COMPARE *(continued)*

HOTEL	MAP NUMBER (pgs. 60-61)	OVERALL QUALITY RATING	ROOM QUALITY RATING	COST ($ = $50)
DISNEYLAND AREA *(continued)*				
Desert Inn & Suites	31	★★★	68	$$$+
Howard Johnson Inn Fullerton Hotel and Conference Center	56	★★★	68	$$$+
Best Western Plus Park Place Inn & Mini-Suites	13	★★★	66	$$$+
Tropicana Inn & Suites	83	★★★	66	$$$+
Eden Roc Inn and Suites	39	★★★	65	$$$+
Alpine Inn	2	★★½	64	$$$
Best Western Courtesy Inn	11	★★½	64	$$$
Extended Stay America Orange County–Anaheim Convention Center	42	★★½	64	$$$+
Travelodge Anaheim Inn & Suites	82	★★½	64	$$$-
America's Best Value Astoria Inn & Suites	3	★★½	63	$$+
Grand Legacy at the Park	45	★★½	63	$$$
del Sol Inn Anaheim Resort	30	★★½	62	$$$$$+
Budget Inn	17	★★½	61	$ x 6
Motel 6 Anaheim Maingate	62	★★½	61	$+
Quality Inn & Suites Anaheim at the Park	66	★★½	60	$$$
Super 8 Anaheim Near Disneyland	80	★★½	60	$$$+
Anaheim Express Inn Maingate	6	★★½	59	$$$$-
Days Inn & Suites Anaheim at Disneyland Park	29	★★½	59	$$$
Days Inn Anaheim West	28	★★½	58	$$$
Anaheim Carriage Inn	5	★★½	57	$$$-
Days Inn Anaheim Maingate	27	★★½	56	$$$+
UNIVERSAL AREA	MAP NUMBER (pg. 62)	OVERALL QUALITY RATING	ROOM QUALITY RATING	COST ($ = $50)
Hilton Los Angeles at Universal City	4	★★★★	86	$- x 7
Sheraton Universal Hotel	7	★★★★	85	$ x 6
Holiday Inn Burbank–Media Center	5	★★★½	82	$$$$-
Tilt Hotel	8	★★★½	80	$$$$$-
Chamberlain West Hollywood	2	★★★½	78	$+ x 8
Marriott Los Angeles Burbank Airport	6	★★★½	78	$ x 6
Best Western Hollywood Plaza Inn	1	★★★	72	$$$$$
Colony Inn	3	★★½	60	$$$$-

HOTEL INFORMATION CHART

Alo Hotel ★★★
3737 W. Chapman Ave.
Orange, CA 92868
☎ 714-978-9168
ayreshotels.com/alo-hotel

ROOM RATING	74
COST	$$$$–
POOL	•
ON-SITE DINING	•
BREAKFAST	Free
WI-FI	Free
PARKING	Free

Anaheim Camelot Inn & Suites
★★★½
1520 S. Harbor Blvd.
Anaheim, CA 92802
☎ 714-635-7275
camelotinn-anaheim.com

ROOM RATING	77
COST	$$$+
POOL	•
ON-SITE DINING	–
BREAKFAST	–
WI-FI	Free
PARKING	Paid

Anaheim Marriott ★★★½
700 W. Convention Way
Anaheim, CA 92802
☎ 714-750-8000
tinyurl.com/anamarriott

ROOM RATING	80
COST	$$$$+
POOL	•
ON-SITE DINING	•
BREAKFAST	Paid
WI-FI	Paid
PARKING	Paid

Ayres Hotel Orange ★★★★
200 The City Dr. N
Orange, CA 92868
☎ 714-919-7940
ayreshotels.com/ayres-hotel-orange

ROOM RATING	83
COST	$$$$+
POOL	•
ON-SITE DINING	–
BREAKFAST	Free
WI-FI	Free
PARKING	Free

Best Western Plus Anaheim Inn
★★★
1630 S. Harbor Blvd.
Anaheim, CA 92802
☎ 714-774-1050
anaheiminn.com

ROOM RATING	74
COST	$$$+
POOL	•
ON-SITE DINING	–
BREAKFAST	Free
WI-FI	Free
PARKING	Free

Alpine Inn ★★½
715 W. Katella Ave.
Anaheim, CA 92802
☎ 714-535-2186
alpineinnanaheim.com

ROOM RATING	64
COST	$$$
POOL	•
ON-SITE DINING	–
BREAKFAST	Free
WI-FI	Free
PARKING	Free

Anaheim Carriage Inn ★★½
2125 S. Harbor Blvd.
Anaheim, CA 92802
☎ 714-740-1440
anaheimcarriagehotel.com

ROOM RATING	57
COST	$$$–
POOL	•
ON-SITE DINING	–
BREAKFAST	Free
WI-FI	Free
PARKING	Free

Anaheim Marriott Suites ★★★★
12015 Harbor Blvd.
Anaheim, CA 92802
☎ 714-750-1000
tinyurl.com/anamarriottste

ROOM RATING	85
COST	$$$$+
POOL	•
ON-SITE DINING	•
BREAKFAST	Paid
WI-FI	Paid
PARKING	Paid

Best Western Courtesy Inn ★★½
1070 W. Ball Rd.
Anaheim, CA 92802
☎ 714-772-2470
bestwesternanaheimhotel.com

ROOM RATING	64
COST	$$$
POOL	•
ON-SITE DINING	–
BREAKFAST	Free
WI-FI	Free
PARKING	Free

**Best Western Plus Park Place Inn &
Mini-Suites** ★★★
1544 S. Harbor Blvd.
Anaheim, CA 92802
☎ 714-776-4800
parkplaceinnandminisuites.com

ROOM RATING	66
COST	$$$+
POOL	•
ON-SITE DINING	–
BREAKFAST	Free
WI-FI	Free
PARKING	Paid

**America's Best Value Astoria
Inn & Suites** ★★½
426 W. Ball Rd.
Anaheim, CA 92805
☎ 714-774-3882
anaheimastoriainn.com

ROOM RATING	63
COST	$$+
POOL	•
ON-SITE DINING	–
BREAKFAST	Free
WI-FI	Free
PARKING	Free

Anaheim Express Inn Maingate
★★½
620 W. Orangewood Ave.
Anaheim, CA 92802
☎ 714-971-9000
anainn.com

ROOM RATING	59
COST	$$$$–
POOL	•
ON-SITE DINING	–
BREAKFAST	Free
WI-FI	Free
PARKING	Free

Ayres Hotel Anaheim ★★★½
2550 E. Katella Ave.
Anaheim, CA 92806
☎ 714-634-2106
ayreshotels.com/ayres-hotel-anaheim

ROOM RATING	82
COST	$$$$
POOL	•
ON-SITE DINING	–
BREAKFAST	Free
WI-FI	Free
PARKING	Paid

Best Western Hollywood Plaza Inn
★★★
2011 N. Highland Ave.
Hollywood, CA 90068
☎ 323-851-1800
bestwesternhollywoodhotel.com

ROOM RATING	72
COST	$$$$$
POOL	•
ON-SITE DINING	•
BREAKFAST	Paid
WI-FI	Free
PARKING	Paid

Best Western Plus Pavilions ★★★
1176 W. Katella Ave.
Anaheim, CA 92802
☎ 714-776-0140
pavilionshotel.com

ROOM RATING	74
COST	$$$
POOL	•
ON-SITE DINING	–
BREAKFAST	Free
WI-FI	Free
PARKING	Free

HOTEL INFORMATION CHART *(continued)*

Best Western Plus Raffles Inn & Suites ★★★
2040 S. Harbor Blvd.
Anaheim, CA 92802
☎ 714-750-6100
bestwesternrafflesinn.com

ROOM RATING	73
COST	$$$$–
POOL	•
ON-SITE DINING	–
BREAKFAST	Free
WI-FI	Free
PARKING	Paid

Best Western Plus Stovall's Inn ★★★½
1110 W. Katella Ave.
Anaheim, CA 92802
☎ 714-778-1880
stovallsinn.com

ROOM RATING	82
COST	$$$$–
POOL	•
ON-SITE DINING	•
BREAKFAST	Free
WI-FI	Free
PARKING	Paid

Budget Inn ★★½
1042 W. Ball Rd.
Anaheim, CA 92802
☎ **714-535-5524**

ROOM RATING	61
COST	$ x 6
POOL	•
ON-SITE DINING	–
BREAKFAST	–
WI-FI	Free
PARKING	Free

Chamberlain West Hollywood ★★★½
1000 Westmount Drive
West Hollywood, CA 90069
☎ 310-657-7400
chamberlainwesthollywood.com

ROOM RATING	78
COST	$+ x 8
POOL	•
ON-SITE DINING	•
BREAKFAST	Paid
WI-FI	Free
PARKING	Paid

Clarion Hotel Anaheim ★★★
616 Convention Way
Anaheim, CA 92802
☎ 714-750-3131
clarionanaheim.com

ROOM RATING	71
COST	$$$+
POOL	•
ON-SITE DINING	•
BREAKFAST	Paid
WI-FI	Free
PARKING	Paid

Colony Inn ★★½
4917 Vineland Ave.
North Hollywood, CA 91601
☎ 818-763-2787
colonyinn.com

ROOM RATING	60
COST	$$$$–
POOL	–
ON-SITE DINING	–
BREAKFAST	Free
WI-FI	Free
PARKING	Free

Courtyard Anaheim Theme Park Entrance ★★★½
1420 S. Harbor Blvd.
Anaheim, CA 92802
☎ 714-254-1442
tinyurl.com/courtyardtpent

ROOM RATING	76
COST	$+ x 7
POOL	•
ON-SITE DINING	–
BREAKFAST	Paid
WI-FI	Free
PARKING	Paid

Courtyard by Marriott Anaheim ★★★½
2045 S. Harbor Blvd.
Anaheim, CA 92802
☎ 714-740-2645
courtyardanaheim.com

ROOM RATING	75
COST	$$$$+
POOL	•
ON-SITE DINING	•
BREAKFAST	Paid
WI-FI	Free
PARKING	Paid

Days Inn & Suites Anaheim at Disneyland Park ★★½
1111 S. Harbor Blvd.
Anaheim, CA 92805
☎ 714-533-8830
tinyurl.com/daysinndland

ROOM RATING	59
COST	$$$
POOL	•
ON-SITE DINING	–
BREAKFAST	Free
WI-FI	Free
PARKING	Free

Desert Inn & Suites ★★★
1600 S. Harbor Blvd.
Anaheim, CA 92802
☎ 714-772-5050
anaheimdesertinn.com

ROOM RATING	68
COST	$$$+
POOL	•
ON-SITE DINING	–
BREAKFAST	Free
WI-FI	Free
PARKING	Paid

Desert Palms Hotel & Suites Anaheim Resort ★★★
631 W. Katella Ave.
Anaheim, CA 92802
☎ 714-535-1133
desertpalmshotel.com

ROOM RATING	69
COST	$$$$+
POOL	•
ON-SITE DINING	•
BREAKFAST	Free
WI-FI	Free
PARKING	Free

Disneyland Hotel ★★★★
1150 W. Magic Way
Anaheim, CA 92802
☎ 714-778-6600
disneyland.disney.go.com/hotels/disneyland-hotel

ROOM RATING	89
COST	$+ x 10
POOL	•
ON-SITE DINING	•
BREAKFAST	Paid
WI-FI	Free
PARKING	Paid

DoubleTree by Hilton Hotel Anaheim–Orange County ★★★★
100 The City Dr.
Orange, CA 92868
☎ 714-634-4500
tinyurl.com/doubletreeana

ROOM RATING	85
COST	$$$$$
POOL	•
ON-SITE DINING	•
BREAKFAST	Paid
WI-FI	Paid
PARKING	Paid

DoubleTree Suites by Hilton Hotel Anaheim Resort–Convention Center ★★★★
2085 S. Harbor Blvd.
Anaheim, CA 92802
☎ 714-750-3000
tinyurl.com/doubletreeanaconv

ROOM RATING	86
COST	$$$$
POOL	•
ON-SITE DINING	•
BREAKFAST	Paid
WI-FI	Free
PARKING	Paid

Eden Roc Inn and Suites ★★★
1830 S. West St.
Anaheim, CA 92802
☎ 714-663-8700
edenrocanaheim.com

ROOM RATING	65
COST	$$$+
POOL	•
ON-SITE DINING	–
BREAKFAST	–
WI-FI	Free
PARKING	Free

Candlewood Suites Anaheim Resort ★★★½
1733 S. Anaheim Blvd.
Anaheim, CA 92805
☎ 714-635-5555
tinyurl.com/candlewoodana

ROOM RATING	82
COST	$$$+
POOL	-
ON-SITE DINING	-
BREAKFAST	-
WI-FI	Paid
PARKING	Free

Candy Cane Inn ★★★
1747 S. Harbor Blvd.
Anaheim, CA 92802
☎ 714-774-5284
candycaneinn.net

ROOM RATING	74
COST	$$$$-
POOL	•
ON-SITE DINING	-
BREAKFAST	Free
WI-FI	Free
PARKING	Free

Castle Inn & Suites ★★★
1734 S. Harbor Blvd.
Anaheim, CA 92802
☎ 714-774-8111
castleinn.com

ROOM RATING	71
COST	$$$+
POOL	•
ON-SITE DINING	-
BREAKFAST	-
WI-FI	Free
PARKING	Free

Comfort Inn & Suites ★★★
300 E. Katella Ave.
Anaheim, CA 92802
☎ 714-772-8713
comfortinnsuitesanaheim.com

ROOM RATING	72
COST	$$$+
POOL	•
ON-SITE DINING	-
BREAKFAST	Free
WI-FI	Free
PARKING	Free

Cortona Inn & Suites ★★★
2029 S. Harbor Blvd.
Anaheim, CA 92802
☎ 714-971-5000
cortonainn.com

ROOM RATING	74
COST	$$$$-
POOL	•
ON-SITE DINING	-
BREAKFAST	Free
WI-FI	Free
PARKING	Free

Country Inn & Suites ★★★½
1640 S. Clementine St.
Anaheim, CA 92802
☎ 714-598-0600
countryinns.com/anaheim-hotel-
ca-92802/usaahca

ROOM RATING	80
COST	$$$$$+
POOL	•
ON-SITE DINING	•
BREAKFAST	Free
WI-FI	Free
PARKING	Free

Days Inn Anaheim Maingate ★★½
2200 S. Harbor Blvd.
Anaheim, CA 92802
☎ 714-750-5211
tinyurl.com/daysinnmaingate

ROOM RATING	56
COST	$$$+
POOL	•
ON-SITE DINING	-
BREAKFAST	Free
WI-FI	Free
PARKING	Free

Days Inn Anaheim West ★★½
1030 W. Ball Rd.
Anaheim, CA 92802
☎ 714-520-0101
tinyurl.com/daysinnanawest

ROOM RATING	58
COST	$$$
POOL	•
ON-SITE DINING	-
BREAKFAST	Free
WI-FI	Free
PARKING	Free

del Sol Inn Anaheim Resort ★★½
1604 S. Harbor Blvd.
Anaheim, CA 92802
☎ 714-234-3411
delsolinn.com

ROOM RATING	62
COST	$$$$$+
POOL	•
ON-SITE DINING	•
BREAKFAST	Free
WI-FI	Free
PARKING	Paid

Disney's Grand Californian Hotel & Spa ★★★★½
1600 S. Disneyland Dr.
Anaheim, CA 92802
☎ 714-635-2300
disneyland.disney.go.com/hotels
/grand-californian-hotel

ROOM RATING	90
COST	$- x 12
POOL	•
ON-SITE DINING	•
BREAKFAST	Paid
WI-FI	Free
PARKING	Paid

Disney's Paradise Pier Hotel ★★★★
1717 S. Disneyland Dr.
Anaheim, CA 92802
☎ 714-999-0990
disneyland.disney.go.com/hotels
/paradise-pier-hotel

ROOM RATING	86
COST	$+ x 7
POOL	•
ON-SITE DINING	•
BREAKFAST	Paid
WI-FI	Free
PARKING	Paid

Dolphin's Cove Resort ★★★
465 W. Orangewood Ave.
Anaheim, CA 92802
☎ 714-980-0830
extraholidays.com/anaheim-california/
dolphins-cove-resort.aspx

ROOM RATING	72
COST	$$$$+
POOL	•
ON-SITE DINING	-
BREAKFAST	-
WI-FI	Free
PARKING	Free

Embassy Suites Anaheim–Orange ★★★★
400 N. State College Blvd.
Orange, CA 92868
☎ 714-938-1111
embassysuitesanaheimorange.com

ROOM RATING	87
COST	$- x 7
POOL	•
ON-SITE DINING	•
BREAKFAST	Free
WI-FI	Paid
PARKING	Paid

Embassy Suites Anaheim–South ★★★★
11767 Harbor Blvd.
Garden Grove, CA 92840
☎ 714-539-3300
anaheimsouth.embassysuites.com

ROOM RATING	83
COST	$$$$$+
POOL	•
ON-SITE DINING	•
BREAKFAST	Free
WI-FI	Paid
PARKING	Paid

Extended Stay America Orange County–Anaheim Convention Center ★★½
1742 S. Clementine St.
Anaheim, CA 92802
☎ 714-502-9988
tinyurl.com/exstayorangeco

ROOM RATING	64
COST	$$$+
POOL	•
ON-SITE DINING	-
BREAKFAST	Free
WI-FI	Free
PARKING	Free

HOTEL INFORMATION CHART *(continued)*

Fairfield Inn Anaheim Resort ★★★
1460 S. Harbor Blvd.
Anaheim, CA 92802
☎ 714-772-6777
tinyurl.com/fairfieldinnana

ROOM RATING	74
COST	$$$$+
POOL	•
ON-SITE DINING	•
BREAKFAST	Paid
WI-FI	Free
PARKING	Paid

Four Points by Sheraton Anaheim ★★★½
1221 S. Harbor Blvd.
Anaheim, CA 92805
☎ 714-758-0900
tinyurl.com/4ptsana

ROOM RATING	77
COST	$$$$
POOL	•
ON-SITE DINING	•
BREAKFAST	Paid
WI-FI	Free
PARKING	Paid

Grand Legacy at the Park ★★½
1650 S. Harbor Blvd.
Anaheim, CA 92802
☎ 714-772-0440
grandlegacyhotel.com

ROOM RATING	63
COST	$$$
POOL	•
ON-SITE DINING	–
BREAKFAST	Free
WI-FI	Free
PARKING	Paid

Hilton Los Angeles at Universal City ★★★★
555 Universal Hollywood Dr.
Universal City, CA 91608
☎ 818-506-2500
tinyurl.com/hiltonuniversal

ROOM RATING	86
COST	$– x 7
POOL	•
ON-SITE DINING	•
BREAKFAST	Paid
WI-FI	Paid
PARKING	Paid

Holiday Inn Burbank–Media Center ★★★½
150 E. Angeleno Ave.
Burbank, CA 91502
☎ 818-841-4770
tinyurl.com/holidayinnburbank

ROOM RATING	82
COST	$$$$–
POOL	•
ON-SITE DINING	•
BREAKFAST	Paid
WI-FI	Free
PARKING	paid

Holiday Inn Express & Suites: Anaheim Resort ★★★½
1411 S. Manchester Ave.
Anaheim, CA 92802
☎ 714-400-2044
hieanaheim.com

ROOM RATING	77
COST	$$$$$
POOL	•
ON-SITE DINING	–
BREAKFAST	Free
WI-FI	Free
PARKING	Paid

Homewood Suites by Hilton Anaheim–Main Gate Area ★★★½
12005 Harbor Blvd.
Garden Grove, CA 92840
☎ 714-740-1800
homewoodsuitesanaheim.com

ROOM RATING	81
COST	$$$$+
POOL	•
ON-SITE DINING	–
BREAKFAST	Free
WI-FI	Free
PARKING	Paid

Hotel Indigo Anaheim ★★★½
435 W. Katella Ave.
Anaheim, CA 92802
☎ 714-772-7755
tinyurl.com/hotelindigoana

ROOM RATING	82
COST	$$$$
POOL	•
ON-SITE DINING	•
BREAKFAST	Paid
WI-FI	Free
PARKING	Free

Howard Johnson Anaheim Hotel & Water Playground ★★★½
1380 S. Harbor Blvd.
Anaheim, CA 92802
☎ 714-776-6120
hojoanaheim.com

ROOM RATING	81
COST	$$$$+
POOL	•
ON-SITE DINING	•
BREAKFAST	Paid
WI-FI	Free
PARKING	Free

Hyatt Regency Orange County ★★★★
11999 Harbor Blvd.
Garden Grove, CA 92840
☎ 714-750-1234
orangecounty.hyatt.com

ROOM RATING	89
COST	$$$$$
POOL	•
ON-SITE DINING	•
BREAKFAST	Paid
WI-FI	Paid
PARKING	Paid

La Quinta Inn & Suites Anaheim ★★★½
1752 S. Clementine St.
Anaheim, CA 92802
☎ 714-635-5000
laquintaanaheim.com

ROOM RATING	75
COST	$$$$
POOL	•
ON-SITE DINING	–
BREAKFAST	Free
WI-FI	Free
PARKING	Paid

Majestic Garden Hotel ★★★½
900 S. Disneyland Dr.
Anaheim, CA 92802
☎ 714-778-1700
majesticgardenhotel.com

ROOM RATING	81
COST	$$$+
POOL	•
ON-SITE DINING	•
BREAKFAST	Paid
WI-FI	Free
PARKING	Paid

Peacock Suites ★★★½
1745 S. Anaheim Blvd.
Anaheim, CA 92805
☎ 714-535-8255
shellhospitality.com/peacock-suites

ROOM RATING	81
COST	$$$
POOL	•
ON-SITE DINING	–
BREAKFAST	–
WI-FI	Free
PARKING	Paid

Portofino Inn & Suites ★★★½
1831 S. Harbor Blvd.
Anaheim, CA 92802
☎ 714-782-7600
portofinoinnanaheim.com

ROOM RATING	75
COST	$$$$
POOL	•
ON-SITE DINING	–
BREAKFAST	–
WI-FI	Free
PARKING	Free

Quality Inn & Suites Anaheim at the Park ★★½
1166 W. Katella Ave.
Anaheim, CA 92805
☎ 714-774-7817
tinyurl.com/qualityinnana

ROOM RATING	60
COST	$$$
POOL	•
ON-SITE DINING	–
BREAKFAST	Free
WI-FI	Free
PARKING	Paid

Hampton Inn & Suites ★★★½
11747 Harbor Blvd.
Garden Grove, CA 92840
☎ 714-703-8800
hamptoninnanaheim.com

ROOM RATING	78
COST	$$$$$+
POOL	•
ON-SITE DINING	–
BREAKFAST	Free
WI-FI	Free
PARKING	Paid

Hilton Anaheim ★★★½
777 W. Convention Way
Anaheim, CA 92802
☎ 714-750-4321
hiltonanaheimhotel.com

ROOM RATING	79
COST	$$$$+
POOL	•
ON-SITE DINING	•
BREAKFAST	Paid
WI-FI	Free
PARKING	Paid

Hilton Garden Inn Anaheim–Garden Grove ★★★
11777 Harbor Blvd.
Garden Grove, CA 92840
☎ 714-703-9100
tinyurl.com/hiltonana

ROOM RATING	74
COST	$$$$$–
POOL	•
ON-SITE DINING	–
BREAKFAST	Paid
WI-FI	Free
PARKING	Paid

Holiday Inn Hotel & Suites Anaheim ★★★
1240 S. Walnut Ave.
Anaheim, CA 92802
☎ 714-535-0300
tinyurl.com/holidayinnana

ROOM RATING	74
COST	$$$$
POOL	•
ON-SITE DINING	•
BREAKFAST	Paid
WI-FI	Free
PARKING	Paid

Holiday Inn–Anaheim Resort Area ★★★½
1915 S. Manchester Ave.
Anaheim, CA 92802
☎ 714-748-7777
tinyurl.com/holidayanaresort

ROOM RATING	82
COST	$$$$–
POOL	•
ON-SITE DINING	•
BREAKFAST	Paid
WI-FI	Free
PARKING	Free

Homewood Suites by Hilton Anaheim Resort–Convention Center ★★★★
2010 S. Harbor Blvd.
Anaheim, CA 92802
☎ 714-750-2010
tinyurl.com/homewoodara

ROOM RATING	84
COST	$$$$$
POOL	•
ON-SITE DINING	–
BREAKFAST	Free
WI-FI	Free
PARKING	Paid

Howard Johnson Inn Fullerton Hotel and Conference Center ★★★
222 W. Houston Ave.
Fullerton, CA 92832
☎ 714-992-1700
hojomaingate.com

ROOM RATING	68
COST	$$$+
POOL	•
ON-SITE DINING	–
BREAKFAST	Free
WI-FI	Free
PARKING	Free

Hyatt House at Anaheim Resort /Convention Center ★★★★
1800 S. Harbor Blvd.
Anaheim, CA 92802
☎ 714-971-1800
anaheimresort.house.hyatt.com

ROOM RATING	85
COST	$$$$$
POOL	•
ON-SITE DINING	–
BREAKFAST	Free
WI-FI	Free
PARKING	Paid

Hyatt Place Anaheim Convention Center ★★★★
2035 S. Harbor Blvd.
Anaheim, CA 92802
☎ 714-750-4000
anaheimresort.place.hyatt.com

ROOM RATING	86
COST	$$$$
POOL	•
ON-SITE DINING	•
BREAKFAST	Free
WI-FI	Free
PARKING	Paid

Marriott Los Angeles Burbank Airport ★★★½
2500 N. Hollywood Way
Burbank, CA 91505
☎ 818-843-6000
marriottburbankairport.com

ROOM RATING	78
COST	$ x 6
POOL	•
ON-SITE DINING	•
BREAKFAST	Paid
WI-FI	Paid
PARKING	Paid

Motel 6 Anaheim Maingate ★★½
100 W. Disney Way
Anaheim, CA 92802
☎ 714-520-9696
motel6-anaheim.com

ROOM RATING	61
COST	$+
POOL	•
ON-SITE DINING	–
BREAKFAST	–
WI-FI	Paid
PARKING	Free

Park Vue Inn ★★★½
1570 S. Harbor Blvd.
Anaheim, CA 92802
☎ 714-772-3691
parkvueinn.com

ROOM RATING	78
COST	$$$$–
POOL	•
ON-SITE DINING	–
BREAKFAST	Free
WI-FI	Free
PARKING	Free

Ramada Anaheim Maingate North ★★★
921 S. Harbor Blvd.
Anaheim, CA 92802
☎ 714-999-0684
tinyurl.com/ramadamainnorth

ROOM RATING	74
COST	$$$
POOL	•
ON-SITE DINING	–
BREAKFAST	Free
WI-FI	Free
PARKING	Free

Ramada Plaza Anaheim Hotel ★★★
515 W. Katella Ave.
Anaheim, CA 92802
☎ 714-991-6868
ramadaanaheim.com

ROOM RATING	74
COST	$$$$$–
POOL	•
ON-SITE DINING	•
BREAKFAST	Free
WI-FI	Free
PARKING	Free

Red Lion Hotel Anaheim ★★★
1850 S. Harbor Blvd.
Anaheim, CA 92802
☎ 714-750-2801
redlion.com/anaheim

ROOM RATING	74
COST	$$$$$–
POOL	•
ON-SITE DINING	•
BREAKFAST	–
WI-FI	Free
PARKING	Paid

HOTEL INFORMATION CHART (continued)

Residence Inn Anaheim Resort Area
★★★½
11931 Harbor Blvd.
Garden Grove, CA 92840
☎ 714-591-4000
tinyurl.com/resinnara

ROOM RATING	76
COST	$$$$$-
POOL	•
ON-SITE DINING	–
BREAKFAST	Free
WI-FI	Free
PARKING	Paid

Residence Inn Anaheim–Maingate
★★★½
1700 S. Clementine St.
Anaheim, CA 92802
☎ 714-533-3555
tinyurl.com/residencemaingate

ROOM RATING	78
COST	$- x 6
POOL	•
ON-SITE DINING	–
BREAKFAST	Free
WI-FI	Free
PARKING	Free

**Residence Inn at Anaheim Resort/
Convention Center** ★★★½
640 W. Katella Ave.
Anaheim, CA 92802
☎ 714-782-7500
tinyurl.com/resinnconvctr

ROOM RATING	81
COST	$$$$$+
POOL	•
ON-SITE DINING	–
BREAKFAST	Free
WI-FI	Free
PARKING	Paid

SpringHill Suites Anaheim Maingate
★★★★
1160 W. Ball Rd.
Anaheim, CA 92802
☎ 714-215-4000
shsanaheim.com

ROOM RATING	86
COST	$$$$$+
POOL	•
ON-SITE DINING	–
BREAKFAST	Free
WI-FI	Free
PARKING	Paid

**SpringHill Suites Marriott at Anaheim
Resort/Convention Center** ★★★★
1801 S. Harbor Blvd.
Anaheim, CA 92802
☎ 714-533-2101
springhillanaheim.com

ROOM RATING	88
COST	$$$$+
POOL	•
ON-SITE DINING	•
BREAKFAST	Free
WI-FI	Free
PARKING	Paid

Stanford Inn & Suites ★★★
2171 S. Harbor Blvd.
Anaheim, CA 92802
☎ 714-703-1220
stanfordinnanaheim.com

ROOM RATING	69
COST	$$$$
POOL	•
ON-SITE DINING	–
BREAKFAST	Free
WI-FI	Free
PARKING	Free

Tilt Hotel ★★★½
3241 Cahuenga Blvd. W
Los Angeles, CA 90068
☎ 323-845-1600
tilthotelhollywood.com

ROOM RATING	80
COST	$$$$$-
POOL	•
ON-SITE DINING	–
BREAKFAST	–
WI-FI	Free
PARKING	Paid

**TownePlace Suites Anaheim Main-
gate Near Angel Stadium** ★★★½
1730 S. State College Blvd.
Anaheim, CA 92806
☎ 714-939-9700
tinyurl.com/towneplacemaingate

ROOM RATING	78
COST	$$$$$
POOL	•
ON-SITE DINING	–
BREAKFAST	Free
WI-FI	Free
PARKING	Free

Travelodge Anaheim Inn & Suites
★★½
1057 W. Ball Rd.
Anaheim, CA 92802
☎ 714-774-7600
travelodgedisneyland.com

ROOM RATING	64
COST	$$$-
POOL	•
ON-SITE DINING	–
BREAKFAST	Free
WI-FI	Free
PARKING	Free

Continued from page 63

THE TOP 30 BEST DEALS

IN ADDITION TO LISTING THE BETTER ROOMS in town, we also take a look at the best combinations of quality and value in a room. The rankings are made without consideration of location or the availability of restaurants, recreational facilities, entertainment, or amenities.

The Disneyland Hotel, you may notice, is not one of the best deals. This is because you can get more for your money at other properties. The Disneyland and Grand Californian Hotels, however, are two of the most popular hotels in the area, and many guests are willing to pay a higher rate for their convenience, service, and amenities.

Sheraton Garden Grove–Anaheim South Hotel ★★★½
12221 Harbor Blvd.
Garden Grove, CA 92840
☎ 714-703-8400
sheratonanaheimsouth.com

ROOM RATING	80
COST	$$$$$–
POOL	•
ON-SITE DINING	•
BREAKFAST	Free
WI-FI	Free
PARKING	Paid

Sheraton Park Hotel at the Anaheim Resort ★★★★
1855 S. Harbor Blvd.
Anaheim, CA 92802
☎ 714-750-1811
sheratonparkanaheim.com

ROOM RATING	83
COST	$$$+
POOL	•
ON-SITE DINING	•
BREAKFAST	Paid
WI-FI	Paid
PARKING	Paid

Sheraton Universal Hotel ★★★★
333 Universal Hollywood Dr.
Universal City, CA 91608
☎ 818-980-1212
sheratonuniversal.com

ROOM RATING	85
COST	$ x 6
POOL	•
ON-SITE DINING	•
BREAKFAST	Paid
WI-FI	Paid
PARKING	Paid

Staybridge Suites Anaheim at the Park ★★★★
1050 W. Ball Road
Anaheim, CA 92802
☎ 714-860-4660
tinyurl.com/staybridgeanapark

ROOM RATING	88
COST	$$$$–
POOL	•
ON-SITE DINING	–
BREAKFAST	Free
WI-FI	Free
PARKING	Paid

Staybridge Suites Anaheim Resort ★★★½
1855 S. Manchester Ave.
Anaheim, CA 92802
☎ 714-748-7700
sbsanaheim.com

ROOM RATING	82
COST	$$$$–
POOL	•
ON-SITE DINING	–
BREAKFAST	Free
WI-FI	Free
PARKING	Free

Super 8 Anaheim Near Disneyland ★★½
415 W. Katella Ave.
Anaheim, CA 92802
☎ 714-778-6900
tinyurl.com/super8nrdland

ROOM RATING	60
COST	$$$+
POOL	•
ON-SITE DINING	–
BREAKFAST	Free
WI-FI	Free
PARKING	Free

Tropicana Inn & Suites ★★★
1540 S. Harbor Blvd.
Anaheim, CA 92802
☎ 714-635-4082
tropicanainn-anaheim.com

ROOM RATING	66
COST	$$$+
POOL	•
ON-SITE DINING	•
BREAKFAST	Paid
WI-FI	Free
PARKING	Paid

Wyndham Anaheim Garden Grove ★★★★
12021 Harbor Blvd.
Garden Grove, CA 92840
☎ 714-867-5555
anaheimwyndham.com

ROOM RATING	86
COST	$$$$–
POOL	•
ON-SITE DINING	•
BREAKFAST	Paid
WI-FI	Free
PARKING	Free

We once had a reader complain to us that he had booked one of our top-ranked rooms for value and had been very disappointed in the room. On checking we noticed that the room the reader occupied had a quality rating of ★★½. We would remind you that the value ratings are intended to give you some sense of value received for your lodging dollar spent. A ★★½ room at $100 may have the same value rating as a ★★★★ room at $160, but that does not mean that the rooms will be of comparable quality. Regardless of whether it's a good deal or not, a ★★½ room is still a ★★½ room.

THE TOP 30 BEST DEALS

RANK	HOTEL | PHONE	MAP NUMBER (pgs. 60-61)	OVERALL QUALITY RATING	ROOM QUALITY RATING	COST ($ = $50)
1	Sheraton Park Hotel at the Anaheim Resort | 714-750-1811	74	★★★★	83	$$$+
2	Staybridge Suites Anaheim at the Park | 714-860-4660	78	★★★★	88	$$$$-
3	Wyndham Anaheim Garden Grove | 714-867-5555	84	★★★★	86	$$$$-
4	Peacock Suites | 714-535-8255	64	★★★½	81	$$$
5	Candlewood Suites Anaheim Resort | 714-635-5555	18	★★★½	82	$$$+
6	DoubleTree Suites by Hilton Hotel Anaheim Resort–Convention Center | 714-750-3000	38	★★★★	86	$$$$
7	Majestic Garden Hotel | 714-778-1700	61	★★★½	81	$$$+
8	Hyatt Place Anaheim Convention Center | 714-778-1700	58	★★★★	86	$$$$
9	Anaheim Camelot Inn & Suites | 714-635-7275	4	★★★½	77	$$$+
10	SpringHill Suites Marriott at Anaheim Resort/Convention Center | 714-533-2101	76	★★★★	88	$$$$+
11	Staybridge Suites Anaheim Resort | 714-748-7700	79	★★★½	82	$$$$-
12	Best Western Plus Stovall's Inn | 714-778-1880	16	★★★½	82	$$$$-
13	Holiday Inn–Anaheim Resort Area | 714-748-7777	49	★★★½	82	$$$$-
14	Anaheim Marriott Suites | 714-750-1000	8	★★★★	85	$$$$+
15	Ayres Hotel Orange | 714-919-7940	10	★★★★	83	$$$$+
16	Park Vue Inn | 714-772-3691	63	★★★½	78	$$$$-
17	Ayres Hotel Anaheim | 714-634-2106	9	★★★½	82	$$$$
18	Best Western Plus Pavilions | 714-776-0140	14	★★★	74	$$$
19	Ramada Anaheim Maingate North | 714-999-0684	67	★★★	74	$$$
20	Hyatt Regency Orange County | 714-750-1234	59	★★★★	89	$$$$$
21	Hotel Indigo Anaheim | 714-758-0900	54	★★★½	82	$$$$
22	Four Points by Sheraton Anaheim | 714-758-0900	44	★★★½	77	$$$$
23	Hyatt House at Anaheim Resort/Convention Center | 714-971-1800	57	★★★★	85	$$$$$
24	Portofino Inn & Suites | 714-782-7600	65	★★★½	75	$$$$
25	DoubleTree by Hilton Hotel Anaheim–Orange County | 714-634-4500	37	★★★★	85	$$$$$
26	Homewood Suites by Hilton Anaheim Resort–Convention Center | 714-750-2010	53	★★★★	84	$$$$$
27	Best Western Plus Anaheim Inn | 714-774-1050	12	★★★	74	$$$+
28	La Quinta Inn & Suites Anaheim | 714-635-5000	60	★★★½	75	$$$$
29	Howard Johnson Anaheim Hotel & Water Playground | 714-776-6120	55	★★★½	81	$$$$+
30	Motel 6 Anaheim Maingate | 714-520-9696	62	★★½	61	$+

Listed on the opposite page are the top 30 room buys for the money, regardless of location or star classification, based on rack rates. Note that sometimes a suite can cost less than a hotel room.

MAKING *the* MOST *of* YOUR TIME

ALLOCATING TIME

THE DISNEY PEOPLE RECOMMEND spending two to four full days at Disneyland Resort. While this may seem a little self-serving, it is not without basis. Disneyland Resort is *huge*, with something to see or do crammed into every conceivable space. In addition, there are two parks, and touring requires a lot of walking, and often a lot of waiting in line. Moving in and among large crowds all day is exhausting, and often the unrelenting Southern California sun zaps even the most hardy, making tempers short.

During our many visits to Disneyland, we observed, particularly on hot summer days, a dramatic transition from happy, enthusiastic touring on arrival to almost zombielike plodding along later in the day. Visitors who began their day enjoying the wonders of Disney imagination ultimately lapsed into an exhausted production mentality ("We have two more rides to do in Fantasyland; then we can go to the hotel").

If your schedule and budget permit, try building in a day of rest to break up your theme park visits, as this mom from Folsom, California, suggests:

> You are SPOT ON *when you emphasize how exhausting a Disney-land Resort trip is. If I could go back and do the trip again, I would spend one day at Disneyland, have a day of rest at the motel (with the kids swimming and me being in the shade and off my feet), and then go to California Adventure on our third day in Anaheim.*

A family from Vancouver, Canada, concurs:

> *With a four- or five-day pass, I strongly recommend a day's break in between where you can sleep in, swim, read a book, and have a day off from theme parks. In hindsight I think this would have made the back end of our holiday that much more enjoyable.*

OPTIMUM TOURING SITUATION

WE DON'T BELIEVE THAT THERE IS ONE IDEAL ITINERARY. Tastes, energy levels, and perspectives on what constitutes entertainment and relaxation vary. This understood, here are some considerations for developing your own ideal itinerary.

Optimum touring at Disneyland requires a good game plan, a minimum of three to five days on-site (excluding travel time), and a fair amount of money. It also requires a fairly prodigious appetite for Disney entertainment. The essence of optimum touring is to see the attractions in a series of shorter, less-exhausting visits during the cooler, less-crowded times of day, with plenty of rest and relaxation between excursions.

Because optimum touring calls for leaving and returning to the theme parks, it makes sense to stay in one of the Disney hotels or in one of the non-Disney hotels within walking distance. If you visit Disneyland during busy times, you need to get up early to beat the crowds. Short lines and stress-free touring are incompatible with sleeping in. If you want to sleep in *and* enjoy your touring, visit Disneyland when attendance is lighter.

THE CARDINAL RULES FOR SUCCESSFUL TOURING

MANY VISITORS DON'T HAVE THREE DAYS to devote to Disneyland Resort. For these visitors, efficient touring is a must. Even the most time-effective plan, however, won't allow you to cover both Disney theme parks in one day. Plan to allocate at least an entire day to each park. We provide a "best of" one-day park-hopper plan for those who insist on seeing the resort's highlights, but it's an expensive and exhausting option. Instead, if your schedule permits only one day of touring, we recommend that you concentrate on one theme park and save the other for another visit.

One-Day Touring

A comprehensive one-day tour of Disneyland Park or Disney California Adventure is possible, but it requires knowledge of the parks, good planning, and plenty of energy and endurance. One-day touring doesn't leave much time for full-service meals, prolonged shopping, or lengthy breaks. One-day touring can be fun and rewarding, but allocating two days per park, especially for Disneyland Park, is always preferable if possible.

Successful touring of Disneyland Park or Disney California Adventure hinges on three rules:

1. DETERMINE IN ADVANCE WHAT YOU REALLY WANT TO SEE What rides and attractions most appeal to you? Which additional rides and attractions would you like to experience if you have any time left? What are you willing to forgo?

To help you establish your touring priorities, we have described every attraction in detail. In each description, we include the author's critical evaluation of the attraction as well as the opinions of Disneyland Resort guests expressed as star ratings. Five stars is the highest (best) rating possible.

Finally, because Disneyland Resort attractions range in scope from midway-type rides and horse-drawn trolleys to colossal, high-tech extravaganzas spanning the equivalent of whole city blocks, we have developed a hierarchy of categories for attractions to give you some sense of their order of magnitude:

SUPER-HEADLINERS The best attractions that the theme park has to offer. They are mind-boggling in size, scope, and imagination and represent the cutting edge of modern attraction technology and design.

HEADLINERS Full-blown, multimillion-dollar, full-scale, themed adventure experiences and theater presentations. They are modern in their technology and design and employ a full range of special effects.

MAJOR ATTRACTIONS Themed adventure experiences on a more modest scale but incorporating state-of-the-art technologies, or larger-scale attractions of older design.

MINOR ATTRACTIONS Midway-type rides, small-scale dark rides (spook house–type rides), minor theater presentations, transportation rides, and elaborate walk-through attractions.

DIVERSIONS Exhibits, both passive and interactive. Also include playgrounds, video arcades, and street theater.

Though not every attraction fits neatly into the above categories, the categories provide a relative comparison of attraction size and scope. Remember, however, that bigger and more elaborate does not always mean better. Peter Pan's Flight, a minor attraction, continues to be one of the park's most beloved rides. Likewise, for many small children, there is no attraction, regardless of size, that can surpass Dumbo the Flying Elephant.

2. ARRIVE EARLY! ARRIVE EARLY! ARRIVE EARLY! This is the single most important key to touring efficiently and avoiding long lines. With your admission pass in hand, be at the gate ready to go at least 30 minutes before the theme park's stated opening time. There are no lines and relatively few people first thing in the morning. The same four rides you can experience in 1 hour in the early morning will take more than 3 hours to see after 11 a.m. Have breakfast before you arrive, so you will not have to waste prime touring time sitting in a restaurant. This advice is especially important at Disneyland Resort, where locals arriving after work tend to swell queues in the afternoon and evening, the opposite of typical attendance patterns at Walt Disney World.

From a Cincinnati, Ohio, mom:

> Arriving early made a tremendous difference. But I'll admit that at 6:15 in the morning when I was dragging our children out of bed, I thought that we'd lost our minds. But we had so much fun that morning riding rides with no waiting in line. It was worth the early arrival.

A couple from Austin, Texas, waxed enthusiastically:

> I tell everyone about your book. It saved my girlfriend and me hours and hours of waiting in line (during spring break no less!). We were first in line for the parks every morning, and boy was it worth it.

Be aware that all park guests must pass through a security checkpoint to enter Disneyland Resort. Security is set up in open tents to the east of the Esplanade between the two parks for guests entering from Harbor Boulevard, and on the west end of Downtown Disney;

additional checkpoints screen guests exiting the Mickey & Friends parking garage and Grand Californian Hotel. The checkpoint for guests from the Disneyland and Paradise Pier Hotels can get especially overwhelmed in the mornings; if the queue is backed up, continue behind ESPN Zone and look for a secondary screening area intended for guests walking from the parking garage. If you arrive before security screening begins and go straight to the turnstiles to await admittance, you will ultimately be directed to abandon your position to go through security. If this occurs, you'll find yourself behind people who arrived 20–30 minutes after you. Therefore, if you arrive before security is set up, wait in one of the open tents for the security folks to arrive. In addition to having your bags inspected, you may be randomly selected for additional screenings. Lucky guests get to empty their pockets and step through a metal detector or be scanned with a handheld wand.

3. AVOID BOTTLENECKS Helping you avoid bottlenecks is what this guide is all about. Bottlenecks occur as a result of crowd concentrations and/ or less-than-optimal traffic engineering. Concentrations of hungry people create bottlenecks at restaurants during the lunch and dinner hours; concentrations of people moving toward the exit near closing time create bottlenecks in the gift shops en route to the gate; concentrations of visitors at new and unusually popular rides create bottlenecks and long waiting lines; rides slow to load and unload passengers create bottlenecks and long waiting lines. Avoiding bottlenecks involves being able to predict where, when, and why they occur. To this end, we provide field-tested touring plans to keep you ahead of the crowd or out of its way (see discussion following). In addition, we provide critical data on all rides and shows that helps you estimate how long you may have to wait in line, compares rides in terms of their capacity to accommodate large crowds, and rates the rides according to our opinions and the opinions of other Disneyland visitors.

TOURING PLANS

OF UTMOST IMPORTANCE: READ THIS!

IN ANALYZING READER SURVEYS we were astonished by the percentage of readers who do not use our touring plans. Scientifically tested and proven, these plans can save you 4 entire hours or more of waiting in line. Four hours! Four fewer hours of standing, 4 hours freed up to do something fun. Our groundbreaking research that created the touring plans has been the subject of front-page articles in the *Dallas Morning News* and *The New York Times* and has been cited in numerous scholarly journals. So the question is, why would you not use them?

We get a ton of e-mail from both our Disneyland and Walt Disney World readers—98% of it positive—commenting on our touring plans. First, from a Puyallup, Washington, woman:

We flew through all the attractions, only waiting in 10- to 15-minute lines all day. The longest line was for Toy Story Midway Mania!, but only because we chose to deviate from the plan and left it until the very end of the day. It proved to my group that the planning really works. (I think they initially thought I was a little loco!)

A family from Stockton, California, descended on Disneyland Park over the Easter holiday:

We're not much for plans and regimentation, so we winged it the first day. It was so awful that the next day we gave one of your itineraries a shot. It worked so well that I was telling strangers about it that night like [I was] some kind of Bible thumper.

From a Salt Lake City, Utah, family of five:

I credit this book for a whine-free, fun-filled, four-day vacation. Several people noticed the book we were using. I seriously felt like we would be lost without it.

A mom from Scottsdale, Arizona:

Your book was INCREDIBLE. On our first visit to Disney, I read it from cover to cover and felt totally prepared! The tips and knowledge you provided were really the difference in making a good trip a GREAT trip! Our relatives, who live in California and go to Disney often, couldn't believe all the stuff they didn't know about that I did!

From a Chicago mom:

I feel strongly that you have to go into a Disney trip with a firm plan or else all you will remember of your vacation will be the squabbles and the long lines! The daily touring plans not only allowed me to see everything that I wanted but also allowed me time to revisit my favorite attractions multiple times! Those who complain that the touring plans are too rigid need a serious reality check. Yes, they are structured, but they save you mountains of time! RELAX and use the touring plans if you are going during a busy part of the year. Not only will it save you the time that you are spending complaining about the plans in the first place, but it will also save you the complaining you will be doing when you are in line for Space Mountain for 90 minutes!

A family of six from Sacramento, California:

The Unofficial Guide was a godsend! I was not so sure how the touring plans would work, but they went over and beyond my expectations. We went to Disneyland during spring break, a very busy time, very crowded, and we hardly spent any time at all in lines for rides (as long as we stuck to the touring plans)! This trip was the first time EVER that my family and I got to do everything we wanted at Disneyland!

From a Portland, Oregon, man:

I hadn't been to Disneyland in 30 years, and it was fantastic and painless to just follow a plan. The FastPass tips were awesome.

From a Missoula, Montana, family:

My wife and I hadn't been to Disneyland in 40 years. I have to admit that I was a little cynical about the costs and the hassle of getting there, the crowds, etc. When we started reading your book, I really got excited. I thought, "Hey, we can do this and we have a friend with us telling us what to do the whole way!" In three days, we rode every ride you told us to (except Roger Rabbit—because it was broken), and we saw two parades, Fantasmic!, and World of Color (don't miss these). We did 61 things in three days. Your book made it all come together for us.

From a reader in Mililani, Hawaii:

With the personalized plans, we were able to hit every ride, show, and parade we wanted to see on the first day at both Disneyland and DCA without EVER waiting in a real line. As I walked by people standing in 70- to 120-minute lines, I felt so relieved that we used your process. It made our trip the most enjoyable week of our entire lives. It was an incredible, stress-free, and enjoyable experience, all thanks to you. Thank you.

WHAT'S A QUEUE?

THOUGH IT'S NOT COMMONLY used in the United States, *queue* (pronounced "cue") is the universal English word for a line, such as one in which you wait to cash a check at the bank or to board a ride at a theme park. There's a mathematical area of specialization within the field of operations research called queuing theory, which studies and models how lines work. Because The Unofficial Guides draw heavily on this discipline, we use some of its terminology. In addition to the noun, the verb *to queue* means "to get in line," and a queuing area is a waiting area that accommodates a line.

TOURING PLANS:
WHAT THEY ARE AND HOW THEY WORK

WHEN WE INTERVIEWED DISNEYLAND VISITORS who toured the theme park(s) on slow days, they invariably waxed eloquent about the sheer delight of their experience. When we questioned visitors who toured on moderate or busy days, however, they talked at length about the jostling crowds and how much time they stood in line. What a shame, they said, that so much time and energy are spent fighting crowds in a place as special as Disneyland.

Given this complaint, our researchers descended on Disneyland to determine whether a touring plan could be devised that would liberate visitors from the traffic flow and allow them to see any theme park in one day with minimal waiting in line. On some of the busiest days of the year, our team monitored traffic into and through Disneyland Park, noting how it filled and how patrons were distributed among the attractions. We also observed which rides and attractions were most popular and where bottlenecks were most likely to occur.

After many years of collecting data, we devised preliminary touring plans, which we tested during one of the busiest weeks of the year. Each day, our researchers would tour the park using one of the preliminary plans, noting how long it took to walk from place to place and how long the wait in line was for each attraction. Combining the information gained on trial runs, we devised a master plan that we retested and fine-tuned. This plan, with very little variance from day to day, allowed us to experience all major rides and attractions and most lesser ones in one day, with an average wait in line of less than 10 minutes at each.

From this master plan, we developed alternative plans that took into account the varying tastes and personal requirements of different Disneyland patrons. Each plan operated with the same logic as the master plan but addressed the special needs and preferences of its intended users.

Finally, after all of the plans were tested by our staff, we selected (using convenience sampling) Disneyland visitors to test the plans. The only prerequisite for being chosen to test the plans was that the guests must have been visiting a Disney park for the first time. A second group of patrons was chosen for a control group. These were first-time visitors who would tour the park according to their own plans but who would make notes about what they did and how much time they spent in lines.

When the two groups were compared, the results were amazing. On days when major theme park attendance exceeded 42,000, visitors touring without our plans *averaged* 2 hours and 36 minutes more waiting in line per day than the patrons touring with our plans, and they experienced 33% fewer attractions. In 2004 the application of a cutting-edge algorithm to our touring plan software increased the waiting time saved to an average of 4 hours. Our latest advancement, introduced in 2012, gives subscribers to **touringplans.com** the ability to build personalized plans online, and then use the Lines smartphone app while inside the parks to optimize their itineraries with real-time wait time data. We expect additional research to continue to improve the performance of the touring plans in future editions.

General Overview of the Touring Plans

Our touring plans are step-by-step guides for seeing as much as possible with a minimum of standing in line. They're designed to help you avoid crowds and bottlenecks on days of moderate to heavy attendance. On days of lighter attendance (see "Selecting the Time of Year for Your Visit," page 25), the plans still save time but aren't as critical to successful touring.

What You Can Realistically Expect from the Touring Plans

Though we present one-day touring plans for both parks, you should understand that Disneyland Park has more attractions than you can see in one day, even if you never wait in line. If you must cram your visit to Disneyland Park into a single day, the one-day touring plans will allow you to see as much as is humanly possible. Under certain circumstances you may not complete the plan, and you definitely won't be able to see everything. For Disneyland Park, the most comprehensive, efficient, and relaxing touring plans are the two-day plans. Though Disney California Adventure has grown recently, you should be able to see everything in one day by following our touring plans.

Variables That Will Affect the Success of the Touring Plans

How quickly you move from one ride to another; when and how many refreshment and restroom breaks you take; when, where, and how you eat meals; and your ability (or lack thereof) to find your way around will all have an impact on the success of the plans. Smaller groups almost always move faster than larger groups, and parties of adults generally can cover more ground than families with young children. Switching off (see page 154), among other things, prohibits families with little ones from moving expeditiously among attractions. Plus, some children simply cannot conform to the "early to rise" conditions of the touring plans. A mom from Nutley, New Jersey, writes:

> [Though] the touring plans all advise getting to parks at opening, we just couldn't burn the candle at both ends. Our kids (10, 7, and 4) would not go to sleep early and couldn't be up at dawn and still stay relatively sane. It worked well for us to let them sleep a little later, go out and bring breakfast back to the room while they slept, and still get a relatively early start by not spending time on eating breakfast out. We managed to avoid long lines with an early morning and by hitting popular attractions during parades, mealtimes, and late evenings.

And a family from Centerville, Ohio, says:

> The toughest thing about your tour plans was getting the rest of the family to stay with them, at least to some degree. Getting them to pass by attractions to hit something across the park was no easy task (sometimes impossible).

A multigenerational family wonders how to know if you are on track or not, writing:

> It seems like the touring plans were very time dependent, yet there were no specific times attached to the plan outside of the early morning. On more than one day, I often had to guess as to whether we were on track.

There is no objective measurement for being on track. Each group's experience will differ to some degree. Regardless of whether your group is large or small, fast or slow, the sequence of attractions in the touring plans will allow you to enjoy the greatest number of attractions in the least possible time. Two quickly moving adults will probably take in more attractions in a specific time period than will a large group comprised of children, parents, and grandparents. However, given the characteristics of the respective groups, each will maximize their touring time and experience as many attractions as possible. That said, if you really want specific times for each step of your touring plan, use the online versions and customize them for your specific day of travel.

Finally, if you have young children in your party, be prepared for character encounters. The appearance of a Disney character is usually sufficient to stop a touring plan dead in its tracks. What's more, while some characters continue to stroll the parks, it is becoming more the rule to assemble characters in some specific venue (such as at Mickey's Toontown), where families must queue for photos of and autographs from Mickey. Meeting characters, posing for photos, and collecting autographs can burn hours of touring time. If your kids are into character-autograph collecting, you will need to anticipate these interruptions to the touring plan and negotiate some understanding with your children about when you will follow the plan and when you will collect autographs. Our advice is to either go with the flow or alternatively set aside a certain morning or afternoon for photos and autographs. Be aware, however, that queues for autographs, especially in Fantasy Faire and Pixie Hollow at Disneyland Park, are every bit as long as the queues for major attractions. The only time-efficient way to collect autographs is to line up at the character-greeting areas first thing in the morning. Because this is also the best time to experience the more popular attractions, you may have some tough decisions to make.

While we realize that following the touring plans is not always easy, we nevertheless recommend continuous, expeditious touring until around noon. After that hour, breaks and diversions won't affect the plans significantly.

Some variables that can profoundly affect the touring plans are beyond your control. Chief among these is the manner and timing of bringing a particular ride to capacity. For example, Big Thunder Mountain Railroad, a roller coaster in Disneyland Park, has five trains. On a given morning it may begin operation with two of the five, and then add the other three if and when they are needed. If the waiting line builds rapidly before operators decide to go to full capacity, you could have a long wait, even in early morning.

Another variable relates to the time you arrive for a show. Usually your wait will be the length of time from your arrival to the end of the presentation in progress. Thus, if the *Enchanted Tiki Room* show is 15 minutes long and you arrive 1 minute after a show has begun, your wait for the next show will be 14 minutes. Conversely, if you arrive as the show is wrapping up, your wait will be only 1 or 2 minutes.

What to Do If You Lose the Thread

Anything from a blister to a broken attraction can throw off a touring plan. If unforeseen events interrupt a plan:

1. If you're following a printed touring plan, skip one step on the plan for every 20 minutes' delay. If, for example, you lose your billfold and spend an hour hunting for it, skip three steps and pick up from there, or

2. Forget the plan; organize the remainder of your day using the standby wait times listed in Lines or the recommended attraction visitation times in each attraction profile.

3. If you're following a touring plan in our **Lines** app (**touringplans.com/lines**), just press the OPTIMIZE button when you're ready to start touring again. Lines will figure out the best possible plan for the remainder of your day.

Flexibility

The attractions included in the touring plans are the most popular attractions as determined by more than 21,000 reader surveys. Even so, your favorite attractions might be different. Fortunately, the touring plans are flexible. If the touring plan calls for an attraction that you don't wish to experience, simply skip it and move on to the next attraction on the plan. Additionally, you can substitute similar attractions in the same area of the park. If the plan calls for riding Dumbo, for example, and you're not interested but would enjoy the Mad Tea Party (which is not on the plan), then substitute the Mad Tea Party for Dumbo. As long as the substitution is a similar attraction (it won't work to substitute a show for a ride) and located pretty close to the attraction called for in the plan, you won't compromise the overall effectiveness of the touring plan.

For the ultimate in flexibility and efficiency, use our Lines smartphone app to check off steps on your plan as you complete them (or delete ones you decide to skip), and then click the OPTIMIZE button to update your itinerary's ideal next destination using the most recent wait times.

A family of four from South Slocan, British Columbia, found that they could easily tailor the touring plans to meet their needs:

> We amended your touring plans by taking out the attractions we didn't want to do and just doing the remainder in order. It worked great, and by arriving before the parks opened, we got to see everything we wanted, with virtually no waits! The best advice by far was to get there early!

A multigenerational family from South Jordan, Utah, found it helpful to use this book in conjunction with **touringplans.com**:

> We didn't follow an exact touring plan, but I used the tips in your book and touring plans to make our own. We decided to see all the major attractions first to do them before the crowds came. We arrived at about 8:05 a.m., and by 11 we were walking on to our eighth attraction. We were able to see all we wanted and then take a more relaxed pace the rest of the day. A downside was that after getting on so many rides so quickly, we didn't want to wait in line for even 20 minutes the rest of the day.

Clip-Out Pocket Outlines of Touring Plans

Select the plan appropriate for your party, and then clip the pocket version from the back of this guide and carry it with you as a quick reference at the theme park. If you're feeling crafty, upgrade your clip-out plans like this lady from London, England:

> I cut out the touring plan; wrote parade times, dining reservations, showtimes, etc., around the side; and then laminated it for our day.

Will the Plans Continue to Work Once the Secret Is Out?

Yes! First, all of the plans require that a patron be there when the theme parks open. Many Disneyland patrons simply refuse to get up early while on vacation. Second, less than 1% of any day's attendance has been exposed to the plans, too little to affect results. Last, most groups tailor the plans, skipping rides or shows according to personal taste.

How Frequently Are the Touring Plans Revised?

Because Disney is always adding new attractions and changing operations, we revise the touring plans every year. Most complaints we receive about them come from readers who are using out-of-date editions of *The Unofficial Guide*. Be prepared, however, for surprises. Opening procedures and showtimes, for example, may change, and you never know when an attraction might break down. Touring plans inside our Lines app are updated even more often and can instantly adapt to any refurbishments or breakdowns during your visit.

Tour Groups from Hell

Tour groups of up to 200 people sometimes use our plans. Unless your party is as large as that tour group, this development shouldn't alarm you. Because tour groups are big, they move slowly and have to stop periodically to collect stragglers. The tour guide also has to accommodate the unpredictability of five dozen or so bladders. In short, you should have no problem passing a group after the initial encounter.

Bouncing Around

Many readers object to crisscrossing a theme park, as our touring plans sometimes require. A woman from Decatur, Georgia, said she "got dizzy from all the bouncing around" and that the "running back and forth reminded [her] of a scavenger hunt." We empathize, but here's the rub.

In Disneyland Park, the most popular attractions are positioned across the park from one another. This is no accident. It's good planning, a method of more equally distributing guests throughout the park. If you want to experience the most popular attractions in one day without long waits, you can arrive before the park fills and see those attractions first thing (which requires crisscrossing the park), or you can enjoy the main attractions on one side of the park first thing in the morning, and then use FastPass for the popular attractions on the other side. All other approaches will subject you to awesome waits at some attractions if you tour during busy times of the year.

The best way to minimize bouncing around at Disneyland Park is to use one of our two-day touring plans, which spread the more popular attractions over two mornings and work beautifully even when the park closes at 8 p.m. or earlier. Using FastPass will decrease your waiting time but will increase bouncing around because you must first go to the attraction to obtain your FastPass and then backtrack later to the same attraction to use your pass.

Disney California Adventure is configured in a way that precludes an orderly approach to touring, or to a clockwise or counterclockwise rotation. Orderly touring is further frustrated by the limited guest capacity of the midway rides in the Paradise Pier/Pixar Pier district of the park. At DCA, therefore, you're stuck with bouncing around, whether you use the touring plan or not, if you want to avoid horrendous waits.

We suggest that you follow the touring plans religiously, especially in the mornings, if you're visiting Disneyland during busy, more crowded times. The consequence of touring spontaneity in peak season is hours of otherwise avoidable standing in line. During quieter times of year, there's no need to be compulsive about following the plans.

Touring Plan Rejection

We've discovered that you can't implant a touring plan in certain personalities without vehement rejection. Some folks just do not respond well to regimentation. If you bump into this problem with someone in your party, it's best to roll with the punches, as did this couple:

> The rest of the group was not receptive to the use of the touring plans. They all thought I was being a little too regimented about planning this vacation. Rather than argue, I left the touring plans behind as we ventured off for the parks. You can guess the outcome. We took our camcorder with us, and when we returned home, we watched the movies. About every 5 minutes there is a shot of us all gathered around a park map trying to decide what to do next.

Finally, as a Connecticut woman alleges, the touring plans are incompatible with some readers' bladders as well as their personalities:

> When you write those day schedules next year, can you schedule bathroom breaks in there too? You expect us to be at a certain ride at a certain time and with no stops in between. The schedules are a problem if you are a laid-back, slow-moving, careful detail noticer. What were you thinking when you made these schedules?

Before you injure your urinary tract, feel free to deviate from the touring plan as necessary to heed the call of nature. If you are using a customized plan in Lines, you can build in as many breaks (bathroom or otherwise) as you like, and the optimizer will plan around them.

A Clamor for Customized Touring Plans

We're inundated by letters urging us to create additional touring plans. These include a plan for 9th- and 10th-graders, a plan for rainy days, a seniors' plan, a plan for folks who sleep late, a plan omitting rides that "bump, jerk, and clonk," a plan for gardening enthusiasts, and a plan for single women.

The touring plans in this book are intended to be flexible. Adapt them to your preferences. If you don't like rides that bump and jerk, skip them when they come up in a touring plan. If you want to sleep in and go to the park at noon, use the afternoon part of a plan. If you're a ninth-grader and want to ride Space Mountain three times in a row, do it. Will it decrease the touring plan's effectiveness? Sure, but the plan was created only to help you have fun. It's your day.

If you really want to tailor your itinerary, we highly recommend subscribing to **touringplans.com,** where you can customize your day's to-do list down to the last snack cart. Our computers will evaluate the efficiency of your chosen attraction order, and try to suggest a better path through the park. From a father of two teens from Superior, Colorado:

> We used a custom touring plan for our day at Disneyland and found it super useful. As always, arriving early was the key to success. It felt a little weird to walk past attractions that had no lines at all.

For a truly personalized experience, some of our team members (including this book's coauthor) offer professional tour-planning services; visit **touringplans.com/disneyland-resort/touring-plans/faq** or **sethkubersky.com** for details.

WHAT TO EXPECT WHEN YOU ARRIVE AT THE PARKS

BECAUSE EACH TOURING PLAN IS BASED on being present when the theme park opens, you need to know a little about opening procedures. Disney transportation to the parks, and the respective theme park parking lots, open 60–90 minutes before official opening time.

Each park has an entrance plaza just outside the turnstiles. Usually you will be held outside the turnstiles until 30 minutes before official opening time. If you are admitted before the official opening time, you will usually be confined to a small section of the park until the official opening time. On Magic Mornings (Tuesday, Thursday, and Saturday), eligible guests are admitted through designated turnstiles 1 hour before official opening and may proceed directly to Fantasyland and Tomorrowland, where select attractions will be operating. All other guests will be admitted later in the hour through the remaining turnstiles and held at the central hub until official opening time. At Disneyland Park you might be admitted to Main Street, U.S.A.; at Disney California Adventure to Buena Vista Street. If you proceed farther into a park, you will encounter a rope barrier manned by Disney cast members who will keep you from entering the remainder of the park. You will remain here until the rope drop, when the rope barrier is removed and the park and all (or most) of its attractions are opened at the official opening time.

A Word About the Rope Drop

Disney has a number of cast members supervising the rope drop in order to suppress the mayhem of anxiously waiting guests. A pleasantly parental prerecorded "Please walk; don't run" announcement seems to have a somewhat subduing effect on the straining crowds. In some cases, the rope is not even dropped. Instead, it's walked back. In other words, Disney cast members lead you with the rope at a fast walk toward the attraction you're straining to reach, forcing you (and everyone else) to maintain their pace. Not until they come within close proximity of the attraction do the cast members step aside.

So here's the scoop. If cast members persist in walking the rope back, the only way you can gain an advantage over the rest of the crowd is to arrive early enough to be one of those close to the rope. Be alert, though; sometimes the Disney folks will step out of the way after about 50 yards or so. If this happens, you can fire up the afterburners and speed the remaining distance to your destination.

FASTPASS

FASTPASS IS A SYSTEM for moderating the waiting time for popular attractions. Here's how it works.

Your handout park map, as well as signs at respective attractions, will tell you which attractions are included. Attractions that use FastPass will have a regular line and a FastPass line. A sign at the entrance will tell you how long the wait is in the regular line. If the wait is acceptable, hop in line. If the wait seems too long, you can scan your park admission pass at a FastPass machine and receive an appointment (for a time later in the day) to come back and ride. When you return at the appointed time, you will enter the FastPass line and proceed directly to the attraction's preshow or boarding area with minimal further wait. There is no extra charge to use FastPass, but you can get an appointment for only one attraction per park at a time (with a few exceptions, noted on page 92).

FastPass works remarkably well, primarily because FastPass holders get amazingly preferential treatment. As a telling indication of their status, Disney (borrowing a term from the airlines) refers to those in the regular line as standby guests. Indeed, we watched guests in the regular line stand by and stand by, shifting despondently from foot to foot, while dozens and sometimes hundreds of FastPass holders were ushered into the boarding area ahead of them. Clearly Disney is sending a message here, to wit: FastPass is heaven; anything else is limbo at best and probably purgatory. In either event, you'll think you've been in purgatory if you get stuck in the regular line during the hot, crowded part of the day.

FASTPASS ATTRACTIONS	
DISNEYLAND PARK	**DISNEY CALIFORNIA ADVENTURE**
Big Thunder Mountain Railroad	California Screamin'
Buzz Lightyear Astro Blasters	Goofy's Sky School*
Fantasmic!	Grizzly River Run
The Haunted Mansion	Guardians of the Galaxy—Mission: Breakout!
Indiana Jones Adventure	Radiator Springs Racers*
Matterhorn Bobsleds	Soarin' Around the World*
Roger Rabbit's Car Toon Spin*	Toy Story Midway Mania!
Space Mountain*	*World of Color*
Splash Mountain*	
Star Tours—The Adventures Continue*	

Denotes rides that routinely issue FastPasses for redemption 3-7 hours later.

FastPass, however, doesn't eliminate the need to arrive at the theme park early. Because each park offers at most 10 FastPass attractions, you still need to get an early start if you want to see as much as possible in a single day. Plus, as we'll discuss later, there's only a limited supply of FastPasses available for each attraction on a given day. So if you don't show up until the middle of the afternoon, you might discover that all the FastPasses have been distributed to other guests. FastPass does, happily, make it possible to see more with less waiting than ever before, and it's a great benefit to those who like to sleep late or who enjoy an afternoon or evening at the theme parks on their arrival day. It also enables you to postpone wet rides such as the Grizzly River Run at Disney California Adventure or Splash Mountain at Disneyland Park until the warmer part of the day.

Understanding the FastPass System

The purpose of the FastPass system is to reduce the waiting time for designated attractions by more equally distributing the arrival of guests at those attractions over the course of the day. This is accomplished by providing a shorter wait in line for guests who are willing to postpone experiencing the attraction until sometime later in the day. The system also, in effect, imposes a penalty—that is, being relegated to standby status—to those who opt not to use it (though spreading guest arrivals more equally decreases waiting time for standby guests too).

When you scan your admission pass at a FastPass machine, it spits out a small slip of paper about two-thirds the size of a credit card, small enough to fit in your wallet (but also small enough to lose easily). Printed on the paper will be the name of the attraction and a specific 1-hour time window—for example, 1:15–2:15 p.m. You can return to enjoy the ride any time from 1:15 to 2:15 p.m. Disneyland Resort strictly enforces the 1-hour FastPass windows, allowing an unpublicized 15-minute grace period and exceptions for ride breakdowns. Pay close attention to the time when you receive your FastPass, and plan your return accordingly. Each person in your party must have his or her own FastPass. Be aware that, as of summer 2017, the printed FastPass tickets only serve as a reminder of your return time and can no longer be traded or given away to another guest. Printed FastPass return tickets may be phased out entirely in the near future.

When you report back to the attraction later, you'll enter a line marked FASTPASS RETURN that will route you more or less directly to the boarding area or preshow area. Each person in your party must have his or her own FastPass and be ready to scan the admission pass at the entrance of the FastPass return line.

You may show up at any time within your FastPass return window, and from our observation, no specific time is better or worse. This holds true because cast members are instructed to minimize waits for FastPass holders. Thus, if the FastPass return line is suddenly inundated (something that occurs more or less by chance), cast members rapidly intervene to reduce the FastPass line. This is done by admitting as many as

25 FastPass holders for each standby guest until the FastPass line is down to an acceptable length. Though FastPass will lop off as much as 80% of the wait you'd experience in the regular line, you can still expect a short wait, but usually less than 20 minutes.

You can obtain a FastPass any time after a park officially opens (not counting early entry, except at select DCA attractions), though most FastPass return lines do not begin operating until about 35–50 minutes after opening. Thus, if the attractions at Disneyland Park open at 9 a.m., the FastPass machines will also be available at 9 a.m., and the FastPass line will typically begin operating at about 9:35 a.m.

Whatever time you obtain a FastPass, you can usually be assured of a period of time between when you receive your FastPass and the beginning of your return window. The interval can be as short as 30 minutes or as long as 7 hours depending on park attendance, the popularity of the attraction, and the attraction's hourly capacity. However, at certain times select attractions—including The Haunted Mansion, Buzz Lightyear Astro Blasters, Roger Rabbit's Cartoon Spin, and California Screamin'—may offer FastPasses with immediate return times. As a general rule, the earlier in the day you secure a FastPass, the shorter the interval between time of issue and the beginning of your return window. On a day that the park opens at 9 a.m., if you pick up a FastPass for Splash Mountain at, say, 9:25 a.m., your recommended window for returning to ride would be something like 10–11 a.m., or perhaps 10:10–11:10 a.m. The exact time will be determined by how many other guests have obtained FastPasses before you.

To more effectively distribute guests over the course of a day, the FastPass machines normally bump the 1-hour return period back 5 minutes for a specific number of passes issued (usually the number is equal to about 6% of the attraction's hourly capacity). When Splash Mountain opens at 9 a.m., for example, the first 125 people to obtain a FastPass will get a 10–11 a.m. recommended return window. The next 125 guests are issued FastPasses that can be used between 10:05–11:05 a.m., with the next 125 assigned a 10:10–11:10 a.m. time slot. And so it goes, with the time window dropping back 5 minutes for every 125 guests. The fewer guests who obtain FastPasses for an attraction, the shorter the interval between the receipt of your pass and the return window. Conversely, the more guests issued FastPasses, the longer the interval. If an attraction is exceptionally popular and/or its hourly capacity is relatively small, the return window might be pushed back all the way to park closing time. When this happens, the FastPass machines stop issuing return times. It would not be unusual, for example, for Guardians of the Galaxy—Mission: Breakout! at Disney California Adventure to distribute an entire day's allocation of FastPasses by 11 a.m. When this happens, the machines simply shut down and a sign is posted saying that FastPasses are all gone for the day.

FASTPASS GUIDELINES

- Park tickets must be activated at the front turnstiles (or Downtown Disney monorail station) before being used to obtain FastPasses, so you can't send one family member into the park while the others snooze. However, once everyone has entered, you can send one person across to the other park with everyone's tickets to retrieve FastPasses there.

- Don't use FastPass unless it can save you 30 minutes or more at an attraction or if the ride is distributing immediate FastPass return times.

- If you arrive after a park opens, obtain a FastPass for your preferred FastPass attraction first thing.

- Always check the FastPass return period before obtaining your FastPass.

- Obtain FastPasses for Star Tours, *Fantasmic!*, Space Mountain, and Splash Mountain at Disneyland Park and for Soarin' Around the World, Radiator Springs Racers, Guardians of the Galaxy—Mission: Breakout!, and *World of Color* at DCA as early in the day as practical.

- Try to obtain FastPasses for rides not mentioned above by 1 p.m.

- Don't depend on FastPasses being available for ride attractions after 2 p.m. during busier times of the year.

- Make sure that everyone in your party has his or her own FastPass. FastPasses are tied to each individual admission pass and may not be transferred.

- You can obtain a second FastPass as soon as you enter the return period for your first FastPass or after 2 hours from issuance, whichever comes first.

- Maximize efficiency by always obtaining a new FastPass for the next attraction before using the first FastPass you already hold.

- Be mindful of your FastPass return time, and plan intervening activities accordingly.

- Attractions don't dispense FastPasses during early entry (with the exception of Guardians of the Galaxy—Mission: Breakout!, Radiator Springs Racers, and *World of Color* at DCA), nor while they are closed for technical difficulties or special events. Don't panic if the FastPass kiosks aren't working immediately at rope drop; alert a cast member, and he or she can quickly activate them.

Disconnected FastPass Attractions

Some attractions' FastPass kiosks are not hooked up to the park-wide FastPass distribution system. Because a disconnected attraction has no way of knowing if you have a FastPass for another attraction, it will issue you a FastPass at any time. There were no disconnected rides at Disneyland Resort at press time, though Buzz Lightyear Astro Blasters and Roger Rabbit's Car Toon Spin at Disneyland Park, and California Screamin' at DCA, have been disconnected at times in the past. *World of Color*'s and *Fantasmic!*'s FastPasses are always disconnected from the other attractions. Disney can connect and disconnect FastPass attractions at will, so the disconnected lineup may vary somewhat during your visit. Finally, Disneyland Park's and DCA's FastPass systems used to not be connected, allowing you to obtain a FastPass at one park and then immediately walk to the other park and obtain another FastPass. However, as of mid-2017 the two parks' computers were integrated, eliminating that useful loophole.

When to Use FastPass

Except as discussed below, there's no reason to use FastPass during the first 30–40 minutes a park is open. Lines for most attractions are quite manageable during this period. In addition, this is the only time of the day when the FastPass attractions exclusively serve those in the regular line. Regardless of time of day, however, if the wait in the regular line at a FastPass attraction is 25–30 minutes or less, we recommend joining the regular line. The exception to this rule is if an attraction is distributing FastPasses that are valid immediately. In this circumstance, you can retrieve a FastPass and use it with less wait than guests entering the standby queue.

Think about it. Using FastPass requires two trips to the same attraction: one to obtain the pass and one to use it. This means that you must invest time to secure the pass (by the way, sometimes there are lines at the FastPass machines!) and then later interrupt your touring and backtrack to use your FastPass. The additional time, effort, and touring modification required, therefore, are justified only if you can save more than 30 minutes. And don't forget: even in the FastPass line, you must endure some waiting.

Tricks of the Trade

Though Disney stipulates that you can hold a FastPass to only one attraction at a time, it's possible to acquire a second FastPass before using the first. Let's say you obtain a FastPass to Star Tours at Disneyland Park with a return time slot of 10:15–11:15 a.m. Any time after your FastPass window begins (anytime after 10:15 a.m.), you will be able to obtain another FastPass, for Splash Mountain, for example. This is possible because the FastPass computer system monitors only the distribution of passes, ignoring whether or when a FastPass is used. Finally, don't forget that you can obtain a second FastPass 2 hours after the time of issuance of the first FastPass if that's sooner than the return time on your first FastPass.

When obtaining FastPasses, it's faster and more considerate of other guests if one person obtains passes for your entire party. This means entrusting one individual with both your valuable park admission passes and your FastPasses, so choose wisely.

FastPass Runners

First, choose a high-energy, inexhaustible member of your party who is quick on his feet and mature and responsible enough not to lose everyone's admission passes. Second, give him all the passes (after you enter the park) and dispatch him to the first attraction to obtain FastPasses for the whole group. Then, about once each hour, the FastPass runner will split from the group to get the next FastPasses. Rinse, repeat. In Disneyland Park, for example, he would speed off to Space Mountain. Because the return time is usually 1 hour or less, it won't be long until he can scoot off again to obtain FastPasses at Splash Mountain. And so it goes. You can even send the runner across the Esplanade to get FastPasses at the other park, provided you have Park

Hopper tickets. Collecting FastPasses this way allows the group to spend the less-crowded early-morning time visiting popular slow-loading attractions that don't offer FastPass. A father from Petaluma, California, shares his technique:

> The trick is to always be holding FastPasses for the next headliner ride. Sending a runner to get the FastPasses is easy to do, as a solo adult can quickly and easily make his/her way across the park and back to rejoin the group. A time-saving maneuver I call the FastPass Daddy Limbo works like this: The main group gets in line for a ride (the line must be at least 15–20 minutes long) while Dad takes off to get FastPasses for another ride. Dad returns 10–15 minutes later and rejoins his group in line by going under/over/through the railing (unclasping a chain if necessary). The dad may need to wait a few minutes to rejoin his group until they are positioned at an easily accessible point. This should be possible at other accessible lines such as Star Tours and Splash Mountain, provided that the line outside is long enough.

MaxPass

Beware FastPass runners! Like so many workers today, your job is threatened by digital technology. After Walt Disney World completed the rollout of FastPass+ in 2014, there was much speculation that the online ride reservation system would eventually migrate west. As of yet, there's still no sign in Anaheim of RFID-based MagicBands or booking attraction appointments months in advance. However, Disneyland is implementing some aspects of FastPass+ in the form of MaxPass, an extra-cost service rolled out in summer 2017.

For $10 per guest per day (included with Signature Plus annual pass; $75/year upgrade for other pass holders), MaxPass users can retrieve FastPass return times using Disneyland's smartphone app. Instead of having to walk to an attraction and pull a printed ticket from a FastPass kiosk, you retrieve a virtual return time from anywhere in the parks on your phone, which will be read by new scanners installed at ride entrances. MaxPass users are still subject to all the usual FastPass restrictions: You can only make one reservation at a time, reservations must be made the same day, and you must have entered a park for the day before reserving a time (though you can use MaxPass to pull a FastPass for a Disneyland ride while inside DCA, or vice versa). Purchase of MaxPass also includes unlimited PhotoPass digital image downloads for the day, which may be even more valuable than the shoe leather you'll save with the service.

SAVING TIME IN LINE BY UNDERSTANDING THE RIDES

THERE ARE MANY DIFFERENT TYPES of rides in Disneyland. Some rides, such as It's a Small World, are engineered to carry several thousand people every hour. At the other extreme, rides such as Dumbo the Flying Elephant can accommodate only around 500 people in an hour. Most rides fall somewhere in between. Lots of factors figure into how long you will have to wait to experience a particular ride: the popularity of the ride, how it loads and unloads, how many people can ride at one time, how many units (cars, rockets, boats, flying elephants, or whatever) of those available are in service at a given time, and how many staff person- nel are available to operate the ride. Let's take them one by one:

1. HOW POPULAR IS THE RIDE? Newer rides such as Guardians of the Galaxy—Mission: Breakout! or Radiator Springs Racers attract a lot of people, as do longtime favorites such as Space Mountain. If you know a ride is popular, you need to learn a little more about how it operates to determine when might be the best time to ride.

2. HOW DOES THE RIDE LOAD AND UNLOAD? A ride need not be especially popular to form long lines. The lines can be the result of less-than- desirable traffic engineering; that is, it takes so long to load and unload that a line builds up. This is the situation at the Mad Tea Party and Dumbo. Only a small percentage of the visitors to Disneyland Park (mostly kids) ride Dumbo, for instance, but because it takes so long to load and unload, this ride can form long waiting lines.

Some rides never stop. They are like a circular conveyor belt that goes around and around. We call these continuous loaders. The Haunted Mansion is a continuous loader. The more cars or ships or whatever on the conveyor, the more people can be moved through in an hour. The Haunted Mansion has lots of cars on the conveyor belt and consequently can move more than 2,400 people an hour.

Other rides are interval loaders. This means that cars are unloaded, loaded, and dispatched at certain set intervals (sometimes controlled manually and sometimes by a computer). Matterhorn Bobsleds is an interval loader. It has two separate tracks (in other words, the ride has been duplicated in the same facility). Each track can run up to 10 sleds, released at 23-second or greater intervals (the bigger the crowd, the shorter the interval). In another kind of interval loader, such as the Jun- gle Cruise, empty boats return to the starting point, where they line up waiting to be reloaded. In a third type of interval loader, one group of riders enters the vehicle while the last group of riders departs. We call these in-and-out interval loaders. Indiana Jones Adventure is a good example of an in-and-out interval loader. As a troop transport pulls up to the loading station, those who have just completed their ride exit to the left. At almost the same time, those waiting to ride enter the troop transport from the right. The troop transport is released to the dispatch point a few yards down the line where it is launched according to what- ever time interval is being used. Interval loaders of all three types can be very efficient at moving people if (1) the release (launch) interval is relatively short and (2) the ride can accommodate a large number of vehicles in the system at one time. Because many boats can be floating through Pirates of the Caribbean at a given time and the release interval is short, almost 3,400 people an hour can see this attraction.

A third group of rides are cycle rides. Another name for these same rides is stop-and-go rides; those waiting to ride exchange places with those who have just ridden. The main difference between in-and-out interval rides and cycle rides is that with a cycle ride, the whole system shuts down when loading and unloading is in progress. While one boat is loading and unloading in It's a Small World, many other boats are proceeding through the ride. But when Dumbo touches down, the whole ride is at a standstill until the next flight is launched.

In discussing a cycle ride, the amount of time the ride is in motion is called ride time. The amount of time that the ride is idle while loading and unloading is called load time. Load time plus ride time equals cycle time, or the time expended from the start of one run of the ride until the start of the succeeding run. Cycle rides are the least efficient of all the Disneyland rides in terms of traffic engineering. Disneyland Park has 6 cycle rides, while Disney California Adventure has 10, an astonishing number for a modern park.

CYCLE RIDES
AT DISNEYLAND PARK
FANTASYLAND • Casey Jr. Circus Train • Dumbo the Flying Elephant • King Arthur Carrousel • Mad Tea Party
MICKEY'S TOONTOWN • Gadget's Go Coaster
TOMORROWLAND • Astro Orbitor
AT DISNEY CALIFORNIA ADVENTURE
A BUG'S LAND • Flik's Flyers • Francis' Ladybug Boogie • Tuck and Roll's Drive 'Em Buggies
PARADISE PIER/PIXAR PIER • Golden Zephyr • Jumpin' Jellyfish • King Triton's Carousel • Mickey's Fun Wheel (Pixar Fun Wheel) • Silly Symphony Swings
CARS LAND • Luigi's Rollickin' Roadsters • Mater's Junkyard Jamboree

3. HOW MANY PEOPLE CAN RIDE AT ONE TIME? This figure is defined in terms of per-ride capacity or system capacity. Either way, the figures refer to the number of people who can ride at the same time. Our discussion above illustrates that the greater a ride's carrying capacity (all other things being equal), the more visitors it can accommodate in an hour.

4. HOW MANY UNITS ARE IN SERVICE AT A GIVEN TIME? A unit is simply a term for the vehicle you sit in during your ride. At the Mad Tea Party the unit is a teacup, and at Alice in Wonderland it's a caterpillar. On some rides (mostly cycle rides), the number of units in operation at a given time is fixed. Thus, there are always 16 elephant units operating on the Dumbo ride, 72 horses on King Arthur Carrousel, and so on. What this fixed number of units means to you is that there is no way to increase the carrying capacity of the ride by adding more units. On a busy day, therefore, the only way to carry more people each hour on a fixed-unit cycle ride is to shorten the loading time (which, as we will see in number 5, is sometimes impossible) or by decreasing the riding time, the actual time the ride is in motion. The bottom line on a busy day for a cycle ride is that you will wait longer and be rewarded for your wait with a shorter ride. This is why we try to steer you clear of the cycle rides unless you are willing to ride them early in the morning or late at night.

Other rides at Disneyland can increase their carrying capacity by adding units to the system as the crowds build. Big Thunder Mountain

Railroad is a good example. If attendance is very light, Big Thunder can start the day by running one of five available mine trains. When lines start to build, more mine trains can be placed into operation. At full capacity, a total of five trains can carry about 2,400 people an hour. Sometimes a long line will disappear almost instantly when new units are brought online. On the other hand, the queue may stop altogether for a few minutes while new units are added, extending the wait for guests who were about to board. When an interval-loading ride places more units into operation, it usually shortens the dispatch interval, so more units are being dispatched more often.

5. HOW MANY CAST MEMBERS ARE AVAILABLE TO OPERATE THE RIDE? Allocation of additional staff to a given ride can allow extra units to be placed in operation, or additional loading areas or holding areas to be opened. Pirates of the Caribbean and It's a Small World can run two separate waiting lines and loading zones. The Haunted Mansion has a short preshow, which is staged in a "stretch room." On busy days a second stretch room can be activated, thus permitting a more continuous flow of visitors to the actual loading area. Additional staff make a world of difference on some cycle rides. Often, if not usually, one attendant will operate the Golden Zephyr. This single person must clear the visitors from the ride just completed, admit and seat visitors for the upcoming ride, check that all zephyrs are properly secured (which entails an inspection of each zephyr), return to the control panel, issue instructions to the riders, and finally, activate the ride (whew!). A second attendant allows for the division of these responsibilities and has the effect of cutting loading time by 25%–50%.

BEWARE OF THE DARK, WET, ROUGH, AND SCARY

OOPS, ALMOST FORGOT: There's a member of our team you need to meet. Called a Wuffo, she's our very own character. She'll warn you when rides are too scary, too dark, or too wet. You'll bump into her throughout the book doing, well, what characters do. Pay attention to her—she knows what she's talking about.

SAVING TIME IN LINE BY UNDERSTANDING THE SHOWS

MANY OF THE FEATURED ATTRACTIONS at Disneyland are theater presentations. While they're not as complex as rides from a traffic-engineering viewpoint, a little enlightenment concerning their operation may save some touring time.

Most Disneyland theater attractions operate in three distinct phases:

1. First, there are visitors who are in the theater viewing the presentation.
2. Next, there are visitors who have passed through the turnstile into a holding area or waiting lobby. These people will be admitted to the theater as soon as the current presentation is concluded. Several attractions offer a preshow in the waiting lobby to entertain the crowd until they are admitted to the main show.
3. Finally, there is the outside line. Visitors waiting here will enter the waiting lobby when there is room and then move into the theater when the audience turns over (is exchanged) between shows.

The theater capacity and popularity of the presentation, along with the level of attendance in the park, determine how long the lines will be at a given theater attraction. Except for holidays and other days of especially heavy attendance, the longest wait for a show usually does not exceed the length of one complete performance.

Because almost all Disneyland theater attractions run continually, only stopping long enough for the previous audience to leave and the waiting audience to enter, a performance will already be in progress when you arrive. If the *Enchanted Tiki Room* show lasts 15 minutes, the wait under normal circumstances should be 15 minutes if you were to arrive just after the show began.

All Disneyland theaters (except the Main Street Cinema and some amphitheater productions) are very strict when it comes to controlling access. Unlike at a regular movie theater, you can't just walk in during the middle of a performance; you will always have at least a short wait.

GUIDED TOURS AT DISNEYLAND PARK AND DCA

ONLY ONE GROUP TOUR is offered year-round, in addition to ultra-expensive private VIP tours. All require a valid park admission in addition to the price of the tour. All Disneyland Resort tours can be booked up to 30 days in advance by calling ☎ 714-781-8687 for the standard tours or ☎ 714-300-7710 for the VIP treatment. All tours are subject to change without notice, and some tours are offered only on certain days, so call ahead. During the Halloween and Christmas seasons, special tours highlighting holiday decorations may be available in addition to the year-round offering. All Disneyland Park tours begin at the Tour Gardens kiosk to the left of City Hall on Main Street, U.S.A. Annual pass holders get a 15% discount on guided tours.

WALK IN WALT'S FOOTSTEPS This 3.5-hour tour offers a historical perspective on both Disneyland Park and the man who created it. It provides a lot of detail, covering Disney's vision and the challenges in bringing the theme park to life. The tour includes a light lunch. You'll take a trip on the Disneyland Railroad (with a look inside the *Lilly Belle* private car if you're lucky), ride two other 1955-vintage attractions, and visit Walt's private apartment above the Main Street firehouse, or the Dream Suite in New Orleans Square, which was to be an apartment for Walt and his family; unfortunately, he died before the furnishings were finished. (The lobby of Club 33 is no longer on the tour.) Cost is $109 for all ages, and the tour is offered every day at 9:30 a.m. and noon, regardless of the park's opening time. (The tour is considered inappropriate for younger children and those who can't walk on their own.) A reader from Superior, Colorado, tried the tour for her birthday and gave a mixed review:

> *The tour was good, but I wouldn't do it more than once. Our guide was a little too rehearsed (read: memorization), and several people on the tour (including my husband and I) knew things she didn't know.*

VIP TOURS For the well-heeled, exclusive VIP tours are available for an eye-popping $400 per hour for up to 10 guests ($550 during peak season) with a 6-hour minimum. VIP guides will arrange special parade and show seating, make dining reservations, dispense Disneyland trivia, and (most crucially) "back door" you past the queues for unlimited expedited boarding at most attractions. You must make reservations 72 hours in advance and cancel at least 48 hours in advance or face a 2-hour cancellation fee.

PART TWO

ESSENTIALS

▐ *The* **BARE NECESSITIES**

CREDIT CARDS

AMERICAN EXPRESS, MASTERCARD, VISA, Discover, and Japan Credit Bureau credit cards are accepted for theme park admission. Disneyland shops, fast-food and counter-service restaurants, sit-down restaurants, and the Disneyland Resort hotels also accept all the cards listed above. Some vendor carts accept credit cards while others do not—ask before you order. Disney Visa cardholders can get a private character meet and greet in Disney California Adventure's Hollywood Land 10:30 a.m.–1:30 p.m., and an exclusive face-to-face with Darth Vader inside Disneyland's Star Wars Launch Bay 2–6 p.m. or 4–8 p.m. depending on the season. Cardholders no longer receive vouchers for free photo prints, but they do get a code to download all their private poses digitally from **disneyphotopass.com** or the Disneyland smartphone app. Disney Visa cardholders also save 10% on merchandise ($50 minimum purchase) and dining at select resort locations and 15% on guided tours. Instant application kiosks can be found in Downtown Disney, with $50 gift cards sometimes offered as an incentive to approved applicants.

Apple Pay is a wireless payment method currently found on the iPhone 6, 6 Plus, and newer models, as well as Apple Watch. Disney was scheduled to start rolling out support for Apple Pay in most of its ticket booths, stores, quick-service restaurants, and outdoor vending carts in 2015, but as of mid-2017 the system was not yet active. Locations that support Apple Pay will have a small black pad with a Contactless Indicator symbol (also known as an EMVCo symbol, which looks like a Wi-Fi symbol turned sideways). When it works, Apple Pay is the swiftest way to pay, even quicker than swiping a hotel key.

RAIN

IF IT RAINS, GO ANYWAY; the bad weather will diminish the crowds. Additionally, most of the rides and attractions at the parks are under cover. Likewise, all but a few of the waiting areas are protected from inclement weather. Some outdoor attractions—such as Tom Sawyer's Island, Mad Tea Party, Alice in Wonderland, Tarzan's Treehouse, and Gadget's Go Coaster at Disneyland Park, and Radiator Springs Racers, Redwood Creek Challenge Trail, and Golden Zephyr at Disney California Adventure (DCA)—may close for safety reasons in inclement weather. Radiator Springs Racers may require hours of downtime after a storm before safely reopening. Roller coasters such as Big Thunder Mountain Railroad and California Screamin' can operate in a drizzle but will close down if lightning is nearby. Fireworks are rarely canceled solely due to rain but may be scuttled by strong winds, and parades may be shortened or modified for safety. A father from Petaluma, California, recommends some supplemental supplies for wet weather, writing:

> Ride operators make a token effort to use a shop vac or towels, but it's good to have your own towel even on sunny days for the water ride seats. For multiday park touring in the rain, have a second pair of shoes to switch off every night at the hotel, allowing 24 hours to dry. We used a small fan to dry shoes and jackets that got wet on rides.

If you get caught in an unexpected downpour, raingear can be purchased at a number of shops. Whatever you do, don't flee for the parking trams during a sudden thunderstorm, or you may find yourself in an unpleasant scene, like this mother of two from Los Angeles:

> It was pouring rain and the park rapidly emptied out. There was complete chaos by the tram loading area [with] hundreds of people pushing and shoving—desperate to get on a tram and get out of there. The trams were arriving very sporadically and tempers were rising.

Instead, wait out the storm inside a self-paced indoor attraction, such as *Great Moments with Mr. Lincoln,* Main Street Cinema, or Star Wars Launch Bay at Disneyland Park, and Boudin Bakery Tour or Disney Animation at DCA.

VISITORS WITH SPECIAL NEEDS

DISABLED VISITORS Rental wheelchairs are available just inside both parks' main gates. Daily wheelchair rentals are $12 (manual) or $50 (electric); a $20 refundable deposit is required. Note that wheelchairs and electric convenience vehicles rented inside the parks are not permitted beyond the Esplanade. A limited supply of nonelectric wheelchairs, which may be taken through the Downtown Disney district, are available to rent at the three Disneyland Resort hotels.

Most rides, shows, attractions, restrooms, and restaurants are engineered to accommodate the disabled. For specific inquiries call ☎ 714-781-7290. If you have an impairment that makes it difficult for you to stand in line and navigate stairs, or otherwise need special assistance, go to City Hall on Main Street in Disneyland Park or Guest Relations in the entrance plaza at DCA and ask to register for Disability Access Service (DAS), which will be electronically attached to your admission ticket. This program is free and available for the disabled visitor and up to five additional guests. You should not have to show a doctor's note or proof of disability.

With the current DAS system, instead of being immediately admitted to an attraction's entrance, users are issued return times based on the current standby wait (minus 10 minutes) from designated kiosks strategically scattered around the parks. In effect, DAS is a special FastPass for disabled guests and can be used in conjunction with the regular FastPass service. A DAS enrollment is valid for 60 days, after which it must be renewed in person, which should be fine for most visitors but can be annoying for local Annual Pass holders. The current system was intended to reduce rampant abuse of the system, which sometimes had hundreds of able-bodied guests skipping the standby line for limited-capacity attractions, but it has proven controversial among autism activists whose children may have meltdowns when told they must wait for their ride. Additional services, such as rider switch and break areas, are available for guests with cognitive disabilities. If you feel you may need the DAS program or other accommodations, be sure to read up on your options in advance at **disneyland.disney .go.com/guest-services/guests-with-disabilities.** A Southern California mom with an autistic daughter had this suggestion:

> *Anyone staying any length of time should go to DCA to get their DAS card—the lines are always shorter there, unless you are in the gates of Disneyland at opening.*

Guests in wheelchairs who do not have additional cognitive or sensory issues do not need to sign up for DAS because all attraction standby queues in Disney California Adventure, and most in Disneyland, are fully wheelchair accessible. At those in Disneyland that are not fully accessible, guests in wheelchairs will go to the ride's main entrance and be issued a return time based on the current wait time (minus 10 minutes), at which point they can report to an alternate accessible entrance. Though similar to DAS, this program is independent of it and does not require preregistration.

For guests with visual or auditory impairments, digital audio and Braille guides, assistive listening devices, captioning, and sign language services are also available through City Hall and Guest Relations. Trained service animals are welcome but must be kept on a leash at all times. Note the special symbol on park maps designating service animal relief areas in both parks.

Close-in parking is available for the disabled; inquire when you pay your parking fee. Parking trams can accommodate guests who bring their own wheelchairs, and a special transportation van is also available (ask a parking lot cast member). Curbside drop-off is only available at the Harbor Boulevard entrance, near the stops for hotel shuttles and local buses. It may be challenging for disabled guests who don't bring their own wheelchairs to walk from there into the parks. If you don't think that you can travel the necessary distance, consider renting a chair or scooter for the length of your vacation from a third-party vendor who can deliver it to your hotel.

If you can afford the room rate, this North Wales, Pennsylvania, reader raved about the convenience of staying on-site at the Grand Californian Hotel:

This was a once-in-a-lifetime trip, and I have some mobility issues. So staying at the Grand Californian for its location and renting an ECV from an off-site company were worth the cost. The Grand Californian is just gorgeous, with Arts & Crafts details everywhere, from the lobby to the hallways to the lighting. I was constantly finding new things to amaze me. It was just a joy to stay here!

Even with all of Disneyland's accommodations for disabled guests, one Claremont, California, woman says that the resort still has a ways to go:

For disabled guests, restrooms are terrible. Usually there is only one handicapped stall, and it is OFTEN used by teens and even cast members, as well as moms taking strollers or multiple kids into the stall.

There are only two companion restrooms in each park (outside of first aid). Other theme parks in Southern California have staff who assist and tell guests not to use these stalls, and other parks have added many more family and companion restroom facilities.

There still are not enough handicapped parking spaces on more crowded days, not enough handicapped restroom stalls, nor adequate seating at many restaurants to accommodate the various types of need.

VISITORS WITH DIETARY RESTRICTIONS Guests on special or restricted diets, including those requiring kosher meals, can arrange for assistance at City Hall at Disneyland Park or at Guest Relations at DCA. These locations can also provide information on gluten-free menu options at restaurants in the resort. For special service at Disneyland Resort restaurants, call the restaurant one day in advance for assistance. See page 170 for more details on allergies and dietary restrictions at Disneyland Resort.

FOREIGN-LANGUAGE ASSISTANCE Translation services are available to guests who do not speak English. Inquire by calling ☎ 714-781-7290 or visiting City Hall at Disneyland Park or at Guest Relations at DCA.

LOST ADULTS Arrange a plan for regrouping with those in your party should you become separated. Failing this, you can leave a message at City Hall or Guest Relations for your missing person. For information concerning lost children, see page 157.

MESSAGES Messages for your fellow group members can be left at City Hall in Disneyland Park or at DCA Guest Relations.

CAR TROUBLE If you elected to decrease the chance of losing your keys by locking them in your car, or decided that your car might be easier to find if you left your lights on, you may have a little problem to deal with when you return to the parking lot. Fortunately, the security patrols that continually cruise the parking lots are equipped to handle these types of situations and can quickly put you back in business.

LOST AND FOUND The lost-and-found office is located in the Guest Services building in the Esplanade to the west of the park entrances. This location services both theme parks and the Downtown Disney complex.

If you do not discover your loss until you have left the parks, call ☎ 714-817-2166 8 a.m.–8 p.m. daily. If you lose your park ticket, Guest Services may be able to retrieve it using the credit card with which it was purchased, but it's far easier for them to reprint if you take a digital photo of the barcode when you first get your pass.

EXCUSE ME, BUT WHERE CAN I FIND . . .

SOME PLACE TO PUT ALL THESE PACKAGES? Lockers are available both outside the entrance of each park, for $7–$15 per day, and inside each park, for $7–$10. Pricing depends on size and includes unlimited in-and-out access throughout the day. A more convenient solution, if you plan to spend 2 or more hours in the park, is to have the salesperson forward your purchases to Package Pickup. When you leave the park, your purchases will be there waiting for you.

GROCERIES? Several convenience stores are on Harbor Boulevard near Disneyland, but no supermarkets are within easy walking distance. The closest store with a good selection is **Food-4-Less** at 1616 W. Katella Ave. about a mile west of Disneyland Resort. **Target** is about a 5-minute drive south of Disneyland on Harbor. The adjacent **Viva Bargain Center** is a good place for cheap supplies. If you don't have a car, **Vons Grocery Delivery** (grocery-delivery.vons.com/ca/anaheim.html) will bring food directly to your hotel with a $49 minimum order. You must be present to receive the delivery but can select a 1- to 4-hour time window when placing your order.

A MIXED DRINK OR BEER? At Disneyland Park, you will have to exit the park and try one of the hotels or Downtown Disney unless you have an ultraexpensive membership to the exclusive Club 33 hidden in New Orleans Square. At DCA alcoholic beverages are readily available.

SOME RAINGEAR? At Disneyland, raingear is available at most shops but is not always displayed. You have to ask for it. Ponchos are $9.50 for adults and $8.50 for kids, and umbrellas are $20 and up.

A CURE FOR THIS HEADACHE? Aspirin and various sundries can be purchased on Main Street at the Emporium in Disneyland Park and at Elias and Co. at the DCA entrance plaza (they're behind the counter, so you have to ask). Basic medical supplies are in each hotel's gift shop.

A PRESCRIPTION FILLED? Unfortunately, there is no place in Disneyland Resort to have a prescription filled. The nearest full-service pharmacy is the **Walgreens** on Harbor Boulevard at Chapman Avenue, about 1.5 miles south of Disneyland.

A DOCTOR? HouseCall Physicians (☎ 800-362-7911) will make house calls to your hotel room 24/7. The fee varies depending on the reason for the visit and the insurance you have, and the fee is payable at the time of the visit. The closest hospital to Disneyland is the **University California Irvine Medical Center,** which is about 2 miles distant at Chapman Avenue and City Drive. For dental emergencies, there is **7 Day Dental** at 637 N. Euclid St. in Anaheim, ☎ 866-856-4335.

If you are staying at a Disneyland on-site hotel, dial 911 on the in-house phone to connect with the resort's medical services, who can send a registered nurse to your room free of charge.

SUNTAN LOTION? Suntan lotion and various sundries can be purchased in Disneyland Park on Main Street at the Emporium and at Elias and Co. at the DCA entrance plaza (they're behind the counter, so you have to ask).

A SMOKE? You won't find cigarettes for sale at Disneyland parks, and smoking is strongly discouraged throughout the parks and resorts. Currently, the only remaining spots in the parks where you may smoke (or use a vaporizer) are near the Tomorrowland train station and Frontierland raft dock in Disneyland, and near Grizzly River Run at DCA. And even though recreational and medical marijuana are now legal in California, it's explicitly prohibited on Disney property.

FEMININE-HYGIENE PRODUCTS? These are available in most women's restrooms at Disneyland Resort.

CASH? Basic banking services and foreign currency exchange are provided at City Hall in Disneyland Park, Guest Relations at DCA, Travelex in Downtown Disney, and the front desks of Disneyland hotels. ATMs can be found in the following places:

AT DISNEYLAND PARK
- Outside the main entrance
- On Main Street, next to the *Disneyland Story* at the Town Square end
- At the entrance to Frontierland on the left
- Near Fantasyland Theatre
- In Tomorrowland, near the exit to Space Mountain

AT DOWNTOWN DISNEY
- Next to Häagen-Dazs
- At the Lego Store

AT DISNEY CALIFORNIA ADVENTURE
- Outside the main entrance
- At the locker complex just inside the main entrance and to the right
- Near the restrooms at Hollywood Land
- Near the restrooms on Pacific Wharf
- Near the restrooms behind Flo's V8 Cafe in Cars Land
- Near Mickey's Fun Wheel (Pixar Fun Wheel) at Paradise Pier/Pixar Pier
- Near the restrooms across from The Little Mermaid: Ariel's Undersea Adventure entrance
- Outside the restrooms near Paradise Gardens Grill

A PLACE TO LEAVE MY PET? Pets are not allowed in the parks (except for service dogs). Kennels and holding facilities are provided for the temporary care of your pets. If you are adamant, the folks at the kennels will accept custody of just about any type of animal. Owners of pets, exotic or otherwise, must themselves place their charge in the assigned cage. Small pets (mice, hamsters, birds, snakes, turtles, alligators, and the like) must arrive in their own escape-proof quarters. Kennels cost

$20 per pet, per day and are located to the right of the Disneyland Park main entrance. For more information, call ☎ 714-781-4565. There are several other details you may need to know:

- Advance reservations for animals are not accepted.
- Kennel employees are not permitted to handle your pet, so you will need to transfer your pet to and from its enclosure and return during the day to walk him or her.
- Cash or credit is accepted.
- Kennels open 30 minutes before and close 30 minutes after theme park operating hours.
- Pets may not be boarded overnight, and none of the on-site Disneyland hotels accept pets.
- Guests leaving exotic pets should supply food for their pet.
- On busy days, there is a 1- to 2-hour bottleneck at the kennel, beginning 30 minutes before the park opens. If you need to use the kennels on such a day, arrive at least 1 hour before the park's stated opening time.
- Pets are fed on request only (yours, not your pet's), and there is no additional charge for food.
- All pets must be at least 4 months old and fully immunized. For dogs, proof of current rabies, distemper, hepatitis, parvovirus, parainfluenza, and Bordetella vaccines is required. For cats, proof of rabies, panleukopenia, rhinotracheitis, and calicivirus vaccines is required. Documentation must include contact info for the owner and veterinarian, a description of the pet, and dates for each type of vaccination.
- Pets are allowed to ride on the Mickey & Friends parking structure tram but are NOT allowed on the Toy Story parking lot buses.

A PLACE TO CHARGE MY CELL PHONE? Disneyland Park offers cell phone charging lockers in the locker facility near Main Street's Market House and in the locker facility inside DCA to the right of the front entrance. They cost $2 per hour, and you can pick one with common connectors built-in (iPhone, Android, and BlackBerry) or a standard power outlet to use with your own charger. A few free accessible power outlets can be found around the parks (our favorites are along the stage in *Great Moments with Mr. Lincoln* and in the balcony in the Golden Horseshoe); just be sure not to block traffic or remove any installed plugs or covers.

Another energy option is the FuelRod, a precharged battery pack sold from a dozen-odd automated kiosks around the parks and inside each on-site hotel. You can find higher-capacity batteries online for less than the $30 FuelRod, but FuelRod's advantage is that, whenever it's drained, you can simply stop at a kiosk and swap it for a full one free of charge. FuelRods can also be found online and in airports and malls for about $20, and all are compatible with Disneyland's kiosks, so save yourself some money by buying them outside the resort. You'll also find FuelRods at Walt Disney World, so bicoastal Mouse fans may get double mileage out of them.

Incidentally, cell phone coverage inside Disneyland can be a crapshoot at best, especially on crowded days. We've watched our AT&T LTE service drop down to an antiquated 3G data stream when transmission towers become overloaded by Instagramming guests.

Fortunately, in 2017 Disneyland finally began rolling out free Wi-Fi access inside its parks to accompany the new MaxPass system. No password is required to join the "Disney Guest" Wi-Fi network, but you will need to open a Web browser and agree to the terms and conditions before accessing the Internet. Connections can be inconsistent, especially inside attraction queues.

CELEBRATION PINS Disneyland first-timers (along with honeymooners and birthday or anniversary celebrants) are rewarded with a special pin, as this Oregon mom relates:

> *The Town Hall on Main Street had pins to proudly announce it was a first visit to DL. I didn't know about this during my older son's first visit. Fortunately, there is no date on it, so I got one for each son.*

You can pick up free celebration buttons from Guest Services inside either park or at any on-site hotel.

CAMERAS AND MEMORY CARDS? You can buy a disposable camera, with or without a flash, as well as digital memory cards and batteries, throughout the parks. If you'd rather let professionals take the pictures, Disney PhotoPass photographers are stationed at scenic spots around the parks. They'll take your snapshot with their camera (and yours, if you request) for free, and then hand you a PhotoPass identification card, which you can continue using during your vacation. Then stop by Main Street Photo Supply Co. in Disneyland Park or Kingswell Camera Shop in DCA (go at midafternoon to avoid long lines), or log onto **disneyphotopass.com** within 45 days of your visit to preview and purchase all your pictures. You can download photos individually for $14.95 each, or get a digital copy and a glossy print for $16.95 and up each. Alternatively, purchase a one-day PhotoPass+ package from **disneyland.com/memories** or the Disneyland app for $39 and get unlimited digital downloads of a single day's photos. A one-week PhotoPass+ package is available online for $78. The PhotoPass+ packages are a great bargain if you take full advantage of the on-ride and character-meal photos, which are included. Better yet, purchase MaxPass for at least one member of your party, and he or she can download unlimited PhotoPass images from the day for a fraction of the regular package price. Finally, if you want up to 45 days worth of photos, along with physical prints of your character-meal pictures and a disc full of stock photos of the resort, you can purchase a Disney PhotoPass Collection package, in person only, from either park's camera center for $99, or $119 including a disc of your personal pictures; activate the package online immediately after your vacation to ensure all your images are included.

All PhotoPass photos expire 45 days after the photo was taken, so remember to download and archive your purchases; a one-time 15-day extension on the expiration date can be purchased for $19.95. Signature, Signature Plus, and Premier Annual Pass holders get unlimited free PhotoPass downloads while their passport is valid, and their pictures don't expire until 365 days after they're snapped.

PART THREE

DISNEYLAND *with* KIDS

I am very grateful for the help your book gave me. The best part was that there were no surprises that spoiled the fun. I was ready for rain, wind, cold, expensive food, small child meltdowns, and 40-minute potty stops for the grandparents (well, maybe not quite ready for the 40-minute potty stops). I did need an hour alone in the Grand Californian bar after the third day.

—Mom from Lompoc, California

The BRUTAL TRUTH *About* FAMILY VACATIONS

IT HAS BEEN SUGGESTED that the phrase *family vacation* is a bit of an oxymoron because you can never take a vacation from the responsibilities of parenting if your children are traveling with you. Though you leave work and normal routine far behind, your children require as much attention, if not more, when traveling as they do at home.

Parenting on the road requires imagination and organization. You have to do all the usual stuff (feed, dress, bathe, supervise, comfort, discipline, and so on) in an atmosphere where your children are hyperstimulated, without the familiarity of place and the resources available at home. Though not impossible—and possibly even fun—parenting on the road is not something you want to learn on the fly.

The point is that preparation, or the lack thereof, can make or break your Disneyland vacation. Believe us: You don't want to leave the success of your expensive Disney vacation to chance. Your preparation can be organized into several categories: mental, emotional, physical, organizational, and logistical. You also need a basic understanding of the two theme parks and a well-considered plan for how to go about seeing them.

MENTAL *and* EMOTIONAL PREPARATION

MENTAL PREPARATION BEGINS with realistic expectations about your Disney vacation and consideration of what each adult and child in your party most wants and needs from his or her Disneyland experience. Getting in touch with this aspect of planning requires a lot of introspection and good, open family communication.

DIVISION OF LABOR

TALK ABOUT WHAT YOU AND YOUR PARTNER NEED and what you expect to happen on the vacation. This discussion alone can preempt some unpleasant surprises mid-trip. If you are a two-parent family, do you have a clear understanding of how the parenting workload will be distributed? We've seen some distinctly disruptive misunderstandings in two-parent households in which one parent is (pardon the legalese) the primary caregiver. Often, the other parent expects the primary caregiver to function on vacation as she (or he) does at home. The primary caregiver, on the other hand, is ready for a break. She expects her partner to either shoulder the load equally or perhaps even assume the lion's share so she can have a real vacation. However you divide the responsibility, of course, is up to you. Just make sure that you negotiate a clear understanding before you leave home.

TOGETHERNESS

ANOTHER DIMENSION TO CONSIDER is how much togetherness seems appropriate to you. For some parents, a vacation represents a rare opportunity to really connect with their children, to talk, exchange ideas, and get reacquainted. For others, a vacation affords the time to get a little distance, to enjoy a round of golf while the kids are enjoying the theme park. The point here is to think about your and your children's preferences and needs concerning your time together. A typical day at a Disney theme park provides the structure of experiencing attractions together, punctuated by periods of waiting in line, eating, and so on, which facilitate conversation and sharing. Most attractions can be enjoyed together by the whole family, regardless of age ranges. This allows for more consensus and less dissent when it comes to deciding what to see and do. For many parents and children, however, the rhythms of a Disneyland day seem to consist of passive entertainment experiences alternated with endless discussions of where to go and what to do next. As a mother from Winston-Salem, North Carolina, reported:

> Our family mostly talked about what to do next with very little sharing or discussion about what we had seen. [The conversation] was pretty task-oriented.

Two observations: First, fighting the crowds and keeping the family moving along can easily escalate into a pressure-driven outing.

Having a plan or itinerary eliminates moment-to-moment guesswork and decision making, thus creating more time for savoring and connecting. Second, external variables such as crowd size, noise, and weather, among others, can be so distracting as to preclude any meaningful togetherness. These negative impacts can be moderated, as previously discussed in Part One, by being selective concerning the time of year, day of the week, and the time of day you visit the theme parks, as well as the number of days of your visit. The bottom line is that you can achieve the degree of connection and togetherness you desire with a little advance planning and a realistic awareness of the distractions you will encounter.

LIGHTEN UP

PREPARE YOURSELF MENTALLY to be a little less compulsive on vacation about correcting small behavioral deviations and pounding home the lessons of life. So what if Matt eats hamburgers for breakfast, lunch, and dinner every day? You can make him eat peas and broccoli when you get home. Roll with the little stuff, and remember when your children act out that they are wired to the max. At least some of that adrenaline is bound to spill out in undesirable ways. Coming down hard will send an already frayed little nervous system into orbit.

SOMETHING FOR EVERYONE

IF YOU TRAVEL WITH AN INFANT, toddler, or any child who requires a lot of special attention, make sure that you have some energy and time remaining for the rest of your brood. In the course of your planning, invite each child to name something special to do or see at Disneyland with Mom or Dad alone. Work these special activities into your trip itinerary. Whatever else, if you commit, write it down so that you don't forget. Remember that a casually expressed willingness to do this or that may be perceived as a promise.

unofficial **TIP**
Try to schedule some time alone with each of your children—if not each day, then at least a couple of times during the trip.

WHOSE IDEA *WAS* THIS, ANYWAY?

THE DISCORD THAT MANY VACATIONING families experience arises from the kids being on a completely different wavelength from Mom and Dad. Parents and grandparents are often worse than children when it comes to conjuring fantasy scenarios of what a Disneyland vacation will be like. It can be many things, but believe us when we tell you that there's a lot more to it than just riding Dumbo and seeing Mickey.

In our experience, most parents and nearly all grandparents expect children to enter a state of rapture at Disneyland, bouncing from attraction to attraction in wide-eyed wonder, appreciative beyond words to their adult benefactors. What they get, more often than not, is not even in the same ballpark. Preschoolers will, without a doubt, be wide-eyed, often with delight but also with a general sense of being overwhelmed by noise, crowds, and Disney characters as big as tool-sheds. We've substantiated through thousands of interviews and surveys that the best part of a Disney vacation for a preschooler is the hotel swimming pool. With some grade-schoolers and pre-driving-age teens, you get near-manic hyperactivity coupled with periods of studied nonchalance. This last phenomenon, which relates to the importance of being cool at all costs, translates into a maddening display of boredom and a "been there, done that" attitude. Older teens are frequently the exponential version of the younger teens and grade-schoolers, except without the manic behavior.

For preschoolers, you can keep things light and happy by limiting the time you spend in the theme parks. The most critical point is that the overstimulation of the parks must be balanced by adequate rest and more-mellow activities. For grade-schoolers and early teens, you can moderate the hyperactivity and false ennui by enlisting their help in planning the

 unofficial **TIP**
The more information your kids have before arriving at Disneyland, the less likely they'll be to act out.

vacation, especially by allowing them to take a leading role in determining the itinerary for days at the theme parks. Putting them in charge of specific responsibilities that focus on the happiness of other family members also works well. For example, one reader turned a 12-year-old liability into an asset by asking him to help guard against attractions that might frighten his 5-year-old sister. Knowledge enhances anticipation and at the same time affords a level of comfort and control that helps kids understand the big picture. The more they feel in control, the less they will act out of control.

BASIC CONSIDERATIONS:
Is Disneyland for You?

ALMOST ALL VISITORS ENJOY Disneyland on some level and find things to see and do that they like. The more salient question, then (since this is a family vacation), is whether the members of your family basically like the same things. If you do, fine. If not, how will you handle the differing agendas?

A mother from Toronto described her husband's aversion to Disney's (in his terms) "phony, plastic, and idealized version of life." Touring the theme parks, he was a real cynic and managed to diminish the experience for the rest of the family. As it happened, however, Dad's pejorative point of view didn't extend to the area golf courses. So Mom packed him up and sent him golfing while the family enjoyed the theme parks.

If you have someone in your family who doesn't like theme parks or, for whatever reason, doesn't care for Disney's brand of entertainment, it helps to get the attitude out in the open. We recommend dealing with the person up front. Glossing over or ignoring the contrary opinion and hoping that "Tom will like it once he gets there" is naive and unrealistic. Either leave Tom at home or help him discover and plan activities that he will enjoy, resigning yourself in the process to the fact that the family won't be together at all times.

DIFFERENT FOLKS, DIFFERENT STROKES

IT'S NO SECRET THAT we at The Unofficial Guides believe that thorough planning is an essential key to a successful Disneyland vacation. It's also no secret that our emphasis on planning rubs some folks the wrong way. Bob's sister and her husband, for example, are spontaneous people and do not appreciate the concept of detailed planning or, more particularly, following one of our touring plans when they visit the theme parks. To them the most important thing is to relax, take things as they come, and enjoy the moment. Sometimes they arrive at 10:30 in the morning (impossibly late for us Unofficial Guide types), walk around enjoying the landscaping and architecture, and then sit with a cup of espresso, watching other guests race around the park like maniacs. They would be the first to admit that they don't see many attractions, but experiencing attractions is not what lights their sparklers.

Not coincidentally, most of our readers are big on planning. When they go to the theme park, they want to experience the attractions, and the shorter the lines, the better. In a word, they are willing to sacrifice some spontaneity for touring efficiency.

We want you to have the best possible time, whatever that means to you, so plan (or not) according to your preference. The point here is that most families are not entirely in agreement on this planning versus spontaneity issue. If you are a serious planner and your oldest daughter and husband are free spirits, you have the makings of a problem. In practice, the way this and similar scenarios shake out is that the planner (usually the more assertive or type-A person) just takes over. Sometimes daughter and husband go along and everything works out, but just as often they feel resentful. There are as many ways of developing a win-win compromise as there are well-intentioned people on different sides of this situation. How you settle it is up to you. We're simply suggesting that you examine the problem and work out the solution before you go on vacation.

unofficial **TIP**
You can have a perfectly wonderful time at Disneyland if you're realistic, organized, and prepared.

THE NATURE OF THE BEAST

THOUGH MANY PARENTS DON'T REALIZE IT, there is no law that says you must take your kids to Disneyland. Likewise, there's no law that says you will enjoy Disneyland. And though we will help you make the most of any visit, we can't change the basic nature of the beast—er, mouse. A Disneyland vacation is an active and physically demanding undertaking. Regimentation, getting up early, lots of walking, waiting in lines, fighting crowds, and (often) enduring the hot

California sun are as intrinsic to a Disneyland vacation as stripes are to a zebra. Especially if you're traveling with children, you'll need a sense of humor, more than a modicum of patience, and the ability to roll with the punches.

KNOW THYSELF AND NOTHING TO EXCESS

THIS GOOD ADVICE WAS MADE AVAILABLe to ancient Greeks courtesy of the oracle of Apollo at Delphi. First, concerning the "know thyself" part, do some serious thinking about what you want in a vacation. Entertain the notion that having fun and deriving pleasure from your vacation may be very different indeed from doing and seeing as much as possible.

Because Disneyland Resort is expensive, many families confuse seeing everything to get your money's worth with having a great time. Sometimes the two are compatible, but more often they're not. So if sleeping in, relaxing with the paper over coffee, sunbathing by the pool, or taking a nap rank high on your vacation hit parade, you need to give them due emphasis on your Disney visit (are you listening?), even if it means that you see less of the theme parks.

Which brings us to the "nothing to excess" part. At the Disneyland parks, especially if you're touring with children, less is definitely more. Trust us: it's tough to go full tilt from dawn to dusk in the theme parks. First you'll get tired, then you'll get cranky, and then you'll adopt a production mentality ("We have three more rides, and then we can go back to the hotel"). Finally, you'll hit the wall because you just can't maintain the pace.

This mom had a great vacation, but not exactly the vacation she had been expecting:

> I was unprepared for traveling with a 2-year-old. All the indoor rides were deemed too dark and scary, and all she wanted to do was see the characters (which I thought she'd be petrified of!). We had a great trip once I threw all my maps and plans out the window and just went with the flow! . . . We all would have appreciated more pool time. Think twice before bringing a 2-year-old. It is one exhausting trip!

Plan on seeing the Disneyland parks in bite-size chunks with plenty of swimming, napping, and relaxing in between. Most Disneyland vacations are short. Even if you have to stay an extra day to build in some relaxation, you'll be happier while you're there and more rested when you get home. Ask yourself over and over in both the planning stage and while you are at Disneyland: what will contribute the greatest contentedness, satisfaction, and harmony? Trust your instincts. If stopping for ice cream or returning to the hotel for a dip feels like more fun than seeing another attraction, do it—even if it means wasting the remaining hours of an expensive admissions pass.

unofficial **TIP**
Get a grip on your needs and preferences before you leave home, and develop an itinerary that incorporates all the things that make you happiest.

The AGE THING

THERE'S A LOT OF SERIOUS COGITATION among parents and grandparents in regard to how old a child should be before embarking on a trip to Disneyland. The answer, not always obvious, stems from the personalities and maturity of the children, and the personalities and parenting style of the adults.

Disneyland for Infants and Toddlers

We believe that traveling with infants and toddlers is a great idea. Developmentally, travel is a stimulating learning experience for even the youngest of children. Infants, of course, won't know Mickey Mouse from a draft horse but will respond to sun and shade, music, bright colors, and the extra attention they receive from you. From first steps to full mobility, toddlers respond to the excitement and spectacle of the Disneyland parks, though of course in a much different way than you do. Your toddler will prefer splashing in fountains and clambering over curbs and benches to experiencing most attractions, but no matter: he or she will still have a great time.

> *unofficial* **TIP**
> Traveling with infants and toddlers sharpens parenting skills and makes the entire family more mobile and flexible, resulting in a richer, fuller life for all.

An Iowa City, Iowa, mother of three says, "Get over it!":

Get over it! In my opinion, people think too much about the age thing. If taking your 3-year-old would make you happy, that's all that counts. It doesn't matter if the trip is really for you or your child. You shouldn't have to jump through hoops to give yourself permission to go.

Somewhere between 4 and 6 years of age, your child will experience the first vacation that he or she will remember as an adult. Though more likely to remember the coziness of the hotel room than the theme parks, the child will be able to experience and comprehend many attractions. Even so, his or her favorite activity is likely to be swimming in the hotel pool.

> *unofficial* **TIP**
> Baby supplies—including disposable diapers, formula, and baby food—are for sale, and rockers and special chairs are available for nursing mothers at each park's Baby Care Center.

As concerns infants and toddlers, there are good reasons and bad reasons for vacationing at Disneyland. A good reason for taking your little one to Disneyland Resort is that you want to go and there's no one available to care for your child during your absence. Philosophically, we are very much against putting your life (including your vacation) on hold until your children are older.

Especially if you have children of varying ages (or plan to, for that matter), it's better to take the show on the road than to wait until the youngest reaches the perceived ideal age. If your family includes a toddler or infant, you will find everything from private facilities for breastfeeding to changing tables in both men's and women's restrooms to facilitate baby's care.

An illogical reason, however, for taking an infant or toddler to Disneyland Resort is that you think Disneyland is the perfect vacation destination for babies. It's not, so think again if you are contemplating Disneyland Resort primarily for your child's enjoyment. For starters, attractions are geared more toward older children and adults. Even designer play areas such as the Pirate's Lair on Tom Sawyer Island in Disneyland Park are developed with older children in mind.

That said, let us stress that, for the well prepared, taking a toddler to Disneyland Resort can be a totally glorious experience. There's truly nothing like watching your child respond to the color, the sound, the festivity, and, most of all, the characters. You'll return home with scrapbooks of photos that you will treasure forever. Your little one won't remember much, but your memories will be unforgettable.

If you elect to take your infant or toddler to Disneyland Resort, rest assured that their needs have been anticipated. The theme parks have centralized facilities for infant and toddler care. Everything necessary for changing diapers, preparing formula, and warming bottles and food is available. At the Disneyland Park, the Baby Care Center is next to the Plaza Inn at the end of Main Street and to the right. At Disney California Adventure (DCA) the Baby Care Center is tucked out of the way next to the Ghirardelli Chocolate Factory in the Pacific Wharf area of the park. Dads in charge of little ones are welcome at the centers and can use most services offered. In addition, men's rooms in the parks have changing tables.

Infants and toddlers are allowed to experience any attraction that doesn't have minimum height or age restrictions. A mother of three from Utah wrote to us, saying:

> We traveled with my 9-month-old, so we did the switching-off option a lot. However, I would appreciate it if you listed a complete list of all the rides that babies can be carried on. I was there alone with all three kids, and it would've been really nice to just look at a list of all the rides that we could've gone on with a baby.

It's actually far easier to list the attractions that you *can't* take a baby on at Disneyland. Unless a minimum height or age requirement is explicitly posted, children of any size—even handheld infants—are welcome on any ride. That includes all the family dark rides, kiddie carnival attractions, and slow-moving boats. On page 116 is a table of all the rides that do impose a height restriction; if a ride isn't listed, you can bring the young 'uns along. But as a Minneapolis mother reports, some attractions are better for babies than others:

> Shows and boat rides are easier for babies (ours was almost 1 year old, not yet walking). Rides where a bar comes down are doable but harder.

unofficial **TIP**
In addition to providing an alternative to carrying your child, a stroller serves as a handy cart for diaper bags, water bottles, and other necessary items.

Peter Pan's Flight was our first encounter with this type, and we had barely gotten situated when I realized that he might fall out of my grasp. The 3-D films are too intense; the noise level is deafening and the images inescapable.

I thought you might want to know what a baby thought (based on his reactions). At Disneyland Park: Jungle Cruise: didn't get into it. Pirates of the Caribbean: slept through it. Mark Twain Riverboat: the horn made him cry. It's a Small World: wide-eyed, took it all in. Peter Pan's Flight: couldn't really sit on the seat. A bit dangerous. He didn't get into it. Disneyland Railroad: liked the motion and scenery. Enchanted Tiki Room: loved it. Danced, clapped, sang along.

The same mom also advises:

We used a baby sling on our trip and thought it was great when standing in the lines—much better than a stroller, which you have to park before getting in line and navigate through crowds. It is impractical to go to the Baby Care Center every time your baby needs to nurse, so moms should be comfortable nursing in public situations.

ATTRACTION MINIMUM HEIGHT REQUIREMENTS

DISNEYLAND PARK

AUTOPIA 32" minimum height (54" to drive unassisted)

BIG THUNDER MOUNTAIN RAILROAD 40" minimum height

GADGET'S GO COASTER 35" minimum height

INDIANA JONES ADVENTURE 46" minimum height

MATTERHORN BOBSLEDS 42" minimum height

SPACE MOUNTAIN 40" minimum height

SPLASH MOUNTAIN 40" minimum height

STAR TOURS—THE ADVENTURES CONTINUE 40" minimum height

DISNEY CALIFORNIA ADVENTURE

CALIFORNIA SCREAMIN' 48" minimum height

GOOFY'S SKY SCHOOL 42" minimum height

GRIZZLY RIVER RUN 42" minimum height

GUARDIANS OF THE GALAXY—MISSION: BREAKOUT! 40" minimum height

JUMPIN' JELLYFISH 40" minimum height

LUIGI'S ROLLICKIN' ROADSTERS 32" minimum height

MATER'S JUNKYARD JAMBOREE 32" minimum height

RADIATOR SPRINGS RACERS 40" minimum height

REDWOOD CREEK CHALLENGE TRAIL 42" minimum height *(rock wall and zip line only)*

SILLY SYMPHONY SPRINGS 40" minimum height (tandem swing) 48" minimum height (single swing)

SOARIN' AROUND THE WORLD 40" minimum height

TUCK AND ROLL'S DRIVE 'EM BUGGIES 36" minimum height

THE AGE THING 117

The rental strollers at the parks are designed for toddlers and children up to 4 and 5 years old but definitely not for infants. Still, if you bring pillows and padding, the strollers can be made to work. You can alternatively bring your own stroller, but only a limited number of non-collapsible strollers fit on each parking tram, and only collapsible strollers are allowed on Toy Story lot's shuttle buses.

Even if you opt for a stroller (your own or a rental), we also recommend that you bring a baby sling or baby/child backpack. Simply put, there will be many times in the theme parks when you will have to park the stroller and carry your child.

Many nursing moms recommend breastfeeding during a dark Disney theater presentation. This only works, however, if the presentation is long enough for the baby to finish nursing. Shows at the Hyperion Theater at DCA are long enough (at least 45 minutes long), but the theater is not as dark as those that show films. Tomorrowland Theater at Disneyland Park is way too loud, as are the 3-D movies at Sunset Showcase Theater at DCA.

unofficial **TIP**
Infants are easy travelers. As long as they are fed and comfortable, there is really no limit to what you can do when on the road with little ones. Food plus adequate rest is the perfect formula for happy babies.

Many Disney shows run back-to-back with only 1 or 2 minutes in between to change the audience. If you want to breastfeed and require more time than the length of the show, tell the cast member on entering that you want to breastfeed and ask if you can remain in the theater while your baby finishes.

If you can adjust to nursing in more public places with your breast and the baby's head covered with a shawl or some such, nursing will not be a problem at all. Even on the most crowded days, you can always find a back corner of a restaurant or a comparatively secluded park bench or garden spot to nurse.

Disneyland for 4-, 5-, and 6-year-olds

Kids in this age group vary immensely in their capacity to comprehend and enjoy Disneyland Resort. With this age group, the go/no-go decision is a judgment call. If your child is sturdy, easygoing, and fairly adventuresome, and demonstrates a high degree of independence, the trip will probably work. On the other hand, if your child tires easily, is temperamental, or is a bit timid or reticent in embracing new experiences, you're much better off waiting a few years. Whereas the travel and sensory-overload problems of infants and toddlers can be addressed and (usually) remedied on the go, discontented 4- to 6-year-olds have the ability to stop a family dead in its tracks, as this mother of three from Cape May, New Jersey, attests:

> My 5-year-old was scared pretty badly on Snow White's Scary Adventures our first day. For the rest of the trip, we had to coax and reassure her before each and every ride before she would go.

If you have a retiring, clinging, and/or difficult 4- to 6-year-old who, for whatever circumstances, will be part of your group, you can sidestep or diminish potential problems with a bit of preparation. Even if your preschooler is plucky and game, the same prep measures (described later in this section) will enhance his or her experience and make life easier for the rest of the family.

Parents who understand that a visit with 4- to 6-year-old children is going to be more about the cumulative experience than about seeing it all will have wonderful memories of their children's amazement.

The Ideal Age

Though our readers report successful trips as well as disasters with children of all ages, the consensus is that children's ages ideal for family compatibility and togetherness at Disneyland are 8–12 years. This age group is old enough, tall enough, and sufficiently stalwart to experience, understand, and appreciate practically all Disney attractions. Moreover, they are developed to the extent that they can get around the parks on their own steam without being carried or collapsing. Best of all, they are still young enough to enjoy being with Mom and Dad. From our experience, ages 10–12 are better than 8–9, though what you gain in maturity is at the cost of that irrepressible, wide-eyed wonder so prevalent in the 8- and 9-year-olds. A reader from Folsom, California, strongly agrees:

> I recommend other families consider waiting until your kids are past the preschooler stage to go. My kids were 12, 10, and 6 (almost 7) on this trip. These were the perfect ages for them to appreciate most of the attractions in both parks and also, generally, have the patience to wait in line and the stamina to tour the parks. They were also tall enough to go on anything.

Disneyland for Teens

Teens love Disneyland, and for parents of teens, Disneyland Resort is a nearly perfect, albeit expensive, vacation choice. Though your teens might not be as wide-eyed and impressionable as their younger sibs, they are at an age where they can sample, understand, and enjoy practically everything Disneyland Resort has to offer.

For parents Disneyland Resort is a vacation destination where you can permit your teens an extraordinary amount of freedom. The entertainment is wholesome, the venues are safe, and the entire complex of hotels, theme parks, restaurants, and shopping is easily accessible on foot. Because most adolescents relish freedom, you may have difficulty keeping your teens with the rest of the family. Thus, if one of your objectives is to spend time with your teenage children during your Disneyland vacation, you will need to establish some clear-cut guidelines regarding togetherness and separateness before you leave home. Make your teens part of the discussion and try to meet them halfway in crafting a decision with which everyone can live. For your teens, touring on their own at Disneyland is tantamount to being independent in an exotic city. In any event, we're not suggesting that you just turn them loose. Rather, we are just attempting to sensitize you to the fact that, for your teens, some transcendent issues are involved. (Children must be at least 14 years old to enter a Disneyland Resort park without an accompanying parent or guardian.)

Most teens crave the company of other teens. If you have a solitary teen in your family, do not be surprised if he or she wants to invite a friend on your vacation. If you are invested in sharing intimate, quality time with your solitary teen, the presence of a friend will make this more difficult, if not impossible. However, if you turn down the request to bring a friend, be prepared to go the extra mile to be a companion to your teen at Disneyland. If you're a teen, it's not much fun to ride Space Mountain by yourself.

One specific issue that absolutely should be addressed before you leave home is what assistance (if any) you expect from your teen in regard to helping with younger children in the family. Once again, try to carve out a win-win compromise. Consider the case of the mother from Indiana who had a teenage daughter from an earlier marriage and two children under age 10 from a second marriage. After a couple of vacations where she thrust the unwilling teen into the position of being a surrogate parent to her half sisters, the teen declined henceforth to participate in family vacations.

Some parents have asked if there are unsafe places at Disneyland Resort or places where teens simply should not be allowed to go. Though the answer depends more on your family values and the relative maturity of your teens than on Disneyland Resort, the basic answer is no. Though it's true that teens who are looking for trouble can find it anywhere, there is absolutely nothing at Disneyland Resort that could be construed as a precipitant or a catalyst. Be advised, however, that adults consume alcohol at most Disneyland Resort restaurants outside of Disneyland Park. Also, be aware that some of the movies available at the cinemas at Downtown Disney demand the same discretion you exercise when allowing your kids to see movies at home.

About **INVITING** *Your* **CHILDREN'S FRIENDS**

IF YOUR CHILDREN WANT TO INVITE FRIENDS on your Disneyland vacation, give your decision careful thought. First, consider the logistics of numbers. Is there room in the car? Will you have to leave something at home that you had planned on taking to make room in the trunk for the friend's luggage? Will additional hotel rooms or a larger suite be required? Will the increased number of people in your group make it hard to get a table at a restaurant?

If you determine that you can logistically accommodate one or more friends, the next step is to consider how the inclusion of the friend will affect your group's dynamics. Generally speaking, the presence of a friend will make it harder to really connect with your own children. So if one of your vacation goals is an intimate bonding experience with your children, the addition of friends will possibly frustrate your attempts to realize that objective.

If family relationship building is not necessarily a primary objective of your vacation, it's quite possible that the inclusion of a friend will make life easier for you. This is especially true in the case of only children, who may otherwise depend exclusively on you to keep them happy and occupied. Having a friend along can take the pressure off and give you some much-needed breathing room.

If you allow a friend to accompany you, limit the selection to children you know really well and whose parents you also know. Your children's friends who have spent time in your home will have a sense of your parenting style, and you will have a sense of their personality, behavior, and compatibility with your family. Assess the prospective child's potential to fit in well on a long trip. Is he or she polite, personable, fun to be with, and reasonably mature? Does he or she relate well to you and to the other members of your family?

A trip to the mall including a meal in a sit-down restaurant will tell you volumes about the friend. Likewise, inviting the friend to share dinner with the family and then spend the night will provide a lot of relevant information. Ideally this type of evaluation should take place early on in the normal course of family events, before you discuss the possibility of a friend joining you on your vacation. This will allow you to size things up without your child (or the friend) realizing that an evaluation is taking place.

By seizing the initiative, you can guide the outcome. For example, Ann, a Redding, California, mom, anticipated that her 12-year-old son would ask to take a friend on their vacation. As she pondered the various friends her son might propose, she came up with four names. One, an otherwise sweet child, had a medical condition that Ann felt unqualified to monitor or treat. A second friend was overly aggressive with younger children and was often socially inappropriate for his age. Two other friends, Chuck and Marty, with whom she had had a generally positive experience, were good candidates for the trip. After orchestrating some opportunities to spend time with each of the boys, she made her decision and asked her son, "Would you like to take Marty with us to Disneyland?" Her son was delighted, and Ann had diplomatically preempted having to turn down friends her son might have proposed.

We recommend that you do the inviting, instead of your child, and that the invitation be extended parent to parent (to avoid disappointment, you might want to sound out the friend's parent before broaching the issue with your child). Observing this recommendation will allow you to query the friend's parents concerning food preferences, any medical conditions, how discipline is administered in the friend's family, how the friend's parents feel about the way you administer discipline, and the parents' expectation regarding religious observations while their child is in your care.

Before you extend the invitation, give some serious thought to who pays for what. Make a specific proposal for financing the trip a part of your invitation; for example: "There's room for Marty in the hotel room, and transportation's no problem because we're driving. So we'll just need you to pick up Marty's meals, theme park admissions, and spending money."

"He Who Hesitates Is Launched!"
TIPS and WARNINGS
for GRANDPARENTS

SENIORS OFTEN GET INTO PREDICAMENTS caused by touring with grandchildren. Run ragged and pressured to endure a blistering pace, many seniors just concentrate on surviving Disneyland rather than enjoying it. The theme parks have as much to offer older visitors as they do children, and seniors must either set the pace or dispatch the young folks to tour on their own. An older reader writes:

> Being a senior is not for wusses. At Disney [parks] particularly, it requires courage and pluck. . . . Half the time, your grandchildren treat you like a crumbling ruin, and then turn around and trick you into getting on a roller coaster in the dark. Seniors have to be alert and not trust anyone. Not their children or even the Disney people, and especially not their grandchildren. When your grandchildren want you to go on a ride, don't follow along blindly like a lamb to the slaughter. Make sure you know what the ride is all about. Stand your ground and do not waffle. He who hesitates is launched!

If you don't get to see much of your grandchildren, you might think that Disneyland is the perfect place for a little bonding and togetherness. Wrong! Disneyland can potentially send children into system overload and precipitates behaviors that pose a challenge even to adoring parents, never mind grandparents. You don't take your grandchildren straight to Disneyland for the same reason you don't buy your 16-year-old son a Ferrari: handling it safely and well requires some experience.

Begin by spending time with your grandchildren in an environment that you can control. Have them over one at a time for dinner and to spend the night. Check out how they respond to your oversight and discipline. Most of all, zero in on whether you are compatible, enjoy each other's company, and have fun together. Determine that you can set limits and that they will accept those limits. When you reach this stage, you can contemplate some outings to the zoo, the mall, or the state fair. Gauge how demanding your grandchildren are when you are out of the house. Eat a meal or two in a full-service restaurant to get a sense of their social skills and their ability to behave appropriately. Don't expect perfection, and be prepared to modify your behavior a little too. As a senior friend of mine told her husband (none too decorously), "You can't see Disneyland sitting on a stick."

If you have a good relationship with your grandchildren and have had a positive one-on-one experience taking care of them, you might consider a trip to Disneyland. If you do, we recommend visiting Disneyland without them to get an idea of what you're getting into. A scouting trip will also allow you to enjoy some of the attractions that won't be on the itinerary when you return with the grandkids.

Tips for Grandparents

1. It's best to take one grandchild at a time, two at the most. Cousins can be better than siblings because they don't fight as much. To preclude sibling jealousy, try connecting the trip to a child's milestone, such as finishing the sixth grade.

2. Let your grandchildren help plan the vacation, and keep the first one short. Be flexible, and don't overplan.

3. Discuss mealtimes and bedtime. Fortunately, many grandparents are on an early dinner schedule, which works nicely with younger children.

4. Gear plans to your grandchildren's age levels, because if they're not happy, you won't be happy.

5. Create an itinerary that offers some supervised activities for children in case you need a rest.

6. If you're traveling by car, this is the one time we highly recommend earbuds. Kids' musical tastes are vastly different from most grandparents'. It's simply more enjoyable when everyone can listen to his or her own preferred style of music, at least for some portion of the trip.

7. Take along a night-light.

8. Carry a notarized statement from parents for permission for medical care in case of an emergency. Also be sure that you have insurance information and copies of any prescriptions for medicines the kids may take. Ditto for eyeglass prescriptions.

9. Tell your grandchildren about any medical problems you may have, so they can be prepared if there's an emergency.

10. Many attractions and hotels offer discounts for seniors, so be sure to check ahead of time for bargains.

11. Plan your evening meal early to avoid long waits. And make reservations if you're dining in a popular spot, even if it's early. Take some crayons and paper to keep kids occupied. If planning a family-friendly trip seems overwhelming, try a tour operator-travel agent aimed at kids and their grandparents.

A **FEW WORDS** *for* **SINGLE PARENTS**

BECAUSE SINGLE PARENTS ARE GENERALLY also working parents, planning a special getaway with your children can be the best way to spend some quality time together. But remember, the vacation is not just for your child—it's for you too. You might invite a grandparent or a favorite aunt or uncle along; the other adult provides nice company for you, and your child will benefit from the time with family members. You might likewise consider inviting an adult friend.

Though bringing along another adult is the best option, the reality is that many single parents don't have friends, grandparents, or favorite aunts or uncles who can make the trip. And while spending time with your child is wonderful, it is very difficult to match the energy level of your child if you are the sole focus of his or her world.

One alternative: Try to meet other single parents at Disneyland. It may seem odd, but most of them are in the same boat as you; besides, all you have to do is ask. Another option, albeit expensive, is to take along a trustworthy babysitter (18 or up) to travel with you.

The easiest way to meet other single parents is to hang out at the hotel pool. Make your way there on the day you arrive, after traveling by car or plane and without enough time to blow a full admission ticket at a theme park. In any event, a couple of hours spent poolside is a relaxing way to start your vacation.

If you visit Disneyland Resort with another single parent, get adjoining rooms; take turns watching all the kids; and, on at least one night, get a sitter and enjoy an evening out.

Throughout this book we mention the importance of good planning and touring. For a single parent, this is an absolute must. In addition, make sure that each day you set aside downtime back at the hotel.

Finally, don't try to spend every moment with your children on vacation. Instead, plan some activities for your children with other children. Then take advantage of your free time to do what you want to do: Read a book, have a massage, take a long walk, or enjoy a catnap.

HOW *to* CHILDPROOF *a* HOTEL ROOM

TODDLERS AND SMALL CHILDREN up to 3 years of age (and sometimes older) can wreak mayhem if not outright disaster in a hotel room. They're mobile, curious, and amazingly fast, and they have a penchant for turning the most seemingly innocuous furnishing or decoration into a lethal weapon. Here's what to look for.

Always begin by checking the room for hazards that you cannot neutralize, such as balconies, chipping paint, cracked walls, sharp surfaces, shag carpeting, and windows that can't be secured shut. If you encounter anything that you don't like or is too much of a hassle to fix, ask for another room.

If you use a crib supplied by the hotel, make sure the mattress is firm and covers the entire bottom of the crib. If there is a mattress cover, it should fit tightly. Slats should be 2⅜ inches (about the width of a soda can) or less apart. Test the drop sides to ensure that they work properly and that your child cannot release them accidentally. Examine the crib from all angles (including from underneath) to make sure that it has been assembled correctly and that there are no sharp edges. Check for potentially toxic substances that your child might ingest. Wipe down surfaces that your child might touch to diminish the potential of infection transmitted from a previous occupant. Finally, position the crib away from drape cords, heaters, wall sockets, and air conditioners.

If your infant can turn over, we recommend changing him or her on a pad on the floor. Likewise, if you have a child seat of any sort, place it where it cannot be knocked over, and always strap your child in.

If your child can roll, crawl, or walk, you should bring about eight electrical outlet covers and some cord to tie cabinets shut and to bind drape cords and the like out of reach. Check for appliances, lamps, ashtrays, ice buckets, and anything else that your child might pull down on him- or herself. Have the hotel remove coffee tables with sharp edges and both real and artificial plants that are within your child's reach. Round up items from tables and countertops such as matchbooks, courtesy toiletries, and drinking glasses and store them out of reach.

If the bathroom door can be accidentally locked, cover the locking mechanism with duct tape or a doorknob cover. Use the security chain or upper latch on the room's entrance door to ensure that your child doesn't open it without your knowledge.

Inspect the floor and remove pins, coins, and other foreign objects that your child might find. Don't forget to check under beds and furniture. One of the best tips we've heard came from a Fort Lauderdale, Florida, mother who crawls around the room on her hands and knees to see possible hazards from her child's perspective.

If you rent a suite, you'll have more territory to childproof and will have to deal with the possible presence of cleaning supplies, a stove, a refrigerator, cooking utensils, and low cabinet doors, among other things. Sometimes the best option is to seal off the kitchen with a folding safety gate.

PHYSICAL PREPARATION

YOU'LL FIND THAT SOME PHYSICAL CONDITIONING, coupled with a realistic sense of the toll that Disneyland takes on your body, will preclude falling apart in the middle of your vacation. As one of our readers put it, "If you pay attention to eat, heat, feet, and sleep, you'll be OK."

As you contemplate the stamina of your family, it's important to understand that somebody is going to run out of steam first, and when they do, the whole family will be affected. Sometimes a cold drink or a snack will revive the flagging member. Sometimes, however, no amount of cajoling or treats will work. In this situation it's crucial that you recognize that the child, grandparent, or spouse is at the end of his or her rope. The correct decision is to get them back to the hotel. Pushing the exhausted beyond their capacity will spoil the day for them—and you. Accept that stamina and energy levels vary, and be prepared to administer to members of your family who poop out. One more thing: no guilt trips. "We've driven 300 miles to take you to Disneyland, and now you're going to ruin everything!" is not an appropriate response.

THE AGONY OF THE FEET

IF YOU SPEND A DAY AT DISNEYLAND PARK, you will walk 3–6 miles! If you walk to the park from your hotel, you can add 1–2 miles, and another couple of miles if you park-hop to DCA. The walking, however, will be nothing like a 5-mile hike in the woods. At Disneyland Park and DCA, you will be in direct sunlight most of the time, navigate through huge jostling crowds, walk on hot pavement, and endure waits in line between bursts of walking. The bottom line, if you haven't figured it out, is that Disney theme parks (especially in the summer) are not for wimps!

Though most children are active, their normal play usually doesn't condition them for the exertion of touring a Disney theme park. We recommend starting a program of family walks six weeks or more before your trip. A Pennsylvania mom who did just that offers the following:

unofficial **TIP**
Be sure to give your kids adequate recovery time between training walks (48 hours will usually be enough), however, or you'll make the problem worse.

> We had our 6-year-old begin walking with us a bit every day one month before leaving. When we arrived, her little legs could carry her, and she had a lot of stamina.

A father of two had this to say:

> My wife walked with my son to school every day when it was nice. His stamina was outstanding.

A Riverside, Utah, dad forgot to train this year:

> I think you really need to stress the importance of starting a walking regimen before going to Disneyland. Last year we had a five-day hopper, and I started walking a month ahead and ran around that place like a champ. This year I didn't walk much at all and was worn out the first day, and we only had a four-day hopper!

The first thing you need to do, immediately after making your hotel reservation, is to get thee to a footery. Take the whole family to a shoe store, and buy each member the best pair of walking, hiking, or running shoes you can afford. When trying on the shoes, wear exactly the kind of socks that you will wear when using them to hike. Do not under any circumstances attempt to tour Disneyland shod in plastic sandals, cheap flip-flops, loafers, or any kind of high heel or platform shoe (though one of our authors swears by high-quality leather sandals or river-rafting footwear, especially for water rides).

unofficial **TIP**
If your child is age 8 or younger, we recommend regular foot inspections whether he or she understands the hot spot idea or not. Even the brightest child will fail to sound off when distracted.

Good socks are as important as good shoes. When you walk, your feet sweat like a mule in a peat bog, and moisture increases friction. To minimize friction, wear a pair of SmartWool or Coolmax hiking socks, available at most outdoor retail (camping equipment) stores, as well as Target and online retailers. To further combat moisture, dust your feet with some antifungal talcum powder.

unofficial **TIP**
If your children (or you, for that matter) think that wearing socks isn't cool, get over it! Bare feet, whether encased in Nikes, Weejuns, Docksides, or Crocs, will turn into lumps of throbbing red meat if you tackle a Disney park without socks.

Now that you have some good shoes and socks, the next thing to do is to break the shoes in. You can accomplish this painlessly by wearing the shoes in the course of normal activities for about three weeks.

Once the shoes are broken in, it's time to start walking. The whole family will need to toughen up their feet and build endurance. Remember that little people have little strides, and though your 6-year-old may create the appearance of running circles around you, consider that (1) he won't have the stamina to go at that pace very long, and (2) more to the point, he probably has to take two strides or so to every one of yours to keep up.

Start by taking short walks around the neighborhood, walking on pavement, and increasing the distance about 0.25 mile on each outing. Older children will shape up quickly. Younger children should build endurance more slowly and incrementally. Increase distance until you can manage a 6- or 7-mile hike without requiring CPR. And remember, you're not training to be able to walk 6–7 miles just once; at Disneyland you will be hiking 3–6 miles or more almost every day of your visit. So unless you plan to crash after the first day, you need to prepare your feet to walk long distances for three to five consecutive days.

Not all feet are created equal. Some folks are blessed with really tough feet, whereas the feet of others sprout blisters if you look at them sideways. Assuming that there's nothing wrong with either shoes or socks, a few brisk walks will clue you in to what kind of feet your family members have. If you have a tender-footed family member, walks of incrementally increased distances will usually toughen up his or her feet to some extent. For those whose feet refuse to toughen, your only alternative is preventive care. After several walks, you will know where your tenderfoot tends to develop blisters. If you can anticipate where blisters will develop, you can cover sensitive spots in advance with moleskin, a friction-resistant adhesive dressing.

When you initiate your walking program, teach your children to tell you if they feel a hot spot on their feet. This is the warning that a blister is developing. If your kids are too young, oblivious, or preoccupied, or don't understand the concept, your best bet is to make regular foot checks. Have your children remove their shoes and socks and present their feet for inspection. Look for red spots and blisters, and ask if they have any places on their feet that hurt.

During your conditioning, and also at Disneyland, carry a foot emergency kit in your day pack or hip pack. The kit should contain gauze, antibiotic ointment, an assortment of blister bandages, a sewing needle or some such to drain blisters, and matches to sterilize the needle. An extra pair of dry socks and talc are optional.

If you discover a hot spot, dry the foot and cover the spot immediately with a blister bandage. If a blister has fully or partially developed, first air out and dry the foot. Next, using a sterile needle, drain the fluid but do not remove the top skin. Clean the area with antibiotic ointment, and place a blister bandage over the blister. If you do not have blister bandages, do not try to cover the hot spot or blister with regular adhesive bandages. Regular bandages slip and wad up. Head to First Aid instead. Moleskin, the old-fashioned hiker's standby for covering blisters, can still be useful for lining the roughened inner surface of shoe heels and toes to prevent further foot damage.

A stroller will provide the child the option of walking or riding, and, if he poops out, you won't have to carry him. Even if your child hardly uses the stroller, it serves as a convenient place for water bottles and other stuff you may not feel like carrying. Strollers at Disneyland are covered in detail beginning on page 141.

unofficial **TIP**
If you have a child who will physically fit in a stroller, rent one, no matter how well conditioned your family is.

SLEEP, REST, AND RELAXATION

PHYSICAL CONDITIONING is important but is not a substitute for rest. Even marathon runners need recovery time. If you push too hard and try to do too much, you'll either crash or, at a minimum, turn what should be fun into an ordeal. Rest means plenty of sleep at night and, if possible, naps during the afternoon and planned breaks in your vacation itinerary. And don't forget that the brain, as well as the body, needs rest and relaxation. The stimulation inherent in touring a Disney theme park is enough to put many children and some adults into system overload. It is imperative that you remove your family from this unremitting assault on the senses and do something relaxing and quiet such as swimming or reading.

The theme parks are pretty big, so don't try to see everything in one day. Even during the off-season, when the crowds are smaller and the temperatures more pleasant, the size of the theme parks will exhaust most children under age 8 by lunchtime. A Texas family underscores the importance of naps and rest:

> Despite not following any of your tours, we did follow the theme of visiting a specific park in the morning, leaving midafternoon for either a nap back at the room or a trip to the pool, and then returning to one of the parks in the evening. On the few occasions when we skipped your advice, I was muttering to myself by dinner. I can't tell you what I was muttering.

When it comes to naps, this mom does not mince words:

One last thing for parents of small kids—take the book's advice and get out of the park and take the nap, take the nap, TAKE THE NAP! Never in my life have I seen so many parents screaming at, ridiculing, or slapping their kids. (What a vacation!) Disney [parks are] overwhelming for kids and adults.

A mom from Rochester, New York, was equally adamant:

You absolutely must rest during the day. Kids went 8 a.m.–9 p.m. in the park. Kids did great that day, but we were all completely worthless the next day. Definitely must pace yourself.

If you plan to return to your hotel at midday and would like your room made up, let housekeeping know before you leave in the morning. If the location of your hotel room makes returning to the room impractical, you should still find alternative ways to take an afternoon break, as this California family advises:

We found it to be less tiring to just get off our feet within a park, have a cool drink, and sit in some shade than to add in an extra trip to and from the hotel.

The Main Street Opera House and old motorboat landing at Disneyland, Disney Animation and the Boudin Bakery Tour at Disney California Adventure, and the lobby of the Grand Californian Hotel are all great places to pause and recharge without leaving the resort.

Routines That Travel

If when at home you observe certain routines—for example, reading a book before bed or having a bath first thing in the morning—try to incorporate these familiar activities into your vacation schedule. They will provide your children with a sense of security and normalcy.

Maintaining a normal routine is especially important with toddlers, as a mother of two from Lawrenceville, Georgia, relates:

The first day, we tried an early start, so we woke the children (ages 2 and 4) and hurried them to get going. BAD IDEA with toddlers. This put them off schedule for naps and meals the rest of the day. It is best to let young ones stay on their regular schedule and see Disney at their own pace, and you'll have much more fun.

DEVELOPING *a* GOOD PLAN

ALLOW YOUR CHILDREN to participate in the planning of your time at Disneyland. Guide them diplomatically through the options, establishing advance decisions about what to do each day. Begin with your trip to Disneyland, deciding what time to depart, who sits by the window, whether to stop for meals or eat in the car, and so on. For the Disneyland part of your vacation, build consensus for wake-up call, bedtime, and naps into the itinerary, and establish ground rules for eating, buying refreshments, and shopping. Determine the order for visiting the two theme parks and make a list of must-see attractions. To help you fill in the blanks of your days, and especially to prevent you from spending most of your time standing in line, we offer a number of field-tested touring plans. The plans are designed to minimize your waiting time at each park by providing step-by-step itineraries that route you counter to the flow of traffic. The plans are explained in greater detail starting on page 78.

Generally, it's better to just sketch in the broad strokes on the master plan. The detail of what to do when you actually arrive at the park can be decided the night before you go, or with the help of one of our touring plans once you get there. Above all, be flexible. One important caveat: Make sure that you keep any promises or agreements that you make when planning. They may not seem important to you, but they will to your children, who will remember for a long, long time if you let them down.

unofficial **TIP**
To keep your thinking fresh and to adequately cover all bases, develop your plan in two or three family meetings no longer than 40 minutes each. You'll discover that all members of the family will devote a lot of thought to the plan both in and between meetings. Don't try to anticipate every conceivable contingency, or you'll end up with something as detailed and unworkable as the tax code.

The more you can agree to and nail down in advance, the less potential you'll have for disagreement and confrontation once you arrive. Because children are more comfortable with the tangible than the conceptual, and also because they sometimes have short memories, we recommend typing up all of your decisions and agreements and providing a copy to each child. Create a fun document, not a legalistic one. You'll find that your children will review it in anticipation of all the things they will see and do, will consult it often, and will even read it to their younger siblings.

By now you're probably wondering what one of these documents looks like, so we've provided a sample on pages 130–131. Incidentally, this itinerary reflects the preferences of its creators, the Shelton family, and is not meant to be offered as an example of an ideal itinerary. It does, however, incorporate many of our most basic and strongly held recommendations, such as setting limits and guidelines in advance, getting enough rest, getting to the theme parks early, and saving time and money by having a cooler full of food for breakfast. As you will

---

THE GREAT DISNEYLAND EXPEDITION

COCAPTAINS Mary and Jack Shelton

TEAM MEMBERS Lynn and Jimmy Shelton

EXPEDITION FUNDING The main Expedition Fund will cover everything except personal purchases. Each team member will receive $40 for souvenirs and personal purchases. Anything above $40 will be paid for by team members with their own money.

EXPEDITION GEAR Each team member will wear an official expedition T-shirt and carry a hip pack.

PREDEPARTURE Jack makes dining reservations at Disneyland restaurants. Mary, Lynn, and Jimmy make up trail mix and other snacks for the hip packs.

see, the Sheltons go pretty much full tilt without much unstructured time and will probably be exhausted by the time they get home, but that's their choice. One more thing—the Sheltons visited Disneyland in late June, when all of the theme parks stay open late.

Notice that the Sheltons' itinerary provides minimum structure and maximum flexibility. It specifies which park the family will tour each day without attempting to nail down exactly what the family will do there. No matter how detailed your itinerary is, be prepared for surprises at Disneyland, both good and bad. If an unforeseen event renders part of the plan useless or impractical, just roll with it. And always remember that it's your itinerary; you created it, and you can change it. Just try to make any changes the result of family discussion

SHELTON FAMILY ITINERARY

DAY 1: FRIDAY

- **6:30 p.m.** Dinner • **After dinner** Pack car • **10 p.m.** Lights out

DAY 2: SATURDAY

- **7 a.m.** Wake up! • **7:15 a.m.** Breakfast
- **8 a.m.** Depart Portland for Hampton Inn Oakland–Hayward; Confirmation #DE56432; Lynn rides shotgun
- **About noon** Stop for lunch; Jimmy picks restaurant • **7 p.m.** Dinner
- **9:30 p.m.** Lights out

DAY 3: SUNDAY

- **7 a.m.** Wake up! • **7:30 a.m.** Breakfast
- **8:15 a.m.** Depart Oakland for Disneyland, Disneyland Hotel; Confirmation #L124532; Jimmy rides shotgun
- **About noon** Stop for lunch; Lynn picks restaurant
- **5 p.m.** Check in, buy park admissions, and unpack
- **6–7 p.m.** Mary and Jimmy shop for breakfast food for cooler
- **7:15 p.m.** Dinner at Rainforest Cafe at Downtown Disney
- **After dinner** Explore Downtown Disney • **10 p.m.** Lights out

DAY 4: MONDAY

- **7 a.m.** Wake up! Cold breakfast from cooler in room
- **8 a.m.** Depart room for Disneyland Park
- **Noon** Lunch at park • **1 p.m.** Return to hotel for swimming and a nap
- **5 p.m.** Return to park for touring, dinner, and *Fantasmic!*
- **9:30 p.m.** Return to hotel • **10:30 p.m.** Lights out

DAY 5: TUESDAY

- **7 a.m.** Wake up! Cold breakfast from cooler in room
- **7:45 a.m.** Depart room for DCA • **Noon** Lunch at park
- **2:30 p.m.** Return to hotel for swimming and a nap
- **6 p.m.** Drive to dinner at Outback Steakhouse
- **7:30 p.m.** Return to DCA for touring
- **10 p.m.** Return to hotel • **11 p.m.** Lights out

and be especially careful not to scrap an element of the plan that your children perceive as something you promised them.

LOGISTIC PREPARATION

WHEN WE RECENTLY LAUNCHED into our spiel about good logistic preparation for a Disneyland vacation, a friend from Phoenix said, "Wait, what's the big deal? You pack clothes, a few games for the car, and go!" So OK, we confess, that will work, but life can be sweeter and the vacation smoother (as well as less expensive) with the right gear.

unofficial **TIP**
Give your teens the job of coming up with the logo for your shirts. They will love being the family designers.

CLOTHING

LET'S START WITH CLOTHES. We recommend springing for vacation uniforms. Buy for each child several sets of jeans (or shorts) and T-shirts, all matching, and all the same. For a one-week trip, for example, get each child three pairs of khaki shorts, three light-yellow T-shirts, and three pairs of SmartWool or Coolmax hiking socks. What's the point? First, you don't have to play fashion designer, coordinating a

---

SHELTON FAMILY ITINERARY *(continued)*

DAY 6: WEDNESDAY

- **ZZZZZZ!** Lazy morning—sleep in! • **10:30 a.m.** Late-morning swim
- **Noon** Check out of Disneyland Hotel • **1 p.m.** Fast-food lunch
- **1:45 p.m.** Depart Anaheim for Hollywood, Sheraton Universal Hotel; Confirmation #3542986X; Lynn rides shotgun
- **7:30 p.m.** Dinner at Universal CityWalk
- **9:15 p.m.** Return to hotel • **10:30 p.m.** Lights out

DAY 7: THURSDAY

- **7 a.m.** Wake up! Cold breakfast from cooler in room
- **7:45 a.m.** Depart for Universal Studios • **11:30 a.m.** Lunch at park
- **4:45 p.m.** Return to hotel for downtime
- **7:30 p.m.** Dinner at Asakuma Rice, 848 N. La Cienga Blvd., West Hollywood
- **10 p.m.** Return to hotel • **11:45 p.m.** Lights out

DAY 8: FRIDAY

- **7:30 a.m.** Wake up!
- **8:30 a.m.** After fast-food breakfast, depart for Vagabond Inn Executive, Old Town Sacramento; Confirmation #SD234; Jimmy rides shotgun
- **About noon** Stop for lunch; Lynn picks restaurant
- **7 p.m.** Dinner • **10 p.m.** Lights out

DAY 9: SATURDAY

- **7 a.m.** Wake up!
- **7:45 a.m.** Depart for home after fast-food breakfast; Lynn rides shotgun
- **About noon** Stop for lunch; Jimmy picks restaurant
- **5:30 p.m.** Home, sweet home!

week's worth of stylish combos. It's simple, it saves time, and there are no decisions to make or arguments about what to wear. Second, uniforms make your children easier to spot and keep together in the theme parks. Third, the uniforms give your family, as well as the vacation itself, some added identity. If you're like the Shelton family who created the sample itinerary in the previous section, you might go so far as to create a logo for the trip to be printed on the shirts.

unofficial **TIP**
Equip each child with a big bandanna. Though bandannas come in handy for wiping noses, scouring ice cream from chins and mouths, and dabbing sweat from the forehead, they can also be tied around the neck to protect from sunburn.

Buy short-sleeve shirts in light colors for warm weather, or long-sleeve, darker-colored T-shirts for cooler weather. All-cotton shirts are a little cooler and more comfortable in hot, humid weather. Polyester-cotton blend shirts are more wrinkle-resistant and dry a bit faster if they get wet.

LABELS A great idea, especially for younger children, is to attach labels with your family name, hometown, the name of your hotel, the dates of your stay, and your cell phone number inside the shirt—for example:

HODDER FAMILY OF DENVER, CO.;
CAMELOT INN; MAY 5–12; 303-555-2108

Instruct your smaller children to show the label to an adult if they get separated from you. Elimination of the child's first name (which most children of talking age can articulate in any event) allows you to order labels that are all the same, that can be used by anyone in the family, and that can also be affixed to such easily lost items as hats, jackets, hip packs, ponchos, and umbrellas. If fooling with labels sounds like too much of a hassle, check out "Lost Children" (see page 157) for some alternatives.

DRESSING FOR COOLER WEATHER Southern California experiences temperatures all over the scale November–March, so it could be a bit chilly if you visit during those months. Our suggestion is to layer: for example, a breathable, waterproof or water-resistant Windbreaker over a light, long-sleeve polypropylene shirt over a long-sleeve T-shirt. As with the baffles of a sleeping bag or down coat, it is the air trapped between the layers that keeps you warm. If all the layers are thin, you won't be left with something bulky to cart around if you want to pull off one or more. Later in this section, we'll advocate wearing a hip pack. Each layer should be sufficiently compactible to fit easily in that hip pack along with whatever else is in it.

ACCESSORIES

FOR YOUR CHILDREN we recommend pants with reinforced elastic waistbands; this eliminates the need to wear a belt (one less thing to find when you're trying to leave). If your children like belts or want to carry an item suspended from their belts, buy them military-style

1½-inch-wide web belts at any Army–Navy surplus or camping equipment store. The belts weigh less than half as much as leather, are cooler, and are washable.

SUNGLASSES Smog notwithstanding, the California sun is so bright and the glare so blinding that we recommend sunglasses for each family member. For children and adults of all ages, a good accessory item is an eyeglass strap for spectacles or sunglasses. The best models have a little device for adjusting the amount of slack in the strap. This allows your child to comfortably hang sunglasses from his or her neck when indoors or, alternately, to secure them fast to his or her head while experiencing a fast ride outdoors.

unofficial **TIP**
If your kids are little and don't mind a hairdo change, consider getting them a short haircut before you leave home. Not only will they be cooler and more comfortable, but— especially with your girls— you'll save them (and yourselves) the hassle of tangles and about 20 minutes of foo-fooing a day.

HIP PACKS AND WALLETS Unless you are touring with an infant or toddler, the largest thing anyone in your family should carry is a hip pack or fanny pack. Each person should have one. The pack should be large enough to carry at least a half-day's worth of snacks and other items deemed necessary (lip balm, bandanna, antibacterial hand gel, and so on) and still have enough room left to stash a hat, poncho, or light Windbreaker. We recommend buying full-size hip packs at outdoor retailers as opposed to small, child-size hip packs. The packs are light; can be made to fit any child large enough to tote a hip pack; have slip-resistant, comfortable, wide belting; and will last for years.

Do not carry billfolds or wallets, car keys, Disney Resort IDs, or room keys in your hip packs because children tend to inadvertently drop their wallet in the process of rummaging around in their hip packs for snacks and other items.

You should weed through your billfold and remove to a safe place anything that you will not need on your vacation (photos, library card, department store credit cards, business cards, and so on). In addition to having a lighter wallet to lug around, you will decrease your exposure in the event that your wallet is lost or stolen. When we are working at Disneyland, we carry a small profile billfold with a driver's license, a credit card, our room key, and a small amount of cash. You don't need anything else.

DAY PACKS We see a lot of folks at Disneyland carrying day packs (that is, small, frameless backpacks) and/or water bottle belts that strap around your waist. Day packs might be a good choice if you plan to carry a lot of camera equipment or if you need to carry baby supplies on your person. Otherwise, try to travel as light as possible. Packs are hot, cumbersome, and not very secure, and they must be removed every time you get on a ride or sit down for a show. Hip packs, by way of contrast, can simply be rotated around the waist from your back to your abdomen if you need to sit down. Additionally, our observation has been that the contents of one day pack can usually be redistributed to two or so hip packs (except in the case of camera equipment).

CAPS Kids pull caps on and off as they enter and exit attractions, restrooms, and restaurants, and—big surprise—they lose them. If your children are partial to caps, purchase a short, light cord with little alligator clips on both ends, sold at ski and camping supply stores. Hook one clip to the shirt collar and the other to the hat.

RAINGEAR Rain is a fact of life, though persistent rain day after day is unusual. Check out the Weather Channel or weather forecasts online for three or so days before you leave home to see if any major storm systems are heading for Southern California. Weather predictions concerning systems and fronts four to seven days out are pretty reliable. If it appears that you might see some rough weather during your visit, you're better off bringing raingear from home. If, however, nothing big is on the horizon weather wise, you can take your chances.

Ponchos sell for about $9.50 adults, $8.50 child, and are available in seemingly every retail shop; they're even cheaper at local discount stores (such as Target). If you do find yourself in a big storm, you'll want to have both a poncho and an umbrella. As one Unofficial reader puts it, "Umbrellas make the rain much more bearable. When rain isn't beating down on your ponchoed head, it's easier to ignore."

And consider this tip from a Memphis, Tennessee, mom:

Scotchgard your shoes. The difference is unbelievable.

MISCELLANEOUS ITEMS

MEDICATION Some parents of hyperactive children on medication discontinue or decrease the child's normal dosage at the end of the school year. Be aware that the Disneyland parks might overly stimulate such a child. Consult your physician before altering your child's medication regimen. Also, if your child has attention deficit disorder, remember that especially loud sounds can drive him or her right up the wall. Unfortunately, some Disney theater attractions are almost unbearably loud.

unofficial **TIP**
Several companies, such as Neutrogena and California Baby, make sunscreens that won't burn your eyes. Look for a product *without* the active ingredient avobenzone, which is usually the culprit when it comes to stinging and burning.

SUNSCREEN Overheating and sunburn are among the most common problems of younger children at Disneyland. Carry and use sunscreen of SPF 30 or higher. Be sure to put some on kids in strollers, even if the stroller has a canopy. Some of the worst cases of sunburn we've seen were on the exposed foreheads and feet of toddlers and infants in strollers. Protect skin from overexposure. To avoid overheating, rest regularly in the shade or in an air-conditioned restaurant or show.

WATER BOTTLES Don't count on keeping young children hydrated with soft drinks and water fountains. Long lines may impede buying refreshments, and fountains may not be handy. Furthermore, excited children may not realize or tell you that they're thirsty or hot. We recommend carrying bottles of water and sports drinks. Bottled water is about $3 in all major parks, or bring your own water bottle and strap from home.

COOLERS AND MINI-FRIDGES If you drive to Disneyland, bring two coolers: a small one for drinks in the car and a large one for the hotel room. If you fly and rent a car, stop and purchase a large Styrofoam cooler, which can be discarded at the end of the trip. If you will be

RESPECT FOR THE SUN

Health and science writer **Avery Hurt** sheds some light on the often confusing products and methods for avoiding sunburn. Here's the basic advice from the medical experts.

• **Choose a sunscreen that is convenient for you to use.** Some prefer sprays, others lotions. The form of sunscreen doesn't matter as much as the technique of applying it.

• **Apply sunscreen a half hour before going out,** and be sure to get enough on you. One ounce per application is recommended—that means a full shot glass worth each time you apply. The 1-ounce amount was calculated for average adults in swimsuits; an average 7-year-old will probably take two-thirds of an ounce (20 cc). It's a good idea to measure that ounce in your hands at home, so you'll be familiar with what an ounce looks like in your palms. It's far more sunscreen than you tend to think.

• **Get a generous covering on all exposed skin.** Then reapply (another full shot glass) every 2 hours or after swimming or sweating. No matter what it says on the label, water resistance of sunscreen is limited. And none of them last all day.

• **There is very little difference in protection** between 30 or so SPF and 45 or 50 or greater. There is no need to spend more for higher SPF numbers. In fact, it is much safer to choose a lower (and typically less expensive) SPF (as long as it is at least 30) and apply it more often. However, do be sure to choose a product that has broad-spectrum coverage, meaning that it filters out both UVA and UVB rays. As long as the SPF is at least 30 and offers broad-spectrum protection, one brand can serve the whole family. There's no need to pay extra for special formulas made for children.

• **It is best to keep babies under 6 months old covered** and out of the sun. However, the American Academy of Pediatrics condones a small amount of sunscreen on vulnerable areas, such as the nose and chin, when you have your baby out. Be very careful to monitor your baby even if he is wearing a hat and sitting under an umbrella.

• **Use a lip balm** with an SPF of 15 and reapply often to your own lips and those of your kids. Again, the brand is less important than choosing something that you will use—and remembering to use it.

• **Sunglasses are also a must.** Too much sun exposure can contribute to age-related macular degeneration (among other things). Not all sunglasses filter out damaging rays. Be sure to choose shades (for adults and kids) that have 99% UV protection. Large lenses and wraparound styles might not look as cool, but they offer much better protection. You may have to spend a little more to be sure you are getting adequate protection, but you don't want to skimp on this.

• **If you do get a burn,** cool baths, aloe gels, and ibuprofen usually help ease the suffering. Occasionally sunburns can be as dangerous in the short term as they are in the long term. If you or your child experience nausea, vomiting, high fever, severe pain, confusion, or fainting, seek medical care immediately.

without a car, book a hotel with mini-fridges in each room. All on-site Disneyland hotels provide free mini-fridges and coffee makers. If mini-fridges aren't provided, rent one from the hotel.

Coolers and mini-fridges allow you to have breakfast in your hotel room, store snacks and lunch supplies to take to the theme parks, and supplant expensive vending machines for snacks and beverages at the hotel. To keep the contents of your cooler cold, freeze a 2-gallon milk jug full of water before you head out. In a good cooler, it will take the jug five or more days to thaw. If you buy a Styrofoam cooler, you can use bagged ice and ice from the ice machine at your hotel. Even if you have to rent a mini-fridge, you will save a bundle of cash as well as significant time by reducing dependence on restaurant meals and expensive snacks and drinks purchased from vendors.

unofficial **TIP**
About two weeks before arriving, ship a box to your hotel containing food, plastic cutlery, and toiletries, plus pretty much any other consumables that might come in handy during your stay. If you fly, this helps avoid overweight fees and problems with liquid restrictions for carry-on luggage.

FOOD-PREP KIT If you plan to make sandwiches, bring along condiments and seasonings from home. A typical travel kit will include mayonnaise, ketchup, mustard, salt and pepper, and packets of artificial sweetener or sugar. Also throw in some plastic knives and spoons, napkins, plastic cups, and plastic zip-top bags. For breakfast you will need some plastic bowls for cereal. Of course, you can buy this stuff in Anaheim, but you probably won't consume it all, so why waste the money? If you drink bottled beer or wine, bring a bottle opener and corkscrew.

ENERGY BOOSTERS Kids get cranky when they're hungry, and when that happens, your entire group has a problem. Like many parents you might, for nutritional reasons, keep a tight rein on snacks available to your children at home. At Disneyland, however, maintaining energy and equanimity trumps snack discipline. For maximum zip and contentedness, give your kids snacks containing complex carbohydrates (fruits, crackers, nonfat energy bars, and the like) before they get hungry or show signs of exhaustion. You should avoid snacks that are high in fats and proteins because these foods take a long time to digest and will tend to unsettle your stomach if it's a hot day.

An experienced and wise grandma underscores the point:

> Children who get cranky during a visit often do so from all that time and energy expended without food. Feed them! A snack at any price goes a long way to keeping the little kids happy and enjoying the parks, and keeping parents sane. Oh, and the security people are very nice about you taking snacks or drinks in, but DO NOT bring glass containers! That is apparently what they are really looking for.

ELECTRONICS Regardless of your kid's ages, always bring a night-light. Flashlights are handy for finding stuff in a room after the kids are asleep. Tablets, iPods, and handheld video games are often controversial gear for a family outing. We recommend compromise. Earbuds allow kids to create their own space even when they're with others, and that can be a safety valve. That said, try to agree before the trip on some parameters, so you don't begin to feel as if they're being used to keep other family members and the trip itself at a distance. If you're traveling by car, take turns choosing the radio station or playlist for part of the trip.

Likewise, cell phones are a mixed blessing. On the one hand, they can be invaluable in an emergency or if your party wants to split up, and if you have a smartphone, you can use our Lines app to see current wait times in the parks. Unfortunately, they also lead to guests missing out on what's around them and bumping into each other because they're glued to a tiny screen. Disneyland's free Wi-Fi is still somewhat unreliable, and local cell towers become overloaded on busy days, so posting social media from the parks may drain your phone in a matter of hours.

Be especially cautious about taking expensive iPads or other tablets into the parks, and for Mickey's sake, beware while using them as cameras during shows and parades, lest you blind or block everyone behind you. Also, selfie sticks are not allowed in Disney parks, though collapsible monopods and tripods are OK. Any friendly cast member will be happy to take your photo for you the old-fashioned way.

DON'T FORGET THE TENT When Bob's daughter was preschool age, he almost went crazy trying to get her to sleep in a shared hotel room. She was accustomed to having her own room at home and was hyperstimulated whenever she traveled. Bob tried makeshift curtains and room dividers and even rearranged the furniture in a few hotel rooms to create the illusion of a more private, separate space for her. It was all for naught. It wasn't until she was around 4 years old and Bob took her camping that he seized on an idea that had some promise. She liked the cozy, secure, womblike feel of a backpacking tent and quieted down much more readily than she ever had in hotel rooms. So the next time the family stayed in a hotel, he pitched his backpacking tent in the corner of the room. In she went, nested for a bit, and fell asleep.

Modern tents are self-contained with floors and an entrance that can be zipped up for privacy but cannot be locked. Affordable and sturdy, many are as simple to put up as opening an umbrella. Some tents are even specifically made to turn a bed into a fort. Kids appreciate having their own space and enjoy the adventure of being in a tent, even one set up in the corner of a hotel room. Sizes range from children's play tents with a 2- to 3-foot base to models large enough to sleep two or three husky teens. Light and compact when stored, a two-adult-size tent in its own storage bag (called a stuff sack) will take up about one-tenth or less of a standard overhead bin on a commercial airliner. Another option for infants and toddlers is to drape a sheet over a portable crib or playpen to make a tent.

THE BOX Bob here: On one memorable Disneyland excursion when my children were younger, we began each morning with an immensely annoying, involuntary scavenger hunt. Invariably, seconds before our scheduled departure to the theme park, we discovered that some combination of shoes, billfolds, sunglasses, hip packs, or other necessities were missing. For the next 15 minutes we would root through the room like pigs hunting truffles in an attempt to locate the absent items. I finally swung by a local store and mooched a big empty box. From then on, every time we returned to the room, I had the kids deposit shoes, hip packs, and other potentially wayward items in the box. After that the box was off-limits until the next morning, when I doled out the contents.

PLASTIC GARBAGE BAGS At the Grizzly River Run raft ride at DCA and at Splash Mountain in Disneyland Park, you are certain to get wet and possibly soaked. If it's really hot and you don't care, then fine. But if it's cool or you're just not up for a soaking, bring a large plastic trash bag or a cheap poncho to the park. By cutting holes in the top and on the sides of a trash bag, you can fashion a sack poncho that will keep your clothes from getting wet. On the raft ride, you will also get your feet wet. If you're not up for walking around in squishing, soaked shoes, bring a second, smaller plastic bag to wear over your feet while riding. Even if you don't mind getting wet yourself, a small zip-top bag (or free plastic bag from a gift shop) is handy for saving your cell phone and wallet from a fatal soaking.

SUPPLIES FOR INFANTS AND TODDLERS

BASED ON RECOMMENDATIONS from hundreds of Unofficial Guide readers, here's what we suggest that you carry with you when touring with infants and toddlers:

- A disposable diaper for every hour you plan to be away from your hotel
- A cloth diaper or kitchen towel to put over your shoulder for burping
- Two receiving blankets: one to wrap the baby and one to lay the baby on or to drape over you when you nurse
- Ointment for diaper rash
- A package of wipes
- Prepared formula in bottles if you are not breastfeeding
- A washable bib, baby spoon, and baby food if your infant is eating solids
- For toddlers, a small toy for comfort and to keep them occupied during attractions

Baby Care Centers at the theme parks will sell you just about anything that you forget or run out of. Like all things Disney, prices will be higher than elsewhere, but at least you won't need to detour to a drugstore in the middle of your touring day.

REMEMBERING *Your* TRIP

1. Purchase a notebook for each child and spend time each evening recording the day's events. If your children have trouble getting motivated or don't know what to write about, start a discussion; otherwise, let them write or draw whatever they want to remember from the day.

2. Collect mementos along the way and create a treasure box in a small tin or cigar box. Months or years later, it's fun to look at postcards, pins, or ticket stubs to jump-start a memory.

3. Add inexpensive postcards to your photographs to create an album; then write a few words on each page to accompany the images.

4. Give each child a disposable camera to record his or her version of the trip. One 5-year-old snapped an entire series of photos that never showed anyone above the waist—his view of Disneyland (and the photos were priceless).

5. Many families travel with a digital camera or camera phone, though we recommend using one sparingly—parents end up viewing the trip through the lens rather than being in the moment. If you must, take it along, but only record a few moments of major sights (too much is boring anyway). And let the kids record and narrate. On the topic of narration, speak loudly so as to be heard over the not-insignificant background noise of the parks. Make use of lockers at all of the parks when the equipment becomes a burden or when you're going to experience an attraction that might damage it or get it wet. Unless you have a camera designed for underwater shots or a waterproof carrying case, leave it behind on Splash Mountain, the Grizzly River Run, and any other ride where water is involved. Don't forget extra batteries or external battery chargers.

6. Consider using Disney's PhotoPass service for some professional-quality pictures; it's free to use and you only pay for the images you want to keep (see page 107 for details).

Finally, when it comes to taking photos and collecting mementos, don't let the tail wag the dog. You are not going to Disneyland to build the biggest scrapbook in history. Or as this Houston mom put it:

Tell your readers to get a grip on the photography thing. We were so busy shooting pictures that we kind of lost the thread. We had to look at our pictures when we got home to see what all we did [while on vacation].

TRIAL RUN

IF YOU GIVE THOUGHTFUL CONSIDERATION to all areas of mental, physical, organizational, and logistical preparation discussed in this chapter, what remains is to familiarize yourself with the Disneyland parks and, of course, to conduct your field test. Yep, that's right, we want you to take the whole platoon on the road for a day to see if you are combat ready. No joke—this is important. You'll learn who tuckers out first, who's prone to developing blisters, who has to pee every 11 seconds, who keeps losing her cap, and, given the proper forum, how compatible your family is in terms of what you like to see and do.

For the most informative trial run, choose a local venue that requires lots of walking, dealing with crowds, and making decisions on how to spend your time. Regional theme parks and state fairs are your best bets, followed by large zoos and museums. Devote the whole day. Kick off the morning with an early start, just like you will at Disneyland, paying attention to who's organized and ready to go and who's dragging his or her butt and holding up the group. If you have to drive 1 or 2 hours to get to your test venue, no big deal. You may have to do some commuting at Disneyland too. Spend the whole day, eat a couple of meals, and stay late.

Don't mess with the outcome by telling everyone that you are practicing for Disneyland. Everyone behaves differently when they know that they are being tested or evaluated. Your objective is to find out as much as you can about how the individuals in your family, as well as the family as a group, respond to and deal with everything they experience during the day. Pay attention to who moves quickly and who is slow; who is adventuresome and who is reticent; who keeps going and who needs frequent rest breaks; who sets the agenda and who is content to follow; who is easily agitated and who stays cool; who tends to dawdle or wander off; who is curious and who is bored; who is demanding and who is accepting. You get the idea.

Discuss the findings of the test run with your spouse the next day. Don't be discouraged if your test day wasn't perfect; few (if any) are. Distinguish between problems that are remediable and problems that are intrinsic to your family's emotional or physical makeup (no amount of hiking, for example, will toughen up some people's feet).

Establish a plan for addressing remediable problems (further conditioning, setting limits before you go, trying harder to achieve family consensus) and develop strategies for minimizing or working around problems that are a fact of life (waking sleepyheads 15 minutes early, placing moleskin on likely blister sites before setting out, or packing familiar food for the toddler who balks at restaurant fare). If you are an attentive observer, a fair diagnostician, and a creative problem solver, you'll be able to work out many of the problems you're likely to encounter at Disneyland before you leave home.

ABOUT THE UNOFFICIAL GUIDE TOURING PLANS Parents who embark on one of our touring plans are often frustrated by the various interruptions and delays occasioned by their small children. In case you haven't given the subject much thought, here is what to expect:

1. Many small children will stop dead in their tracks whenever they see a Disney character. Our advice: Live with it. An attempt to haul your children away before they have satisfied their curiosity is likely to precipitate anything from whining to a full-scale revolt.

2. The touring plans call for visiting attractions in a specified sequence, often skipping certain attractions along the way. Children do not like skipping anything! If they see something that attracts them, they want to experience it now. Some children can be persuaded to skip attractions if parents explain things in advance. Other kids severely flip out at the threat of skipping something, particularly something in Fantasyland. A mom from Charleston, South Carolina, had this to say:

   Following the touring plans turned out to be a train wreck. The main problem is that the plan starts in Fantasyland. When we were on Dumbo, my 5-year-old saw eight dozen other things in Fantasyland she wanted to see. After Dumbo, there was no getting her out of there.

3. Children seem to have a genetic instinct when it comes to finding restrooms. We have seen perfectly functional adults equipped with all manner of maps search

interminably for a restroom. Small children, on the other hand, including those who cannot read, will head for the nearest restroom with the certainty of a homing pigeon. While you may skip certain attractions, you can be sure that your children will ferret out (and want to use) every restroom in the park.

STROLLERS

STROLLERS ARE AVAILABLE for about $15 per day for a single, $25 per day for two; the rental covers the entire day and is good at both parks. If you rent a stroller and later decide to go back to your hotel for lunch, a swim, or a nap, turn in your stroller but hang on to your rental receipt. When you return to either park later in the day, present your receipt. You will be issued another stroller at no additional charge. The rental procedure is fast and efficient, and a central stroller rental facility is in the Main Entrance Plaza between Disneyland and DCA, to the right of the Disneyland Park entrance. Likewise, returning the stroller is a breeze. Even in the evening, when several hundred strollers are turned in following the fireworks or water show, there is no wait or hassle. *Note:* Rented strollers are not permitted in Downtown Disney.

The strollers come with sun canopies and small cargo compartments under the seat. For infants and toddlers, strollers are a must, and we recommend a small pillow or blanket to help make the stroller more comfortable for your child during what may be long periods in the seat. We have also observed many sharp parents renting strollers for somewhat older children. Strollers prevent parents from having to carry children when they run out of steam and provide an easy, convenient way to carry water, snacks, diaper bags, and the like.

unofficial **TIP**
Strollers are also great for older kids who tire easily.

When you enter a show or board a ride, you will have to park your stroller, usually in an open, unprotected area. If it rains before you return, you'll need a cloth, towel, or spare diaper to dry off the stroller.

unofficial **TIP**
Often little ones fall asleep in their strollers (hallelujah!). Bring a large lightweight cloth to drape over the stroller to cover your child from the sun. A few clothespins will keep it in place.

Bringing Your Own Stroller

You are allowed to bring your own stroller to the theme parks. However, only collapsible strollers are allowed on the monorail and Toy Story parking lot buses. Your stroller is unlikely to be stolen, but mark it with your name. We strongly recommend bringing your own stroller. In addition to the parks, there is the walk from and to your hotel, the parking lot bus, or the bus/hotel-shuttle boarding area, not to mention many other occasions at your hotel or during shopping when you will be happy to have a stroller handy.

If you do not want to bring your own stroller, you may consider buying one of the umbrella-style collapsible strollers. You may even consider ordering online and shipping it right to your hotel, or consider renting a stroller from a third party. Make sure you leave enough time between your order and arrival dates.

Having her own stroller was indispensable to this mother of two toddlers:

How I was going to manage to get the kids from the parking lot to the park was a big worry for me before I made the trip. I found that, for me personally, since I have two kids ages 1 and 2, it was easier to walk to the entrance of the park from the parking lot with the kids in my own stroller than to take the kids out of the stroller, fold the stroller (while trying to control the two kids and associated gear), load the stroller and the kids onto the bus, etc. No matter where I was parked, I could always just walk to the entrance. It sometimes took a while, but it was easier for me.

An Oklahoma mom, however, reports a bad experience with bringing her own stroller:

The first time we took our kids we had a large stroller (big mistake). It is so much easier to rent one in the park. The large [personally owned] strollers are nearly impossible to get on [airport shuttle] buses and are a hassle at the airport. I remember feeling dread when a bus pulled up that was even semifull of people. People look at you like you have a cage full of live chickens when you drag heavy strollers onto the bus.

Stroller Wars

Sometimes strollers disappear while you are enjoying a ride or a show. Do not be alarmed. You won't have to buy the missing stroller, and you will be issued a new stroller for your continued use. Lost strollers can be replaced at the main rental facility near the park entrances.

unofficial **TIP**
Beware of stroller stealers. With so many identical strollers, it's easy to grab the wrong one. Mark yours with a bandanna or some other easily identifiable flag.

While replacing a ripped-off stroller is not a big deal, it is an inconvenience. One family complained that their stroller had been taken six times in one day. Even with free replacements, larceny on this scale represents a lot of wasted time. Through our own experiments and suggestions from readers, we have developed several techniques for hanging on to your rented stroller:

1. Write your name in permanent marker on a 6-by-9-inch card, put the card in a transparent freezer bag, and secure the bag to the handle of the stroller with masking or duct tape.

2. Affix something personal (but expendable) to the handle of the stroller. Evidently most

strollers are pirated by mistake (because they all look the same) or because it's easier to swipe someone else's stroller (when yours disappears) than to troop off to the replacement center. Because most stroller theft is a function of confusion, laziness, or revenge, the average pram-pincher will balk at hauling off a stroller bearing another person's property. After trying several items, we concluded that a bright, inexpensive scarf or bandanna tied to the handle works well, and a sock partially stuffed with rags or paper works even better (the weirder and more personal the object, the greater the deterrent).

A multigenerational family tried this:

We decorated our stroller with electrical tape to make it stand out. We also zip-tied an unused, small, insulated diaper bag to the handle to make carrying things easier. One of your readers mentioned using a bike chain or cable lock to insure their stroller was not stolen but said the Disney cast members were a little disturbed. So I took an extra firearm lock (looks like a mini-bike lock) to lock a wheel to the frame while parked. My son added a small cowbell to make it clang if moved. The stroller could then be moved easily for short distances by lifting the back, but trying to go farther would be uncomfortable and noisy.

We receive quite a few letters from readers debating the pros and cons of bringing your own stroller versus renting one of Disney's. A mother with two small children opted for her own pram:

I took my own stroller because the rented strollers aren't appropriate for infants (we had a 5-year-old and a 5-month-old). No one said anything about me using a bike lock to secure our brand-new Aprica stroller. However, an attendant came over and told us not to lock it anywhere because it's a fire hazard! (Outside?) When I politely asked the attendant if she wanted to be responsible for my $300 stroller, she told me to go ahead and lock it but not tell anyone! I observed the attendants constantly moving the strollers. This seems very confusing—no wonder people think their strollers are getting ripped off!

As the reader mentioned, Disney cast members often rearrange strollers parked outside an attraction. Sometimes this is done simply to tidy up. At other times the strollers are moved to make additional room along a walkway. In any event, do not assume that your stroller is stolen because it is missing from the exact place you left it. Check around. Chances are that it will be neatly arranged just a few feet away.

BABYSITTING

CHILDCARE SERVICES ARE UNAVAILABLE in the Disney parks. The Grand Californian Hotel used to offer a paid childcare facility for resort guests, but it was removed during the 2017 renovation with no plans to replace it.

Fullerton Child Care Agency, an independent organization, provides in-room sitting for infants and children. The basic rate for in-room sitting for one or two children is $48 for the first 4 hours, with a 4-hour minimum, and $10 each hour thereafter. The charge for each additional child varies with the sitter. There is no transportation fee, but the client is expected to pay for parking when applicable. All fees and charges must be paid in cash at the end of the assignment. To reserve a sitter, one or two days' advance notice is requested. They fill up quickly, so a couple of weeks' notice is ideal. You can reach the Fullerton Child Care Agency by calling ☎ 714-528-1640.

DISNEY, KIDS, *and* SCARY STUFF

DISNEYLAND PARK and Disney California Adventure are family theme parks. Yet some of the Disney adventure rides can be intimidating to small children. On certain rides, such as Splash Mountain and the roller coasters (California Screamin', Space Mountain, Matterhorn Bobsleds, and Big Thunder Mountain Railroad), the ride itself may be frightening. On other rides, such as The Haunted Mansion and Snow White's Scary Adventures, it is the special effects. We recommend a little parent-child dialogue coupled with a "testing the water" approach. A child who is frightened by Peter Pan's Flight should not have to sit through The Haunted Mansion. Likewise, if Big Thunder Mountain Railroad is too much, don't try Space Mountain or California Screamin'. Just because a child in your party isn't ready for a ride doesn't mean that the grown-ups have to miss out; learn about Disney's "baby swap" system on page 154.

Disney rides and shows are adventures. They focus on the substance and themes of all adventure, and indeed of life itself: good and evil, beauty and the grotesque, fellowship and enmity, quest, and death. Though the endings are all happy, the impact of the adventures, with Disney's gift for special effects, is often intimidating and occasionally frightening to small children.

There are rides with menacing witches, rides with burning towns, and rides with ghouls popping out of their graves, all done tongue in cheek and with a sense of humor, provided you are old enough to understand the joke. And there are bones, lots of bones—human bones, cattle bones, and whole skeletons are everywhere you look. There have to be more bones at Disneyland Park than at the Smithsonian and the School of Medicine at UCLA combined. A stack of skulls is at the headhunter's camp on the Jungle Cruise; a veritable platoon of skeletons sails ghost ships in Pirates of the Caribbean; a macabre assemblage of skulls and skeletons are in The Haunted Mansion; and more skulls, skeletons, and bones punctuate Snow White's Scary Adventures, Peter Pan's Flight, and Big Thunder Mountain Railroad.

One reader wrote us after taking his preschoolers on Star Tours:

We took a 4- and 5-year-old, and they had the *#%! scared out of them at Star Tours. We did it in the morning, and it took hours of Tom Sawyer Island and It's a Small World to get back to normal.

Preschoolers should start with Dumbo and work up to the Jungle Cruise in the late morning, after being revved up and before getting hungry, thirsty, or tired. Pirates of the Caribbean is out for preschoolers. You get the idea.

The reaction of young children to the inevitable system overload of Disney parks should be anticipated. Be sensitive, alert, and prepared for almost anything, even behavior that is out of character for your child at home. Most small children take Disney's variety of macabre trappings in stride, and others are quickly comforted by an arm around the shoulder or a little squeeze of the hand. For parents who have observed a tendency in their kids to become upset, we recommend taking it slowly and easily by sampling more benign adventures such as the Jungle Cruise, gauging reactions, and discussing with children how they felt about the things they saw. A mother of two reported this:

We pressured our kids into going on Pirates of the Caribbean because my husband and I wanted us all to ride as a family. Big mistake! I had not read enough about what the ride would be like. My 12-year-old (who is very sensitive) balked when we were in the queue, but still we pressured her to go on. Well, both her and her 6-year-old sister ended up sobbing through the whole ride.

Sometimes, small children will rise above their anxiety in an effort to please their parents or siblings. This behavior, however, does not necessarily indicate a mastery of fear, much less enjoyment. If children come off a ride in ostensibly good shape, we recommend asking if they would like to go on the ride again (not necessarily right now, but sometime). The response to this question will usually give you a clue as to how much they actually enjoyed the experience. There is a lot of difference between having a good time and mustering the courage to get through something.

Evaluating a child's capacity to handle the visual and tactile effects of the Disney parks requires patience, understanding, and experimentation. Each of us, after all, has his own demons. If a child balks at or is frightened by a ride, respond constructively. Let your children know that lots of people, adults as well as children, are scared by what they see and feel. Help them understand that it is OK if they get frightened. Take pains not to compound the discomfort by making a child feel inadequate; try not to undermine self-esteem, impugn courage, or subject a child to ridicule. Most of all, do not induce guilt, as if your child's trepidation is ruining the family's fun. When older siblings are present, it is sometimes necessary to restrain their taunting and teasing.

A visit to a Disney park is more than an outing or an adventure for a small child. It is a testing experience, a sort of controlled rite of passage. If you help your little one work through the challenges, the time can be immeasurably rewarding and a bonding experience for both of you.

The Fright Factor

While each youngster is different, there are essentially seven attraction elements that alone or combined can push a child's buttons:

1. THE NAME OF THE ATTRACTION Small children will naturally be apprehensive about something called The Haunted Mansion or Snow White's Scary Adventures.

2. THE VISUAL IMPACT OF THE ATTRACTION FROM OUTSIDE Splash Mountain, Guardians of the Galaxy—Mission: Breakout!, and Big Thunder Mountain Railroad look scary enough to give even adults second thoughts. To many small kids, the rides are visually terrifying.

3. THE VISUAL IMPACT OF THE INDOOR QUEUING AREA Pirates of the Caribbean with its dark bayou scene and The Haunted Mansion with its "stretch rooms" are capable of frightening small children before they even board the ride.

4. THE INTENSITY OF THE ATTRACTION Some attractions are so intense as to be overwhelming; they inundate the senses with sights, sounds, movement, and even smell. *It's Tough to Be a Bug!,* for instance, combines loud music, tactile effects, lights, and 3-D cinematography to create a total sensory experience. For some preschoolers, this is two or three senses too many.

5. THE VISUAL IMPACT OF THE ATTRACTION ITSELF As previously discussed, the sights in various attractions range from falling boulders to lurking buzzards, from underwater volcanoes to attacking hippos. What one child calmly absorbs may scare the owl poop out of another child the same age.

6. DARK Many Disneyland attractions are dark rides—that is, they operate indoors in a dark environment. For some children, this fact alone is sufficient to trigger significant apprehension. A child who is frightened on one dark ride, for example Snow White's Scary Adventures, may be unwilling to try other indoor rides.

7. THE RIDE ITSELF; THE TACTILE EXPERIENCE Some Disney rides are downright wild—wild enough to induce motion sickness, wrench backs, and generally discombobulate patrons of any age.

A Bit of Preparation

We receive many tips from parents relating how they prepared their children for the Disneyland experience. A common strategy is to acquaint kids with the characters and the stories behind the attractions by reading Disney books and watching Disney DVDs at home.

Thanks to half the population of California walking around the parks with video cameras, you can view a clip of every attraction and show on **youtube.com**. Videos of dark rides aren't stellar but are good enough to get a sense of what you're in for. The mother of a

Continued on page 150

SMALL-CHILD FRIGHT-POTENTIAL TABLE

As a quick reference, we provide this table to warn you which attractions to be wary of and why. The table represents a generalization, and all kids are different. It relates specifically to kids 3–7 years of age. On average, as you would expect, children at the younger end of the age range are more likely to be frightened than children in their 6th or 7th year.

Disneyland Park

MAIN STREET, U.S.A.

- **DISNEYLAND RAILROAD** Tunnel with dinosaur display frightens some small children.
- *THE DISNEYLAND STORY, PRESENTING GREAT MOMENTS WITH MR. LINCOLN* Brief battle sound effects may surprise small children.
- **MAIN STREET CINEMA** Not frightening in any respect.

ADVENTURELAND

- *ENCHANTED TIKI ROOM* A small thunderstorm momentarily surprises very young children.
- **INDIANA JONES ADVENTURE** Visually intimidating, with intense effects and a jerky ride. Switching-off option (see page 154).
- **JUNGLE CRUISE** Moderately intense, with some macabre sights; a good test attraction for little ones.
- **TARZAN'S TREEHOUSE** Not frightening in any respect.

NEW ORLEANS SQUARE

- **THE HAUNTED MANSION** Name of attraction raises anxiety, as do sights and sounds of waiting area. An intense attraction with humorously presented macabre sights. The ride itself is gentle.
- **PIRATES OF THE CARIBBEAN** Slightly intimidating queuing area; an intense boat ride with gruesome (though humorously presented) sights and two short, unexpected slides down flumes.

CRITTER COUNTRY

- **DAVY CROCKETT'S EXPLORER CANOES** Not frightening in any respect.
- **THE MANY ADVENTURES OF WINNIE THE POOH** Not frightening in any respect.
- **SPLASH MOUNTAIN** Visually intimidating from the outside. Moderately intense visual effects. The ride itself, culminating in a 52-foot plunge down a steep chute, is somewhat hair-raising for all ages. Switching-off option (see page 154).

FRONTIERLAND

- **BIG THUNDER MOUNTAIN RAILROAD** Visually intimidating from the outside; moderately intense visual effects. The roller coaster may frighten many adults, particularly seniors. Switching-off option (see page 154).
- *FANTASMIC!* Loud and intense with fireworks and some scary villains, but most young children like it.
- **FRONTIERLAND SHOOTIN' EXPOSITION** Frightening to children scared of guns.
- **THE GOLDEN HORSESHOE—LAUGHING STOCK CO.** Not frightening in any respect.
- *MARK TWAIN* RIVERBOAT Not frightening in any respect.
- **PIRATE'S LAIR ON TOM SAWYER ISLAND** Some very small children are intimidated by dark walk-through tunnels that can be easily avoided.
- **SAILING SHIP** *COLUMBIA* Not frightening in any respect.

FANTASYLAND

- **ALICE IN WONDERLAND** Pretty benign but frightens a small percentage of preschoolers.
- **CASEY JR. CIRCUS TRAIN** Not frightening in any respect.

SMALL-CHILD FRIGHT-POTENTIAL TABLE

FANTASYLAND (continued)

- **DUMBO THE FLYING ELEPHANT** A tame midway ride; a great favorite of most small children.
- **FANTASYLAND THEATRE** Not frightening in any respect.
- **IT'S A SMALL WORLD** Not frightening in any respect.
- **KING ARTHUR CARROUSEL** Not frightening in any respect.
- **MAD TEA PARTY** Midway-type ride can induce motion sickness in all ages.
- **MATTERHORN BOBSLEDS** The ride itself is wilder than Big Thunder Mountain Railroad but not as wild as Space Mountain. Switching-off option (see page 154).
- **MR. TOAD'S WILD RIDE** Name of ride intimidates some. Moderately intense spook house–genre attraction with jerky ride. Frightens only a small percentage of preschoolers.
- **PETER PAN'S FLIGHT** Not frightening in any respect.
- **PINOCCHIO'S DARING JOURNEY** Less frightening than Alice in Wonderland but scares a few very young preschoolers.
- **PIXIE HOLLOW** Not frightening in any respect.
- **ROYAL HALL AT FANTASY FAIRE** Not frightening in any respect.
- **ROYAL THEATRE AT FANTASY FAIRE** Not frightening in any respect.
- **SLEEPING BEAUTY CASTLE** Not frightening in any respect.
- **SNOW WHITE'S SCARY ADVENTURES** Moderately intense spook house–genre attraction with some grim characters. Absolutely terrifying to many preschoolers.
- **STORYBOOK LAND CANAL BOATS** Not frightening in any respect.

MICKEY'S TOONTOWN

- **CHIP 'N DALE TREEHOUSE** Not frightening in any respect.
- **GADGET'S GO COASTER** Tame as far as coasters go; frightens some small children.
- **GOOFY'S PLAYHOUSE** Not frightening in any respect.
- **MICKEY'S HOUSE AND MEET MICKEY** Not frightening in any respect.
- **MINNIE'S HOUSE** Not frightening in any respect.
- **MISS DAISY, DONALD'S BOAT** Not frightening in any respect.
- **ROGER RABBIT'S CAR TOON SPIN** Intense special effects, coupled with a dark environment and wild ride; frightens many preschoolers.

TOMORROWLAND

- **ASTRO ORBITOR** Waiting area is visually intimidating to preschoolers. The ride is a lot higher, but just a bit wilder, than Dumbo.
- **AUTOPIA** The noise in the waiting area slightly intimidates preschoolers; otherwise, not frightening.
- **BUZZ LIGHTYEAR ASTRO BLASTERS** Intense special effects plus a dark environment frighten some preschoolers.
- **DISNEYLAND MONORAIL SYSTEM** Not frightening in any respect.
- **FINDING NEMO SUBMARINE VOYAGE** Being enclosed, as well as certain ride effects, may frighten preschoolers.
- **JEDI TRAINING: TRIALS OF THE TEMPLE** Not frightening in any respect.
- **SPACE MOUNTAIN** Very intense roller coaster in the dark; Disneyland's wildest ride and a scary roller coaster by anyone's standards. Switching-off option (see page 154).
- **STAR TOURS—THE ADVENTURES CONTINUE** Extremely intense visually for all ages; one of the wildest in Disney's repertoire. Switching-off option (see page 154).
- **TOMORROWLAND THEATER** Extremely intense visual effects and the loud volume scare many preschoolers. Stationary seating is offered.

SMALL-CHILD FRIGHT-POTENTIAL TABLE
Disney California Adventure

BUENA VISTA STREET

- **RED CAR TROLLEY** Not frightening in any respect.

A BUG'S LAND

- **FLIK'S FUN FAIR** Not frightening in any respect.
- *IT'S TOUGH TO BE A BUG!* Loud and extremely intense with special effects that will terrify children under 8 years or anyone with a fear of insects.

GRIZZLY PEAK

- **GRIZZLY RIVER RUN** Frightening to guests of all ages. Wet too!
- **REDWOOD CREEK CHALLENGE TRAIL AND WILDERNESS EXPLORER CAMP** Trail is a bit overwhelming to preschoolers but not frightening.
- **SOARIN' AROUND THE WORLD** Frightens some children 7 years and under, especially anyone afraid of heights. Really a very sweet ride.

HOLLYWOOD LAND

- **ANNA & ELSA'S ROYAL WELCOME** Not frightening in any respect.
- **DISNEY ANIMATION** Not frightening in any respect.
- *DISNEY JUNIOR DANCE PARTY* Not frightening in any respect.
- *FROZEN—LIVE AT THE HYPERION* Very intense and loud; otherwise not frightening.
- **GUARDIANS OF THE GALAXY—MISSION: BREAKOUT!** Frightening to guests of all ages.
- **MONSTERS, INC. MIKE & SULLEY TO THE RESCUE** May frighten children under 7 years of age.
- **SUNSET SHOWCASE THEATER** Intense and loud with a lot of special effects. Frightens some preschoolers.
- *TURTLE TALK WITH CRUSH* Not frightening in any respect.

PACIFIC WHARF

- **BAKERY TOUR** Not frightening in any respect.

PARADISE PIER/PIXAR PIER

- **CALIFORNIA SCREAMIN'** Frightening to guests of all ages.
- **GOLDEN ZEPHYR** Frightening to a small percentage of preschoolers.
- **GOOFY'S SKY SCHOOL** Frightening to the under-8 crowd.
- **JUMPIN' JELLYFISH** The ride's appearance frightens some younger children. The ride itself is exceedingly tame.
- **KING TRITON'S CAROUSEL** Not frightening in any respect.
- **THE LITTLE MERMAID: ARIEL'S UNDERSEA ADVENTURE** Moderately intense effects; Ursula may frighten children under 7 years of age.
- **MICKEY'S FUN WHEEL (PIXAR FUN WHEEL)** The ride in the stationary cars is exceedingly tame. The ride in the swinging cars is frightening to guests of all ages.
- **SILLY SYMPHONY SWINGS** Height requirement keeps preschoolers from riding. Moderately intimidating to younger grade-schoolers.
- **TOY STORY MIDWAY MANIA!** Loud and intense but not frightening.
- *WORLD OF COLOR NIGHTTIME SPECTACULAR* Not frightening for most children, but it is very loud with bursts of flame and a chance of getting wet.

CARS LAND

- **LUIGI'S ROLLICKIN' ROADSTERS** Not frightening, aside from some brief moderate spinning at the end.
- **MATER'S JUNKYARD JAMBOREE** Can induce motion sickness in all ages.
- **RADIATOR SPRINGS RACERS** Moderately intense effects, with high-speed sections that may frighten younger children. Switching-off option (see page 154).

Continued from page 146

7-year-old found YouTube quite effective:

> *We watched every ride and show on YouTube before going, so my timid 7-year-old daughter would be prepared, and we cut out all the ones that looked too scary to her. She still did not like, and cried at, It's Tough to Be a Bug.*

A mother from Gloucester, Massachusetts, handled her son's preparation a bit more extemporaneously:

> *The 3½-year-old liked It's a Small World but was afraid of The Haunted Mansion. We just pulled his hat over his face and quietly talked to him while we enjoyed the ride.*

A Word About Height Requirements

A number of attractions require children to meet minimum height and age requirements, usually 40 inches tall to ride with an adult, or at least 40 inches and 7 years of age or older to ride alone. If you have children too short or too young to ride, you have several options, including switching off (described on page 154). Though the alternatives may resolve some practical and logistical issues, be forewarned that your smaller children might nonetheless be resentful of their older (or taller) siblings who qualify to ride. A mom from Virginia bumped into just such a situation, writing:

> *You mention height requirements for rides but not the intense sibling jealousy this can generate. Frontierland was a real problem in that respect. Our very petite 5-year-old, to her outrage, was stuck hanging around while our 8-year-old went on Splash Mountain and Big Thunder Mountain with Grandma and Granddad, and the nearby alternatives weren't helpful [too long a line for rafts to Tom Sawyer Island, and so on]. If we had thought ahead, we would have left the younger kid back in Mickey's Toontown with one of the grown-ups for another roller coaster or two and then met up later at a designated point. The best areas had a playground or other quick attractions for short people near the rides with height requirements.*

The reader makes a valid point, though splitting the group and then meeting later can be more complicated in practical terms than she might imagine. If you choose to split up, ask the Disney greeter at the entrance to the height-restricted attraction(s) how long the wait is. If you tack 5 minutes for riding onto the anticipated wait, and then add 5 or so minutes to exit and reach the meeting point, you'll have an approximate sense of how long the younger kids (and their supervising adult) will have to do other stuff. Our guess is that even with a long line for the rafts, the reader would have had more than sufficient time to take her daughter to Tom Sawyer Island while the sibs rode Splash Mountain and Big Thunder Mountain with the grandparents. For sure she had time to tour Tarzan's Treehouse in adjacent Adventureland.

Additionally, children under age 7 must be accompanied on all attractions by another guest age 14 or older, who must sit in the same ride vehicle in the same row or an adjacent one. While this shouldn't pose a problem on most attractions, some with small vehicles (such as Gadget's Go Coaster) may require use of a baby swap (see page 154) if your party has an uneven ratio of little members to big ones; ask a cast member at the ride entrance for assistance if you have questions.

Attractions that Eat Adults

You may spend so much energy worrying about Junior's welfare that you forget to take care of yourself. If the ride component of the attraction (that is, the actual motion and movement of the conveyance itself) is potentially disturbing, persons of any age may be adversely affected.

Several attractions likely to cause motion sickness or other problems for older children and adults are listed in the table below. Fast, jerky rides are also noted with icons in the attraction profiles.

POTENTIALLY PROBLEMATIC ATTRACTIONS FOR ADULTS
DISNEYLAND PARK
ADVENTURELAND Indiana Jones Adventure
CRITTER COUNTRY Splash Mountain
FANTASYLAND Mad Tea Party | Matterhorn Bobsleds
FRONTIERLAND   Big Thunder Mountain Railroad
TOMORROWLAND Space Mountain | Star Tours—The Adventures Continue
DISNEY CALIFORNIA ADVENTURE
CARS LAND Mater's Junkyard Jamboree | Radiator Springs Racers
GRIZZLY PEAK Grizzly River Run
HOLLYWOOD LAND Guardians of the Galaxy—Mission: Breakout!
PARADISE PIER/PIXAR PIER California Screamin' | Goofy's Sky School Mickey's Fun Wheel (Pixar Fun Wheel) (swinging)

WAITING-LINE STRATEGIES *for* ADULTS *with* SMALL CHILDREN

CHILDREN HOLD UP BETTER through the day if you minimize the time they have to spend in lines. Arriving early and using the touring plans in this guide will reduce waiting time immensely. There are, however, additional measures that you can employ to reduce stress on little ones.

1. LINE GAMES Smart parents anticipate how restless children become waiting in line and know that a little structured activity can relieve the stress and boredom. In the morning, kids handle the inactivity of waiting in line by discussing what they want to see and do during the course of the day. Later, however, as events wear on, they need a little help. Watching for, and counting, Disney characters is a good diversion. Simple guessing games such as 20 Questions also work well. Lines for rides move so continuously that games requiring pen and paper are cumbersome and impractical. Waiting in the holding area of a theater attraction, however, is a different story. Here, tic-tac-toe, hangman, drawing, and coloring can really make the time go by.

For Apple and Android smartphone users, our favorite new queue distraction is Ellen DeGeneres's Heads Up, a Taboo-style game where one player holds a phone against his or her forehead, and the others help him or her guess the phrase displayed before the timer counts down. The app costs 99¢ and includes several starter "decks" of clues to play. If you're inside Disneyland Resort, you can unlock a deck featuring Disney characters and attractions for free. Don't be surprised if you see several shouting families playing Heads Up in any given line.

2. LAST-MINUTE ENTRY If a ride or show can accommodate an unusually large number of people at one time, it is often unnecessary to stand in line. The *Mark Twain* Riverboat in Frontierland is a good example. The boat holds about 450 people, usually more than are waiting in line to ride. Instead of standing uncomfortably in a crowd with dozens of other guests, grab a snack and sit in the shade until the boat arrives and loading is well under way. After the line has all but disappeared, go ahead and board.

In large-capacity theaters, such as Tomorrowland Theater, ask the entrance greeter how long it will be until guests are admitted to the theater for the next show. If the answer is 15 minutes or more, use the time for a restroom break or to get a snack; you can return to the attraction just a few minutes before the show starts. You will not be permitted to carry any food or drink into the attraction, so make sure you have time to finish your snack before entering.

To help you determine which attractions to target for last-minute entry, we provide the table below.

ATTRACTIONS YOU CAN USUALLY ENTER AT THE LAST MINUTE
DISNEYLAND PARK
• **ADVENTURELAND** *Enchanted Tiki Room*
• **FANTASYLAND** Fantasy Theater
• **FRONTIERLAND** *Mark Twain* Riverboat | Sailing Ship *Columbia*
• **MAIN STREET, U.S.A.** *Disneyland Story,* presenting *Great Moments with Mr. Lincoln*
• **TOMORROWLAND** Tomorrowland Theater
DISNEY CALIFORNIA ADVENTURE
• **A BUG'S LAND** *It's Tough to Be a Bug!*
• **HOLLYWOOD LAND** Disney Animation | Sunset Showcase Theater

3. THE HAIL MARY PASS Certain waiting lines are configured in such a way that you and your smaller children can pass under the rail to join your partner just before boarding or entry. This technique allows the kids and one adult to rest, snack, cool off, or tinkle, while another adult or older sibling does the waiting. Other guests are understanding when it comes to using this strategy to keep small children content. You are likely to meet hostile opposition, however, if you try to pass older children or more than one adult under the rail. Attractions where it is usually possible to complete a Hail Mary pass are listed on the table below.

ATTRACTIONS WHERE YOU CAN USUALLY COMPLETE A HAIL MARY PASS
DISNEYLAND PARK
• **FANTASYLAND** Casey Jr. Circus Train | Dumbo the Flying Elephant King Arthur Carrousel | Mad Tea Party | Mr. Toad's Wild Ride | Peter Pan's Flight Snow White's Scary Adventures | Storybook Land Canal Boats
• **TOMORROWLAND** Autopia

ATTRACTIONS WHERE YOU CAN USUALLY COMPLETE A HAIL MARY PASS

DISNEY CALIFORNIA ADVENTURE

- **PARADISE PIER/PIXAR PIER** Golden Zephyr | Jumpin' Jellyfish | King Triton's Carousel
- **CARS LAND** Luigi's Rollickin' Roadsters | Mater's Junkyard Jamboree

---

4. SWITCHING OFF (ALSO KNOWN AS RIDER SWAP, BABY SWAP, OR CHILD SWAP) Several attractions have minimum height and/or age requirements (see the table on page 116). In addition, all children must be at least 7 years old and 40 inches tall to ride any attraction without an accompanying adult. Some couples with children too short or too young forgo these attractions, while others take turns riding. Missing some of Disneyland's best rides is an unnecessary sacrifice, and waiting in line twice for the same ride is a tremendous waste of time.

Instead, take advantage of the switching-off option, also called the Rider Swap, Baby Swap, or Child Swap. To switch off, there must be at least two adults. At a few attractions, adults and children wait in line together. When you approach the queue, tell the first ride attendant you see (known as a greeter) that you want to switch off. The worker will allow everyone, including young children, to enter the attraction. When you reach the loading area, one adult rides while the other stays with the kids. Some attractions offer waiting areas for this purpose. Then the riding adult disembarks and takes charge of the children while the other adult rides. A third adult (or a child who meets the minimum height or age requirement) in the party can ride twice, once with each switching-off adult, so the switching-off adults don't have to ride alone.

On FastPass attractions, the park may handle switching off somewhat differently. When you tell the worker that you want to switch off, he or she may issue you a special rider-exchange pass good for up to three people. One parent and the nonriding child (or children) will, at that point, be asked to leave the line and are free to do other things while the riding adult is waiting in line and experiencing the attraction. When those riding reunite with the waiting adult, the waiting adult and two other persons from the party can ride using the special ticket. This system eliminates confusion and congestion at the boarding area while sparing the nonriding adult and child the tedium and physical exertion of waiting in line.

There is no cost to use the switching-off option. The attractions where switching off is routinely practiced, often oriented to more mature guests, are listed on page 155. Sometimes it takes a lot of courage for a child just to move through the queue holding Dad's hand. In the boarding area, many children suddenly fear abandonment when one parent leaves to ride. Prepare your children for switching off, or you might have an emotional crisis on your hands. A mom from Edison, New Jersey, writes:

> *Once my son understood that the switch off would not leave him abandoned, he did not seem to mind. I would recommend practicing*

the switch off at home, so your child is not concerned that he will be left behind. At the very least, explain the procedure in advance, so little ones know what to expect.

A Philadelphia, Pennsylvania, mother discovered that the switching-off procedure varies among attractions. She says:

Most rides did not require the entire group to stand in line together. Some rider-switch passes were handed out by the first attendant, others by the last attendant. The most common procedure involved me holding a lanyard and giving it to the very last attendant we saw (the one loading the cars) in exchange for a rider-switch pass.

In addition, the rider-switch pass was good for up to three riders and did not have a time restriction like FastPasses. There were two babies in our party (two separate families), so each time we requested two rider-switch passes, we split up to return later. Because we also got a FastPass for each person with a ticket, we had two leftover FastPasses (because of the two adults who waited outside with the babies). Therefore, we could ride the ride, and then eight of us could reenter the ride immediately via the two switch passes (good for three people each) and the two extra FastPasses. This was a good alternative to the Chuck-Bubba Relay [see below] since we had several children in our group.

ATTRACTIONS WHERE SWITCHING OFF IS COMMON

DISNEYLAND PARK

- **ADVENTURELAND** Indiana Jones Adventure
- **CRITTER COUNTRY** Splash Mountain
- **FANTASYLAND** Matterhorn Bobsleds
- **FRONTIERLAND** Big Thunder Mountain Railroad
- **TOMORROWLAND** Space Mountain | Star Tours—The Adventures Continue

DISNEY CALIFORNIA ADVENTURE

- **CARS LAND** Radiator Springs Racers
- **GRIZZLY PEAK** Grizzly River Run | Soarin' Around the World
- **HOLLYWOOD LAND** Guardians of the Galaxy—Mission: Breakout!
- **PARADISE PIER/PIXAR PIER** California Screamin' | Goofy's Sky School

5. HOW TO RIDE TWICE IN A ROW WITHOUT WAITING Many small children like to ride a favorite attraction two or more times in succession. Riding the second time often gives the child a feeling of mastery and accomplishment. Unfortunately, repeat rides can be time-consuming, even in the early morning. If you ride Dumbo as soon as Disneyland Park opens, for instance, you will only have a 1- or 2-minute wait for your first ride. When you come back for your second ride, your wait will be about 12 minutes. If you want to ride a third time, count on a 20-minute or longer wait.

The best way for getting your child on the ride twice (or more) without blowing your whole morning is by using the Chuck-Bubba Relay (named in honor of a reader from Kentucky):

1. Mom and little Bubba enter the waiting line.

2. Dad lets a certain number of people go in front of him (32 in the case of Dumbo) and then gets in line.

3. As soon as the ride stops, Mom exits with little Bubba and passes him to Dad to ride the second time.

4. If everybody is really getting into this, Mom can hop in line again, no less than 32 people behind Dad.

The Chuck-Bubba Relay will not work on every ride because of differences in the way the waiting areas are configured (that is, it is impossible in some cases to exit the ride and make the pass). The rides where the Chuck-Bubba Relay does work, along with the number of people to count off, appear on the table below.

When practicing the Chuck-Bubba Relay, if you are the second adult in line, you will reach a point in the waiting area that is obviously the easiest place to make the handoff. Sometimes this point is where those exiting the ride pass closest to those waiting to board. In any event, you will know it when you see it. Once there, if the first parent has not arrived with little Bubba, just let those behind you slip past until Bubba shows up.

ATTRACTIONS WHERE THE CHUCK-BUBBA RELAY USUALLY WORKS

DISNEYLAND PARK   *Number of people between adults*

- **ALICE IN WONDERLAND** (tough, but possible)   38 people
- **CASEY JR. CIRCUS TRAIN**   34 people, if 2 trains are operating
- **DAVY CROCKETT'S EXPLORER CANOES**   94 people, if 6 canoes are operating
- **DUMBO THE FLYING ELEPHANT**   32 people
- **KING ARTHUR CARROUSEL**   70 people • **MAD TEA PARTY**   53 people
- **MR. TOAD'S WILD RIDE**   32 people • **PETER PAN'S FLIGHT**   25 people
- **SNOW WHITE'S SCARY ADVENTURES**   30 people

DISNEY CALIFORNIA ADVENTURE   *Number of people between adults*

- **GOLDEN ZEPHYR**   64 people • **JUMPIN' JELLYFISH**   16 people
- **KING TRITON'S CAROUSEL**   64 people
- **LUIGI'S ROLLICKIN' ROADSTERS**   40 people

6. LAST-MINUTE COLD FEET If your small child gets cold feet at the last minute after waiting for a ride (where there is no age or height requirement), you can usually arrange with the loading attendant for a switch-off; see the table on page 155. This situation arises frequently at Pirates of the Caribbean—small children lose their courage en route to the loading area.

There is no law that says you have to ride. If you get to the boarding area and someone is unhappy, just tell a Disney attendant that you have changed your mind, and one will show you the way out. Older children and adults who are unable or unwilling to ride an attraction may also experience the queue with their party and exit before boarding without embarrassment.

7. THROW YOURSELF ON THE GRENADE, MILDRED! For by-the-book, do-the-right-thing parents who are determined to sacrifice themselves on behalf of their children, we provide a one-day touring plan for Disneyland Park called the Dumbo-or-Die-in-a-Day Touring Plan for Parents with Small Children. This plan, detailed on page 373, will ensure that you run yourself ragged. Designed to help you forfeit everything of personal interest for the sake of your children's pleasure, the plan is guaranteed to send you home battered and exhausted with extraordinary stories of devotion and heroic perseverance. Anyone under 8 years old will love it.

8. DISNEY CALIFORNIA ADVENTURE This is not a great park for little ones. With the exception of Flik's Fun Fair, The Little Mermaid: Ariel's Undersea Adventure, two play areas, and a carousel, the remaining attractions are either boring or too frightening for most preschoolers. Elementary school–age children will fare better but will probably be captivated by the low-capacity/long-line rides in Paradise Pier/Pixar Pier. Though designed to be appealing to the eye, these attractions are simply gussied-up versions of midway rides your kids can enjoy less expensively and with a fraction of the wait at a local amusement park or state fair.

9. AUTOPIA Though Autopia at Disneyland Park is a great treat for small children, they must be 54 inches tall to drive unassisted. To work around the height requirement issues, after getting into the car, shift your child over behind the steering wheel. From your position you will still be able to control the foot pedals. To your child, it will feel like driving. Because the car travels on a self-guiding track, there is no way your child can make a mistake while steering.

LOST CHILDREN

LOST CHILDREN NORMALLY do not present much of a problem at Disneyland Resort. All Disney employees are schooled in handling such situations. If you lose a child while touring, report the situation to a Disney employee; then check in at City Hall (Disneyland Park) or Guest Relations (DCA) where lost-children logs are maintained. In an emergency, an alert can be issued throughout the park through internal communications. If a Disney cast member encounters a lost child, the cast member will escort the child to the Baby Care Center located at the central-hub end of Main Street in Disneyland Park and at the entrance plaza in DCA. Guests age 11 or under are taken to the Baby Care Center in the Pacific Wharf area at DCA. Guests age 12 and older may leave a written message at City Hall or the Guest Relations lobby or wait there.

unofficial **TIP**
We suggest that children younger than 8 years old be color coded by dressing them in purple T-shirts or equally distinctive clothes.

It is amazingly easy to lose a child (or two) at a Disney park. It is a good idea to sew a label into each child's shirt that states his or her name, your name, and the name of your hotel. The same task can be accomplished by writing the information on a strip of masking tape;

hotel security professionals suggest that the information be printed in small letters, and that the tape be affixed to the outside of the child's shirt 5 inches or so below the armpit.

HOW KIDS GET LOST

CHILDREN GET SEPARATED FROM PARENTS every day at the Disney parks under remarkably similar (and predictable) circumstances.

1. PREOCCUPIED SOLO PARENT In this scenario the only adult in the party is preoccupied with something such as buying refreshments, adjusting the camera settings, or using the restroom. Junior is there one moment and gone the next.

2. THE HIDDEN EXIT Sometimes parents wait on the sidelines while allowing two or more young children to experience a ride together. As

TIPS FOR KEEPING TRACK OF YOUR BROOD

- Same-colored T-shirts for the whole family will help you gather your troops in an easy and fun way. Opt for just a uniform color or have the T-shirts printed with a logo such as The Brown Family's Assault on the Mouse. You might also include the date or the year of your visit. Light-colored T-shirts can even be autographed by the Disney characters.

- Clothing labels are great. If you don't sew, buy labels that you can iron on the garment. Include your cell phone number or the number of the hotel where you'll be staying on the label.

- An easier option is a temporary tattoo with your child's name and your phone number. Unlike other methods, the tattoos cannot fall off or be lost. Temporary tattoos last about two weeks, won't wash or sweat off, and are not irritating to the skin. They can be purchased online at **safetytat.com** or **tattooswithapurpose .com.** Special tattoos are available for children with food allergies or cognitive impairment such as autism.

- In pet stores you can have name tags printed for a very reasonable price. These are great to add to necklaces and bracelets, or attach them to your child's shoelaces or a belt loop.

- When you check into the hotel, take a business card of the hotel for each member in your party, especially those old enough to carry wallets and purses.

- Always agree on a meeting point before you see a parade, fireworks, or nighttime spectacles. Make sure the meeting place is in the park (as opposed to the car or some place outside the front gate).

- If you have a digital camera or camera phone, take a picture of your kids every morning. If they get lost, the picture will show what they look like and what they are wearing.

- If all members of your party have cell phones, it's easy to locate each other. However, the noise in the parks is so loud that you probably won't hear your cell phone ring. Carry your phone in a front pants pocket and program the phone to vibrate. Or communicate via text message. If any of your younger kids carry cell phones, secure the phones with a strap.

- Save key tags and luggage tags for use on items you bring to the parks, including your stroller, diaper bag, and backpack or hip pack.

- Don't underestimate permanent markers. They are great for labeling pretty much anything. Mini-Sharpies are useful for collecting character autographs.

it usually happens, the parents expect the kids to exit the attraction in one place, and, lo and behold, the young ones pop out somewhere else. The exits of some Disney attractions are considerably distant from the entrances. Make sure that you know exactly where your children will emerge before letting them ride by themselves.

3. AFTER THE SHOW At the completion of many shows and rides, a Disney staffer will announce, "Check for personal belongings and take small children by the hand." When dozens, if not hundreds, of people leave an attraction at the same time, it is easy for parents to temporarily lose contact with their children unless they have them directly in tow.

4. RESTROOM PROBLEMS Mom tells 6-year-old Tommy, "I'll be sitting on this bench when you come out of the restroom." Three situations: One, Tommy exits through a different door and becomes disoriented (Mom may not know there is another door). Two, Mom belatedly decides that she will also use the restroom, and Tommy emerges to find her absent. Three, Mom pokes around in a shop while keeping an eye on the bench but misses Tommy when he comes out. A restroom adjacent to Rancho del Zocalo Restaurante in Frontierland accounts for many lost children. Because it's located in a passageway connecting Frontierland and Fantasy Faire, children can wander into a totally different area of the park from where they came by simply making a wrong turn out of the restroom.

If you can't be with your child in the restroom, make sure that there is only one exit. Designate a meeting spot more distinctive than a bench, and be specific in your instructions: "I'll meet you by this flagpole. If you get out first, stay right here." Have your child repeat the directions back to you.

5. PARADES There are many special parades and shows at the theme park during which the audience stands. Children, because they are small, tend to jockey around for a better view. By moving a little this way and a little that way, it is amazing how much distance kids can put between themselves and you before anyone notices.

6. MASS MOVEMENTS Another situation to guard against is when huge crowds disperse after shows, fireworks, or parades, or at park closing. With 5,000–12,000 people suddenly moving at once, it is very easy to get separated from a small child or others in your party. Extra caution is recommended following the evening parades, fireworks, and *Fantasmic!* Families should develop specific plans for what to do and where to meet in the event they are separated.

7. CHARACTER GREETINGS A fair amount of activity and confusion is commonplace when the Disney characters are on the scene. See the next section on meeting the Disney characters.

The DISNEY CHARACTERS

FOR YEARS THE COSTUMED, walking versions of Mickey, Minnie, Donald, Goofy, and others have been a colorful supporting cast at Disneyland and Walt Disney World. Known unpretentiously as the Disney characters, these large and friendly figures help provide a link between Disney animated films and the Disney theme parks.

Audiences, it has been observed, cry during the sad parts of Disney animated films and cheer when the villain is vanquished. To the emotionally invested, the characters in these features are as real as next-door neighbors; never mind that they are simply cartoons. Likewise, the theme park personifications of Disney characters have become real to us. For thousands of visitors, it is not just some person in a mouse costume they see—it is really Mickey. Similarly, running into Goofy or Snow White in Fantasyland is a memory to be treasured, an encounter with a real celebrity.

About 250 of the Disney animated-film characters have been brought to life in costume. Of these, a relatively small number (about 50) are greeters (the Disney term for characters who mix with the patrons). The remaining characters are relegated exclusively to performing in shows or participating in parades. Some appear only once or twice a year, usually in holiday parades.

CHARACTER ENCOUNTERS

CHARACTER WATCHING has developed into a pastime. Where families were once content to stumble across a character occasionally, they now pursue them armed with autograph books and cameras. For those who pay attention, some characters are more frequently encountered than others. Mickey, Minnie, and Goofy, for example, are seemingly everywhere, while Thumper rarely appears. Other characters are seen regularly but limit themselves to a specific location.

The fact that some characters are seldom seen has turned character watching into character collecting. Mickey Mouse may be the best-known and most-loved character, but from a collector's perspective, he is also the most common. To get an autograph from Mickey is no big deal, but Daisy Duck's signature is a real coup. Commercially tapping into the character-collecting movement, Disney sells autograph books throughout the parks. One *Unofficial Guide* reader offers this suggestion regarding character autographs:

> Young children learn very quickly! If they see another child get an autograph, they will want an autograph book as well. I recommend buying an autograph book right away. My 4-year-old daughter saw a child get Goofy's autograph, and right away she wanted to join the fun.

PREPARING YOUR CHILDREN TO MEET THE CHARACTERS Because most small children are not expecting Minnie Mouse to be the size of a forklift, it's best to discuss the characters with your kids before you go. Almost all of the characters are quite large, and several, such as Br'er Bear, are huge! All of them can be extremely intimidating to a preschooler.

On first encounter, it is important not to thrust your child upon the character. Allow the little one to come to terms with this big thing from whatever distance the child feels safe. If two adults are present, one should stay close to the youngster while the other approaches the character and demonstrates that the character is safe and friendly. Some kids warm to the characters immediately, while some never do. Most take a little time and often require several different encounters.

There are two kinds of characters: those whose costume includes a face-covering headpiece (animal characters plus some human characters such as Captain Hook), and face characters, or actors who resemble the cartoon characters to such an extent that no mask or headpiece is necessary. Face characters include Mary Poppins, Ariel, Jasmine, Aladdin, Cinderella, Mulan, Tarzan, Jane, Belle, Snow White, and Prince Charming, to name a few.

unofficial **TIP**
Don't underestimate your child's excitement at meeting the Disney characters—but also be aware that very small kids may find the large, costumed characters a little frightening.

Only the face characters are allowed to speak. Headpiece characters, called furs in Disney-speak, do not talk or make noises of any kind. Because the cast members could not possibly imitate the distinctive voice of the characters, the Disney folks have determined that it is more effective to keep them silent. Lack of speech notwithstanding, the headpiece characters are extremely warm and responsive, and they communicate very effectively with gestures. As with the characters' size, children need to be forewarned that the characters do not talk. The only exceptions are the costumed stars of some newer shows and parades, who boast articulated facial features that blink and flap in sync with the sound tracks.

Parents need to understand that some of the character costumes are very cumbersome and that cast members often suffer from very poor visibility. You have to look closely, but the eyeholes are frequently in the mouth of the costume or even down on the neck. What this means in practical terms is that the characters are sort of clumsy and have a limited field of vision. Children who approach the character from the back or the side may not be noticed, even if the child is touching the character. It is perfectly possible in this situation for the character to accidentally step on the child or knock him or her down. The best way for a child to approach a character is from the front, and occasionally not even this works. For example, the various duck characters (Donald, Daisy, Uncle Scrooge, and so on) have to peer around their bills. If it appears that the character is ignoring your child, pick your child up and hold her in front of the character until the character responds.

unofficial **TIP**
Explain to your children that the headpiece characters do not talk. Keep in mind, too, that the characters are clumsy and have a limited field of vision.

It is OK to touch, pat, or hug the character if your child is so inclined. Understanding the unpredictability of children, the characters will keep their feet very still, particularly refraining from moving backward or to the side. Most of the characters will sign autographs or pose for pictures. Once again, be sure to approach from the front so that the character will understand your intentions. If your child collects autographs, it is a good idea to carry a big, fat pen about the size of a Magic Marker. The costumes make it exceedingly difficult for the characters to wield a smaller pen, so the bigger the better.

THE BIG HURT Many children expect to bump into Mickey the minute they enter a park and are disappointed when he is not around. If your children are unable to settle down and enjoy things until they see Mickey, simply ask a Disney cast member where to find him. If the cast member does not know Mickey's whereabouts, he or she can find out for you in short order.

"THEN SOME CONFUSION HAPPENED" Be forewarned that character encounters give rise to a situation during which small children sometimes get lost. There is usually a lot of activity around a character, with both adults and children touching the character or posing for pictures. In the most common scenario, the parents stay in the crowd while their child marches up to get acquainted. With the excitement of the encounter, all the milling people, and the character moving around, a child may get turned around and head off in the wrong direction. In the words of a Salt Lake City mom:

> Milo was shaking hands with Dopey one moment, then some confusion happened, and he [Milo] was gone.

Families with several small children, and parents who are busy fooling around with cameras, can lose track of a youngster in a heartbeat. Our recommendation for parents of preschoolers is to stay with the kids when they meet the characters, stepping back only long enough to take a picture, if necessary.

MEETING CHARACTERS You can *see* the Disney characters in live shows and in parades. For times, consult your *Times Guide*. If you have the time and money, you can share a meal with the characters (more about this later). But if you want to *meet* the characters, get autographs, and take photos, it's helpful to know where the characters hang out.

Disneyland Resort includes information about characters in its mobile app, handout park maps, and entertainment *Times Guide*. A listing specifies where and when certain characters will be available and also provides information on character dining. On the maps of the parks themselves, Mickey's gloved hand is used to denote locations where characters can be found.

At DCA, look for characters in Hollywood Land near the Animation Building, in parades, and in shows at the Hyperion Theater. In Cars Land, you'll find interactive incarnations of the series' automotive stars. Anna and Elsa from *Frozen* hold court inside the Disney Animation attraction, while Olaf the Snowman gives warm hugs in Hollywood Land. Marvel's Captain America and Spider-Man also appear in Hollywood Land, near the entrance to the Hyperion Theater, and Sofia the First and Doc McStuffins roam the adjacent boulevard. Oswald the Lucky Rabbit (a long-lost forerunner of Mickey Mouse) meets guests near the park entrance. Nick and Judy from *Zootopia* stake out the San Francisco street near Ariel's ride, and Princess Elena of Avalor holds court in a pavilion at Paradise Gardens. Elsewhere around the park, characters will be less in evidence than at Disneyland Park, but they will make periodic appearances at Flik's Fun Fair and Buena Vista Street (the central hub).

The last few years have seen a number of Disney initiatives aimed at satisfying guests' inexhaustible desire to meet the characters. At Disneyland Park, Mickey and Minnie have all-day tours of duty in their Toontown homes. All of the "fab five" (including Goofy, Pluto, and Donald), along with Chip 'n' Dale and Daisy, also make morning appearances in Main Street, U.S.A.'s Town Square. Likewise, Pooh, Tigger, and Eeyore can usually be found in Critter Country, and *Toy Story*'s Woody hangs around Frontierland. The Fantasy Faire plaza adjacent to Sleeping Beauty Castle is the prime place to meet Aladdin and Jasmine, Ariel, Aurora, Cinderella, Belle, Merida, and Rapunzel with Flynn Rider. Tinker Bell and her fairy friends draw long lines at their Pixie Hollow area off the central hub between Tomorrowland and the Matterhorn. Star Wars celebrities can be spotted in and around Tomorrowland's Star Wars Launch Bay. Tiana and Dr. Facilier (occasionally accompanied by Louis and Prince Naveen) from *The Princess and the Frog* appear in New Orleans Square or at Frontierland's riverboat dock.

*un*official **TIP**
Characters make appearances in all the "lands" but are especially thick in Fantasyland, Mickey's Toontown, and Town Square on Main Street.

While making the characters routinely available has taken the guesswork out of finding them, it has likewise robbed character encounters of much of their surprise and spontaneity. Instead of chancing on a character as you turn a corner, it is much more common now to wait in a queue to meet the character. However, you are still far more likely to encounter free-range characters in Disneyland than at Walt Disney World, especially in the slower morning hours when they are given a longer leash to roam. Be aware that lines for face characters move much more slowly than lines for nonspeaking characters do, as you might surmise. Because face characters are allowed to talk, they do, often engaging children in lengthy conversations, much to the consternation of the families stuck in the queue.

If you believe that Disneyland Park already has quite enough lines, and furthermore, if you prefer to bump into your characters on the run, here's a quick rundown of where the bears and chipmunks roam. In the morning, there is almost always a princess or two posing in front of the Mickey flower bed just inside the park entrance. There will almost always be a character in Town Square on Main Street and often at the central hub; for example, Mary Poppins and Bert are frequently found near Coke Corner. Snow White hangs out near her wishing well in the courtyard of the castle; and Alice and her Wonderland friends, as well as Peter Pan, wander around Fantasyland. Any characters whom we haven't specifically mentioned generally continue to turn up randomly throughout the park. Character selection can vary seasonally, with some (such as Jack Skellington) appearing only around Halloween or Christmas.

Characters are also featured in the afternoon and evening parades, *Fantasmic!,* and Fantasy Faire. Performance times for all of the shows and parades are listed in the Disneyland Park's daily *Times Guide* entertainment listings. After the shows, characters will sometimes stick around to greet the audience.

Mickey Mouse is available to meet guests and pose for photos all day long in his dressing room at Mickey's Movie Barn in Mickey's Toontown. To reach the Movie Barn, proceed through the front door of Mickey's House and follow the crowd. If the line extends back to the entrance of Mickey's House, it will take you about 25–30 minutes to actually reach Mickey. When you finally get to his dressing room, a few families at a time are admitted for a short personal audience with Mickey.

Many children are so excited about meeting Mickey that they cannot relax to enjoy the other attractions. If Mickey looms large in your child's day, board the Disneyland Railroad at the Main Street Station as soon as Toontown opens for the day (usually 1 hour after the rest of the park), and proceed directly to Mickey's Toontown (half a circuit). If you visit Mickey within an hour of Toontown's opening, your wait will be short.

Minnie receives guests at her house in Toontown as well, but only until midafternoon. Also, be aware that the characters bug out for parades and certain other special performances. Check the daily *Times Guide* entertainment listings for performance times and plan your visit to Toontown accordingly.

CHARACTER DINING

FRATERNIZING WITH DISNEY CHARACTERS has become so popular that Disney offers character breakfasts, brunches, and dinners where families can dine in the presence of Minnie, Goofy, and other costumed versions of animated celebrities. Character meals provide a familiar, controlled setting in which young children can warm gradually to the characters. All meals are attended by several characters. Adult prices apply to persons age 10 or older, children's prices to ages 3–9. Little ones under age 3 eat free. Because character dining is very popular, we recommend that you arrange reservations as far in advance (up to 60 days) as possible.

CHARACTER DINING: WHAT TO EXPECT Character meals are bustling affairs, held in hotels' or theme parks' largest table-service or "buffeteria" restaurants. Character breakfasts (there are five) offer a fixed menu served family-style or as a buffet. The typical family-style breakfast includes scrambled eggs; bacon, sausage, and ham; hash browns; waffles, pancakes, or French toast; biscuits, rolls, or pastries; and fruit. The meal is served in large skillets or platters at your table. If you run out of something, you can order seconds (or thirds) at no additional charge. Buffets offer much the same fare, but you have to fetch it yourself.

Whatever the meal, characters circulate around the room while you eat. During your meal, each of the three to five characters present will visit your table, arriving one at a time to cuddle the kids (and sometimes the adults), pose for photos, and sign autographs. Keep autograph books (with pens) and cameras handy. For the best photos, adults should sit across the table from their children. Always seat the children where characters can reach them most easily. If a table is against a wall, for example, adults should sit with their backs to the wall and children should sit nearest the aisle.

You will not be rushed to leave after you've eaten. Remember, however, lots of eager children and adults might be waiting not so patiently to be admitted.

You can dine with Disney characters at Ariel's Grotto at DCA, Disney's PCH Grill at the Paradise Pier Hotel, Goofy's Kitchen at the Disneyland Hotel, the Plaza Inn in Disneyland Park, and Storytellers Café at the Grand Californian Hotel. For information about character meals and to make dining reservations up to 60 days in advance, call ☎ 714-781-DINE (3463).

unofficial **TIP** Arrange dining reservations as far in advance as possible. Your wait for a table will usually be less than 15 minutes.

ARIEL'S DISNEY PRINCESS CELEBRATION Overlooking Paradise Bay, Ariel's Grotto hosts breakfast, lunch, and dinner (until 5 p.m.) with Ariel and friends daily. Breakfast costs $39.87 for adults ($22.63 kids), and lunch (or early dinner) is $43.10 for adults ($26.94 kids). Fixed-price dinners after 5 p.m. include *World of Color* reservations but no characters.

DISNEY'S PCH (PACIFIC COAST HIGHWAY) GRILL PCH Grill at the Paradise Pier Hotel serves a Surf's Up! Breakfast with Mickey & Friends buffet 7–11 a.m. that features traditional Mexican breakfast items such as chilaquiles in addition to the usual American fare. Prices are $38.79 for adults ($22.63 kids). Mickey (wearing beach togs), along with

Stitch, Minnie, and Pluto, entertains you. This is usually the least crowded of the hotel character meals.

GOOFY'S KITCHEN   Located at the Disneyland Hotel, Goofy's Kitchen serves a character breakfast buffet 7–11:30 a.m. (until 1:15 p.m. Saturday–Sunday) and a character dinner buffet 5–8:45 p.m. Breakfast is $38.79 for adults ($22.63 kids). Dinners run $42.02 and $25.86, respectively. Goofy, of course, is the head character, but he's usually joined by Minnie, Pluto, and others.

PLAZA INN   Located at the end of Main Street and to the right, the Plaza Inn character buffet is usually packed because it hosts character breakfasts that are included in vacation packages sold by the Disney Resort Travel Sales Center. Served from park opening until 11 a.m., the buffet costs $35.56 for adults ($19.40 kids). Characters present usually include Minnie, Goofy, Pluto, and Chip 'n' Dale.

STORYTELLERS CAFÉ   Storytellers Café, located at the Grand Californian Hotel, is the most attractive of the character-meal venues. A breakfast buffet is served 7–11:25 a.m., and on weekends brunch is available 11:30 a.m.–2 p.m. The buffet costs $35.56 for adults ($19.40 kids). Chip 'n' Dale, the featured characters, are usually assisted by critters from *Tarzan*, *Brother Bear*, and *Pocahontas*.

"Casting? There's been a mistake. We were supposed to get the Assorted Character Package with one Mickey, one Goofy, one Donald . . . "

PART FOUR

DINING *and* SHOPPING *In and Around* DISNEYLAND

▌ DINING *in* DISNEYLAND RESORT

IN THIS SECTION, we aim to help you find good food without going broke or tripping over one of Disneyland Resort's many culinary land mines. More than 50 restaurants operate in Disneyland Resort, including about 20 full-service restaurants, several of which are inside the theme parks. Collectively, Disney restaurants offer reasonable variety, serving everything from Louisiana Creole to California fusion, but sadly, international cuisines other than Mexican, Asian, Mediterranean, and Italian are not represented.

On the upside, we've seen a dramatic improvement in Disneyland Resort restaurant quality since 2010, though the gains have leveled off lately. Ingredients are fresher, preparation is more careful, and even steam tables and buffets are under almost constant supervision. As a whole, the culinary team has definitely stepped up its game, and we are the winners. Many establishments have undergone complete menu makeovers, with terrific results. On the downside, we've recently seen portion reductions and price increases at some of our favorite eateries. Unlike other attractions and shops inside the resort, the food and beverage operation remains in constant flux. Venues open and close, add and delete menu items, and change decor throughout the year. We strive to provide you with the most accurate information possible; however, we do eventually have to go to press with the most current information we have at the time. Keep this in mind when using the guide. You can find up-to-date Disneyland Resort menu information in our Lines app and the official Disneyland app.

You can expect to pay hefty prices for food within Disneyland Resort. Nearly every entrée, snack, and drink purchased inside the theme parks and resort hotels will cost anywhere from 50% to 300% more than similar items at your hometown eateries. On the concession markup scale, Disneyland falls just behind airports and sports stadiums. As a Vancouver, Washington, reader observed:

After visiting the park several times in the last couple years, I've finally come to accept that the price charged for food, souvenirs, and lodging is probably double what they are actually worth. Sort of like getting charged $10 for a Bud Light at an NBA game.

However, its food is a bargain compared to some regional theme parks, and you can find munchies at more moderate (or at least mall-like) prices in Downtown Disney. To prepare your belly and budget, Disneyland's official app lets you browse the menu (including prices) for every eatery in the resort, from fine dining to the churro carts.

With fine dining offered at California Adventure, you can enjoy a glass of wine, a mug of beer, or even a cocktail inside the resorts without having to exit the park. Downtown Disney offers a wide variety of dining options, from mediocre to awesome, from intimate and adult to wild and kid-friendly. The Grand Californian Hotel is home to **Napa Rose,** one of the finest dining spots in all of Southern California, and even character meals at eateries such as **Ariel's Grotto** and **Disney's PCH Grill** offer better, healthier food than ever before.

Note: Disneyland dining reservations are the Disney-restaurant equivalent of FastPass. This feature, available where noted, gives you the option of picking a time and cutting to the head of the line. You may still have to wait, but it's from the front of the line instead of the back.

DISNEY DINING 101

DISNEYLAND RESORT RESTAURANT RESERVATIONS: WHAT'S IN A NAME

DISNEY TINKERS CEASELESSLY with its restaurant-reservations policy. Disneyland dining reservations issues reservations that aren't exactly reservations. When you call Disney Dining at ☎ 714-781-3463, option 3, your name and essential information are taken, well, as if you were making a reservation. The Disney rep then tells you that you have dining reservations for the restaurant on the date and time you requested, usually explaining that you will be seated ahead of walk-ins—that is, those guests without reservations. Frequent eaters will be thrilled to discover that Disneyland's online dining reservations system has finally caught up with its Orlando sibling and now allows you to book a table without any pesky human interaction. Visit **disneyland.disney.go.com/dining** on your computer or smartphone, or tap "Dining" in the Disneyland app, to see restaurant availability. You will need to create a **disney.com** login account (if you don't already have one) and supply a credit card and phone number to secure a booking (see below). Reservations can be booked 60 days in advance for Disneyland Resort hotel guests and off-site visitors alike,

*un*official **TIP**
Dining reservations are available to all Disneyland visitors—not just guests of the resort hotels. In the theme parks, you can make reservations for later in the day at the door of the restaurant.

starting at midnight PST online or 7 a.m. PST over the phone.

Travelers who have experienced Walt Disney World's dining reservations system (formerly known as Advanced Dining Reservations, or ADR) will be relieved to discover that Disneyland's dining reservations scheme is far less stress-inducing, largely because the Disney Dining Plan is not nearly as popular in Anaheim. Except during the busiest season, most restaurants in the park offer same-week (and often same-day) availability, especially if you are flexible with your mealtimes. If your preferred seatings are unavailable at first, keep checking back, because cancellations are common.

BEHIND THE SCENES AT DISNEYLAND RESORT DINING

DISNEY RESTAURANTS OPERATE on what they call a template system. Instead of scheduling reservations for actual tables, reservationists fill time slots. The number of slots available is based on the average observed length of time that guests occupy a table at a particular restaurant. Disneyland Resort Dining (DRD) tries to fill every time slot for every seat in the restaurant, or come as close to filling every slot as possible. No seats—repeat, none—are *reserved* for walk-ins, though all restaurants accommodate such customers on a space-available basis.

With dining reservations, your waiting time will almost always be less than 20 minutes during peak hours, and often less than 10 minutes. If you just walk in, especially during busier seasons, expect to wait 40–75 minutes.

GETTING YOUR ACT TOGETHER

DRD HANDLES RESERVATIONS for both Disney-owned and independent restaurants at the theme parks, Disney hotels, and Downtown Disney. The sole exception is the **Rainforest Cafe** at Downtown Disney, which makes its own reservations at ☎ 714-772-0413 (though you can make reservations online).

If you fail to make dining reservations before you leave home, or if you want to make your dining decisions spontaneously, your chances of getting a table at the restaurant of your choice are good. Blue Bayou at Disneyland Park, Napa Rose at the Grand Californian Hotel, and the various character-meal venues are the most likely to sell out. If, however, you visit Disneyland during a very busy time of year, it's to your advantage to make dining reservations.

Disneyland collects a credit card number with every dining reservation. If you poop out in the theme park and are a no-show for your meal, you will be charged $10 per person. Your reservation will be voided 15 minutes after the scheduled time, and the penalty will apply unless you call DRD at least 24 hours before your seating (some restaurants or events require more notice). This same cancellation policy also applies to makeover appointments at Bibbidi Bobbidi Boutique, as well as cabanas at the hotel pools. If you've lined up many seatings, it's a good idea to phone DRD a few days before you arrive to make sure that everything is in order. If you stay at a Disney resort, Guest Services can print out a summary of all your dining reservations. If you have a seating for a theme park restaurant at a time before park opening, as is sometimes the case for a character breakfast, simply proceed to the turnstiles and inform a cast member, who will admit you to the park.

DRESS

DRESS IS INFORMAL at all theme park restaurants, but dressy casual is appropriate for resort restaurants such as Napa Rose. That means dress slacks (or dress shorts) with a collared shirt for men and slacks, skirts, or dress shorts with a blouse or sweater (or a dress) for women.

FOOD ALLERGIES AND SPECIAL REQUESTS

WITH MILLIONS OF AMERICANS now reporting sensitivity to certain foods or following specific diets, the restaurants at Disneyland Resort are receiving a record number of special dietary requests. Happily, Disney has responded to this trend and is now able to accommodate most guests' gustatory needs. If you have dietary concerns, call ☎ 714-781-3463 to discuss any special requests when making dining reservations, and ask to speak with a chef or manager before your meal whenever arriving at a restaurant to confirm that your needs can be met.

In 2015 Disneyland rolled out new allergy-friendly menus at many of its table- and quick-service restaurants, both inside and outside the theme parks. These new menus explicitly call out dishes without ingredients such as gluten, dairy, peanuts, tree nuts, eggs, soy, or shellfish. If you have one of these common allergies or are vegetarian, you can be confident of finding something to eat almost anywhere without needing to make special arrangements ahead of time. However, if you have an uncommon or complicated allergy or a metabolic disorder, e-mail **DLRSpecialDiets@email.disney.com** with your needs at least two weeks before your visit.

Kosher meals are available on request at Plaza Inn, Rancho del Zocalo, and Tomorrowland Terrace/Galactic Grill at Disneyland Park, and at Smokejumpers Grill at Disney California Adventure (DCA). Kosher meals can also be delivered to table-service locations with 24 hours' notice (call the above number). About the only diet that can still be challenging to accommodate is vegan. While all locations have vegetarian dishes, they often don't alert you to incidental animal products in things such as cooking oil.

Be warned that, while the Disney folks do their best to meet guests' needs, they don't have separate allergen-free kitchen facilities or dining areas, and inadvertent cross-contamination is always a possibility. Large coolers are prohibited unless your dietary issue is a matter of life or death. However, you are allowed to bring your own food and medication into the parks in small soft-sided coolers, and medication can be refrigerated at First Aid. Glass containers are still prohibited, but snacks and EpiPens are OK; just know that Disney employees aren't allowed to hold or heat up your personal food.

Do Disney's attempts at dietary accommodation work? Well, a Phillipsburg, New Jersey, mom reports her family's experience:

> My 6-year-old has many food allergies, and we often have to bring food with us to restaurants when we go out to eat. I was able to make reservations at the Disney restaurants in advance and indicate these allergies to the reservation clerk. When we arrived at the restaurants, the staff was already aware of my child's allergies and assigned our table a chef who double-checked the list of allergies with us. Each member of the waitstaff was also informed of the allergies. The chefs were very nice and made my son feel very special (to the point where my other family members felt a little jealous).

However, employees at outdoor food carts, as well as at the temporary kitchen kiosks used during special events, may not be as well educated about allergies, as a reader from Salt Spring Island, British Columbia, discovered:

> We were there for the start of Festival of Holidays, and it was impossible to get anything gluten-free. Cast members did not have answers to dietary restrictions.

A FEW CAVEATS

BEFORE YOU BEGIN EATING YOUR WAY through Disneyland, take our advice:

1. However creative and enticing the menu descriptions, avoid fancy food at full-service restaurants in the theme parks. Order dishes that the kitchen is unlikely to botch. Stick with what's familiar in most cases and you won't be disappointed.

2. Don't order baked, broiled, poached, or grilled seafood unless the restaurant specializes in seafood or rates at least ★★★½ in our dining profiles.

3. Theme park restaurants rush their customers to make room for the next group of diners. Eating at high speed may appeal to a family with young, restless children, but for people wanting to relax, it's more like dining in a pressure chamber. The exceptions to this rule may be Wine Country Trattoria and Carthay Circle Restaurant inside DCA, upscale venues that encourage a respite over a glass or bottle of premium wine. But, sadly, you may feel pressure even there in peak season.

   If you want to linger over your expensive meal, don't order your entire dinner at once. Order drinks, study the menu while you sip, and then order appetizers. Tell the waiter you need more time to decide among entrées. Order your main course only after appetizers have been served. Dawdle over coffee and dessert.

4. If you're dining in a theme park and cost is an issue, make lunch your main meal. Entrées are similar to those on the dinner menu, but prices may be slightly lower.

DISNEYLAND RESORT RESTAURANT CATEGORIES

IN GENERAL, food and beverage offerings at Disneyland Resort are defined by service, price, and convenience:

FULL-SERVICE RESTAURANTS Full-service restaurants are in all Disneyland Resort hotels, both parks, and Downtown Disney. Disney operates most of the restaurants in the theme parks and its hotels; contractors or franchisees operate those at Downtown Disney. The restaurants accept Visa, MasterCard, American Express, Discover, and Diners Club.

BUFFETS AND FIXED-PRICE MEALS With set-price character meals, such as Ariel's Grotto at DCA, you can choose one item each from a limited selection of appetizers, salads, main courses, and desserts. Character buffets, such as the one at Goofy's Kitchen in the Disneyland Hotel, have a separate children's menu featuring kid favorites such as hot dogs, burgers, chicken nuggets, pizza, macaroni and cheese, and spaghetti and meatballs, as well as healthier options such as sliced fruit, yogurt, and whole-grain baked goods. Dining reservations are highly recommended for all character meals.

COUNTER SERVICE Counter-service fast food is available at both theme parks and Downtown Disney. The food compares in quality with McDonald's, Long John Silver's, Pizza Hut, or Taco Bell but is more expensive, though it's often served in larger portions.

HARD CHOICES

DINING DECISIONS will definitely affect your Disneyland Resort experience. If you're short on time and you want to see the theme parks, avoid full service. Ditto if you're short on funds. If you want to try a Disney full-service restaurant, arrange dining reservations—this won't reserve you a table, but it will minimize your wait.

Integrating Meals into *The Unofficial Guide* Touring Plans

Arrive before the park of your choice opens. Tour expeditiously, using your chosen plan (taking as few breaks as possible) until about 11–11:30 a.m. Once the park becomes crowded around midday, meals and other breaks won't affect the plan's efficiency. If you intend to stay in the park for evening parades, fireworks, or other events, eat dinner early enough to be finished in time for the festivities.

Character Dining

A number of restaurants, primarily those that serve all-you-can-eat buffets or family-style meals, offer character dining. At character meals, you pay a fixed price and dine in the presence of one to five Disney characters who circulate throughout the restaurant, hugging children, posing for photos, and signing autographs. Character breakfasts, lunches, and dinners are served at restaurants in and out of the theme parks. For an extensive discussion of character dining, see page 164.

FULL-SERVICE DINING FOR FAMILIES WITH YOUNG CHILDREN

unofficial **TIP**
Bottom line: Young children are the rule, not the exception, at Disney restaurants.

NO MATTER HOW FORMAL a restaurant appears, the staff is accustomed to impatient and often boisterous children. In Disneyland Resort's finest dining rooms, it's not unusual to find at least two dozen young diners attired in basic black . . . mouse ears.

Almost all Disney restaurants offer children's menus, and all have booster seats and high chairs. Waiters will supply little ones with crackers and rolls and serve your dinner much faster than in comparable restaurants elsewhere. In fact, letters from readers suggest that being served too quickly is much more common than having a long wait.

QUIET, ROMANTIC PLACES TO EAT

RESTAURANTS WITH GOOD FOOD *and* a couple-friendly ambience are rare in the theme parks. **Blue Bayou** at Disneyland Park satisfies both requirements. In Disney California Adventure, **Wine Country Trattoria** offers one of the quietest and more relaxed environments, along with a California wine country–inspired menu, while the elegant **Carthay Circle Restaurant** ranks as one of the best restaurants in any theme park. Among the hotels at the resort, **Napa Rose** at the Grand Californian Hotel & Spa is the leading candidate for a romantic adult dining experience. At Downtown Disney, try **Ralph Brennan's Jazz Kitchen**; ask for a quiet table, though, if you're not interested in the jazz music. **Catal** in Downtown Disney also offers a quiet ambience and an ambitious gourmet menu geared mostly to adults.

Eating later in the evening and choosing a restaurant we've mentioned will improve your chances for intimate dining; nevertheless, know that children, well behaved or otherwise, are everywhere at Disneyland, and you can't escape them.

FAST FOOD IN THE THEME PARKS

BECAUSE MOST MEALS during a Disneyland vacation are consumed on the run while touring, we'll tackle counter-service and vendor foods first. Plentiful at all theme parks are hot dogs, hamburgers, chicken sandwiches, salads, and pizza. They're augmented by special items that relate to the park's theme or the part of the park you're touring. In the alpine village setting of Fantasyland, for example, counter-service bratwurst and apple strudel are sold; in New Orleans Square, Cajun and Creole dishes are available. Counter-service prices are fairly consistent from park to park. Expect to pay the same amount for your coffee or hot dog at DCA that you would at Disneyland Park.

If you are used to counter-service food at Walt Disney World, the quality and variety in Anaheim may catch you off guard, as it did a Cottleville, Missouri, reader:

> I was surprised that the counter-service food was so excellent. Plaza Inn, Flo's V8 Cafe, and French Market were superb. Selection and quality were clearly better than even table service at WDW.

Getting your act together in regard to counter service is more a matter of courtesy than necessity. Rude guests rank fifth among reader complaints. A mother from Fort Wayne, Indiana, points out that indecision can be as maddening as outright discourtesy, especially when you're hungry:

> Every fast-food restaurant has menus the size of billboards, but do you think anybody reads them? People waiting in line spend enough

time in front of these menus to memorize them and still don't have a clue what they want when they finally get to the order taker. Tell your readers to PULEEEZ get their orders together ahead of time!

Another reader offers a tip about counter-service food lines:

Many counter-service registers serve two queues each, one to the left and one to the right of each register. People are not used to this and will instinctively line up in one queue per register. We had register operators wave us up to the front several times to start a left queue instead of waiting behind others on the right.

Healthful Food at Disneyland Resort

One of the most commendable developments in food service at Disneyland has been the introduction of healthier foods and snacks. Diabetics, vegetarians, weight watchers, those requiring kosher meals, and guests on restricted diets should be able to find something to eat. The same goes for anyone seeking wholesome, nutritious food. Health-conscious choices (including gluten-free bread) are available at most fast-food counters and even from select vendors. A simple request is likely to get you what you need even if it doesn't always appear on the menu.

unofficial **TIP**
Restaurants with a **Mickey Check** logo on their menus (Mickey's head with a check mark) offer special meals for kids ages 3–9. Menu items (including roast turkey, meat loaf, and mac and cheese) are designed to meet balanced nutritional guidelines with zero saturated and trans fats, less sugar, and reduced sodium.

Cutting Your Dining Time at the Theme Parks

Even if you confine your meals to vendor and counter-service fast food, you lose a lot of time getting sustenance in the theme parks. At Disneyland Park and DCA, everything begins with a line and ends with a cash register. When it comes to fast food, *fast* may apply to the time you spend eating it, not the time invested in obtaining it.

Here are suggestions for minimizing the time you spend hunting and gathering food:

1. Don't waste touring time on breakfast at the parks. Restaurants outside Disneyland offer some outstanding breakfast specials. Many hotels furnish small refrigerators in their guest rooms, or you can rent one. If you can get by on cold cereal, rolls, fruit, and juice, having a fridge in your room will save a ton of time. If you can't get a fridge, bring a cooler.

2. After a good breakfast, buy snacks from vendors in the parks as you tour, or stuff some snacks in a hip pack. This is very important if you're on a tight schedule and can't spend a lot of time waiting in line for food.

3. All theme park restaurants are busiest 11:30 a.m.–2:15 p.m. for lunch and 6–9 p.m. for dinner. For shorter lines and faster service, don't eat during these hours, especially 12:30–1:30 p.m.

4. Many counter-service restaurants sell cold sandwiches. Buy a cold lunch (except for drinks) before 11:30 a.m., and carry it until you're ready to eat. Ditto for dinner. Bring small plastic bags in which to pack the food; purchase drinks at the appropriate time from any convenient vendor.

5. Most fast-food eateries have more than one service window. Regardless of the time of day, check the lines at all windows before queuing. Sometimes a window that's staffed but out of the way will have a much shorter line or none at all. Note, however, that some windows may offer only certain items.

6. If you're short on time and the park closes early, stay until closing and eat dinner outside Disneyland before returning to your hotel. If the park stays open late, eat dinner about 4 or 4:30 p.m. at the restaurant of your choice. You should miss the last wave of lunchers and sneak in just ahead of the dinner crowd. Be warned, however, that most eateries at Downtown Disney and the Disneyland Resort hotels stop serving at 10 p.m., even when the parks are open until midnight.

7. Crowds pack nearby eateries before, during, and immediately after special events, parades, and shows such as the wildly popular *World of Color* in DCA. Conversely, dining venues far from the action are almost empty during their run times, and you can typically walk right up to the counter without any wait at all.

Beyond Counter Service: Tips for Saving Money on Food

Though buying food from counter-service restaurants and vendors will save you time and money compared with full-service dining, additional strategies can bolster your budget and maintain your waistline. Over the years, our readers have offered the following suggestions:

1. Go to Disneyland during a period of fasting and abstinence. You can save a fortune *and* save your soul!

2. Wear clothes that are slightly too small and make you feel like dieting. (No spandex allowed!)

3. Whenever you're feeling hungry, ride the Mad Tea Party, California Screamin', or other attractions that can induce motion sickness.

4. Leave your cash and credit cards at your hotel. Buy food only with money your children fish out of fountains and wishing wells.

5. There's no official limit on sourdough bread slices and sample chocolate squares from Boudin Bakery and Ghirardelli at DCA. Test that theory by bouncing back and forth between them until you're sufficiently carb-loaded, or security leads you away.

Cost-conscious readers also have volunteered ideas for stretching food dollars. A Missouri mom writes:

We arrived with our cooler well stocked with milk and sandwich fixings. I froze a block of ice in a milk bottle, and we replenished it daily from the resort ice machine. I also froze small packages of deli meats for later in the week. We ate cereal, milk, and fruit each morning, with boxed juices. I also had a hot pot to boil water for instant coffee, oatmeal, and soup.

Each child had a belt bag of his own, which he filled from a special box of goodies each day. I made a great mystery of filling the box in the weeks before the trip. Some things were actual food, such as packages of crackers and cheese or peanuts and raisins. Some were worthless junk, such as candy and gum. They grazed from their bags at will throughout the day, with no interference from Mom and Dad. Each also had a small, rectangular plastic water bottle that could hang on the belt. We filled these at water fountains before getting into lines and were the envy of many.

We left the park before noon; ate sandwiches, chips, and soda in the room; and napped. We purchased our evening meal in the park at a counter-service eatery. We budgeted for morning and evening snacks from a vendor but often did not need them. It made the occasional treat all the more special. Our cooler had been pretty much emptied by the end of the week, but the block of ice was still there.

The top budget-trimming tip we can offer is to skip the soft drinks and instead order free ice water with every meal. It's far healthier and more hydrating than soda (sugared or artificially sweetened), and at $4 per large fountain drink, you'll be shocked how swiftly the savings add up. The park's drinking fountains are potable in a pinch, but the filtered water that all counter-service restaurants (excluding vending carts) give away tastes as good as the bottled Dasani they sell for $3.50.

A mom from Whiteland, Indiana, who purchases drinks in the parks, offers this suggestion:

One must-take item if you're traveling with younger kids is a supply of small cups to split drinks, which are both huge and expensive.

We interviewed one woman who brought a huge picnic for her family of five packed in a large diaper–baby paraphernalia bag. She stowed the bag in a locker on Main Street and retrieved it when the family was hungry.

Note: Disney prohibits glass containers and alcoholic beverages, as well as coolers and backpacks of a certain size.

READERS' RESTAURANT-SURVEY RESPONSES

FOR EACH DISNEYLAND RESTAURANT PROFILED, we include the results of last year's Reader-Survey Responses. Results are expressed as a percentage of readers who liked the restaurant well enough to eat there again (thumbs-up 👍) versus the percentage who didn't (thumbs-down 👎). (Readers tend to be less critical than we are, for what it's worth.) If you'd like to participate in the ratings, go to **touringplans .com/disneyland-resort/survey.**

Remember that our survey results report overall reader satisfaction, not just food quality. Also, the star ratings of the full-service restaurants represent the opinions of our research team and our dining insider—your experience may vary.

THEME PARK COUNTER-SERVICE RESTAURANT
Mini-Profiles

TO HELP YOU FIND palatable fast-service foods that suit your taste, we have developed mini-profiles of Disneyland Park and DCA counter-service restaurants. The restaurants are listed alphabetically by park.

Detailed profiles of all Disneyland full-service restaurants follow this section, beginning on page 186.

The restaurants profiled in the following pages are rated for quality and portion size as well as value. The value rating ranges from A to F as follows:

A = Exceptional value, a real bargain   **B** = Good value
C = Fair value, you get exactly what you pay for
D = Somewhat overpriced   **F** = Significantly overpriced

Note: Because they offer special or unusual dishes, the following counter-service restaurants are profiled in full and are listed with the full-service restaurants:

French Market Restaurant *Disneyland Park*

Rancho del Zocalo Restaurante *Disneyland Park*

Tangaroa Terrace *Disneyland Hotel*

DISNEYLAND PARK
Bengal Barbecue

QUALITY Good–Excellent   **VALUE** B–   **PORTION** Small   **LOCATION** Adventureland
Reader-Survey Responses   92% 👍   8% 👎

Selections Beef, chicken, pork, or veggie skewers; breadsticks; spring rolls.
Comments Skewers are small, but nothing costs more than $7. The bacon-wrapped asparagus and pork belly skewers are best, proving the old adage that everything tastes better on a stick. Portions have shrunk noticeably over the years, but this is still a good and relatively healthy fast-food alternative to the dine in options inside the park.

Daisy's Diner

QUALITY Fair   **VALUE** C–   **PORTION** Medium   **LOCATION** Mickey's Toontown
READER-SURVEY RESPONSES   17% 👍   83% 👎

Selections Pepperoni and cheese pizzas.
Comments Subpar pizza for eating on the run, with no convenient place to sit.

The Golden Horseshoe

QUALITY Fair   **VALUE** C   **PORTION** Medium   **LOCATION** Frontierland
Reader-Survey Responses   70% 👍   30% 👎

Selections Chicken nuggets, fish-and-chips, crispy chicken salad, chili, and ice cream sundaes.
Comments The Golden Horseshoe hosts live interactive entertainment and fair fried food. Meaty chili is a tribute to Walt and available in an unadvertised side portion perfect for a snack, if you don't want it on a pile of fries or in a bread bowl. Service can be slow; the leftmost open register often has the shortest line. Gazebo-style seating next to the stage is best.

Harbour Galley

QUALITY Good   **VALUE** B   **PORTION** Medium   **LOCATION** Critter Country
Reader-Survey Responses   92% 👍   8% 👎

BEST SNACKS AT DISNEYLAND RESORT

We share our snacking insights on keeping your tummy happy at The Happiest Place on Earth. Call ☎ 714-781-0112 for a recorded message that reveals what candy will be made that week.

DISNEYLAND PARK

- Frozen lemonade *(vending cart)*   • Gourmet doughnuts *(coffee cart near central hub)*
- Stuffed baked potatoes *(Troubadour Tavern)*   • Taffy *(Candy Palace)*
- Honey-pot krispie *(Pooh's Corner)*   • Turkey legs *(vending cart)*
- DL Tigger tails *(Pooh's Corner)*   • *Pommes frites (Café Orléans)*
- Pickles *(Critter Country Fruit Cart)*   • English toffee *(Candy Palace)*
- New Orleans fritters *(Royal Street Veranda)*   • Peanut brittle *(Candy Palace)*
- Apple pie apple *(Pooh's Corner)*   • Mickey-shaped crispy rice treat *(Candy Palace)*
- Pork belly skewer *(Bengal Barbecue)*   • Snickerdoodles *(Pooh's Corner)*
- Mint juleps *(nonalcoholic; Mint Julep Bar)*   • Bratwurst *(Troubadour Tavern)*
- Chocolate-dipped Oreos *(Pooh's Corner)* • Side of chili with cheese *(Golden Horseshoe)*
- Bacon-wrapped asparagus *(Bengal Barbecue)*   • Corn dog *(Little Red Wagon)*
- Mickey-shaped pancakes *(breakfast at Rancho del Zocalo)*
- Mickey-shaped waffles *(breakfast at Carnation Café)*
- Chili-lime corn on the cob *(Edelweiss Snacks)*
- Cinnamon rolls *(cart near Haunted Mansion)*
- Coconut macaroons shaped like the Matterhorn *(Jolly Holiday Bakery Café)*
- Ice cream in a freshly made, chocolate-dipped waffle cone *(Gibson Girl Ice Cream Parlor)*
- Pretzels stuffed with jalapeño cheese *(Refreshment Corner)*
- Pineapple—Dole whips, Dole whip floats, pineapple spears *(Tiki Juice Bar)*

DISNEY CALIFORNIA ADVENTURE

- Red's Apple Freeze *(Cozy Cone Motel)*   • Charcuterie board *(Alfresco Tasting Terrace)*
- Hand-dipped ice cream bars *(Clarabelle's)*   • Corn dog *(Corn Dog Castle)*
- Character-inspired candy apples *(Trolley Treats)*
- Funky flavored popcorn *(Cozy Cone Motel)*
- Ugly crust apple-Cheddar pie *(Flo's V8 Cafe)*
- Edamame with sriracha *(Lucky Fortune Cookery)*
- Chocolate-covered pineapple skewer *(Trolley Treats)*

DOWNTOWN DISNEY

- Fried shrimp po'boy *(Ralph Brennan's Jazz Kitchen Express)*
- Candy unique to Disneyland *(Marceline's Confectionery)*
- Churro ice cream sandwich *(vending cart)*
- Beignets and chicory coffee *(Ralph Brennan's Jazz Kitchen Express)*

RESORT RESTAURANTS

- Carnitas quesadilla *(White Water Snacks at Grand Californian Hotel)*
- Panko-crusted long beans *(Trader Sam's Enchanted Tiki Bar at Disneyland Hotel)*
- Caramel French toast *(character breakfast at Storytellers Café at Grand Californian Hotel)*

Selections Clam chowder or seasonal soup, all served in a sourdough bread bowl; tuna or shrimp salad; lobster roll. Kids' meal includes string cheese, yogurt, and fruit.

Comments The soup-filled bread bowls are always a reliable choice, especially the lobster bisque (when in season). Limited seating, but other seats are available along the dock around the back of the restaurant. The lobster roll is skimpy and overseasoned with Old Bay.

Hungry Bear Restaurant

QUALITY Good   **VALUE** B   **PORTION** Medium–Large   **LOCATION** Critter Country
READER-SURVEY RESPONSES   89% 👍   11% 👎

Selections A huge, one-third-pound chili cheeseburger topped with a fried onion ring (skip the chili; it's pasty and bland), and a fried chicken sandwich with honey mustard. Healthier choices include a turkey Caesar wrap or a Picnic Salad with turkey, berries, Feta, jicama, and almonds with a sweet-tart strawberry vinaigrette. Kids can feast on healthier meals with string cheese, nonfat yogurt, sliced apples, and whole-grain fish crackers.

Comments Popular and crowded during busier times of the year. During slower times, grab a snack and sit on the deck overlooking the Rivers of America, if construction walls for Star Wars construction aren't still obscuring the view during your visit. The Picnic Salad is pretty festive for theme park greens. On nights when *Fantasmic!* is shown, Hungry Bear offers a dining package for $29.99 per adult ($19.99 for kids 3–9), plus tax, that includes an entrée, drink, and a FastPass to *Fantasmic!*

Jolly Holiday Bakery Café

QUALITY Good–Excellent   **VALUE** B   **PORTION** Medium   **LOCATION** Main Street, U.S.A.
Reader-Survey Responses   91% 👍   9% 👎

Selections Chicken and strawberry spinach salad; salad with pecans and Feta; toasted cheese sandwich with tomato soup; turkey, tuna salad, roast beef, or caprese sandwich; grilled vegetable salad; assorted pastries.

Comments Themed to *Mary Poppins,* with stained glass windows featuring penguin waiters, this is a good spot for a light breakfast or lunch, though lines can grow long at peak mealtimes. Seating is outdoors only, and soup portions are small, but the salads and sandwiches are substantial and savory. Don't miss the massive Matterhorn coconut macaroons.

Market House

QUALITY Good   **VALUE** B–   **PORTION** Medium   **LOCATION** Main Street, U.S.A.
Reader-Survey Responses   100% 👍   0% 👎

Selections Starbucks coffee drinks, cocoa, tea, juice, pastries, and breakfast sandwiches.

Comments Starbucks's usual vast array of blended beverages is available (including seasonal flavors), accompanied by its trademark long lines. You can also get a selection of hot breakfast sandwiches in the morning and sweets all day. Starbucks loyalty cards are valid for payment, but you can't earn rewards or redeem freebies here. The expanded coffee shop features a seating area themed after a vintage bookshop. Look for the potbellied stove, checkerboard, and antique party line telephones, all holdovers from the former decor.

Pluto's Dog House

QUALITY Fair–Good **VALUE** C **PORTION** Medium **LOCATION** Mickey's Toontown
Reader-Survey Responses 40% 👍 60% 👎

Selections Hot dog basket, kids' turkey dog, and mac and cheese.

Comments Food's not bad, but there's really no place to sit and eat it.

Redd Rockett's Pizza Port

QUALITY Good **VALUE** C **PORTION** Medium–Large **LOCATION** Tomorrowland
Reader-Survey Responses 63% 👍 37% 👎

Selections Large slices of pizza; pasta with meatballs or chicken; Caesar, Asian chicken, Italian, or cranberry salads.

Comments Redd Rockett's is set up cafeteria-style, so all hot items sit under heat lamps until someone grabs them, but servers will be happy to mix up a fresh bowl of pasta or a pizza on request (a much better choice). The Asian chicken salad is slightly spicy with good flavor. Free drink refills are available. The cafeteria-style setup usually means less waiting. The A/C system is on steroids, making it a really cool place on a hot day. Even on the busiest days, there's ample room to sit on the outdoor patio.

Refreshment Corner

QUALITY Fair–Good **VALUE** C **PORTION** Medium **LOCATION** Main Street, U.S.A.
Reader-Survey Responses 85% 👍 15% 👎

Selections Hot dogs, chili-cheese dogs, and chili in a bread bowl.

Comments Some of the topping selections sound strange (mac and cheese?), but the dogs are good. Limited seating; time it right to catch the ragtime pianist or Dapper Dans performing on the patio.

Royal Street Veranda

QUALITY Good **VALUE** B **PORTION** Medium **LOCATION** New Orleans Square
Reader-Survey Responses 86% 👍 14% 👎

Selections Steak or vegetarian gumbo and clam chowder, all served in a sourdough bread bowl; coffee, espresso, cappuccino; fritters for dessert.

Comments Can get quite crowded, especially around *Fantasmic!* showings, but usually worth the wait. Veggie gumbo and clam chowder are the best, though all are seasoned well. You have to look hard to find any steak in the steak gumbo. Don't miss the fritters with fruit dipping sauce, which now feature a rotating roster of seasonal varieties including sweet potato, apple, and banana.

Stage Door Café

QUALITY Good **VALUE** C **PORTION** Medium **LOCATION** Frontierland
Reader-Survey Responses 88% 👍 13% 👎

Selections Chicken nuggets, fish-and-chips, funnel cakes, and corn dogs.

Comments The corn dogs are nearly as good as those from the Main Street cart, with a shorter line. The fish is edible (albeit previously frozen), but the fries and nuggets are bland. Try the funnel cakes.

Tomorrowland Terrace

QUALITY Fair **VALUE** C+ **PORTION** Large **LOCATION** Tomorrowland
Reader-Survey Responses 68% 👍 32% 👎

Selections Breakfast burrito, egg-and-bacon sandwich, or French toast;

Angus burgers, chicken sandwich, chopped salad with chicken, or veggie wrap; kids' meals of chicken nuggets, turkey sandwich, burger, or smoothie with fruit and crackers.

Comments The food isn't anything special, though the bread is fresh. Seating is available outdoors overlooking the Tomorrowland Terrace stage, which hosts live music and the popular *Jedi Training: Trials of the Temple.*

Troubadour Tavern

QUALITY Fair–Good   **VALUE** C+   **PORTION** Medium   **LOCATION** Fantasyland
Reader-Survey Responses 77% 👍 23% 👎

Selections Bratwurst with sauerkraut, pretzel bites with cheese sauce, stuffed baked potatoes (with bacon and sour cream or broccoli and cheese), cinnamon-apple pastry twists, and ice cream bites.

Comments Built as a concession stand for Fantasyland Theatre, Troubadour Tavern is overwhelmed during shows but overlooked the rest of the day. This and the Village Haus (though not while it's Red Rose Taverne) are the only quick-service sausage vendors serving spicy brown mustard.

Vendor Treats

LOCATIONS Throughout the park   **READER-SURVEY RESPONSES** 83% 👍 17% 👎

Selections Popcorn, fries, smoked turkey legs, ice cream, churros, chimichangas, and more.

Comments We love the smoked turkey legs. There's something delightfully Neanderthal about tucking into a huge, meaty bone. For a quick snack, try Maurice's Treats, close to Fantasy Faire; it serves sweet (if overpriced) strawberry or Grey Stuff pastry twists, as well as a boysenberry apple freeze. Its Cheddar garlic bagel twist is tough and tasteless. Also check out the gourmet doughnuts—including one with a Matterhorn macaroon on top!—at the coffee cart near the central hub.

Village Haus/Red Rose Taverne

QUALITY Good   **VALUE** B–   **PORTION** Medium   **LOCATION** Fantasyland
Reader-Survey Responses 75% 👍 25% 👎

Selections Village Haus: premium cheeseburger, chicken sausage sandwich, veggie burger, pepperoni and cheese pizzas, apple Cheddar salad; mac and cheese kids' meals; seasonal cupcake or apple strudel. The Red Rose Taverne incarnation of the same spot (inspired by the immensely popular live-action movie *Beauty and the Beast*) serves a completely different French-themed menu that includes *pommes frites* and poutine.

Comments Village Haus's flatbread pizzas and heart-stopping pastrami cheeseburger are actually pretty good. Kids love the Pinocchio-themed seating area. Try the salad with fruit and cheese in a tangy yogurt-honey dressing. Vegetarians can rejoice over Red Rose Taverne's hearty grilled cauliflower "steak" sandwich. Movie-themed desserts include Grey Stuff (tastes better than it sounds) and lemon rose cake.

DISNEY CALIFORNIA ADVENTURE
Award Wieners

QUALITY Fair–Good   **VALUE** C   **PORTION** Medium   **LOCATION** Hollywood Land
Reader-Survey Responses 69% 👍 31% 👎

Selections Chili-cheese dogs, grilled sausages, and hot dogs; grilled mushroom, onion, and pepper sandwich.

Comments Award Wieners revamped its menu in 2017 and now offers street dogs topped with bacon, fried onions, or pico de gallo on a potato roll.

Boardwalk Pizza & Pasta

QUALITY Good   **VALUE** B   **PORTION** Medium-Large   **LOCATION** Paradise Pier
Reader-Survey Responses 79% 👍 21% 👎

Selections Pizzas run the gamut from a traditional cheese or pepperoni to a vegetarian with roasted seasonal veggies. Pasta offerings include spaghetti and meatballs, chicken pasta in a sun-dried tomato cream sauce, or pesto ravioli. Freshly tossed salads include a chicken Caesar and a Mediterranean chef salad with salami, fresh mozzarella, roasted peppers, and olives in a red-wine vinaigrette.

Comments Part of Paradise Garden, a Victorian-era outdoor courtyard with freestanding beer and corn dog stands outside the plaza. Salads are large enough to split three ways; say "hold the olives" (or another ingredient) for a fresh-mixed serving. The pesto pasta with pine nuts is our top pick. The uncompelling conventional slices come with steep prices.

Cocina Cucamonga Mexican Grill

QUALITY Good   **VALUE** B-   **PORTION** Large   **LOCATION** Pacific Wharf
Reader-Survey Responses 95% 👍 5% 👎

Selections Tacos, burritos, tamales, grilled chicken, fajita salad, and chicken Caesar salad. Kids' choices include arroz con pollo (chicken with rice), bean and cheese burrito, and chicken quesadillas.

Comments Salads are a safe choice. The chicken is marinated with garlic, cilantro, and citrus, and it comes with flour tortillas. Very tasty. The carne asada has improved but still lacks the full flavor and texture that you would expect. The burritos include a lot of beans.

Corn Dog Castle

QUALITY Good   **VALUE** B   **PORTION** Medium   **LOCATION** Paradise Pier
READER-SURVEY RESPONSES 88% 👍 12% 👎

Selections Corn dogs, Cheddar cheese sticks, fountain beverages.

Comments The corn dogs served here and at the Little Red Wagon on Main Street, U.S.A. have gained a cult following, and deservedly so: they're the freshest, lightest version of the deep-fried fair favorite you'll ever find. This location can draw long lines but is capable of serving more swiftly than its Disneyland cousin, and it offers additional sausage styles, like hot link. All the dogs are priced to include sliced apples or a small bag of chips, but you can save a few dollars by requesting they hold the side.

Cozy Cone Motel

QUALITY Fair-Good   **VALUE** B-   **PORTION** Small-Medium   **LOCATION** Cars Land
Reader-Survey Responses 94% 👍 6% 👎

Selections Chili, ice cream, churros, and pretzel bites. Cone #5 coats popcorn in unusual favors such as dill pickle and sriracha, with multiple rotating varieties offered daily. Signature beverages include a syrupy pomegranate limeade and Red's Apple Freeze, a curiously addictive blend of tart frozen apple juice and sweet toasted marshmallow.

Comments Each conical commissary in this food court, based on Sally's construction-cone motel from the film, serves different snacks and drinks with punny names such as "chili cone queso" and "route beer floats." Each of the five cones vends a different menu.

Fiddler, Fifer & Practical Café

QUALITY Good   **VALUE** B–   **PORTION** Medium   **LOCATION** Buena Vista Street
Reader-Survey Responses   91% 👍   9% 👎

Selections Starbucks coffee, hot breakfast sandwiches, cinnamon rolls with cream cheese icing, premade cold sandwiches, and salads.

Comments This quick-service eatery, named after both the Three Little Pigs and an imaginary songstress trio whose manufactured mementos hang inside, boasts a large open dining area in the Arts & Crafts style. You can get your morning jolt of Starbucks-brand joe and grab-and-go breakfast pastries here, but expect long waits around opening. Starbucks loyalty cards can be used for payment but not for free refills or other rewards.

Flo's V8 Cafe

QUALITY Good-Excellent   **VALUE** B   **PORTION** Medium-Large   **LOCATION** Cars Land
Reader-Survey Responses   90% 👍   10% 👎

Selections At breakfast, try the French toast, which is more like caramel bread pudding. Lunch and dinner offer citrus turkey salad, pork ribs with cola-barbecue sauce, roast beef sandwich, vegetarian shepherd's pie, and fruit pies.

Comments Cars Land's largest eatery serves classic American comfort food with a Southwestern twist. Signature lunch and dinner choices include a vegetarian casserole, with apple-Cheddar and chocolate pies for dessert. The veggie bake is tasty enough to attract meat eaters. Try the pork ribs with a side of mashed potatoes. Kids' meals come in a Lightning McQueen car. Memorabilia from proprietor Flo's past as a famous Motown singer is featured in the decor. Sit on the back patio for a spectacular view of Radiator Springs Racers' high-speed finale.

Lucky Fortune Cookery

QUALITY Fair-Good   **VALUE** C+   **PORTION** Medium   **LOCATION** Pacific Wharf
Reader-Survey Responses   65% 👍   35% 👎

Selections Steamed rice bowls with vegetables and your choice of chicken, beef, or tofu, all with your choice from a variety of pan-Asian sauces, including a popular teriyaki and a sweet, tangy Korean sauce; edamame; mango slices; teriyaki chicken and rice for kids.

Comments The tofu bowl is good, the chicken and beef are average, and the coconut curry sauce is bland. Edamame makes a nice side to share, especially dipped in spicy sriracha sauce.

Pacific Wharf Café

QUALITY Good   **VALUE** A   **PORTION** Medium   **LOCATION** Pacific Wharf
Reader-Survey Responses   94% 👍   6% 👎

Selections Fresh soups and salads served in hollowed-out sourdough loaves from San Francisco's famous Boudin bakery, plus turkey sandwiches and macaroni for the kids. The Chinese chicken salad and broccoli-and-cheese soup are both good, as is the clam chowder, with heaps of clams in a creamy, slightly salty base.

Comments Adults will appreciate the food and ambience as well as the very kid-friendly menu (yogurt smoothie, sliced apples, and whole-grain fish crackers). For dessert, try the candy, hot cocoa, ice cream sundae, or milk shake at Ghirardelli Soda Fountain & Chocolate Shop nearby.

Paradise Garden Grill

QUALITY Good–Excellent   **VALUE** B   **PORTION** Medium   **LOCATION** Paradise Pier
Reader-Survey Responses   89% 👍   11% 👎

Selections During Hispanic festivals such as ¡Viva Navidad! and Asian events like Lunar New Year, the menu offers some excellent ethnic entrées. During the Festival of Holidays and Food & Wine Festival, the fare runs to overpriced appetizers. The grill may serve a less-interesting menu of hamburgers during peak periods or shutter altogether on slow days.

Comments This open-air venue, with a Victorian beer garden theme, shares seating with Boardwalk Pizza. Its excellent standard menu, a selection of Greek-style meat skewers, is sadly rarely seen. This location usually changes its offerings with the season to tie in with whatever event is currently being promoted.

Smokejumpers Grill

QUALITY Fair   **VALUE** C   **PORTION** Medium–Large   **LOCATION** Grizzly Peak
Reader-Survey Responses   64% 👍   36% 👎

Selections Burgers, chicken sandwiches, and grilled chicken salad.

Comments The burgers come with a variety of toppings and sauces, and a separate toppings bar is available in case you need to stack on more. The onion rings are decent, and this is the only place in DCA that serves them. The handsome location, inspired by "brave men and women who fight wildfires in our California forests," features ample seating surrounded by lush pine trees.

DISNEYLAND RESORT RESTAURANTS:
Rated and Ranked

TO HELP YOU MAKE YOUR DINING CHOICES, we've developed profiles of full-service restaurants at Disneyland Resort. Each profile lets you quickly check the restaurant's cuisine, location, star rating, cost range, quality rating, and value rating. Profiles are listed alphabetically by restaurant. In addition to all full-service restaurants, we also list and profile a couple of counter-service restaurants in the theme parks that transcend basic burgers, hot dogs, and pizza. All of the restaurants listed here have disabled access.

PAYMENT All Disney restaurants accept American Express, MasterCard, Visa, Diners Club, Discover, and Japanese Credit Bureau.

STAR RATING The star rating represents the entire dining experience: style, service, and ambience, in addition to taste, presentation, and food quality. Five stars, the highest rating, indicates that the restaurant offers the best of everything. Four-star restaurants are above average, and three-star restaurants offer good, though not necessarily memorable, meals. Two-star restaurants serve mediocre fare, and one-star restaurants are below average. Our star ratings don't correspond to ratings awarded by AAA, Forbes, Zagat, or other restaurant reviewers.

COST RANGE The next rating tells how much an entrée (or, depending on the restaurant, an entrée and side dish) will cost. Appetizers, desserts, drinks, and tips aren't included. We've rated the cost as inexpensive, moderate, or expensive.

INEXPENSIVE	$15 or less per person
MODERATE	$15–$28 per person
EXPENSIVE	More than $28 per person

QUALITY RATING The food quality is rated on a scale of one to five stars, five being the best. The quality rating is based on the taste, freshness of ingredients, preparation, presentation, and creativity of food. There is no consideration of price. If you want the best food available and cost is no issue, look no further than the quality ratings.

VALUE RATING If, on the other hand, you are looking for both quality and value, check the value rating, also expressed as stars.

★★★★★	Exceptional value; a real bargain
★★★★	Good value
★★★	Fair value; you get exactly what you pay for
★★	Somewhat overpriced
★	Significantly overpriced

Ariel's Grotto ★★★½

CHARACTER DINING/AMERICAN   EXPENSIVE   QUALITY ★★★½   VALUE ★★★½
Reader-Survey Responses 85% 👍 15% 👎

Disney California Adventure; ☎ 714-781-DINE

Reservations Recommended. **When to go** Anytime. **Entrée range** Fixed-price meals, $23–$50. **Service** ★★★★. **Friendliness** ★★★★★. **Bar** Cove Bar is upstairs. **Dress** Casual. **Hours** Daily, 9 a.m.–10 p.m.

SETTING AND ATMOSPHERE You're "under the sea" with bright 3-D ocean-themed murals, jellyfish lanterns, and seashell tables, all with views of the wharf, Paradise Bay, and Paradise Pier/Pixar Pier. The overstuffed semi-circular booths along the back wall are the best seats in the house and well worth waiting for. At night, outdoor tables provide picturesque views of the illuminated Fun Wheel.

HOUSE SPECIALTIES At breakfast, Belgian waffles, spinach-artichoke frittatas, and steak and eggs. At lunch and dinner, oak-smoked tri-tip steak, lobster salad, citrus-glazed chicken, corn cakes, and shrimp pasta. Each meal includes soup or salad and finishes with a dessert.

Continued on page 187

DISNEYLAND RESORT RESTAURANTS BY CUISINE

CUISINE	LOCATION	OVERALL RATING	COST	QUALITY RATING	VALUE RATING
AMERICAN					
ARIEL'S GROTTO*	DCA	★★★½	Exp	★★★½	★★★½
THE RIVER BELLE TERRACE	Disneyland Park	★★★½	Mod	★★★½	★★½
TANGAROA TERRACE*	Disneyland Hotel	★★★	Inexp	★★★	★★★½
PLAZA INN*	Disneyland Park	★★★	Mod	★★★	★★★½
CARNATION CAFÉ*	Disneyland Park	★★★	Mod	★★★	★★★
DISNEY'S PCH GRILL*	Paradise Pier Hotel	★★★	Mod/Exp	★★★	★★½
ESPN ZONE	Downtown Disney	★★½	Mod	★★★	★★★
RAINFOREST CAFE*	Downtown Disney	★★½	Mod	★★★	★★½
GOOFY'S KITCHEN*	Disneyland Hotel	★★	Exp	★★	★★½
CALIFORNIA/FUSION					
NAPA ROSE	Grand Californian	★★★★★	V. Exp	★★★★★	★★★½
CARTHAY CIRCLE RESTAURANT	DCA	★★★★½	Exp	★★★★½	★★★½
STORYTELLERS CAFÉ*	Grand Californian	★★★★	Exp	★★★★	★★★½
WINE COUNTRY TRATTORIA	DCA	★★★★	Mod	★★★★	★★★
CAJUN/CREOLE					
FRENCH MARKET RESTAURANT	Disneyland Park	★★★½	Inexp	★★★★	★★★★
CAFÉ ORLÉANS	Disneyland Park	★★★½	Mod	★★★½	★★★
RALPH BRENNAN'S JAZZ KITCHEN*	Downtown Disney	★★★½	Mod	★★★½	★★½
BLUE BAYOU	Disneyland Park	★★★½	V. Exp	★★★½	★★½
CHARACTER DINING					
STORYTELLERS CAFÉ*	Grand Californian	★★★★	Exp	★★★★	★★★½
ARIEL'S GROTTO*	DCA	★★★½	Exp	★★★½	★★★½
PLAZA INN*	Disneyland Park	★★★	Mod	★★★	★★★½
DISNEY'S PCH GRILL*	Paradise Pier Hotel	★★★	Mod/Exp	★★★	★★½
GOOFY'S KITCHEN*	Disneyland Hotel	★★	Exp	★★	★★½
DELI/BAKERY					
NAPOLINI	Downtown Disney	★★★	Inexp	★★★	★★½
LA BREA BAKERY CAFÉ*	Downtown Disney	★★★	Inexp	★★½	★★★
ITALIAN					
NAPLES RISTORANTE E PIZZERIA	Downtown Disney	★★★	Mod	★★★	★★★
NAPOLINI	Downtown Disney	★★★	Inexp	★★★	★★½

DISNEYLAND RESORT RESTAURANTS BY CUISINE

CUISINE	LOCATION	OVERALL RATING	COST	QUALITY RATING	VALUE RATING
MEDITERRANEAN					
CATAL RESTAURANT & UVA BAR*	Downtown Disney	★★★½	Mod/Exp	★★★½	★★★
MEXICAN					
TORTILLA JO'S	Downtown Disney	★★★	Mod/Exp	★★½	★★½
RANCHO DEL ZOCALO RESTAURANTE	Disneyland Park	★★	Inexp	★★	★★½
POLYNESIAN					
TANGAROA TERRACE*	Disneyland Hotel	★★★	Inexp	★★★	★★★½
STEAK HOUSE					
STEAKHOUSE 55*	Disneyland Hotel	★★★★	V. Exp	★★★★½	★★★

*Serves breakfast

Continued from page 185

OTHER RECOMMENDATIONS Surf and turf for dinner and a kids' menu featuring octopus-shaped hot dogs and angel-hair pasta.

SUMMARY AND COMMENTS Ariel's Grotto is *fun* but very pricey; it's also one of the most popular dining spots in DCA. Kids will love the fact that Ariel and two to four other Disney princesses—Snow White, Cinderella, Aurora, or Belle—are on hand for pictures and autographs at breakfast and lunch. One set price buys adults a cup of bacon-topped crab chowder or spring mix salad with dried cranberries and blue cheese (ask your server for one of each), a main course, and shared dessert; the evening-only combo of thinly sliced steak with honey-whiskey glaze and whole grilled lobster tail is the clear winner. Kids' meals are child-friendly standards with cutesy cartoonish presentations, like clam-shaped sandwich rolls. Even toddlers will enjoy the bright surroundings and nonthreatening character visits. Evening diners don't get to meet princesses, but they do receive reserved viewing passes for *World of Color* ($48.58 adults, $26.98 kids ages 3–9, including tax). Demand is high here for obvious reasons, so book your reservations early. Adults (with or without their children) can escape upstairs to the Cove alfresco bar for a glass of wine, cocktail, or bottle of beer. Cove Bar also serves a small selection of appetizers, including enormous lobster nachos. This is a good spot for catching *World of Color* without a FastPass; views of the fountains from here are great, but the oblique angle to the projection screens isn't ideal. Cove Bar is even more popular since its seating area was expanded; it isn't unusual to wait more than an hour for a table in the afternoon, so save time by imbibing early.

Blue Bayou ★★★½

CAJUN/CREOLE   VERY EXPENSIVE   QUALITY ★★★½ VALUE ★★½
READER-SURVEY RESPONSES 94% 👍 6% 👎

Disneyland Park; ☎ 714-781-DINE

Reservations Required. **When to go** Early or late lunch, early evening. **Entrée range** $28–$62. **Service** ★★★. **Friendliness** ★★★. **Dress** Casual. **Hours** Daily, 11 a.m.–10:15 p.m.

SETTING AND ATMOSPHERE The Blue Bayou overlooks Pirates of the Caribbean and maintains an appropriately dark, damp ambience. The best tables ring the perimeter and afford a view of the faux bayou, replete with fireflies flickering among the weeping willows and mangroves, dilapidated houseboats, and soft lantern lights. If you're not lucky enough to get a table bayou-side, there's still enough wrought iron, uneven lighting, and twilight allure to soften the most hardened soul.

HOUSE SPECIALTIES Pan-seared salmon, filet mignon, and Le Special de Monte Cristo sandwich.

OTHER RECOMMENDATIONS Jambalaya or citrus-marinated chicken. Spring for the saffron-infused bouillabaisse if offered as a seasonal special. Entrées include a cup of mild gumbo or a superb side salad with candied pecans and dried cranberries.

SUMMARY AND COMMENTS Easily the best restaurant in Disneyland Park, Blue Bayou is as close to fine dining as you'll get here. The restaurant fills quickly and stays busy, so make reservations before you leave home (up to 60 days in advance) or obtain a same-day reservation at the restaurant door as soon as you get to the park. Though there's a children's menu, this isn't the place to bring wound-up or tired kids for a leisurely meal; they'll be bored. Tables are tightly packed, and nothing disrupts the busy servers more than wild kids up and out of their seats. Blue Bayou is more of a place where adults can escape the noise and happy chaos in the rest of the park without having to exit the gates. For lunch, we love the Monte Cristo sandwich, a deep-fried turkey, ham, and cheese creation that you don't find on many menus these days. Side dishes—including the Blue Bayou au gratin potatoes and fresh vegetables—are quite good as well. The crème brûlée is also a crowd-pleaser. Servers are Disney-pleasant, if a tad harried, but they're more than happy to accommodate the random request. And the dinner rolls are great! If seated at an unromantically over-lit table near the kitchen, don't be shy about requesting a relocation. On nights when *Fantasmic!* is shown, Blue Bayou offers a dining package for $65 per adult ($25 for kids 3–9), plus tax, that includes a starter, entrée, and dessert, as well as a FastPass to *Fantasmic!*'s center viewing section. Unless you order the most expensive items on the prix fixe menu (spiced shrimp, surf and turf), you'll be paying a lot for that FastPass.

La Brea Bakery Café ★★★

DELI/BAKERY	INEXPENSIVE	QUALITY ★★½ VALUE ★★★
Reader-Survey Responses 83% 👍 17% 👎		

Downtown Disney; ☎ 714-490-0233 or 714-781-DINE; labreabakery.com

Reservations Available. **When to go** Breakfast. **Entrée range** $10–$26. **Service** ★★★. **Friendliness** ★★★. **Bar** Limited. **Dress** Casual. **Hours** Sunday–Thursday, 8 a.m.–9 p.m., Friday–Saturday, 8 a.m.–10 p.m. Open 1 hour later in summer.

SETTING AND ATMOSPHERE This indoor-outdoor space is rich with the yeasty aromas of breads and cakes, plus whiffs of herbs and spices. Hardwood floors and large glass display counters distinguish the dining room. A pleasant patio with colorful umbrellas fronting the café is the perfect perch for a quick cappuccino and pastry while you people-watch.

HOUSE SPECIALTIES For brunch, eggs Benedict, chorizo frittata, short rib hash, or the B.E.L.T. sandwich, with eggs over easy, bacon, lettuce, and heirloom tomatoes. For lunch and dinner, entrée salads with shrimp, chicken, or fish; flatbread pizzas; and sandwiches like the spicy barbecue bacon chicken, with sriracha barbecue bacon jam.

OTHER RECOMMENDATIONS Take home one or more loaves of the artisanal breads. If you just want a quick soup or salad, you can get it slightly cheaper from La Brea's express counter.

SUMMARY AND COMMENTS It's all about the bread . . . and the muffins, pastries, desserts, and anything else containing flour and yeast. Breakfast is the obvious time to enjoy La Brea, and if you must supplement your carbohydrate fix, add some smoked salmon or a veggie frittata. At lunch and dinner, the salads, sandwiches, and flatbread pizzas take over. Service has improved markedly in recent years; servers are more attentive and pleasant. Get there early—it's the first eatery at the east end of the resort entrance, and a popular starting (and ending) place for tourists and locals alike. The express counter serves Silverback Coffee, which supports the people and gorillas of Rwanda, with much less waiting than at Starbucks.

Café Orléans ★★★½

CAJUN/CREOLE	MODERATE	QUALITY ★★★½ VALUE ★★★
Reader-Survey Responses	94% 👍	6% 👎

Disneyland Park; ☎ 714-781-DINE

Reservations Recommended. **When to go** Early or late lunch, early evening. **Entrée range** $16–$22. **Service** ★★★★. **Friendliness** ★★★★. **Dress** Casual. **Hours** Daily, 11:30 a.m.–park closing.

SETTING AND ATMOSPHERE Across the alley from Blue Bayou, Café Orléans overlooks the Rivers of America. There's a small patio and limited inside seating, but the table-side service offers a nice break from the serve-yourself and buffet options in the same price range. It's nice to kick back amid the wrought iron and scrolled-wood accents.

HOUSE SPECIALTIES The *pommes frites* have to be among the best sides in the park: traditional thick-cut fries tossed with Parmesan and garlic and served with a mildly spicy Cajun rémoulade sauce. If they aren't served piping hot, send them back. Mickey-shaped beignets are also a treat.

OTHER RECOMMENDATIONS A decent French onion soup with melted Gruyère cheese; an artery-clogging Monte Cristo sandwich in two versions, traditional and three-cheese; and a nice selection of sweet and savory crepes.

SUMMARY AND COMMENTS The *pommes frites* are worth the price of admission. If you don't eat anything else in the park your entire visit, try these. We like to hit Café Orléans for a midafternoon break, kick our feet up for a soda or sweet tea, and pick through a plate of the fries while we people-watch. The small menu makes ordering easy, provided you bring a big appetite and aren't afraid of a little cholesterol and trans fat. The Monte Cristo sandwiches are as good as Blue Bayou's and a few bucks cheaper. Kids will love the three-cheese version: Swiss, mozzarella, and double-cream Brie between thick slices of deep-fried, egg-battered bread. The gumbo is passable, if a little bland, while the Crescent City salad (mixed greens, caramelized pecans, roasted corn, grapes, orange slices, and pan-seared salmon or blackened chicken in an orange-cilantro vinaigrette) is very good. For something different, try the crepes—paper-thin pancakes stuffed with a variety of fillings, including chicken gumbo or beef. A Dixieland jazz band periodically provides lively entertainment.

Carnation Café ★★★

AMERICAN   MODERATE   QUALITY ★★★ VALUE ★★★
Reader-Survey Responses 98% 👍 2% 👎

Disneyland Park; ☎ 714-781-DINE

Reservations Recommended. **When to go** Breakfast or late lunch. **Entrée range** $7–$19. **Service** ★★★★. **Friendliness** ★★★★. **Dress** Casual. **Hours** Daily, 8 a.m.–9 p.m.

SETTING AND ATMOSPHERE A Main Street staple since the park opened in 1955, the Carnation Café serves up an American menu heavy with traditional favorites—hamburgers and meat loaf, eggs Benedict and Mickey-shaped waffles, and fried chicken—in a parlor circa 1890. For those in the know, Oscar Martinez, Disneyland's longest-tenured employee (more than 60 years at the park), is the café's ambassador.

HOUSE SPECIALTIES The loaded baked potato soup (a hot, creamy concoction with Cheddar cheese, chives, and large chunks of baked potato) is a favorite. Other specialties include a spinach and tomato frittata at breakfast and a sourdough bacon melt (with pepper Jack, grilled onions, and spicy sauce) for lunch. Oscar recommends the pan-seared catch of the day. Guy thinks the meat loaf is one of the best entrées in the park.

OTHER RECOMMENDATIONS For starters, try the deep-fried dill pickle spears, dipped in a rémoulade-style sauce. The menu features a beef-and-pork meat loaf, roasted turkey sandwich on a multigrain roll, and warm spinach salad topped with grilled chicken and portobello mushrooms.

SUMMARY AND COMMENTS Here, adults can find a decent plate, the kids can choose from their favorites, and it's easy on the wallet. Because of its location along Main Street, close to bathrooms and across from the lockers, it gets busy—expect to see waiting lines stretching down the street. Service is friendly and unusually patient; someone's briefed these cast members on how an hour's wait and low blood sugar can quickly erode a diner's mood. Once you're seated, the order comes quickly and with a smile.

Carthay Circle Restaurant ★★★★½

CALIFORNIA   EXPENSIVE   QUALITY ★★★★½ VALUE ★★★★½
READER-SURVEY RESPONSES 88% 👍 12% 👎

Disney California Adventure; ☎ 714-781-DINE

Reservations Recommended. **When to go** Lunch or dinner. **Entrée range** $24–$67. **Service** ★★★. **Friendliness** ★★★★. **Bar** Full bar. **Dress** Dressy casual. **Hours** Daily, 11:30 a.m.–9:30 p.m.

SETTING AND ATMOSPHERE Intimate booths, wood paneling, and candle sconces evoke the setting of the opening night in 1937 of *Snow White and the Seven Dwarfs*.

HOUSE SPECIALTIES Crispy firecracker duck wings with chili sauce, grilled Angus steak, sustainable fish with seasonal vegetables, and fried biscuits with Cheddar, bacon, and jalapeño.

OTHER RECOMMENDATIONS The menu here is revamped too frequently to recommend any particular item, but the fish ceviche appetizers and fresh ravioli entrées are reliably delicious. Skuna Bay salmon, Wagyu beef, and truffles are among the upscale ingredients that make frequent appearances on the menu. The signature biscuits (more like cheese-filled fritters) are heavy but have built a fanatical cult following, as have the surprisingly meaty sriracha-laced duck wings. The kids' menu offers fresh fish with veggies, mini crispy tacos, or pasta.

SUMMARY AND COMMENTS The chefs of Napa Rose developed the Southern Californian menu. A downstairs lounge serves appetizers and quick meals, while the larger upstairs restaurant takes reservations. A three-course fixed-price *World of Color* menu is also offered (Lunch: $44.29 adults, $23.76 kids ages 3–9; Dinner: $66.96 adults, $27.01 kids ages 3–9), which includes access to the prime center-stage viewing section. Terrace seating is available. Though service is sometimes unexpectedly inattentive, this is among the finest restaurants found inside the gates of any American theme park (including the vaunted Club 33) and one of the best dining experiences at Disneyland Resort outside of its sibling at the Grand Californian, at a slightly less astronomical price point. If you don't want an entire meal, stop in the downstairs lounge for a classic craft cocktail and Vietnamese tacos or charcuterie tray; it's just a shame duck wings aren't served downstairs. Or for an educational look at the historic photographs that festoon the wall, take the free guided tour offered daily at 10:30 a.m.

Catal Restaurant & Uva Bar ★★★½

MEDITERRANEAN   MODERATE–EXPENSIVE   QUALITY ★★★½ VALUE ★★★
Reader-Survey Responses 91% 👍 9% 👎

Downtown Disney; ☎ 714-774-4442; patinagroup.com/catal

Reservations Recommended. **When to go** Anytime. **Entrée range** $12–$46. **Service** ★★★. **Friendliness** ★★★. **Bar** Full bar and extensive wine list. **Dress** Dressy casual. **Hours** Sunday–Thursday, 8 a.m.–9 p.m. Friday–Saturday, 8 a.m.–10 p.m. Bar is open 2 hours later.

SETTING AND ATMOSPHERE Uva Bar, a circular open-air lounge, sits immediately outside the restaurant and is a good place for a quick bite (sans line) or cocktail while you watch the crowds go by. The outside bistro features a menu focused on Cal-Mediterranean gastropub cuisine. Inside is an elegant Art Deco–inspired restaurant with hardwood floors and spacious dining areas. There are two fireplaces and a large central bar; a narrow balcony with tables wraps around the entire top floor.

HOUSE SPECIALTIES French toast or chilaquiles for breakfast; braised oxtail, lamb roulade, slow-roasted prime rib, and diver scallops with butternut squash purée and crispy kale for dinner. Sample the lamb burger with roasted peppers, arugula, and red onion aioli.

OTHER RECOMMENDATIONS Try a huge and very tasty plate of paella with chicken, chorizo Bilbao, and saffron rice, or the classic Uva street fries with chorizo Bilbao, spicy crema, pickled garlic, and melted cheese.

SUMMARY AND COMMENTS Catal & Uva Bar are a Patina Group pairing, one in a chain of eateries operated by celebrity chef Joachim Splichal. Despite overblown descriptions, the menu is pretty straightforward. The appetizers and salads are better than the rest of the menu and a real value for the money. When the weather cooperates, Uva is the better of the two venues. Be cautious when ordering some of the more complex or unusual offerings; they can be very inconsistent. Side dishes shine though. Price notwithstanding, this is a very adult experience.

Disney's PCH Grill ★★★

CHARACTER DINING/AMERICAN	MOD–EXP	QUALITY ★★★	VALUE ★★½
Reader-Survey Responses 92% 👍	8% 👎		

Disney's Paradise Pier Hotel; ☎ 714-781-DINE

Reservations Accepted. **When to go** Breakfast and dinner. **Entrée range** $23–$39. **Service** ★★★★. **Friendliness** ★★★★. **Bar** Wine and beer. **Dress** Casual. **Hours** Daily, 7–11:30 a.m. and 5:30–9 p.m.

SETTING AND ATMOSPHERE A taste of Southern California beach life: bright primary colors, potted palms, and decorative elements such as surfboards and beach chairs.

HOUSE SPECIALTIES Breakfast: chilaquiles, Mickey-shaped waffles, and smoked salmon. Dinner: shrimp Alfredo with cavatappi pasta and the s'mores bar.

OTHER RECOMMENDATIONS The Surf's Up breakfast is your best bet, with an omelet station for grown-ups and a kids' buffet. The Beach Side Bonfire dinner buffet has some surprisingly good tri-tip beef and baby back ribs.

SUMMARY AND COMMENTS If you can take one more character breakfast, this time with Mickey and friends, get the kids up early and hit the beach. The food has improved in recent years.

ESPN Zone ★★½

AMERICAN	MODERATE	QUALITY ★★★	VALUE ★★★
Reader-Survey Responses 83% 👍	17% 👎		

Downtown Disney; ☎ 714-781-DINE; espnzone.com

Reservations Recommended. **When to go** Lunch or dinner. **Entrée range** $12–$26. **Service** ★★★. **Friendliness** ★★★. **Bar** Full bar. **Dress** Casual. **Hours** Sunday–Thursday, 11 a.m.–4 p.m. and 5–11 p.m.; Friday–Saturday, 11 a.m.–4 p.m. and 5 p.m.–midnight.

SETTING AND ATMOSPHERE Maybe the most entertaining place outside the park walls, with a little something for everyone except the very youngest, the ESPN Zone is a massive, two-story sports enthusiast's dream. Huge flat-panel TVs are everywhere, and there's not a bad seat in the house. There's also a TV and radio broadcast facility inside (from which you can catch live broadcasts, especially when local teams are playing), as well as a massive game and interactive sports arcade.

HOUSE SPECIALTIES A variety of cheeseburgers and sandwiches and the barbecued baby back ribs. Salads are fresher and livelier than they have been in the past.

OTHER RECOMMENDATIONS Sandwiches, appetizers, and most of what comes off the grill are safe bets. The more complicated the dish, the more likely it won't measure up to expectations. Wings and burgers rank as your best options.

SUMMARY AND COMMENTS The ESPN Zone is a three-ring circus—food and beverages oozing from every corner, more televised sports feeds than you can count, and an interactive game zone. Kids will love the manic pace and endless ways to spend more of your money, as well as the kid-friendly fare. Even teens will have a reason to smile here (hoops, a batting cage, and a climbing wall). And adults won't feel guilty over letting the youngsters run amok while they soak up quite possibly the largest televised sports feed on the planet. The food's improved, the service is steady (patient if not a little distracted at times), and you may find yourself in the studio audience for one of the many taped and live sports broadcasts produced right in front of you. When local teams (Lakers, Dodgers, Kings, Angels, Clippers, or Galaxy) are being televised, waits for tables can be excruciatingly long, even with reservations.

French Market Restaurant ★★★½

CAJUN/CREOLE	INEXPENSIVE	QUALITY ★★★★	VALUE ★★★★

Reader-Survey Responses 88% 👍 12% 👎

Disneyland Park; ☎ 714-781-DINE

Reservations Not accepted. **When to go** Lunch and dinner. **Entrée range** $11–$15. **Service** ★★★. **Friendliness** ★★★. **Dress** Casual. **Hours** Daily, 11 a.m.–10 p.m.

SETTING AND ATMOSPHERE In the heart of New Orleans Square, French Market Restaurant suggests a laid-back Southern vibe with lots of wrought iron under the shade of large, mature ficus trees. There's a small indoor dining area, but the best seating is outdoors on a large patio, covered with umbrellas and shadowed further by the trees.

HOUSE SPECIALTIES The menu features a roasted half chicken with citrus and Cajun spices, French dip sandwich, and Cajun meat loaf. The jambalaya is a savory alternative that hits the spot on cooler winter days. Most meals come with a side of rice or mashed potatoes and corn bread.

OTHER RECOMMENDATIONS Hearty soups; a few fresh and flavorful salads (including a roasted potato and bacon salad).

SUMMARY AND COMMENTS French Market Restaurant features comfort food with a Cajun-Creole flair and periodic entertainment from one or more of the roving park musicians or groups. The cafeteria-style service line becomes bottlenecked at the beverage station; see if you can skip to an open cashier at the end if you don't need drinks.

Goofy's Kitchen ★★

CHARACTER DINING/AMERICAN	EXPENSIVE	QUALITY ★★	VALUE ★★½

Reader-Survey Responses 93% 👍 7% 👎

Disneyland Hotel; ☎ 714-781-DINE

Reservations Available. **When to go** Breakfast. **Entrée range** $23–$42. **Service** ★★★★. **Friendliness** ★★★★. **Bar** Wine, beer, and cocktails. **Dress** Casual. **Hours** Daily, 7–11:30 a.m. and 4–8:45 p.m.

SETTING AND ATMOSPHERE Bright, fun, and modern, but also very loud. Goofy, Pluto, and other characters always put a smile to kids' faces.

HOUSE SPECIALTIES It's a buffet and your chef is Goofy, which should tell you everything you need to know. Breakfast features Mickey-shaped waffles, sausages, pancakes, bacon, scrambled eggs, and other traditional breakfast items. Dinner offers everything from prime rib to premium salads.

OTHER RECOMMENDATIONS The kids love Goofy's peanut butter pizza.

SUMMARY AND COMMENTS You come for two reasons: 1) It's convenient, especially if you're staying at the resort, and 2) the youngsters haven't yet had their fill of dining with a rotating cast of Disney characters. Breakfast is your best option for both food and wait times. Goofy's Kitchen has many fans, including this Alpine, Utah, grandmother:

Goofy's Kitchen, even at the staggering price, was well worth it. The food was really good, a lot of the menu is designed for children, and the character visits are worth the price. What a thrill to see my grand-children's delight at being visited by Minnie, Pluto, Chip, and Snow White (with whom my 2-year-old grandson flirted brazenly!).

Napa Rose ★★★★★

CALIFORNIA/FUSION   **VERY EXPENSIVE**   **QUALITY ★★★★★**   **VALUE ★★★½**
Reader-Survey Responses   86% 👍 14% 👎

Grand Californian Hotel; ☎ 714-781-DINE

Reservations Recommended. **When to go** Dinner. **Entrée range** $38–$50; $100 for four courses. **Service ★★★★★. Friendliness ★★★★. Bar** Impressive wine list. **Dress** Dressy casual. **Hours** Daily, 5:30–9:15 p.m.

SETTING AND ATMOSPHERE Napa Rose is Disneyland Resort's flagship fine-dining experience. The Grand Californian's Craftsman theme is carried into this premier room with sweeping views of Disney California Adventure from virtually every table. A large, open demonstration kitchen lets you watch the magic happen, and wine, in all of its glory, is displayed at every turn. Fine linens and china are the norm. This is an absolutely gorgeous room with food and service to match.

HOUSE SPECIALTIES The menu, rotated seasonally, focuses on the cuisine of California's wine region, ranchlands, farm belts, and coastline. Wine finds its way onto most of the menu in sauces, reductions, infusions, and dressings. Dishes may include sautéed portobello mushroom bisque "cappuccino," orange-glazed duck breast, truffle mac and cheese, and braised Angus beef short rib, as well as warm butterscotch bread pudding for dessert.

OTHER RECOMMENDATIONS Game meat, ranch and free-range beef and poultry, and the chef's prix fixe Vintner's Table are constantly changing and always exciting.

SUMMARY AND COMMENTS Napa Rose may be the best restaurant in Orange County and has been at the top of most critics' lists since its debut. Top talent in the kitchen (award-winning chef Andrew Sutton leads the charge) and in the dining room—a beautiful space with panoramic views and a wine cellar second to none—make this an incomparable gustatory experience. Every server has earned sommelier status, a designation that takes years of study and practical experience with wine and winemaking, easing the chore of choosing a wine from its cellar of more than 16,000 bottles. The waitstaff brings the whole experience, from wine rookies to experts, to match your level of knowledge and tastes. Look for unusual ingredients (Tahitian vanilla, smoked sturgeon, truffled quail eggs, lemongrass, almond oil) married to top-notch staples (Colorado lamb, Berkshire pork, pheasant breast, sustainable fresh fish), all deftly handled by a world-class kitchen crew. And though staff are very accommodating in the usual Disney manner, this is definitely not an adventure for the kids. Napa Rose should be on every adult's Disney bucket list, a must-do at least once. If the full menu is too rich for your blood, sit in the cozy lounge and order appetizers. An

Albuquerque, New Mexico, woman tried both Napa Rose and Steakhouse 55 (in the Disneyland Hotel) and offers this comparison:

Prices were quite high, but we had a very good time. Napa Rose was the highlight of the trip, and our waiter was very good. Steakhouse 55 was the biggest letdown. We were expecting to repeat our experience at Napa Rose, but the staff and food didn't come close.

A Suffern, New York, reader with good taste advises:

If you're doing the Napa Rose Chef's Counter, get the tasting menu.

Naples Ristorante e Pizzeria ★★★

ITALIAN **MODERATE** **QUALITY** ★★★ **VALUE** ★★★
Reader-Survey Responses 82% 👍 18% 👎

Downtown Disney; ☎ 714-776-6200 or 714-781-DINE; patinagroup.com/naples

Reservations Recommended. **When to go** Late lunch or early dinner. **Entrée range** $18–$26. **Service** ★★. **Friendliness** ★★★. **Bar** Extensive wine list and full bar. **Dress** Casual. **Hours** Daily, 11 a.m.–10 p.m.

SETTING AND ATMOSPHERE Food aside, this is a really fun restaurant: modern, colorful, and spacious, with tile floors, an open demonstration kitchen, and whimsical design touches that mirror nearby Disneyland. It's also noisy and crowded, typically filled with families. During peak hours, it's difficult to hear yourself think, let alone carry on a meaningful conversation. Nonetheless, it's a great gathering place, and there's something to appeal to everyone from small children to adults.

HOUSE SPECIALTIES Wood-fired Neapolitan-style pizzas: thin, crispy crusts with a hearty, almost spicy red sauce; handmade mozzarella cheese; and fresh toppings of choice.

OTHER RECOMMENDATIONS Some of the non-pasta entrées—pan-seared salmon with roasted tomatoes and green beans, for example—are the real highlights.

SUMMARY AND COMMENTS Another Patina–Joachim Splichal venture where most of the effort went into the design. While the menu seems sophisticated, the recipes are rather bland and uninspired with a few exceptions. The kids will enjoy the colorful decor and activities; adults can get a good glass of wine or a cocktail and feed the entire crew for less than $100.

Napolini ★★★

ITALIAN/DELI **INEXPENSIVE** **QUALITY** ★★★ **VALUE** ★★½
Reader-Survey Responses 87% 👍 13% 👎

Downtown Disney; ☎ 714-781-DINE

Reservations Not accepted. **When to go** Lunch or a quick dinner. **Entrée range** $6–$18. **Service** ★★. **Friendliness** ★★★. **Bar** Wine and beer only. **Dress** Casual. **Hours** Daily, 8 a.m.–11 p.m.

SETTING AND ATMOSPHERE This is next-door Naples's cousin—a quick-in, quick-out deli with most of what you'd expect, from swinging salamis to large jars of peppers. Counter and table service continue to improve, but expect a lapse in attitude once in awhile. They want to get it right, but when frustrated, servers lose patience.

HOUSE SPECIALTIES For breakfast, frittatas and egg sandwiches on focaccia bread. Wood-fired Neapolitan-style pizzas, panini, and salads for lunch and dinner.

OTHER RECOMMENDATIONS Best bets are the panini: grilled sandwiches on thick Italian bread, loaded to order with salami, veggies, peppers, onions, and such.

SUMMARY AND COMMENTS Don't set your expectations too high and you won't be disappointed here. Servers get flustered easily, and order mistakes are common (our guess is that Napolini serves as a training ground for Naples). Noise spills over from Naples on busy nights, as do impatient diners who don't want to wait for a table next door, making for a volatile mix that can have you feeling very uncomfortable in a hurry. But maybe that's the plan: to get you in with the sweet, spicy aromas of Italian cooking and then out quickly. We've noticed an improvement in quality at Napolini in recent years and can now recommend it with some reservations.

Plaza Inn ★★★

CHARACTER DINING/AMERICAN	MODERATE	QUALITY ★★★	VALUE ★★★½
Reader-Survey Responses	90% 👍	10% 👎	

Disneyland Park; ☎ 714-781-DINE

Reservations Recommended. **When to go** When you need a compromise, the kids insist, or you arrive right at the meal switch. **Entrée range** $13–$36. **Service** ★★★. **Friendliness** ★★★. **Dress** Casual. **Hours** Daily, 8 a.m.–park closing.

SETTING AND ATMOSPHERE Probably the high point of your meal at Plaza Inn is the gorgeous Victorian B&B ambience—comfortable, widely spaced tables in a spacious dining room with lots of brocade and brass. The large patio commands a great view of Main Street, where parades, strolling musicians, and the massive variety of visitors endlessly entertain us.

HOUSE SPECIALTIES This buffeteria can be hit-or-miss; see if you can catch something being freshly delivered. Timing is everything. Best bets are the pot roast or the fried chicken (which some claim is better than Knott's famous birds), two items that rarely suffer from sitting on the steam table.

OTHER RECOMMENDATIONS Kids love the daily character breakfast (reservations strongly suggested) hosted by Minnie Mouse and two to four other characters. Adults will suffer through rubbery pancakes and soggy bacon.

SUMMARY AND COMMENTS Don't expect fine dining when you eat at the Plaza Inn, but strides have been made in the quality of the food and the steam table's maintenance, and portions are very generous. Hit this place right when everything comes fresh, during the transitions from breakfast to lunch and from lunch to dinner, but it's still your basic been-in-the-steam-table-too-long scenario.

Rainforest Cafe ★★½

AMERICAN	MODERATE		QUALITY ★★★	VALUE ★★½
Reader-Survey Responses	76% 👍	24% 👎		

Downtown Disney; ☎ 714-772-0413; rainforestcafe.com

Reservations Available. **When to go** Lunch or dinner. **Entrée range** $11–$32. **Service** ★★. **Friendliness** ★★★. **Bar** Full bar. **Dress** Casual. **Hours** Sunday–Thursday, 8 a.m.–10:30 p.m.; Friday–Saturday, 8 a.m.–midnight.

SETTING AND ATMOSPHERE Couldn't get enough of the Jungle Cruise next door *and* you're starving? Exit the park and head to the Rainforest Cafe, a lush tropical experience that attracts a few thousand of your fellow diners on a daily basis. Take a safari through the winding sections of greenery, faux wildlife, and piped-in jungle sounds, and wade through a menu as large as the Orinoco Basin.

HOUSE SPECIALTIES Stick to the basics: burgers, simple sandwiches, and salads. The Volcanic Cobb Salad—a huge mix of romaine and iceberg greens, olives, crumbled blue cheese, chopped egg, bacon, and grilled chicken in a balsamic vinaigrette—is arguably the best one on the menu.

OTHER RECOMMENDATIONS The Mojo Bones (barbecued baby back ribs) are passable; the Volcano chocolate dessert (complete with sparkler top) is gargantuan and irresistible, so invite your posse because you'll never find the bottom of the bowl alone. The sandwich wraps are also a good alternative with some tasty meat and sauce mixes.

SUMMARY AND COMMENTS If the Adventureland experience just doesn't satisfy your lust for all things green, lush, and wildlike, this is the place for you. The menu is massive (maybe a little too large) and mostly palatable, but none of it is truly great. It does make up in quantity for any lack of quality; plates are enough for two in most circumstances. Children love the rain forest theme. All in all, a bit distracting—but maybe that's the point.

Ralph Brennan's Jazz Kitchen ★★★½

CAJUN/CREOLE	MODERATE		QUALITY ★★★½	VALUE ★★½
Reader-Survey Responses	93% 👍	7% 👎		

Downtown Disney; ☎ 714-776-5200; rbjazzkitchen.com

Reservations Available. **When to go** Lunch or dinner. **Entrée range** $14–$39. **Service** ★★★. **Friendliness** ★★½. **Bar** Full bar. **Dress** Casual. **Hours** Sunday, 10 a.m.–10 p.m.; Monday–Thursday, 11 a.m.–10 p.m., Friday–Saturday, 11 a.m.–11 p.m. (*Jazz Kitchen Express:* Daily, 8 a.m.–10 p.m.)

SETTING AND ATMOSPHERE Take a step back in time and space to the 19th-century French Quarter of New Orleans. Almost half the seating area is an open-air courtyard surrounded by wrought iron, hanging ferns, and milled hardwood. Above a small stage where live jazz plays daily, there's a pounded-copper ceiling; to stage left is a beautiful enamel-finished grand piano. You can people-watch from a balcony dining area, but no matter where you sit, you're going to enjoy the ambience and music.

HOUSE SPECIALTIES Gumbo Ya-Ya, blackened fish, and New York steak with horseradish cream sauce.

OTHER RECOMMENDATIONS Barbecue shrimp and grits, grilled filet mignon medallions, and pasta jambalaya are all good.

SUMMARY AND COMMENTS This used to be one of our favorite restaurants in or immediately around the resort, but it seems to have suffered a little through the recession. The Brennan family is still intimately involved with every aspect of the menu, but both quality and presentation decline between visits from the New Orleans crew. Servers, including actual Southerners and even a smattering of Louisiana natives, exude a laid-back (sometimes too laid-back), gracious attitude most of the time but have been known to get a little testy and impatient during the restaurant's busy times. This is a dining experience best suited to adults. Add live jazz to the mix (the zydeco brunch is especially fun), and, all things considered, you have one of Disneyland's better dining experiences. For a quick breakfast after 8 a.m., the sugar-dusted beignets and chicory coffee from the adjoining quick-service counter can't be beat. The Sunday Brunch Fest menu (featuring bananas Foster French toast and Cajun omelets) is offered every Sunday morning 10 a.m.–3 p.m., accompanied by a made-to-order Bloody Mary bar and table-side card tricks.

Rancho del Zocalo Restaurante ★★

MEXICAN	INEXPENSIVE	QUALITY ★★	VALUE ★★½

Reader-Survey Responses 91% 👍 9% 👎

Disneyland Park; ☎ 714-781-DINE

Reservations Not accepted. **When to go** Early lunch or early dinner. **Entrée range** $9–$15. **Service** ★★★. **Friendliness** ★★★. **Dress** Casual. **Hours** Daily, 8 a.m.–9 p.m.

SETTING AND ATMOSPHERE Welcome to the hacienda! Faux adobe, wooden beams, and Mexican tile ring a dark interior and covered outdoor patio. Tucked away from the throngs in the northeast area of Frontierland, this can be a nice, quiet place for a meal.

HOUSE SPECIALTIES The enchiladas are your best bet, probably because they lend themselves to the buffet-style dining here. In the mornings Rancho del Zocalo serves Mickey Mouse pancakes, along with Mexican items such as scrambled egg chilaquiles, chorizo burritos, and a fajita breakfast platter.

OTHER RECOMMENDATIONS Hit or miss: If you can catch a tray of soft tacos, burritos, or grilled chicken fresh from the commissary, you score.

SUMMARY AND COMMENTS Three words sum up the Zocalo: Mexican, cafeteria style. On the bright side, most of the cuisine holds up well under the heat lamps and over the steam tables, the enchiladas and grilled chicken in particular. The rest of the menu—the typical tacos, burritos, Mexican rice, and refried beans—is resolutely average, except at opening or right before the dinner rush, when the food is fresh and uncorrupted. The tortillas, both corn and flour, are consistently good. Anybody not intimately familiar with really good Mexican cuisine may rate this place higher. Zocalo is also a great choice when you can't possibly choke down another hot dog, burger, or pizza slice.

The River Belle Terrace ★★★

AMERICAN	MODERATE	QUALITY ★★★½	VALUE ★★½

Reader-Survey Responses 71% 👍 29% 👎

Disneyland Park; ☎ 714-781-DINE

Reservations Not accepted. **When to go** Lunch and dinner. **Entrée range** $19–$24. **Service** ★★★. **Friendliness** ★★★. **Dress** Casual. **Hours** Daily, 11:30 a.m.–9 p.m.

SETTING AND ATMOSPHERE Situated between New Orleans Square and Frontierland, The River Belle Terrace has an Old South–style exterior replete with wrought iron and wood siding. Large shuttered windows belie a small indoor-dining area; most of the seating is outdoors on a large patio covered with colorful umbrellas.

HOUSE SPECIALTIES Pork spareribs, pulled-pork sandwich, barbecue half chicken, and beef brisket sandwich.

OTHER RECOMMENDATIONS Sustainable fish of the day or the sausage link platter.

SUMMARY AND COMMENTS This 1955 Disneyland original, now a table-service venue, offers homey Southern dishes at lunch and dinner. For fans of the former Big Thunder Ranch Barbecue, River Belle's ribs are the closest they'll find to that all-you-could-eat favorite at the resort, albeit at a much higher cost. While the food quality is acceptable (the pan-seared arctic char we ate was even excellent), entrée pricing places it close behind Blue Bayou on the list of most expensive theme park restaurants, above the average cost at Carnation Café and even Café Orléans, both of which we prefer. The outdoor seating area is good to people-watch or just take in the view of Rivers of America from the patio, but the value proposition is too poor for such uncomplicated fare. The large, buttery cinnamon rolls dripping with buttercream frosting that Disney lore says Walt ate here every morning are now sold from a vendor cart outside The Haunted Mansion. On nights when *Fantasmic!* is shown, River Belle Terrace offers a dining package for $45 per adult ($25 for kids 3–9), plus tax, that includes a starter, entrée, and dessert, as well as a FastPass to *Fantasmic!*'s center viewing section.

Steakhouse 55 ★★★★

STEAK HOUSE	VERY EXPENSIVE		QUALITY ★★★★½	VALUE ★★★
Reader-Survey Responses	91% 👍	9% 👎		

Disneyland Hotel; ☎ 714-781-DINE

Reservations Recommended. **When to go** Breakfast, afternoon tea, or dinner. **Entrée range** $9–$57. **Service** ★★★★. **Friendliness** ★★★★. **Bar** Wine list and full bar. **Dress** Business casual. **Hours** Daily, 7–11 a.m. and 5–10 p.m. *High tea:* Friday–Sunday, noon–3 p.m.

SETTING AND ATMOSPHERE At Steakhouse 55, stylishly Art Deco-inspired hardwood tables, sleek leather chairs, and smaller banquettes decorate this updated classic American steak house. The indirect lighting casts a warm glow over everything, including an impressive collection of black-and-white photographs from Disney's storied past.

HOUSE SPECIALTIES Breakfast is a good value and features eggs Benedict and New York steak and eggs. At dinner it's all about the meat—grilled certified Angus beef seasoned with the restaurant's signature rub—but you can also order one of the fresh seafood choices or delectable lamb, pork, or chicken. Choose a bottle of wine from an impressive wine cellar, or simply engage one of the numerous sommeliers to choose a wine to complement your meal.

OTHER RECOMMENDATIONS The lobster and steak combination is actually very good, but the price can catch you by surprise; always ask up front before ordering unless you have very deep pockets.

SUMMARY AND COMMENTS This underrated eatery has been a well-kept secret for years and matches many of the more well-known steak houses in the area (Morton's and Ruth's Chris) steak for steak. It's alluring and comfortable, a perfect place to spend a grown-up evening over a leisurely meal matched to premium wines. Best to leave the kids behind for this experience; they'll bore easily and may disrupt what could be one of the best adult nights you're likely to have during your stay. The children may enjoy the classic English high tea held three afternoons each week. Traditional scones and finger sandwiches are on the menu, as are adult aperitifs and more kid-friendly items like hot chocolate. However, there are no characters.

Storytellers Café ★★★★

CHARACTER DINING/CALIFORNIA   EXPENSIVE   QUALITY ★★★★   VALUE ★★★½
Reader-Survey Responses   84% 👍 16% 👎

Grand Californian Hotel; ☎ 714-781-DINE

Reservations Recommended. **When to go** Breakfast or dinner. **Entrée range** $9–$36. **Service** ★★★★★. **Friendliness** ★★★★. **Bar** Extensive wine list and full bar. **Dress** Casual. **Hours** Daily, 7 a.m.–9:45 p.m.

SETTING AND ATMOSPHERE The Storytellers Café carries the Grand Californian Hotel's Arts & Crafts theme throughout with large, open beams; natural wood and wood carvings; milled stone; and stained glass. The walls are adorned with impressive murals depicting the state's rich literary history, from Mark Twain's "The Celebrated Jumping Frog of Calaveras County" to Scott O'Dell's *Island of the Blue Dolphins.*

HOUSE SPECIALTIES Children under age 10 will love the character breakfast buffet. Hosted by Chip 'n' Dale, the meal features a complement of woodland friends who visit the tables, sing songs, and pose for photos between bites of omelets, waffles, and caramel French toast. Try the pan-seared salmon for lunch or the roasted chicken for lunch or dinner.

OTHER RECOMMENDATIONS The charred corn chowder with rotisserie chicken is filling. Kids can make their own pizzas.

SUMMARY AND COMMENTS You may experience a little sticker shock at first, but there's real value here. It's not quite on par with Napa Rose across the way, but the same dedication to quality and originality is evident from the menu to the service. Kids will find lots to like about the food, while the adults enjoy California wine country–inspired menu options (from pastas to steaks to fresh fish) and a leisurely cocktail or glass of wine. Dinner gives diners the option to order from the menu or visit the buffet. You'll want to save some room for dessert too—who could pass up warm seasonal skillet pie heaped with vanilla ice cream or a warm s'mores cake? A Manitowoc, Wisconsin, reader recommends the café as an alternative to dining inside DCA, writing:

We ended up eating at Storytellers Café on a spur-of-the-moment decision, and it was one of the best places at which we ate at the park, as far as food, price, and atmosphere. Can share meals too, which costs less than eating in the park. The lemonade with the foam on top was AMAZING!

Tangaroa Terrace ★★★

AMERICAN/POLYNESIAN   INEXPENSIVE   QUALITY ★★★   VALUE ★★★½
Reader-Survey Responses   80% 👍 20% 👎

Disneyland Hotel; ☎ 714-781-DINE

Reservations Not accepted. **When to go** Anytime. **Entrée range** $7–$13. **Service** ★★★★. **Friendliness** ★★★★. **Bar** Beer, wine, and cocktails. **Dress** Casual. **Hours** Daily, 7 a.m.–10 p.m.

SETTING AND ATMOSPHERE This is Disneyland Hotel's poolside tropical retreat.

tiki torches and South Seas music are a dead giveaway that they want to evoke that island feeling.

HOUSE SPECIALTIES Breakfast has French toast with banana-caramel sauce and bacon or cinnamon-spiced oatmeal. Lunch and dinner feature a one-third-pound Hawaiian cheeseburger with teriyaki sauce, bacon, and caramelized pineapple on a brioche bun, or try the chicken salad with black kale, lettuce, and toasted macadamia nuts in a tropical vinaigrette.

OTHER RECOMMENDATIONS Specials get a little more involved with sushi-grade ahi tuna *poke* and shrimp tacos. *Caution:* The sweet potato fries may be habit forming. On request, Tangaroa Terrace will also serve the same bar snacks as Trader Sam's next door, including the exquisite long beans.

SUMMARY AND COMMENTS This eatery has something for everyone, as long as everyone enjoys food with an Asian-Polynesian flare. Adults can enjoy a cocktail (maybe something a little exotic with a fruit garnish and little pink umbrellas) while kids frolic in the nearby pool in between bites. The adjoining Trader Sam's Enchanted Tiki Bar serves exotic cocktails and Asian-inspired appetizers in an intimate and elaborately decorated environment reminiscent of Walt Disney World's extinct Adventurers Club. Order an Uh Oa, Krakatoa Punch, or Shipwreck on the Rocks to see some explosive special effects. The best bet for late-night snacks are Sam's panko-crusted long beans or sweet and spicy Asian wings. If the interior is at capacity (a frequent occurrence on weekends), try the patio, which has live music and a cozy fireplace.

Tortilla Jo's ★★★

MEXICAN	MODERATE–EXPENSIVE	QUALITY ★★½	VALUE ★★½
Reader-Survey Responses	80% 👍	20% 👎	

Downtown Disney; ☎ 714-535-5000; patinagroup.com/tortilla-jos

Reservations Available. **When to go** Lunch or dinner. **Entrée range** $9–$27. **Service** ★★★. **Friendliness** ★★★. **Bar** Full bar. **Dress** Casual. **Hours** Sunday, 9 a.m.–10 p.m.; Monday–Thursday, 11 a.m.–10 p.m.; Friday, 11 a.m.–11 p.m.; Saturday, 9 a.m.–11 p.m.; *taqueria:* Daily, 8 a.m.–11 p.m.

SETTING AND ATMOSPHERE Old Mexico meets California modern. Mexican touchstones such as glazed tiles; thick, crude glass; and wrought iron accent an open dining room with modern, eclectic touches. You can grab a quick bite at the taqueria, and the bartender pours from a huge selection of more than 100 premium and super-premium tequilas at an outdoor cantina. The place goes crazy on the weekends, so gird yourself for a raucous, booze-shooting, beer-chasing good time.

HOUSE SPECIALTIES Start with guacamole made fresh at your table. For an entrée, any one of the gigantic burritos, especially the signature Fajitas Burrito, are good.

OTHER RECOMMENDATIONS Try the enchiladas or the mahi-mahi taco.

SUMMARY AND COMMENTS Another Patina Group eatery from überchef Joachim Splichal, Tortilla Jo's is upscale Mexican with a culinary twist. You can customize any taco or burrito. The eclectic, hybrid menu (and the loosey-goosey crowd) may be too much for the kids, but adults will appreciate a shot of Sauza Silver tequila and a tall glass of Corona beer, complete with a lime wedge. Strolling mariachi musicians fill the dining room and bar with foot-stomping traditional Mexican music.

Wine Country Trattoria ★★★★

CALIFORNIA NOUVELLE	MODERATE	QUALITY ★★★★ VALUE ★★★
Reader-Survey Responses	84% 👍 16% 👎	

Disney California Adventure; ☎ 714-781-DINE

Reservations Recommended. **When to go** Lunch or dinner. **Entrée range** $9–$32. **Service** ★★★. **Friendliness** ★★. **Bar** Wine, beer, and cocktails. **Dress** Casual. **Hours** Daily, 11:30 a.m.–9 p.m.

SETTING AND ATMOSPHERE Arguably one of the better dining options at either park, the trattoria is a leisurely place to park yourself and family away from the frenetic crowds. Whether you choose one of three themed patios outside or the "patio" inside, this spacious bistro captures the California-casual mood with plenty of tile, wood, and trellised greenery, whisking you away from downtown Anaheim and positing you in the middle of California wine country.

HOUSE SPECIALTIES Try the pasta: spaghetti Bolognese or spaghetti with vegetables, lasagna, fettuccine shrimp Alfredo, or linguine with clams.

OTHER RECOMMENDATIONS Try the herb-roasted chicken breast sandwich or salad with chicken or shrimp for lunch.

SUMMARY AND COMMENTS The trattoria is a popular spot for a Mediterranean-style or California-inspired meal, paired with a glass of wine from its extensive cellar. Braised lamb shank and salmon with a dill-butter cream sauce are delicious. And to finish: seasonal *panna cotta.* Wine Country Trattoria appeals more to adults without children, though an improved kids' menu and *World of Color* fixed-price dining packages has made this a more attractive option for families (Lunch: $34.55 adults, $22.66 kids ages 3–9; Dinner: $48.58 adults, $26.98 kids ages 3–9; all including tax). Note that *World of Color* lunch and dinner patrons each receive a center-section viewing ticket. Also note that the fixed-price *World of Color* menu is separate from the posted à la carte selections. The soup or salad and dessert sampler included in the viewing package are all excellent, but some of the entrées can be inconsistent. For a refreshing late-afternoon break, order a glass of wine and plate of sliders or charcuterie at the Alfresco Tasting Terrace on the upstairs patio. From a Richfield, Ohio, mom:

One place we all agreed on was the Wine Country Trattoria at DCA. The service was a bit on the slow side, but the food from start to finish was delicious and fresh. We arrived around 1:30 and enjoyed lunch and the parade, which passed by at 2. Delicious meal and a parade too!

DINING *Outside*
DISNEYLAND RESORT

UNOFFICIAL GUIDE RESEARCHERS LOVE GOOD FOOD and invest a fair amount of time scouting new places to eat. And because food at Disneyland Resort (all of the Disney complex, including the theme parks, hotels, and Downtown Disney) is so expensive, we (like you) have an economic incentive for finding palatable meals off campus.

Redevelopment of the surrounding real estate has attracted a whole new glut of fine-dining and fast-casual options. Choices range from the familiar (**Cheesecake Factory, Roy's Restaurant, Ruth's Chris Steak House**) to local favorites (**Yard House, Umami Burger, The Catch**). Unique dining experiences are also prevalent. While the average Disneyland visitor stays for only two to four nights, there are more than enough fine-dining and fast-casual venues outside Disneyland Resort to keep you happy, if not confused, for that amount of time. Good ethnic dining, however, is woefully underrepresented. Especially hard to find are high-quality Thai, Chinese, Mexican, Japanese, Korean, and Greek restaurants. We've confined our coverage to restaurants that you can reach by car or cab in 15 minutes or less. If you're willing to range farther afield, your choices increase exponentially.

Among restaurants in and out of Disneyland Resort, location and price will determine your choice. For example, a decent Italian restaurant is in Downtown Disney and several independent Italian eateries are within 5 miles of the Disney complex. Which one you select depends on how much you want to spend and how convenient it is.

Better restaurants outside Disneyland Resort cater primarily to adults and aren't as well equipped to deal with children. This is a plus, however, if you're looking to escape children and eat in peace and quiet.

The Anaheim GardenWalk retail and entertainment complex is east of the park. Popular chains such as **The Cheesecake Factory, Roy's Restaurant, California Pizza Kitchen,** and **Bubba Gump Shrimp Co.** are doing brisk business. The best of the lot is probably **McCormick & Schmick's Grille,** which serves well-prepared fresh seafood at outrageous prices (though at happy hour, you can get a cheeseburger and fries for just $5).

BUFFETS AND MEAL DEALS OUTSIDE DISNEYLAND RESORT

BUFFETS, RESTAURANT SPECIALS, AND DISCOUNT DINING abound in the area surrounding Disneyland Resort, especially on Harbor Boulevard and Katella Avenue. The local visitor magazines, which are distributed free at non-Disney hotels, among other places, are packed with advertisements and discount coupons for seafood feasts, buffets (Chinese, Indian, and the like), and a host of combination specials for everything from lobster to barbecue. For a family trying to economize on meals, some of the come-ons are mighty attractive. But are these places any good? Is the food fresh, tasty, and appealing? Are the restaurants clean and inviting? Armed with little more than a roll of Tums, the Unofficial research team tried all the eateries that advertise heavily in the tourist publications. Here's what we discovered.

Chinese Super Buffets

Talk about an oxymoron. If you've ever tried preparing Chinese food, especially a stir-fry, you know that split-second timing is required to avoid overcooking. So it should come as no big surprise that Chinese dishes languishing on a buffet lose their freshness, texture, and flavor in a hurry. On the bright side, however, the super buffets are so cheap that you really can't go wrong. So what if it's not the best Chinese food you've ever had if you can scarf down all you want for $15? All the Chinese buffets serve chicken prepared a dozen different ways but also offer such goodies as peel-and-eat shrimp, various fish and shellfish, the occasional carved meat, salads, soups, and sometimes sushi. Desserts are usually lackluster, but most folks are too stuffed to eat them anyway. The best Chinese buffet within a 15-minute drive of Disneyland Resort is as follows:

HARBOR SEAFOOD BUFFET 12761 Harbor Blvd., Ste. I1, Garden Grove; ☎ 714-636-3338; **theharborseafoodbuffet.net.** Dinner: $15.99 adults, Monday–Thursday; $16.99 adults, Friday–Sunday; $1.40 per year old for children ages 2–10, free for children under age 2. Seniors and military receive 10% off. Discount coupons available. Features Japanese food and sushi in addition to Chinese dishes.

Indian Buffets

Indian food survives the ravages of heat lamps and steam tables much better on a buffet than Chinese food does. The mainstays of Indian buffets are curries. *Curry,* you may be surprised to know, is essentially the Indian word for "stew." In India each curry is prepared with a different combination of spices (dominated by cumin and turmeric). The salient point about Indian buffets is that curries, unlike stir-fries, actually improve with a little aging. If you've ever reheated a leftover stew at home and noticed that it tasted better the second time, it's because the flavors and ingredients continued to marry during the storage period, making the stew richer and tastier.

In the Disneyland Resort area, most Indian restaurants offer buffets at lunch only—not too convenient if you plan on spending your day at the theme parks. If you're out shopping or taking a day off, here is one Indian buffet worth trying:

GANDHI PALACE Ramada Plaza Hotel, 515 W. Katella Ave., Anaheim; ☎ 714-808-6777; **gandhipalaceoc.com.** Lunch buffet: Monday–Saturday, $12. Discount coupons available.

Salad Buffets

The most popular of these in the Disneyland Resort area is **Souplantation** (1901 W. Malvern Ave., Fullerton; ☎ 714-446-0566; **souplantation .com**). The buffet features prepared salads and an extensive array of ingredients to build your own. Souplantation also offers a variety of soups, a modest pasta bar, a baked potato bar, an assortment of fresh fruit, and ice cream sundaes. Dinner runs $11.59 for adults, $5.99 for children ages 6–12, and $2.99 for children ages 3–5. Lunch is $9.99 for adults during the week and $9.59 on weekends; kids eat for the same price as at dinner.

ANAHEIM-AREA FULL-SERVICE RESTAURANTS

SOUTHERN CALIFORNIA IS A MOTHER LODE of wonderful dining, and if we directed you to Newport Beach, La Jolla, or LA, we could guarantee you a fantastic eating experience every night. In that you've chosen Disneyland as your destination, however, we've elected to profile only solid restaurants that you can reach by car or cab in 15 minutes or less. That said, here are our picks; all of them offer disabled access.

ANAHEIM-AREA RESTAURANTS BY CUISINE

CUISINE/LOCATION	OVERALL RATING	COST	QUALITY RATING	VALUE RATING
AMERICAN				
ROSCOE'S HOUSE OF CHICKEN & WAFFLES S. Harbor Blvd.	★★★★½	Inexp	★★★★	★★★½
CLANCY'S AMERICAN GRILL S. Harbor Blvd.	★★★	Mod	★★★	★★★
CAJUN/CREOLE				
HOUSE OF BLUES RESTAURANT & BAR W. Katella Ave.	★★★	Mod	★★★½	★★½
CHINESE				
MAS' CHINESE ISLAMIC RESTAURANT E. Orangethorpe Ave.	★★★½	Mod	★★★	★★★½
GASTROPUB				
HAVEN GASTROPUB S. Glassell St.	★★★	Mod	★★★★	★★★½
GERMAN				
BIERSTUBE GERMAN PUB AT THE PHOENIX CLUB S. Sanderson Ave.	★★★½	Inexp/ Mod	★★★½	★★★★
JÄGERHAUS E. Ball Rd.	★★★	Inexp	★★★½	★★★
ITALIAN				
LUIGI'S D'ITALIA S. State College Blvd.	★★★½	Inexp/ Mod	★★★½	★★★★
CAROLINA'S ITALIAN RESTAURANT Chapman Ave.	★★★	Inexp	★★★	★★★½
MEXICAN				
GABBI'S MEXICAN KITCHEN S. Glassell St.	★★★	Mod	★★★★	★★★½
SEAFOOD				
THE CATCH E. Katella Ave.	★★★½	Exp	★★★★	★★★½
MCCORMICK & SCHMICK'S GRILLE W. Katella Ave.	★★★	Mod/ Exp	★★★	★★★
STEAK				
PARK AVE STEAKS & CHOPS Beach Blvd.	★★★★½	Exp	★★★★	★★★★
MORTON'S S. Harbor Blvd.	★★★★	Exp	★★★½	★★★½
THE CATCH E. Katella Ave.	★★★½	Exp	★★★★	★★★½
PRIME CUT CAFÉ & WINE BAR W. Katella Ave.	★★★	Mod/ Exp	★★★	★★★½

Bierstube German Pub at the Phoenix Club ★★★½

GERMAN   INEXPENSIVE–MODERATE   QUALITY ★★★½   VALUE ★★★★

**1340 S. Sanderson Ave., behind Honda Center, Anaheim;
☎ 714-563-4166; thephoenixclub.com**

Reservations Recommended. **When to go** Lunch or dinner. **Entrée range** $10–
$18. **Service** ★★★. **Friendliness** ★★★★. **Bar** Wine list, extensive draft beer
offerings, and full bar. **Dress** Casual. **Hours** Tuesday–Thursday and Sunday,
11 a.m.–9 p.m.; Friday–Saturday, 11 a.m.–10 p.m.

SETTING AND ATMOSPHERE Once a private club reserved for family members
of the original German settlers of Anaheim and more recent émigrés, this
landmark is now open to the public (members enjoy a few extra privileges). It has more than a half dozen German beers on tap. Its menu is
somewhat limited, trending toward less-fancy preparations, but it's these
basic dishes that keep folks coming back. The pub is conducive to raucous eating, drinking, and carousing. Live music seems omnipresent,
from local and guest polka bands to renowned accordion artists.

HOUSE SPECIALTIES Wursts, kraut, pork roast, mixed platters, and sauer-
braten are the best in a 100-mile radius.

OTHER RECOMMENDATIONS Pork in a creamy mushroom sauce.

SUMMARY AND COMMENTS The bastion of Anaheim's founding families and
subsequent waves of German immigrants, The Phoenix Club offers a little
taste of the *Mutterland* far from home. The food is good, occasionally
great; the beer is always cold; and the help is always ready to show you a
good time, German or not. During Oktoberfest, the place rocks. The kids
will love the early reminders of a rough and rural Anaheim and the oom-
pah bands, Mom and Dad will love the German beers, and everyone will
love the sweet-and-sour flavors of German cuisine.

Carolina's Italian Restaurant ★★★

SOUTHERN ITALIAN   INEXPENSIVE   QUALITY ★★★   VALUE ★★★½

**12045 Chapman Ave., Garden Grove; ☎ 714-971-5551;
carolinasitalianrestaurant.com**

Reservations Recommended. **When to go** Dinner. **Entrée range** $10–$23. **Service**
★★½. **Friendliness** ★★★½. **Bar** Extensive beer and wine lists. **Dress** Casual.
Hours Sunday–Thursday, 11 a.m.–10 p.m.; Friday–Saturday, 11 a.m.–midnight.

SETTING AND ATMOSPHERE A classic Italian family restaurant replete with wall
murals of the motherland, comfortable seating, and the overwhelming
aroma of garlic and olive oil. It's like walking through a time warp.

HOUSE SPECIALTIES You can't go wrong with any one of more than three
dozen hearty pasta dishes, from a very traditional meat sauce to an outstanding lasagna. Try the Atlantic salmon salad.

OTHER RECOMMENDATIONS The Taste of Italy features the colors of Italy's flag
with a combination of chicken penne pesto, shrimp fettuccine Alfredo, and
spaghetti with meatballs. The house-made tiramisu, if you can manage
more food after the large plates, is a treat.

SUMMARY AND COMMENTS Family owned and operated for three generations,
Carolina's also features more than 200 beers from around the globe and
a rather well-selected wine list for such a place. Portions tend toward the
gigantic, so bring your appetite.

The Catch ★★★½

SEAFOOD/STEAK EXPENSIVE   QUALITY ★★★★   VALUE ★★★½

2100 E. Katella Ave., Ste. 104, Anaheim; ☎ 714-935-0101;
catchanaheim.com

Reservations Recommended. **When to go** Lunch or dinner. **Entrée range** $12–
$48. **Service** ★★★. **Friendliness** ★★★½. **Bar** Full bar. **Dress** Business casual.
Hours Monday–Friday, 11:30 a.m.–10 p.m.; Saturday, 5–10 p.m.; Sunday,
5–9 p.m.

SETTING AND ATMOSPHERE Clean, contemporary take on a steak house classic, The Catch exudes urban chic with a comfortable blend of hardwood,
glass, and tile. Expect to see dozens of young urban professionals; old,
die-hard loyalists; and even a smattering of professional athletes who
play for the local Angels baseball or Anaheim Ducks hockey teams dal-
lying at the bar and/or enjoying dinner with friends and family.

HOUSE SPECIALTIES Grilled fresh fish, premium meats, and chops. The top
sirloin may be the best cut you're likely to sample anywhere.

OTHER RECOMMENDATIONS Lunch features butcher-block sandwiches: piles
of thinly sliced meats or fish piled high on fresh slabs of bread, accompanied by all the usual condiments and some not-so-common spreads
such as lemon aioli. For dinner, try the terrific bone-in rib eye.

SUMMARY AND COMMENTS Yes, the place is very expensive, but you're not
likely to find a more beautiful yet comfortable room, attentive service, or
high-quality food prepared with love and care anywhere close by. It has
a vibrant bar scene favored by local luminaries, a beautiful dining room,
and even a nicely appointed patio.

Clancy's American Grill ★★★

AMERICAN MODERATE   QUALITY ★★★   VALUE ★★★

2191 S. Harbor Blvd., Anaheim; ☎ 714-750-7500;
clancysamericangrill.com

Reservations Available. **When to go** Lunch or dinner. **Entrée range** $10–$27. **Service** ★★. **Friendliness** ★★★. **Bar** Full bar. **Dress** Casual. **Hours** Sunday–Thursday,
4–10 p.m.; Friday–Saturday, 4–11 p.m.

SETTING AND ATMOSPHERE Pure sports bar with full, high-definition flat-
panel TVs in every direction, a few booths, and several rooms of tables,
all with a view of the televised action.

HOUSE SPECIALTIES Wings cooked to perfection with all the usual sauces,
plus a very different mango habañero. Make your own burger with beef
or chicken.

OTHER RECOMMENDATIONS The pot roast and fish-and-chips are surprisingly
good for a sports bar.

SUMMARY AND COMMENTS Clancy's is a great alternative to the crammed
insanity of the ESPN Zone in Downtown Disney. Lots of locals and a
friendly vibe; service can be sporadic.

Gabbi's Mexican Kitchen ★★★

GOURMET MEXICAN MODERATE   QUALITY ★★★★   VALUE ★★★½

141 S. Glassell St., Orange; ☎ 714-633-3038; gabbipatrick.com

Reservations Recommended. **When to go** Lunch or dinner. **Entrée range** $10–$27. **Service** ★★★. **Friendliness** ★★★. **Bar** Full bar. **Dress** Casual. **Hours** Sunday–Thursday, 11 a.m.–10 p.m.; Friday–Saturday, 11 a.m.–11 p.m.

SETTING AND ATMOSPHERE Locals flock to Gabbi's vintage storefront that has no sign (look for the *poquito* patio next door to the Army surplus store). Just steps south of Orange's beloved plaza in charming Old Town, Gabbi's adds style to the narrow space with tall ceilings, exposed brick, and giant, colorful Mexican urns.

HOUSE SPECIALTIES Roasted suckling pig with habañero salsa or duck confit tacos.

OTHER RECOMMENDATIONS Chicken enchiladas and signature margaritas made from a tequila collection that would make a desperado blush.

SUMMARY AND COMMENTS In this county teeming with taco stands and burrito counters, chef-owner Gabbi Patrick stands apart with her more refined, regional takes on Mexican food that reflect both her Napa training and her Latino family's roots in the restaurant business.

Haven Gastropub ★★★

GASTROPUB   MODERATE   QUALITY ★★★★   VALUE ★★★½

190 S. Glassell St., Orange; ☎ 714-221-0680; havengastropub.com

Reservations Recommended. **When to go** Lunch or dinner. **Entrée range** $12–$60. **Service** ★★★. **Friendliness** ★★★½. **Bar** Beer and wine. **Dress** Casual. **Hours** Monday–Friday, 11 a.m.–2 a.m.; Saturday–Sunday, 9 a.m.–2 a.m.

SETTING AND ATMOSPHERE The restaurant is in Old Town Orange, a historic area of preserved homes and businesses including this little gem. Like its neighbor, Gabbi's, Haven is housed in a restored brick building. Inside, you'll find a large open dining room packed with tables and booths, framed by a massive bar on one side and an open kitchen on the other.

HOUSE SPECIALTIES House-made potato chips are first soaked in beer, fried, and served with a sprinkling of herbs and a side of garlic aioli. Try the lamb burger with onion jam, *tzatziki,* and onion sprouts on a brioche bun.

OTHER RECOMMENDATIONS Braised beef served poutine style with gravy, Cheddar cheese curds, and *pommes frites*; a whole roasted suckling pig served family style for parties of eight or more (reserve at least one week in advance).

SUMMARY AND COMMENTS Think beer, anything made with beer, and all the food that goes with beer, and you have a grasp of what executive chef Greg Daniels has put together here. More than 200 craft beers on tap and in a bottle—and a service crew who knows every one of them intimately—together with an adventurous menu of faux familiar and exotic foods, and you have Haven. The place is a favorite for the local college students and fills quickly on weekends but stays open late every night until 2 a.m.

House of Blues Restaurant & Bar ★★★

CAJUN/CREOLE   MODERATE   QUALITY ★★★½   VALUE ★★½

321 W. Katella Ave., Anaheim GardenWalk; ☎ 714-520-2334; houseofblues.com/anaheim

Reservations Recommended. **When to go** Dinner. **Entrée range** $10–$25. **Service** ★★★. **Friendliness** ★★★. **Bar** Wine list and full bar. **Dress** Casual. **Hours** Daily, 11 a.m.–9 p.m.

GREAT EATS IN AND AROUND ANAHEIM

BEST BURGER

• **Umami Burger** 338 S. Anaheim Blvd., Anaheim; ☎ 714-991-8626; **umamiburger .com.** Juicy house-ground burgers served mid-rare and topped with truffle cheese, shiitake mushrooms, fried eggs, or other fancy fixin's. Try the homemade pickles.

BEST CHINESE

• **Panda Kitchen** 1770 S. Harbor Blvd., Ste. 120, Anaheim; ☎ 714-999-6888; **panda kitchentogo.com.** For so-bad-it's-good, greasy, late-night lo mein.

BEST INDIAN

• **Punjabi Tandoor** 327 S. Anaheim Blvd., Ste. A, Anaheim; ☎ 714-635-3155; **punjabi tandoor.com.** The fresh tandoori in the evening is exceptional. Offers original dishes and excellent naan.

BEST JAPANESE

• **Sushi Pop** 1105 Euclid St., Fullerton; ☎ 714-278-1062; **www.sushipopus.com.** An unpretentious strip-mall eatery offering all-you-can-eat *nigiri* and unusual *maki* rolls at reasonable prices.

BEST MEDITERRANEAN

• **Zankou Chicken** 2424 W. Ball Rd., Anaheim; ☎ 714-229-2060; **zankouchicken .com.** Forget that this place is a chain, disregard the cheesy ambience, and go for the spit-roasted chicken, hummus, and shawarma beef. Inexpensive and delicious.

BEST MEXICAN

• **La Casa Garcia** 531 W. Chapman Ave., Anaheim; ☎ 714-740-1108; **lacasagarcia .com.** Carnitas, *barbacoa* (beef slow-cooked in a red-chile sauce), and three-flavor chimichangas, all with a Tex-Mex twist, are not to be missed.

• **Los Sanchez** 11906 Garden Grove Blvd., Garden Grove; ☎ 714-590-9300; **lossan chez.com.** This locals-only gem serves authentic Sonoran cuisine at reasonable prices. Fish ceviche, *lengua* (tongue) tacos, seafood soup, and the best chicken mole you've ever had.

BEST PIZZA

• **Pizza Press** 1700 S. Harbor Blvd., Anaheim; ☎ 714-323-7134; **thepizzapress.com.** Excellent artisanal thin-crust pies with upscale toppings for a very reasonable $10–plus tossed-to-order salads, craft beers, and a 1 a.m. closing time—make this tiny independent pizzeria across from Disneyland a perfect post-park pit stop.

SETTING AND ATMOSPHERE The House of Blues closed up shop at Downtown Disney in May 2016 and reopened early 2017 in a larger space at the struggling Anaheim GardenWalk a few blocks away. Think rustic-but-trendy blues club somewhere along the Mississippi River, maybe St. Louis. The restaurant has a more open feel than the previous location, as well as a built-in stage with live music almost every night. The walls feature a fantastic collection of American folk artists, including artworks created especially for the venue.

HOUSE SPECIALTIES Jambalaya, St. Louis–style ribs, pulled pork sandwich, and build-your-own burgers.

OTHER RECOMMENDATIONS Nashville hot fried chicken salad and barbecue short rib tacos with tomatillo salsa.

SUMMARY AND COMMENTS House of Blues is first and foremost a major concert site, with marquee names, up-and-comers, and strong local talent taking the stage every night. Unless stated otherwise, the separately ticketed concert hall is strictly an adult venue (18 and older), though children are always welcome in the restaurant. Happy hour (Monday–Friday, 2–5 p.m., and daily, 10 p.m.–close) offers discounted drinks and cut-price appetizers. You can experience everything the venue has to offer by attending the family-friendly Gospel Brunch, a Sunday-morning event that showcases local gospel singers and features an all-you-can-eat Southern-influenced buffet.

Jägerhaus ★★★

GERMAN   INEXPENSIVE   QUALITY ★★★½   VALUE ★★★

2525 E. Ball Rd., Anaheim; ☎ 714-520-9500; jagerhaus.net

Reservations Recommended only for large parties. **When to go** Breakfast. **Entrée range** $6–$23. **Service** ★★½. **Friendliness** ★★★★. **Bar** Wine list and extensive imported draft beer offerings. **Dress** Casual. **Hours** Monday–Friday, 7 a.m.–9 p.m.; Saturday–Sunday, 8 a.m.–9 p.m.

SETTING AND ATMOSPHERE We don't think that anything has changed since this restaurant opened decades ago. Wood paneling dominates. Pictures of alpine meadows and picturesque Old World villages hang beneath shelves of kitschy accoutrements, from delicate porcelain teapots to hearty beer steins—but it's clean and neat.

HOUSE SPECIALTIES The German pancakes, dense, doughy, platter-size egg cakes flavored with everything from lemon and powdered sugar to fruit jams and even fresh fruit; fat, juicy bratwursts.

OTHER RECOMMENDATIONS Omelets, corned beef hash, and house-made sausage patties.

SUMMARY AND COMMENTS Everyone from recent German émigrés and tourists to descendants of the original German settlers gather here to eat fat, fluffy German pancakes and sausage and gossip over coffee. The huge menu offers something for everyone, from burgers to bratwurst and Wiener schnitzel.

Luigi's D'Italia ★★★½

ITALIAN   INEXPENSIVE–MODERATE   QUALITY ★★★½   VALUE ★★★★

801 S. State College Blvd., Anaheim; ☎ 714-490-0990; luigisditalia.net

Reservations Recommended. **When to go** Lunch or dinner. **Entrée range** $8–$26. **Service** ★★★. **Friendliness** ★★★. **Bar** Wine and beer. **Dress** Casual. **Hours** Monday–Friday, 11 a.m.–10 p.m.; Saturday–Sunday, noon–10 p.m.

SETTING AND ATMOSPHERE The classic tacky Italian decor (think faux grapevines, funky murals, and Chianti-bottle candleholders) was renovated by celebrity chef Gordon Ramsay for an episode of *Kitchen Nightmares* and replaced by a trendy postage-stamp motif, but the generally good food and warm and friendly service are still the same.

HOUSE SPECIALTIES Better-than-average hand-tossed pizzas with all the familiar toppings (pepperoni, mushroom, sausage, and such); a very tasty (and hearty) eggplant Sorrentino.

OTHER RECOMMENDATIONS The pastas, including a superb spaghetti Bolognese, are commendable.

SUMMARY AND COMMENTS When the pocketbook can't take another huge hit no matter how good the menu looks, head to Luigi's. Old-fashioned Italian fare, a welcoming ambience, and friendly smiles await. The pizzas and pastas, Italian staples, are all familiar, hearty, and tasty, if not overly generous in their portions. The kids will love watching the pizzas get tossed, and your credit card will breathe a sigh of relief.

Mas' Chinese Islamic Restaurant ★★★½

NORTHERN CHINESE   MODERATE   QUALITY ★★★   VALUE ★★★½

601 E. Orangethorpe Ave., Anaheim; ☎ 714-446-9553; masislamic.com

Reservations Recommended. **When to go** Lunch or dinner. **Entrée range** $10–$24. **Service** ★★★. **Friendliness** ★★★½. **Dress** Casual but modest (no shorts). **Hours** Monday–Thursday, 11 a.m.–3 p.m. and 5–9:30 p.m.; Friday–Sunday, 11 a.m.–3 p.m. and 5–10 p.m.

SETTING AND ATMOSPHERE One of a small chain of Islamic Chinese restaurants, this is the real deal. Mas' Islamic's dining room is spacious, with comfortable booths and large tables. The decor blends Middle Eastern and Chinese motifs with lots of tile, repetitive patterned mosaics, and lofty arches.

HOUSE SPECIALTIES Get the thick sesame bread with green onions as a starter. Any lamb dish is a sure bet, especially the one served with *sha cha,* a spicy brown sauce.

OTHER RECOMMENDATIONS The warm pots—northern-Chinese stews—are great, as is the beef with green onions.

SUMMARY AND COMMENTS This is a veritable institution among local Muslims (Arabs and East and Southeast Asians), so expect to see women in veils and burkas and men dressed very conservatively; also, note that no alcohol is served. Service is gracious, if a bit English-challenged. Stick to the northern-Chinese specialties—the more familiar Chinese side of the menu is less exciting.

McCormick & Schmick's Grille ★★★

SEAFOOD   MODERATE-EXPENSIVE   QUALITY ★★★   VALUE ★★★

321 W. Katella Ave., Anaheim GardenWalk; ☎ 714-535-9000; mccormickandschmicks.com

Reservations Recommended. **When to go** Lunch or dinner. **Entrée range** $18–$47. **Service** ★★★. **Friendliness** ★★★★. **Bar** Full bar and extensive wine list. **Dress** Business casual. **Hours** Sunday–Thursday, 11:30 a.m.–10 p.m.; Friday–Saturday, 11:30 a.m.–11 p.m.

SETTING AND ATMOSPHERE This large chain of seafood eateries designs each of its units differently to match its local surroundings. In addition to lots of dark hardwoods and spacious booths, the decor here takes its cues from the rich agricultural history of the area.

HOUSE SPECIALTIES The fish is fresh and infinitely variable. The menu changes daily, and each chef is free to choose from among 80 different preparations. You can't miss with king crab, lobster, salmon, or killer fresh swordfish.

SUMMARY AND COMMENTS This is a very popular spot with local business types, and waits without reservations can be long. The menu can be overwhelming; on the other hand, there's something for everyone, even folks who don't eat fish. Happy hour specials (daily, 4–7 p.m.) somewhat soften the sting of expensive entrées; the $7 steamed mussels are an especially good deal.

Morton's ★★★★

STEAK HOUSE   EXPENSIVE   QUALITY ★★★½   VALUE ★★★½

1895 S. Harbor Blvd., Anaheim; ☎ 714-621-0101; mortons.com

Reservations Recommended. **When to go** Dinner. **Entrée range** $24–$88. **Service** ★★★★. **Friendliness** ★★★★. **Bar** Extensive wine list and full bar. **Dress** Dressy casual. **Hours** Monday–Saturday, 5:30–11 p.m.; Sunday, 5–10 p.m.

SETTING AND ATMOSPHERE Classic steak house with overstuffed booths, soft lighting, and dark hardwoods.

HOUSE SPECIALTIES Try the center-cut filet mignon Oscar-style (with lump crab, asparagus, and béarnaise sauce).

OTHER RECOMMENDATIONS The bone-in rib eye is a Chicago staple and beefeater's dream: 22 ounces of prime steak, grilled to order.

SUMMARY AND COMMENTS Morton's is a carnivore's delight—beef, lamb, and chicken dominate the menu. Of course, there's a smattering of fish options, including shrimp in several different iterations, but this place is really about the beef.

Park Ave Steaks & Chops ★★★★½

STEAK HOUSE   EXPENSIVE   QUALITY ★★★★   VALUE ★★★★

11200 Beach Blvd., Stanton; ☎ 714-901-4400; parkavedining.com

Reservations Recommended. **When to go** Dinner. **Entrée range** $14–$50. **Service** ★★★. **Friendliness** ★★★½. **Bar** Full bar. **Dress** Dressy casual/business. **Hours** Tuesday–Friday, 11 a.m.–midnight; Saturday–Sunday, 4 p.m.–midnight.

SETTING AND ATMOSPHERE From the flagstone walls and Sputnik-like lighting to red leather booths, this place exudes 1950s modern chic. There's also an expansive terrace and meticulously maintained grounds, where the chef grows his own herbs, vegetables, and fruit.

HOUSE SPECIALTIES Bone-in rib eye and the five-spiced baked salmon drizzled with honey mustard.

OTHER RECOMMENDATIONS The chef does a marvelous job with a salad featuring marinated skirt steak, dripping with a ginger, molasses, and soy sauce.

SUMMARY AND COMMENTS Park Ave is a throwback to all things mid-20th century—except the menu. The proprietors have managed to avoid the kitsch and concentrate on those things that evoke a simpler, less complicated era—down to a friendly bar shaking up some of the meanest martinis in Orange County. The food is exceptionally good (award winning), but service gets a little sloppy, especially on slower nights. A more casual garden restaurant on the same grounds offers a compact menu of Italian classics.

Prime Cut Café & Wine Bar ★★★

STEAK HOUSE   MODERATE-EXPENSIVE   QUALITY ★★★   VALUE ★★★½

1547 W. Katella Ave. (Stadium Promenade Center), Ste. 101, Orange;
☎ 714-532-4300; primecutcafe.com

Reservations Recommended. **When to go** Lunch or dinner. **Entrée range** $14–
$36. **Service** ★★★. **Friendliness** ★★★. **Bar** Wine and cocktails. **Dress** Casual.
Hours Sunday–Thursday, 11 a.m.–9:30 p.m.; Friday–Saturday, 11 a.m.–10:30 p.m.

SETTING AND ATMOSPHERE Polished but laid-back, this dapper café is a welcome independent in a sea of chain operations. A massive granite bar
anchors the attractive space that also offers a roomy patio overlooking
the center's water fountain.

HOUSE SPECIALTIES Slow-roasted prime rib is offered in two sizes, both part-
nered with good Yorkshire pudding. A huge pork chop is another winner,
paired with pistachios, butter-braised bacon, and apple cider reduction.

OTHER RECOMMENDATIONS Prime rib may hog the spotlight, but steaks, burgers, and entrée salads often outshine the showy star of the menu. Sides
such as potato gratin are scene-stealers, as are from-scratch desserts.

SUMMARY AND COMMENTS Prime Cut Café does a good job of making first-
rate dining affordable and approachable. Sixty-plus wines sold by the
glass or bottle is an attraction for wine lovers, though wine snobs might
find the list a bit lowbrow. The menu offers lots of appetizers and
snacks that pair well with wine, making this a great option for a quick
bite or grown-up get-together. The central location means that crowds
swell or recede according to events at nearby Anaheim Stadium, Honda
Center, or even what's hot at the adjacent multiplex cinema.

Roscoe's House of Chicken & Waffles ★★★★½

AMERICAN INEXPENSIVE   QUALITY ★★★★   VALUE ★★★½

2110 S. Harbor Blvd., Anaheim; ☎ 714-823-4130;
roscoeschickenandwaffles.com

Reservations Not accepted. **When to go** Anytime. **Entrée range** $5–$16. **Service**
★★★. **Friendliness** ★★★. **Dress** Casual. **Hours** Sunday–Thursday, 8 a.m.–11 p.m.;
Friday–Saturday, 8 a.m.–1 a.m.

SETTING AND ATMOSPHERE The outside is a plain, almost featureless, building surrounded by palm trees. The decorations inside are also sparse,
save for the occasional cheap painting or neon sign. Going on only
looks, you'll wonder why there's a huge line to get in, especially on
nights and weekends.

HOUSE SPECIALTIES It's right there in the name: chicken and waffles.

OTHER RECOMMENDATIONS We love the Jeanne Jones Omelette and the macaroni and cheese side dish.

SUMMARY AND COMMENTS Roscoe's is a longtime Los Angeles institution
that finally made its way to Orange County in 2014. Like all the other
locations, locals flock to Roscoe's for its delicious Southern-style comfort
food, including the signature chicken and waffles. While the fried chicken
is good, it may not be the best you'll ever have. But the waffles are excellent, and the macaroni and cheese is a must-try.

▌ SHOPPING *at* DISNEYLAND

SHOPS ADD REALISM AND ATMOSPHERE to the various theme settings and offer souvenirs, clothing, novelties, jewelry, decorator items, and more. Much of the merchandise displayed (with the exception of Disney trademark souvenir items), though, is available back home and elsewhere, so we recommend bypassing the shops on a one-day visit. If you have two or more days to spend at Disneyland Resort, browse in the early afternoon, when many attractions are crowded.

Our recommendations notwithstanding, we realize that for many guests, Disney souvenirs and memorabilia are irresistible. One of our readers writes:

People have a compelling need to buy Disney stuff at Disneyland. When you get home, you wonder why you ever got a cashmere sweater with Mickey Mouse embroidered on the breast, or a tie with tiny Goofys all over it. Maybe they put something in the food?

If you don't want to lug your packages around, you can leave them at the information stand just inside the front gate and pick them up as you exit the park. Retrieving your purchases might take a while if you depart after a parade or fireworks show or at closing, when guests exit en masse. If you're staying at a Disneyland Resort hotel, your loot will be delivered directly to your resort's bellhop desk (by 7 a.m. the following day) on request. If you have a problem with your purchases or need to make a return, call Disneyland Exclusive Merchandise at ☎ 800-760-3566, Monday–Friday, 8 a.m.–5 p.m. PST. If you return home and realize that you forgot to buy those Rastafarian mouse ears or some similarly essential tchotchke, a large selection of park-exclusive merchandise is available to order at **disneyparks.com/store.**

DOWNTOWN DISNEY

DOWNTOWN DISNEY, verdant and landscaped by day, pops alive with neon and glitter at night. The complex offers more than 300,000 square feet of specialty shopping, clubs, restaurants, and movie theaters. Many of the restaurants offer entertainment in addition to dining, including **Ralph Brennan's Jazz Kitchen.** The **ESPN Zone** is a sports bar and restaurant with dozens of giant TV screens. Other restaurant options include **Naples Ristorante e Pizzeria, Tortilla Jo's** Mexican restaurant, **Earl of Sandwich,** and jungle-themed dining at the **Rainforest Cafe.** An elegant **Starbucks,** across from the parking tram stop, serves all the chain's beverages and sandwiches (including beer and wine in the evenings) and offers free Wi-Fi, phone-charging stations, and full loyalty card benefits (though it doesn't accept Disney gift cards). Another Starbucks is across from the monorail station for Disneyland Hotel guests who need to fuel up before launching to Tomorrowland. By the end of 2017, Anaheim will open its own version of Orlando's popular **Splitsville Luxury Lanes,** an improbable but surprisingly successful mash-up of bowling alley and sushi bar.

Downtown Disney

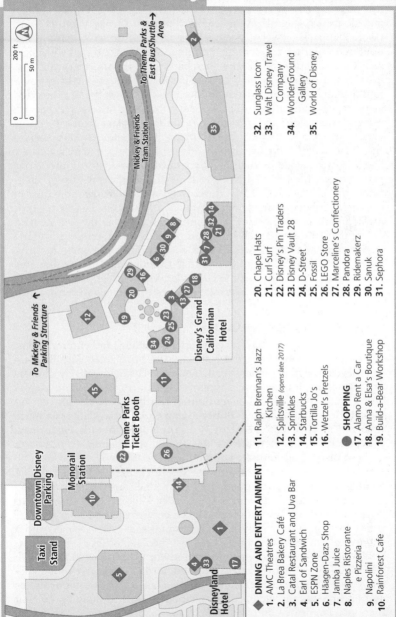

◆ **DINING AND ENTERTAINMENT**
1. AMC Theatres
2. La Brea Bakery Café
3. Catal Restaurant and Uva Bar
4. Earl of Sandwich
5. ESPN Zone
6. Häagen-Dazs Shop
7. Jamba Juice
8. Naples Ristorante e Pizzeria
9. Napolini
10. Rainforest Cafe
11. Ralph Brennan's Jazz Kitchen
12. Splitsville (opens late 2017)
13. Sprinkles
14. Starbucks
15. Tortilla Jo's
16. Wetzel's Pretzels

● **SHOPPING**
17. Alamo Rent a Car
18. Anna & Elsa's Boutique
19. Build-a-Bear Workshop
20. Chapel Hats
21. Curl Surf
22. Disney's Pin Traders
23. Disney Vault 28
24. D-Street
25. Fossil
26. LEGO Store
27. Marceline's Confectionery
28. Pandora
29. Ridemakerz
30. Sanuk
31. Sephora
32. Sunglass Icon
33. Walt Disney Travel Company
34. WonderGround Gallery
35. World of Disney

If you're not hungry, there's always shopping and a 12-theater **AMC Movieplex** with IMAX 3-D to keep you occupied. A 40,000-square-foot **World of Disney** store anchors the shopping scene. Other retailers include **Sanuk,** specializing in comfy flip-flops; **Disney Vault 28,** with fashion apparel, jewelry, handbags, and accessories; **Anna & Elsa's Boutique,** offering hairstyling, braiding, and princess makeovers, as well as a selection of *Frozen* merchandise; **Sephora,** featuring cosmetics; and **Pandora,** which carries jewelry. **D-Street** is where you'll find merchandise from Disney's films and TV shows that are targeted at teenagers and adults, such as Marvel or Star Wars. If expensive designer sunglasses are your thing, head to **Sunglass Icon** for a large variety of shades. For an artistic memento, **WonderGround Gallery** showcases edgy (and expensive) reinterpretations of classic Disney images, often signed by their creators. **LEGO Store** features interactive play tables with LEGO bricks and life-size statues of Disney characters made entirely of LEGOs. At **Build-A-Bear Workshop,** you can customize a teddy bear, starting from scratch with the bearskin, stuffing it, and then accessorizing it. In the same vein as Build-A-Bear, next door there's **Ridemakerz.** But instead of teddy bears, guests can build custom remote-control cars and trucks. During the winter months, look for a holiday village of treat and gift vendors and an extra-charge ice skating rink set up near the Disneyland Hotel.

Our map of Downtown Disney, listing storefronts and restaurants, appears on page 215.

ANAHEIM GARDENWALK

ANAHEIM GARDENWALK is a shopping, dining, and entertainment venue that stretches from West Katella Avenue to Disney Way. Built on three levels and nicely landscaped, the GardenWalk effectively doubles the restaurant, lounge, and shopping choices for Disneyland Resort visitors and attendees of conventions at nearby Anaheim Convention Center. Restaurants include **Bubba Gump Shrimp Co., California Pizza Kitchen, The Cheesecake Factory, House of Blues, Fire + Ice, McCormick & Schmick's Grille, McFadden's Restaurant and Saloon, P.F. Chang's Chinese Bistro,** and **Roy's Restaurant.**

For entertainment, there's an escape room game, a 41-lane bowling complex and nightspot combo, a 24-hour fitness center, a virtual reality arcade, and an ultra lounge. The GardenWalk has long struggled to retain tenants, and several plans the current owners had to resuscitate the venue—such as a Toby Keith restaurant that never opened and a giant escalator that was constructed but then demolished—have sputtered out. The complex's new hopeful savior is **House of Blues,** which relocated from Downtown Disney to the former UltraLuxe movie theater's space in early 2017. A handful of venues, such as **Lush Cosmetics** and an indoor family-entertainment center, are still hanging on, but there are far more shuttered storefronts than open ones, giving the entire venue a depressing *Dawn of the Dead* vibe. For additional information, see **anaheimgardenwalk.com** or call ☎ 714-635-7410.

PART FIVE

DISNEYLAND PARK

ARRIVING *and* GETTING ORIENTED

IF YOU DRIVE, you will probably be directed to the massive Mickey & Friends parking garage on West Street near Ball Road. Parking costs $20 for cars and motorcycles, $25 for RVs. Be sure to make a note of your section, row, and space. A tram will transport you to a loading/unloading area connected to the entrance by a pedestrian corridor. Many locals prefer to park in the Toy Story surface lot on Harbor Boulevard south of Katella Avenue, which offers shuttle service to the east side of the resort entrance Esplanade. Most pedestrians enter the resort from Harbor Boulevard to the east, passing though the bus drop-off area on their way to the ticket booths; on-site hotel guests approach from the west through Downtown Disney. All visitors must pass through security screenings before entering Downtown Disney or the Esplanade. The checkpoint lines can often be lengthy, and there's no bypass for guests without bags. When entering the resort from the east, the far-left security line is often the shortest; feel free to "excuse me" your way through the long queue of folks snaking toward a central checkpoint while you beeline for the briefer wait. Two entrance gates, 14 and 19, are blocked by trees situated in the entrance plaza about 10 feet from the security checkpoint. The trees sometimes inhibit the formation of a line in front of both the obstructed gates. Gates 14 and 19 are staffed nonetheless and draw guests from adjacent lines 13 or 15 and 18 or 20. When this happens, it significantly speeds up the entry process for guests waiting in lines 13 and 20. Our advice on arriving, therefore, is to inspect the lines leading to gates 14 and 19 and join whichever looks to be shortest. Later in the day, the outside gates (1 and 32) tend to be fastest for reentry. Stroller and wheelchair rentals are available in the Main Entrance Plaza between Disneyland and

Continued on page 220

Disneyland Park

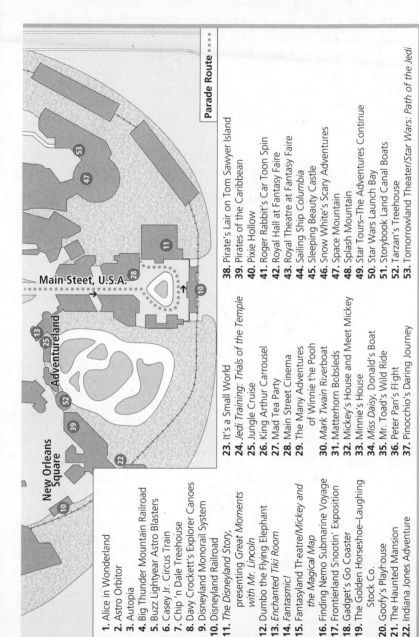

Parade Route ▪▪▪▪

New Orleans Square

Main Steet, U.S.A.

Adventureland

1. Alice in Wonderland
2. Astro Orbitor
3. Autopia
4. Big Thunder Mountain Railroad
5. Buzz Lightyear Astro Blasters
6. Casey Jr. Circus Train
7. Chip 'n Dale Treehouse
8. Davy Crockett's Explorer Canoes
9. Disneyland Monorail System
10. Disneyland Railroad
11. *The Disneyland Story,*
    presenting *Great Moments*
    with Mr. Lincoln
12. Dumbo the Flying Elephant
13. *Enchanted Tiki Room*
14. *Fantasmic!*
15. Fantasyland Theatre/*Mickey and*
    the Magical Map
16. Finding Nemo Submarine Voyage
17. Frontierland Snootin' Exposition
18. Gadget's Go Coaster
19. The Golden Horseshoe—Laughing
    Stock Co.
20. Goofy's Playhouse
21. The Haunted Mansion
22. Indiana Jones Adventure

23. It's a Small World
24. *Jedi Training: Trials of the Temple*
25. Jungle Cruise
26. King Arthur Carrousel
27. Mad Tea Party
28. Main Street Cinema
29. The Many Adventures
    of Winnie the Pooh
30. *Mark Twain Riverboat*
31. Matterhorn Bobsleds
32. Mickey's House and Meet Mickey
33. Minnie's House
34. *Miss Daisy,* Donald's Boat
35. Mr. Toad's Wild Ride
36. Peter Pan's Flight
37. Pinocchio's Daring Journey

38. Pirate's Lair on Tom Sawyer Island
39. Pirates of the Caribbean
40. Pixie Hollow
41. Roger Rabbit's Car Toon Spin
42. Royal Hall at Fantasy Faire
43. Royal Theatre at Fantasy Faire
44. Sailing Ship *Columbia*
45. Sleeping Beauty Castle
46. Snow White's Scary Adventures
47. Space Mountain
48. Splash Mountain
49. Star Tours—The Adventures Continue
50. Star Wars Launch Bay
51. Storybook Land Canal Boats
52. Tarzan's Treehouse
53. Tomorrowland Theater/*Star Wars: Path of the Jedi*

Continued from page 217

NOT TO BE MISSED AT DISNEYLAND PARK
ADVENTURELAND Indiana Jones Adventure
CRITTER COUNTRY Splash Mountain
FRONTIERLAND Big Thunder Mountain Railroad
NEW ORLEANS SQUARE The Haunted Mansion | Pirates of the Caribbean
TOMORROWLAND Space Mountain | Star Tours—The Adventures Continue
LIVE ENTERTAINMENT *Fantasmic!* | *Remember . . . Dreams Come True*

Disney California Adventure. As you enter Main Street, City Hall is to your left, serving as the center for general information, lost and found, and entertainment information.

To combat rampant resales of unexpired tickets, Disneyland Resort has implemented a policy of photographing all guests upon their first park entry. Have your ticket ready for scanning by a cast member just before you enter the turnstiles; if your mug isn't yet in Mickey's mainframe, you'll be asked to pose before proceeding. These added steps can sometimes slow the line at the start of the day, and there's no express lane for returning guests or Annual Pass holders. As long as this plan is imposed, we suggest that you arrive 5 minutes earlier than you otherwise would have, and bring extra patience.

Be sure to pick up a park map as you pass through the turnstiles. Maps are also available in the passages connecting the park entrance to Main Street, U.S.A.; at City Hall; and at a number of shops throughout the park. Also, pick up a *Times Guide*. This pamphlet contains the daily entertainment schedule for live shows, parades, fireworks, and other events and tells you where you can find the characters. If you are attending a special hard-ticket event (like the Halloween party), the daily entertainment schedule may be included in the park map. The park map lists all the attractions, shops, and eateries and provides helpful information about first aid, baby care, assistance for the disabled, and more.

Notice on your map that Main Street ends at a central hub from which branch the entrances to four other sections of Disneyland: **Adventureland, Frontierland, Fantasyland,** and **Tomorrowland.** Two other "lands," **New Orleans Square** and **Critter Country,** can be reached through Adventureland and Frontierland. **Mickey's Toontown** is located on the far side of the railroad tracks from It's a Small World in Fantasyland. **Sleeping Beauty Castle,** the entrance to Fantasyland, is a focal landmark and the visual center of the park. The castle is a great place to meet if your group decides to split up for any reason during the day, and it can serve as an emergency meeting place if you are accidentally separated. Keep in mind, however, that the castle covers a lot of territory, so be specific about *where* to meet at the castle. Also be forewarned that parades and live shows sometimes make it difficult to access the entrance of the castle fronting the central hub. Another good meeting

DISNEYLAND PARK SERVICES

Baby Care Center At the central-hub end of Main Street

Banking Services/Currency Exchange At City Hall at the railroad station end of Main Street

Disneyland and Local Attraction Information At City Hall

First Aid Two doors down from Plaza Inn at the central-hub end of Main Street

Live Entertainment and Parade Information At City Hall

Lost Adults and Messages At City Hall

Lost and Found Lost and Found for the entire resort is located west of the entrance to Disneyland Park

Lost Children At the central-hub end of Main Street

Storage Lockers Down Main Street one block (as you walk toward the castle) and to the right

spot is the *Partners* statue of Mickey and Walt in the central hub.

Ever since the Walt Disney Company acquired Lucasfilm in 2012 for the Death Star–size sum of $4 billion, fans of George Lucas's sci-fi saga have been salivating for a Disney theme park land dedicated to that galaxy far, far away. Disneyland broke ground in early 2016 on its most ambitious and expansive expansion ever, dedicating 14 acres of backstage areas to a new land called **Star Wars: Galaxy's Edge.**

No exact opening date has been announced, but Disney has promised that the project will be complete sometime in 2019. When finished, the new Star Wars land will be carefully concealed from the rest of the park by a mountainous berm built along the north edge of Frontier-land's rerouted Rivers of America. Guests will access the area either via two rocky tunnels branching off from Big Thunder Trail or along a forested path winding north from Critter Country, and discover an exotic Outer Rim spaceport on the fringe of the Galactic frontier. This never-before-seen, yet-unnamed planet incorporates design elements similar to iconic Star Wars locales such as Naboo, Yavin 4, Mos Eisley, and Maz Kanata's hideaway, without re-creating any single familiar setting. Massive attraction buildings reaching as high as 150 feet will be camouflaged by towering rockwork, lush landscaping, and alien architecture, creating a bustling bazaar of trading posts and cantinas teeming with extraterrestrial life.

Two headliner E-tickets will open with Star Wars: Galaxy's Edge. The first is a next-generation simulator where guests get to pilot Han Solo's legendary *Millennium Falcon,* which will feature a full-size replica in front of the attraction. The second signature attraction is a "battle escape" dark ride thrusting visitors into the middle of the war between the heroic Resistance and First Order Stormtroopers from the new Star Wars sequels.

Outside of the two major rides, each of which will sport elaborate scene-setting queues, look for Disney to develop unique Star Wars merchandise and edibles in an effort to match Universal's Harry Potter offerings; expect blue Bantha milk and Rey's self-baking bread to be top-selling menu items.

STARTING THE TOUR

EVERYONE WILL SOON FIND his or her own favorite and not-so-favorite attractions in Disneyland Park. Be open-minded and adventuresome. Don't dismiss a particular ride or show as not being for you until *after* you have tried it. Our personal experience as well as our research indicates that each visitor is different in terms of which Disney offerings he or she most enjoys. So don't miss seeing an attraction because a friend from home didn't like it; that attraction may turn out to be your favorite.

We do recommend that you take advantage of what Disney does best—the fantasy adventures such as Indiana Jones Adventure and The Haunted Mansion and the Audio-Animatronics (talking robots, that is) attractions such as Pirates of the Caribbean. Unless you have almost unlimited time, don't burn a lot of daylight browsing through the shops. Except for some special Disney souvenirs, you can find much of the same merchandise elsewhere. Try to minimize the time you spend on midway-type rides, as you probably have an amusement park, carnival, or state fair close to your hometown. Don't, however, mistake rides such as Splash Mountain and the Big Thunder Mountain Railroad for amusement park rides. They may be of the flume ride or roller coaster genre, but they represent pure Disney genius. Similarly, do not devote a lot of time to waiting in line for meals. Eat a good early breakfast before you come, snack on vendor-sold foods during the touring day, or follow the suggestions for meals incorporated into the various touring plans presented.

SINGLE-RIDER LINES

YOU CAN OFTEN SAVE TIME WAITING IN LINE by taking advantage of single-rider lines, a separate line for people who don't mind riding alone or with a stranger. The objective of single-rider lines is to fill odd spaces left by groups who don't quite fill the entire ride vehicle. Because there aren't many singles and most groups aren't willing to split up, single-rider lines are usually much shorter than the regular line. In Disneyland Park, Indiana Jones Adventure, Matterhorn Bobsleds, and Splash Mountain have single-rider lines. Ask an attraction employee how to enter the single-rider queue; you'll usually be given a paper pass and directed up the exit.

MAIN STREET, U.S.A.

THIS SECTION OF DISNEYLAND PARK is where you'll begin and end your visit. The Disneyland Railroad stops at the Main Street

Station, and you can board here for a grand circle tour of the park, or you can get off the train in New Orleans Square, Mickey's Toontown/ Fantasyland, or Tomorrowland.

Main Street is an idealized version of a turn-of-the-20th-century American small-town street. Many visitors are surprised to discover that all the buildings are real, not elaborate props. Attention to detail is exceptional—interiors, furnishings, and fixtures conform to the period. As with any real Main Street, the Disney version is essentially a collection of shops and eating places, with a city hall, a fire station, and an old-time cinema. A mixed-media attraction combines static exhibits recalling the life of Walt Disney with a patriotic remembrance of Abraham Lincoln. Horse-drawn trolleys, fire engines, and horseless carriages give rides along Main Street and transport visitors to the central hub.

Disneyland Railroad ★★★½

APPEAL BY AGE	PRESCHOOL ★★★★½	GRADE SCHOOL ★★★★	TEENS ★★★½
YOUNG ADULTS ★★★★½	OVER 30 ★★★★		SENIORS ★★★★½

What it is Scenic railroad ride around the park's perimeter; also transportation to New Orleans Square, Mickey's Toontown, Fantasyland, and Tomorrowland. **Scope and scale** Major attraction. **When to go** After 11 a.m. or when you need transportation. **Comments** The Main Street and Tomorrowland Stations are usually the least-congested boarding points. **Duration of ride** About 22 minutes for a complete circuit. **Average wait in line per 100 people ahead of you** 8 minutes; assumes 3 trains operating. **Loading speed** Fast.

Thumbs Up for the Whole Family

DESCRIPTION AND COMMENTS This transportation ride blends an eclectic variety of sights and experiences with an energy-saving way of getting around the park. In addition to providing a glimpse of all the lands except Adventureland, the train passes through the Grand Canyon Diorama (between Tomorrowland and Main Street), a three-dimensional replication of the canyon, complete with wildlife, as it appears from the southern rim. Another sight on the train circuit is Primeval World, a depiction of a prehistoric peat bog and rain forest populated by Audio-Animatronic (robotic) dinosaurs. Opened in 1966 Primeval World uses animatronics recycled from the Disney-designed Ford's Magic Skyway pavilion for the 1964 World's Fair, and it was a precursor to a similar presentation at Epcot's Universe of Energy.

In 2017 the train's path was shifted south over what was once a portion of the Rivers of America to accommodate the new Star Wars land. Passengers' views of the new land are blocked by a mountain range, complete with elevated train trestles and waterfalls that recall the park's original Nature's Wonderland.

TOURING TIPS Save the train ride until after you have seen the featured attractions, or use it when you need transportation. It can also be a helpful way to relax during the peak times of the day when the crowds are swelling. You can get a good estimate of how long you'll wait for the next train by using the posted wait time sign outside each station. It will either list 5 minutes (three trains operating), 10 minutes (two trains), or 20 minutes (only one train). If you have small children who are hell-bent on seeing Mickey first thing in the morning, you might consider taking the train to Mickey's Toontown (a half circuit) and visiting Mickey in his dressing room as soon as you enter the park (note that Toontown opens 1 hour later than the rest of the park). Many families find that this tactic puts the kids in a more receptive frame of mind for the other attractions. On busy days, lines form at the New Orleans Square and Mickey's Toontown/Fantasyland Stations but rarely at the Main Street or Tomorrowland Stations.

The Disneyland Story, presenting *Great Moments with Mr. Lincoln* ★★★½

| APPEAL BY AGE | PRESCHOOL ★★ | GRADE SCHOOL ★★★ | TEENS ★★★ |
| YOUNG ADULTS ★★★ | OVER 30 ★★★★ | | SENIORS ★★★½ |

What it is Nostalgic exhibits documenting the Disney success story followed by an Audio-Animatronics patriotic presentation. **Scope and scale** Minor attraction. **When to go** During the hot, crowded period of day. **Duration of show** 15 minutes including preshow of Disney exhibits. **Probable waiting time** Usually none.

Thumbs Up for the Whole Family

DESCRIPTION AND COMMENTS A warm and well-presented remembrance of the man who started it all. Well worth seeing, and especially touching for those old enough to remember Walt Disney himself. The attraction lobby consists of a museum of Disney memorabilia. Especially interesting are rotating Disney Gallery displays of concept artwork and historical artifacts, most recently featuring the railroads found in every Magic Kingdom around the world and Walt Disney's life-long passion for train travel. A short film starring comedian (and former Disneyland cast member) Steve Martin and Donald Duck screens in the lobby as a preshow. Beyond the Disney memorabilia, guests are admitted to a large theater where *Great Moments with Mr. Lincoln* is presented. The patriotic performance stars an extremely lifelike and sophisticated Audio-Animatronics Abraham Lincoln delivering an amalgamation of his notable speeches (though the over-familiar "Gettysburg Address" is not recited in full) as originally recorded by actor Royal Dano for the 1964 World's Fair. Lincoln's head is stunningly emotive, capable of wrinkling his brow and pursing his lips with unrivaled realism. Surround sound effects and songs borrowed from Epcot's *American Adventure* add to this brief but inspiring biography of America's 16th president.

TOURING TIPS You usually do not have to wait long for this show, so see it during the busy times of day when lines are long elsewhere or as you are leaving the park. Sit up close to best see the detail on the Lincoln figure, or sit a few rows back for a more comfortable view of the screen. For crowd-control reasons, *The Disneyland Story* shuts down during evening parades, a fact often not noted in the *Times Guide*.

Main Street Cinema ★★

| APPEAL BY AGE | PRESCHOOL ★★½ | GRADE SCHOOL ★★ | TEENS ★★ |
| YOUNG ADULTS ★½ | OVER 30 ★★ | | SENIORS ★★ |

What it is Vintage Disney cartoons. **Scope and scale** Diversion. **When to go** Whenever you want. **Comments** Wonderful selection of old-time flicks; audience stands.

Duration of show Runs continuously. **Probable waiting time** None.

DESCRIPTION AND COMMENTS An opening-day attraction, this small theater shows six classic Disney cartoons simultaneously. Early black-and-white Mickey Mouse shorts such as "Steamboat Willie" and "Plane Crazy" are screened, along with the celebrity caricature–stocked oddity "Mickey's Polo Team." The films are played at a low enough volume that the theater remains a quiet respite from the rest of the park.

TOURING TIPS Good place to get out of the sun or rain or to kill time while others in your group shop on Main Street. Fun, but not something you can't afford to miss. Audience stands.

Transportation Rides

DESCRIPTION AND COMMENTS Trolleys, buses, and the like add color to Main Street. One-way only.

TOURING TIPS The rides will save you a walk to the central hub. Not worth waiting in line. If you catch the first trolley of the morning, you may be serenaded onboard by the Dapper Dans.

ADVENTURELAND

ADVENTURELAND IS THE FIRST "LAND" to the left of Main Street and somehow manages to seamlessly combine South Pacific island, Middle Eastern bazaar, and African safari themes. Transitions from one part of Adventureland to another feel quite natural, and the identity crisis inherent in the mixed-theme cocktail never registers in the minds of most guests. Space is tight in Adventureland, however, making for some of the worst pedestrian congestion in any of the Disney theme parks. If you're just passing through Adventureland, say on your way to Splash Mountain, you can avoid the congestion by transiting Frontierland instead.

Enchanted Tiki Room ★★★½

| APPEAL BY AGE | PRESCHOOL ★★★★ | GRADE SCHOOL ★★★½ | TEENS ★★★½ |
| YOUNG ADULTS ★★★★ | OVER 30 ★★★½ | | SENIORS ★★★★½ |

What it is Audio-Animatronics Pacific island musical show. **Scope and scale** Minor attraction. **When to go** Anytime. **Duration of show** 14½ minutes plus preshow of talking totem poles. **Probable waiting time** 11 minutes.

  DESCRIPTION AND COMMENTS An unusual sit-down theater performance in which more than 200 birds, flowers, and tiki-god statues sing and whistle through a Polynesian-style musical program. One of Walt's first large-scale uses of Audio-Animatronics, *Tiki Room* might be more impressive for the technology it took to get the show (ahem) flying in 1963. Beloved by Disneyland fans for its detail and immersive setting, the current version of the show is only slightly altered from the original.

TOURING TIPS One of the most bizarre (yet endearing) of the Disneyland Park entertainments and rarely very crowded. We like it in the late afternoon, when we can especially appreciate sitting for a bit in an air-conditioned theater. Back row seats provide the broadest view with the least neck strain.

The Tiki Juice Bar that straddles the *Tiki Room* entrance dispenses Dole Whip, a delectable blend of pineapple slush and vanilla soft-serve ice cream, one of the park's most popular snacks. Dole sponsors the attraction, so you can enjoy your Tiki Juice Bar treats while watching the show. There are service windows both inside and outside the attraction's waiting area. The line inside is usually much shorter, though it may move slower than the one outside.

Indiana Jones Adventure *(FastPass)* ★★★★★

APPEAL BY AGE	PRESCHOOL ★½	GRADE SCHOOL ★★★★	TEENS ★★★★½
YOUNG ADULTS ★★★★★		OVER 30 ★★★★½	SENIORS ★★★★

What it is Motion-simulator dark ride. **Scope and scale** Super-headliner. **When to go** Before 9:30 a.m. or use FastPass. **Comments** Not to be missed. Must be 46" tall to ride; switching-off option provided (see page 154). **Duration of ride** 3½ minutes. **Average wait in line per 100 people ahead of you** 3 minutes; assumes full-capacity operation with 18-second dispatch interval. **Loading speed** Fast.

DESCRIPTION AND COMMENTS This is a combination track ride and motion simulator. In addition to moving along its path, the military troop–transport vehicle bucks and pitches (the simulator part) in sync with the visuals and special effects. Though the plot is complicated and not altogether clear, the bottom line is that if you look into the Forbidden Eye, you're in big trouble. The Forbidden Eye, of course, stands out like Rush Limbaugh in a diaper, and *everybody* stares at it. The rest of the ride consists of a mad race to escape the temple as it collapses around you. In the process, you encounter snakes, spiders, lava pits, rats, swinging bridges, and the house-size granite bowling ball that everyone remembers from *Raiders of the Lost Ark.*

The Indiana Jones ride is a Disney masterpiece—nonstop action from beginning to end with brilliant visual effects. Elaborate even by Disney standards, the attraction provides a level of detail and variety of action that make use of the entire Imagineering arsenal of high-tech gimmickry. In recent years, the ride was upgraded with dazzling digital projection effects that bring the Chamber of Destiny doors and idol to life.

Sophisticated in its electronic and computer applications, Indiana Jones purports to offer a different experience on each ride. According to the designers, there are veritable menus of special effects that the computer can mix and match. In practice, however, we could not see much difference from ride to ride. There are, no doubt, subtle variations, but the ride is so wild and frenetic that it's hard to apprehend subtlety.

The adventure begins in the queue, which sometimes extends out the entrance of the attraction and over the bridge leading to Adventureland! When you ultimately work your way into the attraction area, you find yourself at the site of an archaeology expedition with the Temple of the Forbidden Eye entrance beckoning only 50 feet away. After crossing a wooden bridge, you finally step into the temple. The good news is that you are out of the California sun. The bad news is that you have just entered Indiana Jones's indoor queuing area, a system of tunnels and passageways extending to within 50 yards of the Santa Monica Pier.

Fortunately, the queuing area is interesting. You wind through caves, down the interior corridors of the temple, and into subterranean rotundas where the archaeologists have been hard at work. Along the way there are various surprises (be sure to disregard any DO NOT TOUCH signs you see on supporting poles or safety ropes), as well as a succession of homilies etched in an "ancient" language on the temple walls. You will eventually stumble into a chamber where a short movie will explain the plot. From there it's back into the maze and finally on to the loading area.

TOURING TIPS Indiana Jones stays fairly mobbed all day. Try to ride during the first hour the park is open or use FastPass. Another alternative, if you don't mind riding alone, is to take advantage of the single-rider line, where the wait is generally about one-third that of guests in the regular queue. Be forewarned that the single-rider line at Indiana Jones is a bit of a maze, requiring you to negotiate your way up the exit ramp, up one elevator, across a walkway over the track, and then down another elevator to the loading area.

During the first hour or so the park is open, Indiana Jones cast members often employ a line-management technique known as stacking. Simply stated, they allow the line for Indiana Jones to form outside the attraction, leaving the cavernous inside queuing area virtually empty. Guests, of course, assume that the attraction is packed to the gills and that the outside line is overflow. Naturally, this discourages guests from getting in line. The reality is that the wait is not nearly as bad as it looks, and that it is probably as short as it will be all day. If you arrive in the park early and the Indiana Jones line appears huge, have the rest of your party get in line while you enter Indiana Jones *through the attraction exit* and check out the inside queue. If it is empty or sparsely populated, stacking is being practiced. Join your party in line and enjoy the attraction; your wait will be comparatively short. If the inside queue is bumper to bumper, try Indiana Jones later or use FastPass or the single-rider line. Stacking is also sometimes practiced during the hour just before the park closes.

Because it is high-tech, the ride breaks down a lot. The Disney people will announce that the ride is broken but usually will not estimate how long repairs will take. From our experience, most glitches are resolved in approximately 15–30 minutes, and probably the best advice is to stick it out.

If you miss Indiana Jones in the early morning and the FastPasses are all gone, use the single-rider line or try again during a parade or *Fantasmic!*, or during the hour before the park closes. Regarding the latter, the Disney folks will usually admit to the attraction anyone in line at closing time. During one visit to Indiana Jones, Disneyland Park closed at 8 p.m. We hopped in the line for Indiana Jones at 7:45 p.m. and actually got on the ride at 8:30 p.m.

Though the Indiana Jones ride is wild and jerky, the motion has been somewhat toned down since its debut, and it is primarily distinguished by its visual impact and realistic special effects. Thus, we encourage the over-50 crowd to give it a chance: we think you'll like it. As for children, most find the ride extremely intense and action-packed but not particularly frightening. We encountered very few children who met the 46-inch minimum-height requirement who were in any way intimidated.

Jungle Cruise ★★★

What it is A Disney outdoor-adventure boat ride. **Scope and scale** Major attraction. **When to go** Before 10 a.m. or after 6 p.m. **Comment** A Disney standard. **Duration of ride** 7½ minutes. **Average wait in line per 100 people ahead of you** 3½ minutes; assumes 10 boats operating. **Loading speed** Moderate–slow.

Thumbs Up for the Whole Family

DESCRIPTION AND COMMENTS On this boat ride through jungle waterways, passengers encounter elephants, lions, hostile natives, and a menacing hippo. It's a long-enduring Disney favorite with the boatman's spiel adding measurably to the fun.

As more technologically advanced attractions have been added to the park over the years, the Jungle Cruise has, by comparison, lost some of its luster. Though still a good attraction, it offers few thrills and no surprises for Disneyland Park veterans, many of whom can rattle off the ride's narration right along with the guide. For park first-timers, however, the Jungle Cruise continues to delight.

A Jingle Cruise holiday makeover runs early November–early January. The seasonal attraction features holiday-themed jokes in the skipper's script, a few holiday items in the queue and around the attraction, and substantially longer waits, as this Anacortes, Washington, family found out:

Jungle Cruise's line can be insanity-inducing long (as in the case of the Jingle Cruise). If the line goes upstairs, expect a very long wait through the grandfather of switchback queues. Nearly every time you expect the queue to turn around back to the ride, it continues into another room.

TOURING TIPS This ride loads slowly, and long lines form as the park fills. To compound problems, guests exiting Indiana Jones tend to head for the Jungle Cruise. Go early, or during a parade or *Fantasmic!* Be forewarned that the Jungle Cruise has an especially deceptive line: just when you think that you are about to board, you are shunted into yet another queuing maze (not visible outside the ride). Regardless of how short the line *looks* when you approach the Jungle Cruise, inquire about the length of the wait—at least you will know what you are getting into. If the second floor of the queue building is in use, you're in for at least a 20-minute wait. When the queue splits before the loading dock, the left lane is often quicker. Finally, many readers consider the Jungle Cruise much better at night. If the Jungle Cruise is closed for refurbishment during your visit, the "Skipper School" and "Land Tour" comedy skits that cast members perform in front of the construction walls are nearly as entertaining as the actual ride (without any waiting required).

Tarzan's Treehouse ★★★

What it is Walk-through tree house exhibit. **Scope and scale** Minor attraction. **When to go** Anytime. **Comments** Requires climbing a lot of stairs; a very creative exhibit. **Duration of tour** 8–12 minutes. **Average wait in line per 100 people ahead of you** 7 minutes.

DESCRIPTION AND COMMENTS Inspired by Disney's 1999 animated film *Tar-

zan, Tarzan's Treehouse replaced the venerable Swiss Family Treehouse that had been an Adventureland icon for 37 years. To enter the attraction, you climb a rustic staircase and cross a suspension bridge. From there, as they say, it's all downhill. Pages from Jane's sketchbook scattered

Thumbs Up for the Whole Family

about tell the story of Tarzan and provide insights into the various rooms and levels of the tree house. At the base of the tree is an interactive play area.

TOURING TIPS This self-guided, walk-through tour involves a lot of climbing up and down stairs but with no ropes or ladders or anything fancy. People who stop during the walk-through to look extra-long or to rest sometimes create bottlenecks that slow crowd flow. We recommend visiting this attraction in the late afternoon or early evening if you are on a one-day tour schedule.

NEW ORLEANS SQUARE

ACCESSIBLE VIA ADVENTURELAND AND FRONTIERLAND, New Orleans Square is one of three "lands" that don't emanate from the central hub. The architecture and setting are Caribbean Colonial, like New Orleans itself, with exceptional attention to detail.

Disneyland Railroad

DESCRIPTION AND COMMENTS The Disneyland Railroad stops in New Orleans Square on its circle tour around the park. See the description on page 223 for additional details regarding the sights en route. This is a pleasant and feet-saving way to commute to Mickey's Toontown/Fantasyland, Tomorrowland, or Main Street. Be advised, however, that the New Orleans Square Station is usually the most congested.

The Haunted Mansion *(FastPass)* ★★★★

APPEAL BY AGE	PRESCHOOL ★★½	GRADE SCHOOL ★★★★	TEENS ★★★★½
YOUNG ADULTS ★★★★½		OVER 30 ★★★★½	SENIORS ★★★★½

What it is Indoor haunted-house ride. **Scope and scale** Major attraction. **When to go** Before 11:30 a.m. or after 6:30 p.m. **Comments** Not to be missed; some of Disneyland's best special effects. Frightens some small children. **Duration of ride** 5½-minute ride plus a 2-minute preshow. **Average wait in line per 100 people ahead of you** 2½ minutes; assumes both "stretch rooms" operating. **Loading speed** Fast.

Dark   Scary

DESCRIPTION AND COMMENTS The Haunted Mansion is a fun attraction more than it is a scary one. An ingenious preshow serves as a vehicle to deliver guests to the ride's boarding area, where they board "doom buggies" for a ride through the mansion's parlor, dining room, library, halls, and attic before descending to an uncommonly active graveyard. Disney employs almost every special effect in its repertoire in The Haunted Mansion, making it one of the most inventive and different of all Disney attractions. Be warned that some youngsters build a lot of anxiety concerning what they think they will see. The actual attraction scares almost nobody. Though this mansion is the original, the ride is somewhat shorter and lacks the interactive queue and some high-tech upgrades that the Walt Disney World version has; however, Disneyland does have the infamous Hat Box Ghost, an impressive new animatronic that "rematerialized" in the mansion's attic in 2015, nearly 45 years after appearing briefly during the attraction's opening days and sparking generations of urban legends. The reimagined figure employs digital projection trickery to make his leering skull vanish from his shoulders and reappear hanging from his outstretched hand, adding an effectively eerie punctuation to the ride's second act.

The Haunted Mansion is one of veteran Unofficial Guide writer Eve Zibart's favorite attractions. She warns:

Don't let the childishness of the old-fashioned Haunted Mansion put you off: this is one of the best attractions in the park. It's jam-packed with visual puns, special effects, hidden Mickeys, and really lovely Victorian-spooky sets. It's not scary, except in the sweetest of ways, but it will remind you of the days before ghost stories gave way to slasher flicks.

Each September, The Haunted Mansion substitutes a special holiday version of the attraction that runs through early January. Inspired by Tim Burton's 1993 stop-motion musical *The Nightmare Before Christmas,* the overlay features characters such as Jack Skellington and Oogie Boogie cavorting among the familiar mansion haunts to songs from Danny Elfman's classic score. *Note:* The attraction closes for several weeks before and after the holiday season to install and remove the overlay.

TOURING TIPS This attraction would be more at home in Fantasyland, but no matter—it's Disney at its best: another not-to-be-missed attraction. Because The Haunted Mansion is in an especially high-traffic corridor (between Pirates of the Caribbean and Splash Mountain), it stays busy all day. Try to see The Haunted Mansion before 11:30 a.m., after 6:30 p.m., or during a parade. In the evening, crowds for *Fantasmic!* gather in front of The Haunted Mansion, making it very difficult to access. FastPass is now offered year-round for The Haunted Mansion but is usually only necessary for the holiday version of this attraction, which is very popular and draws quite a queue.

Pirates of the Caribbean ★★★★★

| APPEAL BY AGE | PRESCHOOL ★★★½ | GRADE SCHOOL ★★★★½ | TEENS ★★★★½ |
| YOUNG ADULTS ★★★★½ | OVER 30 ★★★★½ | | SENIORS ★★★★★ |

What it is A Disney indoor-adventure boat ride. **Scope and scale** Major attraction. **When to go** Before 11:30 a.m. or after 4:30 p.m. **Comments** Our pick as one of Disneyland's very best. Frightens some small children. **Duration of ride** Approximately 14 minutes. **Average wait in line per 100 people ahead of you** 3 minutes; assumes 42 boats operating. **Loading speed** Fast.

Dark   Loud   Scary

DESCRIPTION AND COMMENTS Another boat ride, this time indoors, Pirates of the Caribbean takes you through a series of sets depicting a pirate raid on an island settlement, from the bombardment of the fortress to the debauchery that follows the victory. The attraction includes characters Jack Sparrow and Barbossa in animatronic form, as well as a high-tech mist projection of Davy Jones, from the Pirates of the Caribbean movies.

TOURING TIPS Another not-to-be-missed attraction. Undoubtedly one of the most elaborate and imaginative attractions in Disneyland Park. Though engineered to move large crowds, this ride sometimes gets overwhelmingly busy in the early and midafternoon. Try to ride before noon or while a parade or *Fantasmic!* is in progress. If you have only experienced the Walt Disney World version of Pirates, don't bypass Disneyland's version thinking that it's more of the same: the original ride is far longer, more detailed, and better maintained than its Floridian cousin.

CRITTER COUNTRY

CRITTER COUNTRY, situated at the end of a cul-de-sac and accessible via New Orleans Square, sports a pioneer appearance not unlike that of Frontierland.

Davy Crockett's Explorer Canoes *(seasonal)* ★★★

| APPEAL BY AGE | PRESCHOOL ★★ | GRADE SCHOOL ★★★½ | TEENS ★★★★½ |
| YOUNG ADULTS ★ | | OVER 30 ★★½ | SENIORS ★ |

What it is Scenic canoe ride. **Scope and scale** Minor attraction. **When to go** As soon as it opens, usually 11 a.m. **Comments** Skip if the lines are long; closes at sunset. Most fun way to see Rivers of America. **Duration of ride** 8–10 minutes, depending on how fast you paddle. **Average wait in line per 100 people ahead of you** 12½ minutes; assumes 6 canoes operating. **Loading speed** Slow.

DESCRIPTION AND COMMENTS This paddle-powered ride around Tom Sawyer Island and Fort Wilderness runs the same route with the same sights as the steamboat and sailing ship. The canoes operate only on busier days and close at sunset. The sights are fun and the ride is a little different in that the patrons paddle the canoe. Those with tender rotator cuffs be warned: the trip can give your shoulders quite a workout, unless you slack off and let your fellow passengers handle the hard rowing. Long lines from about 11 a.m. on reflect the popularity of this attraction.

TOURING TIPS The canoes represent one of three ways to see the same waterways. Because the canoes are slower in loading, we usually opt for the larger steamboat or sailing ship. If you're not up for a boat ride, a different view of the same sights can be had by hoofing around Tom Sawyer Island. Try to ride at 11 a.m. or shortly thereafter. The canoes operate on selected days and seasonal periods only. If the canoes are a big deal to you, call ahead to make sure that they are operating.

The Many Adventures of Winnie the Pooh ★★★½

| APPEAL BY AGE | PRESCHOOL ★★★★½ | GRADE SCHOOL ★★★½ | TEENS ★★★ |
| YOUNG ADULTS ★★★½ | | OVER 30 ★★★½ | SENIORS ★★★★ |

Thumbs Up for the Whole Family

What it is Indoor track ride. **Scope and scale** Minor attraction. **When to go** Before 11 a.m. or the late afternoon or evening. **Duration of ride** About 3 minutes. **Average wait in line per 100 people ahead of you** 5 minutes; assumes normal staffing. **Loading speed** Moderate.

DESCRIPTION AND COMMENTS Pooh is sunny, upbeat, and fun—more in the image of Peter Pan's Flight or Splash Mountain. You ride a "hunny pot" through the pages of a huge picture book into the Hundred Acre Wood, where you encounter Pooh, Eeyore, Owl, Rabbit, Tigger, Kanga, Roo, and Piglet too as they contend with a blustery day. There's even a dream sequence with Heffalumps and Woozles, a favorite of this 30-something couple from Lexington, Massachusetts, who think Pooh has plenty to offer adults:

The attention to detail and special effects make this ride worth seeing even if you don't have children in your party. The Pooh dream sequence was great!

TOURING TIPS Though well done, The Many Adventures of Winnie the Pooh is not wildly popular. The wait is rarely more than 15 minutes and is typically less than 5. The only exceptions are on supercrowded days or when Splash Mountain is temporarily closed, which then causes crowds to swarm Winnie the Pooh.

Splash Mountain *(FastPass)* ★★★★½

| APPEAL BY AGE | PRESCHOOL ★★★½ † | GRADE SCHOOL ★★★★½ | TEENS ★★★★★ |
| YOUNG ADULTS ★★★★½ | | OVER 30 ★★★★½ | SENIORS ★★★★ |

†*Many preschoolers are too short to meet the height requirement, while others are intimidated by watching the ride while standing in line. Of those preschoolers who actually ride, most give the attraction high marks.*

What it is Water-flume adventure boat ride. **Scope and scale** Headliner. **When to go** Before 9:45 a.m. or use FastPass. **Comments** A wet winner, not to be missed. Must be 40" tall to ride; those age 7 or younger must ride with an adult; switching-off option provided (see page 154). **Duration of ride** About 10 minutes. **Average wait in line per 100 people ahead of you** 3½ minutes; assumes full-capacity operation. **Loading speed** Moderate.

Scary   Lose Things   Queasy   Muss Your 'Do

DESCRIPTION AND COMMENTS Splash Mountain is a Disney-style amusement park flume ride. The ride combines steep chutes with a variety of Disney's best special effects. Covering more than 0.5 mile, the ride splashes through swamps, caves, and backwoods bayous before climaxing in a 52-foot plunge and Br'er Rabbit's triumphant return home. The entire ride is populated by more than 100 Audio-Animatronics, including Br'er Rabbit, Br'er Bear, and Br'er Fox, all regaling riders with songs, including "Zip-A-Dee-Doo-Dah."

TOURING TIPS This is the most popular ride in Disneyland Park for patrons of all ages—happy, exciting, and adventuresome all at once. Though eclipsed somewhat by newer attractions, Splash Mountain nevertheless builds crowds quickly during the morning, and waits of more than 70 minutes are not uncommon once Disneyland Park fills up on a busy day. Lines persist throughout the day until a few minutes before closing. These words are particularly true on hotter days, as weather affects the wait times significantly.

There are five ways to experience Splash Mountain without a long wait. The first is to be on hand when the park opens and to sprint over and get in line before anyone else. The second way is to allow the initial mob of Splash cadets to be processed through and to arrive at Splash Mountain about

20–40 minutes after the park opens or after riding Peter Pan's Flight and/ or Space Mountain. A third strategy is to get in line for Splash Mountain during a parade and/or a performance of *Fantasmic!* Be advised, however, that huge crowds gathering along the New Orleans Square and Frontierland waterfronts for *Fantasmic!* make getting to Splash Mountain very difficult (if not impossible) just before, during, and just after performances. Fourth, use FastPass, and fifth, use the single-rider line by entering through the exit.

A Disneyland veteran from Layton, Utah, offers this suggestion:

Use FastPass to experience Splash. This lets you visit non-FastPass, slow-loading attractions in the golden early morning. Also, who wants to get wet first thing in the morning?

A Suffolk, Virginia, mom contends that there are more important considerations than beating crowds:

Definitely wait to do Splash Mountain at the end of the day. We were seated in the front of the ride, and we were drenched to the bone. If we had ridden first thing in the morning, I personally would have been miserable for the rest of the day. Parents, beware! It says you will get wet, not drowned.

It is almost a certainty that you will get wet, though probably not drenched, riding Splash Mountain. During the summer months, the water jets are cranked up to 11, practically guaranteeing that you'll get soaked. If you visit on a cool day, you may want to carry a plastic garbage bag. By tearing holes in the bottom and sides, you can fashion a sort of raincoat. Be sure to tuck the bag under your bottom. Though you can get splashed regardless of where you sit, riders in the front seat generally get the worst of it. If you have a camera, either leave it with a nonriding member of your party or wrap it in a plastic bag.

One final word: This is not just a fancy flume ride—it is a full-blown Disney adventure. The scariest part by far is the big drop into the pool (visible from the sidewalk in front of Splash Mountain), and even this plunge looks worse than it really is. Despite reassurances, however, many children wig out after watching it from the sidewalk. A Grand Rapids, Michigan, mother recalls her kids' rather unique reaction:

We discovered after the fact that our children thought they would go underwater after the five-story drop and tried to hold their breath throughout the ride in preparation. They were really too preoccupied to enjoy the clever Br'er Rabbit story.

◼️ FRONTIERLAND

FRONTIERLAND ADJOINS NEW ORLEANS SQUARE as you move clockwise around the theme park. The focus here is on the Old West, with log stockades and pioneer trappings. In 2016 Disney demolished Big Thunder Ranch, with its charming but underutilized petting zoo and barbecue restaurant, to build the anticipated Star Wars: Galaxy's Edge.

Big Thunder Mountain Railroad *(FastPass)* ★★★★

APPEAL BY AGE	PRESCHOOL ★★★	GRADE SCHOOL ★★★★½	TEENS ★★★★★
YOUNG ADULTS ★★★★★		OVER 30 ★★★★½	SENIORS ★★★★

What it is Tame roller coaster with exciting special effects. Scope and scale

Headliner. **When to go** Before 10:30 a.m., after 6:30 p.m., or use FastPass. **Comments** Great effects, though a relatively tame ride. Must be 40" tall to ride; those age 8 and younger must ride with an adult; switching-off option provided (see page 154). **Duration of ride** 3½ minutes. **Average wait in line per 100 people ahead of you** 3 minutes; assumes 5 trains operating. **Loading speed** Moderate-fast.

Scary — Lose Things — Queasy — Rough — Muss Your 'Do

DESCRIPTION AND COMMENTS A roller coaster through and around a Disney "mountain." The idea is that you're on a runaway mine train during gold rush days. Along with the usual thrills of a roller coaster (about a 5 on a "scary scale" of 10), the ride showcases some first-rate examples of Disney creativity: lifelike scenes depicting a mining town, colorful caverns, and a dynamite-chewing goat, all humorously animated.

In 2014 Disneyland replaced the aging track and trains and reconstructed the ramshackle Rainbow Ridge buildings, which dated to 1956. The track layout and vehicle stylings remain the same, but visitors appreciate the smoother ride and enhanced final lift hill, which supplanted the unconvincing old earthquake effects with an explosive fog-fueled finale.

TOURING TIPS A superb Disney experience but not too wild a roller coaster. The emphasis here is much more on the sights than on the thrill of the ride itself. Regardless, it's a not-to-be-missed attraction. Finally, give Big Thunder a try after dark. The lighting gives the attraction a whole new feel.

As an example of how differently guests experience Disney attractions, consider this letter from a reader in Brookline, Massachusetts:

As senior citizens with limited time, my friend and I confined our activities to those attractions rated as 4 or 5 stars for seniors. Because you listed it as not to be missed, we waited an hour to board Big Thunder Mountain Railroad, which you rated a 5 on a scary scale of 10. After living through 3½ minutes of pure terror, I rate that attraction a 15 on a scary scale of 10. We were so busy holding on and screaming and even praying for our safety that we did not see any falling rocks or a mining town. In our opinion it should not be recommended for seniors or preschool children.

A woman from New England discovered that there's more to consider about Big Thunder than being scared:

I won't say it warranted a higher scare rating, but it was much higher on the lose-your-lunch meter. One more sharp turn and the kids in front of me would have needed a dip in Splash Mountain!

DISNEY DISH WITH JIM HILL

DON'T FEEL BAAAH-D FOR BIG THUNDER RANCH'S OLD GOATS It's what every parent tells their kids when an overly rambunctious pet suddenly disappears from the house: they've gone to live on a farm. Well, that's actually what happened to all of the goats and burros that previously interacted with the public in Big Thunder Ranch's petting zoo. When this kid-friendly attraction closed in January 2016 to make way for Star Wars: Galaxy's Edge, all of the much-loved livestock was moved 60 miles away to Murrieta, California, where they joined four goats that had also previously worked at the theme park in their new forever home.

Frontierland Shootin' Exposition ★★

What it is Electronic shooting gallery. **Scope and scale**
Diversion. **When to go** Whenever convenient. **Com-**
ments Costs extra; a nifty shooting gallery.

Thumbs Up for the Whole Family

DESCRIPTION AND COMMENTS A very elaborate
electronic shooting gallery that costs $1 to
play. One of the few attractions in Disneyland
Park not included in the admission pass.

TOURING TIPS Good fun for those who like to shoot, but definitely not a
place to blow time if you are on a tight schedule. Try it on your second
day if time allows.

The Golden Horseshoe—Laughing Stock Co. ★★★

What it is Western dance hall with improvisation comedy show. **Scope and scale**
Minor attraction. **When to go** Catch a show and lunch at the same time; check the
Times Guide for schedule. **Comment** Zany show. **Duration of show** 12 minutes.

DESCRIPTION AND COMMENTS The Golden Horseshoe has always offered a
decent show, hearty snacks, and a nice air-conditioned respite from the
sun. Today, the stage originally headlined by Steve Martin's mentor Wally
Boag, and later Billy Hill and the Hillbillies (who currently perform at
nearby Knott's Berry Farm), is now commanded by the Laughing Stock
Co. comedy troupe.

    Each interactive, semi-improvised Laughing Stock Co. show is different
and includes a set of zany Wild West–style characters. A particular favorite of ours is "find a suitor," where three unsuspecting members of the
crowd are selected to answer questions from the Mayor of Frontierland's
less-than-handsome daughter (played by a man). It's an amusing diversion
when you want a break from big rides, but it isn't a must-see like some of
its predecessors.

TOURING TIPS The Golden Horseshoe has first-come, first-serve seating. We
recommend arriving 30 minutes early if you want to find a table and grab
some grub. Food service can be slow; look for the shortest of the open
service lines, usually on the far left. Absurdly oversize safety railings now
ruin sight lines from the balcony (curse you, OSHA!), so the best view is
from the floor, front and center, but Walt liked the opera box seats best.

Mark Twain Riverboat ★★★

What it is Scenic boat ride. **Scope and scale** Minor attraction. **When to go**
11 a.m.–5 p.m. **Comments** Provides an excellent vantage point. **Duration of ride**
About 14 minutes. **Average wait to board** 10 minutes; assumes normal operations.
Loading speed Fast—en masse.

DESCRIPTION AND COMMENTS This large-capacity paddle-wheel riverboat
navigates the waters around Tom Sawyer Island and Fort Wilderness. A
beautiful craft, the riverboat provides a lofty perch from which to see

Frontierland and New Orleans Square. The *Mark Twain,* Sailing Ship *Columbia,* and Davy Crockett's Explorer Canoes travel through the Rivers of America. The show scenes include a home for Mike Fink (and one of his keelboats, a former Disneyland attraction) and 26 Audio-Animatronic animals; the audio spiel includes a musical nod to the New Orleans–set *The Princess and the Frog.* The river's path was shortened to accommodate construction of the new land, Star Wars: Galaxy's Edge, as well as to provide an impressive new mountain range to admire as you steam by. The *Mark Twain*'s speed has been slowed accordingly, so your total travel time should remain about the same.

TOURING TIPS One of three boat rides that survey the same real estate. Because the Explorer Canoes are slower in loading and the *Columbia* operates seasonally, we think the riverboat makes more efficient use of touring time. If you're not in the mood for a boat ride, many of the same sights can be seen by hiking around Tom Sawyer Island. The riverboat typically operates until 75 minutes before the park closes, except on *Fantasmic!* performance nights, when the voyages end at 5:45 p.m. If you're looking for a new experience aboard the *Mark Twain,* try asking a cast member if you can enjoy the trip from the pilothouse.

Pirate's Lair on Tom Sawyer Island ★★★

APPEAL BY AGE PRESCHOOL ★★★★★ GRADE SCHOOL ★★★★ TEENS ★★★★
YOUNG ADULTS ★★★ OVER 30 ★★½ SENIORS ★★★

What it is Walk-through exhibit and rustic playground. **Scope and scale** Minor attraction. **When to go** Midmorning–late afternoon. **Comments** The place for rambunctious kids; closes at sunset. **Duration of experience** For the raft, a little more than 1 minute one way. As long as you want on the island. **Average wait in line per 100 people ahead of you** For raft, 4½ minutes; assumes 3 rafts operating. **Loading speed** For raft, moderate.

DESCRIPTION AND COMMENTS Pirate's Lair on Tom Sawyer Island manages to impart a sense of isolation from the rest of the park. It has hills to climb, tipsy bridges to cross, paths to follow, and a "rock-climbing" play area. It's a delight for adults but a godsend for children who have been in tow all day. The 2017 realignment of Rivers of America removed a sliver of the island's northern tip, and the tree house and fort are permanently off-limits, but for the most part, this is the same oasis that's been entertaining kids for more than 60 years.

As an aside, a mother of four from Duncan, South Carolina, found Tom Sawyer Island as much a refuge as an attraction, writing:

In the afternoon, when the crowds were at their peak, the weather was hottest, and the kids started lagging behind, our organization began to suffer. We then retreated over to Tom Sawyer Island, which proved to be a true haven. My husband and I found a secluded bench and regrouped. Meanwhile, the kids were able to run freely in the shade. Afterward, we were ready to tackle the park again refreshed and with direction once more.

The island has sets from the Pirates of the Caribbean films, such as William Turner's blacksmith shop, and story artifacts, such as Elizabeth

Swann's love letters, tucked into every nook and cranny. Kids exploring the caverns of Dead Man's Grotto will encounter spooky voices, ghostly apparitions, and buried treasure. Elsewhere, a sunken chest can be discovered by operating a hoist.

Evidently, you can't have a pirate's lair without a bunch of gore. A pop-up head and moving skeletal arm are just the beginning. There's also a "bone cage" and, our favorite, a treasure chest containing Davy Jones's beating heart. The Bootstrappers pirate band occasionally rides the rafts over to administer pirate oaths and lead sing-alongs, and Captain Jack Sparrow can sometimes be spotted stumbling along the island's shoreline.

TOURING TIPS Pirate's Lair on Tom Sawyer Island is not one of Disneyland Park's more celebrated attractions, but it's certainly one of the most well done. Attention to detail is excellent, and kids particularly revel in its adventuresome atmosphere. We think it's a must for families with children ages 5–15. If your party has only adults, visit the island on your second day, or stop by on your first day if you have seen the attractions you most wanted to see. We like the island from about noon until the island closes at sunset. Access is by raft from Frontierland, and you may have to stand in line to board both coming and going. Two or three rafts operate simultaneously, however, and the round-trip is usually pretty time efficient. Tom Sawyer Island takes about 30 minutes or so to see, but many children could spend a whole day there.

Sailing Ship *Columbia* *(seasonal)*   ★★★½

APPEAL BY AGE	PRESCHOOL ★★½	GRADE SCHOOL ★★★½	TEENS ★★★½
YOUNG ADULTS ★★★		OVER 30 ★★★★	SENIORS ★★★★

What it is Scenic boat ride. **Scope and scale** Minor attraction. **When to go** 11 a.m.–5 p.m. **Comments** Pirates on extremely busy days; a stunning piece of workmanship. **Duration of ride** About 14 minutes. **Average wait to board** 10 minutes; assumes normal operations. **Loading speed** Fast—en masse.

Thumbs Up for the Whole Family

DESCRIPTION AND COMMENTS The *Columbia* is a stunning replica of a three-masted 18th-century merchant ship. Both its above- and belowdecks are open to visitors, with belowdecks outfitted to depict the life and work environment of the ship's crew in 1787. The *Columbia* operates only on busier days and runs the same route as the canoes and the riverboat. As with the other rivercraft, the *Columbia* suspends operations at sunset.

TOURING TIPS The *Columbia,* along with the *Mark Twain* Riverboat, provides a short-wait, high-carrying-capacity alternative for cruising the Rivers of America. We found the beautifully crafted *Columbia* by far the most aesthetically pleasing and historically interesting of any of the three choices of boat rides on the Rivers of America. If you have time to be choosy, ride aboard the *Columbia.* After boarding, while waiting for the cruise to begin, tour below. Once the ride begins, come topside and stroll the deck, taking in the beauty and complexity of the rigging.

The *Columbia* does not usually require a long wait, which makes it a good bet during the crowded afternoon hours.

◀ FANTASYLAND

TRULY AN ENCHANTING PLACE, spread gracefully like a miniature alpine village beneath the towers of Sleeping Beauty Castle, Fantasyland is the heart of the park. Fantasyland is the backbone of the Magic Mornings early-entry program, with nine rides open. If your group consists of older kids and adults, ride Peter Pan's Flight first during the early-entry period, followed by Alice in Wonderland and Matterhorn Bobsleds. If you have younger children in your group, start with Peter Pan's Flight and Alice in Wonderland and then ride Dumbo. Certain Fantasyland attractions close for fireworks and may not reopen until the fire marshal gives the all clear, as this Calgary dad discovered:

> A significant number of Disneyland's Fantasyland attractions close before fireworks, and of these, some reopen several minutes later while others remain closed for the night. We arrived at Fantasyland immediately after the fireworks and found very little open.

Alice in Wonderland ★★★½

APPEAL BY AGE PRESCHOOL ★★★★	GRADE SCHOOL ★★★★	TEENS ★★★½
YOUNG ADULTS ★★★★	OVER 30 ★★★½	SENIORS ★★★★

What it is Track ride in the dark. **Scope and scale** Minor attraction. **When to go** Before 11 a.m. or after 5 p.m. **Comment** Good characterization and story line. **Duration of ride** Almost 4 minutes. **Average wait in line per 100 people ahead of you** 12 minutes; assumes 16 cars operating. **Loading speed** Slow.

Dark   Muss Your 'Do

DESCRIPTION AND COMMENTS This attraction recalls the story of *Alice in Wonderland* with some nice surprises and colorful effects. Guests ride nifty caterpillar cars in this Disney spook-house adaptation. Though not a spring chicken, Alice is a third-generation Disney dark ride with more vibrant, evocative, and three-dimensional sets and characters than Pinocchio's Daring Journey or Mr. Toad's Wild Ride. This is also the only two-story Disney dark ride with an outdoor section. In 2014 an extensive refurbishment brought the elevated outdoor track up to modern safety standards; advanced projection effects utilize original hand-drawn animation to bring the static sets to life, reinvigorating the ride without ruining its classic charm.

TOURING TIPS This is a well-done ride in the best Disney tradition, with familiar characters, good effects, and a theme you can follow—too bad it loads very slowly. Do not confuse it with the Mad Tea Party ride. This very popular attraction can build quite a lengthy line as the morning progresses, so we like to ride this as early in the day as possible, usually right after Peter Pan's Flight.

Bibbidi Bobbidi Boutique

This pricey beauty salon for little girls is located in Sleeping Beauty Castle. Here, Fairy Godmothers–in–training make would-be princesses look like prom queens (or vice versa). A range of packages is offered, including everything from hair styling and makeup to princess gowns and accessories (cha-ching). The top-of-the-line package includes skip-the-line VIP access to the nearby Royal Hall princess meet and greet, which may be worth its *wait* in gold. If you have the bucks, the girls love it. For reservations, call ☎ 714-781-7895 up to 60 days in advance. A Winston, Oregon, mom thinks highly of Bibbidi Bobbidi:

> *Bibbidi Bobbidi Boutique is a must if traveling with little girls. Our party had three girls ages 4, 4, and 6, and this was their favorite and most memorable event of the trip. Even though we traveled during the off-season, it was hectic and a little unorganized. We made reservations and still had to wait 30 minutes, but once the girls were matched with their Fairy Godmother–in-training, we were absolutely pleased with the service. It is a little spendy (I think around $60 for a princess hairdo, even more if you want the full service), but it was completely worth it. The hair survived the rest of the day and looked perfect when they put their princess gowns on at night for the fireworks.*

Casey Jr. Circus Train ★★½

APPEAL BY AGE PRESCHOOL ★★★★½ GRADE SCHOOL ★★★ TEENS ★★½
YOUNG ADULTS ★★★ OVER 30 ★★★ SENIORS ★★★

What it is Miniature train ride. **Scope and scale** Minor attraction. **When to go** Before 11 a.m. or after 5 p.m. **Comment** A quiet, scenic ride. **Duration of ride** A little under 4 minutes. **Average wait in line per 100 people ahead of you** 12 minutes; assumes 2 trains operating. **Loading speed** Slow.

DESCRIPTION AND COMMENTS A long-standing attraction and a pet project of Walt Disney, Casey Jr. circulates through a landscape of miniature towns, farms, and lakes. Visible from this ride are some stunning bonsai specimens, as well as some of the most manicured landscaping you are ever likely to see.

TOURING TIPS This ride covers the same sights as the Storybook Land Canal Boats but does it faster and with less of a wait. Accommodations for adults, however, are less than optimal on this ride, with some passengers having to squeeze into diminutive caged cars (after all, it is a circus train). If you do not have children in your party, you can enjoy the same sights more comfortably by riding the Storybook Land Canal Boats, which also benefit from live narration instead of Casey Jr.'s canned sound track.

A father of two toddlers from Menlo Park, California, explains that issues of redundancy were not uppermost in his children's minds.

> *Contrary to your advice, the Casey Jr. Circus Train and Storybook Land Canal Boats are totally different experiences—if you are 4 or younger. Hey, one is a boat, and one is a train! Seems obvious to the mind of a 4-year-old. We did both, and the kids loved both.*

Disneyland Railroad

DESCRIPTION AND COMMENTS The Disneyland Railroad stops in Fantasyland/Mickey's Toontown on its circuit around the park. The station is located to the left of It's a Small World, next to the Fantasyland Theatre. From this often-crowded boarding point, transportation is available to Tomorrowland, Main Street, and New Orleans Square. See the description on page 223 for additional details regarding the sights en route.

Dumbo the Flying Elephant ★★½

APPEAL BY AGE PRESCHOOL ★★★★★ GRADE SCHOOL ★★★★ TEENS ★★★½
YOUNG ADULTS ★★★½ OVER 30 ★★★½ SENIORS ★★★½

What it is Disneyfied midway ride. **Scope and scale** Minor attraction. **When to go** Before 10 a.m. or during late evening parades, fireworks, or *Fantasmic!* performances. **Duration of ride** 1⅔ minutes. **Average wait in line per 100 people ahead of you** 12 minutes; assumes normal staffing. **Loading speed** Slow.

DESCRIPTION AND COMMENTS A nice, tame, happy children's ride based on the lovable Disney flying elephant, this is an upgraded rendition of a ride that can be found at state fairs and amusement parks across the country. Shortcomings notwithstanding, Dumbo is the favorite Disneyland Park attraction of most preschoolers. A lot of readers take us to task for lumping Dumbo in with state-fair midway rides. These comments from a reader in Armdale, Nova Scotia, are representative:

I think you have acquired a jaded attitude. I know Dumbo is not for everybody, but when we took our oldest child (then just 4), the sign at the end of the line said there would be a 90-minute wait. He knew and he didn't care, and he and I stood in the hot afternoon sun for 90 blissful minutes waiting for his 90-second flight. Anything that a 4-year-old would wait for that long and that patiently must be pretty special.

TOURING TIPS This is a slow-loading ride that we recommend you bypass unless you are on a very relaxed touring schedule. If your kids are excited about Dumbo, try to get them on the ride before 10 a.m., during the parades or *Fantasmic!*, or just before the park closes. Also, consider this advice from an Arlington, Virginia, mom:

Grown-ups, beware! Dumbo is really a tight fit with one adult and two kids. My kids threw me out of their Dumbo, and I had to sit in a Dumbo all by myself. Pretty embarrassing, and my husband got lots of pictures.

Fantasyland Theatre / *Mickey and the Magical Map*   ★★★½

APPEAL BY AGE	PRESCHOOL ★★★★★	GRADE SCHOOL ★★★★½	TEENS ★★★½
YOUNG ADULTS ★★★★	OVER 30 ★★★★		SENIORS ★★★★½

What it is Musical stage show. **Scope and scale** Major attraction. **When to go** Check *Times Guide* for schedule; arrive at least 15 minutes before showtime for the best seats. **Duration of show** 22 minutes. **Probable waiting time** 15 minutes.

DESCRIPTION AND COMMENTS This venue is a sophisticated amphitheater where concerts and elaborate stage shows are performed according to the daily entertainment schedule. Better productions that have played here include *Beauty and the Beast Live, Snow White,* and *The Spirit of Pocahontas,* all musical stage adaptations of the respective Disney-animated features.

Mickey and the Magical Map involves apprentice Mickey's accidental adventure into sorcerer Yen Sid's mysterious dream-controlling map. This 22-minute musical adventure combines new songs and classic tunes in a score that skips from India to Hawaii, with a stopover under the sea. Rapunzel, Pocahontas, Mulan, King Louie, Sebastian, and Stitch are among the Disney icons who appear, along with a platoon of dancing paintpots and brushes, but the show is stolen by a mischievous animated paint splotch (brought to life through high-tech video effects).

The opening song is less than memorable, and the computer-generated animation of Yen Sid is disappointingly chunky, but on the whole this is among the park's more entertaining musical productions.

Live singing and energetic choreography influenced by drum corps enliven the somewhat overfamiliar songs, and a gospel-flavored riverboat finale (complete with streamers shot over the audience) brings down the house. Well worth watching once you've experienced the headliners, or on your second day at Disneyland.

TOURING TIPS Performance times are listed in the *Times Guide.* Arrive at least 15 minutes early for optimal seating. Though it's a stage show, the performances are complemented by three giant video screens, each of which spans almost the entire width of the stage, that form a raised platform on which much of the action takes place. For that reason, the best seats are the ones farther back and slightly raised, in the center of the theater. Avoid the seats up front or too far on the sides, where the images on the slanted screen will look distorted.

It's a Small World ★★★★

What it is World brotherhood–themed indoor boat ride. **Scope and scale** Major attraction. **When to go** Anytime except after a parade. **Duration of ride** 14 minutes. **Average wait in line per 100 people ahead of you** 2½ minutes; assumes busy conditions with 56 boats operating. **Loading speed** Fast.

Thumbs Up for the Whole Family

DESCRIPTION AND COMMENTS A happy and upbeat attraction with a world-brotherhood theme and a catchy tune that will stick in your head for weeks. Small boats convey visitors on a tour around the world, with singing and dancing dolls showcasing the dress and culture of each nation. Almost everyone enjoys It's a Small World (well, there are those jaded folks who are put off by the dolls' homogeneous appearance, especially in light of the diversity theme), but it stands, along with the *Enchanted Tiki Room*, as an attraction that some could take or leave but that others consider one of the real masterpieces of Disneyland Park. More than 20 Disney and Pixar characters have been integrated into the classic attraction; tastefully crafted in the style of original artist Mary Blair, the additions don't detract from the ride, except in the tacky U.S.A. tribute added to the end. A mom from Castleton, Vermont, commented:

It's a Small World was like a pit stop in The Twilight Zone. They were very slow unloading the boats, and we were stuck in a line of about six boats waiting to get out while the endless chanting of that song grated on my nerves. I told my husband that I was going to swim for it just to escape one more chorus.

A dad from New Brunswick, Canada, gives this advice for surviving the Happiest Cruise That Ever Sailed:

Ask to sit at the back of the boat. Pull out your iPod with earbuds once you're in the building, and blast some heavy metal. You'd be amazed how different and deceptively funny the ride becomes!

From November through New Year's, the attraction receives an annual holiday overlay inside the attraction as well as outside, featuring "Jingle Bells" and "Deck the Halls" instead of the usual earworm sound track. We particularly enjoy the light show and projection effects outside the attraction that happen every 15 minutes.

TOURING TIPS This fast-loading ride is usually a good bet during the busier times of the day. The boats are moved along by water pressure, which increases as boats are added. Thus, the more boats in service when you ride (up to a maximum total of 60), the shorter the duration of the ride (and wait). Small World is taken off-line in mid-October and reopened in November with a special Christmas holiday theme. Removal of the overlay also keeps the ride closed for several weeks after the holiday season. Two notes: While the loading can be very quick when many boats are running, the unloading can be very slow. Second, the attraction has two loading zones, one that has wheelchair access and one without. Unless you need wheelchair access, we recommend using the loading zone on the far side of the entrance by choosing the right side of the queue when it splits.

King Arthur Carrousel ★★★

APPEAL BY AGE   PRESCHOOL ★★★★½   GRADE SCHOOL ★★★★   TEENS ★★★½
YOUNG ADULTS ★★★½   OVER 30 ★★★½   SENIORS ★★★★

What it is Merry-go-round. **Scope and scale** Minor attraction. **When to go** Before 11:30 a.m. or after 5 p.m. **Comments** A showpiece carousel; adults enjoy the beauty and nostalgia of this ride. **Duration of ride** A little more than 2 minutes. **Average wait in line per 100 people ahead of you** 8 minutes; assumes normal staffing. **Loading speed** Slow.

DESCRIPTION AND COMMENTS A merry-go-round to be sure, but certainly one of the most elaborate and beautiful you will ever see, especially when lit at night. A white horse named Jingles (with bells all over) pays tribute to Julie Andrews and her iconic role in *Mary Poppins*. She's the horse closest to the handicapped ramp.

TOURING TIPS Unless you have small children in your party, we suggest that you appreciate this ride from the sidelines. If your children want to ride, try to get them on before 11:30 a.m. or after 5 p.m. While nice to look at, the carousel loads and unloads very slowly.

Mad Tea Party ★★

What it is Midway-type spinning ride. **Scope and scale** Minor attraction. **When to go** Before 11 a.m. or after 5 p.m. **Comments** You can make the teacups spin faster by turning the wheel in the center of the cup; fun but not worth the wait. **Duration of ride** 1½ minutes. **Average wait in line per 100 people ahead of you** 8 minutes; assumes normal staffing. **Loading speed** Slow.

Queasy · Muss Your 'Do

DESCRIPTION AND COMMENTS Well done in the Disney style, but still just an amusement park ride. *Alice in Wonderland*'s Mad Hatter provides the theme, and patrons whirl around feverishly in big teacups. A rendition of this ride, sans Disney characters, can be found at every local carnival and fair. Colorful LED lighting makes the ride especially attractive after dark.

TOURING TIPS This ride, besides not being particularly special, loads notoriously slowly. Skip it on a busy schedule if the kids will let you. Ride in the morning of your second day if your schedule is more relaxed. A warning for parents: teenagers like to lure adults onto the teacups and then turn the wheel in the middle (which makes the cup spin faster) until the adults are plastered against the side of the cup and on the verge of throwing up.

Matterhorn Bobsleds *(FastPass)* ★★★½

†*Some preschoolers love Matterhorn Bobsleds; others are frightened.*

What it is Roller coaster. **Scope and scale** Major attraction. **When to go** During the first 90 minutes the park is open or during the hour before it closes. **Comments** Fun ride but not too scary. Must be 42" tall to ride. **Duration of ride** 2½ minutes. **Average wait in line per 100 people ahead of you** 7 minutes; assumes both tracks operating with 10 sleds per track with 23-second dispatch intervals. **Loading speed** Moderate.

Scary · Lose Things · Queasy · Rough · Muss Your 'Do

DESCRIPTION AND COMMENTS The Matterhorn is the most distinctive landmark on the Disneyland scene, visible from almost anywhere in the park. Open since 1959, the Matterhorn maintains its popularity and long lines year in and year out. Matterhorn Bobsleds is a roller coaster with an alpine motif. On the scary scale, the ride ranks about 6 on a scale of 10. The special effects don't compare to Space Mountain's, but they do afford a few surprises. In 2012 the Matterhorn completed its first top-to-bottom overhaul since the 1970s, receiving rehabilitated tracks and a more-realistic exterior paint job; that was followed in 2015 by enhancements to the lighting and effects, including a more menacing appearance for the mysterious yeti. You first glimpse the yeti during the initial uphill climb as a menacing silhouette distorted by ice and then cruise past an ominous collection of old ride vehicles (including vintage bobsleds and an antique Skyway bucket) that the beast has hoarded. Finally, you'll come face-to-face with the furry legend not once but twice; the encounters are brief, but he moves with a fluid ferocity that his frozen cousin in WDW's Expedition Everest can only dream of. Added padding has made the ride marginally less murderous on tailbones, but the three-passenger cars with individual seats are unfriendly to the long-legged. Tall riders are advised to ask for the middle or back rows, which have marginally more room, and slide their feet forward into the snug footwells on either side of the seat ahead. For the short-limbed, the front seat is usually the smoothest. But be warned that, wherever you sit, this is the bumpiest coaster in Disneyland's inventory. A Richboro, Pennsylvania, dad disagrees with our scary rating of the Matterhorn:

My biggest disappointment was the Matterhorn. I understand it's iconic, but the notion that it could rate a 6 out of 10 on the scare factor is pure insanity. I'd rate it a 1! After the steep climb in the dark, you basically just go down in circles until you are left baffled that the "roller coaster" ride is over.

TOURING TIPS Lines for the Matterhorn form as soon as the gates open and persist throughout the day. Disneyland added FastPass to the Matterhorn in 2017 as part of the rollout of MaxPass, resulting in an even slower standby queue. The FastPass kiosks are located across from the ride's entrance, near the old motorboat docks. If you don't grab a return time, ride first thing in the morning or just before the park closes. If you are a roller coaster person, ride Space Mountain and then hurry over and hop on the Matterhorn. If roller coasters are not the end-all for you, we recommend choosing one of the other coasters or saving this one for a second day. The Matterhorn's poorly marked single-rider line, which can save you an hour in the queue, is currently one of the park's best-kept secrets. Ask an employee at the Fantasyland side exit how to take advantage of it.

The Matterhorn is actually made up of two separate coasters. Though the two sides are similar, they are not identical; veterans say the left-hand Tomorrowland track is faster with steeper drops, while the Fantasyland side on the right side is slightly longer with sharper turns.

Mr. Toad's Wild Ride ★★½

APPEAL BY AGE **PRESCHOOL** ★★★½ **GRADE SCHOOL** ★★★★ **TEENS** ★★★½
YOUNG ADULTS ★★★½ **OVER 30** ★★★½ **SENIORS** ★★★★

What it is Track ride in the dark. **Scope and scale** Minor attraction. **When to go** Before 11 a.m. **Comment** Past its prime. **Duration of ride** Almost 2 minutes. **Average wait in line per 100 people ahead of you** 9 minutes; assumes 12 cars operating. **Loading speed** Slow.

Dark

DESCRIPTION AND COMMENTS Mr. Toad's Wild Ride is a twisting, curving ride in the dark that passes two-dimensional sets and props. There are a couple of clever effects, but basically it's at the technological basement of the Disney attraction mix. Though Mr. Toad doesn't compare well with newer high-tech attractions, many Disneyland veterans appreciate it because it's one of a handful of attractions remaining from the park's beginning. Hannah, an official Touring Plans Stunt Kid™, summed the ride's appeal up perfectly:

Mr. Toad's Wild Ride is awesome, and everyone should go on it because it's about a toad who goes to hell. I feel like that's a neglected topic in theme parks these days.

TOURING TIPS Not a great but certainly a popular attraction. Lines build early in the day and never let up. Catch Mr. Toad before 11 a.m. Parents beware: there are some loud sound effects as well as a spooky "hell" scene at the end of the attraction.

Peter Pan's Flight ★★★★

APPEAL BY AGE	PRESCHOOL ★★★★½	GRADE SCHOOL ★★★★	TEENS ★★★★
YOUNG ADULTS ★★★★		OVER 30 ★★★★½	SENIORS ★★★★½

What it is Indoor fantasy-adventure ride. **Scope and scale** Minor attraction. **When to go** Immediately at park opening or after 6 p.m. **Duration of ride** Just over 2 minutes. **Average wait in line per 100 people ahead of you** 11 minutes; assumes 13 ships operating. **Loading speed** Slow.

Thumbs Up for the Whole Family

DESCRIPTION AND COMMENTS Though it is not considered one of Disneyland Park's major attractions, Peter Pan's Flight is superbly designed and absolutely delightful, with a happy theme, a reunion with some unforgettable Disney characters, beautiful effects, and charming music. Tiny pirate ships suspended from an overhead track launch you from Wendy's window to fly over nighttime London and on to Never Land and an encounter with Captain Hook, Mr. Smee, and the ubiquitous crocodile. In 2015 Peter Pan celebrated the park's 60th anniversary with a refreshed exterior and brand-new special effects inside, including digital pixie dust projections and floating figures of Wendy and the Darling boys in the nursery scene. The colorful new London flyover and rippling water effects are especially lovely. Though not a major feature of Disneyland Park, we nevertheless classify it as the best attraction in Fantasyland.

TOURING TIPS This attraction has a consistent wait of at least 20 minutes after the first hour of park operation. On the busiest of days, we've seen the wait go up to more than 60 minutes at the extreme. Try to ride right at rope drop (especially on Magic Mornings) or after 6 p.m., during the afternoon or evening parade(s), or during a performance of *Fantasmic!*

Pinocchio's Daring Journey ★★½

APPEAL BY AGE	PRESCHOOL ★★★½	GRADE SCHOOL ★★★½	TEENS ★★★
YOUNG ADULTS ★★★½		OVER 30 ★★★½	SENIORS ★★★½

What it is Track ride in the dark. **Scope and scale** Minor attraction. **When to go** Before noon or after 3:30 p.m. **Comment** A big letdown. **Duration of ride** Almost 3 minutes. **Average wait in line per 100 people ahead of you** 8 minutes; assumes 15 cars operating. **Loading speed** Slow.

Dark

DESCRIPTION AND COMMENTS This is another twisting, curving track ride in the dark, this time tracing the adventures of Pinocchio as he tries to find his way home. The action is hard to follow, and it lacks continuity. Though the sets are three-dimensional and more visually compelling than, say, Mr. Toad, the story line is dull and fails to engage the guest. In the ride's defense, it features some deliciously trippy Pleasure Island imagery, a clever vanishing Blue Fairy effect, and almost always an empty queue.

TOURING TIPS The word must be out about Pinocchio because the lines are seldom very long. Still, the longest waits occur 11:30 a.m.–4:30 p.m.

Pixie Hollow ★★

APPEAL BY AGE	PRESCHOOL ★★★★½	GRADE SCHOOL ★★★★	TEENS ★★½
YOUNG ADULTS ★★½	OVER 30 ★★★½		SENIORS ★★★★

What it is Character-greeting opportunity. **Scope and scale** Minor attraction. **When to go** Before 10 a.m. **Duration of experience** About 10 minutes. **Probable waiting time** 40 minutes or less.

DESCRIPTION AND COMMENTS An elaborate character-greeting area situated on the path connecting Matterhorn Bobsleds to the central hub, Pixie Hollow features Tinker Bell (or one of her fairy friends) in a standard character meet and greet. The line can be deceivingly long.

TOURING TIPS Pixie Hollow accumulates substantial wait times just after opening in the morning that last throughout the day until early evening, when it closes. It also closes temporarily during parades. The best way to visit Tink is to line up near the entrance to Tomorrowland about 15 minutes before the park officially opens.

Royal Hall at Fantasy Faire ★★★

APPEAL BY AGE	PRESCHOOL ★★★★★	GRADE SCHOOL ★★★★½	TEENS ★★★½
YOUNG ADULTS ★★★★★	OVER 30 ★★★★		SENIORS ★★★★★

What it is Princess meet and greet. **Scope and scale** Major attraction. **When to go** If meeting the princesses is important to your little ones, try to arrive 15 minutes before opening. **Comment** Note that Royal Hall doesn't stay open late, even if the park does. **Duration of experience** 5 minutes. **Probable waiting time** 35–60 minutes.

DESCRIPTION AND COMMENTS Once a sleepy corner off the central hub, mainly known since the 1950s for weekend swing-dancing parties, Carnation Plaza Gardens was given a pink-and-purple princess makeover in 2013 and emerged as the Fantasy Faire, which is comprised of Royal Hall and Royal Theatre (see the next profile). Even if you aren't enamored of the princess marketing craze, you can't help but admire the loving details applied throughout this mini-land, from a snoozing animatronic Figaro kitty and crank-operated Clopin's music box to the twinkling hair on the courtyard's *Tangled*-inspired tower.

This indoor meet and greet features three princesses always on duty (usually Ariel, Cinderella, and Snow White). The usual Disneyland queue (mercifully mostly shaded) must be endured to meet and be photographed, but this current incarnation typically sees somewhat shorter waits than the former Fantasy Faire location. The trick is that the Royal Hall's intimate wood-paneled interior actually houses two identical meeting areas with duplicate trios of princesses (perhaps the product of an Epcot cloning experiment?) for double the greeting capacity.

TOURING TIPS Little girls love the Royal Hall, as do boys age 6 and younger. Incidentally, you won't believe how many of the kids come in costume. If you do everything, you'll spend about an hour, not counting shopping time. On busy days, you may be barred from bringing your stroller into Fantasy Faire, unless your child is asleep in it, so teach your kid to play possum on command if you don't want to park.

Royal Theatre at Fantasy Faire ★★★★

APPEAL BY AGE PRESCHOOL ★★★★★ GRADE SCHOOL ★★★★½ TEENS ★★★★½ YOUNG ADULTS ★★★★½ OVER 30 ★★★★½ SENIORS ★★★★

What it is Interactive storytelling show. **Scope and scale** Minor attraction. **When to go** Check the *Times Guide* for showtimes. **Duration of show** 20 minutes. **Probable waiting time** 30 minutes if not using FastPass.

DESCRIPTION AND COMMENTS Royal Theatre, which once hosted jazz greats such as Dizzy Gillespie, now houses a rotating repertory of 20-minute stage shows dramatizing the tales of popular Disney royalty. (Boogie and jive fans, don't get jumpy: the weekend swing-dancing parties return to Disneyland, on its original dance floor, on select Saturday nights; see **tinyurl.com/disneydanceband** for the schedule.) *Tangled* and *Beauty and the Beast* are the featured fables, with Rapunzel and Flynn Rider or Belle joining in their respective reenactments, accompanied by narrators Mr. Smythe and Mr. Jones, milkmaid stagehands, and a live pianist. Rather than straightforward retellings, these fast-paced comic condensations capture the anarchic slapstick of a Renaissance fair trunk show. Witty enough to keep adults far outside the target demographic awake, the Royal Theatre's shows are the sleeper hits of Fantasy Faire. Stick around after the curtain falls for an autograph session with the stars.

The *Beauty and the Beast* show is usually performed at the first three showtimes of the day, with *Tangled* typically taking the stage for the remainder. If you must pick between those two, *Tangled* has the better script.

TOURING TIPS The theater only seats a little more than 200 (with room for 50 kids on the floor up front), so you may want to line up 30 or more minutes before showtime or simply settle for standing right outside the theater.

Sleeping Beauty Castle ★★★

APPEAL BY AGE PRESCHOOL ★★★★ GRADE SCHOOL ★★★½ TEENS ★★★ YOUNG ADULTS ★★★½ OVER 30 ★★★½ SENIORS ★★★½

What it is Walk-through exhibit. **Scope and scale** Minor attraction. **When to go** Anytime. **Comment** Must be able to climb up and down two flights of stairs. **Duration of exhibit** Varies; about 10 minutes. **Average wait** Usually none.

DESCRIPTION AND COMMENTS Disneyland Park's most famous icon, Sleeping Beauty Castle is at the heart of Disneyland and serves as a stage for shows and special events. For the non-claustrophobic, the Sleeping Beauty Castle walk-through exhibit is a miniature 3-D series, arranged along a narrow passage inside the castle, that tells the story of Sleeping Beauty. Originally opened on April 29, 1957, to preview the upcoming 1959 movie *Sleeping Beauty,* and then closed for most of a decade after 9/11, the attraction reopened in 2008 with new dioramas reflecting the style of artist Eyvind Earle, who gave *Sleeping Beauty* its distinctive design. In this version there are animated scenes, interactive elements, and Pepper's Ghost projection effects (as also seen in The Haunted Mansion).

TOURING TIPS The entrance is on the Fantasyland side of the castle near the passageway to Fantasy Faire and Frontierland. The exhibit allows for one-way traffic only. It can get a bit crowded inside, but there should rarely be a line outside the attraction. For guests unable to handle stairs, a small alcove to the left of the bridge to Tomorrowland contains a collection of the animations, as well as music, allowing you to experience the attraction's elements without walking. The viewing location runs on a loop, so you might have to watch it out of order.

Snow White's Scary Adventures ★★★

APPEAL BY AGE	PRESCHOOL ★★★		GRADE SCHOOL ★★★½		TEENS ★★★½
YOUNG ADULTS ★★★½		OVER 30 ★★★		SENIORS ★★★½	

What it is Track ride in the dark. **Scope and scale** Minor attraction. **When to go** Before 11 a.m. or after 5 p.m. **Comments** Quite intimidating for preschoolers; worth seeing if the wait is not long. **Duration of ride** Almost 2 minutes. **Average wait in line per 100 people ahead of you** 9 minutes; assumes 10 cars operating. **Loading speed** Slow.

Dark   Scary

DESCRIPTION AND COMMENTS Here, you ride in a mining car in the dark through a series of sets drawn from *Snow White and the Seven Dwarfs*. The attraction has a *Perils of Pauline* flavor and features Snow White as she narrowly escapes harm at the hands of the wicked witch. The action and effects are a cut above Mr. Toad's Wild Ride but not as good as Peter Pan's Flight. High-tech projection effects enhance the magic mirror and rainstorm scenes.

TOURING TIPS Enjoyable but not particularly compelling. Experience it if the lines are not too long or on a second-day visit. Ride before 11 a.m. or after 5 p.m. if possible. Also, don't take the "scary" part too seriously. The witch looks mean, but most kids take her in stride. Or maybe not. A mother from Knoxville, Tennessee, commented:

The outside looks cute and fluffy, but inside, the evil witch just keeps coming at you. My 5-year-old, who rode Space Mountain three times [and took other scary rides] right in stride, was near panic when our car stopped unexpectedly twice during Snow White. After Snow White, my 6-year-old niece spent a lot of time asking, "Will a witch jump out at you?" before other rides. So I suggest that you explain a little more what this ride is about. It's tough on preschoolers who are expecting forest animals and dwarfs.

It really punches the buttons of the 6-and-under crowd, when other more traditionally scary rides don't. Many kids, once frightened by Snow White's Scary Adventures, balk at trying any other attractions that go into the dark, regardless of how benign they are.

Storybook Land Canal Boats ★★★

APPEAL BY AGE	PRESCHOOL ★★★★		GRADE SCHOOL ★★★★		TEENS ★★★½
YOUNG ADULTS ★★★★		OVER 30 ★★★½		SENIORS ★★★½	

Thumbs Up for the Whole Family

What it is Scenic boat ride. **Scope and scale** Minor attraction. **When to go** Before 10:30 a.m. or after 5:30 p.m. **Comment** Pretty, tranquil, and serene. **Duration of ride** 6½ minutes. **Average wait in line per 100 people ahead of you** 16 minutes; assumes 7 boats operating. **Loading speed** Slow.

DESCRIPTION AND COMMENTS Guide-operated boats wind along canals situated beneath the same miniature landscapes visible from the Casey Jr. Circus Train. This ride—offering stellar examples of bonsai cultivation, selective pruning, and miniaturization—is a must for landscape-gardening enthusiasts. The landscapes include scenes from more recent Disney features—such as the kingdom of Arendelle and Elsa's ice palace from *Frozen,* added in 2014—in addition to those from such classics as *The Wind in the Willows* and *The Three Little Pigs.* We find Storybook Land to be a charming respite from the surrounding overstimulation, but not every guest gets the attraction, as this California reader will attest:

I thought there would be beautiful flowers to see or interesting dioramas, but you just sail past small buildings meant to look like cottages, castles, and so on. There aren't even any little figurines or characters in it.

TOURING TIPS The boats are much more comfortable than the train, the view of the miniatures is better, and the pace is more leisurely. On the downside, the lines are long and, if not long, definitely slow moving. The ride itself also takes a lot of time. Our recommendation is to ride Casey Jr. if you have children or are in a hurry. Take the boat if your party is all adults or your pace is more leisurely. Best of all, the boats' pilots deliver live narration that (depending on the driver) can be delightfully droll. If you ride the boats, try to get on before 10:30 a.m. If the queue isn't prohibitive, this ride is especially appealing after sunset, when the creative lighting adds a whole new dimension. It's closed during parades.

MICKEY'S TOONTOWN

MICKEY'S TOONTOWN IS SITUATED across the Disneyland Railroad tracks from Fantasyland. Its entrance is a tunnel that opens into Fantasyland just to the left of It's a Small World. As its name suggests, Toontown is a fanciful representation of the wacky cartoon community where all the Disney characters live. Mickey's Toontown was inspired by the Disney animated feature *Who Framed Roger Rabbit?,* in which humans were able to enter the world of cartoon characters.

If you want to see characters, Mickey's Toontown is the place to go. In addition to Mickey, who receives guests all day (except during parades) in his dressing room, and Minnie, who entertains in her house, you are likely to bump into such august personages as Goofy and Pluto lurking around the streets. From time to time, horns sound and whistles blow atop Toontown City Hall, followed by a fanfare rendition of *The Mickey Mouse Club* theme song, which indicates that some characters are about to appear.

Mickey's Toontown is rendered with masterful attention to artistic humor and detail. The businesses around the Fireworks Factory have interactive doorbells that elicit audible responses from their occupants. Across the street, the sidewalk is littered with crates containing strange contents addressed to exotic destinations. If you pry open the top of one of the crates (easy to do), the crate will emit a noise consistent with its contents. A box of "train parts," for example, broadcasts the sound of a racing locomotive when you lift the top. Next to Goofy's Playhouse is a Goofy-shaped impact crater marking the spot where he missed his swimming pool while high diving.

Most of the attractions in Mickey's Toontown are for kids, specifically smaller children. Attractions open to adults include a dark ride drawn from *Who Framed Roger Rabbit?* (sort of a high-tech rendition of Mr. Toad's Wild Ride) and a diminutive roller coaster.

Be forewarned that Mickey's Toontown is not very large, especially in comparison to neighboring Fantasyland. A tolerable crowd in most of the other lands will seem like Times Square on New Year's Eve in Mickey's Toontown. Couple this congestion with the unfortunate fact that none of the attractions in Mickey's Toontown are engineered to handle huge crowds, and you come face-to-face with possibly the most attractive traffic jam the Disney folks have ever created.

Mickey's Toontown opens 1 hour after the rest of the park. If you're touring with younger children, hit the Fantasyland attractions during the first hour the park is open, and then head for Toontown.

Finally, be aware that all of Toontown, including Roger Rabbit's Car Toon Spin, will close early before every nighttime fireworks show. It seems that rockets are launched from a building behind the land, showering Mickey's city with fiery embers, which might prove inconvenient for anyone standing below.

Chip 'n Dale Treehouse ★★

APPEAL BY AGE	PRESCHOOL ★★★½	GRADE SCHOOL ★★★	TEENS ★★½
YOUNG ADULTS ★★	OVER 30 ★★		SENIORS ★★½

What it is Imaginative children's play area. **Scope and scale** Diversion. **When to go** Anytime. **Comment** Good exercise for the small fry.

DESCRIPTION AND COMMENTS Play area consisting of a tree house with slides.

TOURING TIPS Located in the most remote corner of Mickey's Toontown and obscured by the crowd waiting to ride the roller coaster next door, the tree house is frequently overlooked. Of all the attractions in Mickey's Toontown, this is the easiest one to get the kids into without much of a wait. Most any child who can fit is allowed to rummage around in the tree house.

Disneyland Railroad

DESCRIPTION AND COMMENTS Mickey's Toontown and Fantasyland share a station on Disneyland Railroad's route around the perimeter of the park. This station becomes fairly crowded on busy days. If you are interested primarily in getting there, it may be quicker to walk. See the description on page 223 for additional details regarding the sights en route.

Gadget's Go Coaster ★★

APPEAL BY AGE	PRESCHOOL ★★★★½	GRADE SCHOOL ★★★½	TEENS ★★★
YOUNG ADULTS ★★★	OVER 30 ★★★		SENIORS ★★★

  What it is Small roller coaster. **Scope and scale** Minor attraction. **When to go** Before 10:30 a.m., during the parades or *Fantasmic!* in the evening, or just before the park closes. **Comments** Great for little ones but not worth the wait for adults. Must be 35" to ride; expectant moms shouldn't ride. **Duration of ride** About 50 seconds. **Average wait in line per 100 people ahead of you** 10 minutes; assumes normal staffing. **Loading speed** Slow.

DESCRIPTION AND COMMENTS Gadget's Go Coaster is a very small roller coaster; the idea is that you are miniaturized and riding around in an acorn shell. The zippy ride is over so quickly that you hardly know that you've been anywhere. In fact, of the 52 seconds the ride is in motion, 32 seconds are consumed in exiting the loading area, being ratcheted up the first hill, and braking into the off-loading area. The actual time you spend careening around the track is a whopping 20 seconds.

TOURING TIPS Gadget's Go Coaster, a beginner roller coaster for young children, is the perfect attraction to gauge the pluckiness of your little ones before tossing them to the coyotes on Big Thunder Mountain Railroad. The coaster cars are not very comfortable for adults, and you can expect a fair amount of whiplash, but as noted, the ride takes less than a minute. The coaster is both slow-loading and visually attractive, so you can expect long waits except during the first 30 minutes that Toontown is open.

Goofy's Playhouse ★★½

APPEAL BY AGE PRESCHOOL ★★★★½ GRADE SCHOOL ★★★★ TEENS ★★★★ YOUNG ADULTS ★★★ OVER 30 ★★½ SENIORS ★★★½

What it is A whimsical children's play area. **Scope and scale** Diversion. **When to go** Anytime.

DESCRIPTION AND COMMENTS Goofy's Playhouse is a small but nicely themed play area for the under-6 set. Usually not crowded, the playhouse is a pleasant place to let preschoolers ramble and parents relax while older sibs enjoy more adventurous attractions.

TOURING TIPS There's not a lot of shade, so visit early or late in the day.

Mickey's House and Meet Mickey ★★★

APPEAL BY AGE PRESCHOOL ★★★★½ GRADE SCHOOL ★★★★½ TEENS ★★★★ YOUNG ADULTS ★★★½ OVER 30 ★★★½ SENIORS ★★★★½

What it is Walk-through tour of Mickey's House and Movie Barn, ending with a personal visit with Mickey. **Scope and scale** Minor attraction. **When to go** Before 10:30 a.m. or after 5:30 p.m. **Duration of tour** 15–30 minutes (depending on the crowd). **Average wait in line per 100 people ahead of you** 20 minutes.

DESCRIPTION AND COMMENTS Mickey's House is the starting point of a self-guided tour that winds through the famous mouse's house, into his backyard, past Pluto's doghouse, and then into Mickey's Movie Barn. This last stop harks back to the so-called "barn" studio where Walt Disney created a number of the earlier Mickey Mouse cartoons. Once in the Movie Barn, guests are entertained by the Disney Channel's current series of retro-styled Mickey Mouse shorts while awaiting admittance to Mickey's Dressing Room.

In small groups of one or two families, guests are ultimately conducted into the dressing room where Mickey awaits to pose for photos and sign autographs. The visit is not lengthy (2–4 minutes), but there is adequate time for all of the children to hug, poke, and admire the star.

TOURING TIPS The cynical observer will discern immediately that Mickey's House, backyard, Movie Barn, and so on are no more than a cleverly devised queuing area to deliver guests to Mickey's Dressing Room for the mouse encounter. For those with some vestige of child in their personalities, however, the preamble serves to heighten anticipation while providing the opportunity to get to know the corporate symbol on a more personal level. Mickey's House is well conceived and contains a lot of Disney memorabilia. You will notice that children touch everything as they proceed through the house, hoping to find some artifact that is not welded or riveted into the set (an especially tenacious child during one of our visits was actually able to rip a couple of books from a bookcase).

Meeting Mickey and touring his house are best done during the first 2 hours that Toontown is open or in the evening during *Fantasmic!* If meeting Mickey is at the top of your child's list, consider taking the Disneyland Railroad from Main Street to the Toontown/Fantasyland Station as soon as you enter the park (note that Toontown opens 1 hour after the rest of the park). Some children are so obsessed with seeing Mickey that they cannot enjoy anything else until they get Mickey in the rearview mirror. (Mickey is not available during parades.)

Minnie's House ★★½

**APPEAL BY AGE   PRESCHOOL ★★★★★   GRADE SCHOOL ★★★★   TEENS ★★★½
YOUNG ADULTS ★★★½   OVER 30 ★★★½   SENIORS ★★★★½**

What it is Walk-through exhibit and character-greeting opportunity. **Scope and scale** Minor attraction. **When to go** Before 10:30 a.m. **Duration of tour** About 10 minutes. **Average wait in line per 100 people ahead of you** 12 minutes.

DESCRIPTION AND COMMENTS Minnie's House consists of a self-guided tour through the various rooms and backyard of Mickey Mouse's main squeeze. Similar to Mickey's House, only predictably more feminine, Minnie's House likewise showcases some fun Disney memorabilia. Among the highlights of the short tour are the fanciful appliances in Minnie's kitchen. Like Mickey, Minnie is usually present to receive guests.

TOURING TIPS Minnie's House can't accommodate as many guests as Mickey's House can. See Minnie early and before Mickey to avoid waiting outdoors in a long queue. Minnie is not available during parades and normally knocks off for the day by midafternoon; check the app or *Times Guide* for her appearance schedule.

Miss Daisy, Donald's Boat ★★

**APPEAL BY AGE   PRESCHOOL ★★★★   GRADE SCHOOL ★★★★   TEENS ★½
YOUNG ADULTS ★★½   OVER 30 ★★½   SENIORS ★★**

What it is Creative play area with a boat theme. **Scope and scale** Diversion. **When to go** Before 10:30 a.m. or after 4:30 p.m.

DESCRIPTION AND COMMENTS Another children's play area, this time with a tugboat theme. Children can climb nets, ring bells, survey Toontown from the captain's bridge, and scoot down slides. The idea is that Donald Duck (who, as everyone knows, lives in Duckburg) is visiting Toontown.

TOURING TIPS Kids more or less wander on and off the *Miss Daisy,* and usually there isn't any sort of organized line or queuing area. Enjoy this play area at your leisure and stay as long as you like.

Roger Rabbit's Car Toon Spin *(FastPass)* ★★★½

**APPEAL BY AGE   PRESCHOOL ★★★½   GRADE SCHOOL ★★★★   TEENS ★★★½
YOUNG ADULTS ★★★★   OVER 30 ★★★½   SENIORS ★★★★**

What it is Track ride in the dark. **Scope and scale** Major attraction. **When to go** Before 10:30 a.m. or after 6:30 p.m. **Comment** Ride with your kids, if you can stomach it. **Duration of ride** A little more than 3 minutes. **Average wait in line per 100 people ahead of you** 7 minutes; assumes full-capacity operation. **Loading speed** Moderate.

Dark   Rough   Queasy

DESCRIPTION AND COMMENTS In this so-called dark ride, guests become part of a cartoon plot. The concept is that you are renting a taxicab for a tour of Mickey's Toontown. As soon as your taxicab gets under way, however, weasels throw a slippery glop (known as dip) on the road, which sends the cab into a more or less uncontrollable spin. This spinning continues as the cab passes through a variety of sets populated by cartoon and Audio-Animatronic characters and punctuated by simulated explosions. As a child of the 1960s put it, "It was like combining Mr. Toad's Wild Ride with the Mad Tea Party while tripping on LSD." The ride features an elaborate indoor queue and some of the best effects of any Disneyland cartoon dark ride, climaxing in a head-scratchingly effective "portable hole" gag that holds up under repeated viewing.

The main problem with the Car Toon Spin is that, because of the spinning, you are often pointed in the wrong direction to appreciate (or even see) many of the better visual effects. Furthermore, the story line is loose. The attraction lacks the continuity and humor of Splash Mountain or the suspense of The Haunted Mansion or Snow White's Scary Adventures.

The spinning, incidentally, can be controlled by the guests. If you don't want to spin, you don't have to. If you do elect to spin, you still will not be able to approach the eye-popping speed attainable by the teacups at the Mad Tea Party. Sluggish spinning aside, our advice for those who are at all susceptible to motion sickness is not to get near this ride if you are touring with anyone under 21 years of age.

A reader from Milford, Michigan, echoed our sentiments, lamenting:

The most disappointing ride to me was Roger Rabbit's Car Toon Spin. I stood in line for 45 minutes for a fun house ride, and the wheel was so difficult to operate that I spent most of my time trying to steer the bloody car and missed the point of the ride.

TOURING TIPS The ride is popular for its novelty, and it is one of the few Mickey's Toontown attractions that parents (with strong stomachs) can enjoy with their children. Because the ride stays fairly thronged with people all day long, ride in the first 90 minutes that Toontown is open, during parades or *Fantasmic!,* or in the hour before the park closes. The best move is to obtain FastPasses before 10:30 a.m., when the return time is an hour or less away, and then let your children enjoy the other Toontown attractions until it's time to ride.

TOMORROWLAND

LOCATED DIRECTLY TO THE RIGHT of the central hub is Tomorrowland. This themed area is a futuristic mix of rides and experiences that relates to technological development and what life will be like in the years to come.

Tomorrowland's design reflects a nostalgic vision of the future as imagined by dreamers and scientists in the 1920s and 1930s. Frozen in time, Tomorrowland conjures up visions of Buck Rogers (whom nobody under age 60 remembers), fanciful mechanical rockets, and metallic cities spread beneath towering obelisks. Disney refers to Tomorrowland as the "Future That Never Was." *Newsweek* dubbed it "retro-future."

Astro Orbitor ★★

APPEAL BY AGE **PRESCHOOL** ★★★★　**GRADE SCHOOL** ★★★★　**TEENS** ★★★
YOUNG ADULTS ★★★½　　　　**OVER 30** ★★½　　　**SENIORS** ★★½

Thumbs Up for the Whole Family

What it is Very mild midway-type thrill ride. **Scope and scale** Minor attraction. **When to go** Before 10 a.m. or during the hour before the park closes. **Comment** Not worth the wait. **Duration of ride** 1½ minutes. **Average wait in line per 100 people ahead of you** 13 minutes; assumes normal staffing. **Loading speed** Slow.

Queasy

DESCRIPTION AND COMMENTS The Astro Orbitor is a visually appealing midway-type ride involving small rockets that rotate on arms around a central axis. Be aware that the Astro Orbitor flies higher and faster than Dumbo, and it frightens some small children.

TOURING TIPS Astro Orbitor is slow to load and expendable on any schedule. If you want to take a preschooler on this ride, place your child in the seat first and then sit down yourself.

Autopia ★★½

APPEAL BY AGE **PRESCHOOL** ★★★★½ **GRADE SCHOOL** ★★★★　**TEENS** ★★★½
YOUNG ADULTS ★★★½　　　　**OVER 30** ★★★　　　**SENIORS** ★★½

What it is Drive-'em-yourself miniature cars. **Scope and scale** Minor attraction. **When to go** Before 10 a.m. or after 5 p.m. **Comments** Boring for adults; great for preschoolers. Must be at least 54" tall to drive unassisted; must be at least 32" tall to ride (and one guest in car must be at least 54" tall). **Duration of ride** Approximately 4½ minutes. **Average wait in line per 100 people ahead of you** 6 minutes; assumes 35 cars operating on each track. **Loading speed** Slow.

Loud

DESCRIPTION AND COMMENTS An elaborate miniature freeway with gasoline-powered cars that travel at speeds of up to 7 miles per hour. In 2016 Autopia was updated with new preshow displays and minimally moving roadside tableaus featuring ASIMO (Honda's humanoid robot that used to perform in Innoventions before it became Star Wars Launch Bay) and his robo-bird buddy, but it still has the same basic appeal it's held for decades. The attraction design—with its sleek cars, auto noises, highway signs, and even an "off-road" section—is quite alluring. In fact, however, the cars poke along on a track that leaves the driver with little to do. Pretty ho hum for most adults and teenagers, but at least it's much more visually stimulating than the unthemed Magic Kingdom version.

TOURING TIPS This ride is appealing to the eye but definitely expendable on a schedule for adults. Preschoolers, however, love it. If your preschooler is too short to drive, place the child behind the wheel and allow him or her to steer (the car runs on a guide rail) while you work the foot pedal.

A mom from North Billerica, Massachusetts, writes:

I was truly amazed by the number of adults in line. Please emphasize to your readers that these cars travel on a guided path and are not a whole lot of fun. The only reason I could think of for adults to be in line was an insane desire to go on absolutely every ride. The cars also tend to pile up at the end, so it takes almost as long to get off as it did to get on. Parents riding with their preschoolers should keep the car going as slow as it can without stalling. This prolongs the preschooler's joy and decreases the time you have to wait at the end.

FastPass was previously offered at Autopia. If it returns, don't bother; it doesn't work very well, with FastPass return lines typically exceeding 20 minutes. Ride early or late in the day instead.

Buzz Lightyear Astro Blasters *(FastPass)* ★★★★

APPEAL BY AGE PRESCHOOL ★★★★½ GRADE SCHOOL ★★★★½ TEENS ★★★★½
YOUNG ADULTS ★★★★ OVER 30 ★★★★ SENIORS ★★★★

What it is Space-travel interactive dark ride. **Scope and scale** Major attraction. **When to go** Before 10:30 a.m. or after 6 p.m. **Comment** A real winner! **Duration of ride** About 4½ minutes. **Average wait in line per 100 people ahead of you** 3 minutes. **Loading speed** Fast.

DESCRIPTION AND COMMENTS Based on the space-commando character Buzz Lightyear from *Toy Story,* the marginal story line has you and Buzz trying to save the universe from the evil Emperor Zurg. The indoor ride is interactive—you can spin your car and shoot simulated laser cannons at Zurg and his minions.

A similar attraction at the Magic Kingdom at Walt Disney World is one of the most popular attractions in the park. The Disneyland version, situated across from Star Tours, is much the same except mobile guns allow more accurate aiming. Don't forget to smile! You can e-mail an on-ride photo to yourself for free from kiosks at the exit.

Praise for Buzz Lightyear is almost universal. This comment from a Massachusetts couple is typical:

Buzz Lightyear was the surprise hit of our trip! My husband and I enjoyed competing for the best score so much that we went on this ride several times during our stay. Definitely a must.

Each car is equipped with two laser cannons and a score-keeping display. Each score-keeping display is independent, so you can compete with your riding partner. A joystick allows you to spin the car to line up the various targets. Each time you pull the trigger, you'll release a red laser beam that you can see hitting or missing the target.

TOURING TIPS Most folks' first ride is occupied with learning how to use the equipment (fire off individual shots as opposed to keeping the trigger depressed) and figuring out how the targets work. The next ride (as with certain potato chips, one is not enough), you'll surprise yourself by how much better you do. *Unofficial Guide* readers are unanimous in their praise of Buzz Lightyear. Some guests, in fact, spend several hours on the attraction, riding again and again. See Buzz Lightyear early in the morning after riding Peter Pan's Flight, Matterhorn Bobsleds, and Star Tours. Buzz Lightyear's FastPasses are dispensed from the two kiosks at the far end of Star Tours' distribution area and are occasionally disconnected from the rest of the FastPass system.

Disneyland Monorail System ★★★

APPEAL BY AGE	PRESCHOOL ★★★★	GRADE SCHOOL ★★★½	TEENS ★★★½
YOUNG ADULTS ★★★½		OVER 30 ★★★½	SENIORS ★★★★

What it is Scenic transportation. **Scope and scale** Major attraction. **When to go** During the hot, crowded period of the day (11:30 a.m.–5 p.m.). **Comments** Nice, relaxing ride with some interesting views of the park; take the monorail to Downtown Disney for lunch. **Duration of ride** 3 minutes one-way to Downtown Disney. **Average wait in line per 100 people ahead of you** 10 minutes; assumes 3 monorails operating. **Loading speed** Moderate-fast.

Thumbs Up for the Whole Family

DESCRIPTION AND COMMENTS The monorail is a futuristic transportation ride that affords the only practical opportunity for escaping the park during the crowded lunch period and early afternoon. Boarding at the Tomorrowland monorail station, you can commute to the Disneyland Resort hotels and Downtown Disney. The monorail provides a tranquil trip with a nice view of Downtown Disney, Disney California Adventure, Fantasyland, and Tomorrowland. The Mark VII monorails have a sleek, retro look but can get quite hot inside during the summer (no air-conditioning!).

TOURING TIPS We recommend using the monorail to commute to Downtown Disney for a quiet, relaxing lunch away from the crowds and the heat. If you only want to experience the ride, go whenever you wish; the wait to board is usually 15–25 minutes except in the 2 hours before closing when everyone tries to leave at once. Also note that to make a round-trip, you may be required to disembark and then queue up to reboard at Downtown Disney. The monorail may suspend services from 1 hour before the Disneyland Park's evening fireworks until 45 minutes afterward, and it ceases to bring guests into the park 30 minutes before closing.

Disneyland Railroad

DESCRIPTION AND COMMENTS The Disneyland Railroad makes a regular stop at the Tomorrowland Station. The wait to board here is usually short. See page 223 for additional details regarding the sights en route.

Finding Nemo Submarine Voyage ★★★★

APPEAL BY AGE	PRESCHOOL ★★★★½	GRADE SCHOOL ★★★½	TEENS ★★★
YOUNG ADULTS ★★★		OVER 30 ★★★	SENIORS ★★★½

What it is Simulated submarine ride. **Scope and scale** Headliner. **When to go** Before 10 a.m. or during evening parades or fireworks. **Duration of ride** 11½ minutes. **Average wait in line per 100 people ahead of you** 7½ minutes; assumes 8 subs operating. **Loading speed** Slow–moderate.

DESCRIPTION AND COMMENTS The Finding Nemo Submarine Voyage ride is based on the story line of the hit Disney-Pixar animated feature *Finding Nemo*. Here you board a submarine in a loading area situated below the Disneyland monorail station in Tomorrowland. After a quick lap of the open-air lagoon, the sub passes through a waterfall and inside to follow the general *Finding Nemo* story. Special effects center on a combination of traditional Audio-Animatronics and, once you're inside the dark interior of the building, what appear to be rear-projection screens, underwater, at a distance of 3–10 feet from the sub's windows. Encased in rock and shipwrecks, the screens are natural looking and allow the animated characters to appear three-dimensionally in the undersea world. Other elements include traveling through a minefield and a sea of jellyfish (very cool) and entering the mouth of a whale. The onboard sound system allows the story to "travel" from front to back of the sub, and the visual experience is different depending on what seat you're in.

The attraction is well done. You don't have to be a Nemo fan to be impressed by the scale and effects. It's not fast-paced but, rather, leisurely in the way that Pirates of the Caribbean is.

TOURING TIPS The attraction's capacity is only about 900 guests per hour, a shockingly small capacity for a headliner attraction. Further, owing to the low carrying capacity, the subs are not a good candidate for FastPass (all FastPasses would be gone before noon).

We've determined that, taking the day as a whole, you make much better use of your time enjoying Space Mountain, Splash Mountain, Peter Pan's Flight, and other popular attractions during the first hour the park is open and saving the subs for later, when a parade, fireworks show, or *Fantasmic!* has siphoned a large number of guests from the line. Incidentally, arriving 15 minutes before a parade or other presentation is not an arbitrary suggestion—during this time window, the Finding Nemo line (or lines at other popular attractions) will be its shortest. The last 30 minutes before park closing is another good time to get in line.

Claustrophobes may not be comfortable with the experience, even though the sub doesn't actually submerge (we saw one 30-ish woman who started hyperventilating before the sub left the dock). Children may be scared of the same thing, or of the encounter with sharks (they keep their distance). The sharks here are a bit less menacing than in the movie too.

The bright-yellow subs use electric power to minimize noise and pollution. The subs fit 40 people. It's not easy to get 40 aboard, however, because the seats are narrow and a few guests take up two. Ideally, large guests should aim to be in one of the four seats at the front or back, but this may be difficult to negotiate.

Wheelchair-bound guests or those who can't get down the spiral staircase into the sub can view the experience from a special topside viewing room (seats about six able-bodied persons plus two wheelchairs). With the exception of one small animated effect, the visual is identical (perhaps faster), but despite a large monitor, the creatures appear smaller than when viewing them through a real porthole. The wait for the alternate viewing area is usually brief (ask a cast member how to bypass the standby line), and there are Mickeys hidden in the dive lockers inside.

A reader from Sydney, Australia, disagrees with our Finding Nemo rating, writing:

Finding Nemo was the most overrated ride. Perhaps it would rate high for those younger than 8 years old, but for our group it was one of the worst rides. It was boring, had rushing water, and moved slowly. What made it worse was that it had a high rating, and this raised expectations.

Jedi Training: Trials of the Temple ★★★½

APPEAL BY AGE	PRESCHOOL ★★★★½	GRADE SCHOOL ★★★★★	TEENS ★★★
YOUNG ADULTS ★★★½	OVER 30 ★★★★		SENIORS ★★★★

What it is Live entertainment where young audience members are trained to be Jedis. **Scope and scale** Minor attraction. **When to go** See *Times Guide* for performance times; go to Star Wars Launch Bay upon park opening to register your child if he or she wants to participate. **Duration of show** 25 minutes.

DESCRIPTION AND COMMENTS Staged at the Tomorrowland Terrace Theater, *Jedi Training: Trials of the Temple* recruits 30 young volunteers and trains them to fight with a light saber (an elegant, if plastic, weapon). The training consists of practicing a surprisingly long set of fencing-style moves while the audience gets to enjoy the minimal comprehension by some of the youngest Jedis. Just when the training ends, Darth Vader and the Seventh Sister (a sinister Inquisitor character from the *Star Wars Rebels* cartoon) arrive, and the young recruits meet them in "battle," with each Jedi getting his or her turn to take a whack at a Darth. The show was updated in 2016 with a new ending, where a Jedi apprentice faces off against Kylo Ren from *The Force Awakens*. The updated finale lacks the acrobatics of the old Darth Maul version, but Ren gets a rise out of the audience with his light saber temper tantrums. It's a great photo op for parents and a major hoot for everyone else.

TOURING TIPS There are two prime viewing locations: standing room on the show floor underneath the overhang, and seating at the Tomorrowland Terrace restaurant. Only 10–20 tables have decent views of the show, so make sure to stake them out early. Otherwise, there is plenty of standing room space around the sides of the stage.

You must register your child in advance if he or she wants to participate in *Jedi Training*. Sign-up is at the entrance to Star Wars Launch Bay and begins at the park's official opening time, though guests begin lining up as soon as early entry begins. Arrive as early as possible if your Padawan wants to test his or her midi-chlorians because all spots typically fill up in well under an hour.

Space Mountain *(FastPass)* ★★★★½

APPEAL BY AGE	PRESCHOOL ★★½	GRADE SCHOOL ★★★★½	TEENS ★★★★★
YOUNG ADULTS ★★★★★		OVER 30 ★★★★½	SENIORS ★★★★

What it is Roller coaster in the dark. **Scope and scale** Super-headliner. **When to go** Right after the park opens or use FastPass. **Comment** Must be 40" tall to ride. **Duration of ride** 2¾ minutes. **Average wait in line per 100 people ahead of you** 3½ minutes. **Loading speed** Moderate.

Dark Scary Lose Things Queasy Rough Muss Your 'Do

DESCRIPTION AND COMMENTS Space Mountain is an indoor roller coaster with a theme of high-speed interstellar travel. It's a designer version of the Wild Mouse, a midway ride that's been around for at least 50 years. There are no long drops or swooping hills as there are on a traditional roller coaster—only quick, unexpected turns and small drops. Disney's contribution essentially was to add a space theme to the Wild Mouse and put it in the dark. And this does indeed make the Mouse seem wilder.

The most surprising thing about Space Mountain is its aesthetic beauty. The vistas of the solar system and the stars, the distant galaxies, and passing comets are intoxicating and very realistic. Because you can't see the track or anticipate where your vehicle will go, your eyes are free to feast on the rich visuals.

In the summer of 2017, Disneyland removed the Star Wars–themed Hyperspace Mountain makeover that was the cornerstone of Tomorrowland's Season of Force promotion and restored Space Mountain's original effects and groovy Michael Giacchino score.

Disney still transforms Space Mountain into Ghost Galaxy for Halloween, adding atmospheric audio and video projections of an angry space ghost (no, not that Space Ghost) chasing you through the cosmos. The interstellar specter is more goofy than genuinely scary, but it makes a fun novelty for the spooky season. Nighttime video projections, which make the iconic conical building look like it's crumbling to dust or crackling with electricity, are the most impressive element of the overlay.

TOURING TIPS Space Mountain is one of the park's most popular attractions, especially during Halloween as Ghost Galaxy. Experience it immediately after the park opens or use FastPass.

Star Tours—The Adventures Continue *(FastPass)* ★★★★

**APPEAL BY AGE PRESCHOOL ★★★½ GRADE SCHOOL ★★★★½ TEENS ★★★★½
YOUNG ADULTS ★★★★½   OVER 30 ★★★★½   SENIORS ★★★★**

What it is Space-flight simulation ride. **Scope and scale** Headliner. **When to go** Before 11 a.m. or use FastPass. **Comments** A blast; not to be missed. Frightens many small children; expectant mothers advised against riding; must be 40″ tall to ride. **Duration of ride** Approximately 7 minutes. **Average wait in line per 100 people ahead of you** 6 minutes; assumes 4 simulators operating. **Loading speed** Moderate.

Scary   Queasy   Rough

DESCRIPTION AND COMMENTS Star Tours features cutting-edge digital 3-D screens (the sharpest and clearest screens in Anaheim) and in-cabin Audio-Animatronic figures of C-3PO, your golden droid pilot. During your inevitably turbulent travels, you'll bump, twist, and dive into a who's who of Star Wars icons, with heroes Master Yoda and Admiral "It's A Trap!" Ackbar on your side, and villains Darth Vader and Boba Fett on your back. You'll be visiting planets from both the classic trilogy—such as icy Hoth and arid Tatooine—and the not-so-classic prequels, including Geonosis (home of the dreaded Death Star) and Naboo (home of the equally dreaded Jar Jar Binks). When the Force awakened with Episode VII, a perilous tour of Jakku's starship graveyard with Finn and the *Millennium Falcon* and a cameo from BB-8 were added to the itinerary, and a trip to Episode VIII's mineral planet Crait will be added in late 2017, providing fan service while shattering the Episode III½ time line continuity the ride had previously observed. The big twist is that the eight possible cosmic destinations and multiple celebrity cameos (look for Han Solo and Chewbacca in the background) are randomly combined into hundreds of different story variations, giving the attraction unprecedented rerideability. A wealth of references to the original Star Tours ride (along with hidden Disney characters and Star Wars inside jokes) can be found inside the detailed queue, and the ride is quite smooth and well synchronized.

TOURING TIPS Star Tours sees hour-plus waits on busy days, so ride as early in the day as possible or grab a FastPass. If you have young children (or anyone) who are apprehensive about this attraction, ask the attendant about switching off (see page 154). You can track the ride combinations you've seen on your phone at **startourspassport.net.**

Star Wars Launch Bay   ★★½

What it is Movie exhibits and character greetings. **Scope and scale** Minor attraction. **When to go** Anytime; open 10 a.m.–8 p.m. **Duration of exhibit** Varies. 30 minutes to examine all exhibits, 30 minutes or more each for meet and greets. **Probable waiting time** 30 minutes for each meet and greet.

Loud   Scary

DESCRIPTION AND COMMENTS Star Wars Launch Bay is a walk-through exhibit housed inside the former Innoventions building (originally the *Carousel of Progress*) that pays homage to the entire Star Wars cinematic series.

A 9-minute introductory film featuring interview snippets with some of the creators of the new Star Wars films—including Lucasfilm president Kathleen Kennedy, *Force Awakens* director J. J. Abrams, and *Rogue One* director Gareth Edwards—runs on an endless loop to the right of the exhibit entrance.

The central display area is devoted to the most recent Star Wars films: *The Force Awakens, Rogue One,* and soon *The Last Jedi*. The room showcases weapons, vehicles, and costumes as seen on-screen, though all are exacting re-creations as opposed to authentic movie props.

Another area displays replica props and models representing the vehicles and weapons of the Rebel Alliance and Galactic Empire, as seen in Episodes IV–VI. The highlight of this area is a detailed scale reproduction of Boba Fett's *Slave I,* with a tiny figure of the infamous bounty hunter visible inside the cockpit.

The back portion of the Star Wars Launch Bay building is dominated by two elaborate meet and greets: one leads to a Rebel base where Chewbacca, the world's favorite Wookie, awaits; the other to an Imperial bunker occupied by Darth Vader, the iconic Dark Lord of the Sith (also known as Kylo Ren's granddaddy). Whichever side you select, you'll find a couple cases of replica helmets and light sabers to look at. The line moves slowly, but the wait is well worth it because both meet and greets use Disney's latest interactive technology to bring these iconic characters to life. Chewbacca can move his mouth and growl in response to your questions, while Vader has a full vocabulary of sinister phrases to taunt you with. The queue is also carefully managed to prevent guests from seeing the encounter ahead of them, so your face-to-face really feels like an intimate experience.

In addition to the two public meet and greets, a private meet and greet with Darth is reserved for Disney Visa credit card holders. It's open for 4 hours every afternoon and always has a shorter wait than the public line, in addition to providing free PhotoPass downloads (see page 107).

Beyond the meet and greets, the Launch Bay includes a small mockup of the Mos Eisley cantina—where you may snap a selfie at the holochess table—and a corner full of video consoles where gamers can test-drive Star Wars games.

To exit, guests pass through the Launch Bay Cargo Shop, stocked with high-end memorabilia aimed at well-heeled collectors. If you want mass-market Star Wars clothes and toys, head over to The Star Trader in Tomorrowland. If, on the other hand, you want to spend $4,000 on an authentically detailed Darth Vader costume (perfect for wearing to any wedding or bar mitzvah) or $3,050 on a life-size Kenner Boba Fett action figure, this is the place.

DISNEY DISH WITH JIM HILL

WATCH THIS SPACE (RIDE) So what happens to Tomorrowland when Star Wars: Galaxy's Edge (the 14-acre "land" under construction behind Fantasyland and Frontierland) opens to guests in 2019? What does that mean for superpopular rides like Star Tours (which first opened to the public in January 1987)? Until recently, it was believed that the four motion-based simulators of Star Tours would be repurposed for a West Coast version of the Iron Man Experience (a 3-D simulator ride that debuted at Hong Kong Disneyland in summer 2016). But Walt Disney Imagineering wants to build a whole Marvel-themed land at DCA behind Hollywood Land and A Bug's Land, so the Southern Californian version of the Iron Man Experience is now slated for that theme park. Well, things are looking kind of terminal for the Star Tours terminal building.

TOURING TIPS Lines can get long for the meet and greets, so be sure to set aside at least 30 minutes each to meet Darth Vader or Chewbacca. Star Wars Launch Bay doesn't open until 10 a.m., but guests line up here from rope drop for *Jedi Training* sign-ups.

Tomorrowland Theater / *Star Wars: Path of the Jedi* ★★½

APPEAL BY AGE PRESCHOOL ★★★★   GRADE SCHOOL ★★★★½   TEENS ★★★½
YOUNG ADULTS ★★★½   OVER 30 ★★★★   SENIORS ★★★★★

What it is Film clips with special effects. **Scope and scale** Minor attraction. **When to go** Anytime. **Comment** The loud, intense show with tactile effects frightens some young children. **Duration of show** Approximately 10 minutes. **Probable waiting time** 15 minutes.

Loud

Scary

DESCRIPTION AND COMMENTS The Tomorrowland Theater, located directly in front of Space Mountain, featured *Captain EO,* a 3-D sci-fi music video starring Michael Jackson, 1986–1987 and 2009–2014, and *Honey, I Shrunk the Audience,* based on the Rick Moranis comedy franchise, 1987–2009.

Rather than a real attraction, the Tomorrowland Theater now promotes Disney's upcoming or recent theatrical releases. Currently, the theater is home to *Path of the Jedi,* a 10-minute montage of memorable moments from all seven of the Star Wars movies.

Rather than try to recap the plot of the first six films, *Path of the Jedi* takes iconic images and dialogue from the saga and stitches them together thematically instead of chronologically. If you haven't already seen all the movies, the result will be visually dazzling but incoherent; for the rest of us, it makes a great memory jog. The classic footage culminates in the death of Darth Vader, which then segues into a 3-minute montage of moments from *The Force Awakens.* The footage from the recent film includes glimpses of an aged Han Solo and Princess Leia, alongside the youthful new heroes.

Path of the Jedi is not presented in 3-D (a shame since 3-D conversions of all the films exist), but it does use in-theater lighting, wind effects, and occasionally moving seats to give the visuals an added punch.

TOURING TIPS The Tomorrowland Theater isn't on our must-do list. But if you are interested in the featured film, it makes a fine air-conditioned distraction, either on your second day in the park or when everything else has too long a line.

Shows usually begin on the hour and continue about every 15 minutes throughout the day. Even during busier times, you should be able to get into the next show without issue.

The sound level can be earsplitting, frightening some young children. Some adults report that the loud sound track is distracting, even uncomfortable. Avoid seats in the first several rows to avoid a stiff neck. If the bouncing floor bothers you, ask for a stationary seat in the last row.

LIVE ENTERTAINMENT *and* SPECIAL EVENTS

LIVE ENTERTAINMENT IN THE FORM OF BANDS, Disney character appearances, parades, singing and dancing, and ceremonies further enliven and add color to Disneyland Park on a daily basis. During the off-season, certain evening spectaculars (such as the fireworks and *Fantasmic!*) may be performed only on weekends. For specific information about what's happening on the day you visit, check the daily entertainment schedule in the *Times Guide*. Be forewarned, however, that if you are on a tight schedule, it is impossible to both see the park's featured attractions and take in the numerous and varied live performances offered. In our one-day touring plans, starting on page 371, we exclude the live performances in favor of seeing as much of the park as time permits. This is a tactical decision based on the fact that the parades and *Fantasmic!,* Disneyland Park's river spectacular, siphon crowds away from the more popular rides, shortening waiting lines.

The color and pageantry of live events around the park are an integral part of the Disneyland Park entertainment mix and a persuasive argument for second-day touring. Though live entertainment is varied, plentiful, and nearly continuous throughout the day, several productions are preeminent.

Fantasmic! (FastPass) ★★★★★

APPEAL BY AGE	PRESCHOOL ★★★★½	GRADE SCHOOL ★★★★½	TEENS ★★★★★
YOUNG ADULTS ★★★★½		OVER 30 ★★★★★	SENIORS ★★★★½

What it is Multimedia water pageant with live characters. **Scope and scale** Super-headliner. **When to go** See *Times Guide* for showtimes; FastPass only. If there's only one show, get a FastPass the first hour the park is open. **Comment** Not to be missed. **Duration of show** 23 minutes. **Probable waiting time** 30–60 minutes for best view.

Loud   Scary

DESCRIPTION AND COMMENTS *Fantasmic!* is a mixed-media show presented one or more times each evening the park is open 10 p.m. or later. Staged at the end of Tom Sawyer Island opposite the Frontierland and New Orleans Square waterfronts, *Fantasmic!* stars Mickey Mouse in his role as the sorcerer's apprentice from *Fantasia.* The production uses lasers, images projected on a shroud of mist, fireworks, lighting effects, and music in combinations so stunning that you can scarcely believe what you have seen.

The plot is simple: good versus evil. The story gets lost in all the special effects at times, but no matter—it is the spectacle, not the story line, that is so overpowering. While *beautiful, stunning,* and *powerful* are words that immediately come to mind, they fail to convey the uniqueness of this presentation, which includes a 45-foot-tall full-bodied fire-breathing dragon (nicknamed Murphy) for the finale. It could be argued, with some validity, that *Fantasmic!* alone is worth the price of Disneyland Park admission. Needless to say, we rate *Fantasmic!* as not to be missed.

Fantasmic! reopened in 2017, after the Rivers of America rerouting, with upgrades to its behind-the-scenes infrastructure, as well as a few updates to the show. Pinocchio's "I've Got No Strings" scene has been replaced with a sequence featuring Aladdin, and Snow White's former spotlight moment now belongs to Rapunzel. Most notable, the Sailing Ship *Columbia* is still the setting for a buccaneer battle, but now the pirates come from the Caribbean instead of Never Land.

TOURING TIPS After years of watching guests stake out prime viewing spots along the edge of the New Orleans Square and Frontierland waterfronts as much as 4 hours in advance, Disney implemented a FastPass-only policy for *Fantasmic!* that is very similar to the one enforced at DCA's *World of Color.* There are now a few ways to see *Fantasmic!*, none of which should require showing up more than an hour before showtime.

The easiest method is to grab a FastPass ticket early in the day. Distribution of *Fantasmic!* FastPass tickets takes place on Big Thunder Trail, the path to the left of Big Thunder Mountain Railroad as you approach Fantasyland from Frontierland. FastPass tickets are distributed until 1 hour before showtime or until they run out, whichever comes first. The return of *Fantasmic!* after more than a year on hiatus has resulted in FastPass tickets running out entirely by noon, but demand for the show should settle down as 2018 progresses. Historically, tickets for the first show are often available until early afternoon, and the second show (when scheduled) can sometimes be snagged until just an hour or so before showtime.

The general FastPass viewing sections (in the order they are distributed) are Yellow, the entrance of which is located near the petrified tree (across from The Golden Horseshoe) in Frontierland; Green, located on the bridge over the Pirates of the Caribbean's entrance; and Blue, in front of The Haunted Mansion in New Orleans Square. The color of the viewing section is printed on the ticket, and that color is the only section the ticket holder is allowed to enter. Yellow, the largest section, watches from along the waterfront to the right of the center island. Guests who purchase dining packages use the center section along the water. The Blue section is located in the center and left, directly behind the dining section, and those in Green stand against the bridge's railing. You can't request a specific section; before pulling your pass, ask a cast member at the FastPass machines which section they are dispensing and which ones are gone.

Fantasmic! general FastPass return windows begin 1 hour before show-time and end when the show begins. If you need to stand right at the railing in the heart of the splash zone, you'll want to be the first inside the viewing pen when it opens. Otherwise, you're best off arriving about 20–30 minutes before curtain and watching from the rear, taking advantage of any available elevation. Entry can be a bit confusing, so pay careful attention to your kids; look for colored lights indicating your section's entrance, and follow the flashlight-wielding cast members' directions.

Fantasmic! FastPasses are disconnected from the rest of Disneyland's FastPass machines, meaning that if you obtain a *Fantasmic!* FastPass, you can also immediately get one for another attraction.

Fantasmic! dining packages are available at Blue Bayou ($65 adults; $25 kids) and River Belle Terrace ($45 adults; $25 kids), both plus tax. Dining packages include a three-course meal and a FastPass ticket for a special preferred viewing area. All FastPass viewing areas are standing room only, but River Belle Terrace diners can pay an extra $15 per person for premium patio seating, from which they can stay and watch the 8 p.m. show. The dinner packages begin at 4 p.m. While the meals are certainly overpriced, especially in comparison to the similar *World of Color* packages next door, the ease of entry and expansive elbow room afforded by preferred Fast-Passes are almost worth the expense.

For those looking to spend a little less money, there is also the *Fantasmic!* On-the-Go Dining Package ($29.99 adults; $19.99 kids) at Hungry Bear Restaurant. This package includes an entrée (salmon, barbecue chicken, pork ribs, or vegetarian frittata), natural soda, and a reserved FastPass ticket for the dining section. On-the-Go Dining Packages can be reserved in advance and may be picked up 3–8 p.m. (varies with show schedule). Reservations for all *Fantasmic!* dining packages can be made online at **disneyland.disney.go.com/dining/disneyland/fantasmic-dinner -packages** or by calling ☎ 714-781-3463.

Fantasmic! viewing spots are first come, first served for all guests, including those in the FastPass dining-experience viewing section, which is located along the waterfront from center stage to Tom Sawyer Island. You can enter the dining section near the Harbour Galley restaurant beginning 30 minutes before each showtime, and the earlier you get in, the better spot you will obtain.

Disney also offers limited standby viewing for all showings. The standby viewing area is not the best spot to see the show due to its location at the far left end of the viewing area. You'll be looking at the side of the show rather than the front of it. The standby line begins 1 hour before showtime and is located between the Harbour Galley restaurant and the Tom Sawyer Island raft dock. The standby viewing section is small and fills up quickly. Plan to get in line as soon as it opens 1 hour before showtime. If you do not have a FastPass ticket, you will be aggressively shooed away from every available vantage point outside the designated standby section.

No matter which method you use, you'll probably spend some time sitting around waiting. A mom from Lummi Island, Washington, dismantled her Disney stroller to make a nest:

We used the snap-off cover on the rental stroller to sit on during Fantasmic! *since the ground was really cold.*

Along similar lines, a middle-aged New York man wrote, saying:

Your excellent guidebook also served as a seat cushion while seated on the ground waiting for the show to begin. Make future editions thicker for greater comfort.

Rain and wind conditions sometimes cause *Fantasmic!* to be canceled. Unfortunately, Disney officials usually do not make a final decision about whether to proceed or cancel until just before showtime. Note that if you purchased a *Fantasmic!* dining package earlier in the day, you will not be refunded if a show is canceled.

If you see the first *Fantasmic!* showing, stay in place afterward for the nightly fireworks, which should start a few minutes later. If attending the second performance, you'll be prevented from entering the New Orleans waterfront until all the earlier guests have exited the viewing areas.

Finally, make sure to hang on to children during *Fantasmic!* and to give them explicit instructions for regrouping in the event that you become separated. Be especially vigilant when the crowd disperses after the show.

Incidentally, if you invested in the Made with Magic light-up ears and other glowing accessories that synchronize with Disney California Adventure's *World of Color* show (see page 313), you'll find that they interact with *Fantasmic!* as well. At times, an exclusive viewing area may be offered for hat holders, intensifying the impact of the illumination effects.

PARADES

DISNEY THEME PARKS ARE FAMOUS THE WORLD OVER for their parades. Currently, there is a parade every day in late afternoon or early evening. On days when the park closes late (10 p.m.–midnight), the parade may run twice. The parades are full-blown productions with some combination of floats, huge balloons of the characters, marching bands, old-time vehicles, dancers, and costumed Disney characters. Themes for the parades vary from time to time, and a special holiday parade is always produced for Christmas. **Mickey's Soundsational Parade,** Disneyland's latest daytime processional, features a whimsical marching band theme with floats dedicated to *The Princess and the Frog, The Little Mermaid,* and Drummer Mickey. The parade is well worth watching, from the stick-twirling drum-line kickoff to the *Mary Poppins* finale. DCA's **Pixar Play Parade** (see page 317) will relocate to Disneyland for 2018's Pixar Fest.

Parades always draw thousands of guests from the attraction lines. We recommend, therefore, watching from the departure point. With this strategy you can enjoy the parade and then, while the parade is continuing on its route, take advantage of the diminished lines at the attractions. Watching a parade that begins in Fantasyland from Small World Mall affords the greatest mobility in terms of accessing other areas of the park when the parade has passed.

Main Street is the most crowded area from which to watch a parade when the route begins at Town Square. The opposite is true when the parade begins in Fantasyland. The upper platform of the Main Street

Station affords the best viewing perspective along the route. The best time to get a position on the platform is when the parade begins in Fantasyland. When this happens, good spots on the platform are available right up to the time the parade begins. When you are at the end of the parade route, you can assume that it will take the parade 15–18 minutes to get to you.

Keep an eye on your children during parades and give them explicit instructions for regrouping in the event that you get separated. Children constantly jockey for better viewing positions. A few wiggles this way and a few wiggles the other, and presto, they are lost in the crowd. Finally, be especially vigilant when the crowd starts dispersing after the parade. Thousands of people suddenly strike out in different directions, creating a perfect situation for losing a child or two.

EVENING PARADE At press time, Disneyland's popular Paint the Night was being transferred to DCA. If and when another nighttime parade replaces it, expect it to draw heavy crowds like its predecessors.

On nights with two scheduled nighttime parades, the first performance will start at It's a Small World, travel past the west side of Matterhorn Bobsleds, go around the Tomorrowland side of Central Plaza, head down Main Street, and then circle Town Square counterclockwise. The second performance will begin at Town Square and run the route in the opposite direction. Most guests watch from Central Plaza or Main Street. The viewing area in front of It's a Small World will fill up last, so we recommend checking there if you need a spot.

The parade route will fill up a couple of hours early for the first showing, so we recommend grabbing a spot for the fireworks, and then immediately getting a spot for the second performance of the evening parade. Any spot along the parade route will offer the same experience, so you shouldn't worry if you can't see the parade on Main Street. Once the parade has started, count on gridlock all along the route, especially on Main Street. Due to aggressive crowd-control restrictions on the sidewalks, you're best off entering or exiting the park via the backstage breezeways (if open) or Emporium shops.

LIVE ENTERTAINMENT THROUGHOUT THE PARK

PARADES AND *FANTASMIC!* MAKE UP only a part of the daily live-entertainment offerings at Disneyland Park. The following is an incomplete list of other performances and events that are scheduled with some regularity and that require no reservations.

DISNEY CHARACTER APPEARANCES Disney characters appear at random throughout the park but are routinely present in Mickey's Toontown, in Fantasyland, and on Main Street. An irregularly used greeting area that sometimes features Aladdin and Jasmine is located at Aladdin's Oasis in Adventureland (see the *Times Guide*). Disney princesses are on call daily at the Royal Hall at Fantasy Faire (see page 246). An elaborate character-greeting area, Pixie Hollow (see page 246) offers a chance to meet Tinker Bell.

DISNEY CHARACTER MEALS Disney characters join guests for breakfast each morning until 11 a.m. at the **Plaza Inn** on Main Street, **Disney's PCH Grill** at Paradise Pier Hotel, and **Storytellers Café** at the Grand Californian Hotel. Disney characters also join guests for breakfast and dinner at **Goofy's Kitchen** at the Disneyland Hotel. **Ariel's Grotto** at Disney California Adventure serves breakfast and lunch with Ariel and friends.

REMEMBER . . . DREAMS COME TRUE ★★★★½ After retiring the acclaimed *Disneyland Forever* fireworks with the conclusion of its Diamond Anniversary celebration, the park resurrected *Remember . . . Dreams Come True*, originally created for the resort's 50th birthday in 2005. The show runs the full gamut of special effects: a rousing score, spectacular firework effects, sophisticated new video projection mapping on the castle, lasers, and an impressive flight from the fairy Tinker Bell. Julie Andrews narrates this pyrotechnic tribute to classic Disneyland attractions—featuring a pirate cannon assault on Sleeping Beauty Castle and audio from Adventure Thru Inner Space—with music from Walt Disney World's former *Wishes* fireworks.

We rate this show as not to be missed, but seeing it poses some serious challenges that you should be aware of. Without a doubt, the area around the central hub is the best vantage point for watching the show; stand too far down Main Street or at the train station and the castle projections will be just postage stamps.

Unfortunately, every guest in the park won't fit in that sweet spot at the same time. Fortunately, the fireworks were specifically designed to look good from multiple locations throughout the park. If you want the ideal view, you'll need to camp out on the curb (possibly for hours) before the evening's first parade and then claim your fireworks position as soon as the parade passes. Alternatively, slowly browse through Main Street's candy shop while the parade is concluding, or linger on the Adventureland side of the hub (where the parade does not pass) and then slip out the exit and into the street following the final float. Our favorite method is to linger outside Main Street Photo Supply and step into the middle of Main Street just as the first parade passes. Cast members will quickly erect a rope barrier to form a crosswalk at that intersection; if you are standing immediately on the south side of it, no one will be allowed to stand directly in front of you during the fireworks and block your view of the castle. Be warned—the crushing crowds can make this aggravating for adults and almost impossible with stroller-bound kids in tow.

The same projections seen on the castle are also projected on the surface of It's a Small World. You'll be missing out on the bevy of fireworks and lasers that shoot out of Sleeping Beauty Castle, but It's a Small World will be your best option if Main Street is full.

Your third option is viewing from the Rivers of America. Fireworks similar to those launched around the castle are shot from Tom Sawyer Island, and video is projected onto the mist screens used in *Fantasmic!*, but they're not as sharp as the ones projected on the other two locations. You'll also miss most or all of the flames and flying. The benefit of viewing from Rivers of America is that, if you have a Fast-Pass for the first showing of *Fantasmic!*, you can stay in your spot through the fireworks. Though you get the least impressive view from here, it's the least stressful way to experience the fireworks and can be very enjoyable if you haven't already seen them from a better location.

Finally, be forewarned that the fireworks may be canceled for safety reasons with only a few minutes' notice if there are stiff winds at upper altitudes, even if the air at ground level seems calm. During one of our weeklong visits, the fireworks were nixed a full 40% of the time, which is a fairly frustrating percentage; you've never heard a collective groan like 50,000 people learning they've waited for nothing. For this reason, we don't recommend that you build your night around the fireworks—as wondrous as they are—if you only have one night at the resort.

In 2017 Disneyland introduced the Tomorrowland Skyline Lounge Experience, which bundles a boxed snack and beverage with access to the upstairs balcony of the Star Wars Launch Bay building, which affords a fine vantage for the fireworks but no view of the castle projections. Admission is $45 per person (age 3 and up), and there are no refunds if the fireworks are canceled; visit **disneyland.disney.go.com /dining/disneyland/tomorrowland-skyline-lounge** or call ☎ 714-781-3463 to make reservations.

Remember . . . Dreams Come True will be preempted in 2018 with a limited-time Pixar fireworks spectacular, which will feature projections of characters like the Little Green Men on Main Street's buildings. Two other first-rate fireworks shows—*Halloween Screams* and *Believe . . . In Holiday Magic*—are performed seasonally and may require paid admission to an after-hours party. *Halloween Screams* is the centerpiece of the extra-cost parties held after regular hours in the fall; it is hosted by Jack Skellington (incarnated as an animated skull projected onto a giant balloon next to the castle) and his flying ghost-dog Zero, along with a rogue's gallery of Disney villains. Tinker Bell does not appear in the winter show, and the sound track selections focus on traditional holiday tunes, making *Holiday Magic* the most dignified and least Disneyfied of the fireworks spectaculars.

DISNEY ROCK GROUPS High-energy Disney rock groups perform seasonally in Tomorrowland according to the *Times Guide*.

FLAG RETREAT CEREMONY Daily at around sunset in Town Square, an honor guard lowers the flag as the Disneyland marching band plays patriotic tunes. Members of the armed forces are encouraged to participate in this respectful ceremony and are called up to be honored by branch.

STREET ENTERTAINMENT Various bands, singers, comics, and strolling musicians entertain in spontaneous (that is, unscheduled) street performances throughout the park. Musical styles include banjo, Dixieland, steel drum, marching, and fife and drum. The Disneyland Band, re-formed in 2015 with younger musicians, now accompanies its repertoire of

Disney tunes with more contemporary orchestrations and some drum corps–style choreography. You'll often find the Bootstrappers, a roving band of musical pirates, roaming the waterfront near New Orleans Square. For a respite from the rides, grab a snack and listen to the ragtime piano player outside the Refreshment Corner on Main Street. You don't want to miss the Dapper Dans, a slapstick barbershop quartet that has been performing on Main Street, U.S.A. in Disneyland since 1959. While the cast changes on a regular basis, the Dans really liven up the street.

UNHERALDED TREASURES *at* DISNEYLAND PARK

UNHERALDED TREASURES are special features found in all of the Disney theme parks that add texture, context, beauty, depth, and subtlety to your visit. Generally speaking, unheralded treasures are nice surprises that should be accorded a little time. Lani Teshima, Unofficial Guide friend and writer for **mouseplanet.com,** knows them all. Her list follows.

TREASURE Snow White's Grotto and Wishing Well | **LOCATION** The front right of Sleeping Beauty Castle

A SLOW STROLL AROUND THE SLEEPING BEAUTY CASTLE can be romantic, but sitting quietly to its right is Snow White's Grotto and Wishing Well. If you stop for a few moments, you can hear the voice of Snow White singing "I'm Wishing" in the area. The grotto includes a trickling waterfall framing statues of Snow White and the Seven Dwarfs, placed on three tiers to make Snow White appear to be off in the distance in an optical illusion that masks the fact that her statue is the same height as those of the dwarfs. Next to the grotto is a wishing well, where you can toss a coin and make a wish. This area is a popular place for Snow White to appear for photos, so don't be surprised to see a group of people milling around.

TREASURE Disneyland Railroad | **LOCATION** Stations in Main Street, U.S.A.; New Orleans Square; Mickey's Toontown/Fantasyland; and Tomorrowland

AFTER A LONG DAY, the Disneyland Railroad offers a nice way to get from one end of the park to another. But trains held a special place in Walt Disney's heart, and the railroad offers much more than just a ride back to the park gates. Pause and turn around before you enter Main Street Station for a beautiful view of the entire length of Main Street, U.S.A. Inside the station, you can enjoy looking at model trains and other little exhibits. If you get off at the New Orleans Square Station, stop and listen— that beeping sound you hear is Walt Disney's 1955 Disneyland Park opening speech in landline telegraphic code. And don't forget to ride from Tomorrowland back to Main Street so you can enjoy an unexpected treat: two large indoor dioramas inside the train tunnel, one depicting the Grand Canyon and another depicting a primeval world, complete with large-scale dinosaurs!

TREASURE Windows on Main Street | **LOCATION** Main Street, U.S.A.

THE NAMES ON THE MAIN STREET WINDOWS represent very special people who have had a profound influence on the park in some way, like guardian angels looking over park guests. The names are also often associated with "professions" related to what the person used to do when he or she worked for Disney. For example, the inscription for a window dedicated to the person who modeled Disneyland's waterways reads, DECORATIVE FOUNTAINS AND WATERCOLOR BY FRED JOERGER. Disneyland still occasionally bestows this window honor in official dedication ceremonies in the park.

TREASURE Frontierland Shootin' Exposition | **LOCATION** Frontierland

SMACK IN THE MIDDLE OF FRONTIERLAND is the shooting gallery where cowpokes can close an eye and squeeze the trigger to try to get their target to ping, ting, move, or light up. Don't discount the Frontierland Shootin' Exposition as just another arcade gimmick. Everything about this well-themed attraction is dusty and rustic—except the laser-powered guns, which are both safe and cause little wear on the targets. About the only things missing are blowing tumbleweeds.

TREASURE Edible Plants | **LOCATION** Tomorrowland

THE DISNEY THEME PARKS are known for their magnificent landscaping, but did you know that many of the plants in Tomorrowland are edible, emphasizing the practicality of a future where the garden plants do double-duty as your vegetable garden? For example, the entryway to Tomorrowland is lined with orange trees, and the bushes along the walkways are planted with leafy vegetables such as lettuce, kale, and rhubarb, as well as herbs such as sage, chives, rosemary, and basil.

TREASURE Flag Retreat Ceremony | **LOCATION** Main Street Square

EVERY DAY IN THE AFTERNOON, THE DISNEYLAND BAND or Dapper Dans vocal group marches to the front of Main Street to perform a number of Americana tunes. Park security guards then lower the American flag as the band plays "The Star-Spangled Banner" in this very respectful ceremony.

TREASURE *Partners* statue | **LOCATION** Central Plaza

AT THE CASTLE END OF MAIN STREET, in the center of the circular hub, is a bronze statue of Walt Disney holding the hand of Mickey Mouse. The statue, simply called *Partners,* pays homage to the two original ambassadors of Disneyland. If you stand in front of the statue, you can get a nice shot of it with Sleeping Beauty Castle in the background. The spot is encircled by a bench, and it's a great place to meet should your family decide to split up to visit different lands. Smaller statues of other popular Disney figures such as Dumbo, Goofy, and Pluto form a ring around this garden oasis in the middle of the park.

QUIET PLACES AT DISNEYLAND PARK

PEACE AND QUIET are anything but the norm at Disneyland. Yet sometimes when you're overwhelmed by it all, a place to decompress is worth a lot, as a reader from Culver City, California, points out:

> *I can't tolerate the hyperstimulation as well as my husband and kids. Sometimes when I'm on my ninth nerve, I'd give anything to put myself in time-out and just collapse for a while. Are there any nice out-of-the-way places in the park where this is possible?*

Actually, there are a few. A **pier** with a canopy and benches, opposite the Matterhorn Bobsleds loading area, overlooks a quiet pool. There's still ambient noise, of course, but the pier is far enough removed from the action to afford both tranquility and a lovely setting. The **Hungry Bear Restaurant** in Critter Country offers upper and lower covered outdoor decks overlooking the Rivers of America. In between major feeding periods, the decks are decidedly low-key. **Snow White's Grotto and Wishing Well** (see page 269) is also very pleasant, though it does have a modest but continuous flow of pedestrian traffic. Finally, the alfresco dining area of **Troubadour Tavern,** adjacent to Fantasyland Theatre, is relaxing between shows.

TRAFFIC PATTERNS
at DISNEYLAND PARK

1. WHAT ATTRACTIONS AND WHICH SECTIONS OF THE PARK DO VISITORS HEAD FOR WHEN THEY FIRST ARRIVE? When guests are admitted, the flow of people to Tomorrowland (Space Mountain, Buzz Lightyear Astro Blasters, Star Tours, and Finding Nemo Submarine Voyage) is heaviest. The next most crowded land is Fantasyland, though the crowds are distributed over a larger number of attractions. Critter Country is likewise crowded with its small area and only two attractions (Splash Mountain and The Many Adventures of Winnie the Pooh). Adventureland, Frontierland, and New Orleans Square fill more slowly, with Mickey's Toontown not really coming alive until later in the morning. As the park fills, visitors appear to head for specific favored attractions that they wish to ride before the lines get long. This, more than any other factor, determines traffic patterns in the mornings and accounts for the relatively equal distribution of visitors throughout Disneyland.

ATTRACTIONS HEAVILY ATTENDED IN EARLY MORNING
ADVENTURELAND Indiana Jones Adventure | Jungle Cruise
CRITTER COUNTRY Splash Mountain
FANTASYLAND Alice in Wonderland | Dumbo the Flying Elephant | Matterhorn Bobsleds | Peter Pan's Flight
TOMORROWLAND Buzz Lightyear Astro Blasters | Finding Nemo Submarine Voyage Space Mountain | Star Tours—The Adventures Continue

2. HOW LONG DOES IT TAKE FOR THE PARK TO REACH PEAK CAPACITY FOR A GIVEN DAY? HOW ARE THE VISITORS DISPERSED THROUGHOUT THE PARK? A surge of early birds arrives before or around opening time but is quickly dispersed throughout the empty park. After the initial onslaught is absorbed, there is a bit of a lull that lasts until about an hour after opening. Following the lull, the park is inundated with arriving guests for about 2 hours, peaking 10–11 a.m. Guests continue to arrive in a steady but diminishing stream until around 2 p.m.

Sampled lines reached their longest length noon–3 p.m., indicating more arrivals than departures in the early afternoon. For general touring purposes, most attractions develop substantial lines 9:30–11 a.m.

In the early morning, Tomorrowland, Critter Country, and Fantasyland fill up first. By late morning and into early afternoon, attendance is fairly equally distributed throughout all of the "lands." Mickey's Toontown, because it is comparatively small, stays mobbed from about 11:30 a.m. on. By midafternoon, however, we noted a concentration of visitors in Fantasyland, New Orleans Square, and Adventureland, and a slight decrease of visitors in Tomorrowland.

In the late afternoon and early evening, attendance continues to be more heavily distributed in Tomorrowland, Critter Country, and Fantasyland. Though Space Mountain, Buzz Lightyear Astro Blasters, Splash Mountain, and Star Tours remain inundated throughout the day, most of the other attractions in Tomorrowland and Critter Country have reasonable lines. In New Orleans Square, The Haunted Mansion, Pirates of the Caribbean, and the multitudes returning from nearby Critter Country keep traffic brisk. Frontierland (except Big Thunder Mountain Railroad) and Adventureland (except Indiana Jones Adventure) become less congested as the afternoon and evening progress.

3. HOW DO MOST VISITORS GO ABOUT TOURING THE PARK? IS THERE A DIFFERENCE IN THE TOURING BEHAVIOR OF FIRST-TIME VISITORS AND REPEAT VISITORS? Many first-time visitors accompany relatives or friends who are familiar with Disneyland and who guide their tour. These tours sometimes proceed in an orderly (clockwise or counterclockwise) sequence. First-time visitors without personal touring guidance tend to be more orderly in their touring. Many first-time visitors, however, are drawn to Sleeping Beauty Castle on entering the park and thus commence their rotation from Fantasyland. Repeat visitors usually proceed directly to their favorite attractions or to whatever is new.

4. WHAT EFFECT DO SPECIAL EVENTS HAVE ON TRAFFIC PATTERNS? Special events such as parades, fireworks, and *Fantasmic!* pull substantial numbers of visitors from the lines for rides. Unfortunately, however, the left hand taketh what the right hand giveth. A parade or *Fantasmic!* snarls traffic flow throughout Disneyland so much that guests find themselves captive wherever they are. Attraction lines in Tomorrowland, Mickey's Toontown, Adventureland, and Fantasyland (behind the castle) diminish dramatically, making Space Mountain, Finding Nemo Submarine Voyage, Buzz Lightyear Astro Blasters, Star Tours, Jungle Cruise, Indiana Jones Adventure, Peter Pan's Flight, and Snow White's Scary Adventures particularly good choices during the evening festivities. The remainder of the park (Critter Country, New Orleans Square, Frontierland, Main Street, and Small World Plaza in Fantasyland) is so congested with guests viewing the parade or *Fantasmic!* that it's almost impossible to move. Conversely, when *Fantasmic!* is on hiatus, the crowds that would otherwise be watching it must go elsewhere, chiefly toward the parade route and attraction queues.

5. WHAT ARE THE TRAFFIC PATTERNS NEAR TO AND AT CLOSING TIME? On our sample days, which were recorded in and out of season, park departures outnumbered arrivals beginning in midafternoon, with a substantial number of guests leaving after the afternoon parade. Additional numbers of visitors departed during the late afternoon as the dinner hour approached. When the park closed early, there were steady departures during the 2 hours preceding closing, with a mass exodus of remaining visitors at closing time.

When the park closed late, departures were distributed throughout the evening hours, with waves of departures following the evening parade(s), fireworks, and *Fantasmic!* Though departures increased exponentially as closing time approached, a huge throng was still on hand when the park finally shut down. The balloon effect of this last throng at the end of the day generally overwhelmed the shops on Main Street, the parking lot, trams, and the hotel shuttles, as well as the exits onto adjoining Anaheim streets. In the hour before closing in the lands other than Main Street, touring conditions were normally uncrowded except at Indiana Jones Adventure in Adventureland and Splash Mountain in Critter Country.

DISNEYLAND PARK TOURING PLANS

THE DISNEYLAND PARK TOURING PLANS are step-by-step plans for seeing as much as possible with a minimum of time wasted standing in line. They are designed to assist you in avoiding crowds and bottlenecks on days of moderate to heavy attendance. On days of lighter attendance (see "Selecting the Time of Year for Your Visit," page 25), the plans will still save you time but will not be as critical to successful touring.

Choosing the Right Touring Plan

If you have two days to spend at Disneyland Park, the two-day touring plans are by far the most relaxed and efficient. The Two-Day Touring Plan A takes advantage of early-morning touring, when lines are short and the park has not yet filled with guests. This plan works well all year and is particularly recommended for days when Disneyland Park closes before 8 p.m. On the other hand, Two-Day Touring Plan B combines the efficiencies of early-morning touring on the first day with the splendor of Disneyland Park at night on the second day. This plan is perfect for guests who wish to sample both the attractions and the special magic of Disneyland Park after dark, including *Fantasmic!*, parades, and fireworks. The Two-Day Touring Plan for Adults with Small Children spreads the experience over two more-relaxed days and incorporates more attractions that both children and parents will enjoy.

For readers who have requested a Three-Day Park-Hopper Touring Plan, we recommend using the Two-Day Disneyland Park Touring Plan of your choice and mixing it with the One-Day Disney California Adventure Touring Plan as you see fit. Enter Disneyland Park first, and then send a runner across the Esplanade to DCA with your entire group's tickets. Because the FastPass systems of the two parks are disconnected, you can collect FastPasses for *World of Color* and Radiator Springs Racers with any you've already claimed in Disneyland Park (such as Space or Splash Mountain). Just keep an eye on your return windows when juggling cross-park FastPasses, as attendants enforce the expiration times.

If you have only one day but wish to see as much as possible, use the One-Day Touring Plan for Adults. This plan will pack as much into a single day as is humanly possible, but it is pretty exhausting. If you prefer a more relaxed visit, try the Author's Select One-Day Touring Plan. This plan features the best that Disneyland Park has to offer (in the author's opinion), eliminating some of the less impressive attractions.

If you have small children, you may want to use the Dumbo-or-Die-in-a-Day Touring Plan for Adults with Small Children. This plan includes most of the children's rides in Fantasyland and Mickey's Toontown and omits roller coasters and other attractions that small children cannot ride (because of Disney's age and height requirements), as well as rides and shows that are frightening for small children. Because this plan calls for adults to sacrifice many of the better Disney attractions, it is not recommended unless you are touring Disneyland Park primarily for the benefit of your children. In essence, you pretty much stand around, sweat, wipe noses, pay for stuff, and watch the children have fun. It's great.

An alternative to the Dumbo plan is the One-Day Touring Plan for Adults or the Author's Select One-Day Touring Plan, taking advantage of switching off, a technique whereby children accompany adults to the loading area of rides with age and height requirements but do not actually ride (see page 154). Switching off allows adults to enjoy the wilder rides while keeping the whole group together.

For guests who really want to burn the candle at both ends (and a bunch of money) by buying a single-day Park Hopper, we offer a one-day/two-park touring plan that touches on the highlights of Disney California Adventure in the morning and Disneyland in the afternoon. See page 323 for details.

Park-Opening Procedures

Your progress and success during your first hour of touring will be affected by the particular opening procedure the Disney people use that day.

A. All guests are held at the turnstiles until the park opens (which may or may not be at the official opening time). On admittance, all "lands" are open. If this is the case on the day you visit, blow right past Main Street and head for the first attraction on whatever touring plan you are following.

B. Guests are admitted to Main Street 30 minutes–1 hour before the remaining "lands" open. Rope barriers block access to the various lands from the central hub on these days. On admittance, move to the rope barrier and stake out a position as follows:

(1) If you are going to Indiana Jones Adventure or Splash Mountain first, take up a position in front of Jolly Holiday Bakery at the central-hub end of Main Street on the left. Wait next to the rope barrier blocking the walkway to Adventureland. When the rest of the park opens, proceed quickly to Adventureland for Indiana Jones, or Critter

Country by way of Adventureland and New Orleans Square for Splash Mountain.

(2) If you are going to Finding Nemo Submarine Voyage, Star Tours, or Space Mountain first, wait on the right side of the central hub. When the rope drops at opening time, bear right and zip into Tomorrowland.

(3) If you are going to Fantasyland or Frontierland first, proceed as far forward in the central hub as allowed and line up at the rope, to the left of Walt and Mickey's central statue.

PRELIMINARY INSTRUCTIONS FOR ALL DISNEYLAND PARK TOURING PLANS

ON DAYS OF MODERATE to heavy attendance, follow the touring plans exactly, deviating only when you do not wish to experience a listed show or ride. For instance, the touring plan may direct you to go next to Big Thunder Mountain Railroad, a roller coaster. If you do not like roller coasters, simply skip that step and proceed to the next activity.

1. Buy your admission in advance (see "Admission Options" on page 20).

2. Call ☎ 714-781-7290 the day before you go for the official opening time.

3. Become familiar with the park-opening procedures (described on page 88) and read over the touring plan of your choice, so you will have a basic understanding of what you are likely to encounter as you enter the park.

DISNEYLAND PARK ONE-DAY TOURING PLAN FOR ADULTS *(page 371)*

FOR Adults without small children. **ASSUMES** Willingness to experience all major rides (including roller coasters) and shows.

If you have only one day but wish to see as much as possible, use this touring plan. It packs as much into a single day as is humanly possible, but it is pretty exhausting. Be forewarned that this plan requires a lot of walking and some backtracking; this is necessary to avoid long waits in line. A little extra walking coupled with some hustle in the morning will save you 2–3 hours of standing in line. Note that you might not complete the tour. How far you get will depend on the size of your group, how quickly you move from ride to ride, how many times you pause for rest or food, how quickly the park fills, and what time the park closes.

ABOUT EARLY ENTRY If you are eligible for early entry, arrive at the turnstiles 45–60 minutes before the early-entry period begins on Tuesday, Thursday, or Saturday (days subject to change) with admission in hand. Upon admission to the park, experience (1) Peter Pan's Flight, (2) Alice in Wonderland, (3) Matterhorn Bobsleds, (4) Star Tours, and (5) Buzz Lightyear Astro Blasters, and then obtain FastPasses for Space Mountain, in that order. If you're not able to enjoy all of the above during the early-entry hour, see as many as you can. When the park opens to the general public, begin the touring plan, skipping any attractions you've already seen.

If you are not eligible for early entry, use the plan on a non-early-entry day (currently Sunday, Monday, Wednesday, or Friday). Do not attempt to use the plan on an early-entry day—Disneyland Park will be packed with early-entry guests before you even make it past the turnstiles. If you wish to tour on an early-entry day but are not eligible for early entry, visit Disney California Adventure and save Disneyland Park for a non-early-entry day.

Note: The success of the touring plan hinges on you entering the park when it first opens. Arrive at the entrance 40 minutes before official opening time.

AUTHOR'S SELECT DISNEYLAND PARK ONE-DAY TOURING PLAN *(page 372)*

FOR Adults touring without small children. **ASSUMES** Willingness to experience all major rides (including roller coasters) and shows.

This touring plan is selective, including only attractions that, in the author's opinion, represent the best that Disneyland Park has to offer. Be forewarned that this plan requires a lot of walking and some backtracking; this is necessary to avoid long waits in line. A little extra walking coupled with some hustle in the morning will save you 2–3 hours of standing in line. Note that you might not complete this tour. How far you get will depend on the size of your group, how quickly you move from ride to ride, how many times you pause for rest or food, how quickly the park fills, and what time the park closes. With a little zip and some luck, it is possible to complete the touring plan even on a busy day when the park closes early.

ABOUT EARLY ENTRY If you are eligible for early entry, arrive at the turnstiles 45–60 minutes before the early-entry period begins on Tuesday, Thursday, or Saturday (days subject to change) with admission in hand. Upon admission to the park, experience (1) Peter Pan's Flight, (2) Alice in Wonderland, (3) Matterhorn Bobsleds, (4) Star Tours, and (5) Buzz Lightyear Astro Blasters, in that order. If you're not able to enjoy all of the above during the early-entry hour, see as many as you can. When the park opens to the general public, begin the touring plan, skipping any attractions you've already seen.

If you are not eligible for early entry, use the plan on a non-early-entry day (currently Sunday, Monday, Wednesday, or Friday). Do not attempt to use the plan on an early-entry day—Disneyland Park will be packed with early-entry guests before you even make it past the turnstiles. If you wish to tour on an early-entry day but are not eligible for early entry, visit Disney California Adventure and save Disneyland Park for a non-early-entry day.

Note: The success of the touring plan hinges on your entering the park when it first opens. Arrive at the entrance 40 minutes before official opening time.

DUMBO-OR-DIE-IN-A-DAY TOURING PLAN FOR ADULTS WITH SMALL CHILDREN *(page 373)*

FOR Parents with children under age 7 who feel compelled to devote every waking moment to the pleasure and entertainment of their small children. **ASSUMES** Periodic stops for rest, restrooms, and refreshment.

The name of this touring plan notwithstanding, this itinerary is not a joke. Regardless of whether you are loving, guilty, masochistic, truly selfless, insane, or saintly, this touring plan will provide a small child with about as perfect a day as possible at Disneyland Park.

If this description has intimidated you somewhat or if you have concluded that your day at Disneyland Park is as important as your children's, use the One-Day Touring Plan for Adults, making use of the switching-off option (see page 154) at those attractions that impose height or age restrictions.

Because the children's attractions in Disneyland Park are the most poorly engineered in terms of handling large crowds, this touring plan is the least efficient of our touring plans. It does represent the best way to experience most of the child-oriented attractions in one day, if that is what you hope to do. We do not make recommendations in this plan for meals. If you can, try to hustle along as quickly as is comfortable until about noon. After noon, it won't make much difference if you stop to eat or take it a little easier.

ABOUT EARLY ENTRY Do not attempt to use the plan on an early-entry day if you're not eligible for early entry—Disneyland Park will be packed with early-entry guests before you even make it past the turnstiles. If you wish to tour on an early-entry day but are not eligible for early entry, visit Disney California Adventure and save Disneyland Park for a non-early-entry day.

If you are eligible for early entry, experience (1) Peter Pan's Flight, (2) Alice in Wonderland, and (3) Dumbo, in that order, and then begin the touring plan, skipping any attractions you've already seen.

Note: The success of this touring plan hinges on you being among the first to enter the park when it opens. Arrive at the entrance 40 minutes before official opening time.

DISNEYLAND PARK TWO-DAY TOURING PLAN FOR ADULTS WITH SMALL CHILDREN *(pages 374–375)*

FOR Parents with children under age 7 who wish to spread their Disneyland Park visit over two days. **ASSUMES** Frequent stops for rest, restrooms, and refreshments.

This touring plan represents a compromise between the observed tastes of adults and the observed tastes of younger children. Included in this touring plan are many of the midway-type rides that your children may have the opportunity to experience at local fairs and amusement parks. These rides at Disneyland Park often require long waits in line, and they consume valuable touring time that could be better spent experiencing the many rides and shows found only at a Disney theme park and which best demonstrate the Disney genius. This touring plan is heavily weighted toward the tastes of younger children. If you want to balance it a bit, try working out a compromise with your kids to forgo some of the carnival-type rides (such as Mad Tea Party, Dumbo, King Arthur Carrousel, and Gadget's Go Coaster) or such rides as Autopia. All of the attractions are appropriate for children 40 inches and shorter.

Another alternative is to use one of the other two-day touring plans and take advantage of the switching-off option (see page 154). This technique allows small children to be admitted to rides such as Space Mountain, Indiana Jones Adventure, Big Thunder Mountain Railroad, Star Tours, and Splash Mountain. The children wait in the loading area as their parents ride one at a time; the nonriding parent waits with the children.

TIMING This two-day touring plan takes advantage of early-morning touring. On each day you should complete the structured part of the plan by 3 p.m. or so. We highly recommend returning to your hotel by midafternoon for a nap and an early dinner. If the park is open in the evening, come back to the park by 7:30 or 8 p.m. for the evening parade, fireworks, and *Fantasmic!*

ABOUT EARLY ENTRY Do not attempt to use day two of the touring plan on early-entry days if you are not eligible for early entry—Fantasyland will be packed with early-entry guests before you even make it past the turnstiles. Day one of the plan begins in Adventureland, which is not affected by early entry. Come back to Disneyland Park on the following non-early-entry day and proceed with day two. You can do day two first (the order makes no difference) as your travel plans dictate.

If you are eligible for early entry, experience (1) Peter Pan's Flight, (2) Alice in Wonderland, (3) Mr. Toad's Wild Ride, and (4) Dumbo, in that order, followed by the other Fantasyland attractions. At the end of the early-entry hour, begin day two of the touring plan, skipping any attractions you've already seen.

Note: Because the needs of small children are so varied, we have not built specific instructions for eating into the touring plan. Simply stop for refreshments or a meal when you feel the urge. For best results, however, try to keep moving in the morning. In the afternoon, you can eat, rest often, and adjust the pace to your liking.

DISNEYLAND PARK TWO-DAY TOURING PLAN A, FOR DAYTIME TOURING OR FOR WHEN THE PARK CLOSES EARLY *(pages 376–377)*

FOR Parties wishing to spread their Disneyland Park visit over two days and parties preferring to tour in the morning. **ASSUMES** Willingness to experience all major rides (including roller coasters) and shows.

TIMING This two-day touring plan takes advantage of early-morning touring and is the most efficient of all the touring plans for comprehensive touring with the least time lost waiting in line. On each day you should complete the structured part of the plan by 3 p.m. or so. If you are visiting Disneyland Park during a period of the year when the park is open late (after 8 p.m.), you might prefer our Two-Day Touring Plan B, which offers morning touring on one day and late afternoon and evening touring on the other day. Another highly recommended option is to return to your hotel around midafternoon for a well-deserved nap and an early dinner, and to come back to the park by 7:30 or 8 p.m. for the evening parade, fireworks, and live entertainment.

ABOUT EARLY ENTRY Do not attempt to use the plan on early-entry days if you are not eligible for early entry—Disneyland Park will be packed with early-entry guests before you even make it past the turnstiles. Do day one of the plan on a non-early-entry day. The next day will be an early-entry day, so visit Disney California Adventure on that day. Come back to Disneyland Park on the following non-early-entry day and proceed with day two.

If you're eligible for early entry, experience (1) Peter Pan's Flight, (2) Alice in Wonderland, (3) Mr. Toad's Wild Ride, and (4) Matterhorn Bobsleds, in that order. If you're not able to enjoy all of the above during the early-entry hour, ride as many as you can. When the park opens to the general public, begin day one of the touring plan, skipping any attractions you've already seen.

DISNEYLAND PARK TWO-DAY TOURING PLAN B, FOR MORNING AND EVENING TOURING OR FOR WHEN THE PARK IS OPEN LATE *(pages 378–379)*

FOR Parties who want to enjoy Disneyland Park at different times of day, including evenings and early mornings. **ASSUMES** Willingness to experience all major rides (including roller coasters) and shows.

TIMING This two-day touring plan is for those visiting Disneyland Park on days when the park is open late (after 8 p.m.). The plan offers morning touring on the first day and late afternoon and evening touring on the other day. If the park closes early, or if you prefer to do all of your touring during the morning and early afternoon, use the Two-Day Touring Plan A.

ABOUT EARLY ENTRY If you are not eligible for early entry, do not try to use day one of the plan on an early-entry day. Disneyland Park will be packed with early-entry guests before you even get past the turnstiles.

If you are eligible for early entry and want to use day one of the plan on an early-entry day, experience (1) Peter Pan's Flight, (2) Alice in Wonderland, (3) Matterhorn Bobsleds, (4) Space Mountain, and (5) Finding Nemo Submarine Voyage, in that order. If you're not able to enjoy all of the above during the early-entry hour, ride as many as you can. When the park opens to the general public, begin day one of the touring plan, skipping any attractions you've already seen.

THE DISNEYLAND NO RIDES, NO QUEUES, NO STRESS ANTI-TOURING PLAN

MOST OF OUR READERS are interested in touring plans to get them through as many attractions as possible in the most efficient manner. But, like the authors, some of you may have siblings, spouses, or other companions who are congenitally opposed to queuing for anything clanking or claustrophobic. What can Disney do to occupy your Aunt Gertie, who is dead set against standing in a line, or sitting in anything with a lap bar?

Disneyland Park is one of the few places where you can experience a full day of entertainment without getting on a ride faster than the railroad, and without waiting more than 15 minutes or so, even during the busiest season.

Yes, you can get your money's worth at Disneyland without sprinting to Space Mountain or spinning in a teacup. You just have to adjust your expectation of what constitutes an attraction. (A handful of sedate activities are available at Disney California Adventure, such as Disney Animation, the winery, and the bakery tour, but not enough to justify a full-price pass.)

Because this "anti-touring" plan is designed to eliminate stress, there is no strict order to follow the steps in, nor instructions to arrive before rope drop (though it doesn't hurt). Simply tour the park as your feet take you, skipping any suggested experiences that don't interest you. If there is more than a 15–20 minute wait for anything you want to do, simply move along and check back later. Most important, take a break after 4 or 5 hours and leave the park for a nap, meal, or swim. The key is to take your time and (literally) stop to smell the roses.

Main Street, U.S.A.

- Ride one of the vintage vehicles up Main Street to the hub, and then take a different one back.
- Look at the memorabilia in the Main Street Station, and then ride the rails for a round-trip or two around the park.
- Explore the Disneyana shop's collectible artwork inside the old Bank of Main Street.
- Peer in the Emporium's high-tech animated window displays.
- See *Great Moments with Mr. Lincoln,* arriving early enough to see the Steve Martin preshow and the lobby's Disney Gallery historical displays.
- Watch the classic short films inside the Main Street Cinema.
- Snoop on the antique party line telephones inside the Market House, and then sit outside at a table on Center Street, listening to the amusing sounds emanating from the windows above.
- Check out the primitive 3-D movie viewers in the Penny Arcade.
- Watch the chefs in the candy store whip up a batch of sweets. On select days during the holidays, the handmade supersize candy canes are a can't-miss. They are in short supply, so you'll need to line up early and receive a numbered wristband to buy one, but anyone can walk up and watch them being made.
- Catch a performance or three of the Dapper Dans, Main Street Marching Band, or Coke Corner ragtime pianist. The daily flag retreat ceremony is not to be missed.
- Try to identify the names of Disney Legends and Imagineers honored on Main Street's windows.
- Stop and watch some artisans—such as the silhouette cutters and glass sculptors—work.
- Ask the prestidigitators at the Magic Shop to demonstrate some tricks for

you, and stare at the creepy optical illusion in the window.
- On the right side of the street next to the silhouette shop, sit in the chairs on the porch.
- Take a picture with the *Partners* statue in the central hub, and appreciate the surrounding flora and fauna.

Adventureland
- See the *Enchanted Tiki Room,* arriving in time to buy a Dole Whip and watch the preshow.
- Jungle Cruise is gentle fun if the line isn't long.
- If stairs aren't an issue, climb Tarzan's Treehouse, or at least enter through the exit and watch the kids going wild on the playground.
- Consider walking through the Indiana Jones Adventure queue at least once, even if you aren't interested in riding; it's an impressive (if exhausting) example of scenic design. When the posted wait time is more than 15 minutes, get a FastPass to skip the boring exterior line. Before you climb the stairs near the loading bay, simply tell a cast member that you want to exit. If you are brave but impatient, Indy's single-rider line often has little to no wait.

New Orleans Square
- Haunted Mansion and Pirates of the Caribbean both move guests through quickly even on busy days, and neither is likely to disturb any but the most delicate constitutions.
- Seek out the jazz and pirate bands that play in the area.
- Poke around the lovingly detailed alleyways around the Pirates of the Caribbean exit.
- Sit outside Café Orléans with a plate of *pommes frites* and watch the crowds go by.

Critter Country
- Stand on the bridge near Splash Mountain and watch riders take the plunge. If you dare to get damp, the single-rider wait is usually bearable.
- Feed the ducks from the porch behind the Hungry Bear Restaurant.

Frontierland
- Take a raft to Tom Sawyer Island, and explore the island.
- Sail on the Sailing Ship *Columbia, Mark Twain* Riverboat, or both. You can usually step on board just before departure time without standing in line, or board early for the best seat at the top front.
- Grab some chili and a box seat for the show in The Golden Horseshoe.
- Look for the petrified tree that was an anniversary gift from Walt to his wife; she donated it to the park. Also try to spot railroad tunnel remains from Mine Train Through Nature's Wonderland, across from Big Thunder Mountain.
- Pump some quarters into the Frontierland Shootin' Exposition.
- Walk through the Rancho del Zocalo patio, especially when decorated for Dia de Los Muertos.

Fantasyland
- Go through the Sleeping Beauty Castle walk-through, or watch the alternative experience video.

- Make a wish at Snow White's well in front of the castle, and gaze at her grotto of handcrafted sculptures.
- Cruise Storybook Land Canal Boats or It's a Small World if lines are short.
- Try on some mouse ears in the Mad Hatter chapeau shop.
- Take a break with a vendor treat (such as an ear of corn) on the benches at the old motorboat dock across from the Matterhorn Bobsleds.
- Stick your head in the Fantasy Faire if a show is scheduled, but don't bother with the massive queue to meet a princess.
- The elevated mall near It's a Small World is a convenient spot to stand for the parade or fireworks show.
- Enjoy the stage musical inside Fantasyland Theatre.

Mickey's Toontown

- Play with the interactive doodads dotted around the building facades.
- Take a tour of Mickey's and Minnie's homes, but bail on the meet and greet if the line is out the door.
- Walk though the cleverly decorated children's playgrounds, being wary of bouncing babes.

Tomorrowland

- Take the monorail to Downtown Disney for a bite or a drink, and then return (remember your park ticket!).
- Watch young Padawans battle Sith Lords on Tomorrowland Terrace in the *Jedi Training: Trials of the Temple* show. Check the schedule for other entertainment on this stage.
- Experience the film clips inside the Tomorrowland Theater. Ask for a nonmoving seat in the back to avoid bouncing.
- The line for Buzz Lightyear Astro Blasters moves swiftly, and almost everyone of all ages loves it.
- Browse the unique Star Wars merchandise (including build-your-own light sabers and droid action figures) in The Star Trader with a life-size X-Wing overhead.
- Search for imaginatively groomed edible plants along the Tomorrowland walkways.
- Explore the Star Wars Launch Bay exhibits.

PART SIX

DISNEY CALIFORNIA ADVENTURE

We enjoyed DCA much more than Disneyland Park. More fun, fewer strollers and little kids, more-adventurous people. Just a different feeling all the way around.

—Mom from Bend, Oregon

A MOST ANTICIPATED SEQUEL

DISNEY CALIFORNIA ADVENTURE held its grand opening on February 8, 2001. Known as DCA among Disneyphiles, the park is a bouquet of contradictions conceived in Fantasyland, starved in utero by corporate Disney, and born into a hostile environment of Disneyland loyalists who believed they'd been handed a second-rate theme park. Its parts are stunningly beautiful yet come together awkwardly, failing to compose a handsome whole. And perhaps most lamentable of all, the California theme is impotent by virtue of being all-encompassing. But after a billion-dollar metamorphosis, DCA overcame its inauspicious debut and emerged as an honorable companion to its storied older sibling across the Esplanade.

The history of the park is another of those convoluted tales found only in Robert Ludlum novels and corporate Disney. Southern California Disney fans began clamoring for a second theme park shortly after Epcot opened at Walt Disney World in 1982. Though there was some element of support within the Walt Disney Company, the Disney loyal had to content themselves with rumors and half-promises for two decades while they watched new Disney parks go up in Tokyo, Paris, and Florida. For years, Disney teasingly floated the Westcot concept, a California version of Epcot that was always just about to break ground. Whether it was a matter of procrastination or simply pursuing better opportunities elsewhere, the Walt Disney Company sat on the sidelines while the sleepy community of Anaheim became a sprawling city and property values skyrocketed. By the time Disney emerged from its Westcot fantasy and began to get serious about a second California park, the

Disney California Adventure

Paradise Pier/
Pixar Pier

Grizzly
Peak

Disney's Grand Californian
Hotel & Spa

Pacific
Wharf

Cars Land

a bug's land

Buena
Vista
Street

Entrance

Hollywood Land

1. Anna & Elsa's Royal
   Welcome
2. Bakery Tour
3. California Screamin'
4. Disney Animation
5. Disney Junior Dance
   Party
6. Flik's Fun Fair
7. Frozen—Live at the
   Hyperion
8. Golden Zephyr
9. Goofy's Sky School
10. Grizzly River Run
11. Guardians of the
    Galaxy—Mission:
    Breakout!
12. It's Tough to Be a Bug!
13. Jumpin' Jellyfish
14. King Triton's Carousel
15. The Little Mermaid:
    Ariel's Undersea
    Adventure
16. Luigi's Rollickin'
    Roadsters
17. Mater's Junkyard
    Jamboree
18. Mickey's Fun Wheel
19. Monsters, Inc.
    Mike & Sulley
    to the Rescue
20. Radiator Springs
    Racers
21. Red Car Trolleys

22. Redwood Creek
    Challenge Trail and
    Wilderness Explorer
    Camp
23. Silly Symphony Swings
24. Soarin' Around the
    World
25. Sunset Showcase
    Theater
26. Toy Story Midway
    Mania!
27. Turtle Talk with Crush
28. World of Color
    Nighttime Spectacular

price tag—not to mention the complexity of integrating such a development into a mature city—was mind-boggling.

Westcot had been billed as a $2- to $3-billion, 100-plus-acre project, so that was what the Disney faithful were expecting when Disney California Adventure was announced. What they got was a park that cost $1.4 billion (slashed from an original budget of about $2.1 billion), built on 55 acres, including a sizable piece carved out for the Grand Californian Hotel. It's quite a small park by modern theme park standards, but $1.4 billion, when lavished on 55 acres, ought to buy a pretty good park.

Then there's the park's theme. Though flexible, California Adventure came off like a default setting, lacking in imagination, weak in concept, and without intrinsic appeal, especially when you stop to consider that two-thirds of Disneyland guests come from Southern California. As further grist for the mill, before the arrival of Cars Land, there was precious little new technology at work in Disney's newest theme park. Of the headliner attractions, only two—Soarin' Over California (now Soarin' Around the World), a simulator ride, and Toy Story Midway Mania!, a "virtual dark ride"—broke new ground. All the rest are recycled, albeit popular, attractions from the Animal Kingdom and Disney's Hollywood Studios. When you move to the smaller-statured second half of the attraction batting order, it gets worse. Most of these attractions are little more than off-the-shelf midway rides spruced up with a Disney story line and facade.

From a competitive perspective, Disney California Adventure was an underwhelming shot at Disney's three Southern California competitors. The Hollywood section of DCA takes a hopeful poke at Universal Studios Hollywood, while Paradise Pier/Pixar Pier offers midway rides à la Six Flags Magic Mountain. Finally, the whole California theme has for years been the eminent domain of Knott's Berry Farm. In short, there's not much originality in DCA, only Disney's now-redundant mantra that "whatever they can do, we can do better."

Finally, after more than eight years of basically being in denial about Disney California Adventure, The Walt Disney Company seemed willing to admit that this theme park (which pulled in only about a third of Disneyland's attendance annually) needed some help. On June 15, 2012, The Mouse held a grand reopening to celebrate the completion of a $1.1 billion effort, originally announced in 2007, to address DCA's problems.

Starting at the park entrance, the Imagineers scoured every inch of DCA, injecting charm, character, and ride capacity wherever they could. The current entryway embraces the legacy of Disneyland's founder with a nostalgic re-creation of 1920s Los Angeles. That freshly poured-on theming flows all the way to Paradise Pier/Pixar Pier, where the tacky seaside amusements were softened with new-old Victorian-era stylings. An original family-friendly dark ride based on a popular Piscean princess was added, and the central lagoon now sports a Vegas-quality water show designed expressly to keep crowds in DCA after dark. The final element of DCA's transformation fell into place with 2012's opening of Cars Land, an entire area dedicated to the best-selling Pixar property.

Some Disneyholics may never forgive DCA's dire beginnings, dismissing its upgrades as expensive attempts to patch over a flawed foundation. The rest of us will have some fun enjoying the park for what it is: the theme park equivalent of a jukebox musical, featuring a greatest hits collection of attractions also found in Walt Disney World's Epcot, Hollywood Studios, and Animal Kingdom, along with just enough exclusive E-tickets to give DCA a unique personality all its own.

While the park spent its first decade as a punch line, today DCA is a legitimate destination in its own right. And as the popular Marvel superheroes increase their presence inside the park, look for it to rival its older brother for turnstile entry bragging rights on busy days—something that was once almost unimaginable.

ARRIVING *and*
GETTING ORIENTED

THE ENTRANCE TO DISNEY CALIFORNIA ADVENTURE faces the entrance to Disneyland Park across a brick-paved pedestrian plaza called the **Esplanade.** If you arrive by tram from one of the Disney parking lots, you'll disembark at the Esplanade. Facing east toward Harbor Boulevard, Disneyland Park will be on your left and DCA will be on your right. In the Esplanade are ticket booths, the group sales office, and resort information.

Seen from overhead, Disney California Adventure is roughly arrayed in a fan shape around the park's central visual icon, Grizzly Peak. At ground level, however, the park's layout is not so obvious.

There are six themed "lands" at DCA, not including **Buena Vista Street.** A left turn at the hub leads you to **Hollywood Land,** celebrating California's history as the film capital of the world. **Grizzly Peak** (which absorbed the former Condor Flats area) is reminiscent of the Pacific Northwest woods, while **Pacific Wharf** nods to Monterey's Cannery Row. You'll find Grizzly Peak by taking the first right as you approach the hub, though you must walk two-thirds of the way around the mountain to reach its namesake raft ride. Pacific Wharf is situated along a kidney-shaped lake and can be accessed by following the walkway emanating from the hub at 7 o'clock and winding around Grizzly Peak. A fourth land, **A Bug's Land,** is situated opposite the Golden Vine Winery and can be reached by taking the same route. The fifth land, **Paradise Pier/Pixar Pier,** recalls seaside amusement parks of the Victorian era. It is situated in the southwest corner of the park, around the large lake. **Cars Land** is the sixth land, claiming a former parking lot behind the Pacific Wharf and A Bug's Land, with its primary entrance across from the Golden Vine Winery.

DISNEY CALIFORNIA ADVENTURE SERVICES

Baby Care Center In Pacific Wharf, near the Ghirardelli Soda Fountain

Banking Services/Currency Exchange At the Chamber of Commerce at Buena Vista Street, immediately to your left upon entering

Disneyland and Local Attraction Information At the Chamber of Commerce

First Aid At the Chamber of Commerce

Live Entertainment and Parade Information At the Chamber of Commerce

Lost Adults and Messages At the Chamber of Commerce

Lost and Found Lost and Found for the entire resort is located west of the entrance to Disneyland Park

Lost Children In Pacific Wharf next to the Baby Care Center

Storage Lockers Immediately to your right upon entering

SINGLE-RIDER LINES

YOU CAN OFTEN SAVE TIME WAITING in line by taking advantage of single-rider lines, a separate line for people don't mind riding alone or with a stranger. The objective of single-rider lines is to fill odd spaces left by groups who don't quite fill the entire ride vehicle. Because there aren't many singles and most groups aren't willing to split up, single-rider lines are usually much shorter than the regular line. Four attractions at DCA offer single-rider lines: California Screamin', Goofy's Sky School, Grizzly River Run, and Radiator Springs Racers.

PARK-OPENING PROCEDURES

DISNEYLAND RESORT HOTEL GUESTS get a 1-hour jump on the public four or more mornings each week through the Extra Magic Hours program (see page 30). You'll be required to show a key card from any of the three on-site hotels before being allowed in early. Disneyland Hotel and Paradise Pier guests must go to the park's main entrance; only Grand Californian guests are allowed through that hotel's private entrance into DCA before 11 a.m. This entrance is often overwhelmed, especially on early-entry days, so you may save time by walking to the front gate. All other guests will be allowed through the main entrance onto Buena Vista Street up to 1 hour early and held there until after a brief rope drop musical fanfare at the official opening time. Guests wishing to ride Radiator Springs Racers first (or retrieve a FastPass) will gather to the right of Carthay Circle, while those headed to Guardians of the Galaxy—Mission: Breakout! line up to the left outside Hollywood Land. The crowd will be walked toward their destination at the appointed hour to avoid a stampede.

BUENA VISTA STREET

FROM THE ESPLANADE, where huge block letters spelling CALIFOR-NIA originally stood, you now pass through a Streamline Moderne

NOT TO BE MISSED AT DISNEY CALIFORNIA ADVENTURE
• **A BUG'S LAND** *It's Tough to Be a Bug!*
• **CARS LAND** Radiator Springs Racers
• **GRIZZLY PEAK** Grizzly River Run | Soarin' Around the World
• **HOLLYWOOD LAND** Hyperion Theater | Guardians of the Galaxy—Mission: Breakout!
• **PARADISE PIER/PIXAR PIER** California Screamin' | Toy Story Midway Mania! | *World of Color*

entrance facade, designed after Los Angeles's fabled Pan Pacific Auditorium. (If it looks familiar, that's because it can also be recognized as the entrance to Disney's Hollywood Studios park in Florida.)

DISNEY DISH WITH JIM HILL

YOU'D NEED A VERY LARGE STAMP TO MAIL THESE LETTERS How many of you recall those enormous "C-A-L-I-F-O-R-N-I-A" letters that once sat in the Esplanade between Disneyland Park and Disney California Adventure? When DCA's entrance was reimagined in 2012, those letters—which each weighed between 5,000 and 13,000 pounds—were donated to Cal Expo, the nonprofit that runs the California Exposition & State Fair. These 11-foot, 8-inch pieces were then carted to Sacramento, where they were placed outside the California State Fairgrounds.

Once past the turnstiles, you'll find yourself on **Buena Vista Street,** a re-creation of 1920s Hollywood as Walt saw it when he first arrived. Immediately upon entering, to your left you'll find **Oswald's Filling Station** (a souvenir shop with a snazzy antique car parked outside) and the **Chamber of Commerce.** The street leading to the central plaza is lined on both sides with a variety of shops and eateries with backstories referring to Disney's early biography. Among the shops on the east side is **Elias & Company Department Store** (the park's largest shop, named after Walt's father). The west side of the street features an indoor shopping arcade that leads to **Kingswell Camera Shop** (a PhotoPass printing location) and the **Trolley Treats** candy shop (check out the Big Rock Candy Mountain model in the window), among others.

The hub area, called Carthay Circle, is home to the *Storytellers* statue (depicting a young Walt Disney with an early version of Mickey Mouse) and a replica of the **Carthay Circle Theater,** where *Snow White and the Seven Dwarfs* premiered in 1937; in this incarnation, it encloses an upscale restaurant and bar.

Winding past the shops and facades, the **Red Car Trolley** transports guests from the park entrance to Mission: Breakout! and back again.

Together, Buena Vista Street and Carthay Circle serve as a point of departure for the park's other various themed areas, as well as bring much-needed charm and warmth to DCA's opening act, forming a fantastic improvement over the flat cartoon-postcard facades that framed the former entryway.

Red Car Trolleys ★★★

| APPEAL BY AGE | PRESCHOOL ★★★½ | GRADE SCHOOL ★★★ | TEENS ★★½ |
| YOUNG ADULTS ★★★½ | OVER 30 ★★★½ | | SENIORS ★★★★½ |

What it is Scenic in-park transportation. **Scope and scale** Minor attraction. **When to go** The first or last 2 hours the park is open. **Duration of ride** About 11 minutes. **Average wait in line per 100 people ahead of you** 12 minutes; assumes both cars in operation. **Loading speed** Very slow.

DESCRIPTION AND COMMENTS Much like the vintage vehicles that travel up and down Main Street, U.S.A., at Disneyland Park, these trolley cars add visual interest to DCA's entrance area but not much entertainment value. Modeled after the Pacific Electric Railway that served the Los Angeles area in the 1920s and 1930s (as seen in *Who Framed Roger Rabbit?*), the trolleys boast authentic details such as narrating conductors who share historical tidbits during your travels, retro-styled interior advertisements, and realistic overhead power lines—unelectrified, as the eco-friendly cars are actually battery-powered. More transportation than attraction, the Red Car Trolleys ferry guests on a one-way trip between Buena Vista Street near the park entrance and Guardians of the Galaxy—Mission: Breakout! (or back the other way), making stops in Carthay Circle and Hollywood Land along the way.

TOURING TIPS It is usually faster to walk the route than to wait for the next Red Car Trolley, but if you wish to experience this nostalgic transportation, do so in the morning. Hop on at the station near the Mission: Breakout! exit; it should be less crowded than the station on Buena Vista Street near the park entrance.

The Red Car briefly stops serving guests several times daily so it can be commandeered as a stage for the Red Car News Boys show (see show schedule for details).

HOLLYWOOD LAND

HOLLYWOOD LAND OFFERS attractions and shopping that are inspired by California's (and Disney's) contribution to television and cinema. Visually, the land is themed as a studio back lot with sets, including an urban street scene, soundstages, and a central street with shops and restaurants that depict Hollywood's golden age. In the coming years, expect more of the soundstage architecture to give way to sci-fi stylings as Disney builds an immersive Marvel Super Heroes universe in this corner of DCA, bringing new Spider-Man- and Avengers-inspired attractions to this area and the adjacent A Bug's Land.

Anna & Elsa's Royal Welcome ★★★

| APPEAL BY AGE | PRESCHOOL ★★★★★ | GRADE SCHOOL ★★★★½ | TEENS ★★ |
| YOUNG ADULTS ★★★½ | OVER 30 ★★★★ | | SENIORS ★★★½ |

What it is Character greeting with the *Frozen* sisters. **Scope and scale** Minor attraction. **When to go** Within the first 90 minutes after park opening, or an hour before closing. **Comment** Located inside Disney Animation. **Duration of experience** 3–5 minutes. **Probable waiting time** 20–30 minutes.

DESCRIPTION AND COMMENTS The insanely popular ladies of Arendelle,

Queen Elsa and Princess Anna, meet guests within the Disney Animation building. As an added bonus, Kristoff and Olaf sometimes take turns accompanying the sisters. Much like Fantasy Faire's Royal Hall, the *Frozen* character encounter is richly appointed and has multiple meeting rooms to increase capacity without ruining the magic.

TOURING TIPS In a sure sign that *Frozen* fever is cooling off, this meet and greet has gone from *requiring* FastPass to manage the maddening crowds to ditching FastPass entirely and still drawing queues of under an hour. Even with the drop-off in demand, the line here isn't particularly efficient, so if your party would like to meet the sisters, you should schedule it early in the day or shortly before closing.

Disney Animation ★★★½

**APPEAL BY AGE PRESCHOOL ★★★★ GRADE SCHOOL ★★★★ TEENS ★★★★
YOUNG ADULTS ★★★★½ OVER 30 ★★★★ SENIORS ★★★★½**

What it is Behind-the-scenes look at Disney animation. **Scope and scale** Major attraction. **When to go** Anytime. **Comment** Quite amusing, though not very educational. **Duration of experience** 40–55 minutes. **Probable waiting time** None.

Thumbs Up for the Whole Family

DESCRIPTION AND COMMENTS The Disney Animation building houses a variety of shows, galleries, and interactive exhibits that collectively provide a sort of crash course in animation. Moving from room to room and exhibit to exhibit, you follow the Disney animation process from concept to finished film, with a peek at each of the steps along the way. Throughout, you are surrounded by animation, and sometimes it's even projected above your head and under your feet!

Because DCA's Animation building is not a working studio, the attraction does not showcase artists at work on real features, and the interactive exhibits are more whimsical than educational. "Sorcerer's Workshop," for example, is an interactive exhibit where you can use a book-shaped touch screen to discover which Disney character you most resemble.

The Animation Academy, hosted by a Disney cartoonist, teaches you how to draw a Disney character; if you have any artistic inclination, you may consider it DCA's best-kept secret and find yourself taking the class repeatedly, as a Salt Lake City reader suggests:

Animation Academy turned out to be one of my absolute favorite things. I did it four times in a row and would have gone more if I wasn't starving. I plan to devote quite a bit of time to it on my next trip.

And from a Sammamish, Washington, mom:

I took three, and they were the highlight of the trip. I have no drawing ability whatsoever, but following along with the instructor, I was able to make a pretty decent Donald, a passable Mickey, and a Pooh bear, though he looked like he was in a car accident. My 4-year-old loved drawing along, my husband loved it, and my 2-year-old loved scribbling on her paper and drawing board. It was fun for the whole family.

The Animation Academy classes normally rotate during the day through a dozen-odd different classic and current Disney characters, but at times it may be devoted to a single theme. New characters, such as Heihei from

Moana, are often added in sync with their film's release.

Both "Sorcerer's Workshop" and Animation Academy provide a good foundation on the animation process and will enhance your appreciation of the other exhibits. Anna & Elsa's Royal Welcome (see page 289) and *Turtle Talk with Crush* (see page 296) are also located here.

TOURING TIPS On entering the Animation building, you'll step into a lobby where signs mark the entrances of the various exhibits. Look up in the lobby for a moment at the ultra-high-definition oversize projections of animations in process, including Disney's and Pixar's latest hits; clips from *Zootopia* set to Shakira's "Try Everything" are a recent addition. It takes 40–55 minutes to do all the interactive stuff and see everything. You probably won't experience much of a wait for the Disney Animation offerings except on weekends and holidays. Even then, the Animation building clears out considerably by late afternoon.

Disney Junior Dance Party ★★★

APPEAL BY AGE	PRESCHOOL ★★★★★	GRADE SCHOOL ★★★★	TEENS ★★
YOUNG ADULTS ★★½	OVER 30 ★★★		SENIORS ★★★

What it is Live show for children. **Scope and scale** Minor attraction. **When to go** Per the daily entertainment schedule. **Comments** Audience sits on the floor. A must for families with preschoolers. **Duration of show** 20 minutes. **Probable waiting time** 25 minutes.

DESCRIPTION AND COMMENTS Tykes can work out their wiggles as their elders develop tinnitus during this exhaustingly exuberant interactive dance party. In 2017 the production (previously known as *Disney Junior—Live on Stage!*) was revamped, replacing the simple plot and elaborate puppets with a concert-style presentation focused on music and video projections.

Two iPad-wielding live hosts sing and dance their way through a structure that quickly becomes familiar: a large video screen displays a long commercial for a Disney Junior series, then a character from that show appears in the flesh (or fur) for an audience participatory dance-along song. The featured shows include *Mickey and the Roadster Racers, Doc McStuffins, Sofia the First,* and *The Lion Guard,* with Mickey and Minnie themselves arriving in time for the grand finale.

The minimalist story line makes this production seem more like a Disney Cruise Line deck party than a coherent piece of theater, but the production values—from slickly edited interactive video segments to squeal-inducing bubbles and streamers—are solid enough to satisfy the toddler target audience.

All the jumping, squirming, and high-stepping is facilitated by having the audience sit on the floor so that kids can spontaneously erupt into motion when the mood strikes. Even for adults without children, it's a treat to watch the tykes rev up. However, solo adults might feel creepy amid this extremely youthful exuberance, especially if they lack familiarity with any of the characters. If you have a younger child in your party, all the better: just stand back and let the video roll.

For preschoolers, *Disney Junior* will be the highlight of their day, as a Thomasville, North Carolina, mom attests:

My 3-year-old loved it. The children danced, sang, and had a great time.

TOURING TIPS The show is headquartered to the right of the entrance to Hollywood Land and has an Art Deco marquee. Because the tykes just can't get enough, it has become a hot ticket. Arrive earlier on Sundays, when all showings sometimes fill to capacity. If you arrive to find a line that extends out of the main queuing area and onto the sidewalk, you might not get into the show. Count two palm trees to the left of the theater entrance; if the line extends to the left of the second palm, you probably won't make the cut. If the line hasn't extended past the second palm tree, go ahead and get in line—chances are about 90% that you'll be admitted to the next show. Once inside, pick a spot on the floor and take a breather until the performance begins.

Frozen—Live at the Hyperion ★★★★

APPEAL BY AGE	PRESCHOOL ★★★★½	GRADE SCHOOL ★★★★½	TEENS ★★★★½
YOUNG ADULTS ★★★★	OVER 30 ★★★★½	SENIORS ★★★★½	

What it is Live musical show. **Scope and scale** Major attraction. **When to go** After experiencing DCA's rides. **Comments** Great venue; not to be missed. **Duration of show** 65 minutes. **Probable waiting time** 30–60 minutes.

Thumbs Up for the Whole Family

DESCRIPTION AND COMMENTS The 2,000-seat Hyperion Theater is DCA's premier venue for live productions based on Disney animated films. Shows exhibit Broadway quality in every sense (except duration of the presentation), and we rate them as must-see. In 2016 DCA retired the long-running *Disney's Aladdin—A Musical Spectacular,* which spawned a Disney cruise ship show and Broadway production. *Aladdin*'s replacement is the first fully produced stage show based on the blockbuster *Frozen* film and arrived in Anaheim two years before a full-length New York version's 2018 debut.

The show is directed by Liesl Tommy, whose previous production on Broadway was *Eclipsed,* with Oscar winner Lupita Nyong'o. In addition to all those insistent earworm songs you know and love from the multiplatinum movie sound track, the production features extensive video effects, not only on the enormous LED screen that serves as the stage's cyclorama but also on the revolving stage, the "aurora borealis" projection curtain that encircles the audience at key moments, and the actors themselves. Even if you're sick to death of "Let It Go," you'll appreciate the showstopping way it's presented: a huge frosty staircase appears from the back of the stage and then rotates and swings over the audience as Elsa is climbing it and singing, while swirling snow and wind effects fill the entire theater. It's all very impressive.

There's a lot to admire about this adaptation, from the talented multiethnic cast to the sumptuous high-tech production values. But *Frozen* has some flaws as a theme park production, principally its hour-plus running time, which will test the patience and potty training of any preschooler. The choreography is busy without being particularly creative, and the script is slavishly faithful to the original screenplay, allowing little room for fresh surprises; without a character like the Genie who is able to improvise, it's hard to imagine ourselves sitting through this show over and over again.

TOURING TIPS The lavish productions at the Hyperion Theater are very popular. FastPass is no longer offered for the show, and guests start filling the standby queue more than an hour before the curtain rises, so if you want to see it, be prepared to invest a good chunk of your afternoon. When three or four shows are scheduled, the middle performances are the most popular, so arrive up to 1 hour early. The first and last shows of the day are less crowded; show up 30 minutes before curtain.

Another option is the *Frozen* dinner package, which combines a three-course lunch at Carthay Circle with priority seating at the Hyperion for $89 per adult ($59 for kids ages 3–9). Make reservations at **disneyland.disney.go.com/dining/disney-california-adventure/frozen-live-at-hyperion-plus-dining.**

Showtimes are listed in the park *Times Guide.* The theater is multilevel. Though all seats provide a good line of sight, we recommend sitting on the ground level relatively close to the entrance doors (if possible) to facilitate an easy exit after the performance. Finally, be forewarned that the sound volume for Hyperion Theater productions would give heavy-metal rock concerts a good run for the money.

DISNEY DISH WITH JIM HILL

I'M NOT LION. *FROZEN* HAS SOME IN-GENIE-OUS TOUCHES Fans of Disney on Broadway's productions may have a real sense of déjà vu when they view *Frozen—Live at the Hyperion.* The script for this theme park show was written by Tony Award nominee Chad Beguelin, who wrote the libretto for *Disney's Aladdin—A Musical Spectacular.* And those Olaf and Sven puppets that have been charming visitors at this venue? They were directly inspired by the Timon and Pumbaa outfits that master puppet designer Michael Curry built for Julie Taymor to use in her long-running Broadway production of Disney's *The Lion King.*

Guardians of the Galaxy—Mission: Breakout!
(FastPass) ★★★★

| APPEAL BY AGE | PRESCHOOL ★ | GRADE SCHOOL ★★★★ | TEENS ★★★★★ |
| YOUNG ADULTS ★★★★★ | | OVER 30 ★★★★½ | SENIORS ★★★★★ |

What it is Sci-fi–themed indoor thrill ride. **Scope and scale** Super-headliner. **When to go** The first hour the park is open or use FastPass. **Comments** Not to be missed. Must be 40" tall to ride; switching-off option provided (see page 154). **Duration of ride** About 2 minutes plus preshow. **Average wait in line per 100 people ahead of you** 4 minutes; assumes all elevators operating. **Loading speed** Moderate.

Dark Scary Rough Lose Things Queasy Muss Your 'Do

DESCRIPTION AND COMMENTS In 2017 Rod Serling was evicted from the abbreviated adaptation of Walt Disney World's terrific Twilight Zone attraction when Disney gave the once-stately Tower of Terror a gaudy cyberpunk makeover, turning it into the first major foothold of Marvel Cinematic Universe's expansion into Anaheim. What was formerly a once-famous Hollywood hotel gone to ruin is now the pipe-festooned futuristic fortress of Taneleer Tivan, also known as The Collector (played here, as in the films, by Benicio del Toro).

The amoral accumulator has invited park guests inside to tour his museum of arcane artifacts from across the universe, which features a rotating display of weapons and armor from multiple Marvel movies (plus some vintage Disney artifacts) to marvel at while you wait. Tivan's greatest treasures are the Guardians of the Galaxy themselves: Peter "Star-Lord" Quill (Chris Pratt), Gamora (Zoe Saldana), Drax (Dave Bautista), and even Baby Groot have all been captured and suspended in display cases hanging over a vast abyss.

Luckily, the wily Rocket Raccoon (Bradley Cooper) has broken free and is crawling around in the ventilation system overhead. While you're waiting in The Collector's Easter egg–filled office (check out the objects on his desk), Rocket enlists you to help liberate his pals. The life-size Audio-Animatronic of the reckless rodent is among the resort's most realistic figures and is a highlight of the revamp.

For the ride itself, guests board a gantry lift (also known as Twilight Zone's service elevators) and are propelled up and down the tower, experiencing multiple free falls while immersed in intense visual effects and rockin' tunes ripped right from Star-Lord's *Awesome Mix* tapes. Like Walt Disney World's Tower of Terror, Guardians of the Galaxy—Mission: Breakout! features multiple randomized ride profiles, with different video sequences and drop patterns synchronized to six different songs. Musical options include the Jackson 5, Pat Benatar, and even Elvis (but unfortunately not Blue Swede's "Ooga Chaka/Hooked on a Feeling"), and each sound track is accompanied by a different combination of comic vignettes depicting our hapless antiheroes' escape. Whichever sequence you get, you can still count on the doors opening at the top of the shaft for a bird's-eye view of the resort.

The hardware behind DCA's tower attraction is very similar to the Walt Disney World version, but they are definitely not clones. Thematic differences in the queues and preshows aside, the two attractions really part company once you are in the ride vehicle. In the Disney World version, the elevator stops at a couple of floors to reveal some eerie visuals, but then actually moves forward out of the shaft and through one of the floors; you don't realize that you've entered the drop shaft until the elevator accelerates vertically. In the DCA attraction, the elevator never leaves the shaft, creating a more straightforward ride experience.

Lacking the eerie atmosphere and lateral disorientation that distinguishes the Florida attraction, DCA instead replaces suspense with non-stop acceleration from the second the doors close, resulting in a rambunctious ride that's in keeping with the spirit of these comically chaotic characters. As long as the superior original East Coast Tower of Terror remains untouched, we don't object to Disney swapping Serling for Star-Lord, especially since the reimagined attraction's wilder drop patterns are much more thrilling than the original version.

Perhaps the most important legacy of Mission: Breakout will be if it leads to Disney building a larger Marvel area (hopefully with an original E-ticket Avengers thrill ride) out of DCA's underutilized Hollywood Land.

This attraction is a whopper at 13-plus stories tall. As a result, it has great potential for terrifying young children and rattling more mature visitors. If you have teenagers in your party, use them as experimental probes—if they report back that they really, really liked it, run as fast as you can in the opposite direction. Seriously, a senior from Shelton, Connecticut, who tried it in its Tower of Terror incarnation, warns:

I am fine with rides like Matterhorn Bobsleds and Big Thunder Mountain Railroad, but . . . there is NO detail on that ride that is worth the multiple stomach-jolting drops. After the first drop, all I could do was hang on and pray that it would be over soon. My legs were shaking as we walked out.

TOURING TIPS Because of its height, the tower is a veritable beacon, visible from outside the park and luring curious guests as soon as they enter. You can count on a footrace to get there when the park opens. Get a FastPass or try standby during the first or last hour of the day. Mission: Breakout! is one of the few attractions that distributes FastPasses during the early-entry hour, and FastPasses may run out for the day by midmorning.

To access the attraction, bear left from the park entrance into Hollywood Land. Continue straight to the Hyperion Theater and then turn right. To save time, when you enter the preshow area, stand in the far back corner across from the door where you entered. When the doors to the loading area open, you'll be one of the first admitted.

Monsters, Inc. Mike & Sulley to the Rescue ★★★½

APPEAL BY AGE   PRESCHOOL ★★★★   GRADE SCHOOL ★★★½   TEENS ★★★½
YOUNG ADULTS ★★★½   OVER 30   ★★★½   SENIORS   ★★★★

What it is Dark ride. **Scope and scale** Major attraction. **When to go** Before 11 a.m. **Comment** Disney's best dark ride in years. **Duration of ride** 3¾ minutes. **Average wait in line per 100 people ahead of you** 4 minutes; assumes 23 cars in operation. **Loading speed** Moderate.

DESCRIPTION AND COMMENTS Based on characters and the story from the Disney-Pixar film *Monsters, Inc.*, the ride takes you through child-phobic Monstropolis as Mike and Sulley try to return baby Boo safely to her bedroom. If you haven't seen the film, the story line won't make much sense. In a nutshell, a human baby gets loose in a sort of parallel universe populated largely by amusing monsters. Good monsters Mike and Sulley try to return Boo to her home before the bad monsters get their hands on her.

The Disney Imagineers did a very good job on the Monsters, Inc. ride, recreating the humor, characters, and setting of the film in great detail. The section of the attraction where you ride through the Door Vault with all of its lifts and conveyors is truly inspired. Special effects are first-rate, and lots of subtle and not-so-subtle jokes are worked into the whole experience. You'll have to ride several times to catch them all. Before disembarking, be sure to banter with sluglike supervisor Roz, an animatronic "living character" that can see and interact with riders.

TOURING TIPS You can usually ride without too much of a wait. Because it's near several theater attractions, the ride is subject to experiencing a sudden deluge of guests when the theaters disgorge their audiences. In a unique twist on the single-rider line operated by other attractions, Monsters, Inc. sometimes offers a Buddy Pass system. If you are a party of one or two adults, with up to two lap-seating small children, you can ask the ride's greeter for a Buddy Pass, which will permit you to enter through the exit. Because Monsters, Inc.'s ride vehicles have three benches, Buddy Pass guests get to fill the otherwise empty back row, resulting in significantly shorter waits.

Monsters, Inc. is an iffy attraction for preschoolers: some love it and some are frightened. Increase your odds for a positive experience by exposing your little ones to the movie before leaving home.

Sunset Showcase Theater ★★★

APPEAL BY AGE	PRESCHOOL ★★½	GRADE SCHOOL ★★★	TEENS ★★★½
YOUNG ADULTS ★★★½		OVER 30 ★★★	SENIORS ★★★

What it is 3-D movie preview with in-theater effects. **Scope and scale** Minor attraction. **When to go** Anytime. **Comment** 3-D effects and loud noises may frighten preschoolers. **Duration of show** 10 minutes. **Probable waiting time** 7 minutes.

DESCRIPTION AND COMMENTS Originally home to the delightful *Muppet-Vision 3-D,* the rechristened Sunset Showcase Theater is now devoted to screening 4-D movie trailers promoting Disney's hopeful cinematic blockbusters, such as *Pirates of the Caribbean: Dead Men Tell No Tales* and the Marvel Cinematic Universe superhero films. The 10-minute previews typically consist of a substantial, yet largely spoiler-free, scene from the film, followed by a montage of clips, all presented in digital 3-D and accompanied by bursts of wind, water, and other in-theater special effects.

TOURING TIPS There's rarely more than a single screening's wait. Check it out if you're interested in a sneak peek at the advertised flick or just need to get off your feet in the air-conditioning for a few minutes.

Turtle Talk with Crush ★★★★

APPEAL BY AGE	PRESCHOOL ★★★★½	GRADE SCHOOL ★★★★	TEENS ★★★★
YOUNG ADULTS ★★★½		OVER 30 ★★★★	SENIORS ★★★★½

What it is An interactive animated film. **Scope and scale** Minor attraction. **When to go** After you see the other attractions in the Animation building. **Duration of show** 17 minutes. **Probable waiting time** 10–20 minutes.

DESCRIPTION AND COMMENTS *Turtle Talk with Crush* is an interactive theater show starring the 150-year-old surfer-dude turtle from *Finding Nemo.* Though it starts like a typical Disney theme park movie, *Turtle Talk* quickly turns into a surprise interactive encounter as the on-screen Crush begins to have actual conversations with guests in the audience. Real-time computer graphics are used to accurately move Crush's mouth when forming words. In summer 2016 Crush was joined in his tank by son Squirt, Dory the blue tang, Destiny the whale shark, Bailey the beluga whale, and Hank the seven-legged octopus. The gang's all here to promote (er, celebrate) the release of the theatrical sequel *Finding Dory.*

A mom from Henderson, Colorado, has a crush on Crush:

Turtle Talk with Crush is a must-see. Our 4-year-old was picked out of the crowd by Crush, and we were just amazed by the technology that allowed one-on-one conversation. It was adorable and enjoyed by everyone from Grammy and Papa to the 4-year-old!

TOURING TIPS The animation is brilliant, and guests of all ages list *Crush* as their favorite Animation building feature. By late afternoon, the building has usually cleared out. Save this for your last stop there.

A BUG'S LAND

THIS LAND IS DISNEY'S RESPONSE to complaints that DCA lacked appeal for younger children with a bug's-eye world of giant objects, children's rides, and the *It's Tough to Be a Bug!* movie.

Flik's Fun Fair ★★★

APPEAL BY AGE	PRESCHOOL ★★★★½	GRADE SCHOOL ★★★½	TEENS ★★★
YOUNG ADULTS ★★★	OVER 30 ★★★		SENIORS ★★★

What it is Children's rides and play areas. **Scope and scale** Minor attraction. **When to go** Before 11:30 a.m. for the rides; anytime for the play areas. **Comment** Preschool heaven. **Duration of tour** About 50 minutes for a comprehensive visit.

DESCRIPTION AND COMMENTS Flik's Fun Fair is a children's park as seen through the eyes of an insect. Children can wander among 20-foot-tall blades of grass, tunnel-size garden hoses, an enormous anthill, and the like. Princess Dot's Puddle Park is a kid's water-maze play area fashioned from giant-size garden sprinklers. Kiddie rides include Flik's Flyers, with a balloon-ride theme; a drive-it-yourself car ride called Tuck and Roll's Drive 'Em Buggies; Heimlich's Chew Chew Train, a miniature train ride; and a mini–Mad Tea Party ride titled Francis' Ladybug Boogie, where you can spin your own "ladybug."

TOURING TIPS Though they're colorful and magnetically alluring to the under-8 crowd, the rides are low capacity, slow loading, and ridiculously brief. Our advice is to ride them before 11 a.m. if you visit on a weekend or during the summer. The play areas can be enjoyed anytime, but then you're faced with the prospect of the kids caterwauling to get on the rides. Following is the relevant data on the kiddie rides (note that waiting times are per 50 people ahead of you as opposed to the usual 100 people):

FLIK'S FLYERS ★★½ *(suspended "baskets" swing around a central axis)*
- **RIDE TIME** Almost 1½ minutes
- **AVERAGE WAIT IN LINE PER 50 PEOPLE AHEAD OF YOU** 6 minutes

FRANCIS' LADYBUG BOOGIE ★★★ *(adaptation of Mad Tea Party)*
- **COMMENTS** Unlike most teacup-style rides, turning the center wheel won't spin you faster. Instead, squeeze together on one side of the car and lean your weight into the turns.
- **RIDE TIME** 1 minute
- **AVERAGE WAIT IN LINE PER 50 PEOPLE AHEAD OF YOU** 8 minutes

HEIMLICH'S CHEW CHEW TRAIN ★★★½ *(train ride)*
- **COMMENTS** Adults as well as children can ride and should enjoy the surreal narration and scent effects.
- **RIDE TIME** Almost 2 minutes
- **AVERAGE WAIT IN LINE PER 50 PEOPLE AHEAD OF YOU** 5 minutes

TUCK AND ROLL'S DRIVE 'EM BUGGIES ★★ *(bumper cars)*
- **COMMENTS** Adults as well as children can ride. Cars are much slower than on normal bumper car rides.
- **RIDE TIME** Almost 2 minutes
- **AVERAGE WAIT IN LINE PER 50 PEOPLE AHEAD OF YOU** 12 minutes

It's Tough to Be a Bug! ★★★★

APPEAL BY AGE   PRESCHOOL ★★★★   GRADE SCHOOL ★★★★½   TEENS ★★★★
YOUNG ADULTS ★★★★   OVER 30 ★★★★½   SENIORS ★★★★½

What it is 3-D movie. **Scope and scale** Major attraction. **When to go** After experiencing DCA's better rides. **Comment** 3-D effects and loud noises frighten many preschoolers. **Duration of show** 8½ minutes. **Probable waiting time** 20 minutes.

   DESCRIPTION AND COMMENTS *It's Tough to Be a Bug!* is an uproarious 3-D film about the difficulties of being a very small creature. It features some of the characters from the Disney-Pixar film *a bug's life. It's Tough to Be a Bug!* combines a 3-D film with an arsenal of tactile and visual special effects. In our view, the special effects are a bit overdone and the film somewhat disjointed. Even so, we rate it as not to be missed.

TOURING TIPS Because this attraction is situated in one of the sleepier themed areas, *Bug* is not usually under attack from the hordes until late morning. This should make *It's Tough to Be a Bug!* the easiest of the park's top attractions to see. Lately, *It's Tough to Be a Bug!* has periodically been preempted in favor of 4-D feature-film previews promoting Disney's latest potential blockbusters, like *Moana* and *Cars 3*. Check it out if you're interested in a supersized trailer of an upcoming movie, accompanied by bursts of wind and water.

Be advised that *It's Tough to Be a Bug!* is very intense; the special effects will do a number on young children, as well as anyone who is squeamish about insects. First, from a mother of two from Mobile, Alabama:

It's Tough to Be a Bug! was too intense for any kid. Our boys are 5 and 7, and they were scared to death. They love bugs, and they hated this movie. All of the kids in the theater were screaming and crying. I felt like a terrible mother for taking them into this movie. It is billed as a bug movie for kids, but nothing about it is for kids.

But a Williamsville, New York, woman had it even worse:

We almost lost the girls to any further Disney magic due to It's Tough to Be a Bug! *It was their first Disney experience, and it was almost their last. The story line was nebulous and difficult to follow—all they were aware of was the torture of sitting in a darkened theater being overrun with bugs. Total chaos, the likes of which I've never experienced, was breaking out around us. The 11-year-old refused to talk for 20 minutes after the fiasco, and the 3½-year-old wanted to go home—not back to the hotel room, but home.*

Most readers, however, loved the movie, including this mom from Brentwood, Tennessee:

The bugs are cartoonlike instead of realistic and icky, so I can't understand what all the fuss is about. Disney has conditioned us to think of rodents as cute, so kids think nothing of walking up to a mouse the size of a portable toilet but go nuts over some cartoon bugs. Get a grip!

▌ PARADISE PIER/PIXAR PIER

WRAPPED AROUND THE SOUTHERN SHORE of the kidney-shaped lake, Paradise Pier is Disney's version of a seaside amusement park from the Victoria era. It covers about one-third of Disney California Adventure and contains almost one-third of the attractions.

Paradise Pier's original tacky mid-20th-century theme at DCA was ironic, and in a perverse way it brought the story of Walt Disney and Disneyland full circle. Walt, you see, created Disneyland Park as an alternative to parks with a carnival atmosphere, simple midway rides, carny games, and amply available alcohol. Amazingly, corporate Disney had made just such a place the centerpiece of Disneyland's sister park. The 2012 refurb's clapboard buildings and retro carnival games gave the area much-needed charm, and in 2018 the area will be reimagined as Pixar Pier, DCA's new home for all Pixar characters. Existing rides like Mickey's Fun Wheel will be given a Pixar paint job, characters such as *Inside Out*'s Bing Bong will get their own shops, and a vaudeville-inspired Pixar Pals Theater will be built beneath California Screamin'. Also look for A Bug's Land to close so that Marvel may expand, with some of Flik's small-fry rides relocating here.

Incidentally, those aforementioned carnival games aren't as avaricious as their unfair fair ancestors. If you and a companion play together, you can win a stuffed animal for only $5 (less than you'd pay in the park's gift shops). Some games let you combine multiple wins for an impressive prize. The fishing and racehorse games seem easiest.

Note: Most of the attractions (except Toy Story Midway Mania!) in Paradise Pier close early for *World of Color* performances.

California Screamin' *(FastPass)* ★★★★

| APPEAL BY AGE | PRESCHOOL ★★ | GRADE SCHOOL ★★★★½ | TEENS ★★★★★ |
| YOUNG ADULTS ★★★★★ | | OVER 30 ★★★★½ | SENIORS ★★★★ |

What it is Big, bad roller coaster. **Scope and scale** Super-headliner. **When to go** Ride first thing in the morning, or use FastPass. **Comments** Long and smooth; may induce motion sickness. Must be 48″ tall to ride; switching-off option provided (see page 154). **Duration of ride** 2½ minutes. **Average wait in line per 100 people ahead of you** 2½ minutes; assumes 24-passenger trains with 36-second dispatch interval. **Loading speed** Moderate–fast.

Scary   Lose Things   Queasy   Muss Your 'Do

DESCRIPTION AND COMMENTS This apparently antiquated wooden monster is actually a modern steel coaster, and at 6,072 feet, it's the third longest steel coaster in the United States. California Screamin' gets off to a 0-to-55-mph start by launching you up the first hill like a jet fighter plane off the deck of a carrier (albeit with different technology). From here you will experience tight turns, followed by a second launch that sends you over the crest of a 110-foot hill with a 107-foot drop on the far side. Next, you bank and complete an elliptical loop. A diving turn followed by a series of camelbacks brings you back to the station. Speakers play a synchronized sound track complete with recorded canned screaming and a carnival barker cameo by actor Neil Patrick Harris.

We were impressed by the length of the course and the smoothness of the ride. From beginning to end, the ride is about 2½ minutes, with 2 minutes of actual ride time. En route the coaster slows enough on curves and on transition hills to let you take in the nice view. On the scary-o-meter, Screamin' is certainly worse than Space Mountain but doesn't really compare with some of the steel coasters at nearby Magic Mountain. What Screamin' loses in fright potential, however, it makes up for in variety. Along its course, Disney has placed every known curve, hill, dip, and loop in roller coaster design.

A Carlsbad, California, woman found the ride to be a smooth operator:

California Screamin' was WONDERFUL, and I am a 57-year-old mom, not an adrenaline-crazed young adult! It was my first ever upside-down ride, but it was so smooth and quick that I only felt a gentle pressure pushing me into the seat. It was so fun that I went again! Don't miss this one, at any age!

A Texas woman agrees, writing:

I hate roller coasters, and I love California Screamin'. Very smooth.

TOURING TIPS California Screamin' is a serious coaster, one that makes Space Mountain look like Dumbo. Secure any hats, cameras, eyeglasses, or anything else that might be ripped from your person during the ride. Stay away completely if you're prone to motion sickness.

Engineered to run several trains at once, California Screamin' does a better job than any roller coaster we've seen at handling crowds, at least when the attraction is running at full capacity. The coaster is sometimes shut down two or more times a day for technical problems. Early in the morning, however, it's usually easy to get two or three rides under your belt in about 15 minutes. Ride in the first hour the park is open or use FastPass or the single-rider line (enter up the ramp to the left of the queue).

Golden Zephyr ★★

APPEAL BY AGE	PRESCHOOL ★★★½	GRADE SCHOOL ★★★½	TEENS ★★★½
YOUNG ADULTS ★★★		OVER 30 ★★★	SENIORS ★★★★

What it is Zephyrs spinning around a central tower. **Scope and scale** Minor attraction. **When to go** Any time it is operating. **Comment** Can't operate on breezy days. **Duration of ride** 2 minutes. **Average wait in line per 100 people ahead of you** 8½ minutes; assumes normal operations. **Loading speed** Slow.

Queasy

DESCRIPTION AND COMMENTS First, a *zephyr* is a term often associated with blimps. On this attraction, the zephyrs look like open-cockpit rockets. In any event, each zephyr holds about a dozen guests and spins around a central axis with enough centrifugal force to lay the zephyr partially on its side. As it turns out, the Golden Zephyrs are very touchy, as zephyrs go: they can't fly in a wind exceeding 10 miles per hour. Needless to say, the attraction is shut down much of the time. While the Golden Zephyr does not have a height requirement, babies must be able to sit up in order to board, and no lap sitting is allowed.

TOURING TIPS This colorful attraction is another slow-loading cycle ride. Despite its inefficiency, it rarely attracts more than a cycle or two wait to ride, assuming it's even operating (a bold assumption).

Goofy's Sky School *(FastPass)* ★★★

APPEAL BY AGE	PRESCHOOL ★★★½	GRADE SCHOOL ★★★★	TEENS ★★★★
YOUNG ADULTS ★★★½		OVER 30 ★★★½	SENIORS ★★½

What it is Disney's version of a Wild (or Mad) Mouse ride. **Scope and scale** Major attraction. **When to go** During the first few hours the park is open. **Comments** Space Mountain with the lights on. May induce motion sickness; must be 42" tall to ride; switching-off option provided (see page 154). **Duration of ride** About 1½ minutes. **Average wait in line per 100 people ahead of you** 6¼ minutes; assumes 15-second dispatch interval. **Loading speed** Slow–moderate.

Scary   Lose Things   Queasy   Muss Your 'Do

DESCRIPTION AND COMMENTS Themed as Goofy teaching new pilots how to fly, Goofy's Sky School is a designer Wild Mouse (sometimes also called a Mad Mouse). If you're not familiar with the genre, it's a small, convoluted roller coaster where the track dips and turns unexpectedly, presumably reminding its inventor of a mouse tearing through a maze. To define it more in Disney terms, the ride is similar to Space Mountain, only outdoors and therefore in the light. Goofy's Sky School is an off-the-shelf midway ride in which Disney has invested next to nothing in spiffing up. In other words, fun but nothing special. One Denver, Colorado, woman who otherwise loves the park feels even that middling assessment is too generous, writing:

I think Goofy's Sky School deserves a significant demotion. It doesn't deserve to be called a roller coaster. It jerked us around so much that we were aching afterward.

TOURING TIPS A fun ride but also a slow-loading one, and one that breaks down frequently. Ride during the first few hours the park is open, or use FastPass or the single-rider line (when open).

Jumpin' Jellyfish ★½

APPEAL BY AGE	PRESCHOOL ★★★★	GRADE SCHOOL ★★★½	TEENS ★★★½
YOUNG ADULTS ★★½	OVER 30 ★★★		SENIORS ★★

What it is Parachute ride. **Scope and scale** Minor attraction. **When to go** The first 90 minutes the park is open or just before closing. **Comments** All sizzle, no meat; can't operate on breezy days. Must be 40" tall to ride. **Duration of ride** About 45 seconds. **Average wait in line per 100 people ahead of you** 20 minutes; assumes both towers operating. **Loading speed** Slow.

DESCRIPTION AND COMMENTS On this ride, you're raised on a cable to the top of the tower and then released to gently parachute back to earth. Mostly a children's ride, Jumpin' Jellyfish is paradoxically off-limits to those who would most enjoy it because of its 40-inch minimum-height restriction. For adults, the attraction is a real snore. Oops, make that a real bore—the paltry 45-second duration of the ride is not long enough to fall asleep.

TOURING TIPS The Jellyfish, so called because of a floating jellyfish's resemblance to an open parachute, is another slow-loading ride of very low capacity. Get on early in the morning or prepare for a long wait.

King Triton's Carousel ★★★

APPEAL BY AGE	PRESCHOOL ★★★★★	GRADE SCHOOL ★★★★	TEENS ★★★½
YOUNG ADULTS ★★★	OVER 30 ★★★½		SENIORS ★★★

What it is Merry-go-round. **Scope and scale** Minor attraction. **When to go** Before noon. **Comment** Beautimus. **Duration of ride** A little less than 2 minutes. **Average wait in line per 100 people ahead of you** 8 minutes; assumes normal staffing. **Loading speed** Slow.

DESCRIPTION AND COMMENTS On this elaborate and stunningly crafted carousel, dolphins, sea horses, seals, and the like replace the standard prancing horses.

TOURING TIPS Worth a look even if there are no children in your party. If you have kids who want to ride, try to get them on before noon.

The Little Mermaid: Ariel's Undersea Adventure   ★★★½

APPEAL BY AGE	PRESCHOOL ★★★★½	GRADE SCHOOL ★★★★	TEENS ★★★½
YOUNG ADULTS ★★★½		OVER 30 ★★★½	SENIORS ★★★★

What it is Track ride in the dark. **Scope and scale** Headliner. **When to go** Anytime. **Duration of ride** 6¼ minutes. **Average wait in line per 100 people ahead of you** 3 minutes; assumes normal operations. **Loading speed** Fast.

DESCRIPTION AND COMMENTS The Palace of Fine Arts dome was incorporated into an impressive lagoon-facing facade modeled on early-20th-century aquariums. The seafoam-trimmed building, topped by a statue of King Triton, conceals Disney's 21st-century take on an old-school dark ride. The basics of The Little Mermaid: Ariel's Undersea Adventure are similar to Disneyland's Haunted Mansion: a continuously loading ride system transports you through a series of elaborately themed, darkened scenes with sophisticated special effects. In this case, The Little Mermaid attraction takes you to the bottom of the ocean in clam shell cars, where the ride recaps Ariel's journey from her father's undersea kingdom to marrying Prince Eric. After Scuttle the seagull recaps the backstory for you, your vehicle descends backward beneath the simulated sea surface with a spritz of cool air. Assuming that you haven't drowned, you'll then meet a cutting-edge animatronic Ariel (featuring "floating" hair); party down "Under the Sea" with Sebastian the crab; and be menaced by a 12-foot-wide, 7½-foot-tall undulating figure of Ursula, the evil sea witch. The adventure is all set to newly orchestrated versions of Alan Menken and Howard Ashman's classic songs, and original animator Glen Keane and actress Jodi Benson both returned to lend their talents.

The ride greatly benefited from a 2014 upgrade, which added more figures and enhanced the "Under the Sea" scene with vibrant black light. However, though the ride is colorful and kinetic, it still suffers from short-changed storytelling, especially in the unsatisfyingly abrupt finale. While it's a welcome addition to DCA's short roster of kid-friendly indoor rides, anyone expecting a modern-day classic to compete with Haunted Mansion and Pirates of the Caribbean may come away somewhat disappointed. But this family from Arvada, Colorado, thinks the ride serves its supporting role well:

Head for The Little Mermaid ride when you need a break. It's well done, and it's air-conditioned.

TOURING TIPS As one of the first additions from the park's major makeover, The Little Mermaid has slipped in popularity since the debut of Cars Land and Guardians of the Galaxy. This attraction does not have FastPass, and the Omnimover ride system is capable of efficiently handling more than 2,000 guests per hour, keeping lines moving swiftly even on busy days. If the posted wait is more than 20 minutes, check back in the late afternoon, when you will often be able to walk on with little wait.

Mickey's Fun Wheel (Pixar Fun Wheel) ★★½

APPEAL BY AGE PRESCHOOL ★★★ GRADE SCHOOL ★★★★ TEENS ★★★★
YOUNG ADULTS ★★★½ OVER 30 ★★★½ SENIORS ★★★

What it is Ferris wheel. **Scope and scale** Major attraction. **When to go** The first 90 minutes the park is open or just before closing. **Comments** The world's largest chicken coop; may induce motion sickness. **Duration of ride** 9 minutes. **Average wait in line per 100 people ahead of you** 6¼ minutes; assumes all 24 cabins in use. **Loading speed** Slow.

DESCRIPTION AND COMMENTS Higher than the Matterhorn Bobsleds at Disneyland Park, this whopper of a Ferris wheel tops out at 150 feet. Absolutely spectacular in appearance, the Fun Wheel offers stunning views in all directions. Unfortunately, however, the view is severely compromised by the steel mesh that completely encloses the passenger compartment. In essence, Disney has created the world's largest revolving chicken coop. As concerns the ride itself, some of the passenger buckets move laterally from side to side across the Fun Wheel in addition to rotating around with the wheel. Because it feels like your bucket has become unattached from the main structure, this lateral movement can be a little disconcerting if you aren't expecting it. If the movement proves too disconcerting, motion sickness bags are thoughtfully provided in each swinging car.

TOURING TIPS Ferris wheels are the most slow loading of all cycle rides, but the Fun Wheel has a platform that allows three compartments to be loaded at once. The lateral sliding buckets are loaded from the two outside platforms, while the stationary compartments are loaded from the middle platform. Loading the entire wheel takes about 6½ minutes, following which the Fun Wheel rotates for a single revolution. And speaking of the ride, the Fun Wheel rotates so slowly that the wonderful rising and falling sensations of the garden-variety Ferris wheel are completely absent. For our money, the Fun Wheel is beautiful to behold but terribly boring to ride. If you decide to give it a whirl, ride the first hour the park is open or in the hour before the park closes.

Silly Symphony Swings ★★★

APPEAL BY AGE PRESCHOOL ★★★½ GRADE SCHOOL ★★★★ TEENS ★★★★½
YOUNG ADULTS ★★★★ OVER 30 ★★★★ SENIORS ★★★½

What it is Swings rotating around a central tower. **Scope and scale** Minor attraction. **When to go** The first 90 minutes the park is open or just before closing. **Comments** Simple but fun. Must be 40" tall to ride (48" tall to ride solo). **Duration of ride** Less than 1½ minutes. **Average wait in line per 100 people ahead of you** 6 minutes; assumes normal staffing. **Loading speed** Slow.

DESCRIPTION AND COMMENTS The theme pays tribute to the 1935 Mickey Mouse cartoon *The Band Concert,* the first color Mickey cartoon released to the public, with guests seated in swings flying around a tower. In the scary department, it's a wilder ride than Dumbo, but SSS is still just swings going in circles. A number of tandem swings are available to allow children 40–48 inches to ride with a parent; look for a separate tandem line to the left as you approach the attraction.

TOURING TIPS This is a fun and visually appealing ride, but it's also one that loads slowly and occasions long waits unless you ride during the first hour or so the park is open. Be aware that it's possible for the swing chairs to collide when the ride comes to a stop—Bob once picked up a nice bruise when an empty swing smacked him during touchdown.

Toy Story Midway Mania! *(FastPass)* ★★★★½

APPEAL BY AGE	PRESCHOOL ★★★★	GRADE SCHOOL ★★★★½	TEENS ★★★★★
YOUNG ADULTS ★★★★★		OVER 30 ★★★★½	SENIORS ★★★★½

What it is 3-D ride through indoor shooting gallery. **Scope and scale** Headliner. **When to go** First 30 minutes the park is open or use FastPass. **Comment** Not to be missed. **Duration of ride** About 6½ minutes. **Average wait in line per 100 people ahead of you** 9 minutes; assumes both tracks operating. **Loading speed** Moderate.

DESCRIPTION AND COMMENTS Toy Story Midway Mania! ushered in a whole new generation of Disney attractions: virtual dark rides. Since Disneyland opened in 1955, ride vehicles had moved past two- and three-dimensional sets often populated by Audio-Animatronics (AA); these detailed sets and robotic figures literally defined the Disney creative genius in attractions such as Pirates of the Caribbean, The Haunted Mansion, and Peter Pan's Flight. Instead, Toy Story Midway Mania! has long corridors, totally empty, covered with reflective material. There's almost nothing there . . . until you put on your 3-D glasses. Instantly, the corridor is full and brimming with color, action, and activity, thanks to projected computer-graphic imagery (CGI).

Conceptually, this is an interactive shooting gallery much like Buzz Lightyear Astro Blasters (see page 255), but in Toy Story Midway Mania!, your ride vehicle passes through a totally virtual midway, with booths offering such games as ring tossing and ball throwing. You use a cannon on your ride vehicle to play as you move along from booth to booth. Unlike the laser guns in Buzz Lightyear, however, Toy Story Midway Mania's pull-string cannons take advantage of CGI technology to toss rings, shoot balls, and even throw eggs and pies. Each game booth is manned by a Toy Story character who is right beside you in 3-D glory cheering you on. In addition to 3-D imagery, you experience various smells, vehicle motion, wind, and water spray. The ride begins with a training round to familiarize you with your cannon and the nature of the games and then continues through a number of "real" games in which you compete against your riding mate. The technology has the ability to self-adjust the level of difficulty so that every rider is challenged, and there are plenty of easy targets for small children to reach. *Tip:* Let the pull-string retract all the way back into the cannon before pulling it again. If you don't, the cannon won't fire.

Also of note, a 6-foot-tall Mr. Potato Head interacts with and talks to guests in real time in the preshow queuing area of Toy Story.

TOURING TIPS Much of the queuing area for Toy Story Midway Mania! is across the pedestrian walkway from the attraction's entrance. The queuing is covered, which is good, but it's not air-conditioned, which is very bad, with temperatures escalating into the 90s and higher. Not roasting in this oven is a great incentive to experience Toy Story Midway Mania! in the early morning, before it gets crowded.

As you might expect, Toy Story Midway Mania! is addictive, and though it's great fun right off the bat, it takes a couple of rides before you really get the hang of the pull-string cannon and the way the targets are presented. To rack up a high score, you must identify and shoot at high-value targets: high-value targets are small and often moving, while low-value targets are larger and easier to hit. Toward the end of the ride, the top score of the day and the top scores of the month are posted. If you're a newbie and you'd like to ride several times to gain experience and get your skill level up, consider making the attraction your first stop after the park opens.

In 2017 Disney added FastPass to Toy Story Midway Mania! in conjunction with its MaxPass program, installing the kiosks across the boardwalk from the ride's entrance. We bemoaned this move, after years of praising how much swifter DCA's FastPass-free queue moved in comparison to the molasses-like mess at Disney's Hollywood Studios version, which had to add a third track to tame wait times. Because Anaheim's ride still has only two tracks, it's now essential to either grab a FastPass or ride standby as early in the day as possible. If you're eligible for early entry, the attraction is often a walk-on while everyone else is speeding to Cars Land or Guardians of the Galaxy.

CARS LAND

CARS LAND IS THE CROWNING CAPSTONE on DCA's transformation, and the first major "land" in an American Disney theme park devoted solely to a single film franchise. Tucked in the park's southeast corner on 12 acres of repurposed parking lot, Cars Land's main entrance is across from the Golden Vine Winery, though there are secondary gateways in A Bug's Land and in Pacific Wharf (the vista through the latter's stone archway entrance is especially scenic). A massive mountainous backdrop topped with 125-foot-high peaks patterned after 1950s Cadillac Pinnacle tail fins, known as the Cadillac Range, cradles Ornament Valley, home to a screen-accurate re-creation of Radiator Springs. That's the sleepy single-stoplight town along Route 66 populated by Pixar's anthropomorphized automobiles. Along its main drag, in addition to three rides, you'll find eateries themed to the film's minor characters and souvenir shops selling Cars-themed and Route 66 merchandise.

Walking through the aesthetically astounding area is uncannily like stepping into the cinematic universe, and well worth the wait even if you weren't particularly enamored of the merchandise-moving movies. As striking as Cars Land is by daylight, it is even more stunning after sunset; the nightly neon-lighting ceremony set to the doo-wop classic "Life Could Be a Dream" is a magical must-see (showtimes are not publicized but occur promptly at sundown, so ask a Cars Land cast member and arrive early). Finally, a word to the wise from a Dallas, Texas, family:

Tip: *Cars Land has NO shade. Literally none. Wear a hat.*

Luigi's Rollickin' Roadsters ★★★

APPEAL BY AGE   PRESCHOOL ★★★★   GRADE SCHOOL ★★★½   TEENS ★★★½
YOUNG ADULTS ★★★½   OVER 30 ★★★½   SENIORS ★★★★

What it is Outdoor "dancing" car ride. **Scope and scale** Minor attraction. **When to go** During the first or last hours of the day. **Comment** Must be 32" to ride. **Duration of ride** About 1½ minutes. **Average wait in line per 100 people ahead of you** 10 minutes. **Loading speed** Slow.

DESCRIPTION AND COMMENTS When Cars Land opened in 2012, one of its three attractions was Luigi's Flying Tires, a reincarnation of Disneyland Park's Flying Saucers, a Tomorrowland attraction that lasted five years in the early 1960s. Imagineers retreaded the concept of hovercraft bumper cars, using a system similar to an air hockey table, as the basis for a tribute to the Radiator Springs resident Ferrari fanatic.

Luigi's Flying Tires turned out to be an example of nostalgia being better than reality; the tires accelerated very gradually and were tricky for first-time riders to control. Lines dwindled substantially in the years after the tires debuted, despite how glacially slow the attraction was to load.

In early 2015 Disney shuttered Luigi's to reimagine the attraction, which reopened in 2016 as Luigi's Rollickin' Roadsters. Guests still first queue inside the Casa Della Tires shop (where memorabilia from Luigi's and Guido's careers is on display), and then pass through a garden of automotive-inspired topiaries before approaching the attraction itself, which occupies the same outdoor arena. However, instead of giant tires, 20 small open-top faux Fiats (with the franchise's signature cartoon faces) serve as the ride vehicles. And instead of controlling their destiny, this time, passengers are just along for the ride, as the cars spin and "dance" autonomously around each other in unpredictable patterns, thanks to trackless GPS technology.

With a library of Italian tunes like "Volare" and "Mambo Italiano" for the cars to dance to, each ride experience is a little different (you may even get a solo in the center of the floor while everyone else swirls around you), though each routine ends with a brief but brisk bout of spinning. But the cars' movements are surprisingly jerky, sometimes feeling like a shopping cart with a stuck wheel, and it's impossible to appreciate the choreographic patterns while you're in the middle of it. Much like its predecessor, Luigi's Rollickin' Roadsters may actually be more fun to watch than to ride, so it's fortunate that benches are provided near the exit.

TOURING TIPS Luigi's capacity is limited. Try to ride during the first or last hours of the day, especially if you are eligible for early entry.

Mater's Junkyard Jamboree ★★★

APPEAL BY AGE	PRESCHOOL ★★★★½	GRADE SCHOOL ★★★★	TEENS ★★★½
YOUNG ADULTS ★★★★		OVER 30 ★★★★	SENIORS ★★★½

What it is Midway-type whip ride. **Scope and scale** Minor attraction. **When to go** Before noon. **Comment** Must be 32" tall to ride. **Duration of ride** About 1½ minutes. **Average wait in line per 100 people ahead of you** 10 minutes; assumes both sides operating. **Loading speed** Slow.

Queasy

DESCRIPTION AND COMMENTS On the outskirts of town sits the junkyard home of Mater, the redneck tow truck voiced by Larry the Cable Guy. In his yard sit 22 baby tractors, each towing an open-air two-seater trailer. While Mater's voice emerges from a jury-rigged jukebox singing one of seven specially composed square-dancing tunes (plus one hilarious hidden song that plays only once per hour), the tractors travel in overlapping figure eight patterns along interlocking turntables. The vehicles are transferred from one revolving turntable to another, creating near-miss moments much like Francis' Ladybug Boogie. The difference is that Mater's trailers swing freely from side to side, creating a centripetal snapping sensation similar to vintage whip carnival rides. Mater's may look like a simple kiddie ride, but it supplies an unexpected kick that draws us back for repeated spins. This London, Ontario, dad echoed our assessment:

Mater's Junkyard Jamboree was surprisingly good. It doesn't look like much, but you have to ride it. We saw a woman lose her sunglasses because she wasn't prepared for how it swings around. The mechanically inclined adults exiting the ride were impressed with the engineering that allowed for the figure eight movement.

TOURING TIPS Mater is the breakout hit character of the Cars franchise, and his namesake ride is visually attractive but slow loading. Still, it typically has the shortest queue of the three Cars Land attractions.

Radiator Springs Racers *(FastPass)* ★★★★★

APPEAL BY AGE	PRESCHOOL ★★★½	GRADE SCHOOL ★★★★★	TEENS ★★★★★
YOUNG ADULTS ★★★★★		OVER 30 ★★★★★	SENIORS ★★★★

What it is Automotive dark ride with high-speed thrills. **Scope and scale** Super-headliner. **When to go** The first 30 minutes the park is open or use FastPass. **Comments** Not to be missed. Must be 40″ tall to ride; switching-off option provided (see page 154). **Duration of ride** About 4 minutes. **Average wait in line per 100 people ahead of you** 4 minutes; assumes normal operations. **Loading speed** Moderate–fast.

Dark   Scary   Lose Things   Muss Your 'Do

DESCRIPTION AND COMMENTS To the right of the Radiator Springs Courthouse at the end of Route 66 lies the entrance to the most ambitious attraction built at Disneyland Resort in more than a decade. Disney's Imagineers wedded an enhanced version of the high-speed slot cars developed for Epcot's Test Track with immersive sets and elaborate animatronics. The ride, which covers nearly 6 of Cars Land's 12 acres, mixes slow indoor sections with thrilling open-air acceleration in a way that appeals to every demographic.

You begin your road trip by walking through Stanley's Oasis, the town's original 1909 settlement, and end up in a cavernous loading station. There you board a six-passenger convertible, each with a smiling face on its front grille, and you're off on a scenic tour of stunning Ornament Valley, on your way to compete in today's big race.

After a leisurely drive past massive rock formations and a majestic waterfall, you enter the show building for a series of indoor scenes depicting the residents of Radiator Springs. These environments don't quite match the awe-inspiring scale of scenes in Pirates of the Caribbean or Indiana Jones Adventure, but they are a big step up from the old-fashioned Fantasyland dark rides and feature movie-accurate animatronics with impressively expressive eyes and mouths (achieved through a combination of digital projections and practical effects). Along your tour, you'll be sidetracked by a tractor-tipping expedition with Mater, which leads to a run-in with an angry harvester. Before reaching the starting line, you'll need some new tires or a fresh coat of paint. Then it's time to line up alongside another carload of guests as you await Luigi's countdown. The last third of the ride is a flat-out race over camelback hills, under outcrops, and around banked curves, with a randomly chosen car crossing the finish line first. Radiator Springs Racers's top speed of 40 miles per hour falls short of Test Track's 60-plus peak, but the winding turns and airtime-inducing humps supply an exhilarating rush. After a final swing past the glowing stalactites of Tail Light Cavern and some parting praise from Lightning McQueen and Mater, you'll exit your vehicle and inspect your obligatory on-ride photo.

TOURING TIPS While the new Guardians of the Galaxy—Mission: Breakout! has diverted some demand, Radiator Springs Racers is still a massive draw from the minute the park opens every day. With a carrying capacity of about 1,500 riders per hour, the attraction sees standby waits of up to 3 hours during peak season, and FastPasses may all be claimed for the day by noon; even the single-rider queue can run 45 minutes or more. Your best options are to secure a FastPass within the first few hours after park opening, or step into the standby queue shortly before closing. If time permits, try to ride once by day and again after dark; evening illumination makes the outdoor portions especially enchanting.

Note that FastPasses for Radiator Springs Racers are distributed outside of Cars Land proper, near *It's Tough to Be Bug!,* with the queue being routed toward A Bug's Land. You may be tempted to rush to the standby queue at rope drop instead of getting a FastPass, but be warned that the ride regularly opens late due to daily maintenance, potentially wasting your valuable morning touring time. The ride also shuts down for long periods after any substantial rainstorm. Unlike at most attractions, hotel guests using early-entry privileges may retrieve a FastPass for Radiator Springs Racers before regular park hours start. Day guests are currently only allowed into the FastPass queue after official park opening, with guests gathering in a disorganized blob to the right of Carthay Circle before rope drop. This can cause quite a traffic jam as hundreds of people rush to get in line. Send one member of your party with all the tickets to get Fast-Passes, and keep your kids clear of the mob. Don't be scared off by the size of the crowd queuing for FastPasses, says a Superior, Colorado, reader:

The FastPass line for RSR was amazingly efficient. A cast member at every kiosk was shoving tickets in and getting FastPasses out—none of that "which-way-do-I-put-these-in" thing. The line wove down the street, but I was out in less than 5 minutes!

Perhaps the best option is to follow this Suffern, New York, reader's advice and bypass Radiator Springs Racers' FastPass and standby queues:

Don't waste your time waiting to get a Radiator Springs FastPass. It's much faster to just go right to the single-rider line at rope drop.

If you try this technique, be aware that the ride's singles queue often doesn't open until the standby line has built up a bit. You may have time for a quick spin on Luigi's and Mater's and still be among the first into Racers' single-rider entrance.

◼ PACIFIC WHARF

THIS LAND INCORPORATES a Cannery Row–inspired eatery area adjacent to Paradise Bay with a diminutive winery, situated at the base of Grizzly Peak and across from A Bug's Land, making it the smallest of the Golden State–themed areas. At the base of the winery you'll find **Blue Sky Cellar,** a seldom-used building that is occasionally opened as an annual pass holder lounge or promotional preview center. It would be a stretch to call it an attraction, much less a themed area.

In 2016 Disney California Adventure resurrected its **Food & Wine Festival** after a half-decade absence, planting a handful of vending kiosks along the Pacific Wharf performance corridor between Carthay Circle and the bridge to Paradise Pier/Pixar Pier. The booths, which operate only on select spring days in March and April, are comparable to those found at the similarly named Epcot event, though far fewer in number, and likewise serve tasty but tiny plates and thimbles of alcohol at indigestion-inducing prices. Items such as ahi *poke* can be found cheaper elsewhere at the resort; your best bet is to stick with the vegetarian offerings, which are filling and fairly priced. Be warned that the festival booths halt alcohol sales a full hour before DCA closes. Also during the festival, Sonoma Terrace and Hollywood Land host free culinary demonstrations on outdoor stages, as well as extra-fee seminars with celebrity chefs. See **disneyland.com/foodand wine** for more details.

Bakery Tour ★★½

APPEAL BY AGE	PRESCHOOL ★★★		GRADE SCHOOL ★★★½		TEENS ★★★
YOUNG ADULTS ★★★½		OVER 30 ★★★½		SENIORS ★★★★	

What it is Free bread! (Plus a short film and walking tour.) **Scope and scale** Diversion. **When to go** Anytime. **Comment** Visitors get a free bite-size sample of fresh sourdough bread. **Duration of tour** 9 minutes. **Probable waiting time** None.

DESCRIPTION AND COMMENTS The Bakery Tour (hosted by Boudin Bakery) is a walk-through attraction featuring hosts Rosie O'Donnell and Colin Mochrie via video. It takes visitors through the history of the Boudin Bakery and also explains how the bread is baked for various restaurants across Disneyland Resort.

TOURING TIPS There's never any wait to enter this attraction, and you get a small bread sample as soon as you walk in. The tour is a great way to kill 10 minutes. See this when you have some downtime, perhaps after a meal, while on the way back to Paradise Pier/Pixar Pier, or before watching *Frozen—Live at the Hyperion.*

If the bread sample whets your appetite, you can buy a full-size loaf (including ones shaped like Mickey) at the café adjoining the exit. Next door is the Ghirardelli Soda Fountain and Chocolate Shop, where you can indulge in diabetes-inducing ice cream sundaes (or snag a free sample of candy) while admiring an animated diorama of San Francisco.

GRIZZLY PEAK

GRIZZLY PEAK, a huge mountain shaped like the head of a bear, is home to **Grizzly River Run,** a whitewater raft ride, and the **Redwood Creek Challenge Trail,** an outdoor playground that resembles an obstacle course. In 2015 Grizzly Peak absorbed the adjacent area originally known as Condor Flats, rechristening the area around **Soarin' Around the World** as Grizzly Peak Airfield and adding woodsy theming appropriate to a national park in the High Sierras, as opposed to its former desolate desert look.

Grizzly River Run *(FastPass)* ★★★★½

APPEAL BY AGE   PRESCHOOL ★★★   GRADE SCHOOL ★★★★½   TEENS ★★★★★
YOUNG ADULTS ★★★★½   OVER 30 ★★★★½   SENIORS ★★★★

What it is Whitewater raft ride. **Scope and scale** Super-headliner. **When to go** First hour the park is open, or use FastPass. **Comments** Not to be missed; you are guaranteed to get wet, and possibly soaked. Must be 42" tall to ride. **Duration of ride** 5½ minutes. **Average wait in line per 100 people ahead of you** 5 minutes; assumes 32 rafts operating. **Loading speed** Moderate.

Scary   Wet   Lose Things   Rough   Muss Your 'Do

DESCRIPTION AND COMMENTS Whitewater raft rides have been a hot-weather favorite of theme park patrons for decades. The ride consists of an unguided trip down a man-made river in a circular rubber raft, with a platform mounted on top seating six to eight people. The raft essentially floats free in the current and is washed downstream through rapids and waves. Because the river is fairly wide with numerous currents, eddies, and obstacles, there is no telling exactly where the raft will go. Thus, each trip is different and unpredictable. The rafts are a little smaller than those used on most rides of the genre. Because the current can buffet the smaller rafts more effectively, the ride is wilder and wetter.

What distinguishes Grizzly River Run from other theme park raft rides is Disney's trademark attention to visual detail. Where many similar rides essentially plunge down a concrete ditch, Grizzly River Run winds around and through Grizzly Peak, the park's foremost visual icon, with the great rock bear at the summit. Featuring a 50-foot climb and two drops—including a 22-footer where the raft spins as it descends—the ride flows into dark caverns and along the mountain's precipitous side before looping over itself just before the final plunge. Period-appropriate props support the mid-century national parks theme.

Grizzly River Run is a heart thumper, one of the best of its genre anywhere. And at 5½ minutes from load to unload, it's also one of the longest. The visuals are outstanding, and the ride is about as good as it gets on a man-made river. While it's true that theme park raft rides have been around a long time, Grizzly River Run has set a new standard, one we don't expect to be equaled for some time.

TOURING TIPS This attraction is hugely popular, especially on hot summer days. Ride the first hour the park is open, after 4:30 p.m., or use FastPass or the single-rider line. Make no mistake—you will certainly get wet on this ride. Our recommendation is to wear shorts to the park and bring along a jumbo-size trash bag, as well as a smaller plastic bag. Before boarding the raft, take off your socks and punch a hole in your jumbo bag for your head. Though you can also cut holes for your arms, you will probably stay drier with your arms inside the bag. Use the smaller plastic bag to wrap around your shoes. If you are worried about mussing your hairdo, bring a third bag for your head.

A Shaker Heights, Ohio, family who adopted our garbage-bag attire, however, discovered that staying dry on a similar attraction at Walt Disney World is not without social consequences:

The Disney cast members and the other people in our raft looked at us like we had just beamed down from Mars. We didn't cut armholes in our trash bags because we thought we'd stay drier. The only problem was that once we sat down, we couldn't fasten our seat belts. The Disney person was quite put out and asked sarcastically whether we needed wet suits and snorkels. After a lot of wiggling and adjusting and helping each other, we finally got belted in and off we went, looking like sacks of fertilizer with little heads perched on top. It was very embarrassing, but I must admit that we stayed nice and dry.

If you forget your plastic bag, ponchos are available at the adjacent Rushin' River Outfitters. If you don't mind walking around in wet underwear, a Vancouver, Washington, reader advises availing yourself of the free short-term lockers found near Grizzly River Run's entrance:

The first time we rode Grizzly River Run, we wore ponchos per your advice. We looked ridiculous and the cast members looked at us like we were aliens. Our last two trips, we left our bags with others in our party, wore flip-flops on the ride, and had a blast! Not having to worry about our stuff getting soaked makes the ride way more enjoyable.

About 50 lockers are located near the bear statue that marks the ride's entrance; use is complimentary for up to 2 hours.

Redwood Creek Challenge Trail and Wilderness Explorer Camp ★★★½

APPEAL BY AGE	PRESCHOOL ★★★★	GRADE SCHOOL ★★★★½	TEENS ★★★★
YOUNG ADULTS ★★★½		OVER 30 ★★★	SENIORS ★★★½

What it is Elaborate playground and obstacle course. **Scope and scale** Minor attraction. **When to go** Anytime. **Comments** Very well done; plan to spend about 20 minutes here. Must be 42" tall.

DESCRIPTION AND COMMENTS An elaborate maze of rope bridges, log towers, and a cave, the Redwood Creek Challenge Trail is a scout camp combination of elements from Tarzan's Treehouse and Tom Sawyer Island. Built into and around Grizzly Peak, the Challenge Trail has eye-popping appeal for young adventurers. A mom from Salt Lake City writes:

Most underrated . . . If this were a city park, it would be packed every day. In Disneyland it seems to be the least popular thing. The kids, young and older, just loved it. The adults were able to run for FastPasses, change diapers, get snacks for all the kids, and sit down while the kids had a great time.

Grab a map near the entrance and complete the self-guided activities to earn your own Wilderness Explorer merit badge sticker.

TOURING TIPS The largest of several children's play areas in the park, and the only one that is dry (for the most part) and relatively shady, the Challenge Trail is the perfect place to let your kids cut loose for a while. Though the Challenge Trail will be crowded, you should not have to wait to get in. Experience it after checking out the better rides and shows. Be aware, however, that the playground is quite large; you will not be able to keep your children in sight unless you tag along with them.

Soarin' Around the World (FastPass) ★★★★½

APPEAL BY AGE   PRESCHOOL ★★★★   GRADE SCHOOL ★★★★½ TEENS ★★★★★
YOUNG ADULTS ★★★★★   OVER 30 ★★★★★   SENIORS ★★★★★

What it is Flight-simulation ride. **Scope and scale** Super-headliner. **When to go** The first 30 minutes the park is open, or use FastPass. **Comments** The park's best ride for the whole family. Must be 40" tall to ride; switching-off option provided (see page 154). **Duration of ride** 4½ minutes. **Average wait in line per 100 people ahead of you** 4 minutes; assumes 2 concourses operating. **Loading speed** Moderate.

Thumbs Up for the Whole Family

DESCRIPTION AND COMMENTS Soarin' Around the World is a thrill ride for all ages, as exhilarating as a hawk on the wing and as mellow as swinging in a hammock. If you've ever experienced flying dreams, you'll have a sense of how Soarin' feels. Once you enter the main theater, you're secured in a seat not unlike the ones used on inverted roller coasters (in which the coaster is suspended from above). Once everyone is in place, you are suspended with your legs dangling. Thus hung out to dry, you embark on a hang glider tour around the world with IMAX-quality images projected below you, and with the simulator moving your seat in sync with the movie. The immersive images are well chosen and drop-dead beautiful, and special effects include wind, sound, and even smell.

A new ride film debuted at Soarin' in summer 2016, featuring film clips from flights around the world. Instead of being geographically constrained to California, the new film—which was created for the debut of Shanghai Disneyland—glides around the globe from the Matterhorn (the one in Switzerland, not Anaheim) and an arctic glacier to the Taj Mahal and Great Wall of China. Exclusive to DCA is a finale filmed in 2014 over the Disneyland Resort. The visuals are stunningly sharp, thanks to laser IMAX projectors, and computer-animated animals are employed to create clever transitions, an improvement over the original's jarring location changes. Jerry Goldsmith's memorable musical theme returned with updated orchestrations, as did Patrick Warburton's flight attendant preshow, but there's a new trio of scents to inhale along the way; we're growing partial to Eau de Africa. While some of the computer-generated imagery is distractingly artificial, and we still miss the orange-scented original's subtler moments, on balance we feel the updated Soarin' constitutes an upgrade over what was already one of DCA's top-rated rides.

The ride itself is thrilling but also perfectly smooth, exciting, and relaxing. We think Soarin' is a must-experience for guests of any age who meet the height requirement. And yes, seniors we interviewed were crazy about it. But a North Carolina mom says:

*Wait a minute! Soarin' was VERY cool but definitely on the scary side for peo-
ple afraid of heights or who don't like that "unsteady" feeling. While we were
"soaring" up, I was fine, but when we were going down, I had to continually say
to myself, "This is only an illusion, I cannot fall out, this is only an illusion . . . "*

TOURING TIPS Aside from being a true technological innovation, Soarin'
Around the World also happens to be located near the entrance of the
park, thus ensuring heavy traffic all day. It should be your very first attraction in the morning after securing FastPasses for Guardians of the Galaxy,
or, alternatively, use FastPass. If you arrive later and elect to use FastPass,
obtain your FastPass before noon. Later than noon and you're likely to
get a return period in the hour before the park closes, or worse, find that
the day's supply of FastPasses is gone. Unfortunately, the attraction's
single-rider line was removed during the 2016 upgrade, eliminating that
time-saving option.

The new Soarin' film features a number of vertical landmarks like the
Eiffel Tower that look comically distorted from seats on the far ends. Once
directed toward one of the two theaters, politely request to wait an extra
cycle for seats in row B1 to have an ideal view.

PARADES *and*
LIVE ENTERTAINMENT

Disney's World of Color Nighttime Spectacular *(FastPass)*
★★★★½

APPEAL BY AGE   PRESCHOOL ★★★★   GRADE SCHOOL ★★★★½   TEENS ★★★★½
YOUNG ADULTS ★★★★½   OVER 30 ★★★★½   SENIORS ★★★★½

What it is Fountain show with special effects. **Scope and scale** Super-headliner.
When to go See *Times Guide* for showtimes; FastPass only. If there's only one show,
get your FastPass within the first 30 minutes the park is open. **Duration of show** 28
minutes. **Probable waiting time** Up to an hour if you want the best view.

DESCRIPTION AND COMMENTS The 1,200 high-pressure water
nozzles installed under the surface of DCA's Paradise Bay are
the infrastructure for Disney's $75-million attempt to keep
guests in the park (and spending money) until closing time.

Muss Your 'Do   Wet

If you've seen or heard about the spectacular fountain show at the Bel-
lagio in Las Vegas, *World of Color* is similar but larger, with more special
effects and themed to Disney movies. The show includes a musical score
and incorporates dozens of Disney films and characters in its 28-minute
performance. The show's backdrop includes the Fun Wheel, which is fit-
ted with special lighting effects for use in the show. Giant projection surfaces sculpted by sprayed water—even larger than those used in
Fantasmic!—display custom-made animations, and flamethrowers spew
almost enough heat to dry off guests standing in the splash zones.
What's most remarkable about the show is how the flashing colored
lights and pulsating fountains combine to look like low-level fireworks.
The effects are astounding, the colors are vibrant and deep, and the

music includes some of Disney's best songs without being overloaded by overly sentimental ballads. You can even invest $25 in Made with Magic mouse ear hats, wands, gloves, or headbands that illuminate in sync with the show; better yet, stand toward the rear and freeload by eyeballing others who bought them.

But while *World of Color* is aesthetically entrancing, dramatically speaking it's a bit of a dud. Disney spectacles have never needed especially strong story lines, but *World of Color* is so plotless that it makes *Fantasmic!* next door look like a Russian novel. The show is essentially a 30-minute montage of movie moments with awkwardly edited segues straining to tie them together. Despite the show's titular association with Uncle Walt's 1960s NBC TV show, and the retro theme of DCA's overall rebranding, there's precious little vintage Disney referenced in *World of Color*. Aside from a brief cameo by 1937's *The Old Mill*, almost all the featured films are drawn from the last three decades, with lots of mist-screen time given to modern Pixar heroes such as Buzz Lightyear and Wall-E, and Second Golden Age stalwarts like Aladdin and Ariel, as well as footage from the fourth Pirates of the Caribbean film. There's also a handful of obscurities mysteriously tossed in: was there a fan club somewhere clamoring for more of *Fantasia 2000*'s flying whales? Ultimately, there's enough dazzling eye candy to overwhelm any underlying emotional emptiness in the narrative. Finally, *World of Color* has more false finales than the last Lord of the Rings film, so stay put until you're absolutely sure that the show is over.

During the 2016 holiday season, a special "Season of Light" edition of *World of Color* was introduced. The show focuses on clips of Disney cartoons with wintery themes—from *Bambi* to *Frozen*—synced with a sound track of classy Christmas classics. Highlights include a *Fantasia* ballet backed by the brilliant a cappella ensemble Pentatonix and Goofy's Trans-Siberian Orchestra–fueled lighting display. In the interest of equal time for warmer climes, Hawaii's Stitch and Latin America's Three Amigos even get in on the seasonal action via Bing Crosby's "Mele Kalikimaka" and José Feliciano's "Feliz Navidad." The montage of princesses trying to evade their princes, set to Michael Bublé and Idina Menzel's cover of "Baby, It's Cold Outside," is deliciously ironic, and a skit with *Inside Out*'s Sadness being serenaded by Elvis's "Blue Christmas" draws big laughs. But the stirring climax, featuring soaring hymns sung by Broadway's Heather Headley, is guaranteed to put a lump in your throat.

TOURING TIPS Entertainment value aside, *World of Color* is an operational nightmare. The effects were expressly designed to be viewed from Paradise Park, the tiered area along the lagoon in front of The Little Mermaid attraction. Unfortunately, only about 4,500 people—less than a quarter of the park's average daily attendance—are permitted to stand there for each show. Getting a decent view for *World of Color* requires time, planning, and/or money, and therefore can almost seem to be more trouble to see than it's worth, but we still consider it not to be missed. A couple from San Jose writes:

Though the [World of Color] *FastPass line was horrible and waiting for the show was horrible, the show itself was simply amazing.*

An Austin, Texas, mom found *World of Color* challenging:

World of Color was fantastic but hard for kids and shorter adults to see unless they are standing right in front facing Mickey's Wheel. My son could not see the preshow at all, and I had to put him on my shoulders for the 28-minute production. My back has not recovered. They need amphitheater reserved seating. We arrived 1½ hours prior to DCA opening to get a FastPass and waited 1½ hours for the show to start when admitted.

If you want anything approaching a decent view of *World of Color*, you'll need a special FastPass, the securing of which can be an annoying adventure in and of itself. Here are your options for obtaining FastPasses, beginning with the easiest (and most expensive) method.

World of Color meal packages are offered by Ariel's Grotto, Carthay Circle Restaurant, and Wine Country Trattoria. The fixed-price dinner runs $48.58 per adult ($26.98 for kids) at Ariel's Grotto and Wine Country Trattoria, and $66.96 per adult ($27.01 for kids) at Carthay Circle Restaurant. Lunch packages (not available at Ariel's) are $44.29 per adult ($23.76 for kids) at Carthay Circle and $34.55 per adult ($22.66 for kids) at Wine Country Trattoria. (The above prices include tax but not tip.)

All viewing-package meals include an appetizer, your choice of entrée, dessert, and nonalcoholic beverage; selections are from a limited list that is separate from the restaurant's à la carte menu. After your meal, you'll receive special FastPasses for each member of your party, permitting entry into a preferred viewing area reserved for dining-package patrons. Note that you don't actually watch the show from the restaurant, so you'll want to eat early enough to make it to the viewing area. There is also a *World of Color* dessert party for $79 per person (tax and tip included), where you snack on upscale sweets and sip sparkling wine (or nonalcoholic cider) while sitting at tall cocktail tables during the show. Note that in the event *World of Color* is canceled due to technical difficulties or inclement weather, there are no refunds or rain checks for dinner or dessert packages. The viewing sections for premium dining and dessert party patrons are dead center along the waterline. Ariel's Grotto and Wine Country Trattoria diners get the closest section to the water, and those standing at the front railing are likely to get soaked; Carthay Circle and dessert party guests get the elevated section slightly farther back, which affords a better (and drier) view. To enter the dining FastPass area, look for the illuminated White (Ariel's Grotto and Wine Country Trattoria), Green (Carthay Circle), or Purple (dessert party) entrance signs between the Blue and Yellow sections, directly across from The Little Mermaid ride. Though expensive, the dining and dessert packages are the only way to be guaranteed a central viewing spot with minimal crowding. On nights when there are multiple *World of Color* performances, early eaters receive passes to the first show, while those eating later get tickets to the later viewing; be sure to confirm when booking your meal which showing you'll be scheduled to attend.

Free FastPasses are distributed on a first-come, first-serve basis from machines located near the entrance to Ariel's Undersea Adventure (tickets are available early to Disneyland Resort hotel guests during Extra Magic Hour). Make sure that you get passes for your whole party at once, or you may end up in different sections or showings. These machines are disconnected from the rest of the park's FastPass system, so your *World of Color* ticket won't interfere with other attractions. On busy days, they may all be claimed by early afternoon. If seeing the first *World of Color* show of the night is a priority for you, we suggest getting a FastPass within the first 30 minutes the park is open. When a second show is scheduled, FastPasses for the late performance can often be had well into the afternoon.

Once you have your FastPass, you'll notice that you've been assigned one of two color-coded sections. Yellow stretches from the right side of the premium viewing section toward the Golden Zephyr, and Blue includes the left side and bridge to Paradise Pier/Pixar Pier. A special section is available by request for disabled guests, and the prime areas in the middle are reserved for VIPs and dining-package purchasers.

Your FastPass also includes a return-time window. You won't be allowed into Paradise Park before the start time, but the best viewing spots will all be claimed shortly after opening, so don't be surprised to see people lining up an hour before the area opens. Once inside the viewing area, try to move to the front of an elevated area. You're best off at the front of an elevated tier farther back, rather than at the rear of a lower section, as these readers from Langley, British Columbia, discovered:

World of Color *was great, but even with FastPass, it was hard for me to see (wearing flat shoes and being 5'5"). My husband, who is 6'4", also found himself bobbing around trying to see. When we got there, we had good line of sight, but as people stood up and put their kids on their shoulders, it became difficult.*

If you stand close to the railing, pay attention to the SPLASH ZONE signs; on a calm night, you'll be seriously spritzed, and if the wind blows the wrong way, you'll get soaked.

If all else fails, it's theoretically possible to view the show from various points around the park, but employees with flashlights will vigorously shoo you away from all the obvious vantage points. The best ticketless viewing spot is next to the Golden Zephyr, to the right of the Yellow section. Unticketed viewing is also available immediately in front of The Little Mermaid attraction. You can see many of the fountain and lighting effects from the opposite side of Paradise Pier/Pixar Pier, near the bases of the Fun Wheel and Silly Symphony Swings, but the mist projections are illegible from that angle, so we can't recommend it for first-time viewers. On nights when there are multiple performances, you have better odds finding a good spot for the last show.

You can also watch *World of Color* from the Cove Bar. The view of the projections is less than ideal, but no reservations are required, and you can sit down with an adult beverage during the show, provided you can secure a perch in this popular watering hole.

While waiting for the show to start, connect your smartphone to the park's free "PierGames" Wi-Fi network and launch any Web browser to join in the Fun Wheel Challenge. Follow the pattern of flashing colored lights on the Fun Wheel, and duplicate them Simon Says–style on your device; points are awarded for speed and accuracy, with the winner of each round awarded 30 seconds of control over the giant wheel's light display. The game starts 45 minutes prior to the evening's first *World of Color* show and stops about 7 minutes before the performances.

The mass movement toward the exits that immediately follows each performance can be exhausting. Instead, relax and enjoy the musical encore that follows each fountain show; though not as explosive as the main performance, it's a colorful capper to the night, and it's much nicer exiting the park after the initial exodus has subsided. After the show, if you are headed to the hotels or Downtown Disney, you can bypass the crowd at the main entrance by exiting through the Grand Californian Hotel.

AFTERNOON AND EVENING PARADES **Pixar Play Parade** features characters from *a bug's life; Cars; Finding Nemo; Monsters, Inc.; The Incredibles;* and *Toy Story*. Lively, very funny, and as varied as the Pixar characters, Pixar Play Parade should be on your must-see list. In 2018 the Pixar Play Parade will move to Disneyland Park as part of the limited-time Pixar Fest.

The parade route runs from a gate to the left of Guardians of the Galaxy—Mission: Breakout!, through Hollywood Land toward the fountain in Carthay Circle, around Grizzly Peak past A Bug's Land and Cars Land, and through Pacific Wharf toward Paradise Pier/Pixar Pier, where it disappears backstage through a gate to the left of Boardwalk Pizza. Note that for the second parade or on other occasions, the direction may be reversed. On days when the crowds are light, any place along the parade route will suffice. On days of heavy attendance, try to score a viewing spot on the elevated courtyard or steps of the Golden Vine Winery. The upstairs Alfresco Tasting Terrace offers an excellent bird's-eye perspective. Parades may be suspended due to construction or during special events like the springtime Food & Wine Festival. In their stead, Mr. Incredible, Elastigirl, and Frozone may do a mini-parade along the performance corridor as The Incredibles H.I.T. Squad.

In 2018 Disneyland Park's previous nighttime parade, **Paint the Night** (★★★★★), will be revived at DCA. The parade is patterned after the processional that debuted at Hong Kong Disneyland in 2014 (with a few new additions). Inspired in part by the original Main Street Electrical Parade, these floats are covered in 1.5 million LEDs. Each float represents a classic Disney or Pixar film, as scenes from *Monsters, Inc., Cars, Toy Story, Beauty and the Beast, The Little Mermaid,* and *Frozen* are brought to life by a cast of more than 75 performers, who bounce down the route to the upbeat sound track of *Wreck-It Ralph's* "When Can I See You Again?" by pop artist Owl City. Keep an ear out for musical nods to "Baroque Hoedown," the old Electrical Parade's synth-tastic theme song.

These superbright displays go far beyond earlier nighttime pageants and include character puppets with digitally animated faces, a tractor-trailer full of floating 3-D designs, and a kinetic Sorcerer's Apprentice sculpture whose twisting motion defies description. In our opinion, Paint the Night is one of Disney's best nighttime parades ever—not to be missed.

The parade route will fill up a couple of hours early for the first showing, so we recommend riding rides during the first run, and then immediately getting a spot for the second performance of Paint the Night. Any spot along the parade route will offer the same experience. Once the parade has started, count on gridlock all along the route.

GUARDIANS OF THE GALAXY: AWESOME DANCE OFF! In 2017 DCA ended its long-running evening dance parties, which requisitioned a portion of Hollywood Land near the Monsters, Inc. ride for family-friendly techno-raves themed after everything from *Tron* to *Alice in Wonderland.* In their place, DCA introduced an interactive dance show staged a dozen times during the day outside the new Guardians of the Galaxy ride, featuring three of the attraction's stars. Star-Lord and Gamora arrive on a mission to retrieve Star-Lord's beloved boom box and engage guests in a boogie-off to 1970s disco classics "for the sake of the universe." Stick around until the end or you'll miss the meet and greet with Groot, everyone's favorite anthropomorphic foliage.

HOLLYWOOD BACKLOT STAGE This open-air stage, one of our favorite venues in the park, features small productions and Disney characters. During the summer of 2017, the *Avengers Training Initiative* took over the venue with a cute, kid-focused interactive Marvel superhero show similar to Disneyland's *Jedi Training.* During the off-season, visiting school bands, glee clubs, and dance teams frequently use this stage. Check the *Times Guide* to see what's playing.

STREET ENTERTAINMENT You'll frequently find a period-appropriate klezmer, Irish, or other ethnic band playing outside Paradise Garden Grill. On Buena Vista Street, a gang of singing **Red Car News Boys** (and one newsgirl), loosely inspired by the cult film and Tony-winning Broadway musical *Newsies,* uses the Red Car Trolleys as a roving stage for exuberant song-and-dance performances (look for the high-tech talking Mickey Mouse to make an extended cameo appearance). Also on Buena Vista Street, the **Five and Dime** musical sextet (accompanied by a zoot suit–clad Goofy) sings jazz standards of the 1920s and 1930s, such as "Million Dollar Baby," "I Got Rhythm," and "Bye Bye Blackbird"; this is one of the best street shows in Disney's repertoire. You may also bump into interactive improvisation actors portraying police officers, bicycle messengers, or other eccentric **Citizens of Buena Vista,** a troupe similar to the popular Streetmosphere characters at Disney's Hollywood Studios in Orlando. Along Cars Land's main drag, **Red the Firetruck** shows up in the morning with sirens blazing to spray down the crowds, and **DJ's Dance and Drive** features the "ultimate party car" hosting afternoon oldies dance parties with the help of interactive carhop waitresses. The **Mariachi Divas** is a fabulous all-female mariachi musical group that plays sets in the Pacific Wharf area, walking between the seating areas of the counter-service restaurants. They are probably the only multiple Grammy Award–winning recording artists (most recently Best Regional Mexican Music Album of 2014) with a regular theme park gig. We particularly enjoy the Divas' rendition of "It's a Small World." *Operation: Playtime!* in Paradise Pier is a Blue Man Group–esque street show of another color, featuring Toy Story's Green Army Man banging up a storm on improvised drums.

DISNEY CHARACTERS Character appearances are listed in the daily *Times Guide.* In addition, Olaf and Kristoff from *Frozen,* as well as Sofia the First and Doc McStuffins from Disney Junior, make appearances in

Hollywood Land, as do Captain America, Spider-Man, and Groot, the talking tree from *Guardians of the Galaxy*; Princess Elena of Avalor holds court in Paradise Gardens; and Ariel's Grotto restaurant at Paradise Pier/Pixar Pier offers character dining featuring Ariel and her princess friends. Oswald the Lucky Rabbit (an old-school Disney cartoon from before Mickey's creation) greets guests on Buena Vista Street, and the "fab five" can be found around Carthay Circle in dapper Roaring Twenties duds. Mater and Lightning take turns posing for photos near the Cozy Cone Motel; these life-size vehicles can deliver quips recorded by the original voice actors to grinning guests.

SEASONAL EVENTS Following in Epcot's footsteps, Disney California Adventure has been expanding its seasonal festival lineup, offering an ever-increasing array of events featuring temporary food kiosks and additional live entertainment. In January the **Lunar New Year** celebration brings a brief processional led by Mulan and Mushu, plus a special 6-minute *World of Color* preshow with music made for Shanghai Disneyland. The spring **Food & Wine Festival** hosts celebrity chefs and beverage experts, who appear in exclusive cooking demonstrations and tasting seminars (additional fees required), along with free presentations and hands-on kids' activities. In the fall, Cars Land's residents celebrate **Haul-O-Ween** with special decorations and costumes on the car characters. And **¡Viva Navidad!** honors the holidays with Hispanic flair from November through Three Kings' Day with a festive street celebration, live storytellers, and traditional musicians, all centered on the Paradise Garden Grill area. Visit **disneyland.disney.go.com/events-tours/disney-california -adventure** to stay up to date on DCA's seasonal event schedule.

UNHERALDED TREASURES
at DCA

TREASURE: Cove Bar | **LOCATION:** On the bridge to Paradise Pier/Pixar Pier

ARIEL'S GROTTO IS A FIXED-PRICE character-meal restaurant on the span connecting Paradise Pier to the Pacific Wharf. Instead of heading downstairs to the restaurant from the entrance, though, go around the walkway. There, you'll find the Cove Bar, where you can enjoy a full-service bar and a small selection of food. This is also one of the best places to enjoy the view. It's a bit too sunny during the day, but as the sun sets and the evening lights come on, the Cove turns into a mellow hideaway where you can enjoy a beautiful view of Paradise Pier. In the background, you hear music, laughter, and the occasional sounds of a roller coaster, while watching small waves lap against the pier that houses a brightly lit carousel—enough to make you forget that you're sitting in the middle of a completely artificial environment.

TREASURE: Redwood Creek Challenge Trail | **LOCATION:** Opposite Grizzly Peak

MAYBE A VISIT TO A THEME PARK was your kid's idea, and you prefer a quiet walk in the woods. If you want to take a break from the hectic rush of a trip to DCA, hop over to the Redwood Creek Challenge Trail. You probably assume that this is just a playground designed for kids, but the area is actually a good representation of a wilderness park. OK, so you don't really need to bring your bird-watching book, but there are various nooks and crannies, as well as a few "ranger buildings," that are very well themed (down to the wildlife books on the shelves). You could easily spend a portion of your day just enjoying the decidedly rustic feel of Redwood Creek.

TRAFFIC PATTERNS *at* DISNEY CALIFORNIA ADVENTURE

AS SOON AS THE PARK OPENS, most guests head straight for Radiator Springs Racers in Cars Land (or the Racers FastPass machines) or to Hollywood Land for Guardians of the Galaxy—Mission: Breakout!

On days of lighter attendance, waits of more than an hour will form within a few minutes at Racers; waits of 2 hours or more appear on holidays and other days of peak attendance. FastPasses for Radiator Springs Racers will typically be gone by midday on most days. Fast-Passes for Guardians of the Galaxy disappear as fast or faster, and that ride regularly posted a standby wait of 3 hours during its debut summer.

Of the other attractions in Cars Land, waits for Luigi's Rollickin' Roadsters will typically be 25–40 minutes as soon as the park opens, while Mater's Junkyard Jamboree's waits will be low for the first hour or two that DCA is open.

Cars Land's attractions' wait times will usually peak 11 a.m.–2 p.m. Radiator Springs Racers will have consistent 75- to 120-minute waits throughout the day, possibly higher if the attraction has to shut down for unscheduled maintenance, a common occurrence. Waits for Mater's Junkyard Jamboree will start to drop by 4 p.m., and lines at Luigi's Rollickin' Roadsters will start to diminish around dinnertime.

Our advice (for parties of adults and older kids) is to obtain Fast-Passes for Mission: Breakout! immediately at rope drop, then get FastPasses for Radiator Springs Racers as soon as you're eligible. If FastPasses are all gone, consider using the single-rider line for RSR. If possible, wait until the last 2 hours the park is open to try Luigi's and Mater's.

As crowded as Cars Land and Guardians of the Galaxy—Mission: Breakout! get, the good news is that traffic to the rest of DCA is relatively light for the first hour the park is open. When DCA opens before 10 a.m., lines for Soarin' Around the World, California Screamin', and Toy Story Midway Mania! are usually less than 20 minutes, even during holidays.

At Grizzly Peak, Soarin's wait times start to climb about an hour after the park opens and peak 11 a.m.–2 p.m. Once the crowds are in the park, Soarin' will have waits of at least 30–35 minutes for the rest of the day during most times of year. Next door, wait times at Grizzly

River Run are relatively low for the first hour the park is open. During summer and warm holidays, lines grow quickly about an hour after the park opens, peaking at around noon. Waits grow more slowly when the weather is cooler but still peak around noon. Expect waits to start dropping around 4 p.m. regardless of the time of year.

In Hollywood Land, waits at Mission: Breakout! and Monsters, Inc. usually peak 11 a.m.–noon. Mission: Breakout!'s waits don't drop off until close to closing time, while the wait times at Monsters, Inc. typically drop off at 4 p.m. most days and 6 p.m. on holidays. *Disney Junior Dance Party* and *Frozen—Live at the Hyperion* each draw good-size crowds throughout the late morning and afternoon.

Lines at A Bug's Land typically do not exceed 10–15 minutes at any time, except on the most crowded days of the year.

Toward the back of the park, long waits develop fastest at Toy Story Midway Mania!—still about an hour after the park opens—and peak by 11 a.m. Like Soarin' Around the World, Toy Story will remain popular for the rest of the day, regardless of season. Secondary attractions, including Goofy's Sky School and California Screamin', won't usually be too crowded until about 2 hours after the park opens. Like the attractions at Hollywood Land, most lines at B-list Paradise Pier/Pixar Pier attractions start to drop after 4 p.m. Lines at The Little Mermaid seem to be low throughout the day and on any day of the year.

Park departures begin around 3 p.m., when families with small children start heading home. However, 9-to-5 workers with annual passes start coming into the park around 6 p.m. and generally stay for the evening. It's common to see waits hold steady or even rise from early evening until the park closes, undoubtedly because of Cars Land, Guardians of the Galaxy—Mission: Breakout!, and *World of Color*.

World of Color FastPasses are generally available until 11 a.m. or noon most days. Guests with *World of Color* FastPasses will begin queuing in the Pacific Wharf, Grizzly Peak, and Paradise Pier/Pixar Pier walkways an hour or more before showtime. The largest wave of departing guests occurs at the end of *World of Color*. Just before closing, crowd levels are thin except, of course, at Cars Land, Soarin' Around the World, and Mission: Breakout!

CALIFORNIA ADVENTURE TOURING PLANS

PRELIMINARY INSTRUCTIONS FOR ALL DISNEY CALIFORNIA ADVENTURE TOURING PLANS

ON DAYS OF MODERATE to heavy attendance, follow the touring plans exactly, deviating only when you do not wish to experience a listed show or ride.

1. Buy your admission in advance (see "Admission Options" on page 20).

2. Call ☎ 714-781-7290 the day before you go for the official opening time.

3. Become familiar with the park-opening procedures (described on page 88) and read over the touring plan of your choice, so you will have a basic understanding of what you are likely to encounter as you enter the park.

DCA ONE-DAY TOURING PLAN FOR ADULTS
(page 380)

FOR Adults without small children. **ASSUMES** Willingness to experience all rides and shows.

Height and age requirements apply to many attractions. If you have kids who aren't eligible to ride, try switching off (see page 154) or use the One-Day Touring Plan for Parents with Small Children. This touring plan includes most of the amusement park rides on Paradise Pier/Pixar Pier. If you're short on time or wish to allocate more of the day to DCA's theatrical attractions, forgo a few of the slow-loading rides in Paradise Pier/Pixar Pier. This plan prioritizes obtaining FastPasses for the new Guardians of the Galaxy—Mission: Breakout! attraction over Radiator Springs Racers. Note that Disney hotel guests get into DCA 1 hour earlier on Monday, Wednesday, and Friday.

ABOUT EARLY ENTRY If you are eligible for early entry, experience (1) Guardians of the Galaxy—Mission: Breakout!, (2) Toy Story Midway Mania!, and (3) California Screamin', in that order, followed by (4) Soarin' Around the World (time permitting). Pick up FastPasses from the (5) Radiator Springs Racers kiosks before official park opening. Pick up the plan after picking up your FastPasses, skipping any attractions you've already seen, and return to ride Radiator Springs Racers once your FastPass window starts.

DCA normally hosts early entry on Sunday, Monday, Wednesday, and Friday. Unlike Disneyland, DCA's early entry is for hotel guests only; Magic Morning ticket holders may not enter early. If you are not eligible for early entry, try not to use the plan on an early-entry day. Cars Land will be packed with early-entry guests before you even get past the turnstiles.

DCA ONE-DAY TOURING PLAN FOR ADULTS WITH SMALL CHILDREN *(page 381)*

FOR Adults with small children who wish to experience all major rides and shows. **ASSUMES** Willingness to experience all rides and shows.

Height and age requirements apply to many attractions. If you have kids who aren't eligible to ride, try switching off (see page 154). This touring plan includes most of the amusement park rides on Paradise Pier/Pixar Pier. If you're short on time or wish to allocate more of the day to DCA's theatrical attractions, forgo a few of the rides in A Bug's Land. Crowds are smaller at DCA on Tuesday, Thursday, and Saturday when Disneyland Park has early entry. This plan prioritizes obtaining FastPasses for Radiator Springs Racers over Guardians of the Galaxy—Mission: Breakout! If your party is more interested in the latter, swap Guardians of the Galaxy for Radiator Springs Racers in the plan.

ABOUT EARLY ENTRY If you are eligible for early entry, experience (1) Guardians of the Galaxy—Mission: Breakout! and then head over to Cars Land to ride (2) Luigi's Rollickin' Roadsters and (3) Mater's Junkyard Jamboree, in that order, followed by (4) Toy Story Midway Mania! If you have time before the park officially opens, ride (5) Soarin' Around the World. Pick up FastPasses from the (6) Radiator Springs Racers kiosks before official park opening. Pick up the plan after picking up your FastPasses, skipping any attractions you've already seen, and return to ride Radiator Springs Racers once your FastPass window starts.

DCA normally hosts early entry on Sunday, Monday, Wednesday, and Friday. Unlike Disneyland, DCA's early entry is for hotel guests only; Magic Morning ticket holders may not enter early. If you are not eligible for early entry, try not to use the plan on an early-entry day. Cars Land will be packed with early-entry guests before you even get past the turnstiles.

THE BEST OF DISNEYLAND RESORT IN ONE DAY
(pages 382–383)

FOR Guests who really want to burn the candle at both ends (and a bunch of money) by buying a single-day Park Hopper. **ASSUMES** Willingness to experience all major rides (including roller coasters) and shows in both parks and to walk a lot.

This plan is for groups who wish to visit both Disneyland and Disney California Adventure in one day. Most of the major, must-see attractions are included for each park. The plan starts in DCA with Guardians of the Galaxy—Mission: Breakout!, switching over to Disneyland in the afternoon, and finishes the night with Disneyland's fireworks spectacular. This plan is only recommended on days when the parks open early and stay open late. Try to finish up the DCA portion of this plan by 1 p.m., so you have enough time to ride everything in Disneyland.

ABOUT EARLY ENTRY If you are eligible for early entry, experience (1) Guardians of the Galaxy—Mission: Breakout!, (2) Luigi's Rollickin' Roadsters, (3) Mater's Junkyard Jamboree, and (4) Toy Story Midway Mania!, in that order, followed by (5) Soarin' Around the World (time permitting). Pick up FastPasses from the (6) Radiator Springs Racers kiosks before official park opening. Pick up the touring plan after picking up your FastPasses, skipping any attractions you've already seen, and return to ride Radiator Springs Racers once your FastPass window starts.

DCA normally hosts early entry on Sunday, Monday, Wednesday, and Friday. Unlike Disneyland, DCA's early entry is for hotel guests only; Magic Morning ticket holders may not enter early. If you are not eligible for early entry, try not to use the plan on an early-entry day. Cars Land will be packed with early-entry guests before you even get past the turnstiles.

PART SEVEN

UNIVERSAL STUDIOS HOLLYWOOD

UNIVERSAL STUDIOS HOLLYWOOD was the first film and TV studio to turn part of its facility into a modern theme park. By integrating shows and rides with behind-the-scenes presentations on moviemaking, Universal Studios Hollywood created a new genre of theme park, stimulating a number of clone and competitor parks. First came Disney-MGM Studios (now Disney's Hollywood Studios) at Walt Disney World, followed shortly by Universal Studios Florida, also near Orlando. Where Universal Studios Hollywood, however, evolved from an established film and TV venue, its cross-country imitators were launched primarily as theme parks, albeit with some production capability on the side. Disney is also challenging Universal in California with Disney California Adventure (DCA). While DCA does not have production facilities, one of its themed areas focuses on Hollywood and the movies.

Located just off US 101 north of Hollywood, Universal Studios operates on a scale and with a quality standard rivaled only by Disney, SeaWorld, and Busch Gardens parks. Unique among American theme parks for its topography, Universal Studios Hollywood is tucked on top of, below, and around a tall hill. The studios consist of an open-access area and a controlled-access area. The latter contains the working soundstages, back lot, wardrobe, scenery, prop shops, postproduction facility, and administration offices. Guests can visit the controlled-access area by taking the Studio Tour. The open-access area, which contains the park's rides, shows, restaurants, and services, is divided into two sections. The main entrance provides access to the upper section, the Upper Lot, on top of the hill. Four theater shows and four rides (including The Wizarding World of Harry Potter), as well as two walk-through attractions and the loading area for the Studio Tour, are located in the Upper Lot. The Lower Lot, at the northeastern base of the hill, is accessible from the Upper Lot via escalators. There are three rides and a couple of meet and greets in the Lower Lot.

On April 7, 2016, Universal Studios Hollywood capped a half-decade of redevelopment with the grand opening of The Wizarding

World of Harry Potter, a West Coast annex of the wildly popular Hogsmeade area originally found at Orlando's Islands of Adventure. The parapets of Hogwarts Castle that now tower over the Upper Lot, forming a beacon visible for miles around, are merely the most visible effect of Universal's ambitious Evolution expansion plan, which completely overhauled three-quarters of the park in under five years. Casualties of the expansions included the old Wild West arena, *Terminator 2: 3-D,* the tram tour's Mummy tunnel, the Curious George playground, and Gibson Amphitheater, with the *Special Effects Show* still potentially on the chopping block. But the extreme makeover has brought USH a beautiful new Art Deco entry corridor and central plaza, upgraded points of interest along the tram tour, and the global attention that comes with The Wizarding World. Universal isn't stopping there in its bid to attract Disneyland guests who've grown weary of waiting for the Mouse to add new E-tickets; two new Universal Studios Hollywood on-site hotels have been proposed, and additional attractions are in the works on both the Upper and Lower Lots.

The park offers all standard services and amenities, including stroller and wheelchair rental, lockers, diaper-changing and nursing facilities, car assistance, and foreign-language assistance. Most of the park is accessible to disabled guests, and TDDs are available for the hearing impaired. Almost all services are in the Upper Lot, just inside the main entrance.

GATHERING INFORMATION

THE MAIN UNIVERSAL STUDIOS information number is ☎ 818-622-3801. To short-circuit the operating-hours litany, dial 3. If you have problems, try calling ☎ 818-622-3735 or 818-622-3750. Universal Studios' website, **universalstudioshollywood.com,** is easy to navigate. Once inside the park, use the Universal Studios Hollywood official iPhone and Android app, or visit **ushwaittimes.com** with your smartphone to see current wait times and show schedules. Incidentally, USH offers free public Wi-Fi (look for SSID "Universal"), but it quickly gets overloaded on busy days, and cell reception can be spotty depending on which side of the hill you're on.

WHAT MAKES UNIVERSAL STUDIOS HOLLYWOOD DIFFERENT

WHAT MAKES UNIVERSAL STUDIOS HOLLYWOOD different is that the attractions, with a couple of exceptions, are designed to minimize long waits in line. The centerpiece of the Universal experience is the Studio Tour. While on the tram, you experience a high-speed car chase and come face-to-face with King Kong, among other things. In other parks, including Universal's sister park in Florida, each of these is presented as an individual attraction with its own long queue. At Universal Studios Hollywood, by contrast, you suffer only one wait to board the tram and then experience all of these events as part of the tour.

Universal Studios Hollywood

Back Lot

The Wizarding World of Harry Potter

Upper Lot

Lower Lot

Stairway/Escalator

Universal CityWalk

Entrance

Ticket Booths

Ticket Booths

1. Despicable Me
   Minion Mayhem
2. DreamWorks Theatre
3. Flight of the Hippogriff
4. Harry Potter and the
   Forbidden Journey
5. Jurassic Park—The Ride
6. Ollivanders
7. Revenge of the
   Mummy—The Ride
8. The Simpsons Ride
9. *Special Effects Show*
10. Studio Tour
11. Transformers:
    The Ride 3-D
12. *Universal's Animal
    Actors*
13. The Walking Dead
    Attraction
14. *WaterWorld*

.03mi
.03 km

In addition to the time saving and convenience provided by the tram tour, most of the live shows at Universal Studios Hollywood are performed in large theaters or stadiums. Instead of standing in line outside, guests are usually invited to enter the theater and wait in seated comfort for the production to begin.

One more distinguishing feature of Universal is that it's *loud*. Unlike Disney's background music, which is carefully curated to create a relaxing ambience, Universal insists on blasting high-energy sound tracks at full volume through every available speaker. When you're lucky, you'll only be exposed to one oppressive score at a time; if you linger too long in spots where competing sound systems overlap, you could quickly lose your sanity. And we haven't even addressed the rides themselves, which typically feature frequent explosions and other ear-splitting sound effects played at decibel levels that would make Spinal Tap shudder. As a father from Petaluma, California, put it:

> *Universal Studios loves its sound tracks. Every ride had blaring sound effects, and even as we just walked around the park, the music was blaring from various attractions so loud that you had trouble talking to the person next to you. Crowd noise was so loud that you couldn't hear the magical effects in the windows at Hogsmeade Village! We were frazzled by the end of the day. I highly recommend putting in earplugs when you arrive and keeping them in for the whole day.*

A Vancouver, Canada, visitor was even blunter:

> *Universal is an assault on the senses. Where Disney is so often quaint and genteel, Universal is brash, loud, and in your face.*

TIMING *Your* VISIT

CROWDS ARE LARGEST IN THE SUMMER (Memorial Day–Labor Day) and during specific holiday periods during the rest of the year. December 25–January 1 is extremely busy, as are Thanksgiving weekend, the week of Presidents Day, spring break for schools and colleges, and the two weeks bracketing Easter. The least busy time is from after Thanksgiving weekend until the week before Christmas. The next slowest times are September through the weekend preceding Thanksgiving, January 4 through the first week of March, and the week following Easter to Memorial Day weekend. We don't currently maintain a crowd calendar for Universal Studios Hollywood, but you'll find a useful free one at **californiainformer.com/universal-hollywood/crowd-calendar.**

SELECTING THE DAY OF THE WEEK FOR YOUR VISIT

WEEKENDS ARE MORE CROWDED than weekdays year-round. Saturday is the busiest day. Sunday, particularly Sunday morning, is the best bet if you have to go on a weekend, but it is still extremely busy. During the summer, Friday is very busy; Monday, Wednesday, and Thursday are usually less so; Tuesday is normally the slowest of all.

During the off-season (September–May, holidays excepted), Tuesday is usually the least-crowded day, followed by Thursday.

HOW MUCH TIME TO ALLOCATE

THOUGH THERE'S A LOT TO SEE and do at Universal Studios Hollywood, you can (unlike at Disneyland) complete a comprehensive tour in one day. If you follow our touring plan, which calls for being on hand at park opening, you should be able to check out everything before the park closes, even on a crowded day.

Never mind that Universal Studios Hollywood claims to cover 400 acres; the area you will have to traverse on foot is considerably smaller. In fact, you will do much less walking and, miracle of miracles, much less standing in line at Universal Studios than at Disneyland.

Increased attendance since the opening of the Harry Potter attractions has helped transform USH from a half-day attraction to one that merits a full day's visit. And just as he did in Orlando, Potter has propelled USH's attendance to new peaks, with a 13.9% increase in guests in 2016 and a stunning 60% boost in the first quarter of 2017. A record 45,000 guests packed into the park on January 2, 2017, and on some peak days the park has had to close its ticket windows and hang SOLD OUT signs as Hogsmeade becomes mobbed from opening until evening.

UNIVERSAL STUDIOS HOLLYWOOD FOR YOUNG CHILDREN

WE DO NOT RECOMMEND UNIVERSAL STUDIOS HOLLYWOOD for preschoolers. Of 14 major attractions, all but 3 (DreamWorks Theatre, Ollivanders, and *Universal's Animal Actors*) have the potential for flipping out sensitive little ones. See the Small-Child Fright-Potential Table on the opposite page.

All Universal rides with a height requirement offer child switch, which is similar to Disney's rider swap; most attractions allow everyone to wait in line together and have a quiet room where the nonriding parent can wait with the kids while his or her partner rides. Ask the greeter at each attraction's entrance how to take advantage of child switch.

COST

JUST AHEAD OF The Wizarding World's debut, Universal Studios Hollywood did away with its old single-day and annual pass admission structures, instituting its own version of demand-based tiered pricing even before Disneyland did, and sharply increasing prices and blackout dates for pass holders. The new ticket system, dubbed EZ Rez, strongly encourages guests to select the date of their visit in advance. One-day adult tickets are $120 at the gate but can be purchased online for as low as $105 if you select your visit date in advance. Tickets for kids ages 3–9 cost $6 less than adult tickets; children 2 and under are free. In addition to saving you money and time by avoiding the ticket booths, purchasing your Universal Studios Hollywood admission online also grants you

UNIVERSAL STUDIOS HOLLYWOOD
SMALL-CHILD FRIGHT-POTENTIAL TABLE

DESPICABLE ME MINION MAYHEM Loud with some intense 3-D effects.

DREAMWORKS THEATRE Special effects may frighten preschoolers.

FLIGHT OF THE HIPPOGRIFF Frightens a small percentage of preschoolers.

HARRY POTTER AND THE FORBIDDEN JOURNEY Extremely intense special effects and macabre visuals with wild simulated movement that may frighten and discombobulate guests of any age.

JURASSIC PARK—THE RIDE Intense water-flume ride. Potentially terrifying for people of any age.

OLLIVANDERS Not frightening in any way.

REVENGE OF THE MUMMY—THE RIDE Scares guests of all ages.

THE SIMPSONS RIDE Motion simulator too intense for many children age 7 and younger tall enough to ride.

SPECIAL EFFECTS SHOW Some intense special effects. Shows how bloody fake wounds are created, and someone is (safely) set on fire.

STUDIO TOUR Certain parts of the tour are too frightening and too intense for many preschoolers.

TRANSFORMERS: THE RIDE 3-D Too intense for children younger than age 7, and potentially terrifying for visitors of any age.

UNIVERSAL'S ANIMAL ACTORS Not frightening in any way.

THE WALKING DEAD ATTRACTION Potentially traumatizing to young children, grown adults, and all sentient creatures. Not appropriate for anyone under age 13 or those afraid of being eaten by zombies.

WATERWORLD Fighting, gunplay, and explosions may frighten children age 4 and younger.

access to early entry, giving you a 1 hour head start in The Wizarding World of Harry Potter (see page 341 for details).

A pass that allows you to skip the regular line at all attractions (including Harry Potter and the Forbidden Journey) using the Gate A express entrance runs $189–$264 (depending on season) for adults or children, including admission. Save $10 by buying online in advance.

Locals can buy a California Neighbor Pass for $149 at the gate or $129 online. It's valid for 9 months after your first visit but has so many blackout dates (including many weekends and most of the summer) that it's only valid 181 days of the year; however, you can use it on any day for your first visit. The Gold Annual Pass is good for 12 months after your first visit, offers 344 valid days (including 88 weekend days), and costs $299 ($10 less if purchased online). The Silver Annual Pass is $179 ($169 online) for 275 valid days, including 59 weekend days. Finally, the Platinum Annual Pass ($599, $589 online) is the only pass valid 365 days a year with no blackouts. Silver, Gold, and Platinum Passes can be purchased on interest-free monthly installments with FlexPay. The Gold and Platinum Passes include free self-parking before 5 p.m. and also provide 15% discounts on most in-park food and merchandise. The Platinum Pass also throws in a Halloween Horror Nights ticket and priority access to all rides and shows that offer Gate A, including the Studio Tour.

For Hollywood-happy high rollers, USH offers a VIP Experience ($359–$409, depending on season; $10 off if ordered online) that includes admission, valet parking, escorted queue-cutting at all attractions, off-tram walking tours of sets and soundstages, light breakfast and gourmet lunch, and amenities such as ponchos and bottled water. The quality of service provided by the VIP touring guides is exceptional, and you'll get to explore places—like Universal's gargantuan prop warehouse or the *War of the Worlds* airliner crash site—that are otherwise inaccessible to guests. Best of all, you travel in style, in a luxury air-conditioned bus that beats the heck out of the standard Studio Tour trams. If you have the spare dough, it's undoubtedly a better deal than Disney's pay-per-hour VIP guides, and with The Wizarding World now open, this service is worth its weight in goblin gold. Reservations are required; call ☎ 818-622-8477 to book or visit **universal studioshollywood.com/tickets/vip-experience** for more information.

In addition to the website discounts, admission discounts are sometimes offered in area freebie publications available in hotels. Admission discounts are also periodically offered to AAA members.

While Universal's team members don't have a reputation for the exceptionally sunny service their pixie-dusted counterparts at Disneyland are famous for, they do excel at guest recovery when things go wrong. For example, when rides at Universal Studios Hollywood break down (as they inevitably seem to do), the operators sometimes hand out free jelly beans to guests stuck in the queue, a policy we wish every park would adopt.

STAYING ON-SITE AT UNIVERSAL STUDIOS HOLLYWOOD

HILTON AND SHERATON both operate hotels on Universal Studios Hollywood's property, but if you've experienced the exceptional perks offered to guests at Universal Orlando's Loews hotels, lower your expectations before booking an on-site room at USH. Both on-property hotels are pricey for the room size and service quality, the parks are a poorly marked 10-minute hike away, and no theme park bonuses—such as front-of-the-line passes or even early entry (unless you purchase a designated vacation package)—are included. You can also walk into Universal from a handful of off-site hotels along Cahuenga Boulevard (we can vouch for The Tilt), though it's a 15-minute hike up an extremely steep slope.

THE SHUTTLE

UNIVERSAL CITY is on the Red Line of **Los Angeles Metro Rail,** which makes it relatively easy to commute by light rail from downtown LA and many other places, though not from Anaheim. Across the street from the subway station and the bus stop, at Lankershim Boulevard and Universal Hollywood Drive, is a free Universal Studios shuttle bus that will conveniently take you to the main entrances of Universal Studios Hollywood and CityWalk. The bus runs daily, beginning at 7 a.m., with pickups about every 10–15 minutes; service continues until about 2 hours after the theme park closes. Refer to the posted times at each shuttle stop for information on the last departing shuttle. For rail and bus schedules and additional public transportation information, call the Los Angeles Metropolitan Transportation Authority at ☎ 800-COM-MUTE or 213-626-4455, or visit **metro.net.**

Alternatively, you can reach Universal Studios Hollywood by taxi, Uber, or bus tours like Starline Tours (**starlinetours.com/anaheim-tours .asp**), which combine round-trip transportation from Disneyland-area hotels with park admission. Just beware that shuttle services must pick up at multiple hotels and might not get you to the park before rope drop.

ARRIVING *and* GETTING ORIENTED

MOST FOLKS ACCESS UNIVERSAL STUDIOS by taking US 101, also called the Hollywood Freeway, and following the signs to the park. If the freeway is gridlocked, you can also get to the Studios by taking Cahuenga Boulevard and then turning north toward Lankershim Boulevard. If you are coming from Burbank, take Barham Boulevard toward US 101, and then follow the signs.

Universal Studios has a number of big, multilevel parking garages at the top of the hill, including a massive *E.T.*-inspired facility that opened in 2016. Signs directing you to the garages have improved but can still be a bit confusing, so pay attention as you come up the hill. Even after you have made it to the pay booth and shelled out $20 to park, it is still not exactly clear where you go next. (Preferred parking costs $30, $40 for even closer front-gate parking; parking costs extra if your RV is more than 15 feet long. All parking rates except valet are discounted by $10 after 6 p.m.) Drive slowly, follow other cars proceeding from the pay booths, and avoid turns onto ramps marked EXIT. You may become a bit disoriented, but ultimately you will blunder into the garage. Once parked, make a note of your parking level and the location of your space. Valet parking ($15 for the first 2.5 hours, $35 for more than 2.5 hours) is located inside the Frankenstein parking structure and is even more bewildering to navigate to; take the Lankershim exit off US 101 for easier access to valet and the on-site hotels.

Walk toward the opposite end of the garage from where you entered and exit into Universal CityWalk, a shopping, dining, and entertainment complex (no admission required) situated between the parking structure and the main entrance of the park. As an aside, CityWalk is much like Downtown Disney at Disneyland. Some of Universal's better restaurants and more interesting shops are at CityWalk, and it's so close to the theme park entrance that you can conveniently pop out of the park to grab a bite (don't forget to have your hand stamped for reentry). If "riding the movies" at the theme park inspires you to watch one, the 19-screen AMC IMAX Cineplex was recently upgraded with plush reclining seats, Dolby Atmos surround sound, and razor-sharp Christie RGB laser projectors.

Universal Studios' ticket booths and turnstiles are about 100 yards from the main parking garage. Before approaching the ticket booths and turnstiles, you'll have to pass through an expansive TSA-style security checkpoint; fortunately, Universal's setup is far more efficient than Disneyland's inspections. If you need cash, an ATM is outside and to the right of the main entrance. There are also ATMs inside the park at the Kwik-E-Mart, near the Jurassic Cove Cafe on the Lower Lot, and even a Gringotts money machine in Hogsmeade. Nearby is a guest-services window. As you enter the park, be sure to pick up a park map and a daily entertainment schedule.

THE UPPER LOT

THE UPPER LOT is essentially a large, amorphous pedestrian plaza. In-park signage (which is inordinately confusing) references street names such as New York Street and Baker Street and place names such as Cape Cod and Moulin Rouge, but on foot these theme distinctions are largely lost and placement of buildings appears almost random. The park's previously utilitarian entry corridor was rejuvenated in 2016 with fresh facades recalling the Golden Age of Hollywood (look for tributes to the studio's past talents, like makeup artist Jack Pierce), and an Art Deco tower serves as a central "weenie" to navigate by, but outside of The Wizarding World of Harry Potter, don't expect Disneyland's dedication to thematic integrity.

Inside the main entrance, stroller and wheelchair rentals are on the right, as are rental lockers. Straight ahead is a TV Audience Ticket Booth, where you can obtain free tickets to join the audience for any TV shows that are taping during your visit (subject to availability).

Attractions in the Upper Lot are situated around the perimeter of the plaza. Near The Simpsons Ride (straight ahead) are the escalators and stairs that lead to the Lower Lot.

THE LOWER LOT

THE LOWER LOT is accessible only via the escalators and stairs descending from the back left section of the Upper Lot. Configured roughly in the shape of the letter *T*, the Lower Lot is home to Transformers, Jurassic Park, and Revenge of the Mummy, all headliner attractions at Universal Studios Hollywood. Look for further developments on the Lower Lot in the next few years; rumored upcoming additions include an animatronic-filled *Secret Life of Pets* dark ride using trackless vehicles and Super Nintendo Land, featuring a Mario Kart ride. Be aware that the Lower Lot typically opens 1 hour after the rest of the park, though its attractions remain operating 15 minutes after closing time.

UNIVERSAL STUDIOS HOLLYWOOD ATTRACTIONS

UPPER LOT ATTRACTIONS

Despicable Me Minion Mayhem ★★★★

APPEAL BY AGE	PRESCHOOL ★★★★	GRADE SCHOOL ★★★★★	TEENS ★★★★★
YOUNG ADULTS ★★★★		OVER 30 ★★★★	SENIORS ★★★

What it is Motion simulator with 3-D projection. **Scope and scale** Major attraction. **When to go** The first hour the park is open or after 4 p.m. **Comment** Must be 40" tall to ride. Single-rider line available. **Duration of ride** 5 minutes, plus 10-minute preshow. **Average wait time per 100 people ahead of you** 3½ minutes. **Loading speed** Moderate–slow.

DESCRIPTION AND COMMENTS Despicable Me Minion Mayhem is a 3-D motion simulator ride similar to The Simpsons Ride and Disneyland's Star Tours. You're seated in a ride vehicle that faces a large video screen, on which the attraction's story is projected. When the story calls for you to drop down the side of a mountain, your ride vehicle tilts forward as if you were falling; when you need to swerve left or right, your ride vehicle tilts the same way. The main difference between Minion Mayhem and other simulators is that most other simulators usually provide one video screen per ride vehicle, while Minion Mayhem arranges all of its eight-person vehicles in front of one large IMAX-size video screen. The ride vehicles are set on raised platforms, which get slightly higher toward the back of the theater, affording good views for all guests.

The preshow area is inside the home of adorably evil Gru (voiced by Steve Carell), where you see his unique family tree and other artifacts. The premise of the ride is that you're turned into one of Gru's yellow Minions. Once converted you must navigate the Minion training grounds, where your "speed, strength, and ability not to die" is tested. Something soon goes amiss, though, and your training turns into a frenetic rescue operation.

The ride is a fast-paced series of dives, climbs, and tight turns through Gru's Rube Goldberg–esque machines. Like The Simpsons Ride, there are more sight gags and interesting things to see here than anyone possibly could in a single ride. Guests exit the ride into a colorful carnival-themed gift shop, where they may find the opportunity for a photo with some Minions.

TOURING TIPS Minion Mayhem, a hit import from Universal Studios Florida, features a much more elaborate facade (try ringing doorbells on the homes neighboring the attraction entrance) than the Orlando ride; this version is also blessed with a second theater and preshow, effectively doubling the attraction's capacity. Unfortunately, unlike Orlando's version, Hollywood's ride lacks stationary seating, making the attraction inaccessible to those who don't meet the height requirement or can't handle the shaking simulators. Even so, it can accrue a long queue thanks to the franchise's popularity. Ride it as early in the day as possible, preferably before the Lower Lot opens. If the line for Despicable Me exceeds 30 minutes, try late afternoon or the hour before the park closes. Adjacent to the ride's exit, the Super Silly Fun Land area should help small tykes burn off some steam, with wet and dry playgrounds, carnival mid-way games, and Silly Swirly (★★½), a simple Dumbo-style spinning ride sporting wacky bug-shaped vehicles and Minion-ized disco music.

DreamWorks Theatre, Featuring *Kung Fu Panda* (opens mid-2018)

What it is 4-D theater show. **Scope and scale** Headliner. **When to go** The first hour the park is open or after 4 p.m. **Duration of show** About 20 minutes. **Probable waiting time** About 20 minutes.

DESCRIPTION AND COMMENTS In 2017 Universal Studios Hollywood shuttered its long-in-the-tooth *Shrek 4-D* attraction and transformed it into the Art Deco DreamWorks Theatre, which screens 4-D shorts featuring franchises from the computer-animation studio Universal purchased. When DreamWorks Theatre debuts in 2018, it will screen an all-new 3-D adventure starring Master Po, the portly protagonist of the Kung Fu Panda series, and his Furious Five friends. The show should incorporate the usual slate of multisensory 4-D effects—water, wind, fog, more water—augmented with LED lighting and advanced projection-mapping effects that extend the action beyond the edges of the screen. The venue will launch with all-day screenings of *Kung Fu Panda* but is equipped to rotate programming, perhaps to present seasonal shows themed to Halloween or Christmas.

TOURING TIPS With an hourly capacity of 2,400 guests an hour, there was rarely a wait for *Shrek 4-D.* The new *Kung Fu Panda* film may prove more popular, so pop in early or check back in the afternoon until wait times drop to 20 minutes.

The Simpsons Ride ★★★★

APPEAL BY AGE	PRESCHOOL ★★★½	GRADE SCHOOL ★★★★	TEENS ★★★★
YOUNG ADULTS ★★★★		OVER 30 ★★★★	SENIORS ★★★½

What it is Mega-simulator ride. **Scope and scale** Super-headliner. **When to go** Before the Lower Lot opens. **Comment** Must be 40" tall to ride; not recommended for pregnant women or people prone to motion sickness; switching-off option provided (see page 154). **Duration of ride** 4⅓ minutes, plus preshow. **Average wait time per 100 people ahead of you** 5 minutes. **Loading speed** Moderate.

Queasy

DESCRIPTION AND COMMENTS This ride is based on the Fox animated series that is TV's longest-running sitcom. Featuring the voices of Dan Castellaneta (Homer), Julie Kavner (Marge), Nancy Cartwright (Bart), Yeardley Smith (Lisa), and other cast members, the attraction takes a wild and humorous poke at thrill rides, dark rides, and live shows "that make up a fantasy amusement park dreamed up by the show's cantankerous Krusty the Clown."

Two preshows involve *Simpsons* characters speaking sequentially on different video screens around the line area. Their comments help define the characters for guests who are unfamiliar with the TV show. The attraction is a simulator ride similar to Star Tours at Disneyland Park, but with a larger domed Omnimax-type screen more like that of Soarin' at Disney California Adventure. The interior queue in Hollywood's Simpsons has slightly more breathing room than is found at the same attraction in Orlando, and the ride has been upgraded with 4K projectors and a photo op at the end, but the

East and West Coast versions are otherwise indistinguishable.

The story line has the conniving Sideshow Bob secretly arriving at Krustyland, the aforementioned amusement park, and plotting his revenge on Krusty and Bart, who, in a past *Simpsons* episode, revealed that Sideshow Bob had committed a crime for which he'd framed Krusty. Sideshow Bob gets even by making things go wrong with the attractions that the Simpsons (and you) are riding.

Like the show on which it's based, The Simpsons Ride definitely has an edge, and more than a few wild hairs. There will be jokes and visuals that you'll get but will fly over your children's heads—and most assuredly vice versa. A mom from Huntington, New York, had this to say:

The ride is lots of fun and suitable for all guests. I'm not a fan of wild motion simulators, but I was fine on this ride.

TOURING TIPS Expect large crowds all day. We recommend arriving at the park before opening and making the ride your last stop before the Lower Lot attractions open. Though not as rough and jerky as its predecessor, it's a long way from being tame. Several families we interviewed found the humor a little too adult for their younger children. Don't miss the neighboring Simpson-ized carnival games and Kwik-E-Mart gift shop for more snarky Simpsons sight gags, as well as an expansive strip of Springfield-inspired shops and eateries (partially patterned after Universal Studios Florida's popular Fast Food Boulevard). Featured destinations include Krusty Burger, Luigi's Pizza, Phineas Q. Butterfat's Ice Cream, Moe's Tavern, and Duff Brewery Beer Garden. You'll also find funny facades of iconic cartoon locations such as Springfield's police station, elementary school, and nuclear power plant; try pressing the button outside Homer's workstation for an explosive surprise.

Special Effects Show ★★★½

APPEAL BY AGE	PRESCHOOL ★★½	GRADE SCHOOL ★★★	TEENS ★★★½
YOUNG ADULTS ★★★½		OVER 30 ★★★½	SENIORS ★★★½

What it is A theater presentation on special effects. **Scope and scale** Major attraction. **When to go** Anytime. **Comments** Predictable but still interesting; may frighten young children. **Duration of show** 30 minutes. **Probable waiting time** 15 minutes.

DESCRIPTION AND COMMENTS Guests view a fast-paced presentation on special effects, with elements borrowed from both the old Special Effects Stages (formerly on the park's Lower Lot) and the *Horror Make-Up Show* found in Universal Studios Florida. Audience members participate in demonstrations of green screens, computer-generated imagery (CGI), and motion capture. For the finale, a volunteer is apparently attached to a flying rig (left over from the short-lived *Creature of the Black Lagoon* musical that once occupied this space) and sent sailing above the crowd. The educational content will already be familiar to anyone who has ever watched a DVD making-of documentary, and the show lacks *Horror Make-Up* humor and spontaneity. But a 2016 update eliminated the tired "old school versus new school" story line, substituting straightforward stunt demonstrations, including a spectacular opportunity to watch a full-body fire burn in person.

TOURING TIPS The best seats seem to be in the center of the theater, not directly up front. Or try the seats to the left or right of the center runway.

Studio Tour, Including *Fast & Furious: Supercharged*
★★★★★

| APPEAL BY AGE | PRESCHOOL ★★★ | GRADE SCHOOL ★★★★ | TEENS ★★★★ |
| YOUNG ADULTS ★★★★ | | OVER 30 ★★★★ | SENIORS ★★★★ |

What it is Indoor-outdoor tram tour of soundstages and back lot. **Scope and scale** Headliner. **When to go** After experiencing the other rides. **Duration of tour** 45–60 minutes, depending on studio productions. **Average wait time per 100 people ahead of you** 2½ minutes. **Loading speed** Fast.

Loud   Scary

DESCRIPTION AND COMMENTS The Studio Tour is the center-piece of Universal Studios Hollywood and is one of the longest attractions in American theme parks. The tour departs from the tram boarding facility to the *right* of The Simpsons Ride and down the escalator. (Note that there's also an escalator to the left of The Simpsons Ride, so don't get confused.)

Tonight Show host and former *Saturday Night Live* star Jimmy Fallon is the tour's prerecorded host. All trams are equipped with high-definition monitors showing clips from actual movies that demonstrate how the sets and soundstages were used in creating the films.

The tour circulates through the various street scenes, lagoons, special effects venues, and storage areas of Universal's back lot. The tram passes several soundstages where current films and TV shows such as *The Voice* are in production and actually enters three soundstages where action inspired by *Earthquake, King Kong,* and *The Fast and the Furious* is presented. Other famous sets visited include those from *Psycho, Jaws, War of the Worlds,* and *The Grinch Who Stole Christmas.* A simulated flash flood, long a highlight of the tour, has been enhanced with new sound effects. *Back to the Future* fans will spot the restored Lyon Estates gateway on the tour.

The award-winning *King Kong 360/3-D* is a virtual experience inspired by Peter Jackson's 2005 remake. Guests enter a darkened tunnel where tram-length curved projection screens transform into the jungles of Skull Island. A family of hungry *V. rexes* decides to dine on your tour group, and Kong himself swings to save you, with hydraulic lifts under the cars simulating the sensations of their tug-of-war. The experience is visceral and visually stunning, especially when seen from the middle of a row (sitting on the outside exposes the top of the screen, spoiling the illusion). At only about 90 seconds, *King Kong* is too short to be a satisfying stand-alone attraction (it was substantially expanded for the Orlando incarnation), but it's a terrific addition to the overall tour.

In 2015 Universal debuted *Fast & Furious: Supercharged,* a new finale to the tram tour, featuring Vin Diesel (Dominic "Dom" Toretto), Dwayne Johnson (Luke Hobbs), Michelle Rodriguez (Letty Ortiz), Tyrese Gibson (Roman Pearce), and Luke Evans (Owen Shaw) from the long-running car-racing franchise. Inside a 50,000-square-foot soundstage built on the site of the old avalanche-effect tunnel, the "3D-HD thrill ride" uses hydraulic platforms, 400-foot-long screens, and 34 4K 3-D projectors to make it appear as if your tram is in the midst of a high-stakes car chase, pursuing an international crime cartel at 100-plus miles per hour through the streets of Los Angeles. The *Fast & Furious* finale begins when your tram driver spots Dom's iconic Dodge Charger along your path, prompting the revelation that a member of your party is a crime witness being sought by both the bad guys and the FBI. Your tram shelters in an industrial warehouse, where a rave is in full swing until the feds crash the party. The F&F crew come to your rescue and escort you on a virtual high-speed highway chase filled with CGI car crashes and simulated explosions. After so much hype, *Supercharged* is frankly somewhat disappointing, failing to advance the *Kong 360* technology in a meaningful way or capture the visceral thrill that made the Fast & Furious films so popular. The dialogue and visual effects are shockingly cheesy (even by theme park standards), but it all goes by in such a nitro-fueled blur that audiences emerge applauding.

Nighttime tram tours were introduced in 2015 to mark the Studio Tour's 50th anniversary, and they continue to run seasonally during summer evenings with extended operating hours. The nighttime tour still showcases additional lighting on the back lot sets, but live encounters with "celebrities" such as Frankenstein's monster have been discontinued.

The great thing about the Studio Tour is that you see everything without leaving the tram—essentially experiencing four or five major attractions with only one wait.

TOURING TIPS Though the wait to board might appear long, do not be discouraged. Each tram carries several hundred people and departures are frequent, so the line moves quickly. We recommend taking the tram tour after experiencing the rides on the Lower Lot.

Including your wait to board and the duration of the tour, you will easily invest an hour or more at this attraction. Remember to take a restroom break before queuing up. This is one of the few attractions that allows food and beverages to be brought on board. Though the ride as a whole is gentle, some segments may induce vertigo or motion sickness—especially the *Kong* encounter and *Fast & Furious* finale. Finally, be aware that several of the scenes may frighten small children.

Universal's Animal Actors ★★★½

APPEAL BY AGE	PRESCHOOL ★★★★½	GRADE SCHOOL ★★★★	TEENS ★★★½
YOUNG ADULTS ★★★½	OVER 30 ★★★½		SENIORS ★★★½

What it is Trained animals stadium performance. **Scope and scale** Major attraction. **When to go** After you have experienced all rides. **Comment** Warm and delightful. **Duration of show** 20 minutes. **Probable waiting time** 15–20 minutes.

Thumbs Up for the Whole Family

DESCRIPTION AND COMMENTS *Universal's Animal Actors* features various critters, including some rescued from shelters, demonstrating behaviors that animals often perform in the making of motion pictures. The live presentation is punctuated by clips from films and TV shows, including *The Secret Life of Pets*. Of course, the animals often exhibit an independence that frustrates their trainers while delighting the audience.

TOURING TIPS Presented five or more times daily, the program's schedule is in the daily entertainment guide. Go when it's convenient for you; queue about 20 minutes before showtime. If you purchased front-of-the-line access through a Gate A or VIP ticket, stick around after select show-times for a personal audience with some of the furry stars.

The Walking Dead Attraction ★★★½

APPEAL BY AGE	PRESCHOOL —	GRADE SCHOOL —	TEENS ★★★★
YOUNG ADULTS ★★★★		OVER 30 ★★★	SENIORS ★★

What it is A fun house–style walk-through of scenes based on AMC's *The Walking Dead,* incorporating animatronics, live actors, and special effects. **Scope and scale** Major attraction. **When to go** After seeing the headliner rides. **Comments** Not suitable for children age 13 and younger. Switching-off option provided (see page 154). **Duration of experience** About 4 minutes. **Average wait time per 100 people ahead of you** 5 minutes.

Dark   Loud   Scary

DESCRIPTION AND COMMENTS This attraction is an extremely elaborate horror maze inspired by AMC's top-rated zombie drama *The Walking Dead.* Designed in cooperation with series executive producer and horror makeup guru Greg Nicotero, it's a more permanent and elaborate version of the walk-through haunted houses you see around Halloween. Guests walk in the footsteps of Rick Grimes and the show's other survivors, battling through iconic locations such as the Atlanta hospital, the moonshine cabin, and the West Georgia Correctional Facility. As you pick your way through the dark, there are lots of gruesome sights, disorienting devices such as faux fire and lurching animatronics, and, worst of all, live people springing out of dark corners to startle you. If you don't like being startled but really want to see the attraction, follow some teenage girls through. The leaping, growling, menacing ghouls will expend lots of extra energy on the girls and be in a state of relative depletion when you pass through.

TOURING TIPS The Walking Dead is located very near the main entrance to the park. It doesn't take long to tour (as the length of the experience depends on how badly you want out), but once a line builds, it moves very slowly. This attraction usually opens at 11 a.m. or noon and closes by 8 p.m. Wait times are often minimal in the evening.

WaterWorld ★★★★

APPEAL BY AGE	PRESCHOOL ★★★	GRADE SCHOOL ★★★★	TEENS ★★★★
YOUNG ADULTS ★★★★		OVER 30 ★★★½	SENIORS ★★★½

Thumbs Up for the Whole Family

What it is Arena show featuring simulated stunt-scene filming. **Scope and scale** Major attraction. **When to go** After experiencing all the rides and the tram tour. **Duration of show** 15 minutes. **Probable waiting time** 15–30 minutes.

DESCRIPTION AND COMMENTS Drawn from the film *WaterWorld,* this outdoor theater presentation features stunts and special effects performed on and around a small man-made lagoon. The action involves various watercraft and, of course, a lot of explosions and falling from high places into the water. Fast-paced and well adapted to the theater, the production is in many ways more compelling than the film that inspired it. The show was revamped in 2014 with a restructured climax featuring additional stunts and pyrotechnics, making for an even more rousing finale.

TOURING TIPS Wait until you have experienced all the rides and the tram tour before checking out *WaterWorld*. Because the show is located near the main entrance, most performances are filled to capacity. Arrive at the theater about 30 minutes before the showtime listed in the daily entertainment schedule. Be careful if you sit in on a green bench; when this show says "splash zone," it means it. The stunt team reveals some behind-the-scenes secrets in an interesting show-and-tell seminar for Gate A and VIP guests after select shows.

THE WIZARDING WORLD OF HARRY POTTER

UNIVERSAL STUDIOS HOLLYWOOD'S Wizarding World of Harry Potter, a close copy of the original "land" at Orlando's Islands of Adventure with some subtle upgrades, is an amalgamation of landmarks, creatures, and themes that are faithful to the films and books. You access the area through its main entrance, an imposing gate adjacent to the DreamWorks Theatre that leads to The Wizarding World's primary shopping and dining area, **Hogsmeade,** a village depicted in winter and covered in snow. (A secondary entryway is found between The Simpsons Ride and the Studio Tour escalator, but it may be restricted to exit-only traffic.) The towering castle houses **Hogwarts School of Witchcraft and Wizardry,** flanked by the **Flight of the Hippogriff** kiddie coaster and **Hagrid's Hut.** The grounds and interior of the castle contain part of the queue for the super-headliner **Harry Potter and the Forbidden Journey.** Universal went all out on the castle, with the intention of creating an icon even more beloved and powerful than Sleeping Beauty Castle at Disneyland.

In front of the gate, the **Hogwarts Express** locomotive sits belching steam, and a small station houses a train-themed gift shop. The village setting is rendered in exquisite detail: stone cottages and shops have steeply pitched slate roofs, bowed multipaned windows, gables, and tall, crooked chimneys. Add cobblestone streets and gas streetlamps, and Hogsmeade is as reminiscent of Sherlock Holmes as it is of Harry Potter. Your first taste—literally—of the Harry Potter universe comes courtesy of **Honeydukes.** Specializing in Potter-themed candy such as Acid Pops (no flashbacks, guaranteed), Tooth Splintering Strong Mints, and Fizzing Whizzbees, the sweet shop offers no shortage of snacks that administer an immediate sugar high. The big draw is the elaborately boxed Chocolate Frogs; the packaging looks as if it came straight from a Harry Potter film, complete with wizard trading card. Taking up a small corner of Honeydukes is **Zonko's Joke Shop,** selling toys such as Fanged Flyers (Frisbees with teeth) and adorable Pygmy Puff dolls.

Next door to Honeydukes and set back from the main street is **Three Broomsticks,** a rustic tavern serving English staples such as fish-and-chips, shepherd's pie, bangers and mash, and Guinness stew. To the rear of the tavern is the **Hog's Head** pub, which serves a nice selection of beer and is the quickest place to get The Wizarding

World's signature nonalcoholic brew, **Butterbeer** (vanilla soda with butterscotch–marshmallow foam, available cold, frozen, or, in cooler months, hot). There's even Butterbeer fudge (tooth-shatteringly sweet) and Butterbeer potted cream (like butterscotch pudding in a jar), though Butterbeer soft-serve ice cream wasn't imported from Orlando's Diagon Alley. For the adults, exclusive beers are available; we like the Wizard's Brew, a rich chocolate stout. If all that imbibing inspires you to heed nature's call, be warned that Moaning Myrtle haunts both the men's and ladies' sides of the land's only facilities; hearing her cries while you're trying to go can be distracting to say the least.

On the far side of the pub is **Ollivanders,** where young wizards are matched with magic wands (see the full description on page 345) in a brief but charming show. Adjoining the wand shop (where you can browse without queuing for the show) is **Wiseacre's Wizarding Equipment,** where you can buy binoculars or telescopes.

Roughly across the street from the pub, you'll find benches in the shade at the **Owlery,** where animatronic owls (complete with lifelike poop) ruffle and hoot from the rafters. Next to the Owlery is the **Owl Post,** where you can have mail stamped with a Hogsmeade postmark before dropping it off for delivery. The Owl Post also sells stationery, school supplies, and toy owls. Here, once again, a nice selection of owls preens on the timbers overhead. The Owl Post is attached to **Dervish and Banges,** a magic supplies shop selling brooms and Quidditch equipment, and **Gladrags Wizardwear,** ground zero for getting outfitted in fashionable school robes.

Finally, at the exit of Hogwarts Castle is **Filch's Emporium of Confiscated Goods,** which offers all manner of Potter-themed gear, including Marauder's Maps, magical creature toys, film-inspired chess sets, and, of course, Death Eater masks (breath mints extra). In keeping with the stores depicted in the Potter films, the shopping venues in The Wizarding World of Harry Potter–Hogsmeade are small and intimate—so intimate, in fact, that they feel congested when they're serving only 12–20 shoppers. USH also sells most of its Potter merchandise, including wands, at two easily accessible stores near the park entrance.

For those who have been to the original Wizarding World in Orlando, visiting Hollywood's version is somewhat surreal. Though at first glance everything is superficially the same—except for the obvious absence of the Dragon Challenge roller coaster—there are numerous disorienting differences, starting with the fact that you can see neighboring attractions poking up between the buildings of Hogsmeade, as well as majestic California mountains (standing in for the Scottish Highlands). Universal's scenic artists (led by film series art director Alan Gilmore) have compensated for the location's lack of immersiveness by layering additional details throughout the land, from rockwork and cinematic murals on exposed show buildings to extra grit and grime on the buildings. Orlando-based Potter fans should be a bit jealous of the upgraded interactive shop windows and much-needed elbow room afforded by a new pedestrian area behind the Owlery, and first-time visitors to The Wizarding World will be blown away by Hollywood's thrice-refined iteration of the acclaimed area.

After a somewhat slow start, Hollywood's Potter attractions have attracted a stampede of interest from locals and tourists alike. Prepare for the land to be packed to the gills if you visit during a peak period. Guests who purchase advance tickets online or book a vacation package, including admission and a room at a designated Preferred Hotel (see **universalstudioshollywood.com/hotels** for details), are granted early park admission to The Wizarding World 1 hour before the general public; if you are eligible for this perk, it's your best way to experience the headliner ride and browse the shops with minimal waiting. If the Hogsmeade area reaches maximum capacity (a little more than 6,000 guests), you may need to queue just to enter the land, and then queue again for the individual attractions once inside. If you can't use early entry, your best bet for experiencing Harry Potter may be to bypass the daytime rush and wait until after sundown, when you should be able to enter without waiting. The evening illumination makes Hogwarts even more magical, and wait times are often minimal in the hour before closing.

Flight of the Hippogriff ★★★

APPEAL BY AGE	PRESCHOOL ★★★½	GRADE SCHOOL ★★★★	TEENS ★★★
YOUNG ADULTS ★★½		OVER 30 ★★★½	SENIORS ★★★

What it is Kiddie roller coaster. **Scope and scale** Minor attraction. **When to go** First 90 minutes the park is open or after 4 p.m. **Comment** Must be 39" tall to ride. Single-rider line available. **Duration of ride** 1 minute. **Average wait time per 100 people ahead of you** 14 minutes. **Loading speed** Slow.

DESCRIPTION AND COMMENTS Below and to the right of Hogwarts Castle, next to Hagrid's Hut, the Hippogriff is short and sweet but not worth much of a wait. This outdoor, elevated coaster is designed for children old enough to know about Harry Potter but not yet tall enough to ride Forbidden Journey. The ride affords excellent views of the area within Wizarding World and of Hogwarts, and the theming is also very good, considering that this isn't a major attraction. As a children's coaster only slightly taller and longer than Gadget's Go Coaster in Disneyland, there are no loops, inversions, or rolls: it's just one big hill and some mild turns, and almost half of the 1-minute ride time is spent going up the lift hill. Hollywood's coaster has a layout similar to the Orlando original, but this one is a brand-new model manufactured by Mack (rather than an aging Vekoma) and gives a much smoother and somewhat snappier ride.

For fans of Harry Potter, there are two gorgeous items in this attraction that you will want to see. The first is a faithful re-creation of Hagrid's Hut in the queue (complete with the sound of Fang howling) while the second is an incredible animatronic of Buckbeak that you pass by while on the ride. Remember that when Muggles (also known as humans) encounter hippogriffs like Buckbeak, proper etiquette must always be maintained to avoid any danger. Hippogriffs are extremely proud creatures and must be shown the proper respect by bowing to them and waiting for them to bow in return.

TOURING TIPS If you are eligible for early entry, have your kids ride soon after the park opens while older siblings enjoy Forbidden Journey, or save it for late in the day.

Harry Potter and the Forbidden Journey ★★★★★

What it is Motion-simulator dark ride. **Scope and scale** Super-headliner. **When to go** Immediately after park opening or just before closing. **Comments** Expect long waits in line. Must be 48" tall to ride; switching-off option provided (see page 154). Single-rider line is available. All bags must be placed in a free locker. **Duration of ride** 4¼ minutes. **Average wait time per 100 people ahead of you** 4 minutes. **Loading speed** Fast.

Dark Loud Scary Lose Things Queasy

DESCRIPTION AND COMMENTS This ride provides the only opportunity at Universal to come close to Harry, Ron, Hermione, and Dumbledore as portrayed by the original actors. Half the attraction is a series of preshows, setting the stage for the main event, a thrilling dark ride. You can get on the ride in only 10–25 minutes using the singles line, but everyone should go through the main queue at least once. The characters are incorporated into the queue and serve as an important element of the overall experience, not merely something to keep you occupied while you wait for the main event.

From Hogsmeade you reach the attraction through the imposing Winged Boar gates and progress along a winding path past the Weasleys' crashed Ford Anglia from *The Chamber of Secrets.* Entering the castle on a lower level, you walk through a sort of dungeon festooned with various icons and prop replicas from the Potter flicks, including the Mirror of Erised from *Harry Potter and the Sorcerer's Stone.* You later emerge back outside and in the Hogwarts greenhouses. The greenhouses compose the larger part of the Forbidden Journey's queuing area, and despite some strategically placed mandrakes, there isn't much here to amuse beyond the majestic view of the mountains. If you're among the first in the park and in the queue, you'll move through this area pretty quickly.

Having finally escaped horticulture purgatory, you reenter the castle, moving along its halls and passageways. One chamber you'll probably remember from the films is a multistory gallery of portraits, many of whose subjects come alive when they take a notion. You'll see for the first time the four founders of Hogwarts: Helga Hufflepuff holding her famous cup, Godric Gryffindor and Rowena Ravenclaw nearby, and the tall, moving portrait of Salazar Slytherin straight ahead. The founders argue about Quidditch and Dumbledore's controversial decision to host an open house at Hogwarts for Muggles (garden-variety mortals). Don't rush through the gallery—the effects are very cool, and the conversation is essential to understanding the rest of the attraction.

Next, after you've navigated some more passages, is Dumbledore's office, where the wizard principal appears on a balcony and welcomes you to Hogwarts. The headmaster's appearance is your introduction to Musion Eyeliner technology—a high-definition video-projection system that produces breathtakingly realistic, three-dimensional, life-size moving holograms. After his welcoming remarks, Dumbledore dispatches you to the Defence Against the Dark Arts classroom to hear a presentation on the history of Hogwarts.

As you gather to await the lecture, Harry, Ron, and Hermione pop out from beneath an invisibility cloak. They suggest that you ditch the lecture in favor of joining them for a proper tour of Hogwarts, including a Quidditch match. After some repartee among the characters and a couple of special effects surprises, it's off to the Hogwarts Official Attraction Safety Briefing and Boarding Instructions Chamber—OK, it's actually the Gryffindor common room, but you get the picture. The briefing and instructions are presented by animated portraits, including an etiquette teacher. Later on, even the famed Sorting Hat gets into the act. All this leads to the Room of Requirement, where hundreds of candles float overhead as you board the ride.

After all the high-tech stuff in your queuing odyssey, you'll naturally expect to be wowed by your ride vehicle. Surely it's a Nimbus 3000 turbobroom, a phoenix, a hippogriff, or at least the Weasleys' flying car. But no, what you'll ride on the most technologically advanced theme park attraction in America is . . . a bench? Yep, a bench.

A bit anticlimactic, perhaps, but as benches go, this one's a doozy, mounted on a Kuka robotic arm. When not engaged in Quidditch matches, a Kuka arm is a computer-controlled robotic arm similar to the kind used in heavy manufacturing. If you think about pictures you've seen of automotive assembly plants, Kuka arms are those long metal appendages that come in to complete welds, move heavy stuff around, or fasten things. With the right programming, the arms can handle just about any repetitive industrial tasks thrown at them (see **kuka-robotics.com** for more info).

High-tech high jinks aside, is the attraction itself ultimately worthy of the hype? In a word, yes! Your 4¼-minute adventure is a headlong sprint through the most thrilling moments from the first few Potter books: you'll soar over Hogwarts Castle, narrowly evade an attacking dragon, spar with the Whomping Willow, get tossed into a Quidditch match, and fight off Dementors inside the Chamber of Secrets. Scenes alternate between enormous physical sets (complete with animatronic creatures), elaborate lighting effects, and high-definition video-projection domes that surround your field of view, similar to Soarin' Around the World or The Simpsons Ride. Those Kuka-powered benches really do "levitate" in a manner that feels remarkably like free flight, and while you don't go upside down, the sensation of floating on your back or being slung from side to side is certainly unique.

unofficial **TIP**
Even if your child meets the height requirement, consider carefully whether Forbidden Journey is an experience he or she can handle—because the seats on the benches are compartmentalized, kids can't see or touch Mom or Dad if they get frightened.

Following in the footsteps of Universal Studios Japan, USH's Forbidden Journey was the first version in America to feature 3-D visuals in the ride, but the heavily advertised upgrade was quietly yanked shortly after its debut because guests found it blurry at best and barf-inducing at worst. Instead, the ride's now-flat projections have been polished up to 120 frames per second, reducing flicker and motion blur to create a sharper, more lifelike image. Even without the extra dimension, Forbidden Journey can be a lunch-liberating experience. We recommend that you not ride with a full stomach. If you start getting queasy, fix your gaze on your feet and try to exclude as much from your peripheral vision as possible.

Other adjustments from Orlando have also made what was already one of the world's best attractions even better. Interior sets, which were monumental to begin with, are even more massive in Hollywood, with expanded scenery in the Forbidden Forest and Chamber of Secrets scenes, while lighting and sound effects were amped up to 11 for maximum impact. Of particular note is the expanded army of Dementor animatronics, which have regained the outstretched limbs deemed too spooky for Orlando's audiences.

The seamless transitions between screens and sets, and the way the domes appear to remain stationary in front of you while actually moving, serve to blur the boundary between actual and virtual better than any attraction before it. The greatest-hits montage plotline may be a bit muddled, but the ride is enormously effective at leaving you feeling as though you just survived the scariest scrapes from the early educational career of The Boy Who Lived.

To understand the story line and get the most out of the attraction, you really need to see and hear the entire presentation in each of the preshow rooms. This won't happen unless, contrary to the admonishments of the team members, you just park yourself and watch a full run-through of each preshow. Try to find a place to stop where you can let those behind you pass and where you're as far away from any staff as possible. As long as you're not creating a logjam, the team members will leave you alone as often as not.

Hollywood's Hogwarts has a private secondary queue (complete with its own enchanted portrait gallery) as a Gate A entrance for guests who paid extra to skip the line. However, if you bring any bags, you may still need to wait in the external queue for an open locker before reaching the Gate A entrance. The Gate A queue also doubles as a castle walk tour, providing nonriding guests a way to see the preshow without waiting in line; ask the greeter inside for a ticket that will permit you into the secondary queue.

The dialogue in the preshows is delivered in English accents of varying degrees of intelligibility, and at a very brisk pace. Add an echo effect owing to the cavernous nature of the preshow rooms, and it can be quite difficult for Yanks to decipher what's being said. This is especially evident in the staccato repartee between Harry, Ron, and Hermione in the Defence Against the Dark Arts classroom.

TOURING TIPS The best way to ride Forbidden Journey with a reasonable wait is to be one of the first through the turnstiles in the morning (especially if eligible for early entry) or to visit in the final hours of the evening.

Upon approaching Forbidden Journey's front gates, those who have bags or loose items and therefore require a free locker may be directed into an extended outdoor queue. The Forbidden Journey locker area in Hollywood is much more open and accessible than the one in Orlando, but it can still be crowded and confusing, so send only one member of your party to stow everyone's stuff while the rest of the family waits farther ahead. Alternatively, have one member of your party hold your bags for you in the child swap area.

Universal warns you to secure or leave behind loose objects, which most people interpret to mean eyeglasses, purses, ball caps, and the like. However, the ride makes a couple of moves that will empty your trousers faster than a master pickpocket—ditto and worse for shirt pockets. When these moves occur, your stuff will clatter around like quarters in a slot-machine tray.

Whereas on most attractions the wait in the singles line is one-third the wait in the standby line, at Forbidden Journey it can be as much as one-tenth. Because the individual seating separates you from the other riders whether your party stays together or not, the singles line is a great option, as this wife from Edinburgh, Scotland, discovered:

Trust me—sitting next to hubby on Forbidden Journey, romantic though it may be, is not as awesome as having to wait only 15 minutes as a single rider.

To get there, keep left all the way into the castle. Past the locker area, take the first left into the singles line.

If you see a complete iteration of each preshow in the queue and then experience the ride, you'll invest 25–35 minutes even if you don't have to wait. If you elect to skip the preshows (the Gryffindor common room, where you receive safety and loading directions, is mandatory) and use the singles line, you can get on in about 10–25 minutes at any time of day. At a time when the posted wait in the regular line was 2 hours, we rode and were out the door in 15 minutes using the singles line.

The end seats on each flying bench are designed to accommodate a wider variety of body shapes and sizes. Though these modified seats allow many more people to ride, it's still possible that guests of size can't fit in them. The best way to figure out whether you can fit in a regular seat or one of the modified ones is to sit in one of the test seats outside the queue. After you sit down, pull down on the safety harness as far as you can. One of three safety lights will illuminate. A green light indicates that you can fit into any seat, a yellow light means that you should ask for one of the modified seats on the outside of the bench, and a blue light means that the harness can't engage enough for you to ride safely.

In addition, USH team members select guests of all sizes "at random" to plop in the test seats, but they're really looking for large people or those who have a certain body shape. Team members handle the situation as diplomatically as possible, but if they suspect you're not the right size, you'll be asked to sit down for a test. For you to be cleared to ride, the overhead restraint has to click three times; once again, it's body shape rather than weight (unless you're over 300 pounds) that's key. Most team members will let you try a second time if you don't achieve three clicks on the first go. Passing the test by inhaling sharply is not recommended unless you can also hold your breath for the entire 4-plus minutes of the ride.

Ollivanders ★★★★

APPEAL BY AGE	PRESCHOOL ★★★★	GRADE SCHOOL ★★★★★	TEENS ★★★★
YOUNG ADULTS ★★★★		OVER 30 ★★★½	SENIORS ★★★½

What it is Combination wizarding demonstration and shopping op. **Scope and scale** Major attraction. **When to go** After riding Harry Potter and the Forbidden Journey. **Comment** Audience stands. Enchanting. **Duration of presentation** 6 minutes. **Average wait time per 100 people ahead of you** 12 minutes.

DESCRIPTION AND COMMENTS Ollivanders, located in Diagon Alley in the books and films, somehow sprouted a branch location in Hogsmeade. Potter purists have pointed out this misplacement, but the wand shop was franchised with J. K. Rowling's blessing. Inside this musty store stacked high with dusty boxes, 24 guests at a time can experience the little drama where wands choose a wizard (rather than the other way around). Orlando's original Ollivanders experience became a horrible bottleneck because of its limited capacity, but at USH, the shop has two separate choosing chambers and a blissfully shaded queue, changing it from a popular curiosity into an actual attraction.

Every few minutes, following a script from the Potter books, a wand-selection show takes place in which a random customer (often a child dressed in Potter regalia) is selected to take part in a wand-choosing ceremony. Usually just one person in each group gets to be chosen by a wand, though occasionally siblings are selected together. This is one of the most truly imaginative elements of The Wizarding World: a Wandkeeper sizes you up and presents a wand, inviting you to try it out; your attempted spells produce unintended, unwanted, and highly amusing consequences. Ultimately, a wand chooses its wizard, with all the attendant special effects. The Celtic zodiac-inspired wands ($50) presented in the ceremony interact with shop windows throughout The Wizarding World (see below).

After the presentation, guests exit into a gift shop, where interactive wands are available for purchase, along with noninteractive "famous wizard" replica wands ($44) for a vast variety of characters and toy "learner" wands ($25) for li'l wizards.

TOURING TIPS To increase your odds of being picked, be a cute kid, stand up front, and make eye contact. If your young 'un is selected to test-drive a wand, be forewarned that you'll have to buy it if you want to take it home. You do not need to see the wand-selection show to purchase a wand at Ollivanders—just enter the store directly rather than wait in the long outdoor queue.

INTERACTIVE WANDS AND SPELL-CASTING LOCATIONS

INTERACTIVE WANDS ($50) are available in 13 Ollivanders Original styles inspired by the Celtic calendar; interactive wands modeled after those wielded by a variety of characters (including Harry, Hermione, Dumbledore, Sirius Black, and Luna Lovegood) are also available. The widest selection of wands is found in the Ollivanders shop, but stores outside of The Wizarding World at the entrance of the park, as well as CityWalk's Universal Studios Store, carry a limited variety of interactive and noninteractive wands. Wands can also be ordered from Universal Orlando's merchandise website; wands from Florida are fully compatible with Hollywood's effects.

Medallions embedded in the ground designate a dozen locations around The Wizarding World where hidden cameras in storefront windows can detect the waving of these special wands and respond to the correct motions with special effects both projected and practical. You might use the swish and flick of Wingardium Leviosa to levitate one object or the figure four Locomotor spell to animate another. It can take some practice to get the hang of spell casting. Wizards wander around the area to assist novices and demonstrate spells (though they may not loan their wands), but queues to trigger certain effects can grow to a dozen deep at peak times. A map provided with each wand purchase details the location and movement for the effects.

Note that the price of the interactive wands includes unlimited activations of the hidden effects; you don't have to pay to recharge your wand on subsequent visits or even replace a battery. If you encounter a spell-casting location with a sign saying it currently has an anti-jinx in place, just move along to the next one; that's Potter-speak for "it's broken." Damaged wands are cheerfully "repaired" for free at Ollivanders, even without a receipt.

We've received positive feedback so far on the interactive wands, like this praise from a New York, New York, family:

> We took our interactive wand and map and explored all the many interactive surprises for well over an hour and had a fantastic time. An interactive wand is highly recommended. Our girls (12 and 14) had a blast making the wand motions and watching the windows come to life.

On the other hand, some guests have found the wands maddeningly difficult to master, as a father from Petaluma, California, warns:

> After getting their wands, my boys were soon frustrated to tears that the wands didn't work and that they had wasted their saved allowance money on "a piece of plastic junk," in my oldest son's words. We searched desperately for one of the robed employees to assist us, but it seemed they were all on break somewhere. After a long while we finally located one. He gave a quick tutorial on where to point the wand, how much to move it, where to stand, and so on, and my boys were able to get their wands to work. My best advice is that, after buying the wand, keep it in the box until you find someone helping at one of the magic windows, and get a lesson on how to use it. Many of the magic spells worked the opposite of how you would think, or were so subtle that you weren't sure if the spell had worked or not. The best windows for beginners are (in order) #11 Dominic Maestro's, #2 Three Broomsticks, and #1 Honeydukes.

LOWER LOT ATTRACTIONS

Jurassic Park—The Ride ★★★★

APPEAL BY AGE	PRESCHOOL ★★★	GRADE SCHOOL ★★★★½	TEENS ★★★★½
YOUNG ADULTS ★★★★		OVER 30 ★★★★	SENIORS ★★★★

What it is Indoor-outdoor adventure ride based on the movie *Jurassic Park*. **Scope and scale** Super-headliner. **When to go** The first hour the Lower Lot is open or after 4 p.m. **Comments** Must be 42" tall to ride; switching-off option provided (see page 154). Single-rider line is available. **Duration of ride** 6 minutes. **Loading speed** Fast.

Scary   Wet   Lose Things   Queasy   Rough

DESCRIPTION AND COMMENTS Guests board boats for a water tour of Jurassic Park. Everything is tranquil as the tour begins; the boat floats among large herbivorous dinosaurs such as apatosaurus and stegosaurus. Then word is received that some of the carnivores have escaped their enclosure, and the tour boat is accidentally diverted into Jurassic Park's water-treatment facility. Here the boat and its riders are menaced by an assortment of hungry meat-eaters led by the ubiquitous *T. rex.* At the climactic moment, the boat and its passengers escape by dropping over a waterfall.

Jurassic Park is impressive in its scale, but the number of dinosaurs is a little disappointing. The big herbivores are given short shrift to set up the plot for the carnivore encounter, which leads to floating around in what looks like a brewery. When the carnivores make their appearance, though, they definitely get your attention. The final drop down a three-story flume to safety is a dandy, though not as impressive as its Orlando sibling.

TOURING TIPS You can get very wet on this ride, and extra jets enabled during hot weather practically ensure a soaking. Once the ride is under way, there's a little splashing but nothing major until the big drop at the end. When you hit the bottom, enough water will cascade into the boat to extinguish a three-alarm fire. Bring along an extra-large garbage bag and (cutting holes for your head and arms) wear it like a sack dress. If you forget to bring a garbage bag, you can purchase a poncho at the park for about $10, or rent a locker to stow your stuff for a few bucks less.

Young kids must endure a double whammy. First, they are stalked by giant, salivating reptiles and then are catapulted over the falls. Wait until your kids are fairly stalwart before you spring Jurassic Park on them, or let them sit out the ride inside the fossil-themed playground near the entrance.

Jurassic Park is no longer one of the park's top draws, but it stays jammed on warm days. Ride early in the morning after Revenge of the Mummy.

Revenge of the Mummy—The Ride ★★★½

APPEAL BY AGE	PRESCHOOL —	GRADE SCHOOL ★★★½	TEENS ★★★★½
YOUNG ADULTS ★★★★½		OVER 30 ★★★★	SENIORS ★★★½

What it is High-tech dark ride. **Scope and scale** Super-headliner. **When to go** The first hour the Lower Lot is open or after 4 p.m. **Comments** Must be 48" tall to ride; switching-off option provided (see page 154). Single-rider line is available. All bags must be placed in a free locker. **Duration of ride** About 2 minutes. **Loading speed** Slow.

Dark Scary Lose Things Queasy Rough

DESCRIPTION AND COMMENTS Revenge of the Mummy is an indoor dark ride based on the Mummy flicks, where guests fight off "deadly curses and vengeful creatures" while flying through Egyptian tombs and other spooky places on a high-tech roller coaster.

The queuing area serves to establish the story line: you're in a group touring a 1944 archeological dig of an Egyptian tomb when evil Imhotep decides to make another comeback. The theming includes authentic hieroglyphics as the queue makes its way to the loading area, where you board a somewhat clunky, jeep-looking vehicle. The ride begins as a slow, elaborate dark ride passing through various chambers, including one where golden treasures are offered in exchange for your soul. Suddenly you're shot at high speed straight forward into a minute of pitch-black hills and tight curves, dead-ending in an encounter with leg-tickling scarab beetles. We don't want to divulge too much, but the roller coaster part of the ride has no barrel rolls or any upside-down stuff.

After an all-too-brief backward section, the attraction anticlimaxes in a darkened dome, where the mummy moans and then blinds you with a strobe. Compared to Universal Studios Florida's ride of the same name, this abbreviated attraction severely disappoints with shorter drops, simpler Audio-Animatronics, and no pyrotechnics.

TOURING TIPS Revenge of the Mummy has a very low riders-per-hour capacity for one of the park's top draws. Your only prayer for a tolerable wait is to be on hand when the park opens and sprint to the Mummy immediately after riding Transformers. If you can ride Space Mountain without getting sick, you should be fine on this.

Transformers: The Ride 3-D ★★★★½

APPEAL BY AGE PRESCHOOL ★★★ GRADE SCHOOL ★★★★★ TEENS ★★★★★
YOUNG ADULTS ★★★★★ OVER 30 ★★★★★ SENIORS ★★★★

What it is Multisensory 3-D dark ride. **Scope and scale** Super-headliner. **When to go** The first hour the Lower Lot is open or after 4 p.m. **Comments** Must be 40" tall to ride; single-rider line is available. **Duration of ride** 4½ minutes. **Average wait time per 100 people ahead of you** 3 minutes. **Loading speed** Moderate–fast.

Dark

Loud   Scary

Rough

DESCRIPTION AND COMMENTS Hasbro's Transformers—those toy robots from the 1980s that you turned and twisted into trucks and planes—have been around long enough to go from commercial to kitsch to cool and back again. Thanks to director Michael Bay's recent movies, "Robots in Disguise" are again a blockbuster global franchise. Recruits to this cybertronic war enlist by entering the N.E.S.T. Base (headquarters of the heroic Autobots and their human allies) beneath a massive dimensional mural depicting Optimus Prime and his nemesis Megatron locked in mortal metal combat. Inside an extensive, elaborately detailed queue, video monitors catch you up on the backstory. Basically, the Decepticon baddies are after the AllSpark, source of cybernetic sentience. We're supposed to safeguard the shard by hitching a ride aboard our friendly Autobot ride vehicle Evac, presumably without getting smooshed like a Lincoln in a souvenir penny press when he shifts into android form. Needless to say, Megatron and his pals Starscream and Devastator won't make things easy, but you'll have Sideswipe and Bumblebee (sadly, the modern Camaro version instead of an old-school VW Beetle) backing you up. For the ride's 4½ minutes, you play human Ping-Pong ball in an epic battle between these Made in Japan behemoths. To do justice to this Bay-splosion–packed war of good versus evil, Universal has harnessed the same ride system behind Islands of Adventure's Amazing Adventures of Spider-Man ride, blending motion simulation and live effects with 3-D.

Transformers ups the ante with photo-realistic high-definition imagery, boosted by dichroic 3-D glasses (the same kind used in the upgraded Star Tours) that produce remarkably sharp, vivid visuals. The plot amounts to little more than a giant game of keep-away, and the uninitiated will likely be unable to tell one meteoric mass of metal from another, but you'll be too dazzled by the debris whizzing by to notice. Fanboys will squeal with delight at hearing original cartoon actors Peter Cullen and Frank Welker voicing the pugilistic protagonists, and then spill into the postride gift shop to purchase armloads of exclusive merchandise, while the rest of us might need a bench on which to take a breather afterward. We'll admit slight disappointment at not getting to see an actual four-story-tall animatronic transform, but the ride's mix of detailed (though largely static) set pieces and video projections was likely a much more maintenance-friendly solution for bringing these colossi to life. Either way, this is one of the most intense, immersive thrill rides found in any theme park.

TOURING TIPS Though the opening of The Wizarding World has taken some of the heat off, Transformers still draws heavy crowds, so ride immediately upon arriving on the Lower Lot. The single-rider entrance will often let you walk on the attraction, even when the standby wait is an hour, but its queue lacks any theming, so be sure to take at least one trip through the regular line. It can be difficult for your eyes to focus on the fast-moving imagery from the front row; center seats in the second and third rows provide the best perspective. And be sure to say hello to the towering robots posing for photos outside the entrance; they can talk back to you!

LIVE ENTERTAINMENT *at* UNIVERSAL STUDIOS HOLLYWOOD

THE THEATER ATTRACTIONS operate according to the entertainment schedule available with handout park maps. The number of daily performances of each show varies from as few as 3 a day during less busy times of year to as many as 10 a day during the summer and holiday periods. Characters like Gru's Minions, The Simpsons, and the Transformers can be spotted hanging out near their respective rides. Characters from DreamWorks films—including the Shrek, Kung Fu Panda, and Madagascar series, as well as *Trolls*—greet guests at designated photo ops around the central Universal Plaza, while others (SpongeBob SquarePants, Dora the Explorer, Beetlejuice, Dracula, and Scooby-Doo) frequently wander the Upper Lot. Don't miss bantering with the New York apartment dwellers leaning out of the second-story windows above the candy shop. Near the Jurassic Park ride, you can take a selfie with a real-life velociraptor (actually an actor inside an impressive full-body puppet) and her wry wrangler.

Two brief street entertainments are staged in a raised outdoor alcove at the Forbidden Journey end of Hogsmeade. Showtimes aren't listed in the park map, but performances usually start every 30 minutes on the hour and half hour.

THE FROG CHOIR (★★★) is composed of four singers, two of whom are holding large amphibian puppets sitting on pillows. Inspired by a brief scene in *Harry Potter and the Prisoner of Azkaban,* the group sings three or four a cappella wizarding-related songs, including "Hedwig's Theme" and "Something Wicked This Way Comes." The 13-minute show concludes with a photo op. Though cute, *The Frog Choir* isn't much more than filler for USH's attraction list and probably not worth going out of your way for.

THE TRIWIZARD SPIRIT RALLY (★★★½) showcases a group of three men performing martial arts–type moves including jumps, kicks, and simulated battle with sticks, as well as a group of five women performing rhythmic gymnastics. The entire performance lasts about 6 minutes. After each show, the students of Beauxbatons Academy of Magic and the Durmstrang Institute are available for group photos. Hollywood's version of this show is more exciting than Orlando's, with some impressive acrobatics, but is still only a must-do for major Potter fans.

THE NIGHTTIME LIGHTS OF HOGWARTS CASTLE (★★★★) is a dazzling digital projection show introduced in the summer of 2017 that transforms The Wizarding World's central icon through magical video mapping effects, synchronized to a newly recorded score of John Williams's symphonic themes. The Sorting Hat narrates the show, which honors each of the four Hogwarts houses with colorful creatures that seem to soar across the castle walls. There are no fireworks, but the stirring music and spectacular lighting effects make it worth staying late for. The 5-minute performances repeat every 15 or 20 minutes after sunset; check the park map for showtimes. People tend to camp out for views of the first two showings of the evening, making it a perfect time to ride the Potter attractions; you should have plenty of elbow room if you stick around for the final runs of the night. During the holiday season, the standard light show is swapped for one with a Christmas theme.

DINING *at* UNIVERSAL STUDIOS HOLLYWOOD

THE COUNTER-SERVICE FOOD at Universal Studios runs the gamut from burgers and hot dogs to pizza, fried chicken, crepes, and Mexican specialties. We rank most selections marginally better than fast food, though executive chef Eric Kopelow has made great strides in creativity and ingredient quality recently. Prices are comparable to those at Disneyland. **The Three Broomsticks** is the best restaurant at USH by far and ranks with the finest quick-service food found in any theme park, but the wait to order during mealtimes can be 30 minutes or more.

Our other favorites in the park outside The Wizarding World are the gourmet sandwiches at **Palace Theatre Café** and the soups and salads at **French Street Bistro. Mel's Diner** has upgraded its burgers and decor, but the franchised fast food on the Lower Lot still leaves much to be desired. **Gru's Lab Café** (near Despicable Me Minion Mayhem) serves grilled cheese sandwiches with pulled pork, El Macho nachos, fried mac and cheese, and banana-flavored desserts to mollify your Minions' munchies. The Simpsons eateries are a great bet; give Cletus's chicken and waffles, Bumblebee Man's tacos, or a Krusty burger a try, with a Duff beer to wash it down.

In 2017 USH introduced a Coca-Cola Freestyle souvenir soda cup. For $14.99 (or as low as $11.99 each when purchased in bulk; reactivate for $6.99 per day) you get a large sipper cup and one day of unlimited refills from the park's 21 Freestyle fountains, each of which can mix 100-plus varieties of soft drinks; try the Orange Coke!

If you're looking for full-service dining, try **Wolfgang Puck Bistro, Buca di Beppo, Wasabi, Dongpo Kitchen,** or the **Hard Rock Cafe** in Universal CityWalk just outside the park entrance. **Jimmy Buffett's Margaritaville,** a longtime crowd-pleaser at Orlando's CityWalk, opened a Hollywood branch in 2017, serving signature laid-back libations and Floribbean bar food. If you prefer counter service, an upstairs food court is full of well-known franchises, plus some more-adventuresome eateries like **Voodoo Doughnut** and **LudoBird.** If you leave the park for lunch, be sure to have your hand stamped for reentry. To service your caffeine addiction, there are now **Starbucks** outlets on both the Upper and Lower Lots, as well as in CityWalk.

UNIVERSAL STUDIOS HOLLYWOOD ONE-DAY TOURING PLAN *(page 384)*

THIS PLAN IS FOR GROUPS OF ALL SIZES and ages and includes thrill rides that may induce motion sickness or get you wet. If the plan calls for you to experience an attraction that does not interest you, proceed to the next step. The plan calls for minimal backtracking.

Before You Go

1. Call ☎ 818-622-3801 the day before your visit for the official opening time. If you can't get through, call ☎ 818-622-3735 or 818-622-3750. On all numbers, press 3 for a live attendant.

2. If you have young children in your party, consult the Universal Studios Hollywood Small-Child Fright-Potential Table on page 329.

APPENDIX

READERS' QUESTIONS *to the* AUTHORS

QUESTION:
> *When you do your research, are you admitted to the park for free? Do the Disney people know you are there?*

ANSWER:
We pay the regular admission, and usually the Disney people do not know we are on site. Both in and out of Disneyland, we pay for our own meals and lodging.

QUESTION:
> *How often is* The Unofficial Guide to Disneyland *revised?*

ANSWER:
We publish a new edition once a year but make corrections every time we go to press.

QUESTION:
> *I have an older edition of* The Unofficial Guide to Disneyland. *How much of the information in it is still correct?*

ANSWER:
Veteran travel writers will acknowledge that 5%–8% of the information in a guidebook is out of date by the time it comes off the press! Disneyland is always changing. If you are using an old edition of *The Unofficial Guide to Disneyland,* the descriptions of attractions existing when the guide was published should still be generally accurate. Many other things, however—particularly the touring plans and the hotel and restaurant reviews—change with every edition. Finally, and obviously, older editions of *The Unofficial Guide to Disneyland* do not include new attractions or developments.

QUESTION:

Do you write each new edition from scratch?

ANSWER:

We do not. With a destination the size of Disneyland, it's hard enough keeping up with what is new. Moreover, we put great effort into communicating the most salient and useful information in the clearest possible language. If an attraction or hotel has not changed, we are very reluctant to tinker with its coverage for the sake of freshening up the writing.

QUESTION:

Do you stay at Disneyland hotels? If not, where do you stay?

ANSWER:

We do stay at Disneyland-area hotels from time to time, usually after a renovation or management change. Since we began writing about Disneyland in 1984, we have stayed in more than 70 different properties in various locations around Anaheim.

QUESTION:

How many people have you interviewed or surveyed for your age-group ratings on the attractions?

ANSWER:

Since the publication of the first edition of *The Unofficial Guide* in 1985, we have interviewed or surveyed more than 21,000 Disneyland patrons.

QUESTION:

How are your age-group ratings determined? I am 42 years old. During Star Tours, I was quite worried about hurting my back. If the senior citizens rating is determined only by those brave enough to ride, it will skew the results.

ANSWER:

The reader makes a good point. Unfortunately, it's impossible to develop a rating unless the guest (of any age group) has actually experienced the attraction. So yes, all age-group ratings are derived exclusively from members of that age group who have experienced the attraction. Health problems, such as a bad back, however, can affect guests of any age, and Disney provides more-than-ample warnings on attractions that warrant such admonitions. But if you are in good health, our ratings will give you a sense of how much others your age enjoyed the attraction.

QUESTION:

I have heard that when there are two lines to an attraction, the left line is faster. Is this true?

ANSWER:

In general, no. We have tested this theory many times and usually have not gained an advantage of even 90 seconds by getting in one line versus another. The few rare exceptions are noted in the ride descriptions. What *does* occasionally occur, however, is that after a second line has *just been opened,* guests ignore the new line and persist in standing in the established line. Generally, if you encounter a two-line waiting configuration with no barrier to entry for either and one of the lines is conspicuously less populated than the other, get in it.

AND FINALLY . . .

To end on a high note, consider this compliment from a Redding, California, reader:

> *Thanks to your book, this trip turned out much better than our last, so much in fact that I required only half as much Valium.*

And so it goes . . .

INDEX

IN 35

T

tablets, iPods, 136–137

Tangaroa Terrace restaurant, 46, 200–201

Target, 104

Tarzan's Treehouse, 228–229

taxis, 331

tents, 137

theater attractions, saving time, 97–99

themeparkinsider.com, 18

theunofficialguides.com, 14

Three Broomsticks (USH), 339, 351

Tiki Juice Bar, 226

Tilt Hotel, 66, 72

time, making the most of your, 75–78

Times Guide entertainment listings, 162–163, 220

timing your visit, 25–32

Tivan, Taneleer, 294

toilets, 159

Tommy, Liesl, 292

Tomorrowland, 9, 293
  Disneyland Park vs. Walt Disney World, 12
  location of, 220
  profiled rides, 253–262
  small-child fright-potential table, 148
  touring quickly, 282

Tomorrowland Skyline Lounge Experience, 268

Tomorrowland Terrace, 180–181

Tomorrowland Theatre/*Star Wars: Path of the Jedi*, 261–262

Tom Sawyer Island, 236–237

Toro, Benicio del, 294

Tortilla Jo's, 201, 214

touring
  avoiding bottlenecks, 78
  optimal situation, 75–76
  plans, 78–99, 172, 273–282, 321–323
  rules for successful, 76–78

touringplans.com, 14, 15, 16, 24, 82, 87, 176

TownePlace Suites Anaheim—Maingate Near Angel Stadium, 65, 72

Toy Story Midway Mania! (DCA), 304–305

Trader Sam's, 46

traffic
  around Disneyland, Anaheim area, 39
  patterns at Disney California Adventure, 320–321
  patterns at Disneyland Park, 271–273
  problems, avoiding, 34–35

trams from hotels, motels, 37–38

Transformers: The Ride 3-D (USH), 349–350

transportation rides, 225

travel agents, 52

traveling to Disneyland, 32–39

Travelocity.com, 53–54

Travelodge Anaheim Inn & Suites, 66, 72

travel packages, 56–57

Triwizard Spirit Rally, The (USH), 351

Tropicana Inn & Suites, 41, 66, 73

Troubadour Tavern, 181, 271

Turtle Talk with Crush (DCA), 296

Twitter feeds, best Disney, 19

two-day touring plan, 277–279

U

Uber, 35, 331

Umami Burger, 203

Universal Studios Hollywood (USH)
  arriving, getting oriented, 331–332
  attractions, 333–350
  dining at, 351–352
  live entertainment at, 350–351
  map, 326
  one-day touring, 352
  overview, 324–327
  for small children, 328
  timing your visit, 327–331

universalstudioshollywood.com, 17–18, 325, 340

One-Day Plan for Adults

Disneyland Park

1. Arrive at the entrance 40 minutes before official opening time.
2. Ride Peter Pan's Flight in Fantasyland.
3. Ride Alice in Wonderland.
4. Go to Tomorrowland and obtain FastPasses for Space Mountain.
5. Ride Star Tours—The Adventures Continue.
6. Ride Finding Nemo Submarine Voyage.
7. Try Buzz Lightyear Astro Blasters.
8. Ride Space Mountain using the FastPasses you received earlier.
9. Go to Big Thunder Trail in Critter Country and get FastPasses for *Fantasmic!*
10. Obtain FastPasses for Splash Mountain.
11. Take the Jungle Cruise in Adventureland.
12. Eat lunch at French Market in New Orleans Square.
13. Experience Pirates of the Caribbean.
14. Visit The Haunted Mansion.
15. Return to ride Splash Mountain in Critter Country using the FastPasses obtained earlier.
16. Ride The Many Adventures of Winnie the Pooh.
17. Get FastPasses for Indiana Jones Adventure in Adventureland.
18. Ride the Matterhorn Bobsleds in Fantasyland.
19. Ride It's a Small World.
20. Experience Indiana Jones Adventure in Adventureland using the FastPasses obtained earlier.
21. Explore Tarzan's Treehouse nearby.
22. Obtain FastPasses for Big Thunder Mountain Railroad in Frontierland.
23. See *Enchanted Tiki Room* in Adventureland.
24. Eat dinner. Try Plaza Inn on Main Street, U.S.A.
25. See *The Disneyland Story*, presenting *Great Moments with Mr. Lincoln*, on Main Street, U.S.A.
26. Ride Big Thunder Mountain Railroad in Frontierland, using the FastPasses obtained earlier.
27. Check the *Times Guide* for parades, fireworks, and *Fantasmic!*

Author's Select One-Day Plan

Disneyland Park

Mickey's Toontown

Fantasyland

Critter Country

Frontierland

Tomorrowland

New Orleans Square

Adventureland

Main Street, U.S.A.

1. Arrive at the entrance 40 minutes before official opening time.
2. Ride Peter Pan's Flight in Fantasyland.
3. Ride Alice in Wonderland.
4. Experience the Matterhorn Bobsleds.
5. Ride Star Tours—The Adventures Continue in Tomorrowland.
6. Obtain FastPasses for Indiana Jones Adventure in Adventureland.
7. Ride Big Thunder Mountain Railroad in Frontierland.
8. See The Many Adventures of Winnie the Pooh in Critter Country.
9. Ride Splash Mountain.
10. See The Haunted Mansion in New Orleans Square.
11. Experience Pirates of the Caribbean.
12. Experience Indiana Jones Adventure in Adventureland using the FastPasses obtained earlier.
13. Obtain FastPasses for Space Mountain in Tomorrowland.
14. Take the Finding Nemo Submarine Voyage.
15. Eat lunch.
16. Try Buzz Lightyear Astro Blasters.
17. Ride It's a Small World in Fantasyland.
18. Ride Space Mountain in Tomorrowland using the FastPasses obtained earlier.
19. See *The Disneyland Story*, presenting *Great Moments with Mr. Lincoln*, on Main Street, U.S.A.
20. Check the *Times Guide* for parades, fireworks, and *Fantasmic!*

Dumbo-or-Die-in-a-Day Plan

Disneyland Park

1. Arrive at the entrance 40 minutes before official opening time.
2. Ride Peter Pan's Flight in Fantasyland.
3. Ride Dumbo the Flying Elephant.
4. Ride Alice in Wonderland.
5. Send a party member to Big Thunder Trail in Critter Country to get FastPasses for *Fantasmic!*
6. Ride the King Arthur Carrousel.
7. Take Pinocchio's Daring Journey.
8. Ride the Casey Jr. Circus Train.
9. Take a spin on the Mad Tea Party.
10. Ride the Storybook Land Canal Boats.
11. In Mickey's Toontown, ride Roger Rabbit's Car Toon Spin. Obtain FastPasses if the wait exceeds 30 minutes.
12. Ride Gadget's Go Coaster.
13. Tour Minnie's House.
14. Let the kids blow off some steam at Goofy's Playhouse.
15. Take the It's a Small World boat ride in Fantasyland.
16. Experience the Royal Hall princess meet and greet.

17. In Tomorrowland, ride Autopia.
18. Try Buzz Lightyear Astro Blasters.
19. See the *Enchanted Tiki Room* in Adventureland.
20. Ride Pirates of the Caribbean in New Orleans Square.
21. Eat lunch.
22. Obtain a Fastpass for The Haunted Mansion.
23. Take The Many Adventures of Winnie the Pooh ride in Critter Country.
24. Take a raft to explore the Pirate's Lair on Tom Sawyer Island.
25. See The Haunted Mansion in New Orleans Square.
26. Explore Tarzan's Treehouse in Adventureland.
27. If time permits, let the kids play at *Miss Daisy*, Donald's Boat, in Mickey's Toontown.
28. Also check out the Chip 'n Dale Treehouse.
29. Eat dinner.
30. Visit any attractions you may have missed earlier.
31. Check the *Times Guide* for parades, fireworks, and *Fantasmic!*

Two-Day Plan for Adults with Children: Day One

Disneyland Park

1. Arrive at the entrance 40 minutes before official opening time.
2. As soon as the park opens, ride Indiana Jones Adventure in Adventureland.
3. Go to Big Thunder Trail in Critter Country and get FastPasses for *Fantasmic!*
4. Take the Jungle Cruise in Adventureland.
5. Try Splash Mountain in Critter Country.
6. Ride The Many Adventures of Winnie the Pooh.
7. Experience the Royal Hall princess meet and greet in Fantasyland.
8. In Mickey's Toontown, tour Mickey's House.
9. Ride Gadget's Go Coaster.
10. Let the kids blow off some steam at Goofy's Playhouse.
11. Try Roger Rabbit's Car Toon Spin. Obtain Fast-Passes if the wait exceeds 30 minutes.
12. In Fantasyland, ride It's a Small World.
13. Ride Pirates of the Caribbean in New Orleans Square.
14. See The Haunted Mansion. Obtain FastPasses if the wait exceeds 30 minutes.
15. Eat lunch and take the Disneyland Railroad from New Orleans Square to Toontown.
16. In Mickey's Toontown, see Minnie's House.
17. Try the Chip 'n Dale Treehouse.
18. Check out *Miss Daisy*, Donald's Boat.
19. Ride Autopia in Tomorrowland.
20. If time permits, take a round-trip on the Disneyland Monorail.
21. Eat dinner.
22. Visit any attractions you may have missed earlier.
23. Check the *Times Guide* for parades, fireworks, and *Fantasmic!*

Two-Day Plan for Adults with Children: Day Two

1. Arrive at the entrance 40 minutes before official opening time.
2. As soon as the park opens, ride Peter Pan's Flight in Fantasyland.
3. Ride Alice in Wonderland.
4. Send a party member to obtain FastPasses for Space Mountain in Tomorrowland.
5. Experience Dumbo the Flying Elephant.
6. Take Mr. Toad's Wild Ride.
7. Try the Storybook Land Canal Boats.
8. Take a spin on the Mad Tea Party.
9. Ride the Matterhorn Bobsleds.
10. Obtain FastPasses for Star Tours—The Adventures Continue in Tomorrowland.
11. Ride Space Mountain.
12. Take the Finding Nemo Submarine Voyage.
13. Try Buzz Lightyear Astro Blasters.
14. In Fantasyland, ride Pinocchio's Daring Journey.
15. Take a spin on the King Arthur Carrousel.
16. Ride Big Thunder Mountain Railroad in Frontierland.
17. See the *Enchanted Tiki Room* in Adventureland.
18. Ride Star Tours in Tomorrowland, using the FastPasses obtained earlier.
19. Eat lunch.
20. Visit any attractions you may have missed earlier.
21. Check the *Times Guide* for parades, fireworks, and *Fantasmic!*

Two-Day Plan A: Day One

1. Arrive at the entrance 40 minutes before official opening time.
2. As soon as the park opens, ride Peter Pan's Flight in Fantasyland.
3. Experience Alice in Wonderland.
4. Ride the Matterhorn Bobsleds.
5. Go to Big Thunder Trail in Critter Country and get FastPasses for *Fantasmic!*
6. Take a cruise on the Storybook Land Canal Boats.
7. Take Mr. Toad's Wild Ride.
8. Ride Snow White's Scary Adventures.
9. Take Pinocchio's Daring Journey.
10. In Tomorrowland, take the Finding Nemo Submarine Voyage.
11. Obtain FastPasses for Space Mountain.
12. Ride Buzz Lightyear Astro Blasters.
13. Eat lunch.
14. Ride Space Mountain using the FastPasses obtained earlier.
15. See the *Enchanted Tiki Room* in Adventureland.
16. See *The Disneyland Story,* presenting *Great Moments with Mr. Lincoln* on Main Street, U.S.A.
17. Send one member of your party to obtain FastPasses for Big Thunder Mountain Railroad in Frontierland.
18. Climb through Tarzan's Treehouse in Adventureland.
19. Ride Big Thunder Mountain Railroad using the FastPasses obtained earlier.
20. Eat dinner.
21. Revisit favorite attractions or visit any attractions you may have missed earlier.
22. Check the *Times Guide* for parades, fireworks, and *Fantasmic!*

Two-Day Plan A: Day Two

1. Arrive at the entrance 40 minutes before official opening time.
2. As soon as the park opens, take the Indiana Jones Adventure in Adventureland.
3. Ride Star Tours—The Adventures Continue in Tomorrowland.
4. In Mickey's Toontown, visit Mickey's House.
5. See Minnie's House.
6. Try Roger Rabbit's Car Toon Spin. Use FastPass if the wait exceeds 30 minutes.
7. Ride It's a Small World in Fantasyland.
8. Take the Jungle Cruise in Adventureland.
9. Ride The Haunted Mansion in New Orleans Square.
10. Obtain FastPasses for Splash Mountain in Critter Country.
11. Experience The Many Adventures of Winnie the Pooh.
12. Take a round-trip on the Disneyland Railroad from the New Orleans Square Station.
13. Ride Pirates of the Caribbean.
14. Take the monorail from Tomorrowland to Downtown Disney, and eat lunch.
15. Ride Splash Mountain in Critter Country using the FastPasses obtained earlier.
16. See the *Jedi Training: Trials of the Temple* in Tomorrowland.
17. Revisit any favorite attractions or visit any attractions you may have missed earlier.
18. Check the *Times Guide* for parades, fireworks, and *Fantasmic!*

Two-Day Plan B: Day One

Disneyland Park

1. Arrive at the entrance 40 minutes before official opening time.
2. Ride Peter Pan's Flight in Fantasyland.
3. Experience Indiana Jones Adventure in Adventureland.
4. See The Haunted Mansion in New Orleans Square.
5. Experience Pirates of the Caribbean.
6. Enjoy The Many Adventures of Winnie the Pooh in Critter Country.
7. Obtain FastPasses for Space Mountain in Tomorrowland.
8. Ride the Finding Nemo Submarine Voyage.
9. Eat lunch.
10. See It's a Small World in Fantasyland.
11. Ride Space Mountain in Tomorrowland using

the FastPasses obtained earlier.
12. Obtain FastPasses for Star Tours—The Adventures Continue.
13. Ride Alice in Wonderland in Fantasyland.
14. Take a spin on the Mad Tea Party.
15. Experience Matterhorn Bobsleds.
16. Try Mr. Toad's Wild Ride.
17. Eat dinner.
18. Ride Star Tours—The Adventures Continue in Tomorrowland using the FastPasses obtained earlier.
19. Watch the *Remember . . . Dreams Come True* fireworks. Find a spot on Main Street or near Sleeping Beauty Castle to watch the fireworks.
20. Enjoy the Paint the Night parade.

Two-Day Plan B: Day Two

Disneyland Park

Mickey's Toontown

Fantasyland

Critter Country

Frontierland

Tomorrowland

New Orleans Square

Adventureland

Main Street, U.S.A.

1. Arrive at Disneyland Park around noon.
2. Go to Big Thunder Trail in Critter Country and get FastPasses for *Fantasmic!*
3. Ride Splash Mountain.
4. Take Davy Crockett's Explorer Canoes around Tom Sawyer Island.
5. Obtain FastPasses for Big Thunder Mountain Railroad in Frontierland.
6. Eat a late lunch. A good choice is Jolly Holiday Bakery Café.
7. Try Buzz Lightyear Astro Blasters in Tomorrowland.
8. Ride Big Thunder Mountain Railroad in Frontierland using the FastPasses obtained earlier.
9. See *Mickey and the Magical Map* in Fantasyland.
10. See the *Enchanted Tiki Room* in Adventureland.
11. Experience Tarzan's Treehouse.
12. Enjoy Mickey's Soundsational Parade.
13. On Main Street, U.S.A., see *The Disneyland Story*, presenting *Great Moments with Mr. Lincoln.*
14. In Frontierland, ride the *Mark Twain* Riverboat or Sailing Ship *Columbia*, whichever boards first.
15. Take the Jungle Cruise in Adventureland.
16. Eat dinner. The Plaza Inn is a good choice.
17. Check the *Times Guide* for parades, fireworks, and *Fantasmic!*

One-Day Plan for Adults

Disney California Adventure

1. Arrive at the entrance 40 minutes before official opening time.
2. As soon as the park opens, obtain FastPasses for Guardians of the Galaxy—Mission: Breakout! in Hollywood Land.
3. Ride Soarin' Around the World in Grizzly Peak.
4. Obtain FastPasses for *World of Color*. Fast-Passes are distributed to the right of the entrance of The Little Mermaid: Ariel's Under-sea Adventure in Paradise Pier/Pixar Pier.
5. Try Toy Story Midway Mania!
6. Obtain FastPasses for Radiator Springs Racers. FastPasses are distributed outside of Cars Land near *It's Tough to Be a Bug!*
7. Ride Guardians of the Galaxy—Mission: Break-out! in Hollywood Land using the FastPasses obtained earlier.
8. Ride Mater's Junkyard Jamboree in Cars Land.
9. Ride Goofy's Sky School in Paradise Pier/Pixar Pier.
10. Try the Silly Symphony Swings.
11. Check the daily entertainment schedule for the next showing of *Frozen—Live at the Hyperion*

in Hollywood Land. Work in this show around lunch.
12. Get FastPasses for California Screamin' in Paradise Pier/Pixar Pier.
13. See *It's Tough to Be a Bug* in A Bug's Land.
14. Ride The Little Mermaid: Ariel's Undersea Adventure in Paradise Pier/Pixar Pier.
15. Ride Radiator Springs Racers in Cars Land using the FastPasses obtained earlier.
16. Take the Bakery Tour in the Pacific Wharf.
17. Ride California Screamin' in Paradise Pier/Pixar Pier using the FastPasses obtained earlier.
18. Ride Monsters, Inc. Mike & Sulley to the Rescue in Hollywood Land.
19. See the Disney Animation exhibit, including Animation Academy and *Turtle Talk with Crush*.
20. Eat dinner.
21. Ride Grizzly River Run in Grizzly Peak.
22. Repeat any favorite attractions or see any missed attractions.
23. Check your daily entertainment schedule for parades, and check your *World of Color* Fast-Pass for the performance time.

One-Day Plan for Adults with Small Children

Disney California Adventure

1. Arrive at the entrance 40 minutes before official opening time.
2. As soon as the park opens, obtain FastPasses for Radiator Springs Racers in Cars Land. FastPasses are distributed outside of Cars Land near *It's Tough to Be a Bug!*
3. Ride Luigi's Rollickin' Roadsters.
4. Ride Mater's Junkyard Jamboree.
5. Ride Radiator Springs Racers using the Fast-Passes obtained earlier.
6. Obtain FastPasses for *World of Color*. Fast-Passes are distributed to the right of the entrance of The Little Mermaid: Ariel's Under-sea Adventure in Paradise Pier/Pixar Pier.
7. Ride Soarin' Around the World in Grizzly Peak.
8. Obtain FastPasses for Guardians of the Galaxy—Mission: Breakout! in Hollywood Land.
9. Try Francis' Ladybug Boogie in A Bug's Land.
10. Ride Tuck and Roll's Drive 'Em Buggies.
11. Ride Flik's Flyers.
12. Check the daily entertainment schedule for the next showing of *Frozen—Live at the Hyperion* in

Hollywood Land. Work in this show around lunch
13. See the Disney Animation exhibit, including Animation Academy and *Turtle Talk with Crush*.
14. Try the Silly Symphony Swings in Paradise Pier/ Pixar Pier.
15. Try Toy Story Midway Mania!
16. Experience King Triton's Carousel.
17. Explore the Redwood Creek Challenge Trail in Grizzly Peak.
18. See *It's Tough to Be a Bug!* in A Bug's Land.
19. Ride Monsters, Inc. Mike & Sulley to the Rescue in Hollywood Land.
20. Ride Guardians of the Galaxy—Mission: Break-out! using the FastPasses obtained earlier.
21. Eat dinner.
22. Ride The Little Mermaid: Ariel's Undersea Adventure in Paradise Pier/Pixar Pier.
23. Repeat any favorite attractions or see any missed attractions.
24. Check your daily entertainment schedule for parades, and check your *World of Color* Fast-Pass for the performance time.

382 CLIP-OUT TOURING PLANS

The Best of Disneyland Resort in One Day

Disney California Adventure

1. Arrive at the entrance 40 minutes before official opening time.
2. As soon as the park opens, obtain FastPasses for Guardians of the Galaxy—Mission: Breakout! in Hollywood Land.
3. Ride Radiator Springs Racers in Cars Land.
4. Ride Guardians of the Galaxy—Mission: Breakout! in Hollywood Land using the FastPasses obtained earlier.
5. Try Toy Story Midway Mania! in Paradise Pier/Pixar Pier.
6. Ride California Screamin'.

7. Ride Goofy's Sky School.
8. Ride The Little Mermaid: Ariel's Undersea Adventure.
9. Ride Grizzly River Run in Grizzly Peak.
10. Experience Soarin' Around the World.
11. In Hollywood Land, ride Monsters, Inc. Mike & Sulley to the Rescue!
12. Eat lunch.
13. If you have time, ride Mater's Junkyard Jamboree in Cars Land.
14. Leave DCA and head to Disneyland Park.

(continued on next page)

The Best of Disneyland Resort in One Day

Disneyland Park

Mickey's Toontown

Fantasyland

Critter Country

Frontierland

Tomorrowland

New Orleans Square

Adventureland

Main Street, U.S.A.

(continued from previous page)

15. Get FastPasses for Indiana Jones Adventure in Adventureland.
16. Ride Peter Pan's Flight in Fantasyland.
17. Ride Star Tours—The Adventures Continue in Tomorrowland.
18. Ride the Finding Nemo Submarine Voyage.
19. Try Buzz Lightyear Astro Blasters.
20. Ride Alice in Wonderland in Fantasyland.
21. Ride Dumbo the Flying Elephant.
22. See It's a Small World.
23. Obtain FastPasses for Big Thunder Mountain Railroad in Frontierland.
24. Ride Indiana Jones Adventure in Adventure-

land using the FastPasses obtained earlier.
25. Ride Big Thunder Mountain Railroad in Frontierland using the FastPasses obtained earlier.
26. Watch the *Remember . . . Dreams Come True* fireworks. Find a spot on Main Street or near Sleeping Beauty Castle to watch the fireworks.
27. Ride Pirates of the Caribbean in New Orleans Square.
28. Take the Jungle Cruise in Adventureland.
29. See The Haunted Mansion in New Orleans Square.
30. Ride Splash Mountain in Critter Country.
31. Ride the Matterhorn Bobsleds in Fantasyland.
32. Ride Space Mountain in Tomorrowland.

Universal Studios One-Day Touring Plan

1. If you are eligible for early entry, arrive 1 hour and 20 minutes before official opening time, and enjoy The Wizarding World of Harry Potter until the park opens to the general public. Otherwise, arrive 40 minutes before opening time.

2. In the Upper Lot, ride Despicable Me Minion Mayhem.

3. Experience The Simpsons Ride.

4. As soon as the Lower Lot opens, descend the escalators and ride Transformers: The Ride 3-D.

5. Ride Revenge of the Mummy—The Ride.

6. Check out Jurassic Park—The Ride, and say hello to the velociraptor.

7. Return to the Upper Lot and eat an early lunch in Springfield.

8. Take the Studio Tour. Allocate an hour and 10 minutes for the tour.

9. See a 4-D film at DreamWorks Theatre (opens 2018).

10. Check your daily entertainment schedule for a) *WaterWorld*, b) the *Special Effects Show*, and c) *Universal's Animal Actors* showtimes.

11. Experience The Walking Dead, if you dare.

12. When crowds begin to die down as closing approaches, enter Hogsmeade Village. Explore the shops and experience the wand ceremony in Ollivanders.

13. Check the daily entertainment schedule for *The Frog Choir* and *Triwizard Spirit Rally* shows on the stage outside Hogwarts. Work in the shows around dinner at The Three Broomsticks.

14. Get into line for a) Harry Potter and the Forbidden Journey and/or b) Flight of the Hippogriff during the first two performances of the Hogwarts Castle projection show.

15. Watch one of the final performances of the Hogwarts Castle show, then revisit your favorites or see attractions you missed.